THE pep REVOLUTION

Inside Guardiola's Manchester City

MARTÍ PERARNAU

EBURY
SPOTLIGHT

Ebury Spotlight, an imprint of Ebury Publishing
20 Vauxhall Bridge Road
London SW1V 2SA

Ebury Spotlight is part of the Penguin Random House group of companies
whose addresses can be found at global.penguinrandomhouse.com

Penguin
Random House
UK

First published in English by Ebury Spotlight in 2024
First published in Spanish as *Dios salve a Pep* in 2023
by Roca Editorial de Libros, S. L.

www.penguin.co.uk

A CIP catalogue record for this book is available from the British Library

Hardback ISBN 9781529937305
Trade paperback ISBN 9781529937312

Printed and bound in Great Britain by Clays Ltd, Elcograf S.p.A.

The authorised representative in the EEA is Penguin Random House Ireland,
Morrison Chambers, 32 Nassau Street, Dublin D02 YH68.

Penguin Random House is committed to a sustainable future for our
business, our readers and our planet. This book is made from
Forest Stewardship Council® certified paper.

MIX
Paper | Supporting
responsible forestry
FSC
www.fsc.org   FSC® C018179

Contents

SEASON 3: 2018–19

Chasing the Red Rabbit

Months

SEASON 4: 2019–20

Five Dinners and a Funeral

SEASON 5: 2020–1

Sisyphus on Top of the World (the City of the Yugoslavs)

Moments

SEASON 6: 2021–2

5 minutes and 36 seconds

SEASON 7: 2022–3

Moving On

Scenes

*The secret of success is that none of us is
the same as we were the first day.*

Pep Guardiola

The secret of success is that we hate to lose.

Scott Carson

Prologue

The solitary figure stands at the towering window of an attic apartment gazing down at the city spread before him. A single candle casts a bluish hue over his reflection as he contemplates the city lights.

Far below, Manchester sleeps. Conquered.

A glass of red wine in his hand, Pep Guardiola paces the huge living room back and forth, just as he's done so many times over the last seven years. He's looking at Deansgate, the city's main artery, but his thoughts are elsewhere.

Miles away, on the football pitch.

He's puzzling over how to apply old concepts in new ways, how best to tackle the many challenges he'll face in the next few games, how to make sure his team is progressing, moving forward …

This unfiltered book lays out the many faces of Pep, every facet of his character.

The meticulous, punctilious artisan, zealous in his pursuit of perfection.

The champion many times over, a serial winner who fights tooth and nail for every title, no matter how insignificant it might appear to others.

The perpetual innovator, bound in equal measure to his ideas and doubts and constantly searching for the single gambit that will change a game.

The mercurial maestro, sometimes affable, sometimes enraged, equally capable of putting up a wall between him and his players or throwing his door open for them, ready and willing to help.

The brilliant tactician who can find the perfect solution in the darkest of moments and guide his squad safely through uncharted territory.

The Sisyphus determined to scale the tallest peak, even as the Fates predict his downfall.*

---

* The Greek gods punished Sisyphus by making him push a huge boulder up a hill for eternity; the boulder would roll back down every time he almost reached the top.

The obsessive workaholic, convinced that only even *harder* work can overcome a nagging worry that he lacks natural talent, and who pushes everyone around him to the point of exhaustion.

The charismatic leader whose team talks captivate his foot soldiers, because he's proven time and again that his way is the only guaranteed route to success.

Spikey, disagreeable, engaging, aggravating, vacillating, ironic, histrionic, stoical, euphoric, passionate, cerebral and, of late, increasingly relaxed about life.

These are the many sides of Pep.

• • •

As this, the third era of Pep's coaching career, approaches its completion, it's a good time to take stock. Back in 2016, Guardiola understood that Manchester City would be a colossal undertaking. With no clear idea of exactly what awaited him, the Catalan approached his new job as if it were a blank canvas upon which to stamp his mark. Bringing his vast experience to the role, he continued to learn and develop, drawing on the triple stimuli of high risk, extreme pressure and complete freedom to fire up his creativity and imagination.

Eight years and 17 titles later, it's clear that Manchester City has become Pep's magnum opus.

During that time, the most demanding, difficult, complex and exhausting years of his life, we've seen Pep at his innovative, paradoxical, anarchic, fertile best. He's steered City through the calamitous times, watched them produce epic comebacks and countless goals, and revelled in their sensational performances on the pitch. A seven-season saga of dizzying highs and demoralising lows. Much like life itself.

'It's not about titles. It's how you make people feel. Legacy consists of the emotions you generate. The important thing is how you make people feel!'

This book is the last in my trilogy about Pep Guardiola. The first, *Pep Confidential* (2014), chronicles his debut season at Bayern. Pep welcomed me into the dressing room and has continued to give me exclusive behind-the-scenes access ever since. In the second book, *Pep Guardiola: The Evolution* (2016), I explained Pep's next two years in Munich, focusing specifically on the way Germany changed him and examining how that transformation might manifest itself later, in Manchester. This third book describes how he has conquered the hostile, difficult terrain of the English Premier League and imposed his own brand of football upon it.

Pep's approach has changed constantly over the years (although it may be more accurate to say that he has responded to the changing circumstances of life itself) and the book's structure reflects this. Each of the following seven chapters varies in length, format and depth of analysis. They have all been written in real time and I report my own and others' observations, analysis and predictions exactly as they were expressed, without revisions or retrospective corrections.

Seven years of raw emotion. Pep can't hide the intensity of his feelings, even if he wants to. Manchester has humanised Pep in every sense.

The circumspection of the first months and those crushing losses; that dreadful, dispiriting first season; the panic he felt during the tragic Manchester Arena terrorist attack in 2017; the boundless energy he brings to his pursuit of success; the joy of victory; the brutal defeats that rip open old wounds; his obsessive quest for perfection; his unstoppable determination to scale that mountain time and again; reaching the apogee of success by winning the treble and then celebrating with a cigar on the main road of Manchester, standing in the pouring rain, yet somehow appearing not to get wet …

This is the story of a coronation, a faithful account of seven rollercoaster years of raw emotion.

Nights of agony, days of glory.

God save Pep.

Season 1: 2016–17

'Do You Really Want to Be a Coach?'

SCENE 1. 'REMEMBER HIS NAME: PHIL FODEN'

Manchester, 12 October 2016

Pep and Cris stroll through Deansgate. Nobody seems to recognise City's coach even though Pep hasn't bothered wearing the cap he uses when he wants to fly under the radar. He doesn't need it this evening. They're both wrapped up in black winter coats and nobody gives them a second glance. Just an ordinary couple out for a stroll and looking for somewhere to have a romantic dinner.

Then we bump into them. My wife Loles and I are looking for somewhere to eat too. This will be my first of many visits to Manchester and, having learned from some of my experiences in Munich, these days I too prefer to travel incognito.

It could be a scene straight out of a Hollywood movie. Both couples are peering into a restaurant in Deansgate when we realise exactly who the 'strangers' beside us are and suddenly it's dinner for four. Just like the old days in Munich. We greet each other, four kisses on the cheek, and then Pep's off:

'I just couldn't work out how to deal with the way Tottenham set themselves up in that game. I went over and over it but couldn't come up with the right thing to turn the game for us. That's why I cancelled the trip to Oktoberfest in Munich, so I could spend some time working out what I should have done. The international break has given me ten days to analyse what has been going well for us … and where we've been lacking. We need to get back to basics: control the game. We need four men in the centre of the pitch so that we control matches and force our opponents to chase after the ball.'

Pep has made a declaration of intent and, judging by the expression on her face, Cristina is already resigned to the fact that their 'romantic dinner' has now become a 'football dinner'. Pep wants to find a quieter place to talk, a back street where he can explain in detail what he plans to do from now on. Deansgate, Manchester's main commercial thoroughfare, is far too busy for such discussions.

He finds the perfect spot in Brazennose Street, just beside the statue of Abraham Lincoln, and embarks on a detailed, animated description of how he anticipates his changes will work. He explains how and where he wants each player to move, how they'll occupy the centre of the pitch while at the same time causing maximum disorganisation in their opponent's ranks.

'I've decided to play a 3–4–3 against Everton. Like a 3–2–2–3 or a WM formation. Four in the centre of the pitch. We've already practised it but only with the kids from the youth side because our senior players were away with their national teams. Tomorrow we'll try it with the first team in an 11-a-side game and then we'll field a 3–4–3 on Saturday. The objective is "control" and getting back to basics; disorganise our opponents with pass after pass after pass.'

It's a chilly night, though, and Cristina and Loles are desperate to find somewhere to eat. Pep suggests Wings, a Chinese restaurant he knows isn't too far away. We set off just as Pep remembers something he's desperate to communicate. He grabs my arm and starts to explain enthusiastically, almost shouting,

'Listen … everyone's talking about Jadon Sancho and Brahim Díaz. And, don't get me wrong, they're great. Really. I love them. But there's another name I want you to remember. Phil Foden. I swear, he's an astounding player. I'm putting him in the team very soon. In fact, if the League Cup game had been against anyone except Manchester United, that's where he'd have made his debut. He's your typically pale-faced English footballer, left-footed, skinny as a rake with bandy legs, but he protects the ball brilliantly and has a *fantastic* vision of the game. Foden, remember that name. He's going to be outstanding.'

Our dinner at Wings is delicious.

SCENE 2. THE BEST TEAM IN THE PREMIER LEAGUE
Manchester, 15 October 2016

Ronald Koeman makes light work of Pep's 3–2–2–3.

Despite City's absolute domination of the pitch, the final score doesn't reflect the superiority of their game. Everton's keeper Maarten Stekelenburg has made sure of that. He's played out of his skin.

Pep, as planned, fields a 3–2–2–3 despite the absence of two of his key players (John Stones and Leroy Sané) from Thursday's training session. Problems with their return flights from international duty have meant that

Friday is their first day back, making it the only chance for the team to try out the new game plan. Despite the lack of practice time, the coach is still sure about the personnel he wants – and the team's tactical shape. Claudio Bravo in goal; a back three of Nicolás Otamendi, Stones and Gaël Clichy; Fernandinho, Kevin De Bruyne, İlkay Gündoğan and David Silva will form the midfield diamond; Sané and Raheem Sterling as inverted wingers and the striker is Kelechi Iheanacho. On the whiteboard the 3–2–2–3 reminds me of the WM formation introduced by Herbert Chapman (1925) but in action it's much more of a Cruyff-inspired 3–4–3.

City's performances in their last few games are worrying Pep. It's not just that loss to Tottenham, his first defeat of this new era, but also the lack of control they displayed against Celtic, in Glasgow, where a poor performance left them with a 3–3 draw in a key Champions League match. The thing that most irritates the Catalan, however, is if his team fails to control the game, yet that's exactly what's happened over their last 180 minutes of competitive football. And it's why he's decided to change his system from the more ortho- dox 4–3–3 with which they started the season to this 3–4–3, which he hopes will allow them 'to control the play'. Four midfielders forcing the opposition players out of position as City pass and move the ball around and around.

And his men pull it off. Well, sort of.

Under the attentive gaze of Sir Alex Ferguson, City make 661 passes against Everton's 255. The Sky Blues have almost double the touches of the ball of their opponent (878 and 478 respectively), 19 shots at goal compared to the visitors' 3, and take 13 corners to Everton's 1. City domi- nate completely: 73 per cent possession.

Koeman, who knew Cruyff well and played alongside Pep for many years at Barcelona, was under no illusions about the brutal pressure City would put them under at the Etihad Stadium. He's planned various defen- sive strategies with which to try and slow down the home team's playing style. Every attacking move City make is met with at least eight Everton players behind the ball. In total Everton clear the ball out of their penalty area, and away from the danger zone, 49 times.

Despite these ultra-defensive tactics, Pep's men impose a fluid rhythm, controlling the pace of the game and patiently constructing almost non-stop attacking movements. They make several clear-cut chances, all of which are saved by Stekelenburg. It's a masterclass in smooth, well-coordinated attacking play, which enraptures the home support. They're loving this exhibition of first-class football.

But City's positional superiority doesn't produce a goal, not even from De Bruyne's 43rd minute penalty resulting from Phil Jagielka's foul on Silva. The Belgian shoots hard at mid-height to the keeper's left but Stekelenburg stretches full-length and punches it away with both hands.

Then, just when a City goal seems inevitable, Everton score.

It's all down to, as Pep often points out, a failure to properly mark opponents who hang around higher up the pitch, waiting for quick transitions and breakaway chances.

City press Everton as the visitors try to bring the ball out and even Otamendi pushes up to add to the general press – hoping to prevent Romelu Lukaku getting service. Everton abandon their methodical approach and Yannick Bolasie thumps the ball long. Stones tries but fails to intercept and now Lukaku is on the charge with only the fragile Clichy in front of him.

Caught out of position, Otamendi and Fernandinho sprint back but don't manage to stop Lukaku slamming it past Claudio Bravo. It's the kind of calamity that will be repeated many times this season and, to a lesser extent, over the next few years. Poor man-marking of wide players sitting high on the pitch will cost City a lot of time and many painful goals. Only once Rúben Dias and Rodrigo Hernández – Rodri – start to make their mark on the team in 2020 will this defect become a more sporadic occurrence, although it's impossible to completely neutralise the possibility of a successful counterattack by a strong opponent.

One–nil down, Pep's men are now looking for the equaliser. Just five minutes later Jagielka commits another foul, this time on Sergio Agüero, who then takes the penalty. His shot is a carbon copy of De Bruyne's. Same spot, equal power, identical height. But Stekelenburg is just as agile and defiant as before. Making the most of his impressive long-limbed stretch (he's 1.97m/ 6 ft 6 in tall), the Dutch international once again palms the ball away with both hands.

The Dutchman stubbornly continues his exhibition of defiance and saves several more big chances. Then, finally, there's a breakthrough. Silva sends in a cross from the left wing and Nolito heads it home beautifully.

Stekelenburg is finally beaten ... but Everton have their 1–1 draw.

A point at the Etihad is a huge result for the Toffees, who celebrate accordingly while City act – long faces and slumped shoulders – as if they've just suffered a huge defeat. Pep is dismayed. Three consecutive games without a win and a Champions League clash with Messi's Barcelona at the Camp Nou just four days away.

His men have clearly mastered the 3–4–3 and have controlled the game with brilliant, fluid passing but it hasn't been effective. As ever in football, it's the final score that tells you whether or not your system is doing its job. En route to the dressing room, Domènec Torrent, Pep's assistant, wishes Koeman good luck for the rest of the season. Koeman laughs. 'I think today we've had a full year's worth of luck. I don't expect to get so lucky for the rest of the season ...'

Post-match, the Dutch coach is crystal clear in his analysis:

City are the best team I have ever faced as a coach. When I saw that they were fielding three defenders I told my men that we'd play with three forwards and try to get the second balls. City played brilliantly: high pressing, high tempo. But my defenders were heroic today and our keeper had the game of his life.

City are the best team in the Premier League: their attacking and movement, their control of the centre of the pitch, the way they recuperate the ball ... And today they've produced that same level of play from the first minute to the 95th. Without taking a breath. It's been an incredible exhibition of elite European football. It won't be easy but if they play like that against Barcelona they've definitely got a good chance of winning. I'll say it again so everyone is clear: City is the best team I have played against in my entire coaching career.

As we leave the stadium I share Koeman's comments with Pep. He's chuffed:

'He said that? Bloody hell, Ronald's a gem. I couldn't ask for better feedback. The trophies and titles aren't what *really* count. It's getting praise like that from people you rate.'

The following morning Guardiola's technical team have a long debate as they prepare for the recuperation session. They're already planning for the game against Barcelona. They won't be going with the 3–4–3 because it's clear that the players aren't yet 100 per cent comfortable with it despite executing it so well against Everton.

Dome Torrent makes the first suggestion: 'We'll need one extra man in defence at all times in the Barça match. We can't use the line of three because they'll tear us apart. We'll need one more. Four defenders because they'll definitely attack with three.'

Pep is even firmer. 'We'll need one more in defence *and* another in midfield. That's the only way to maintain possession. If we don't do that it will be impossible. They've got a "monster" up front. Let's see how we can stop him …'

They agree the focus of the match that will see Guardiola return to the site of his greatest triumphs so far. Four in defence, giving them numerical superiority in the middle of the pitch. Stopping Messi? That's another thing entirely.

Pep's German friend Michael Reschke, head of scouting at Bayern, is with us for Sunday training. It's a low-key training session, just the substitutes practising positional play. I take the opportunity to give copies of my recently published book, *Pep Guardiola: The Evolution*, to a couple of the coaching team whom I haven't previously met: Xabier Mancisidor, the goalkeeping coach, a serious, meticulous Basque, and Mikel Arteta, who, having just hung up his football boots, has immediately stepped into this role as Pep's assistant. Definitely another superb football coach in the making. I want to know what Arteta makes of the magnificent Sportcity (the multipurpose sports complex that houses the Etihad Stadium) and his response confirms my initial assessment. He has the kind of football philosophy that will take him to the elite levels of world football management in the years to come.

'It's an outstanding set-up but you have to fill it with substance and only the right quality of people can do that. Football clubs are made up of people.'

It's a sunny day and we stroll round the training fields with Manel Estiarte (who has worked with Guardiola since Barcelona) chatting about the coaching team.

'We're really happy. Dome Torrent is brilliant, Carles Planchart is an incredibly modest guy who can't do enough to help and Mikel Arteta has all the makings of a fantastic coach. He's really got his head screwed on.'

I ask him about Pep, about whether the three-year contract he's signed will give him enough time to dominate English football and, above all, build a true legacy at Manchester City.

'Pep will probably stay in coaching for another six to ten years, although I reckon six is more likely than another ten. Then again, with Pep you never know. He doesn't make long-term plans. It's all about focusing on the here and now rather than thinking too much about the future.'

We also chat about my new book, which describes the ways in which Pep's time in Germany changed him and how that might impact this new stage in England.

Estiarte: 'Munich was a great experience for Pep. It was his first time coaching abroad, away from Barcelona. Experiences like that toughen you up and make you mature very quickly. Pep gave you complete access to the dressing room and training at Bayern for your books because it was all so new and fresh, an adventure, and he was prepared to allow things he didn't allow in Barcelona.'

It's the perfect moment to tell him what I'm planning. 'Maybe it's not possible to say how long Pep will stay in Manchester but if he's here for any length of time, I think I'll write one more book. My third and final book about him.'

Estiarte's all for it, as I thought he would be. 'A trilogy. That sounds just right.'

So far so good. Prior to losing at Spurs, Guardiola has made an outstanding start to his first season at City.

The trilogy continues.

Good things come in threes … right?

SCENE 3. ON PEP'S SOFA …

Four months earlier, Barcelona, 27 June 2016

We're sitting on Pep's sofa staring at a TV screen, which he actually switched off quite some time ago.

It's a huge, grey sofa but, somehow, we're crushed up together. But not speaking. Just gazing at a blank screen …

Our only companions are the 87 packing cases and 15 suitcases piled up in one corner of the room, waiting to make their journey to Manchester next week.

I push Pep on what he thinks Manchester City will be like.

No response.

By now, what seems an endless, claustrophobic silence has filled the room.

Until, at last, Pep punctures it: 'I don't know … I just can't tell you what my team will be like, how we'll play. I can't visualise it as yet – I don't even know what players I'll have!'

It's the middle of my first visit chez Pep in Barcelona and here we are – sitting on his extremely comfortable couch, ploughing our way through a couple of litres of water.

Reason? Pep has his annual health check with Dr Albert Estiarte tomorrow and thus isn't allowed any solid food today.

Neither of us has moved for four hours.

We've watched Italy unceremoniously bundle Spain out of the European Championship (2–0).

Pep is unashamedly fascinated by the way the Italians are playing under coach Antonio Conte.

'Conte's version of positional play is outstanding! It's not the traditional model we're used to, it's much more about vertical. But he executes it brilliantly!'

Pep anticipates that the coming decade is going to unleash countless innovations in football and he's on alert to pick up ideas from other coaches: 'None of us can afford to stand still. Football is constantly changing and we have to change with it. I mean, Italy, playing positional football!'

'It's different from what I do with my teams but the mere fact that they're playing it at all … I really admire Conte for that! And his players, Buffon, Bonucci, Chiellini … the rest of them.'

City's incoming coach is transfixed by Conte's passion for his work and by the aggressive, intense style of football he demands of his teams.

They always fight to the death. In Pep's mind there's no question that Conte's Chelsea are favourites to win the league this season.

Chelsea have all the ingredients: a superb coach, outstanding players and no European matches to distract them from their rigorous training schedule and match preparation.

The 5–3–2 formation Conte is likely to use has another great advantage. It's easier, thus quicker, to learn and apply than Pep's more complicated model.

Ergo, Pep is sure that Chelsea will be favourites for the title: 'It's always a total nightmare trying to attack a 5–3–2.'

Even more so if you still have no idea what your own team is going to be like. 'I honestly can't visualise it yet! I don't even know who'll be our key players. All I know is what Txiki [Begiristain, the sports director] has told me. He says that we have a talented bunch of footballers and speaks very highly of Fernandinho, who's versatile positionally and could be very important to us. Txiki also really rates Fernando, who's a great team-mate apparently. But I've still no idea who I'll be able to sign or indeed whether the squad is going to change at all. So, you can see, it's basically impossible for me to visualise what my team will look like.'

I catch Pep's reflection in the blank TV screen and his glum expression indicates that something is bothering him. I'm reminded of a conversation we had in Munich in the summer of 2014, just after his bosses at Bayern had informed him that they were selling Toni Kroos despite Pep's heated opposition to the idea.

'Clubs promise you the earth when you're negotiating!' he'd told me then. 'But the minute the contract's signed all that's forgotten. And by then, of course … you're trapped.'

I suspect City initially promised him a total squad renovation but, now he's on board, they're imposing only a partial renovation via small changes. Pep is currently facing far too many unknown factors. Far more than he expected. He's got his work cut out in the weeks to come.

Then, suddenly, he rouses himself. 'I'll tell you this, though … any player who isn't prepared to run his legs off and work like a beast will be out and I'll put one of the kids in his place! There's outstanding talent in our youth team.'

Hours later, making my way home, I decide to jot down a few notes from our day together. And I never really stop.

Those notes are the basis for this book. My observations of seven years of life at Manchester City. The worst days and the moments of sheer joy, the matches – official and friendlies – the team talks and training sessions.

I've been there for it all, filling hundreds of pages with my observations on the technical and tactical aspects of City's football; their playing models and tactical variants, the way they take corners, how they defend set pieces, their counterattacking, successful or otherwise, and how they've dealt with opposition counterattacks.

Seven thick notebooks full.

I've had the privilege of countless conversations with Pep and most of his assistants. Usually after a game, rather than before.

I've observed City's tactical evolution and attempted to truly understand the hearts and minds of Pep's players. The very soul of the team. What you're reading is the culmination of that work. A finely drawn portrait of the legacy of Pep Guardiola's Manchester City.

Two days later, Pep gets his check-up results. He's as fit as a fiddle – although the hernia in his back is troubling him. And will continue to do so.

SCENE 4. WE CAN'T CHANGE THE SQUAD THE WAY YOU WANTED
Manchester, 3 July 2016

Guardiola has inherited 12 players over the age of 30. More than half City's squad. And 17 players are at least 28 or over – only 4 are 25 or under. This group urgently needs a radical overhaul – a swift injection of the youthful energy City need in order to achieve the competitive edge he's determined to instil.

Back in early June, Guardiola met Khaldoon Al Mubarak and Txiki Begiristain in Dubai. The coach requested ten new players but was told that City could only stretch to half that number. There were good reasons for their reluctance to do more. The club was keen to respect the contracts of current players and determined to keep the salary spend under control. Above all, it was important to continue their policy of amortisation, which would allow them to make bigger investments in key players further along the road.

City's directors view Guardiola's appointment as the start of a long-term project and know that he's eventually going to need serious financial backing to successfully replace the 'golden generation' of Agüero, Silva, Vincent Kompany, Joe Hart, Fernandinho, Yaya Touré etc.

And to elevate City to a higher dimension.

Essentially, Pep's employers reckon that his first season will be a transition phase during which current contracts and pending amortisations will come to an end. There will then be plenty of opportunities to finance high-value signings.

Pep gets it. But this is nowhere near what he's hoped for. He's certain he requires a new keeper, two full-backs, two central defenders, two midfielders, two wingers and a striker but has had to settle for a keeper, one defender, one midfielder and two wingers instead.

A substantial sacrifice. Fifty per cent.

Nor is Pep content with the specifics of who he's able to sign. He had set his sights on Marc-André ter Stegen and is gutted when, despite the German sweeper-keeper's own desire to leave … Barcelona refuse to sell him.

The Catalan club does agree to the transfer of Claudio Bravo, who was their starting keeper last season. On paper at least, the Chilean has exactly the right profile for the kind of goalkeeper Pep wants. Frustratingly, Pep can't pull off the signing of left-footed centre-back Aymeric Laporte from Athletic Club (Athletic Bilbao). For now at least.

But City do manage to sign three of Guardiola's key targets: right-sided centre-back John Stones, who will play a key role in bringing the ball out in the build-up phase; midfielder İlkay Gündoğan, whom Pep has dreamed of signing since coaching Bayern and whose metronomic skills will control the rhythm and pace of the team's play; plus Leroy Sané, the promising young winger from Schalke 04 in whom Pep hopes to find another Arjen Robben. There's also a bargain buy in the shape of veteran Spanish winger Nolito.

Unfortunately, the club's strategy has precisely the effect Pep suspected it would. Their decision to delay making the major squad improvements that Pep knew were vital results in a lacklustre season in footballing and economic terms. Those gaps and imperfections in City's squad just get more obvious.

The new goalkeeper proves vulnerable, they lack a left-footer at the heart of the defence, plus the technical abilities and physical energy of the full-backs are sadly lacking. Worse, Gündoğan suffers a bad injury in December so the centre of the pitch loses a gifted playmaker. Sadly, after a promising start, Nolito's form dips significantly and the general lack of goals forces the club to add striker Gabriel Jesus to their number during the winter transfer market. (The Brazilian striker was in fact signed in August but remained at Palmeiras until January 2017.)

All entirely predictable.

But the fact that it's understandable in context does absolutely zero to diminish Guardiola's frustration. Being forced to 'struggle' through the transition season really rankles.

Given that City only acceded to half his wishes to redesign the squad, Guardiola, more than ever, wants to keep things low-key in Manchester. His years coaching in Munich taught him that maintaining a low profile is the best way to go and, here in England, it's going to be more important than ever, if somewhat challenging.

The club's aim is to use the presentation of their new coach to really connect with City's fans. Above all, they want to begin creating a strong bond between Guardiola and their supporters. Any false perception that Pep thinks of himself as some kind of football Messiah coming here with 'highfalutin ideas' to singlehandedly save the club needs to be stamped out.

No, the Catalan needs to be viewed as just one more cog in what is already a highly efficient trophy-winning machine.

The presentation is a relaxed, informal affair. There's something of a party atmosphere and Pep is obviously enjoying himself. He fields a few questions from the fans but is very careful not to make any lofty claims, focusing instead on his excitement at the idea of experiencing first-hand the might and power of the Premier League.

He's genuinely relishing the prospect of visiting historic stadia, from small and idiosyncratic to globally famous, and testing himself in this footballing culture. He's excited by the thought of measuring 'his' City against the giants of English football.

Naturally for Pep, he's also very clear about his priorities.

'My main objective is creating an exceptional team spirit. We want City to play the kind of entertaining football that our fans will really enjoy. That's what we will try to produce but first we must create something special within the team: a real spirit of unity.'

Pep is choosing his words precisely.

He wants everyone to be crystal clear about his order of priorities.

To succeed in producing great football you must first create a strong sense of team spirit. You can't achieve the former without the latter.

From this day forward, team unity will be at the absolute core of the Cityzen universe ('Cityzens' is the name City fans have adopted for themselves).

Legendary US basketball coach John Wooden talked about something similar in his famous 'pyramid of success'. In Wooden's model, 'team spirit' is placed roughly halfway up but, Pep makes very clear, here in Manchester it will be the foundation of everything they do.

In reality, the seeds of this new focus were sown several months previously when, under Manuel Pellegrini, City reached the Champions League semi-finals only to be beaten by Real Madrid.

This was a historic achievement for the club, no question. But the matches also exposed a worrying lack of competitive spirit in the team. Pellegrini's men seemed apathetic – physically and mentally exhausted. City's president, Khaldoon Al Mubarak, was worried and told City TV: 'Losing to Madrid didn't anger me but I'd like to think that the players are giving it 100 per cent and that's not what I saw out there.'

The level of apathy he observed has become a fundamental concern for all the club's directors. They concur with Pep that building exceptional team spirit has to be the top priority of this new era – the cornerstone of everything.

'I want people to be proud of the way Manchester City play. I want our supporters to come to our games, spend two entertaining hours and then go home knowing that they've just watched some brilliant football. That's our huge challenge – to produce first-class football.'

Pep really wants to stress that everything will depend on these two priorities. 'First you build team spirit, then you produce great football. Then win one game, then another, and another …'

Having only given Pep half of his requested players, the club's directors want to protect him by moderating people's expectations about how much he can realistically achieve in the short term.

Khaldoon explains, 'There's no doubt in my mind that Pep is going to transform this team and take us to another level. His passion and dedication mean that we anticipate great things from him. Our great objectives for the next few years are to fight hard every year to win the Premier League and, of course, do our best to win the Champions League as well.'

Chief executive Ferran Soriano is also at pains to temper fan and media expectations. 'We want to get into a position to be able to compete for everything in the months when titles are decided.'

Having denied Pep his much-desired renovation of the squad, the club does as much as possible to protect him from the unrealistic expectations of starry-eyed supporters. Nevertheless, none of his employers are going public on the degree to which their decision has upset the Catalan's plans.

Pep's second-in-command, Domènec Torrent, an avid student of military strategy, has his own acerbic take on how this first season is likely to turn out, given the club's intransigence.

'The best generals win the biggest battles. But only because they're given the best weapons.'

SCENE 5. A BRILLIANT START
Swansea, 24 September 2016

City win their first ten official games with Pep in charge.

Ten out of ten. Thirty scored, just six conceded.

It's a brilliant start – so much better than Pep anticipated after his request to overhaul the team was rejected. And the two priority objectives, strong team spirit and first-class football, are also being achieved. Not a day goes by that one of the players doesn't comment on the 'team spirit'.

City's football is superb. Compliments flood in.

Manchester City are a force to be reckoned with.

This all began in Munich back in June when Karl-Heinz Rummenigge and Pep agreed it would be a cool 'transition' idea to kick off the new era with a friendly between Bayern, managed by incoming coach Carlo Ancelotti, and Manchester City.

The game is in the Allianz Arena on 20 July. Tens of thousands of fans have turned up to say goodbye to, and salute, their ex-coach. Pep's top players, most of whom have just competed in the Euros, aren't yet available and he takes the chance to try out youth team regulars like Pablo Maffeo, Tosin Adarabioyo, Angeliño, Brandon Barker, Iheanacho, Bersant Celina and Sinan Bytyqi. Plus there's room for a certain baby-faced, fair-haired youngster called Oleksandr Zinchenko.

On paper, it's pretty clear that Bayern are likely to dominate the game. Their lineup is incomparably stronger with the likes of Philipp Lahm, David

Alaba, Xabi Alonso, Franck Ribéry, Rafinha, Juan Bernat and Javi Martínez in the starting 11. Things are made even more complicated for the visitors when their bus gets caught in a traffic jam en route to the stadium, resulting in a 30-minute delay to kick-off.

Bayern's supporters are exuberant about their 1–0 victory (Erdal Öztürk's shot is deflected into the net by Clichy) and will undoubtedly be spending the next couple of days delightedly analysing their team's performance. This is a very passionate fan base who are always true to their favourite chant.

'Einmal Bayern, Immer Bayern' (Once Bayern, Always Bayern).

And the local supporters turn out in their thousands for City's training session at Säbener Strasse the next day. They've come to watch the Manchester City players work out and to catch a last glimpse of the great man – even in new colours. It's this, the huge support and dedication Bayern's fans have shown him, that will stay with Pep.

The happiest memory of his time in Munich.

But two City players have piled on the pounds and it's spoiling Pep's good mood. Anyone who has read my previous books will know that ongoing weight-control monitoring has always been a fundamental part of fitness management in Pep's teams. At Barcelona, still more so at Bayern and, now, here at City.

Before the summer holidays Pep requested a detailed chart showing the weight of every player at City and worked with the fitness coaches to set an ideal weight range for each man. Txiki Begiristain then sent the information to the players asking them to make sure that they came back for the new season fit and ready to start training with their weight well within the agreed parameters.

Today, it's obvious to everyone that two of the players are carrying extra weight. They're puffing and panting as they tackle fitness coach Lorenzo Buenaventura's exercises. Both of them have come back around 6 kilograms overweight! Pep takes one look at them and immediately decides that City needs to bring in a nutritionist to oversee the dietary changes that are clearly desperately needed. Of the various specialists available, he opts for Silvia Tremoleda, a fantastic Catalan nutritionist who, over the next two years, will introduce nutrition guidelines and standards, as well as a range of different menu plans which allow the players to maintain a healthy weight while enjoying the great food served up in City's canteen.

Essentially, Pep's first few weeks at Manchester aren't very different from the same period at Bayern. It's all about teaching and learning. And it's not easy. Understanding and assimilating so much new information are always tough, and he needs the team to change a lot of their routines and habits. His men have to learn a new model of football, develop a different rhythm and dynamic, and start to play as a cohesive unit. They need to find the competitive spirit that has been lacking and, of course, consistently produce good performances. In reality, Pep and his coaching staff aren't just building a culture of unity and team spirit. They're working to establish a whole new identity.

It's a bit like downloading a whole load of new, complicated software. Pep and his coaching staff require boundless patience as they calmly correct and redirect the players over and over again. They know that there are no shortcuts. Great oaks grow at the speed nature intends, and you can't argue with nature. It's just so frustrating when it feels likes some new instruction isn't going in. But it's the only way to make a success of this. Slow and steady.

Months later, when I ask him for his assessment of those early weeks, he tells me tersely, 'Let's just say there's still a lot of room for improvement and a lot of new things to assimilate.'

Having spent intensive time with his men during City's short, calamitous, pre-season tour of China, during which their match against José Mourinho's Manchester United had to be cancelled because of the dreadful weather and the Borussia Dortmund game ended in a disappointing draw (although the Cityzens won the penalty shoot-out), Pep has a pretty accurate idea of the strengths and weaknesses of each of his players.

He understands their technical/tactical abilities, their attitude to their physical health and the process of rehabilitation post-injury. In other words, he knows how each man trains, looks after himself and manages his recuperation. He also has a good idea of what drives each of them. Guardiola has already carried out a radical shake-up of the club's medical care and physiotherapy. He's recruited a team of top nutritionists and brought in new fitness coaches and video analysts. Sportcity's facilities are extraordinary and all he needs now is to get it all working like a well-oiled machine so that he can get on with creating the team ethos they badly need. He's going to be ultra-demanding towards his squad. Intense hard work all-round.

As Arteta said: 'clubs are made up of people.' Pep knows that if he develops the right environment the results will follow, even if this first season has to be a transition period before the complete renovation of the squad can take place.

It's not just what the players are learning that matters, it's how they approach their work, their attitude.

Pep is eagle-eyed for a desire to shake off the inertia and apathy that has dogged the squad. He wants guys who are hungry, willing to buy in to all the positive habits and dynamics he's committed to instilling. City's new boss makes it brutally clear from the outset that nobody is guaranteed a first-team place, and that whoever earns it will find himself in the starting 11.

Several players are loaned out or released in August. Jason Denayer, Samir Nasri, Wilfried Bony all go, as does the iconic Joe Hart, who Pep doesn't believe has the required skills and characteristics. Hart has been a first-class goalkeeper but has limited ability with his feet. Pep is totally upfront about what's happening. The England international will have to go. Hart's gutted, of course, but accepts the firmness of Guardiola's reasoning and becomes convinced that the door, here, is shut. Later on, he'll only have good things to say about Pep, specifically about the Catalan's honesty and clarity.

With those departures, plus the arrivals of Bravo, Stones, Gündoğan, Sané and Nolito, Guardiola has a squad of 23, although at the moment only 20 of his men are able to play. Gündoğan, Kompany and Sané are all still afflicted by injuries from last season.

Their first Premier League game looks straightforward. At home to David Moyes's Sunderland. Pep fields what appears, on paper, to be a classic 4–3–3.

Willy Caballero in goal, centre-backs Stones and Aleksandar Kolarov … but the 'pivot' Fernandinho in central midfield has the two full-backs, Bacary Sagna and Clichy, positioned either side of him. It's a repeat of the innovative strategy he introduced at Bayern. In front of these five players, De Bruyne and David Silva need to move freely between lines, finding creative space, while Sterling and Nolito use both wings to 'stretch' the opponent. Agüero is the centre-forward. This is 4–3–3 in appearance, 2–3–2–3 in effect.

The positional organisation of his men in this first challenge reveals four of Pep's fundamental principles in English football:

1. Centre-backs who bring the ball out well.
2. Inverted full-backs.
3. Attacking, 'inside' midfielders with freedom to roam.
4. Wingers who remain open and pegged to the touchlines.

1. THE CENTRE-BACKS

Guardiola's centre-backs have to protect their area just like any defender, but above and beyond their defensive abilities they must be exceptional at bringing the ball out in the build-up. Without passing precision from the back, City's positional play will be short-circuited and it'll be impossible to move possession into their opponent's half with the order needed to dominate them.

The centre-backs create the framework of the attack, establishing the path the ball takes in the build-up stage and initiating the movement towards their opponent's penalty area. But Guardiola asks even more of them. Once the ball is around the opposition's area, his game plan demands that the centre-backs remain close to the centre circle, 50m from their own goal, so that they can continue to press the play forward. Meaning there's a good chance they'll be out of position if there's a sudden counterattack. It's high risk, requires nerves of steel and a super-fast turn of speed.

Although Otamendi is a significantly more experienced centre-back, his passing isn't nearly as good as Kolarov's. For Pep, the Serb's passing ability with his left foot is a huge plus (the need for this skill is why he insisted, without success, on buying Aymeric Laporte). So the Serb, not Otamendi, starts today. This means that Stones – who was signed specifically for his superb control of the ball – can bring the ball out on the right and Kolarov on the left. Over the next few games, Stones will partner alternately with Kolarov or Otamendi. One of them defends better, the other moves the ball more skilfully.

2. THE FULL-BACKS

Full-backs now have a fundamental role in Guardiola's playing philosophy and bear no resemblance to the old-school defenders who defend from the touchline and only occasionally join the attack down the wings. No, these guys have to act as deep midfielders who move between supporting the attacking midfielders in the centre of the pitch and defending on the touchline when necessary.

At least that's the idea.

What Pep discovers in Manchester are four players who just can't get their heads around his vision of how a full-back should perform. Bacary Sagna, Pablo Zabaleta, Gaël Clichy and Aleksandar Kolarov are all hugely experienced and very talented, but seem unable to get to grips with this 'new' idea of becoming deep midfielders who support the attacking midfielders. In that sense, they're nowhere near as good as his wonderful Bayern quartet of Lahm, Alaba, Rafinha and Bernat. As Pep explains it:

'Using "interior" or "inverted" full-backs allows me to field five attacking players [three forwards plus two advanced midfielders]. The full-backs play a vital role, forming a line of three with the central midfielder, thereby maximising my other midfielders' attacking potential. This positional play hopefully means that my creative midfielders need to be on the ball and circulating possession less in the middle of the pitch than they are in or around the opposition penalty area to create or score because they know that their backs are always covered.'

3. CENTRAL MIDFIELDERS

Pep has found the perfect 'positional' central midfielder in İlkay Gündoğan. This was Guardiola's role in his own playing days and his up-to-date version of this concept flows naturally from what he used to do on the Camp Nou pitch. So it's only players with similar abilities as he himself possessed who make the cut; Sergio Busquets and Yaya Touré at Barcelona … Philipp Lahm and Xabi Alonso at Bayern.

It's no coincidence that Gündoğan is Pep's first signing on taking over at City. This is an organising midfielder who facilitates the game's 'construction' in the centre of the pitch, allowing forwards to 'move up together' into the box. Crucially, he's also a magnificent playmaker, equally capable of drawing opponents away from City's forwards or breaking up their lines of pressure through pinpoint accurate passing. Effectively, Gündoğan's range of skills and versatility make him either an outstanding organising midfielder or an attacking, creative inside-forward.

Unfortunately, an old back injury begins to act up at the beginning of the season and Gündoğan is out of action for the first few weeks. Touré's not yet match-fit so Guardiola deploys Fernandinho in central midfield.

The coach has total faith that the Brazilian can handle it: 'Fernandinho is so talented that I could put him in any one of ten positions.' The coming months will prove Guardiola right.

Both of Pep's attacking midfielders are extraordinary players whose skills enhance and complement each other. David Silva brings that rare skill where things go quiet and still in his brain while everyone else is thundering around, and then the pint-sized Spaniard does the smart thing over and over again. Kevin De Bruyne is forward looking and forward thinking. He makes City's play 'vertical' and elevates everything.

The coach gives them the freedom to roam between the lines at all stages of the build-up, to initiate joint attacking moves, seek to score goals and establish the rhythm of play at any given time. Like two 'free electrons' they run at the opposition, smashing their lines of defence and generating chances for City's forwards.

4. WINGERS

During his time in Germany, Pep's use of wingers evolved and changed. At Barcelona he demanded that his wingers stay as wide as possible, stretching opponents' lines of defence to provide attacking chances on the inside, where the unbeatable Leo Messi could work his magic. At Bayern the magnificent dribbling abilities of Robben, Ribéry, Kingsley Coman and Douglas Costa gave Pep a wide range of options for tactical adjustments to his wingers' role.

Now, here in Manchester, Pep wants to combine the two approaches. His wingers will stay wide, still 'opening' the game as much as possible, but waiting ultra-patiently for the ball to reach them so that they can dribble forward, beating defenders and getting into a position to make chances for a teammate or take the shot themselves. They are told to be daring on the ball, urged to go one-on-one.

'In my playing model, the wingers have to spend a lot of time alone on the wing, almost immobile, without getting involved in the action, without touching the ball. Just waiting. A bit like the keeper who can spend 40 minutes without a sniff of the ball and then, all of a sudden, has to leap into action to make a miraculous save. In my teams the wingers have to have a unique perspective on the game, much like the keeper.'

• • •

In Pep's master plan his keeper decides the initial direction of play, the central defenders bring the ball out until it is in their opponent's half, the pivot and the roaming midfielders move possession closer to the opposition box, while the wingers lie in wait, looking for the chance to score or give assists.

Against Sunderland however, not everything goes to plan. Willy Caballero's passing is poor and the forwards are nowhere near as effective as Pep would like. Although Agüero scores a penalty three minutes into the game, City struggle to get past the visitors' banked defence – Sunderland have 'parked the bus'. Twenty minutes before the end, City's defence appears to disintegrate and Sunderland gleefully make it 1–1.

It's looking like Pep's 'glorious' reign is about to get off to a very bumpy start.

But, in the dying moments of the game, Jesús Navas, in a perfect demonstration of what Pep wants his wingers to do, dribbles the ball towards Sunderland's goalmouth, where defender Paddy McNair, in an attempt to block Fabian Delph, deflects the ball into his own net. A last minute, skin-of-the-teeth triumph but a triumph nonetheless. Things have begun.

A couple of hours later, once Pep has recovered from the high emotion of the game, I ask what he thought of his team's performance.

'We started very well and did brilliantly bringing the ball out. Our attacking wasn't great, though. We should have focused on pressurising their central defence more … It's a decent first step though.'

• • •

Pep spends time the following morning analysing the game with Domènec Torrent and Mikel Arteta. As always he's happy to give credit where it's due: 'Dome, you won that match for us when you suggested we change to a three-man defence. When we swapped Clichy for Iheanacho, we broke Sunderland.'

During the game, with City in a muddle, Pep had pushed Torrent for suggestions on how to turn things around. The assistant had argued that they had too many defenders on the pitch – Sunderland were *so* defensive that moving to three at the back would immediately mean more players, numerical superiority, in attacking, creative areas. It worked perfectly and brought City their win. Pep's keen to acknowledge his second-in-command in front of Arteta. For Guardiola, recognising his people's successes is a fundamental part of building good team spirit.

Pep's in a great mood today. He's been watching the Rio Olympics and is bowled over by the performance of Katie Ledecky, the fabulous US swimmer who has won numerous Olympic medals and world championships in everything from the 200m to the 1,500m freestyle. She's become one of his sporting idols and he tells anyone who will listen all about Ledecky getting up before 5am to train every day for years, in all kinds of weather. He knows how gruelling her training schedule is, and he is evangelically impressed. 'I'm a huge fan. What she's achieved is amazing!'

City win their next nine games and the team keeps improving. There are powerful scorelines, like the 0–5 against Steaua Bucharest in the qualifying round of the Champions League first leg, where Agüero gets a hat-trick – as well as missing two penalties – and City hit the woodwork four times. And the 4–1 victory at Stoke's bet365 Stadium where the pundits had been predicting Pep's ideas would end in disaster. Because it's windy there. The doom-merchants don't trouble Pep, however – he's more inspired than ever to prove them wrong. He tells me later, not without sarcasm: 'A breeze like that couldn't stop us. Talk about the answer being "blowin' in the wind"! It was actually quite bracing. It kept their eyes clear and helped our play.'

And it's in Stoke that he hears the Cityzen supporters' new chant for the first time. They've adapted the words of the Dave Clark Five's 1964 hit 'Glad All Over' and are roaring Guardiola's praises: 'Coz we've got Guardiola, yes, it's Guardiola, baby it's Guardiola. So glad your mine.'

The goal difference isn't quite as impressive in their next two clashes: they knock Steaua out with another win, 1–0, then brush West Ham aside, 3–1 at home.

The international break gives Pep the chance to take a breather and review his first month. 'We're really happy so far. Things are going much better than we anticipated. Let's see whether or not they all come back fit from their international duty so that we can then do a really good job of preparing for the Champions League game against Borussia Mönchengladbach. That's going to be our biggest game of the year so far and we have to beat them to go through to the knockout round. I think we can do it. It'll be the next step in our process of building something extraordinary here.'

It's no surprise to hear him describe the 14 September match as their biggest so far. City's Champions League group now includes FC Barcelona, Celtic and Borussia Mönchengladbach. Of the three, Messi's Barcelona will definitely be the hardest to beat and Celtic probably the easiest. Which is why Pep is focusing on the Germans. He's sure that if they win at least one of their games against Mönchengladbach, City will make it through to the next stage.

Just four days before that vital match, already highlighted on his white-board, Guardiola faces another huge test. A Manchester derby – at Old Trafford. And he's extremely tense. This is going to be his first derby in England and he'll be facing none other than his old enemy: José Mourinho.

If that wasn't enough, he's going to have to do it without Sergio Agüero, who's serving a three-match ban for elbowing West Ham defender Winston Reid in the face during that 3–1 win. Although the ref missed the foul, and Agüero escaped any punishment at the time, the English FA later decided to sanction him for 'violent conduct' and issued the ban five days after the match. It all means that Pep is noticeably uptight about the upcoming clash. A Manchester derby is certain to be a significant change from the relatively straightforward wins so far.

United play a 4–2–3–1, with Paul Pogba and Marouane Fellaini behind Henrikh Mkhitaryan, Wayne Rooney and Jesse Lingard in the attacking trident and Zlatan Ibrahimović up front. Guardiola deploys his usual 4–3–3 with Claudio Bravo making his debut in goal. Stones and Otamendi are his centre-backs, Sagna and Kolarov the full-backs, whom he's asked to play open/wide; Fernandinho, De Bruyne and Silva are City's midfield; Sterling and Nolito the wingers, and Iheanacho is at centre-forward.

Guardiola's men play with positional daring against formidable rivals and are two goals up within 30 minutes. Kolarov launches a long ball down-field; Iheanacho and Eric Bailly both jump for it but the Nigerian wins the clash and heads it towards the box, where it looks like it's going straight to Daley Blind's feet. De Bruyne, much more alert, beats him to the 40:60 challenge and slots home from his position on the edge of David De Gea's area. This isn't the kind of goal you'll see a lot from the Cityzens. Instead of culminating a sequence of precision passes, this is the result of a very, very long pass of more than 60m fired from deep within their own half. Kelechi and De Bruyne have gone off script. To great effect.

Minutes later, the same two players are involved in the visitors' second goal. De Bruyne's curving shot comes off the post and Iheanacho, totally alone in the six-yard box having been played onside by the hapless Blind, calmly tucks it away.

Mourinho can't be happy with his team's performance but, as coach, he shares responsibility for his team's inability to contain City.

Silva and De Bruyne constantly draw United's midfielders out of position and Fellaini, in particular, is being run off his feet as he chases around like a headless chicken. Pogba just looks bemused, as if he has no idea what's happening. The two slow, confused United players are totally outclassed by Silva and De Bruyne, who establish complete dominance. De Bruyne, in particular, moves across the lines of attack ensuring that none of the defenders manage to mark him effectively.

Unfortunately for City's calm procession to victory there's a road bump, when a bad Claudio Bravo mistake just before half-time radically changes the mood of the game. From a free kick launched in towards the middle of his box, the Chilean goalkeeper tries to catch a ball Stones is about to head away. The Bravo-inspired tango only results in giving an easy volley to Ibrahimović, who halves City's lead. A maladroit, badly timed error – the first of many Bravo will make in the months to come.

Five minutes later, another moment of indecision from the keeper gives Ibrahimović another chance and only a timely intervention from Stones stops him scoring a second. Then, moments into the second half, Bravo fails to control the ball with his feet and ends up in a head-to-head with Rooney. He manages to avoid giving away a penalty, but only just, and it's clear that the Chilean's lack of confidence is unsettling the rest of his team. (Note to the reader: I comment on errors made on the pitch throughout this book. It's not my intention to criticise or embarrass the players, coaches or teams that commit these mistakes but simply to mention important moments in the games I describe. For me, making mistakes is an essential part of all sports and I know that Johan Cruyff, who always said that football would be a very dull game if nobody ever made a mistake, felt the same. Cruyff, a genius of football strategy, considered mistakes the price one had to pay in the pursuit of excellence. In this book, I apply that same perspective to my descriptions of errors and missteps.)

On the visitors' bench Guardiola and Domènec Torrent put their heads together: 'Dome, we need to change what we're doing. They've got us on the run.'

Torrent doesn't think that Bravo's errors are City's biggest problem. 'They've outnumbered us in the centre of the pitch ever since Ander Herrera came on [at half-time, for Mkhitaryan],' he argues. The two men know that they must regain City's midfield domination immediately, or else lose their lead. Pep puts Fernando at pivot and takes Iheanacho off. Fernandinho moves up beside De Bruyne and Silva is now the team's striker. The effect is immediate. United lose their numerical superiority in the centre of the pitch and equilibrium is restored. Tactically, Mourinho has made a good move but Pep and his staff have successfully countered it. Pep decides to send Leroy Sané on. The young German, one of Guardiola's first signings in Manchester, who has been recuperating from an injury, hasn't played a competitive game this season. Pep reckons he might just clinch the match for them.

Sané gallops on to the Old Trafford pitch and launches himself into the fray as if this is the last game he'll ever play. He's giving it 120 per cent but, unfortunately, his first sprint leaves him panting for breath, lungs screaming. It's too much too soon and he's already struggling. Domènec Torrent has seen it all before: 'It's so common for a player who's been out for months to overdo it in his first match back. Leroy got a bit carried away. He went out there desperate to prove how good he is but used up all his energy in that first move so that he was running on empty thereafter. But nobody should think less of him because of today's performance. Leroy is an excellent player – he's going to do great things for us.'

Truth be told, very little of that excellence is on display in Old Trafford and Sané produces only one real chance for City when, after a sprint down the right wing, he crosses to De Bruyne who thumps it off the post. The last 20 minutes see the advantage seesaw from City's sustained bombardment of United's goal – while producing seven clear chances, none go in – to the home side's assault on City's goal after Mourinho sends on a new striker (Anthony Martial for Shaw). Guardiola switches to a five-man defence and then, when Fellaini abandons the midfield to join his team's assault on goal as the fifth striker, De Bruyne comes off and Zabaleta joins his teammates to complete City's block of six in defence! To Pep's obvious relief, City's unheard of six-man defensive line holds United at bay until the final whistle.

It's a fantastic result. This first away game in the challenging, hostile territory of Old Trafford hasn't brought City's winning streak to a shuddering halt. And none of the old tension between the two coaches has been in evidence. Mourinho's behaviour has been welcoming and friendly, with Pep responding in kind. Crucially, Agüero's absence hasn't been the disaster Pep worried it might be.

Pep does come away with two serious doubts. Claudio Bravo's mistakes have really worried him. Moreover, his defenders, Stones, Otamendi and the full-backs, often looked nervous out there and, when they did, it clearly affected the rest of the team. But these remain relatively minor points in the great scheme of things and Guardiola leaves the stadium beaming from ear to ear, telling Torrent how pleased he is, despite the hiccups. 'And we did it using eight players I inherited from last season!'

It's the determination and courage of his defenders in the face of sustained attack in those final ten minutes that has impressed him. 'We defended like animals. It was amazing!'

Despite not having played in the derby, it's Gaël Clichy who sums up Pep's strategy for us. 'Pep wanted us to play very offensively and so he told us defenders to give constant support in pressing and recuperation of the ball. It was a total change for us because in the past we've tended to be very open and have conceded a lot of goals from counterattacks. Pep wants us to play attacking football and maintain an organised solid defensive structure.'

Good defending has been one of Pep's principal obsessions since he began coaching – it thrills him when his players turn in a rigorous defensive performance. All over the pitch. Under Guardiola, Barcelona conceded an average of just 0.73 goals per match over a total of 247 games. In his four years in charge, the Catalan club won three league titles and only once finished in second place, behind José Mourinho's Real Madrid. And across each of those four seasons Barça were the La Liga team that conceded the fewest goals. His record at Bayern was even more impressive. Out of 161 games, the Bavarians conceded just 0.69 goals per match over his three seasons in Germany. Effectively, Guardiola's teams have conceded the fewest goals in every league he has competed in since becoming a coach. And it's very nearly the achievement of which he's most proud. 'People tend to focus on my attacking record but I'm more interested in our defensive stats. That's where a coach's skills are really tested.'

It's been magical watching these two great coaches go head to head, each of them demonstrating superb tactical instincts in the heat of battle. This is a subject close to Pep's heart: 'Tactical ability isn't about number-crunching, it's about knowing exactly what to do in every moment of the game.'

• • •

City play their most important game of the season on 14 September when they host Borussia Mönchengladbach at the Etihad. Making it into the last eight of the Champions League might well depend on the outcome of this game. It's the second consecutive year these teams have met in the group stage, with City winning both games last season, 1–2 in Mönchengladbach and 4–2 in Manchester.

The match, originally planned for Tuesday, 13 September, has been postponed due to the massive storm that has battered Manchester. The Metrolink, which transports the fans to and from the stadium, is off and the pitch is a quagmire after hours and hours of rain. There's thunder and lightning too and UEFA have no choice but to postpone the game until the next day, when the weather is due to calm down.

Meanwhile, over in Barcelona, Messi and Co. have reduced Celtic to their knees with a 7–0 drubbing at the Camp Nou. Meaning that City vs Gladbach will definitely be the game that decides second place. All of which just makes Pep even more tense than usual. He's decided on four changes from the team he fielded for the derby.

Zabaleta comes in at full-back in place of Sagna; Gündoğan makes his much-awaited debut in midfield, replacing Silva, who's carrying an injury from the Old Trafford game; plus Agüero's back at centre-forward – dumping Iheanacho to the bench; Navas replaces Nolito on the right wing.

City dominate the game from start to finish with Agüero grabbing the starring role. He scores quickly. Shaking off his marker, Andreas Christensen, he receives a perfect left wing cross from Kolarov and thumps the ball into the net. Then, 30 minutes in, he converts the penalty awarded to City for Christoph Kramer's foul on Gündoğan. From 12 yards he puts the ball one way … Yann Sommer goes the other. Fifteen minutes from the end, he produces his best goal, when Sterling sends a lovely through ball into space for him to control and dribble past the keeper for his third. Another Agüero hat-trick – the second he's scored in the Champions League in less than a month. His last was in City's 5–0 thumping of Steaua in Bucharest on 16 August. It's also his third in the Champions League, the first coming in the 3–2 defeat of Bayern in November 2014.

All eyes are on Agüero but in reality his performance owes everything to City's total dominance. The Cityzens get 23 shots on target against the visitors' 3. Guardiola is still tense, he won't allow himself to relax until the final whistle. But he hasn't missed how well today's formation is working. The Stones–Otamendi partnership is well-entrenched at the back; Kolarov is doing superbly, moving constantly from the wing to the inside; Fernandinho, De Bruyne and Silva/Gündoğan are shaping up to be an unbeatable trio in midfield; and Agüero … is Agüero.

Guardiola does have doubts at right-back. The squad lacks technical ability in that position. And he has growing concerns about his wingers. Nolito started well but it looks like he's running on empty now. Navas is in great physical shape and is also an intelligent player but Pep isn't yet convinced he possesses the right level of skill. Sterling at least does look like he can cope playing wide and, alternatively, get in behind the striker to create and support in the middle. Twice, against United and Borussia Mönchengladbach, he's proven this. And Pep still expects big things from Sané despite his performance against United. There's still deep confidence in the ultra-quick young German.

Sané produces a brilliant assist for City's fourth goal, combining with De Bruyne as he moves the ball into the penalty area, dribbles past Christensen, nutmegs Kramer and gifts an assist for Iheanacho to slot home. A breathtaking display, particularly considering he's played only the last ten minutes of the game, and a positive indication that Pep was right to sign him. But is the fledgling Sané/Sterling partnership about to become Pep's new Robben/Ribéry combo?

'It's a difficult process. You can't just talk to them and expect everything to happen just like that. You have to consider their egos too. That's why a kid of 18 who has the humility to do what the team needs of him and is fast on his feet can sometimes adapt better than older players. My first challenge is to convince them. Just stay there on the wing, stay wide. Bide your time, be patient and your moment will come. Then, when you do get your chance, think about it: "How many opponents am I going to have to get past?" The answer? Just one. We've come up with this whole strategy so that you, the winger, only have to dribble past one man and sometimes there will be nobody in your way. On the other hand, if you stop paying attention and drift into the middle, how many will you have to get past? Four!'

During those ten minutes of playing time, Sané has followed Pep's instructions to the letter. He's stayed on the wing and doggedly waited for the ball to come to him, only then driving it past the sole defender in his way to provide a scintillating assist.

The coaching team is cautiously pleased with the way things have gone. Seven victories in seven games, including their triumph at Old Trafford plus a blistering defeat of their main Champions League rival. There's obvious room for improvement in the team's game and some aspects of the positional play need work, but they're definitely moving at cruising speed in the right direction.

Pep and Torrent keep reminding everyone: 'We're having to play with eight players we inherited from last season and only three of our own new signings. Which just shows how well the guys who're being asked to change are assimilating this new model of play.'

There's just one real 'fly in the ointment'.

Pep has decided not to include Yaya Touré in his Champions League squad list. He's unimpressed with Touré's lax approach to training and with his lack of match fitness due to the extra weight he's carrying. Dimitri Seluk, the player's agent, decides to go public with his disgust at the coach's decision, which inevitably just hardens Pep's resolve. 'As coach I will not tolerate the agent of every player who doesn't get a game going to the media to protest every decision I make.' Touré won't be back in the team until his agent makes a formal apology to the club.

Pep's successful early stage of his debut season culminates in City's victory at home against Eddie Howe's Bournemouth on 17 September. Just five seconds in, De Bruyne's effort looks like it's flying in but is expertly batted away by Polish goalkeeper Artur Boruc. Over the next 90 minutes City bombard the penalty area, producing 20 shots, 11 of which are on target, to end the afternoon with a resounding 4–0 win. The Bournemouth game highlights three fundamental landmarks, which haven't featured in previous wins: a counterattack that culminates in a goal; a goal from a free kick; and a pattern of City's attacking midfielders arriving in scoring positions having made well-timed late runs into the box. Green shoots, but dazzling ones.

De Bruyne sets the tone: 1–0 thanks to a direct free kick not far outside the opponent's penalty area. He's cute about it too. The Belgian shoots hard and low, a real daisycutter, so that when the wall jumps in unison the ball slides under their feet, leaving Boruc bemused and beaten. Anyone looking for clues only needed to watch Pep turn in euphoric exaltation towards Domènec Torrent, hugging him for having been the author of this neat trick. Until this point in the season De Bruyne has taken various free kicks without scoring – albeit two he crossed into the goalmouth ended with headed goals (from Agüero and Fernandinho). The other move that stands out is City's fast, precise and lethally effective counterattacking. Twice, Iheanacho picks the ball up in deep areas then, once via Nolito and the other time after a direct run himself, sets up De Bruyne, who is positioned at the top point of City's attack. The rosy-cheeked Belgian uses two of his standout skills to great effect: the speed with which he drives forward in possession and the precision of his passing. De Bruyne hardly seems to touch the ball at all as he advances … he's unstoppable. The first of these counterattack goals, which so please Pep, comes as De Bruyne feeds Sterling, whose cross lets Iheanacho score. City's second scoring counterattack is a carbon copy of the previous goal, except with the provider of the assist and the finisher switching places. Iheanacho provides, Sterling scores. Pep's properly chuffed and celebrates the goals in the happy certainty that his team has just added a new weapon to their armoury. With De Bruyne's speed on the ball and exceptional passing, City's counterattacking could become one of their most effective moves. Meanwhile, Iheanacho has quietly gone about scoring his tenth goal in the Premier League, an impressive ratio given that the Nigerian has only shot at goal 14 times.

Gündoğan popping up in scoring positions, having made clever, well-timed runs, is the third impressive development. When he was at Dortmund the German international wasn't prolific by any means – 15 goals in 157 appearances. Today, his Premier League debut brings his Premier League debut goal. De Bruyne spots that Iheanacho's decoy run has cleared a space and 'Gündo' has nipped into it. Belgian service, German efficiency: 4–0. Guardiola's intuition told him that Gündoğan has all the instincts and 'smarts' to let him score a lot more regularly – here's proof.

De Bruyne is the one who gets the hero-gram however. 'Kevin's had an outstanding game. Out of possession he fights for every ball and then when he's got the ball at his feet, he seems clairvoyant. He misses nothing.' Pep's found 'his' guy. At Barça it was Xavi, at Bayern it was Lahm and here at City it looks like De Bruyne is the chosen one.

Swansea's Liberty Stadium welcomes the Cityzens twice over four days: a League Cup game on 21 September then league duty on the 23rd. City win each time but at the cost of two injuries. Captain Vincent Kompany, who damaged his right thigh muscle at the start of May, has just come back after nearly five months out – including missing the European Championship. In added time, just as Gylfi Sigurdsson's goal gives Swansea faint hope at 2–1, the Belgian centre-back suffers yet another injury, his sixth in 12 months. This time it's his groin. A downcast Kompany limps off, devastated at this latest disaster, while his teammates restart the match. Pep's already made all three changes, City are down to ten. Swansea are hungry but Kompany clearly can't last another second. The final whistle goes so swiftly that City preserve their win. It's not been an easy three points for City, particularly because they've played with a reserve lineup, including five under-20s (Angeliño, Adarabioyo, Brahim Díaz, Aleix García and Iheanacho).

The second injury happens on City's Premier League return to Swansea and has far-reaching consequences; 79 minutes into City's decisive 3–1 win Kevin De Bruyne's hamstring suddenly tightens painfully. The injury mars an otherwise brilliant Kun Agüero display. The burly Argentinian scores twice, taking him to an impressive total of 11 in 6 matches (having missed three others because of that ban for violent conduct). He's been on fire – tucking away four of the six penalties he's taken: negotiations to renew his contract are almost finished.

Sterling's goal, City's third, also comes from a De Bruyne-inspired counterattack – as fast and precise as before – and convinces Pep that his instincts are spot-on: City's counterattacking can be devastating as long as De Bruyne assumes a central role. By contrast, Pep's not too happy with

Bacary Sagna's performance. Sagna provides the assist for Agüero's goal just three minutes in but is also victim to an unfortunate slip, which leads to Fernando Llorente's goal for the Welsh team.

All in all, though, Pep's reign is up and running – in style. Six consecutive wins means he's matched the current Premier League record for a new coach, set by Carlo Ancelotti on joining Chelsea in 2009.

Once back in Manchester the Catalan has a chance to reflect on what's been achieved so far – prior to travelling to Glasgow to face Celtic. City have won all 10 games, scoring 30 goals and conceding just 6. They've also hit the post 11 times. Pep's never had such a successful start before – neither in Barcelona nor in Munich. He's extremely satisfied. Deservedly so.

He and his son Màrius are planning a trip to Munich during the impending 'international break'. Màrius wants to catch up with friends there and Pep quite fancies the effervescence of Oktoberfest. Domènec Torrent hears of their plans and decides to join them with his son Arnau. The four of them will fly out of London on 2 October.

City look set to continue their record-breaking run. If they win at Celtic Park next Wednesday, they'll have equalled the historic record set by Tottenham Hotspur in the 1960–1 season. That side, led by the legendary Bill Nicholson, won 11 consecutive games, scoring 36 goals while doing so. They went on to win the title. Strangely enough, it was Manchester City who brought their winning streak to an end after holding them to a 1–1 draw at White Hart Lane on 10 October 1960. The team that day included club legends like German keeper Bert Trautmann as well as the great Denis Law. Pep fancies equalling Spurs' record on Wednesday.

But a chill wind awaits them in Scotland. A storm's brewing.

SCENE 6. THE FIRST BIG CRISIS
West Brom, 29 October 2016

A month has passed since that horrible night in Glasgow.

Just a month.

In those four weeks they haven't won a single game and Guardiola looks like he's aged years.

Despite City's tremendous start under their new coach and their incredible run of ten consecutive victories, they've only managed three draws and three defeats in their last six games.

A black month.

But here, today, victory at last. Pep's men leave the Hawthorns with their heads held high. They'd almost forgotten what winning feels like.

And there are lots of other positives.

On paper at least.

Despite their dismal October, City are still at the top of the league, sitting jointly with Arsenal and Liverpool on 23 points, one ahead of Chelsea. They're also joint top with Liverpool in terms of goals scored – 24 – with just 9 conceded. Spurs are the only side to have conceded fewer goals than City, having let in just 5 so far, but they've also only managed to score 14, a whopping 10 fewer than the Cityzens. All in all, City's stats are pretty good, despite their recent run of bad luck. One of Pep's maxims is that a league is lost in the first eight weeks, so, given that they're in the top spot after 10 league matches, he doesn't have too much to complain about.

Or so you'd think.

In actual fact, Pep's very troubled.

All his coaching staff are feeling it too. There's a real sense of foreboding. The last few results have brought them to a crisis point and Pep has even begun to be concerned about his job security. Six tough, punishing games without a win: that inauspicious draw in Glasgow, losing away to Spurs and then enduring another galling draw, at home to Everton. After suffering a lacerating defeat at the hands of a prolific Barcelona at the Camp Nou, they'd scraped another miserable draw at home against Southampton and had humiliatingly been eliminated from the League Cup by none other than city rivals, Manchester United. Six matches without a win. It's unprecedented for Guardiola. Today's superb victory has managed to staunch the bleeding but there's another massive test looming. In just 72 hours, Barcelona will be in Manchester for the return leg of their Champions League clash.

Pep's extremely worried.

He's genuinely concerned that the club might sack him if his team lose badly to Barcelona. It would be his first dismissal. Ever. I've never seen Pep in such a tight spot before.

City's 'black month' actually started back in September.

It's a freezing night in Glasgow. City arrive at Celtic Park knowing that the Scottish club has just suffered a devastating 7–0 loss to Barcelona, but if anyone's expecting Brendan Rodgers's men to be intimidated by the prospect of facing Man City, they're about to get the biggest shock of their lives. The Hoops start the game with all guns blazing, their aggression catching City totally by surprise. Even Pep, who prides himself on his careful match preparation, isn't ready for such a blistering attack. The home side go ahead in the first ten minutes and look all set to keep hammering away at Claudio Bravo's goal for the rest of the night. Pep and his men are stymied by this green-and-white hurricane.

Then Fernandinho rallies. He equalises quickly, only to have an own goal from Sterling put Celtic ahead again. Then, half an hour in, Sterling redeems himself and snatches City's second goal. It's turning into the toughest game City have had for a long time and, although you could put it down to De Bruyne being out with an injury or to Stones's absence from the centre of defence as a result of normal squad rotation, there's a deeper problem here. He can't quite put it into words yet, but Pep's intuition tells him there's something lacking.

He's realising that periods of high stress really accentuate the weaknesses he's already identified in his team and, indeed, in the squad as a whole. His full-backs are only just up to scratch, his centre-backs have limited abilities, his midfield isn't yet capable of dominating the centre of the pitch as he would like and the team's finishing needs work. But above all, in tense, aggressive clashes like this one, his men haven't yet shown the competitive aggression he needs. There's strong team spirit but, as a group, they still lack strength of character.

Strength of character is vital for any ambitious sports team; history is full of examples of teams whose resilience and sheer force of character have taken them far beyond the level to which they could reasonably aspire based on talent alone. Sadly, there are also countless cases of teams who have never realised their full potential despite their evident talent.

Both Barcelona and Bayern possessed the level of 'character' he's looking for, at an individual and a collective level. And the strength of those teams' competitive spirit was always, at the very least, on a par with their talent. Two tough, dynamic sides, cool-headed in moments of acute stress, confident in their abilities even when they go behind, unflappable in the most volcanic of arenas, with the kind of true grit that keeps you on your feet when you've just been punched in the mouth. Everyone has a plan until they get punched in the face. That's when the truly great teams stand their ground.

Here at Celtic Park, Pep begins to worry. His more experienced players like Bravo, Pablo Zabaleta, Otamendi, Kolarov, Clichy, Fernandinho, Silva, Gündoğan and Agüero are struggling to compete with the passion and energy of the locals. The game ends in a 3–3 draw, although City miss a good chance to snatch victory in the dying seconds. Pep leaves the stadium concerned. Even more than the poor result, it's because of his intuition that the steep learning curve his men have been on has just plateaued.

Four days later, at White Hart Lane, his worst fears are realised when City suffer their first official defeat of the season.

It's Sunday, 2 October. Matchday seven dawns bright and warm. Spurs, who are second, run rings around the Premier League leaders. A Danny Rose cross deflects in off Kolarov to put Mauricio Pochettino's men in front. It's City's second own goal in as many games and the fifth goal conceded in the last six matches as a direct result of a clear defensive error. Then, 30 minutes in, a succession of poor clearances and bad marking by Kolarov, Fernando, Zabaleta and Otamendi allow Son Heung-min and Dele Alli to combine with military precision to deliver the second goal. Agüero does manage to hit the post, but other than that City fail to impose themselves and there are only fleeting moments of the dominance Pep's looking for. Claudio Bravo saves Erik Lamela's penalty 60 minutes in but it's cold comfort. City look incapable of mounting any kind of comeback.

The defeat is disheartening but Pep's not yet clear if the bad results are circumstantial or if there's something wrong at a structural level. Guardiola and Torrent decide to cancel their trip to Munich and Oktoberfest. They're acutely aware that the optics of them slugging back beer in Munich while things at home aren't looking great would be damaging. They return to Manchester, planning to use this international break to formulate where City's game goes from here.

Pep and I meet over breakfast the next morning and I suggest that his players were perhaps just mentally exhausted after the game in Glasgow.

It's common for elite teams who have to play a game every three days to end up totally drained. Game after game of relentless, brutally hard top-level football can leave players with a kind of cognitive fatigue that prevents them from performing at their best.

Pep doesn't agree. 'It's more about our problems with the second balls and how we react to long balls that opponents launch into our area when we've been squeezing them high up the other end of the pitch. We're not good at defending long balls.'

I mention a recent interview the journalist Axel Torres did with the brilliant José Luis Mendilibar in which the Basque coach talked about how he wants his players to defend against long balls:

> Obviously there are teams who always use long balls whether or not their strikers can reach or control them. In such situations I want my defenders to jump against their forwards. Why? Because if I send one of my midfielders in to head the ball (which is what usually happens), we're almost guaranteed to lose possession because those "second balls" go to a midfield gap which you've just freed up to your opponents. I won't have any men in a position to recuperate the ball. So, it's one of my centre-backs who goes up for the aerial dual and my midfielders move closer ready to intercept and prevent our opponents getting a "second ball". And the nearest full-back will have taken up position in the space left by my centre-back.

Pep sees potential in Mendilibar's approach: 'That's really interesting. I'm definitely going to consider it. I always send a midfielder in for the aerial dual and leave my centre-backs to provide cover in behind. But, it's true, we lose almost all the second balls, particularly if our opponents are using a 4–3–3. In those cases their organising deep midfielder will win all the loose balls because we don't have an attacking midfielder or no. 10 who can challenge for them. Playing with a diamond shape in the middle sometimes solves that problem for us because then we tend to win the second balls. It's definitely something to think about. I'm always interested in learning from other coaches and even more so when the coach in question is one of the good ones, like Mendilibar.'

I'm keen to unpick other aspects of their game and tell Pep that, having watched the Celtic and Spurs matches, it seems to me that teams who press hard in the centre of the pitch are more difficult to beat.

'It's also probably because we're also having a lot of problems bringing the ball out, particularly on the smaller pitches where opponents crowd in on us. We also don't have the kind of tall forwards who can easily be spotted from the other end of the pitch. All of this is something I'm going to have to think hard about.'

I ask him how worried he is by City's recent results.

'When you've played 12 games in the league and Europe and only lost one, against a team like Spurs, and drawn another, you're doing pretty well. We've won six of the seven league games we've played, which isn't bad either. But we need to do much better. It took me a while to understand German football, particularly the strength of their counterattacking, and it's the same here. I still don't fully understand English football. In yesterday's game, whenever Tottenham gave us space to play the ball out, we completely dominated them but it was a different story when they began to press us, man on man. We couldn't cope. And it was the same against Celtic. But none of this was entirely unexpected. You have to go through this stuff so that you can then come up with the solutions. It's just as well I've got the next ten days to go over it all again so that I can work out what to do. Thank goodness for the international break. It'll give me the time to get to the root of the problem.'

Pep and his technical team make full use of the next ten days to review the formation he's using and he eventually opts to go with a 3–4–3 for the Everton game. He also takes advantage of the first team players' absence to get better acquainted with the youngsters from City's academy. He spends a week and a half training the likes of Jadon Sancho, Phil Foden, Brahim Díaz, Lukas and Felix Nmecha, Tosin Adarabioyo and Rabbi Matondo. He's impressed by all the youngsters but one player in particular stands out: 'Remember his name: Phil Foden. He's going to be extraordinary.'

The 3–4–3 Pep plays against Everton gives City numerical superiority in the midfield with Fernandinho, Gündoğan, De Bruyne and Silva, and offers several different channels for the build-up stage. It also gives his inverted wingers Sané and Sterling more options. City are electric and play a dynamic, elastic game. They're unrecognisable from the team we watched struggle through their last two games. If Pep's aim in using the 3–4–3 was to transform his team and ensure City's total domination, then he's pulled it off beautifully. Unfortunately he doesn't get the win he was hoping for and the team merits. Everton hunker down in their own area and hold City to a draw. At home at the Etihad, it's another blow for Pep.

But there's no time to feel sorry for himself. The Barcelona game is in three days.

'We'll need one more in defence and another in midfield. That's the only way to maintain possession …' Having one more in defence and in the midfield means that the 3–4–3 is replaced by a 4–4–2 with the midfielders in a diamond shape. If he wants to continue using the two wingers, he can't have a central striker too. This is the plan that Pep, Torrent and Arteta come up with three days before their men take on the most powerful attacking lineup in the world: Neymar, Lionel Messi and Luis Suárez.

• • •

It's Wednesday, 19 October, and Sergio Agüero is sitting on the bench in the Camp Nou. Pep has stuck to the plan and the team is without a striker today. Instead, De Bruyne is the point of the midfield diamond in front of Fernandinho, Gündoğan and Silva. Sterling and Nolito are stationed on the wings just behind the Belgian international and there are four in defence: Zabaleta, Otamendi, Stones and Kolarov. Inevitably as soon as the lineup is released the criticism starts. The pundits, most of whom have no idea of the tactical reasoning behind Pep's decision, can't believe he's left Agüero on the bench.

The game ends with a crushing defeat for City. Barcelona win 4–0, although the match hasn't been quite as one-sided as the scoreline would suggest. City have shown none of the stage fright they suffered in Glasgow and have retained possession for significant periods of the game, although less so than Barcelona. It's only the third time in his career a Guardiola side has achieved less time on the ball than the opposition. The first was in 2010 when Barça beat Getafe despite achieving only 49.2 per cent possession, and on the second occasion, in 2015, Bayern managed 49.9 per cent possession and beat Borussia Dortmund away, one goal to nil. Today, Pep's men have had 47.2 per cent of possession. Just the third time this has happened in the 422 games Pep has disputed since becoming a coach.

Barcelona's attacking trio are at their devastating best tonight with Messi producing a hat-trick and Neymar providing their fourth goal. Fortunately Willy Caballero prevented another by saving the Brazilian's penalty. Luis Suárez plays his part, making his signature sprints up front and peppering City's goal with shots. City play audaciously and manage to control much of the game but there's no doubt that the farcical circumstances that lead to the first goal have a huge impact psychologically. Zabaleta intercepts Andrés Iniesta's run into the penalty area and the ball lands at Fernandinho's feet. The Brazilian goes to clear it and somehow loses his footing, collapses on the ground and leaves Messi free to tuck the opening goal away. It feels like a ridiculous way to concede a goal but that's football for you. We are barely 15 minutes in to the test of fire.

Pep's men fight for every last ball. This is the competitive spirit and personality he was desperate for. They're constantly looking for the ball, they move it with speed and accuracy, generating several terrific chances which tonight are all, unfortunately, saved by Ter Stegen. The German keeper is Barcelona's best player, saving shots from De Bruyne, Nolito and Gündoğan, all of which look certain to go in and give City the equaliser. An even clearer chance is Stones's 45th minute header, which he puts wide when it's easier to score. There's another break for Barça when Lucas Digne's handball on Sterling's cross is missed by the refereeing team.

In the dressing room, Pep repeats what he told them hours earlier, 'Be bold, don't worry about the score, take the ball, pass the ball.' His men have played impeccably, regardless of what the scoreboard says. De Bruyne has handed the position at the top of the midfield diamond to Silva and alternates with Sterling on the right wing, From there, he makes constant attacks on the Barcelona defence, assiduously looking for City's equaliser. Fernandinho's inexplicable slip for Messi's first goal felt disastrous at the time but in the 52nd minute things get exponentially worse. Claudio Bravo messes up on a simple pass and, outside his penalty area, paws at Luis Suárez's opportunistic lob to stop it going over his head.

There's no argument. It's an immediate red card. To add to City's woes, Zabaleta gets injured almost simultaneously. His game plan in tatters, Pep takes Nolito off so that Caballero can come on as replacement keeper. Clichy then replaces the injured Argentinian full-back and City's whole defensive line has to take a step to the right – Otamendi as full-back and Kolarov one in at left centre-back so that Clichy fits in at left-back. It's the best Pep can do in a bad situation.

City are overwhelmed by a re-energised Messi who, taking full advantage of Barcelona's numerical advantage, finds the net twice in only eight minutes. Impressively, the visitors stick to the game plan and produce several dangerous shots at Ter Stegen's goal, most of them courtesy of De Bruyne. Caballero is also kept busy by Neymar and saves two goal-bound shots, one of which is the penalty. 'Third time lucky' for the Brazilian, who dribbles extravagantly around several opponents and slams the ball home. Barça go 4–0 up.

City have played entertaining, skilful stuff today, better in fact than in most of their victories. But such is football and it's results that matter. In the post-match press conference Pep is unrepentant and insists that his game plan was the right way to go, despite the loss. His detractors – and there are many of them – seem to consider this a ridiculous response. And they sneer at him.

'I'm responsible for our loss because I'm responsible for the team. But I'm not going to change my philosophy and ideas. I'd rather pack up and go home before I'd do that.'

The press pack insist that surely now he has to change his playing style. But, particularly in Munich, Pep's seen this many times before and is unde-terred. 'I've won 21 titles in seven seasons using this playing style. That's three trophies per season. So, no, I don't think that I'm going to change the way I do things. I can assure you that I considered all the alternatives but none of them seemed better than the game plan I went with. If it ends up that it doesn't work out for this club, then, fine, I'll walk away. But, there's no doubt in my mind. Today we played the game that gave us the best chance of winning. One of my friends, Ronald Koeman, said publicly that he's never encountered a team that plays as well as Manchester City. As far as I'm concerned, that says it all. I couldn't ask for better feedback.'

City have now gone four games without a win. It's just the third time such a thing has happened to Guardiola in his coaching career. But at dinner later in the W Hotel, looking out over the Mediterranean with the twinkling lights of Barcelona behind him, Pep, sitting with his brother Pere and his three trusted assistants, Torrent, Arteta and Planchart, raises his glass of red wine and proposes a toast. To his football philosophy.

'We've won an incredible amount of trophies but I don't want people to admire us just for winning. I want them to love the way we play too. If you look at the "greats" of history, they weren't always victorious. Hungary in '54, Holland in '74, Brazil in '82 … all of them loved and admired throughout the world and yet, they lost. Staying true to your ideas, your own ethics. That's more important than the biggest of wins. Staying true to yourself. With titles you accumulate pieces of metal. But by playing a certain kind of football, you can win people's hearts. Don't lose faith. We're sticking with our own ideas. No matter what.'

Having sat down for dinner feeling totally dispirited, Pep's assistants are delighted with Guardiola's ideological manifesto. He wants to win with Manchester City but he'll do it his way, regardless of the difficulties. Winning trophies is still a key objective, of course, but he's convinced that they'll only achieve that by playing his style of football. Pep has huge respect for other coaches' ideas and approaches but, for him, his is the playing philosophy likely to bring both the success the club wants while also entertaining and delighting people at the same time.

The following morning there's a board meeting at FC Barcelona. All is not well and several key board members are deeply worried. Barça has enjoyed ten years of unrivalled success in Spanish and, to a certain extent, European football. Between 2006 and 2015 the club has won four Champions League titles (one with Frank Rijkaard, two under Guardiola and one with Luis Enrique) as well as six league titles. Barça's thrilling style of play has also left an indelible mark on the history of the game. But 12 hours after watching their side beat City 4–0, several board members are deeply worried about what they saw the night before. Later, one of them will tell me exactly what had them so worried: 'You could see from the football they played that City have a genuine identity. And we don't. They may have lost the game but we're at danger of losing all sense of our identity.'

Of course, on 20 October 2016, nobody could have imagined how prophetic these words would be. Things were going to take a positive turn for City. Not so for Barcelona.

As the City contingent leaves the Camp Nou, one of the press pack wants to know what the coach said to them in the dressing room after the final whistle. He addresses his question to Nolito, who mutters that he has no idea, given that Pep had spoken in English. Everyone around him has heard and the player's response is quietly noted by the management team.

· · ·

Back at the Eithad, City's first game is against Southampton. Pep returns to his tried and tested 3–4–3 and a disappointing 1–1 draw once again belies the quality of the flowing, finely tuned football City have played. Pep's men are controlling and meticulous across all zones, moving the ball with precision and effortlessly dominating the midfield. Today the four midfield positions form a rectangle with Fernandinho and Gündoğan at the base and Silva and De Bruyne higher up. Sané and Sterling are the inverted wingers and Agüero's back as striker. Stones, Kompany and Kolarov form the backline. Everything is going swimmingly on this sunny Sunday afternoon until the 26th minute when Stones makes a disastrous mistake as he tries to pass to his keeper. Southampton's lightning-fast forward Nathan Redmond sees his chance and takes it. Another defensive error that has cost City dearly.

They're swimming against the tide. Again. Just like the last four matches when they've gone behind. Worse follows when Stones's equaliser is mistakenly given as offside. City boss the second half. Ten minutes after the break Iheanacho, on for De Bruyne at half-time, equalises with a panache Agüero would admire. City batter Saints for the remainder of the match – but 2m-tall (6ft 7 in) Fraser Forster repels everything. Five games, no win and, grouped together in the centre circle at the end of the draw, City's staff and players try to drag their morale up from the ground. This is when team spirit needs to meet with character head-on.

Another potential negative is that his 3–2–2–3 formation, in which he's had such faith and which lets City play the brand of football he wants, yet again hasn't produced the ultimate product: victory.

For their return to Old Trafford in the League Cup Pep returns to a 4–3–3: 'It's all about knowing exactly who we're up against and adapting our tactics accordingly. Every single guy in my team has to be absolutely clear about our opponent's style of play and know what to do at all times.'

There's another reason for changing the formation for this match: Pep wants to use his non-regulars: Maffeo, Clichy, Aleix García, Fernando and Jesús Navas. United win the derby thanks to a Juan Mata goal but it feels like it could have gone either way. Both teams have produced outstanding foot-ball, matching each other in terms of possession, chances, shots on goal and passes. In the end, the combined might of Ibrahimović, Marcus Rashford, Mata and Pogba win the day, and although Pep has been impressed with his chosen players today, he's also acutely aware that this is their sixth game without a win. He's never had a run of bad results like this.

For the West Bromwich Albion game on 29 October, Pep fields more or less his top side, minus De Bruyne, who starts on the bench. Although Barça's visit to Manchester for the return leg is looming, Pep doesn't want to risk another bad result, and has therefore chosen almost all of his best players for the visit to the Hawthorns.

Only the use of Fernando at right-back raises eyebrows. West Brom play 5–4–1; City counter with 2–3–2–3 when bringing the ball out from the back and then 2–4–4 whenever they move into the Baggies' half of the pitch.

Fernando and Kolarov, the full-backs, close ranks around Fernandinho in the middle of the pitch leaving Otamendi and Stones as the only 'real' defenders when City have possession. It works: City have 81 per cent posses-sion in the first half, then 70 per cent during the next 45 minutes. City tear West Brom apart. The score is 4–0 but there is an infinite number of good goal chances (amidst 21 shots at goal).

Sergio Agüero has gone six without scoring but, during the cascade of chances, hits two. Gündoğan, so good as a provider, begins to show real quality in his finishing too.

At long last the team has something to celebrate. And they do so. Despite their bad run, they are still at the top of the Premier League, but Pep isn't ready for self-congratulations just yet and plays things down a bit for the media at the press conference. 'When you don't win a game, it's not just the number of points lost, it's the blow to your self-confidence that risks affecting your next game. It doesn't matter how well you play, how many things you do perfectly, if you don't win, all your explanations sound like excuses.'

As we leave the Hawthorns it's clear that Pep is still in no mood to cele-brate. He doesn't even want to talk about the resounding victory they've just pulled off. His mind is already focused on the Barça game. I've never seen him so exhausted after a game and wonder if he still believes that his job is hanging by a thread. He's been through this before, back in the summer of

2008 when his Barça side lost his debut game against Numancia (1–0) and then only managed a draw at home against Racing Santander (1–1). Back then, the great Johan Cruyff was there to support and defend him against the people who were calling for his head. Now it's Txiki Begiristain who has his back, but only time will tell if Begiristain has the kind of weight and influence at City that Cruyff had at Barcelona.

Pep's voice trembles a bit as he bids me goodbye.

'If we lose on Tuesday they're going to kick my arse so hard that you'll have to go all the way to Australia to pick up the pieces …'

SCENE 7. 'IT'S BEEN TORTURE'

Düsseldorf, 23 November 2016

'These past few months have been a complete nightmare. I've been a nervous wreck.'

Pep's face is expressionless.

As if almost gagging, his hand to his chest, the words rush out. 'It's been total torture ever since we drew against Celtic in Glasgow.'

It's only then, having got it out, that he picks up his wine glass. He's liberated the demons that have harried him since September, and the start of the Champions League group phase. Nerves and worry initially; anguish and torture as the weeks passed. Two months haunted by a level of anxiety that no one except his family was properly aware of. A gnawing feeling of disquiet that made him sick to the stomach and kept him awake night after night.

They've only managed a draw tonight but, right now, on this cold November night in Germany, it's a huge relief for Pep. They're into the last eight of the Champions League. In the eyes of the world, it's probably no big deal.

The very least they'd expect of Pep Guardiola's Manchester City.

But Pep knows different.

His team is coming apart at the seams.

Their defence is a disaster, as was only too evident against Borussia Mönchengladbach. The two full-backs who should really be first choice, Sagna and Clichy, have been benched and even when Pep decides to move from three to four at the back it's Jesús Navas he opts to use as an improvised right-back.

The weaknesses he's seeing in central defence – Otamendi's sluggishness, Stones's lack of physicality in one vs one clashes and Kolarov's poor marking – are costing the team dearly. They've conceded goals in 11 of the last 12 games. Nor is his midfield functioning with the harmony the coach envisaged when he formed his quartet of Fernandinho, Gündoğan, De Bruyne and Silva.

Fernandinho is in the process of completing his metamorphosis to organising midfielder but it's precisely that process that has created another problem. The Brazilian ends up out of position far too often. He's terrific in one-on-one battles, tackles, man-marking, he carries out transitions with speed and energy, and is great on the ball. But when he drifts out of position, the whole balance of the team suffers.

Gündoğan works even harder to compensate for this but there's another problem. De Bruyne, a naturally vertical player, prefers to stick to the wing, thereby leaving middle spaces empty, particularly since David Silva likes to push into the opposition penalty area as much as possible.

So, ironically enough, it's the natural tendencies of these unquestionably great players that dilutes the impact of what should be City's aimed-for numerical superiority in midfield. Result? They don't always manage to impose as tight control as they would like in some of their big matches, including this one in Mönchengladbach.

Up front, Pep hasn't yet found the ideal partner for Agüero – the only player he currently considers 'untouchable'. Sterling always performs well and as a result is the player with the most playing time, but Nolito's initial impressive contribution has become less consistent, perhaps because his limited range of dribbling and dummies is now too familiar to opponents. He's a bit predictable.

Leroy Sané is yet to hit full form: he's only started three games so far and, including tonight, hasn't played a single minute in the last five matches. In Mönchengladbach, Pep picked Jesús Navas as his other winger. Navas isn't an extraordinary player but he never produces a poor performance and Pep is happy to use him more and more. In fact, the following day, talking to Juanma Lillo (who managed Guardiola at Dorados in Mexico at the end of his playing career and would later join City's backroom staff), I mention how well Navas did as a full-back. Lillo tells me, 'Pep's delighted with Navas, 100 per cent. He never gives the ball away and anything he does, he does well.'

Borussia Mönchengladbach expose City's weaknesses. Nevertheless the 1–1 draw leaves Pep's team guaranteed to qualify for the knockout round and they only look properly overwhelmed in the 22nd minute when Raffael takes advantage of a moment of weakness from Stones, who is grabbed and pushed to the ground by Lars Stindl, to put the home side 1–0 up.

The goal knocks City's confidence and they suddenly look nervous and clumsy. Guardiola addresses this by moving Navas to full-back so that City are now using a four-man defence. De Bruyne replaces the Spaniard down the right wing. And it's he who provides Silva with the assist for his 45th minute equaliser.

First Stindl and then Fernandinho are sent off so Pep is forced to keep altering his format. His first move, when it's 11 vs 10, is to move Navas and Kolarov inside, flanking Fernandinho, with De Bruyne and Gündoğan as attacking 'inside' midfielders plus Sterling and Silva on the wings. Then, six minutes later, when the Brazilian is red-carded, Pep puts Sagna on, using him and Kolarov as traditional full-backs in a flat four, Navas, Gündoğan, De Bruyne and Silva in the middle of the pitch and Agüero up front alone. At 10 vs 10, City generate three excellent chances but in the end have to settle for the draw. The result means they've achieved what they set out to do and the mood in the dressing room is celebratory.

At dinner later, in Düsseldorf's Meliá Hotel, flanked by Domènec Torrent and Mikel Arteta, Guardiola explains that he won't be able to solve the team's problems in the short term. Having only been permitted to renew 50 per cent of the squad, it's been impossible to compensate for the serious structural faults solely with tactical solutions. But today's game, specifically the result, has bought them some time before February. As far as the Champions League is concerned at least. It's then that he owns up to how hard things have been for him.

'It's been torture ever since we drew against Celtic in Glasgow. Or really since the Champions League Draw and having to qualify for the last eight. These past few months have been a nightmare … I've been a nervous wreck.'

He warms to his theme: 'Thank goodness a draw is enough to get us through. We've lost fluidity, we aren't bold enough when we bring the ball out, it's like we don't dare to really play … my players only really go all out when they're losing! Then they become the kind of ballsy team we had in Bayern! They pull out all the stops, create lots of chances and produce great football. But when they become too risk averse, it's very difficult and they look stiff and wooden. I think the same thing that happened at Bayern will happen here. It's going to be tough to find a balance between maintaining control and playing ballsy, daring football. But at least we're guaranteed two Champions League games in February. Now we can focus completely on the Premier League.'

Torrent is keen to point out that City's position in the league is more positive than it looks: 'Chelsea and Liverpool are very strong but bear in mind one crucial factor. We've played seven games more than them in three and a half months: the two qualifying games against Steaua and the five group matches. Seven games more than Chelsea and Liverpool in 14 weeks. Yet we're more or less in the same position as them. It's definitely a good sign.'

Pep has the last word: 'Let's see if we can keep pace with them until March and April when we can launch our sprint for the tape!'

City slip from the top of the league during the month of November. After the win at West Brom on the last Saturday in October they're in pole position but then lose two points at home when Middlesbrough equalise in the 91st minute after another defensive error, this time because of Clichy's poor marking of Marten de Roon. Despite the scoreline, City dominate the game with 25 shots on goal and triple the number of passes produced by the visitors.

A wonderful, weighted pass from De Bruyne, rapidly becoming the formidable Belgian playmaker's signature move, sets up Agüero's goal but isn't enough to maintain City's position at the top of the league before the next international break.

Once league football restarts, City visit Selhurst Park and get a good win (1–2), which allows them to make it to the end of November tied with Jürgen Klopp's Liverpool and just a point behind Conte's Chelsea, who lead with 28 points. The Crystal Palace match sees the return of three players: Bacary Sagna, out through injury since the end of September; Yaya Touré, who's been frozen out by Pep since 24 August; and captain Vincent Kompany, who has suffered perpetual injury problems and has only managed 213 minutes in 19 games.

Kompany and Touré are the headline names in the beating of Palace. For very different reasons. City's captain is unfortunately knocked out by Claudio Bravo in an accidental clash around the 25th minute and Touré delivers both of City's goals, the first courtesy of a fantastic one–two with Nolito. City's second is an oddity: De Bruyne's daisycutter, fizzing low across the turf from the corner, and Touré side-footing home first time, unmarked, and with Palace all over the place.

Yaya Touré's return to the team sheet was contingent on the player agreeing to the conditions outlined by Pep weeks ago. It's taken him until 4 November to finally get round to issuing a statement apologising to the club and the coach. 'I wish to apologise – on behalf of myself and those who represent me – to the management team and all those working at the club for past misunderstandings. Those statements [by his agent Dimitri Seluk] do not represent my views on the club or the people who work there. I have nothing but respect for Manchester City and only wish the best for the football club.'

Despite being conscious that Touré has used face-saving euphemisms, and equally aware that Seluk himself has not apologised, Pep decides to let it go and puts the big, talented Ivorian in his starting 11 at the first opportunity – Selhurst Park.

Just a few weeks previously, Pep had faced his first 'match-ball' – Barça's visit to the Etihad. An all-or-nothing clash. The coach instinctively believes that another defeat could mean the end of his role in the City project. But, typically, the fact that it's make or break seems to give the team wings and on 1 November they beat Barcelona 3–1 despite their magnificent attacking trident of Messi, Neymar and Suárez.

Although City come away with an impressive result, it's a brutal test for Guardiola's men, who press hard when Barcelona bring the ball out with the sharp, aggressive front three of Sterling, Agüero and De Bruyne. Fernandinho, Gündoğan and Silva make up the midfield with Zabaleta and Kolarov at full-back; Otamendi and Stones make up the backline.

The aggressive ambition of the home side almost pays off ten minutes in when the referee fails to penalise Digne for his penalty-box foul on Sterling – no spot kick. Instead, the visitors are about to grab the initiative. Agüero takes a shot, which is blocked by Samuel Umtiti. Messi picks up possession just outside Barça's box and sends a long ball to Neymar, who's not well marked by Gündoğan. Meanwhile Messi is sprinting up the pitch to finish his counterattack – De Bruyne unable to do anything to stop it.

With 20 minutes gone, Guardiola feels the noose beginning to tighten. Barça assert increasing control of the game and the only thing preventing them running away with it is the gigantic figure of Willy Caballero filling the goalmouth. The coach's heart is in his mouth. Again.

But football is a sport of errors and just one slip-up from Barcelona turns the game. They lose the ball to Agüero as they bring it out from the back. He plays it to Sterling who sends it straight to the centre of the box into the path of Gündoğan, who slots it away for the equaliser 38 minutes in.

The final scoreline won't reflect the respective quality of the two sides today. Barcelona will end the game having had 72 per cent possession while City have spent much of the game chasing shadows. But it's been a gutsy performance and Pep's men have played with self-belief and determination.

City go ahead in the 58th minute thanks to a superb free kick taken by De Bruyne. Ter Stegen appears not to see the ball's trajectory, his view blocked by his own side's defensive wall as well as City players. With the crowd now 'believing' and adding considerable vocal support, City get their second wind and produce several more chances. But neither Agüero's two opportunities nor De Bruyne's counterattack pay off. Fortunately, André Gomes misses a good chance when his shot hits the crossbar after a serious error from Stones.

In the end, it's Gündoğan, who has been perfecting his goalscoring, who bursts forward from the centre of the pitch and finishes a magnificent action sparked by Agüero, continued by De Bruyne and served up by Navas. Winning 3–1 is a huge achievement. Overcoming this massive obstacle becomes Pep's second major triumph after beating United in the derby at Old Trafford. The victory is also precisely what's been needed to reinforce the players' self-belief.

That evening, even despite defeating Barcelona, Pep's still very uptight. He's got that same knot of anxiety in his stomach that he's had since the draw in Glasgow but at least he no longer feels like there's a noose around his neck. He can breathe again.

'It's fantastic, fantastic. If they'd got a second goal in the first half I'd be in Australia right now. But that's football for you. The first 30 minutes were a Barça extravaganza, a fucking spectacle. We couldn't lay a glove on them.

But then in the second half, once we'd equalised, it really lifted us and just knowing how much we needed the points made all the difference. I think we could have scored even more goals. It gives us new life. If we don't do anything stupid, we're almost there. If we manage to get out of this group everything will feel calmer, more straightforward.'

The Mönchengladbach game is just around the corner. City will get the draw they need to go through.

Pep will be able to stop worrying and start sleeping again.

Or so he thinks …

SCENE 8. DRINKING FROM A BITTER CUP

Manchester, 5 December 2016

There are a lot of positives.

After City's strong start to the new season, they've managed to get through their first big crisis and save the match against Barcelona. The Mönchengladbach result meant Pep could begin to rid himself of the desperate anxiety that had plagued him for months. But things still feel pretty shaky – Pep hasn't yet achieved the level of stability he believes he should have. When he signed up for this project at City he never imagined things would be so tough – days and nights of stress and worry.

He's drinking from a bitter cup.

We chat about everything he's going through and, as he often does, he explains that he's found inspiration outside the world of football: 'I've just read a good interview with Gregg Popovich in which he says that people always want immediate victories and don't understand what it takes to create and develop a winning team. Patience, that's what we need. Patience.'

Statistically speaking this is the lowest point of Guardiola's career. After winning away to Burnley (1–2) and losing at home to Chelsea (1–3), City are seven points behind the leaders. They've played 24 games, won 14, drawn 6 and lost 4. They've scored 50 goals and conceded 27 (2.08 in favour, 1.12 against), which compares badly with Pep's past average. They've won 64.3 per cent of their league games and just 50 per cent of their Champions League clashes.

Pep's asking for patience but he's absolutely exhausted.

Luckily for Guardiola, his right-hand man Manel Estiarte, who's usually happy to stay quietly in the background, has a clear-headed, analytical perspective on whatever they're going through. 'I've told Pep not to worry, not to compare his third year at Bayern with what he's going through just now. Bayern's football wasn't always as impressive as it was in that third season. At the start, we played even worse than City are just now but it's not something we remind him of. Memory can play tricks on you. The big difference is that in Munich it was often the talent of individual Bayern players which won us games. We won a lot of points thanks to one of our guys producing a last-minute moment of genius. We just don't have the same level of talent here and we also haven't had a single piece of good luck since we started. We could have easily beaten Chelsea 3–1 but ended up losing 1–3 despite the fact that they only had one chance in 60 minutes.'

Estiarte has always been able to retain a certain amount of detachment and tends not to get swept up in the emotion of the team's latest result. He doesn't get distracted and remains focused on the path ahead. For him it's all about the 'process'. 'The really important thing is that we're doing a good job. Everyone's pulling in the same direction and we're on the right path. Winning the Premier League is a tough proposition but we're going to give it our best shot. The Champions League is an even bigger ask but if we're lucky with the draw, we might have a chance.'

'But the crucial thing is that we get the process right. Perhaps it's difficult to keep believing in the process when you're not getting the results you want but that's exactly what we must do: place less importance on the results and judge ourselves on whether or not the process is going well. And it is. There are no excuses. We have to continue on this same path. And I'll tell you this, if we'd had a bit of luck in just one of our games, we'd not be talking about the process at all. We'd be sitting here congratulating ourselves on how quickly the team has adapted to Pep's philosophy.'

Of course, Estiarte isn't blind to the weaknesses and faults that undoubtedly exist. 'Obviously we shouldn't kid ourselves. We definitely have weaknesses in certain positions. And the players we've signed haven't yet fully come into their own. John Stones, for example, is having a bad time personally but let's not forget that he's only 21 and is a player with a lot of talent. Pep is really concerned that his signings haven't yet met his expectations but I've told him not to worry. Stones is going to be a great player for us, as will Sané. Even if it all happens gradually. We're already seeing them produce some special stuff, which bodes really well for the future. And Gündoğan is a superb player. None of them are performing at their true level as yet but we need to be patient. They'll come through for us. I keep telling Pep that he has nothing to blame himself for. He needed to make some signings and we didn't go mad and spend a fortune for any of them.'

Only time, the great sculptor, will tell if Estiarte is right to remain focused on the medium term and to continue to believe in the process and in the players Pep has signed. For the time being, though, they're drinking from a bitter cup.

SCENE 9. 'DO I REALLY WANT TO BE A COACH?'
Manchester, 16 January 2017

His first Christmas in Manchester has been bleak and miserable. The kind of Christmas you don't forget – for all the wrong reasons. They've lost to Chelsea at home (1–3), been held to a draw by Celtic (1–1) and allowed Leicester to tear them to pieces (4–2). They've handed Liverpool a win at Anfield (1–0), and taken a beating from Everton at Goodison Park (4–0). It's a nightmare. A Nightmare Before Christmas.

The only bright spot is their thrilling fightback against Arsenal after the London side go ahead at the Etihad with an early goal, leaving City trailing behind at half-time. Their eventual 2–1 victory represents the kind of comeback City hasn't achieved since November 2012. A brief high point in a disastrous run of games.

Pep's on his knees. So is the team.

Their punchy start to the season is a distant memory and right now it feels like they're wading through mud. They're well and truly stuck. Their coach is struggling under the weight of all the defeats and his players are beginning to understand what Marcelo Bielsa meant when he said, 'Defeat gives you a bad odour.' The stink seems to have seeped into every corner of the dressing room in the winter of 2016, and Pep's even considering giving up. Leaving it all behind … Every defeat chips away at his determination to continue as City's coach.

Gündoğan has torn the cruciate ligaments in his knee, bringing his season to a short, sharp and very painful end. The German international is the cornerstone of Pep's project. He needs him for it to be a success and Gündo's loss is a massive blow. City's captain, Kompany, is still struggling with successive injuries – Sané and Fernando are also absent. To add insult to injury, Agüero and Fernandinho are each serving four-match bans.

The pundits are scathing in their criticism of City's coach. They want him gone. 'Go home,' is the unanimous message. And it's repeated ad nauseam.

City are lying fifth in the league, out of the places for next year's Champions League, and ten points behind league leaders Chelsea. For the first time in his coaching career, Pep's team is out of contention for the title at this early stage of the season.

At the start of the new year, he tells me, a little sarcastically but also as if he's deadly serious: 'It's the beginning of the end of my career.' He's only been coaching for seven and a half years but already he's considering calling it a day …

Just thinking about where he goes from here brings to mind something Juanma Lillo said to him a few months ago: 'Pep, you need to lose a lot more games before you can be sure that you genuinely want to be a coach.' It was March 2016 and the two men were having coffee together just a few hours after Bayern had eliminated Juventus from the Champions League after an agonisingly hard-fought game in which the Munich side were themselves a minute away from being knocked out. Lillo was keen to temper Pep's euphoria by warning him of the harsh reality of life as a football coach.

Now, only nine months later, Pep is staring this reality square in the face. 'Lillo's not the only one who's said this to me. Dome has also been telling me for a while that I'll only know how committed I am to this career when I start losing.'

And here in Manchester he's learned all about defeats. They've rained down on him, unrelenting and brutal.

He's not used to losing – it only happened in 8.5 per cent of his games with Barcelona and 11.8 per cent with Munich. In Manchester, he's lost 22.5 per cent of his games. And it hurts. Every loss feels like a dagger to the heart. He's not used to losing but he's having to learn to live with it, with the physical pain he suffers every time they fail.

And yet it seems that this is the best way for him to decide if he really wants to be a coach.

One evening in December, Pep climbs the stairs to Torrent's apartment, a bottle of red wine in his hand. The two men are neighbours. They, along with several other members of City's technical team, live at No.1 Deansgate, a tall building that presides over the city's main artery. Txiki Begiristain lives in apartment 11, Torrent in no. 10, with Mikel Arteta and Pep residing at 8 and 9 respectively. Dome opens the bottle and the two men sit on his couch together, drinking and chatting until the wee small hours.

The two old friends talk about everything but football; their kids and their studies, their parents, health problems … For the first time in years, football's off the agenda. Life with all its ups and downs, is their focus tonight (although arguably the two things are often synonymous). Dome has almost ten years on Pep, who, at 45, is facing some of the family milestones and worries that his friend has already put behind him. Different life experiences. Different perspectives.

As the festive season drags on, Pep and Dome get together for a heart-to-heart whenever possible. They open a bottle of red and put the world to rights. All thoughts of football momentarily forgotten. And, somehow, that's all it takes. No grand declarations or eureka moments required, Pep begins to shake off the stench of defeat and drag himself out of the mire. By focusing on and valuing the process, he'll make it to the other side.

There will be more losses and more triumphs, for sure. But Pep's perspective is gradually changing. He's always placed too much importance on winning, seeing it almost as a moral imperative, as if the world were judging him solely in terms of his successes and failures. Winning has been everything.

Now he's realising that it's more important to focus on the journey than the destination, just as Estiarte has been saying. One should never fear defeat. It's letting oneself down that holds the real threat.

Weeks later, with his nightmare before Christmas and his chats with Dome behind him, Pep's back on form, full of energy and brimming with optimism. He's banished all thoughts of throwing in the towel and hasn't forgotten Lillo's words: 'You know, losing used to equal disaster for me. Although I suppose I shouldn't use the past tense because I'm still crushed every time we lose. It's like something just clicks in my head. Defeat is not something I'm used to. But it's part of the process, a normal part of sport. Intellectually I accept it completely but, deep down, it's still very hard to stomach …'

SCENE 10. JESUS IN, KUN OUT

Manchester, 19 January 2017

Agüero's becoming a problem for Pep. Put simply, Agüero, the undisputed idol of Manchester's Citizens, is getting far too comfortable. And Pep doesn't want anyone in his squad feeling that way.

For Pep football has never been about ten men plus one, with possibly the unique exception of Lionel Messi, the only footballer in a class of his own. But no one else comes close. Not even El Kun.

Sergio Agüero is a superb player, a prolific goalscorer, a lethal predator in the opposition's box, and the legend who scored that epic 93rd-minute-and-20-seconds goal in the nerve-shredding 2012 Premier League finale. A City legend. But he's not Messi and Pep will not tolerate his team becoming 10+1. Pep expects the same commitment from his star striker as he does from De Bruyne, Fernandinho or Sterling. The coach is quite sure: Agüero has become too comfortable. It's unacceptable.

The two men get on, professionally and personally. There's genuine affection there and it's nothing like the relationship Pep had had with Ibrahimović and Mario Mandžukić. However, the coach wants a lot more out of Agüero and needs to see him put as much effort as his teammates into creating and developing the strong sense of team spirit City need.

Over Christmas the technical team check the stats. Agüero has scored 33 goals in the last 34 league games. Impressive. But he's also been sent off twice, earning himself a total sanction of seven matches. City can't afford their main striker to keep messing up like that. In his absence, Pep has trialled various players in his position: transitory solutions like Iheanacho, Nolito, De Bruyne and even Sterling.

Then Agüero returns and nothing changes. The dynamics of their play don't improve and at Goodison Park in mid-January City are smashed by

Everton, 4–0: the worst league defeat of Guardiola's entire career. Koeman's men are relentless. City are like a groggy boxer on the ropes for most of the game. Bravo fails to stop a single dangerous effort and City concede the first chance their opposition creates (disastrously, they've done this four times in the last seven games). The backline is chaotic, and their defensive transitions are appalling. The team's emotional fragility is brutally obvious and Agüero's return has added nothing: no goals, none of the fighting spirit the team needs and zero commitment to City's press.

Gabriel Jesus has been at City since the start of January, but has had to wait two weeks for his work permit to come through. He's been training with the first team and is performing well. Just 19, he's been hailed as the most promising new Brazilian striker of the current era. Txiki Begiristain signed him for around €33 million (£27 million) back in August on the condition that he stay with Palmeiras until December. Pep is delighted with the young Brazilian, who seems to have everything he's looking for in a striker. A natural team player who works well with the rest of the squad, he brings the kind of all-out aggression and indefatigable pressing that City need up front. The only question is whether or not he can match Agüero's capacity for goalscoring. Pep still has a lot of faith in Kun. He just doesn't want him taking anything for granted. He needs Gabriel Jesus to provide the impetus for City's local hero to wake up and buckle down.

Unsurprisingly Jesus's arrival puts Kun out. Not only is Pep aware of this, but it's exactly what he intended all along. Just a few weeks ago, he'd been singing Agüero's praises but he'd also laid out exactly what he needed from him: 'Sergio has been hugely important to us. He's a special player and I want him to understand just how important he is for us. We need him. We need him a lot. When he's aggressive on the pitch, and shows that he's hungry to score and determined to press our rivals hard, at that moment Sergio is immense.' However, when he fails to play like that, the team becomes 10+1.

Pep wants Gabriel Jesus to make his debut but not at the cost of leaving Agüero on the bench. It's vital that the two men have a positive relationship. He wants his players to compete for their place in the team, sure, but he also needs them to cooperate so that they play as a unit of 11 players. Just as he's done many times in the past, Guardiola decides to resolve the situation over dinner.

They meet in Salvi's, a small, glass-fronted pizzeria at 19 John Dalton Street in the centre of Manchester. Pep knows that the food is delicious here, although he usually eats at the other Salvi's in the Corn Exchange, where there's more privacy to be had. I get the impression that the venue has been chosen quite deliberately by Agüero's agent. Slap bang in the city centre, not far from the busy area around the town hall, there's no chance that the meeting will go unnoticed. The player's agent probably wants the public to be aware that there's some kind of conflict and that both he and Agüero are keen to resolve the situation.

No real surprises emerge over dinner. Agüero wants to stay in Manchester for a few more years and is keen to maintain the status he's already achieved. He loves being City's superstar. Guardiola doesn't want him to leave either and has no problem with his elevated status but he wants him to become more of a team player. He wants him to break out of his comfort zone and become the team's first line of defence. Pep has always believed that the best defence begins in a good offence, led by aggressive strikers who block their opponents' attempts to bring the ball out, thereby making life much easier for their teammates.

Agüero, idolised by the fans and the club alike, is used to being the team's standout striker and feels that he can't offer any more. Pep recognises his brilliance but believes that he's become too comfortable and can give a lot more. He tells him that he wants more effort and even better performances. More goals, for sure, but also greater participation in the team's play and, specifically, in pressing opposition defenders.

Agüero has been worried about the suggestion that Pep no longer sees him as his number one up front now that a new, young, dynamic striker has arrived, but Pep reassures him that the opposite is true. He's still counting on Kun but he's looking for the 2.0 version who will perform better and participate more.

'Sergio, it feels like sometimes you're 100 per cent with us but sometimes you're not. That's not good enough. It's got to be all the time. Even if you only manage 60 minutes I want maximum effort for those 60 minutes. I don't want Kun on autopilot. I want Kun firing on all cylinders.'

Two days later, Agüero is City's striker when they draw 2–2 with Spurs at home. Gabriel Jesus makes his debut but only in the 82nd minute when he comes on for Sterling. However, seven days after that the Brazilian starts in their 0–3 FA Cup victory against Crystal Place and performs so well that he's also in the starting 11 for their routing of West Ham in London (0–4). Agüero, who's on the bench for both games, can only sit and watch as the young Brazilian scores and provides an assist. Four days later, it all happens again, Gabriel Jesus scores both goals in City's triumph against Swansea (2–1), with Agüero only coming on in the 83rd minute.

If Pep was keen for Kun to understand his message, it's now coming through loud and clear: up your game or be prepared to play second fiddle.

There's a new kid in town.

SCENE 11. 'IF YOU DON'T LEARN ENGLISH, YOU DON'T PLAY'
Manchester, 2 February 2017

As always, Pep saves his criticism for the good days. If his players are having a bad time, he'll usually try to give them a boost and cheer them up, not hammer them with a lecture. He saves the reprimands for the good days when he'll point out any flaws or weaknesses he's spotted or highlight the ways in which his players can improve. Which is why he's chosen the morning after City's victory away to West Ham to raise an issue that's been bothering him.

Gabriel Jesus, making his debut yesterday, was the standout star of the match. The young Brazilian is now the first player in the club's history to score and assist on his debut. This kid brings an almost electric charge to the team, which by the 40th minute is already 3–0 up. Pep picked an unorthodox combination of players for his lineup, fielding veterans like Caballero, Sagna, Kolarov, Touré and Silva alongside his younger players – Stones, Sterling, Sané and Gabriel Jesus. Agüero's on the bench and stays there until the 70th minute when the game is in the bag. Pep's deadly serious. If Agüero isn't prepared to try harder and show more commitment, Gabriel Jesus will take his place.

But the team as a whole is on a high after the win and it's the perfect time for Pep to have a stern word with six of his players. 'Guys, you need to integrate more into the culture of the country you're living in and where you earn your money. To do that, you need to learn the language. As a priority.'

The six men know exactly what he's talking about. None of them have been making use of the one-to-one English classes offered by the club for some years now. The teacher comes in to Sportcity almost every day to help the foreign players either learn the language from scratch or improve their existing level. And lots of their teammates have made the most of this opportunity. Fernandinho, Zabaleta and Caballero have all been keen to invest time in learning the language, as have, to a lesser extent, Fernando and David Silva. Other players, however, haven't bothered to turn up to a single lesson and can barely say half a dozen words in English.

There's little that irritates Guardiola more than a player with no interest in integrating into the city and country he lives in. Mastering the language is vitally important. You need to be able to communicate with your teammates, chat to them at mealtimes, give each other support when you're feeling down or things are going badly. It's also fairly important for a professional footballer to understand the instructions the coach is giving him!

But Pep also sees it as a vital part of adapting fully to a new place and situation. Soon after taking over at Bayern he'd discovered that the club expected the players to meet with supporters clubs from all over Germany. The meetings happened annually and all squad players were involved. Pep heartily approved of the initiative and made huge efforts himself to learn German so that he could communicate with his players, the club's directors and local journalists. Although he was criticised on occasion for failing to provide sufficiently fluent answers on controversial topics or tactical details, there's no doubt that the Catalan made every effort to integrate fully into life in Munich.

Pep can't understand how some of his players can barely say 'Good morning' in English despite having lived in Manchester for some time. The meeting doesn't last long and his message is short and sharp. 'If you don't learn English, you don't play.' He's not bluffing, but it's a threat he sincerely hopes he won't have to carry out.

The six men get the message. Some of them take it on board and start attending English classes and making an effort to integrate more into Manchester life. Others don't. They've made their choice …

SCENE 12: 'WE LACK CHARACTER'
Nice, 16 March 2017

The seat in Nice Airport feels like an instrument of torture. It's a reddish brown colour and as hard as stone. Pep has had a herniated disc for years and this kind of seating is particularly uncomfortable for him. He's looking haggard and hollow-eyed, like he hasn't slept a wink.

It looks like it's going to be a beautiful day on the Côte d'Azur and in other circumstances he'd be enjoying it but instead he feels like he's just woken up after a bad dream. A disastrous night, no sleep and now this interminable wait for the flight back to Manchester.

They're out of Europe.

Pep went through the same thing last year with Bayern, who were knocked out in the semi-finals, losing to Atlético Madrid. This time, it's Monaco who go through, winning on the away-goal rule after a 6–6 result. (Against all expectations, Monaco will get as far as the semi-finals, where they'll lose to Juventus.) The two-leg tie has transfixed anyone lucky enough to have seen all 180 minutes of it. Just three weeks ago, in the first leg at the Etihad, City pulled off victory in a colossal match (5–3) against the French side.

It's been a wild ride, an emotional rollercoaster, an exhausting game of Russian roulette.

This time three weeks ago, almost to the minute, Pep was in a different airport, Manchester, on his way to Abu Dhabi for a few days' break. During his time at Bayern he'd spent the international breaks coaching the youth players but since coming to City he's decided to do the opposite. Thailand, Morocco, the Maldives and now Abu Dhabi – all great places to play some golf and enjoy the sun. Back then, sitting in the departure lounge, he was on cloud nine, thrilled with the game, which had finished barely two hours before. 'What a brilliant match. So emotional!'

It was a historic night for the club, not least because of the gutsy performance delivered by his players. The game had been an explicit homage to Johan Cruyff with two ferociously combative teams unleashed onto the pitch to bombard the opposition with goals. Much like the previous year's Bayern–Juventus Champions League quarter-final clash, the game featured an avalanche of attacking fervour. That night the Italians went ahead by two goals only to have Pep's men equalise in the final minute and score two more in extra-time.

'We were so strong today, especially when you consider our lack of self-confidence. This performance will re-energise us, just you wait and see. We can still correct the mistakes we're making. And if we can sign some good defenders next year, that will really improve our game. This year we're just getting by …'

Pep was on edge throughout the frenetic game. First, Sterling scored, then Radamel Falcao equalised. Disastrously Spanish referee Mateu Lahoz messed up and failed to give Agüero a penalty. City lost the ball to Leonardo Jardim's men and then 18-year-old Kylian Mbappé, about to become a world superstar, scored. Fernandinho was doing the best he could at left-back and Willy Caballero kept City's hopes alive by saving Falcao's penalty. Then Agüero equalised, and Zabaleta came on for Fernandinho and staunched the flood of counterattacks by the French side. Falcao tucked away a second goal, but so did Agüero, followed in rapid succession by Stones and Sané. And Caballero then saved Falcao's goal-bound effort in the dying minutes of the game. City won 5–3.

Pep's players – and Monaco's – were brave, combative and merciless in their attacking, but both sides seemed overwhelmed in defence. They were like wild mustangs – capable of incredible actions and appalling mistakes. They showed the kind of team spirit that Pep identified as essential for the project's success. He was proud of his men, but even then, in the moment of pure euphoria, he had doubts about the return leg.

'We'll need to score a few goals in Monaco. They're bound to get at least two because they're fucking beasts. If I could, I'd sign five of those "monstrous" players right now.'

He didn't name the players he was talking about but I can make a good guess: Djibril Sidibé, Benjamin Mendy, Fabinho, Bernardo Silva and Mbappé. The whole of Europe had seen how talented these five players were. And witnessed just how bad Mateu Lahoz's refereeing was.

'Don't even talk about that … At this level of competition, where there are such tiny margins between teams, the tiniest details can kill you.'

That was 20 days ago. Now Pep is in a different airport. With a different result. And in a very different state of mind.

This is Nice with its hard, brown seats, where he sits, depressed and sleep-deprived with huge black bags under his eyes, remembering the pale, strained faces of his men as the Champions League anthem began. How nervous they looked. Just more evidence that they lack the character to compete at the highest level.

'I've tried but I haven't been able to instil in them the strength of character you need to win these kinds of games …'

Monaco dismantle City in the first half. So-so at the back and a bit lost up front with Agüero failing to control the ball, Guardiola's men go into the break having lost all their advantage (2–0) from the last game and showing none of the ambition or courage they have demonstrated in other games.

They improve exponentially in the second half and create numerous chances, which neither Agüero nor Sané convert until the 70th minute, when Sané gets City a goal and reinstates a sense of optimism. At 2–1 it looks like City are through to the quarter-finals, but their dreams are shattered six minutes later when Tiémoué Bakayoko makes it 3–1, thereby eliminating Pep and his underperforming team.

Now, a desolate Pep sits waiting in the airport: 'I don't know which is worse – today's result or the time Madrid beat Bayern 0–4 when I was in charge there. I remember I worked on the Bayern players for three days before that game, trying to ensure they had the right level of aggression and were prepared to attack and attack. Then Madrid's first goal just seemed to deflate us completely! But here …'

I try to reassure him that this is only to be expected given that he's not been able to renew the team as he wanted. It will take time and the young, fresh legs and fighting spirits of new signings to turn things around.

'Character is far more important than any stats. I've not managed to give them the kind of character they need for the big events. They don't believe in themselves. It's like they're scared of playing, they're not comfortable with taking the initiative. They're much happier being reactive. I don't think they really want to take the lead role. I really thought I could give them these qualities but I haven't been able to.'

But it's only mid-March and there are still a lot of tough challenges in store.

'Now we just have to pick ourselves up and fight to earn our place in next year's Champions League. It's not going to be easy and nothing's guaranteed. We're pretty low right now but it will all feel a bit better tomorrow and we'll get over it eventually. We'll get our mojo back and move on from this and there will be fantastic days ahead, I'm certain of it!'

I remind him that his mentor, Johan Cruyff, had a horrible first season at Barcelona in 1989, and that he resisted all the pressure to change what he was doing until eventually he was able to impose his own philosophy on the team's game.

'What really bugs me is that I don't think we're actually that far off where we need to be! There have been times when we've played really well. Better than anything I ever achieved at Bayern. But we're like some kind of charitable organisation in both boxes. We struggle to score and we concede far too easily.'

The plane takes off for Manchester where City will face Liverpool at home in four days. Then they're off to Arsenal and Chelsea. They're facing three of the biggest clubs in the Premier League when the whole team is still reeling from the Monaco defeat and struggling without Gündoğan and Gabriel Jesus. The promising Brazilian striker was injured against Bournemouth on 13 February, meaning he's only played three games since joining City. There are good and bad results in the weeks ahead.

Pep's men defy expectations by continuing to play bold, aggressive football. There is none of the poor morale and lacklustre performances that might have been expected after being knocked out by Monaco in the manner they were.

First, they draw with Liverpool (1–1). Pep's delighted: 'This is one of the best days I've had as a coach. I'm so proud of these players. We trained yesterday in almost total silence. After the trauma of Monaco, we could barely speak. But today they've gone out there and shown that they believe in my style of play.'

The players' performance has confirmed that they're on the right track, heading in the right direction. More and more players have adapted fully to Pep's ideas: first Sané, Gündoğan and Gabriel Jesus, and now Stones has made a huge leap forward. And what a player he is! I don't know if he'll ever be the kind of central defender Gerard Piqué was (perhaps if he finds a Carles Puyol of his own) but he's a tremendously courageous player. In Monaco, he held on to the ball surrounded on all sides by rapacious animals and he had done the same thing here against Liverpool.

His coach agrees: 'Stones has shown more personality than anyone. My style of game makes the central defender's role very difficult but he's got big balls, that guy!' But Pep isn't blind to his team's faults: 'We created lots of clear chances and didn't convert them, which is why we can't compete with the top sides. Today we created a lot and conceded very little … but we didn't win. That's nothing new. But, I'll also say this: I want to stick with these lads for a long time to come – I was so impressed by the way they attacked and ran their legs off till the very last minute.'

The next few weeks will see City draw away to Arsenal (2–2) and lose to league leaders Chelsea at Stamford Bridge. Antonio Conte and his men's brilliant campaign will in due course win them the league title.

By the start of April City have scored 24 goals in a row from low crosses into the box, typical of Pep's idea about how City should play. But they've also added to City's horrible run of 21 years without managing to come back to win in a game away from home if they're losing at half-time. Ninety-five times they've been behind at half-time and have only managed a draw in 11 of them. To end that self-destructive pattern, Guardiola desperately needs more players with the character to cope with the pressure of high-level competition. Everything looks bleaker when City are knocked out of the FA Cup by Arsenal (2–1). For the first time in his coaching career, Pep will end the season without a trophy. He'd known there was a good chance of finishing empty-handed but it's a bitter pill to swallow. The club didn't let him renew the squad as he'd wanted to. It's become an absolute priority for next season.

Manel Estiarte shares his own thoughts: 'We knew it would take two years to get this project up and running – that was pretty obvious – but we would have liked to have won some silverware this year, so that the whole thing would feel less of an uphill struggle. Now we really need to get on with renovating the squad.' He then goes into detail on which players City need: 'Next season we'll need a goalkeeper, two full-backs, a midfielder and a striker.'

The management team have very clear ideas about who they want to sign for certain positions, but by no means all of them. In terms of the keeper, it will be up to Claudio Bravo whether or not he wants to stay, despite the difficulties he's been suffering. City must sign a really good goalkeeper and Bravo's answer will be the deciding factor as to whether Willy Caballero stays or goes. As far as the full-backs are concerned, things are clearer. Pep wants one or two of Monaco's current players, or maybe Kyle Walker from Tottenham, because Sagna and Clichy have to go. It's also possible that they'll sign a centre-back given that Kompany's recovery has been pretty sporadic – preventing him from being a consistent part of the team.

And there's no doubt that they need to bring in another midfielder. Silva, Touré and Fernandinho are all now over 30. Fernando is leaving and Pep has his sights set on Bernardo Silva. Estiarte explains, 'Everyone wants to sign Monaco's midfielder but he would be very expensive.'

Up front it's planned that Navas, Nolito and Iheanacho can leave, meaning there'll be three kids, Sané, Sterling and Jesus, plus Kun Agüero. That's insufficient.

In total, between five and six new signings are needed to complete a process the club wouldn't back as a one-off exercise last summer. Now it's on. Pep has no fears that club owner Sheikh Mansour won't be true to his word. It was given as a guarantee.

Before the end of April, I ask Guardiola about his plans and expectations for next season. His response is clear: 'We need more time. We still aren't able to compete strongly against the big Premier League and European clubs. Let's see if we can turn that around next year. There are a lot of older guys in the team and they've been together for a long time. We had to face Monaco with nine players who've been at the club for ages and we weren't able to make the changes we wanted. We haven't been able to buy all the players we would have liked, just a few. We're already doing some things much better than I expected but we're not strong enough in either box and that costs us a lot. But we'll get there. I didn't come to Manchester for six months. I came for three years. It's going to be hard work but we'll get there in the end. I've no doubt at all.'

By the time negotiations have been completed, the words of Estiarte and Guardiola are borne out. Txiki Begiristain makes several signings. Ederson comes in as the new keeper; Walker, Danilo and Mendy are brought in as full-backs; Bernardo Silva, a player who can transition easily between playing as a midfielder and a forward, comes onboard, and in January 2018 City have a new centre-back: Aymeric Laporte. The first team also have three youngsters joining their ranks: Phil Foden, Brahim Díaz and Oleksandr Zinchenko. It's precisely the radical shake-up of his squad that Pep has been demanding.

SCENE 13. A WALL OR A BRIDGE?

Manchester, 8 May 2017

'Which do you want to be? A Karajan or a Bernstein?'

The question's out there. Across the table of Salvi's trattoria in the Corn Exchange, Manchester.

Pep has been at City for almost a year but still finds himself in uncharted territory: eliminated from the Champions League, the FA Cup, the League Cup and currently battling Liverpool and Arsenal even to finish in the top four. This first season in England has been much grimmer than he could have possibly imagined. The squad is still a long way from what he wants. More than half of the players are well over 30 and his new recruits haven't completely found their feet yet (Sané, Jesus, Stones) or else have turned out to be a massive disappointment (Bravo, Nolito).

But Pep has shaken off the winter blues and is determined to finish the season strongly so that he can put it behind him and move on. He's looking forward to next season and the fresh blood he plans to bring in. New, young players who hopefully will allow him to fully impose his football philosophy on City's game.

I'm with Pep for a family lunch so we won't be discussing any of the serious issues facing City at the moment. Pep's demolishing the delicious pasta dish he's ordered while trying to record a video message for Luis Enrique, whose birthday it is today. By the time we're on to dessert, the conversation has turned to music and to the psychological profiles of two of the best orchestra conductors of the twentieth century: Herbert von Karajan and Leonard Bernstein.

Neither Pep nor Cristina are huge aficionados of classical music but they're intrigued by my descriptions of the two maestros: 'Karajan was a genius who conducted with his eyes closed because he knew the music by heart. He didn't need to look at the scores. Which is why you'll often see photos of him with his eyes shut. Bernstein, also an absolute genius, was the complete opposite with his huge expressive eyes, flamboyant gestures, constant animation and overflowing, vital energy.'

It's striking how two great conductors, each blessed with boundless creative brilliance and artistic excellence, should have such different styles.

'Karajan essentially erected an impregnable wall between himself and the members of his orchestra. He believed that this "barrier" between the conductor and his musicians would stimulate the synergy between then and allow them to produce the highest quality of music. Bernstein, on the other hand, was a genius who preferred to build a bridge between himself and the orchestra so that the music would flow through it.'

In the dim light of the Italian trattoria Pep's face lights up. He looks like he does when he's about to come up with a new idea. I've seen that keen, intelligent expression before, like an animal about to pounce on its prey. He repeats the idea aloud, perhaps just to make sure he's fully understood. 'So, Karajan builds a wall to separate himself from the orchestra and Bernstein constructs a bridge that makes him more connected to the orchestra?'

'That's it exactly.'

Pep just smiles …

No prizes for guessing what happens next.

Throughout his career Pep has repeatedly been told about the importance of creating a feeling of 'closeness' with his players. But it's exactly the kind of tight bond that he's struggled to establish in the dressing room – in Barcelona and, initially, in Munich. At Bayern he gradually managed to develop a warmer relationship with his players, who had seemed cold and standoffish at the start but who, by the end, absolutely adored the Catalan.

He's come to Manchester determined to change this aspect of his behaviour but the stress of competition, the bitterly disappointing results, his emotional setback over Christmas and the low expectations with which he's entering the final weeks of the season combine to distract him from his good intentions. He hasn't built that connection with his players or done away with the protective shell that stops him 'opening himself up' to them without worrying about the consequences. Pep's still conducting his men from behind the 'wall' that divides him from them. But now he sees things more clearly. He's listened and understood. He needs to find a way to tear down the wall and build a bridge to his players.

Our chat about Karajan and Bernstein stimulates Pep to keep working on this aspect of his relationship with his players. Sure enough, months after that family lunch in Salvi's, as Pep begins his second season, it's clear that he's becoming more of a Bernstein and less of a Karajan.

SCENE 14. THE TERRORIST ATTACK

Manchester, 22 May 2017

City trounce Watford 0–5. The score in this last match of Pep's first season in England reflects his growing belief that, at last, all the pieces are falling into place. May has been a great month for them: 4 wins, 15 goals and just 2 conceded.

After a grim campaign in which they've failed to win a single trophy City have finished the league on a high note, in third. Sure, well behind champions Chelsea and runners-up Spurs, but two points ahead of Klopp's Liverpool and thus guaranteed qualification for the Champions League group stage next season.

Pep has had to endure a rocky first year. Initially frustrated by the club's stubborn insistence on giving him just 50 per cent of the new signings he'd demanded in order to make the project an immediate success, he'd none-theless found hopeful signs early in his work with this squad. Then things began to go wrong. The constant highs and lows took a psychological toll and, for the first time, caused him to question his choice of this high-stress, energy-sapping career.

He faced weeks of anguish and worry with the feeling of a noose tight-ening around his neck, then the joy of pulling off what Pep considered a project-saving win followed by a winter of excruciating defeats plus a miser-able Christmas. The elation of the highs when it looks like the fightback has begun, only to be consistently dragged back into the depths of despair. He's been knocked down. And picked himself up again. Time after time. And been forced to accept, after defeat in Monaco, that too many of his men lack the character needed to triumph in the biggest arenas. Now City's strong performance in the final weeks of the season has produced a significant boost. All the suffering over the past 12 months suddenly seems worth it. This is definitely the job for him. He's going nowhere.

Then their world explodes.

A moment of terror, blind panic, horror … and then, waiting fearfully.

An explosion shakes their entire building. It's 10.30 at night. Pep and his son Màrius are waiting for Cristina and their daughters Maria and Valentina to return before having dinner. Cris and the girls have been at the Ariana Grande concert in the Manchester Arena, just around the corner.

The shockwaves shatter windows, spreading confusion, panic and fear. The whole world seems to shake.

Pep assumes: *It's a terrorist attack!*

He's on his feet and running. Down ten flights of stairs and, once outside, off in the direction of the cathedral. Then his phone rings.

It's Cristina: 'I don't know what's happened but we're coming home now. As fast as we can.'

Then the line goes dead – the mobile reception's gone.

Pep takes a deep breath and stops running. He waits in front of their building until, after several agonising, interminable minutes, Cristina calls back, 'We're OK. We've made it out. We've made it out!'

A suicide bomber has blown himself up in the foyer of the Manchester Arena just as the concert came to an end while fans began to leave through the vestibule. There were also families arriving, there to pick up their loved ones after a brilliant night out. Twenty-three are dead, 116 injured.

Cristina and the girls had decided to leave before the encores. Valentina was obviously exhausted and half-asleep as the concert was coming to a close. Maria saw that her kid sister was struggling and was happy enough to head home. It was a decision that would save their lives. The three of them crossed the vestibule just one minute before the suicide bomber detonated the explosive device attached to his body.

None of them – Pep, Cristina or their kids – will ever forget the horror of those hours.

The next day, Cristina and Pep quietly join the crowds gathered in Albert Square to honour the victims of the attack. Tony Walsh reads a long, emotional poem called 'Choose Love, Manchester'.

The first and last lines, 'This is the place … Always remember. Never forget. Forever Manchester. Choose Love', seem to speak directly to them. They are deeply moved. In this, the most heartbreaking of moments, they feel like they truly belong.

'This is the place. Manchester.'

This is their place.

The home they've chosen.

STATS 2016–17

	P	W	D	L	GF	GA
Premier League	38	23	9	6	80	39
Third						
League Cup	2	1	0	1	2	2
Fourth round						
FA Cup	6	1	1	1	16	1
Semi-finalists						
Champions League	10	5	3	2	24	16
Knockout round						
Total	56	33	13	10	122	60

- 58.9 per cent victories all season
- 60.5 per cent victories in Premier League matches (81.6 per cent at Barça; 85.3 per cent at Bayern)
- 2.17 goal average per match in the entire season (Barça 2.58; Bayern 2.46)
- 2.10 goal average per match scored in the Premier League
- 1.07 goal average per match conceded in the entire season (Barça 0.73; Bayern 0.69)
- 1.02 goal average per match conceded in the Premier League
- 62 positive goal difference across the whole season
- 78 points in the Premier League (champions Chelsea, 93 points)
- 20 efforts off the post in the Premier League (9 De Bruyne)
- 63.3 per cent possession in the entire season (Barça 66.1 per cent; Bayern 70.5 per cent)
- 65 per cent possession in the Premier League
- 77.9 per cent highest level of possession (vs Leicester, December 2016)
- 34.6 per cent lowest level of possession (vs Barcelona, November 2016)
- 597 average number of passes per match
- 718 highest number of passes (vs Sunderland, March 2017)
- 86 per cent completed passes per match
- 15.7 shots at goal per match/5.6 on target
- 8.3 shots at goal conceded per game/3 on target
- 6 best run of consecutive wins in the Premier League (Barça 16; Bayern 19)
- 33 top goalscorer: Sergio Agüero (20 in the Premier League)
- 19 most assists: Kevin De Bruyne (18 in the Premier League)
- 49 most appearances: Kevin De Bruyne (36 in the Premier League)
- 5–0 biggest win (vs Crystal Palace, Norwich, Steaua and West Ham)
- 4–0 biggest defeat (vs Everton and Barcelona)

Season 2: 2017–18

The Centurions

ACT 1. 'WE'VE BOUGHT ENERGY'

Barcelona/Manchester, June–September 2017

Pep's plans for the summer holidays? Sunshine and golf.

Given that sunny days are few and far between in Manchester, Pep takes any chance to head somewhere hot and, if possible, play a few holes while he's there. The combination always does him the world of good, and it's a great way to recharge the batteries and get ready for the challenges ahead.

But the business of football doesn't stop for the summer holidays and Txiki Begiristain calls daily to discuss whatever problems they're having signing new players. The club has promised Pep that they'll replace the remaining 50 per cent of the squad, which they refused to do last season, so City's sports director is having a frenetic summer.

Nine first team players are leaving (Caballero, Sagna, Zabaleta, Clichy, Kolarov, Iheanacho, Nolito, Fernando and Navas) and a dozen lower category players are being loaned out or transferred to other clubs. Among them is Jadon Sancho, one of the academy's stars who, during his contract renewal negotiations, had insisted on a guaranteed place in the first team, something Pep never agrees to, no matter how good the player is.

So Sancho has decided to sign for Borussia Dortmund, where they have promised him a first-team place. City have received very little compensation for losing him – just €10 million (£8 million). Pep would have preferred to hold on to the talented 17-year-old winger, to bring Sancho through gradually, like he's doing with Brahim Díaz and Phil Foden who are now going to be training with the first team.

Between holes Pep tells me how excited he is about Foden: 'Foden's a genius. He's going to be a star. One of the best young players I've ever seen. I want him to come on the pre-season tour and play in the big friendlies we have planned. If he does well I'll keep him in the first team. He's fantastic.'

Beyond his plans for the youngsters, Pep has clear objectives for the summer transfer market. He needs five players to fully replenish the squad: a keeper, two full-backs, a midfielder and a striker.

Progress is slow but steady and Txiki keeps him informed of each new signing. On the recommendation of Xabi Mancisidor, he's signed Ederson Santana de Moraes as keeper. It has cost City €40 million (£35 million), a bargain given the extraordinary potential of the player who Pep first came across just over a year ago when Bayern played Benfica. Begiristain and Mancisidor agree that Ederson has the perfect profile for the goalkeeper Guardiola needs. And this deal means they don't have to get embroiled in cut-throat multimillion-pound negotiations for bigger names like the Italian keeper Gianluigi Donnarumma.

Just a week ago, when Pep was still in Manchester waiting for the schools to break up for the summer, City also signed Bernardo Silva. This, alone, guaranteed that Pep could embark on his summer break with a skip in his step. He has big plans for Silva, whom he intends to play as an inverted winger or, when feasible, as a false 9.

Pep is bowled over by Bernardo's talent and is convinced the Portuguese has the potential to become a truly great player. Among mere mortals Bernardo is probably the footballer who most closely resembles Messi, although it's never occurred to Pep to compare them. Obviously there are immense differences between the two but Pep's delighted to have signed such a versatile attacking midfielder and he thinks that the Portugal international has a lot more to give. In terms of ability and profile, eventually he'll be an ideal replacement for David Silva.

With their new keeper and a creative player sorted out, Txiki focuses on the full-backs. It's only the beginning of June but City have lost each of the four men who played in that position last season.

Unfortunately, other clubs are perfectly aware of this and, as a result, hike their prices up to pretty unacceptable levels, especially when negotiations for Dani Alves collapse at the last minute and he signs for PSG.

In the end Kyle Walker, Danilo Luiz da Silva and Benjamin Mendy are signed for a combined total of €140 million (£120 million). It's good business. City are getting two defenders who are in superb physical shape (Walker and Mendy) and one who has outstanding technical talent (Danilo). Someone who, in fact, caught Pep's eye back in April 2015 during a Bayern–Porto game.

Txiki has been instructed not to sign anyone else. Just a month ago the president, Khaldoon Al Mubarak, called the entire squad together and told them, 'A few years ago I promised to build this sports city and that's what we've done. Today I'm making another promise – to build a world-beating team.' But even City's budget has its limits and Txiki's already overspent.

Despite that, he tries for one last, low-cost signing: young Brazilian midfielder Douglas Luiz. Pep believes this kid has loads of talent and is keen on getting him. But the UK's department of immigration has other ideas and refuses to issue a work permit. Luiz must go on loan to Girona.

It's not quite the squad Pep was looking for. He's not got the extra midfielder he wanted but he does have one more full-back than planned. He's also missed out on the left-footed centre-half he's still sure the team needs – Begiristain pushes him to wait for the next transfer window when there'll be a new budget.

They mutually decide to confront the first half of the season by bringing back some of the players who are out on loan: central defender Eliaquim Mangala will strengthen their backline where they've currently only got Stones, Otamendi and Kompany, and young Zinchenko will be given an opportunity in the midfield.

The window's closed and summer's over.

It's back to work.

• • •

'THE BALL'S MINE. IT BELONGS TO ME'

'Don't call it work. Training isn't work. It's practice.'

For Paco Seirul·lo words matter. Using inexact, imprecise or incorrect terminology for the concepts we're trying to explain just confuses people. And ourselves. Which is why Seirul·lo insists on using exactly the right words.

Seirul·lo has been a key part of Barcelona's success from the days of Johan Cruyff onwards. He worked at first with the legendary Dutchman, then with Louis van Gaal, and all the club's coaches right up to Frank Rijkaard. His career took a leap forward with Guardiola's appointment as first team coach in 2008 when he added the management of club methodology to his portfolio. Pep wanted the football philosophy Paco had developed over the previous 20 years to be ingrained not just in the first team but in every category below that. He continued in that role until Pep, sick of the disrespectful treatment meted out by President Sandro Rosell, decided to leave. At that point, Seirul·lo was slowly and deliberately marginalised by the club, who changed his role so that he was no longer involved in the work on the training pitches preparing teams for competition.

By 2017, with Ernesto Valverde in charge, Seirul·lo was back working closely with the first team, particularly with the core group of players from Pep's great Barcelona side: Iniesta, Messi, Piqué, Sergio Busquets and Javier Mascherano. In collaboration with Joan Vilà, he painstakingly created an approximation of the game Barça had played when Pep was at the helm. In his role as fitness trainer, he'd developed his own methodology: 'structured micro-cycles' and 'simulated preferential situations'. As the director of methodology his remit covered every aspect of Barça's game and he developed 'phase spaces' as the foundation of his tactical vision.

With his first season in Manchester over, Pep is back in Barcelona and we get together with Seirul·lo and Vilà to discuss all things football. During the season Pep doesn't have time for these kinds of lengthy conversations but he likes to touch base during the holidays with the people from whom he's learned so much. It's a great way to revisit old ideas and absorb new ones.

With his usual precision and care, Seirul·lo explains:

The so-called four phases of a game (or six if you add set pieces) don't actually exist. Football is all about one thing and one thing only. Sometimes I have the ball and sometimes I don't have it and have to try to get it back. When I have it I'm sometimes attacking and sometimes I'm defending. And the same when I don't have the ball. Without it sometimes I'm defending and at others I'm attacking. What is key to my understanding of the game is that I always initiate.

In my mind, the ball is mine. It belongs to me and when the opposition has it I have to take back what is mine. It's not about stealing the ball because that would mean I don't see it as belonging to me. It's someone else's ball. And that's not the case, it's just the opposite.

We divide the pitch into four advancing zones which, starting at our goal and working up to the opposition end, we call: alarm (the area closest to our goal), wellbeing, control and definition/finishing (the area closest to their goal).

So, as we advance vertically up the pitch we move from alarm to wellbeing, through control until finally we reach definition/finishing. We can advance up any of the four (or five) vertical lanes available on the pitch. At the same time, we always think of the players doing their work in three zones, depending on their proximity to the ball: intervention, mutual support and cooperation.

We define it as BSTS [BECA in Spanish], which stands for ball, space, teammates and support. These are four essential elements that condition the development of play. There are numerous variables: the position of the players and the ball, the distance between teammates with respect to the ball and opposition players, plus their respective trajectories, their orientation and organisation.

All of which leads us to define the phase spaces as the core elements of a match in which we are constantly reorganising ourselves. Every hundredth of a second we are reorganising again because the play in a match isn't a series of individual actions but a stochastic succession of phase spaces.*

Our team organises itself according to the phase spaces I've described with all their variables, zones, lanes and defined elements. And it does it with universal players – everyone does everything – who are constantly reorganising.

We aim to retain superiority at all times, whether it's numerical, positional, socio-affective, qualitative or dynamic (to do with space and time). We see our game as a 'game of intention', which we can sum up in the four Ps: perception, position, possession and pressing (to recuperate the ball). And we practise it in the training sessions. Training isn't work. It's practising moving through the successive phase spaces and constantly reorganising.

'WE HAVE TO MAKE A LOT MORE PASSES'

The concepts Seirul·lo has developed inspire Pep to make some improvements in his second season at City. The idea of 'the ball is ours and it's not about stealing it. We're just recuperating what is ours already' is at the fore-

---

* In 2013, in collaboration with Joan Vilà and Marcel Sans, Paco Seirul·lo developed the ideological concept of phase spaces (EdF in Spanish), a concept taken from physics which explains the internal dynamics of complex systems. The theory involves observing the game according to the internal variability of teams, while bearing in mind the complex nature of the situations they encounter in football. (Definition taken from *Phase Spaces: How Seirul·lo Changed Tactics Once and For All*, published by Agustín Peraita in 2020.)

front of his mind as he plans the pre-season preparation. Pep's not a great fan of stats but one number is burned into his brain.

Last season his team made an average of 597 passes per game with 86 per cent accuracy. Not a bad number. Unless you compare it with their average the season before. Under Manuel Pellegrini they made 539 passes with 83 per cent accuracy. Not a great improvement from one year to the next. Under Pep, Bayern averaged 726 passes per game with 87.9 per cent accuracy – significantly better than City managed in Pep's first year. In other words, the team made some progress with respect to the previous season but remains too far away from Bayern's figures, a comparison that convinces Pep this must become one of his main objectives for his second season.

'We need to make a lot more passes. Passes, passes, passes! The more passes we accumulate, the fewer chances we give the opposition. If we hold on to the ball and keep passing it among ourselves, our opponents will have fewer opportunities to do us damage and we'll be the ones with the initiative. We must find a way to make more passes.'

This idea underpins everything they do at training starting right from the first day of pre-season. For Pep, tactical training should always be a significant part of the pre-season. He works closely with Lorenzo Buenaventura to produce a highly effective training schedule in Sportcity, focusing on the development of tactical concepts, positional play exercises, looking for the 'third man', holding on to possession and the other 'tools' he uses to instil his model of the game.

The work to improve the players' fitness takes second place to developing their tactical abilities. This has always been Pep's philosophy and he is rigorous about applying it. According to Buenaventura, 90 per cent of the pre-season training they do involves working with the ball while the remaining 10 per cent is dedicated to injury prevention training.

Each week they'll focus on different aspects of injury prevention, individual weight training and on a variety of general training sessions that aim to adjust and balance the players' ability to cope with what's ahead. But their core focus is perfecting the fundamentals of the game the coach wants them to play.

Pep explains the thinking behind this training model: 'You only learn tactical concepts by putting them into practice through play. We want to see them make decisions during training sessions. That's how we convince the players that these concepts are the right ones. Through training.'

Pep reckons that it takes 20 months to imbue this complex philosophy in his men but he may need more time given that they have to do this work at the same time as competing for titles. This isn't some training academy teaching abstract tactical ideas. It's a football club, intent on winning trophies. And that's what Pep always focuses on: he's playing to win. If he doesn't win, he'll be out, regardless of how beautiful the football is. As a result, their ongoing learning must be absorbed into their campaign, and Pep will therefore probably have to stay on longer than originally intended in order to fully complete this project to the standard he wants.

It's pretty clear that three years will not be enough to achieve everything he wants to do. This is something I pointed out in my previous book, *Pep Guardiola: The Evolution*, in 2016:

> His playing model is pro-active and constructive. It's not about exploiting the gaps left by his opponents or destroying the other team, it's an attacking model that's based on the slow, careful construction of the game backed up by a well-organised defence. The effective execution of this style of game isn't learned quickly, under pressure and the players must be allowed to learn at the right pace. We must have the patience to allow them to fully grasp the demands of the game of position and to master it completely. It's another question entirely whether it's possible to fully realise Guardiola's and the club's objectives in three years. It certainly seems to me that this won't be long enough for Pep to finish the complex and ambitious project he's started. He may well need more time and it will be for him to make that decision when the time comes. I'm not speculating here about a contract extension, this is definitely not the moment for that, but merely expressing the opinion that three years will not be sufficient to achieve everything he's set out to do: implant a defined and detailed playing model, develop team spirit in a unified and competitive group, establish a clear football identity at City, establish a unique 'language' in the City academy and win trophies. These are ambitious plans that he must realise in a high-pressure demanding league and it's therefore not impossible that Guardiola will change his mind and stay on longer.

Twelve months later the situation hasn't changed as Pep concludes a short, intense pre-season, which has focused on teaching his players the best tactical concepts.

Passes, passes and more passes.

That's their aim for the coming season.

• • •

On a sunny afternoon in Manchester, Manel Estiarte, another great sun worshipper, is enjoying his ristretto coffee on a Corn Exchange terrace, near Deansgate. His bags are packed, ready for tomorrow's flight to the USA, where the team have three friendlies lined up plus a load of commercial obligations to fulfil. He takes the chance to explain his thoughts on the start of the season: 'What was really frustrating about our first season was that we created a lot of chances, which we failed to convert, but our opponents somehow managed to score at the first opportunity. We should have made a lot more of the chances we had and we failed to do that. There's another important factor in all of this. Pep is perceived as a threat in English football, and that's absolutely not our intention. But it's very obvious. It's as if Pep is attacking their customs and traditions, their way of doing things. The pundits, referees, the press … they all see him as a threat to the status quo. When we took over at Barcelona there was a similar reaction but that team scored a lot more goals so we won people over. But so far we haven't managed to do that here. In fact, everything that could possibly go wrong has gone wrong. Everything has gone against us and it feels like we keep losing the toss of the coin. City's shirt still doesn't have the kind of status in England that Barça's or Bayern's or Manchester United's have. You just have to look at the different criteria that are applied depending on who is playing. There's also no culture here of clubs intervening and offering their opinions on referees, opponents or other issues. And that leaves Pep on his own to face up to the people who're gunning for him. In any case, this isn't what really matters. It's not about luck or refereeing decisions. It's not even about the days when everything seems to go wrong. What's really important is that our players are highly motivated, that they are willing to stick with Pep to the death. I've no doubt at all: we'll never convince anyone just by talking. We need to stick to our process and win.'

Process, process, process …

The three US friendlies take place in Houston, Los Angeles and Nashville against three big hitters: Manchester United, who beat City 2–0, Real Madrid and Tottenham, whom they beat 4–1 and 3–0 respectively. City then go on to play West Ham in Reykjavik, beating them 3–0.

Pep uses those four matches to try out a formation he experimented with in Munich, and which he's considering using this season at City. It involves playing with three central defenders who organise bringing the ball out. 'This way I can ensure that their passes will be tight and short and there will be less chance of losing the ball. We can cover the entire width of the pitch with those three players and bring the ball out cleanly.'

They'll be able to use this technique with three pure central defenders or two centre-backs and a full-back or by pulling one of the midfielders back between the centre-backs. Pep uses this last option in the first friendly, with Yaya Touré positioned between Kompany and Adarabioyo. But for the next three games he opts for three centre-backs: Kompany, Stones and Otamendi. It's an interesting declaration of intent. Pep wants to play a 3–3–2–2. Three centre-backs in the first line of defence and a midfielder plus two full-backs in front of them. That's the basic plan, which is then completed by two holding midfielders who are free to roam plus two strikers at the front. This formation applies almost all of the coach's fundamental principles of the game. The three centre-halves guarantee good defensive structure and a precise, secure bringing-out of the ball. The organising midfielder and full-backs make up the 'protective wall' Pep wants in the centre. They act as a firewall against opponents' counterattacks. This then allows the creative midfielders to act as 'free electrons' who create chances for the strikers to convert. But there are no wingers. Without them, the defenders are the ones who have to cover the flanks when City attacks. This role demands enormous physical stamina, which is why City have brought in three of the best defenders in the world who are also in peak physical condition. Pep reckons that Walker and Mendy in particular are more than capable of taking on the triple role of defending without the ball, acting as midfielders as City push up into the opposition's area and becoming wingers in the final stage of attack. The formation will adapt to the different stages of the match. So at times the 3–3–2–2 will become a 3–1–4–2 in which both full-backs move up a level, or a 3–4–3, with a diamond-shaped midfield, when one of the full-backs moves up as a winger. When City don't have the ball it will oscillate between a 4–1–4–1 and a 5–4–1.

The players are totally comfortable with the 3–3–2–2, in which Agüero and Gabriel Jesus make up the attacking line and De Bruyne and David Silva act as roaming creative midfielders.

It's this last role that Pep wants Phil Foden to fulfil and the youngster gets his first chance in these friendlies. The young left-footed midfielder gives a gutsy, creative performance and Pep can see that he's better on the right than on the left. The whole coaching team can see that he has all the potential to become a substitute for David Silva in the long term. Ederson's in goal and his performances confirm outstanding talent. He's definitely going to give the team precisely the sense of security they lacked last season. Sané and Sterling aren't enjoying the tour. Pep gives them playing time but asks them to play in positions that are different from last season. He uses Sterling as a second striker and Sané as a left wing-back. The young German doesn't perform well but that's the only discordant note of the whole trip.

Pep gives me a review of the US tour when he gets back to Manchester: 'We played well. We've bought energy on the outside and our game is much more complete on the inside. I absolutely loved our training sessions. They were playing so well. We did well in the friendlies too and now we just need to make sure that we can maintain that level under pressure. If we manage that, there will be nobody else playing football like us. If we don't manage it, I'll be out on my backside.'

Pep Guardiola doesn't do things by half …

· · ·

As the Premier League starts, Pep duly introduces all his planned innovations: three centre-backs (Kompany, Stones and Otamendi), a central 'wall' made up of one holding midfielder, Fernandinho, and, on either side of him, two full-backs (Walker and Danilo), who are tasked with the triple role of defenders, ball-winners and wingers. 'I'm asking a lot from the full-backs,' Pep tells me, but he's determined to continue with this strategy because it gives David Silva and De Bruyne the freedom to move around the pitch. Up front, Agüero and Gabriel Jesus combine brilliantly, playing with unexpected harmony. Agüero has come back fitter and sharper than he was and is totally focused on pressing the opposition. It seems that teaming up with Gabriel Jesus has brought out the best in Kun.

Brighton play a super-defensive 4–4–2, which quickly becomes a protective line of six players at the back. City batter away at Brighton's backline over and over again with one of the full-backs moving high up the pitch depending on which side the action's on. Pep's men produce an incredible number of passes – 768 in total, which is 50 more than their highest tally last season (718 against Sunderland) – and achieve 78 per cent possession. But Brighton's two tight defensive lines manage to frustrate City's attempts to score until the last 20 minutes when they go 2–0 up. It's a decisive victory. They've implemented Pep's new strategy to perfection. Mission accomplished.

Their next two games are much tougher, not so much because of the quality of the opposition but because both Everton and Bournemouth use highly defensive formations. They know that this new, improved City is more dangerous, more direct and more vertical than last season and therefore focus all their energy on two tasks: creating and maintaining tight defensive lines close to their area and being ultra-aggressive when pressing City. Pep uses a 3–3–2–2 against Everton and plays Sané as a left wingback in what is more or less a carbon copy of their last game, except for the fact that Everton go ahead thanks to a Wayne Rooney goal, the result of Everton's counterattack after David Silva hits the post. Walker's sending off for a second yellow card complicates matters further for Pep who, after half-time, makes several changes, effectively transforming the formation into an unusual 2–3–3–1. He retains two centre-backs, Kompany and Otamendi, but creates a diamond shape in the centre with De Bruyne at the base, Sterling at the tip and the two Silvas on either side.

Agüero's now alone up front and Danilo and Fernandinho are the fullback/wingers. Pep's asking a lot of his men but they take it in their stride, dominating the second half completely despite being one man down. Their efforts are rewarded in the 82nd minute when Danilo's cross sets up Sterling to score.

Five days later Bournemouth, under the direction of the young and brilliant Eddie Howe, bring a formidable amount of aggression to bear and succeed in opening the scoring with an extraordinary shot from Charlie Daniels. Not to be outdone, Gabriel Jesus then produces a goal for City. One-all. Today Pep's set aside the 3–3–2–2, only using two centre-backs (Kompany and Otamendi), while Danilo, Fernandinho and

Mendy – who's making his debut – form the midfield line with support from De Bruyne. Today Pep has asked the Belgian international to take on the new task of continually linking City's defence and attack in the opposition's half. Despite the fact that Bournemouth score first, City have clearly dominated today. They've achieved 604 passes and taken 19 shots at goal, with the two Silvas moving constantly on the inside, Sterling and Jesus attacking the box and the full-backs bringing depth with their extra work as auxiliary wingers. The frustration grows as the minutes pass and the score is stuck at a draw. Then Pep sends on Sané and Agüero; the team changes to a 2–1–3–4 and begins to impose complete domination. Then, at the 97th minute, Sterling scores from another Danilo cross, securing a victory for the Citizens. Overjoyed, the team starts celebrating on the pitch with many of City's players running to hug their fans in the stands. Unfortunately Sterling's over-enthusiasm earns him his second booking and a red card. It can't dampen the mood, though, and, as they celebrate their last-minute win, there's a real sense of the strong team spirit that they had begun building last season. City are flying. They're playing well and right now they feel that they can cope with any setback. This has been one of those small steps that are such a vital part of creating a winning dynamic.

The team looks unbeatable during the first week of competition in September: 15 goals in favour, none against. In the space of seven days they see off Liverpool, Feyenoord and Watford. Premier League or Champions League, it makes no difference, they feel unstoppable. Ederson's out, recovering from the facial injuries caused by Liverpool winger Sadio Mané's high boot to his face, so Claudio Bravo's back in goal and performing brilliantly, repelling all attacks on goal while his teammates slam goal after goal away.

Guardiola is having to tinker with the 3–3–2–2 he's planned to use. In practice, its disadvantages are clear. On the plus side, it gives them defensive solidity, allows his midfielders to roam freely and lets him have two strikers up front. But it also demands huge physical effort from his full-backs, reduces the role of the wingers in the squad – thereby violating one of the fundamental principles he learned in Munich – and encourages their opponents to pile defenders into their own box and park the bus. It's a dilemma that he knows will take a lot of patience to resolve. He goes with the 3–3–2–2 for the Liverpool game but isn't overimpressed, despite the 5–0 scoreline. His men play with less fluidity than in their previous matches and it's obvious that their tally of 730 passes owes much to the fact that Mané is sent off in the 36th minute for his kung-fu kick on Ederson. Kompany has also been sidelined again, having sustained a calf injury at the end of August. The medical prognosis isn't good – the damage will take a while to heal – which makes it pretty hard for Pep to field three centre-backs given that he now only has two available, Stones and Otamendi, with Danilo as an option. Mangala, back from being on loan at Valencia last season, is still a long way from what the coach is looking for in a centre-back.

He uses a 2–3–2–3 in the next two games, which City smash, pulling off a 4–0 away victory against Feyenoord in the Champions League and beating Watford 6–0 at Vicarage Road in a Premier League game, the latter becoming his biggest winning margin since moving to England. His game plan ensures that the team revert to the 3–3–2–2 when they bring the ball out, with Fernandinho moving back to position himself between the two central defenders and David Silva also dropping back, to where Fernandinho was, between the full-backs. The coach therefore manages to maintain his preferred formation when they bring the ball out and only modifies it once his men have moved the ball past the centre circle, when the players who have moved back return to their original positions. The added flexibility lets him incorporate his wingers thereby gaining extra support in City's high pressing. Bernardo Silva plays against Feyenoord and Sterling is in the team for the Watford game. The team produces some excellent performances and is also given a welcome boost in the shape of İlkay Gündoğan, who's just come back after the serious injury he sustained last season. City dominate. They control the game beautifully and produce flowing, effective football. They press high and concede very little. And the following week they're still on a roll. They eliminate West Brom from the League Cup (1–2) in a game Pep has used to give some playing time to Mangala, Fabian Delph, Yaya Touré and Gündoğan. They then follow that up with a goal fest against Crystal Palace (5–0) in a match that will have huge consequences for the rest of their season.

The coach repeats the flexible game plan he used against Watford, although this time he puts Sterling and Sané up front in attack with Kun, and playing on their favoured sides. Gabriel Jesus starts the game on the bench. The dynamic of the game goes exactly to plan with Fernandinho joining Stones and Otamendi to bring the ball out and David Silva taking up position between Walker and Mendy in their second line of defence. With Sané also moving back beside Kevin De Bruyne, City are temporarily back to 3–3–2–2. Once the ball crosses the centre line the team reforms itself into a 2–3–2–3 but are met with a rigid 4–4–2. The Londoners have shut down all the vertical lanes. Sané and Sterling promptly change sides and are now playing as inverted wingers but City are finding it difficult to break through the Eagles' defences. Roy Hodgson has been in post for just a few days at Palace but he's already bringing his vast experience to bear.

Then, disaster strikes.

Twenty-seven minutes in, Benjamin Mendy is injured in an Andros Townsend challenge. He's taken a hard knock to his left shin and has to be taken off. Pep puts Danilo on in his place and alters his wingers' positions again. Sané goes back to the left flank in order to provide greater depth on the outside. Despite City's total dominance (724 passes and 72 per cent possession) the scoreboard doesn't change until the 44th minute when Sané puts Pep's team one–nil up. City then add four more in a glorious second half in which Danilo plays at right-back while Walker and Otamendi stay in central defence. Talented midfielder Fabian Delph supports Fernandinho bringing out the ball and scores the fifth goal.

City become the first English club to win three consecutive matches by a margin of five or more goals since Blackburn Rovers achieved it in the 1958–9 season. However, back in the dressing room Dr Eduard Mauri's face suggests anything but good news. He obviously fears the worst for Mendy's knee. Pep looks worried. All that energy they bought is already at risk …

ACT 2. FROM 3–3–2–2 TO 2–3–2–3 BECAUSE OF TWO INJURIES

Manchester/Naples/Huddersfield, September–November 2017

There's a camera recording most of what happens in the dressing room from the first day of the new season. Back at the start of the summer, Manel Estiarte explained to me the thinking behind this new project: 'The club received a very lucrative offer from Amazon and Pep agreed to open up the dressing room. Just a few years ago this kind of thing would have been unimaginable but, after his experience in Munich with your two books, he can see the value in being a bit more open. There are no major disadvantages to showing the world what happens behind the scenes. Obviously there will be things that don't go well but you lose nothing by being open about it. And then, all the things that go well more than compensate for the hiccups. The end result is that our fans end up with a much better idea of what happens in the dressing room of an elite club.'

Once completed, the hours of recordings are then edited to create the magnificent documentary *All or Nothing*, released in August 2018 by Amazon Prime Video, which tells the story of everything that happens in Pep's second season. Injuries, which have a huge impact on the life of any football team, play a prominent role in the documentary. This is not surprising given that preventing and managing injuries are as important as a team's training programme, their game plan and tactics, and the analysis of opposition teams. It is one of the factors that determine the success of the team in terms of the seriousness of the injuries the players suffer and their impact as a circuit-breaker of the plans and dynamics of the team. Sometimes it's possible to predict injuries, sometimes not. The kind of things that happen in the heat of a game, either in competition or training,* are impossible to predict. Unintended knocks, mistimed tackles and pure bad luck play a huge role in these incidents. Predictable injuries are the ones that one can antic- ipate based on the player's personal injury record and on whether or not the demands of the training schedule are disproportionate or the excessive number of competitive games is taking too much of a toll.

Lorenzo Buenaventura, City's fitness trainer, tells me, 'An elite team mustn't have more than one or two players, in terms of regular starters, rather than substitutes, who are especially vulnerable to injury. Having more than two top players with a high risk of injury is far too dangerous to the wellbeing of the team.'

This makes it pretty obvious that a series of injuries in a team – whether they're predictable or unpredictable – increases the risk of other players

---

* The study on injury patterns carried out by Jak Ekstrand, Martin Hägglund and Markus Waldén for UEFA in 2011 concluded that on average there are 50 injuries per team per season, which equates to approximately 2 injuries per player, of which 57 per cent are sustained during matches and 43 per cent during training.

getting injured, given that the core group of healthy players has to cope with increased demands as a result of their teammates' absences. The risk of further physical problems therefore rises greatly.

Captain Vincent Kompany injures his calf at the end of August and the doctors tell the club he won't be back before mid-November. Two and a half months without their captain or, to put it another way, with only two top-level centre-backs (Stones and Otamendi). Kompany's injury record makes him a high-risk player. He'll suffer 23 injuries in the 11 seasons he spends at City, from his arrival in the summer of 2008 until his departure at the end of the 2018–19 season. The majority of his injuries are to his lower legs and calves but also to his groin, knees, abductor muscles, quadriceps and hamstrings. Kompany has an extraordinary physique for a defender but his physical fragility has increased over time, resulting in him spending 880 days out through injury in his time with City, for whom he's played 265 games and missed out on 152. The recent diagnosis after his latest injury plus the previous incidents all serve to confirm just how fragile he is. Pep therefore no longer has three fit, top-class centre-backs in the squad and has to rethink his plans.

Four days later, things look even grimmer when Barcelona-based doctor Ramon Cugat confirms that Benjamin Mendy has torn the cruciate ligament of his right knee. Mendy has played 387 minutes but he's going to be out for the rest of the season. The Frenchman is the only pure left-back in the team and one of the most important signings this season. He's like a living embodiment of atomic energy and an essential piece of the tactical formations that Pep has planned. But this injury makes Pep's plans unworkable. Mendy's torn his ligament and Pep's had to tear up his game plan. Back to the drawing board.

His planned formation of three centre-backs and two full-back/wingers either side of a midfielder is unsustainable now that two key players are out. And reconfiguring the first two lines of defence means Pep is obliged to alter the other lines too. Around half past three on the afternoon of Saturday, 23 September 2017, the 3–3–2–2 ceases to exist. Pep's gutted: 'This destroys all our plans. We've scored so many goals in this first part of the season [27 in eight games] because Mendy gave us width. Both him and Walker have been like missiles running up and down non-stop. Do you remember me saying in Munich that I see full-backs as inside midfielders? I still think that, but if you have two rockets you can launch up the flanks, you've got to use them. Walker and Mendy are what you might call "old-school" defenders who run up and down the flanks, giving the team extra width. They're beasts when they defend and human missiles when they attack. Mendy's absence destroys 50 per cent of the plan and we'll have to change our thinking. Danilo is a different kind of full-back. He can definitely play on the outside but he's right-footed and his tendency will inevitably be to cut inside. Delph is the player I'll use to replace Mendy but he doesn't have his stamina and we'll have to help him adapt. He's got a different playing profile. He's a midfielder who arrives in the opposition half with good timing but he's going to have to learn to defend. And we can't expect miracles from him. So the question remains, who have we got who can give us extra width on the left?'

The answer is pretty obvious and Pep doesn't spend a lot of time thinking about it. Leroy Sané is the man to give them that extra width. Pep finds this solution in the fundamental principles of his own philosophy, one of which is the use of 'open' wingers to give greater width. If he no longer has access to a human missile like Mendy, he'll use another kind of missile, although in this case the play is only in the direction of the attack. He can't expect the young German winger to take on the French full-back's defensive duties as well.

Pep therefore adopts the 'Italian method', which is a 2–3–2–3 formation in an attempt to salvage something from what has worked so well up to now. He distributes his men in four rows: two centre-backs form the first defensive line, next come the two full-backs who create a central wall alongside the 'pivot' midfielder; two creative midfielders occupy the intermediary spaces between the opposition players and there is one centre-forward who will, occasionally, drop further back, as a 'false 9'. There are also two wingers playing on their favoured side. There is one qualification. The line of three in the middle is different from the one fielded when Mendy was still available. Now it's more asymmetric. The right-back (Walker or Danilo) will continue to attack on the outside but the left-back (Delph) will stay inside, beside Fernandinho, leaving the attack on the left flank to Sané. The new plan may lack symmetry, but it's organised and executed with absolute precision. On the left the winger (Sané) provides depth and the full-back covers the inside while on the right it's the full-back (Walker) who creates depth and width while the winger (Sterling) cuts inside. In exchange, Pep has to sacrifice the 'double 9' partnership of Agüero and Gabriel Jesus.

The 2–3–2–3 is known to be the playing model introduced to the Italy team by Vittorio Pozzo and Carlo Carcano in 1925 and is widely considered to be what allowed the Azzurri to win the World Cups of 1934 and 1938 plus the Olympic gold in 1936. Historically, it was known as the 'method' and underpinned all the extraordinary success of the Italy team in the 1930s. By using it, Pozzo and Carcano intended to maintain the basic foundation of the 'Cambridge Pyramid' with two centre-backs and three in the middle, but breaking up the line of five 'pure' attackers into two midfielders and three forwards in order to try and reduce how exposed the team is when attacking.

Guardiola's version of the 2–3–2–3 creates a very special dynamic. Once the team is established in the opposition's area – thus the build-up is already completed – attacking readiness combines with defensive alertness, and the first and last lines respond in similar ways: both of the centre-backs and the two wingers slow down almost to a standstill, 'waiting' for the action to develop. It's the six 'inside men' in the middle lines that circulate the ball looking for space to break through their opponents' defensive structure. These six men (the defensive midfielder plus the full-backs, the creative midfielders and the central striker) adapt their baseline positions and their movements depending on the type of opposition they're playing. It can often look like the players are distributed in different ways but in reality the basic 2–3–2–3 never changes. The inside men move the ball and the remaining four sit tight, waiting for their chance to intervene, either as points of defensive support or to finish off an attacking move. The two creative midfielders are principally responsible for the quality, speed and direction of the passing sequences within a flexible hexagon shape, which they, the pivot/organising midfielder, both full-backs plus the central striker create, and which constantly breaks down into small or large triangles in order to disorganise the opponent. (I specifically refer to small or large triangles for an obvious reason: the team forms small triangles on the left [where the full-back stays inside] and big triangles on the right [where his duty is to give width and depth].)

Pep does it this way because of the characteristics of the particular players he's got: on the left David Silva (or, in his absence, Gündoğan) builds long sequences of short passes which facilitates his advance up the pitch along-side the full-back and the winger; on the right De Bruyne (or Bernardo or Foden) then has much more sizeable space in which to form bigger triangles with the other full-back or corresponding winger. In this way, although the triangles on the left are much smaller than those on the right, the creative process is similar. The two wingers wait, positioned ahead of wherever the ball is, for exactly the right moment to join the action, while behind them the midfielder and the two full-backs, plus the slightly deeper centre-backs, combine to protect City's area from possible counterattacks. Guardiola's 2–3–2–3 formation is a variant of the traditional pyramid shape and as soon as a full-on attack is launched and they're going for the opponent's throat, it shifts itself into the classic 2–3–5. Using this model allows City to dominate in the opponent's half while maintaining a protective wall against counters via their five men who, theoretically, remain behind the ball. It also means that their six players based in the middle of the pitch can create intense pressure by circulating the ball while forming different triangles in order to advance. It's not unusual for the final attacking line to consist of five men.

Pep's men are totally at home in the 2–3–2–3 and could find their required positions with their eyes shut. The model requires high levels of collective commitment and cooperation but also gives them the fluidity and freedom to perform at their best. The 2–3–2–3, and its many variants, causes City to achieve an average of 70 per cent possession and feel almost unbeatable.

Pep continues to apply the tactical changes he's made through the end of September and into October. September ends on a high note as City add two key wins to the five they've already accumulated: 2–0 against Shakhtar in the Champions League and 0–1 against reigning champions Chelsea. The winning goal is scored by none other than Kevin De Bruyne, who had been unceremoniously dumped by the London club in the winter of 2012 after playing just three games.

The same playing model is still in place throughout October. No matter the variety of tactics their opponents choose, they use it against Burnley's 5–4–1, against West Brom and against the 4–3–3 Napoli decide to play. For every game Pep's men are distributed across the pitch in the same shape, with eight 'untouchable' players: Ederson, Walker, Stones, Otamendi, Delph, Fernandinho, De Bruyne and David Silva. Up front, Pep chooses different permutations from the squad's five attacking players. Bernardo Silva is still adapting to this style of play and it's a gradual process. Pep is slowly increasing his playing time as well as that of Germany international Gündoğan, whom he hopes will soon be back to the kind of amazing form he demonstrated at Borussia Dortmund. To everyone's surprise Fabian Delph is performing brilliantly as an interior full-back. His formidable partnership with Fernandinho in the organisation of the game has added relentless speed to the team's arsenal while Sané heads up the blistering attacks on the opposition's goal.

Yet this has all come about by accident. Having been forced to abandon his original plans, Guardiola has done away with the use of two strikers, has 'improvised' a new full-back and begun to make Sané an automatic starter. Meanwhile, the team has continued to produce excellent football, far beyond what anyone could have expected. They remain unbeaten throughout October, adding four and a half victories (City draw with Wolves in the League Cup but win on penalties) to the nine previously achieved this season.

Mid-October, a brilliant game against Maurizio Sarri's Napoli showcases City's strengths but also exposes weaknesses. An initial breathtaking half-hour sees City produce superlative football and two goals, plus a shot off the crossbar and a beautiful strike by Gabriel Jesus, which doesn't quite make it across Pepe Reina's goal-line. Then the Italians launch their fightback. They block the avalanche of City's attacks and take control for the next 30 minutes. Sarri's men are now the dominant force and their efforts produce a penalty, which Ederson manages to save. After the game Pep's full of praise for the Italians: 'This Napoli side are the best I've come across in terms of their ability to produce sequences of short, accurate passes.'

This is the second time in a row that John Stones has achieved an almost 100 per cent success rate in his passing (108 of 109 passes against Stoke; 83 out of 85 against Napoli) and Pep congratulates him publicly, saying, 'John has made a huge leap forward in terms of his performance.' Txiki Begiristain goes even further, 'John's already one of the best centre-backs in the world and one day he's going to be the best.' Gabriel Jesus has also impressed. So far, he has played a part in 21 of City's goals in the 20 games he's started and has scored his last 10 goals with his first touch.

City's amazing performance against Stoke City (7–2) means they've scored 29 goals in their first 8 games, bringing them a hair's breadth away from the record Everton set in 1894 by scoring 30 goals in their first 8 games. It also marks Pep's 300th league game as a coach. He's won 76 per cent of those games with an average of 2.58 goals per match.

Sergio Agüero sets another record in the Burnley game. He's scored 177 goals to equal the record set by City's legendary striker Eric Brook, but has done it in 259 games, significantly fewer than Brook, who took 493 games over 11 years (1928 to 1939) to achieve the same total.

The team has also matched the record number of consecutive victories achieved in the club's history (11) and a few days later shatter several Premier League records in their performance against West Bromwich Albion: a total of 843 passes, 1,111 touches and 72 per cent possession. They end their tenth league game of the season with 28 points out of a possible 30. The best start to a league competition in history.

Domènec Torrent, who's been Pep's assistant coach since 2013, explains that Pep 'came to England to contribute and share ideas, not to change English football or give lessons to anyone. Just to bring new ideas. Let me repeat it so that nobody misunderstands. Pep's not the Messiah or some kind of evangelist on a mission to change football. He's here to offer his vision of the game, learn from those who have other ideas and then create effective, entertaining football.'

For the past few weeks Sané and Sterling have been alternating wings. They're either playing on their favoured sides, to create width, or, as inverted wingers, looking to cut inside onto their stronger foot so that they can assist or shoot directly on goal. Sané's playing out of his skin. He's scored 8 and given 5 assists in 15 matches. Mikel Arteta always spends a bit of time at the end of training to go through specific attacking routines with Sané, Sterling and Gabriel Jesus. It's really paying off.

Guardiola maintains the asymmetrical positioning of his full-backs but in some games Walker and Delph play in parallel on the inside, leaving the wingers to handle the attack on the outside. These changes are made according to the kind of opponent they're playing. At difficult moments, Pep makes alterations to the 2–3–2–3, reorganising the team into a 2–1–4–3 or a 2–4–4, and even into a pyramid shape (2–3–5) when he decides that all-out attack is inevitable. He'll also ask De Bruyne and David Silva to play different roles depending on the needs of the moment. Their versatility means they can act as single organising midfielders, attacking midfielders or wingers. At the same time Bernardo Silva is really coming into his own in the dual role of winger/creative midfielder. He's playing brilliantly.

City are still unbeaten in November, winning six more games, and continuing to break records. After a difficult start to the Napoli game – 25 excruciating minutes of constant pressure – Pep's men find their rhythm, and, despite going 1–0 down, begin to boss the game. Napoli lose left-back Faouzi Ghoulam after he sustains a bad injury, a big plus for City. In the end, Pep's team dominate the game and beat a very strong opponent 2–4. It's the first time an English team has beaten Napoli in the San Paolo Stadium in a Champions League game and Sarri's side hasn't lost at home since April. Agüero scores his 178th goal and becomes the top goalscorer in the club's history (264 matches, 0.67 goals/match).

When they don't have the ball, the team tends to reconfigure into a 4–1–4–1, in which Fernandinho showcases his excellent defensive aerial skills. Given that the team only spends 25 per cent of the time without the ball, Pep doesn't vary his defensive organisation too much. They've also reduced the number of direct shots at goal taken by opposition teams: 6.2 shots on goal (compared to 8.2 last season) of which only 2.2 are on target. It's the lowest figure of any team in the league. By some margin.

What is now officially the best start in the history of the Premier League culminates in a 3–1 victory over Arsenal. This has also been Guardiola's best-ever start to a season: 11 games, 10 victories, 1 draw, 38 goals, 7 conceded. Pep's players are clearly comfortable with his playing model. Each of them knows he can play his own role with total security, knowing that his teammates will be exactly where they're meant to be at all times, that every position will be covered. They're also confident in their ability to switch smoothly between bold, aggressive attacks and the periods of calm, measured control needed in every game.

Nobody handles transitioning between the two rhythms of play better than De Bruyne, an innately talented playmaker with the freedom to roam all over the pitch. Multiskilled and capable of playing in any one of six different positions, De Bruyne is having a monumental season, controlling and guiding play, dominating all phases of the game and taking the team to previously unsuspected levels of excellence. De Bruyne's success represents the triumph of permanent mobility and the concept of capitalising on players' natural abilities rather than being limited by clichéd ideas of fixed positions.

Halfway through November, John Stones tears his hamstring. It is one of the few hamstring injuries that the team will suffer all season but it breaks up the Stones–Otamendi partnership, which has been pretty much unbeatable and has played a huge part in City's success so far this season. Coincidentally, Stones injures himself on the same day that City's captain, Vincent Kompany, returns after an absence of 77 days. Kompany therefore partners up with Otamendi. Conscious of his captain's fragility, Pep also gives Mangala a handful of starts so he can alternate with Kompany. It's now that Otamendi's performance moves up a gear. He's improved dramatically in several aspects of his game relating to position, anticipation, driving the attack and accurate passing. The coaching team know how ambitious the player is and attribute this improvement to his single-minded determination to progress. And to two other key factors. The distribution of City's players on the pitch creates lots of passing lines and their long hours of practising positional play have paid dividends.

Dome Torrent explains this unexpected improvement in Otamendi: 'Players have a natural style of play, which they themselves sometimes don't even know they possess. But if you manage to create the right environment, you often find that suddenly, to everyone's surprise, they produce a kind of football from deep within themselves that they didn't believe was possible. That's what's happening with Otamendi. He's become a master of positional drills and the rondos.'

Unfortunately Otamendi will be responsible for the first goal from a set piece that the team concede this season. It results from a corner taken by Huddersfield, which the Argentine defender knocks into his own goal in the 45th minute. It's a bad sign. Not since April 1995 have City won away from home having gone into half-time a goal or more behind. During the exhausting second half Huddersfield defend with an impenetrable 5–4–1. The Sky Blues make 295 passes during this period against 16 from the home side and have 85 per cent possession. Then, just as a draw seems inevitable, the 'Sterling factor' comes into play. It's a phenomenon much like the

'Cesarini zone'.* The young striker snatches the winning goal in the 84th minute having done a similar thing against Feyenoord in the 88th minute five days previously and against Everton (82nd minute) and Bournemouth (96th minute) in the weeks before that. If Sané stands out playing wide, Sterling does the same thing, just in a different way. Last season he scored 11 goals in 47 games. He's matched that tally this season already, having played just 17 times. His improvement is down to geometry.

Despite all this, the coaching team always want more. After having beaten Feyenoord 1–0 in the Champions League, City have qualified, arithmetically at least, top of their group. They've also played 25 games without defeat. But Dome Torrent isn't happy with how they play when the opposition parks the bus. 'I think it's a mistake to play inverted wingers against the tight defensive lines we had today. If we want to avoid creating our own log jam, they should be on the side that suits their favoured foot.'

Today is Pep's 50th win as City coach and it's also Phil Foden's official debut. He's the third player born in 2000 to compete in the Champions League and the youngest City player ever to do so. City's other young future star, Brahim Díaz, also comes on in the final minutes. The 5–4–1 has become the go-to formation for City's opposition. It's the formation they think is their best 'anti-City' tactic. Mauricio Pellegrino's Southampton defends with ten men in their own area and it seems to be working for them until the 96th minute when, for the third game in a row, Sterling scores and wins the game for City, just as the clocks are showing 'time's up'.

Out on the pitch in the Etihad Stadium, Pep's men go wild …

ACT 3. THE SHARK TEAM: 18 STRAIGHT WINS

Manchester/London, December 2017

Txiki has invited the doctor for a coffee this morning – 11 hours after an agonising win over Southampton. On his mind is whether what Mendy did

---

* The Italian Argentine player Renato Cesarini had a peculiar ability to score in the closing minutes of games and this became known as the 'Cesarini zone'. The nickname was first used on 13 December 1931 in Turin when Italy beat Hungary 3–2 in the Dr Gerö Cup, and he scored in the 90th minute.

last night will impact on his knee recovery process. Dr Mauri doesn't think
so ... but it's too soon to be absolutely sure.

Southampton, full of top-class players like Virgil van Dijk, Pierre-
Emile Højbjerg, Oriol Romeu, Fraser Forster, Ryan Bertrand and Nathan
Redmond, squeeze every last drop out of City. So when Sterling tucks away
the winner there is an explosion of collective joyful 'madness'.

Pep's team go one up thanks to De Bruyne's free kick, which van Dijk
deflects into the Southampton net. But they squander copious chances, with
Jesus and Gündoğan particular sinners. Saints duly equalise from Romeu's
free kick 15 minutes before the final whistle, leading to a frantic cavalry
charge from the home side, desperate to conserve their superb start to the
season. They get there, but it takes until the 96th minute when Sterling whips
the ball into the top corner of Forster's goal – the fifth time he's scored in
the dying stages and the third straight match in which he's conjured up a
last-minute match-winner.

Emotions spill over. City's entire staff are leaping about on the playing
surface, Sterling is buried under a pile of exuberant teammates. Amidst it
all, Mendy has chucked his crutches aside and jogged-limped half the length
of the pitch as if he hasn't just undergone knee surgery. The Frenchman
is the self-appointed cheerleader and team-spirit guru of the squad – even
more so since his knee-ligament injury. From the surgeon's table onwards
he's begun to send upbeat 'cheer-up' messages to all his teammates. The
frequency has gone up, as has the optimistic, cheeky tone – to the point that
his nickname for the team becomes contagious. In short order, the club will
launch a run of 'Shark Team' merchandising with the predator's jaws wide
open, and across the stadium's stands there are scores of inflatable sharks
popping up everywhere. 'We are the Shark Team and when any team tries
to swim with us we'll eat them up!' is Mendy's boast. He comes up with the
idea in September – two months later, the team is still insatiable.

Full of beans from the win, City's 12th in the league already, Guardiola's
upbeat with the media as he wisecracks about Mendy's crazy sprint: 'He's
mad! He's in a six-month recovery process and there he is sprinting across
the pitch. Disaster!' Said with a resigned grin. But Txiki's preoccupied with
what extra damage may have been done and wants to pin the doctor down
– although their chat doesn't lead to any firm conclusions. Except, naturally,

that Mendy needs to be told to keep a lid on his emotions if they're going to worsen his injury. Time to avoid unnecessary risks.

They have nine matches in December. It's going to be tough and Pep intends to mitigate the impact on his men by trying some daring team rotations (Mangala's back in the equation so Kompany, for example, can be protected), all the while maintaining the 2–3–2–3 structure. First up: West Ham. Not unexpectedly the east London team park the bus. A 5–4–1, which plays deep, squeezes space between lines and allows City up to 80 per cent possession. But Pep's team doesn't really create the right amount of clear chances despite such high levels of possession. It's a trend. After the likes of Huddersfield, Feyenoord and Southampton have tried to create a wall between their goal and City's attack force, other teams decide to copy them. It seems the ideal way to frustrate City's efforts.

A minute before the break, West Ham expose a City weakness: a corner to the front post and a super header from Angelo Ogbonna. It's only the second goal that City have conceded from a corner this season but now the Hammers build their wall still deeper having gone 1–0 up – it's horrible trying to break it down.

But, eventually, goals from Otamendi then David Silva give the home side their 13th straight win – equalling a record previously set by Preston and Sunderland in 1891–2 and 1892–3, respectively.

Fifteen matches into the season the sky blue team in Manchester have 43 points, which is a Premier League record and Pep's high-water mark throughout his entire coaching career. Typically, even in the midst of such record-breaking success Pep has a real bee in his bonnet about how much it's costing him, and more importantly his team, to break down hermetically sealed defensive opponents. His verdict: 'These last matches have suggested to me that it's important to attack differently when you're facing a side which has opted to park the bus. I think the way forward is two central strikers [Kun and Jesus] plus two "open" wingers – De Bruyne and David Silva – serving them from wide. We've learned things in the last three or four weeks which'll serve us well in the future.'

City are comfortable league leaders and have won their Champions League group so the away trip to Shakhtar, with nothing serious riding on it, obviously invites team rotation. It'll be 3–4–3 this time, Fernandinho in between Adarabioyo and Mangala in the backline, Yaya Touré at pivot (since the summer friendlies he's only played 207 competitive minutes across three matches), with young Foden as one of the two full-back/wingers. The team swaps to a 5–2–3 formation at key moments and, late in the match, Pep puts Brahim Díaz on who, in a short space of time, tries 18 dribbles and pulls off 8 of them. Impressive.

All the same, the night brings City's first defeat this season (2–1) and ends a run of 28 unbeaten matches (5 at the end of last term and 23 this season) of which 24 have been wins. That Pep's 100th Champions League match as coach is stained by defeat matters not one jot to the Catalan. His absolute priorities were to rotate his players and to experiment with the team shape, not to add another win to their stats, which are already the best in the competition's history: 61 wins, 23 draws and, now, just 16 defeats. This is in comparison to the numbers for Mourinho (54 wins), Ferguson (53) and Ancelotti (50).

By happenstance, Mourinho's Manchester United is next up – four days after defeat in Kharkiv it's United at Old Trafford. Trying to curveball his old rival, Pep has Sterling at false 9, Leroy Sané wide right and Gabriel Jesus on the left touchline. This is not at all how they lineup for kick-off but three minutes in, all three City forwards change positions and there's something for Mourinho and his back four to puzzle over while the derby rages on. United don't like it. Mourinho copies those who've gone immediately before him and parks the bus. Until City find the winning goal in the 54th minute (1–2), they've had a 72 per cent share of possession, which is a record high for an away team at Old Trafford.

While it's up as high as 75 per cent domination of the ball in the first half, Sterling gives an absolute recital of how a false 9 is supposed to play. It's 15 months and 40 matches since United lost at the Theatre of Dreams but this is turning into a nightmare for them. Their last defeat? Pep's first Manchester derby. And, while today's scoreline is the same, there are a thousand more details in this win to savour.

So total is the away team's domination of the match that, for example, they win the aerial duels (19 vs 14) despite the average height of the two teams being 6cm in United's favour. It's a derby, though, and Ederson needs to pull off three good saves. On two occasions, Delph messes up and fails to clear a United long ball, and from one of the rebounds Rashford squares the game after Silva's opener. Kompany is hit by muscular problems at half-time and needs to come off. Fernandinho replaces him in the middle of the backline with Gündoğan taking the organising position in central midfield. Once City re-establish their lead, thanks to Otamendi bang in front of David De Gea's goalmouth, Pep really shakes things up – starting with Mangala on for Gabriel Jesus. Now it's Otamendi and Mangala at the back, Fernandinho flanked by Walker and Delph in the middle, Gündoğan and De Bruyne the floating creative men plus David Silva now at false 9 with Sané and Sterling the wingers.

This win gives City an 11-point lead on United, 14 on Chelsea and 16 on Liverpool. After only 16 matches. Now the outright record for consecutive wins belongs to Manchester City – 14. This is Pep's second victory at Old Trafford and brings his record against Mourinho to 9 wins out of 20 head-to-head contests as coaches (4 draws, 7 defeats). City's party in the Old Trafford dressing room raises the roof and Graeme Souness, the star of that all-conquering Liverpool side of the 1970s, wraps up the day with the phrase: 'Not even in the most powerful era of Liverpool's greatness did we manage to dominate at Old Trafford like City have done today.'

City's triumphal march continues into the last month of 2017. It's only three days later that David Silva produces his best game in many months in the 0–4 destruction of Swansea. Pre-match, Mikel Arteta tells his boss: 'Pep, you can't believe the shape they're in today – they've handled the warm-up like raging animals.'

Another record falls, one set by Arsenal's 'Invincibles' in 2003–4. City make 831 successful passes, they're on the ball 1,006 times and, because they dominate 78.2 per cent of possession, the coach decides to give match time to both Touré and Zinchenko. Swansea coach Paul Clement is unhesitating: 'if you support City it must be an absolute joy to watch them play. That's one of the best teams I've ever seen …'

Life is tough, however, and, barely a day after Silva's display of outright genius, there comes a hammer blow. His son, Mateo, is born prematurely, at only six months, and everyone's priorities are reordered. Nevertheless, the Premier League is relentless. Spurs, under Mauricio Pochettino, are beaten 4–1 on 16 December and it's another record-breaking game for City – they've now beaten every club from the second to the ninth position in the league. It's also a breakthrough moment for De Bruyne who, in Silva's absence, will step forward, in thrilling, driving form, over the next three months. Against Spurs the Belgian does it all: he presses, sets the match tempo, drives with the ball, passes and passes, shoots, scores … Pep's offered him a structure where he's an 8 but with total freedom of movement. He earns another Man of the Match award to add to those he's already accrued against Chelsea, Manchester United, Liverpool, Arsenal … 'I really don't have the vocabulary to sum up what Kevin's done today,' Pep tells me after the game.

Prior to us heading off into the city the entire squad poses in the dressing room with a 'Silva' shirt, including young Phil Foden, the man Pep hopes will become the 'next David Silva'. He's just made his Premier League debut, exactly 27 years to the day after a young Pep Guardiola played his first game in the Spanish league. It's no coincidence. Pep has become Foden's mentor. The Catalan wants Foden to fulfil his destiny as a potential great of English football.

But there's work to do. 'We've performed the right way for this team today, the system gives our players confidence, strength and very few self-doubts on the pitch. But tomorrow I'm going to review the game – I saw a few minor details I want them to correct.' For Guardiola, even winners can't afford to relax.

• • •

When the League Cup visit to Leicester comes around City show up with a mix of veterans and young players (Bravo and Touré are both 34 but there are eight who are younger than 21: Zinchenko, Adarabioyo, Foden, Brahim and, during extra-time, Lukas Nmecha and Fisayo Dele-Bashiru). All the youngsters are familiar with the first team's usual playing model and the game doesn't differ greatly from most City performances. They dominate but then lose an equaliser to a 97th-minute penalty. After a solid performance in the extra half-hour, Pep's men win the shoot-out thanks to Bravo's save from Riyad Mahrez. For the second time in a row, the Chilean has done his stuff when facing opponents from 12 yards away. This group are in the semi-finals. After knocking Leicester out, the dressing room is buzzing with the idea that if the 'big' team is the 'Shark Team' then this is the 'Zinchenko Team'. The baby brother.

Two days before Christmas David Silva comes back to play a game, as he'll often do over these three very testing months. Bournemouth are, as anticipated, a tight 5–4–1, determined to extinguish any creative space for City to have fun in. So Pep puts the Spanish 'Magician' in a midfield diamond-four: Sterling at the tip, Fernandinho at the base with Silva and De Bruyne either side. During the second half City produce stunning football, overwhelming the visitors with 80 per cent possession. It's encouraging to hear that the crowd understand just how technically brilliant their game is. There's applause for Otamendi turning to pass backwards to Ederson so that the Brazilian keeper can quickly change the line of City's attack. And there are cheers when City press Bournemouth into immediately surrendering the ball on the rare occasion they have it. The result is that, for the first time in his career, Kun scores two headers in the same match.

The year 2017 is ushered out with a terrific home record. Twenty-six matches, no defeats, 101 goals – the first English team to beat the century mark in a calendar year since Liverpool (106) in 1982. Right now, City's Premier League stats are: 18 wins, 1 draw, 60 goals (3.1 on average per match), 12 conceded (0.6) and 55 points out of a possible 57. Those are outstanding numbers, but I want to explore one other relevant detail: the number of times this team threads ten or more passes together.

When City are winning they put together these longer sequences 13.4 per cent of the time and when they are losing it's 6.8 per cent. In other words, the number of continuous passes doubles when City are in a positive situation compared to a negative one: a clear indication of passing and possession being used as a means of controlling matches. When City are winning those longer passing sequences finish with an effort on goal 9 per cent of the time. When they're losing that figure goes up to 27 per cent. Triple the number.

As Christmas approaches, Pep is in a very different state of mind from the same time last year. He's thrilled with the team's success – they're 13 points ahead of second-placed United, which is the greatest margin ever between the first- and second-placed teams in the Premier League. He's also delighted with his men: 'this dressing room is like a dream come true.'

City increase their lead on 27 December at St James' Park with their 18th straight win. Kompany is injured three minutes in and Pep surprises just about everyone by bringing on Jesus for the central defender. Now City have two central strikers and the formation is 2–3–1–4. Given that Newcastle are using a 5–4–1 Fernandinho can alternate between centre-back and pivot.

Otamendi makes more passes individually (122) than the entire Newcastle team (115). City now have 58 points from a possible 60 after 20 matches (19 wins, 1 draw), 61 scored, 12 conceded, and it's becoming the best start to a campaign in any of the five top European leagues. Of the Shark Team's 18 wins, 11 have been away from home. Now City have 15 points on United and 16 on reigning champions Chelsea.

Even if, inevitably, fatigue gnaws at these remarkable players, there's little to no doubt that the title will be sky-blue coloured by the end of the season. With zero recovery time it's down to London, where, on the final day of the year, City draw 0–0 at Palace. No David Silva, De Bruyne worn out and Sané's form irregular. Nothing here is a surprise. In the Premier League, 29 per cent of all 0–0 draws come in the last week of the year – the one where Boxing Day and New Year matches squeeze creativity out of players. Competitive stress has emptied too many players of their mental and physical best. Pep tries everything against yet another 4–5–1 but his creative players don't produce a goal for the first time since January (vs Everton). Even dropping the run of straight wins for this tiring goalless draw isn't the thing that stings. It's the injuries. Gabriel Jesus has twisted ligaments in his left knee – out until the end of February. Kompany's calf problem means he's out for three weeks. De Bruyne has taken a really nasty kick on the ankle, the fourth properly bad one an opponent has dealt out on a City player in recent matches: Dele Alli on De Bruyne, Harry Kane on Sterling, Jacob Murphy on Gündoğan and, today, Jason Puncheon on De Bruyne again. Guardiola speaks directly to the refereeing community when he says: 'Protect the players please – not just mine but all of them!' But nobody's listening …

Those who can't keep up can kick all they want but it won't derail City. Liverpool, 18 points behind City when 2018 dawns, manage to sign a player Guardiola was keen on: Virgil van Dijk. Southampton accept £75 million for the talented defender – at that price City are out. All this triggers Txiki going back to Athletic Bilbao and laying out the €65 million (£57 million) they want for Aymeric Laporte. Finally, finally, Pep has the left-footed centre-back he's craved.

ACT 4. THE FIRST TROPHY OF THE GUARDIOLA ERA

Liverpool/Manchester/Basel/London, January–March 2018

In January, City suffer their first league defeat. To add salt to the wound, it happens at Anfield.

An action-packed game, during which City's centre-backs make four serious mistakes that cost their team dearly. Klopp's using his favoured, asphyxiating gegenpressing style and a 4–2–3–1 formation with which he likes to hurt Guardiola's teams. It's lethally effective, as ever, but it also exposes a psychological weakness in Pep's men. The team has an almost congenital tendency to panic at certain moments. City lose focus and organisation during a nine-minute period in which the Reds score three times. Stones, Otamendi and Ederson, three of the standout players of the season so far, mess up badly.

Just minutes into the game, Fernandinho loses the ball as they bring it out. Stones fails to close down the space that's opened up and Alex Oxlade-Chamberlain crosses from distance, angling the ball so that Ederson can't stop it. Pep's men aren't thrown, though, and they stick to the philosophy they've used the whole season. They're creating a lot of danger for Liverpool who respond with a series of fierce counterattacks.

Klopp's men remain tight on the inside but are vulnerable on the wing, which is precisely where Sané makes his move 40 minutes in when he controls the ball with his chest, dribbles past two opponents and shoots the ball in off the near post. All square at half-time. Each of these two mighty Premier League sides is playing to type: Liverpool with their powerful pressing and ferocious counterattacking and City maintaining high possession despite their passing being slightly less accurate than usual (83 per cent).

Delph injures his right knee 30 minutes in – he'll be out for several weeks as a result – so Danilo replaces him at left-back.

Immediately as the second half starts, City have a corner and Otamendi's header bounces off the crossbar. But, just when everything seems to be going according to Pep's plan, his central defenders switch to panic mode between the 59th and 68th minutes. First, Firmino wins a duel with Stones in City's penalty box and then beats Ederson to score. Within seconds, Fernandinho messes up as he brings the ball out, effectively gifting it to Mané, whose shot hits the post.

Almost immediately, Otamendi fluffs an easy tackle on Mo Salah, who feeds Mané. This time his shot is right on target. The horror show concludes with a disastrous clearance from Ederson, which lands straight at Salah's feet. The Liverpool winger lofts the ball towards City's goal and it's number four for the home side. Late in the game, Bernardo Silva and Gündoğan both score (84, 91) but it's not enough. The league leaders have been soundly beaten. It's City's first defeat in the 23 league games they've played so far this season. They've won 20 and drawn 2, achieving 62 of a possible 69 points, thereby matching records set by Spurs in 1960–1 and Chelsea in 2005–6.

It's exactly a year since Pep's men conceded four goals in a league game. That defeat also took place in Liverpool, at Goodison Park, where Everton won 4–0. Their run of 30 games without defeat has lasted 283 days, from 5 April 2017, during which time they've won 26 and drawn 4. Klopp now edges ahead of Pep in the battle of the coaches. He's just pulled off his 6th victory in 12 encounters against Pep's 5 wins and 1 draw.

Bookending the Anfield debacle, City continue relentlessly in January. They start the new year against Watford at the Etihad on the 2nd. Thirty-eight seconds in, Sterling sends a killer pass to Sané who immediately converts it. The fastest goal of the season so far.

Stones is back, having recovered from his torn hamstring. Pep's players are clearly exhausted, though, and, for the first and only time this season, he decides to skip the pre-match team talk. 'It's not the moment to fill their heads with more stuff. They're exhausted. I want them going out with clear heads at least.'

Four days later, City eliminate Burnley from the FA Cup (4–1) but a bad error from Stones gives the visitors the opening goal and mars his triumphant return. Pep leaps to his player's defence: 'The important thing is not John's error but his reaction to it. Instead of putting his head down, letting it throw him off and stop looking for the ball, John came back stronger. That's what's so admirable. It's not the mistakes that matter, it's how you react and adapt after making them.'

After the break, a double whammy from Gündoğan and Agüero (two assists from the German matched by two more goals from the little Argentine) drives the Citizens' fightback, which culminates with two more from Sané and Bernardo Silva. David Silva produces a standout performance but after today his time will now be much more taken up with his premature baby, who's still very delicate. The influential and much-loved Spaniard needs to spend as much time with his son as possible until he's out of danger and will miss the majority of matches and all training sessions until that moment arrives. It's only once little Mateo Silva has been given the all-clear that his father will be able to refocus his efforts on the team. This forced absence accelerates Gündoğan's recuperation. He gets more playing time, which helps enormously in getting him back to full match fitness and form.

With their audacious, high-pressing football, Bristol City become one of the toughest opponents City face in the League Cup. Across the two-legged semi-final, City beat them 2–1 at home with a late goal from Agüero (91st minute) and then at Ashton Gate where Kevin De Bruyne finds another late winner (95th) to give the visitors a 3–2 win on the night and a 5–3 passage overall.

Guardiola completes his 500th match as coach with an impressive tally: 365 victories (73 per cent), 83 draws, 52 defeats, 1,252 goals scored (average 2.5) and 381 conceded (average 0.76). But the real significance of the result is that beating Lee Johnson's team means it's time for Pep's first final in charge of City. David Silva has also reached an extraordinary milestone. This is his 24th victory in 24 consecutive games. It's the longest winning streak a player has achieved in English football since 1863.

Towards the end of January, with the Anfield defeat now a distant memory, City play Newcastle and Agüero produces his 11th hat-trick for the club. It's sublime. In fact, it's 'perfect'. First a header, then a right-foot finish and, finally, he tucks the ball away off his left. Kun is also celebrating his 200th game for City. Meanwhile, Pep gives Brahim Díaz his first league appearance.

Their next game, Cardiff in the FA Cup, sees De Bruyne convert a free-kick, which he directs low, under Cardiff's jumping wall. He dedicates the idea, if not the execution, to Dome Torrent and Carles Planchart: 'It was all thanks to our team of analysts. They warned me that Cardiff's defensive wall always jumps when the opposition take a free kick!' Unfortunately, even if predictably, an opponent cuts Sané down as he starts one of his amazing sprints. It's a brutal tackle and Sané's left with a damaged ankle that swells up like a tennis ball. Pep's furious with the referee and calls for better protection for players, 'That's what the referee's there for. To protect the players.' As usual, nobody listens …

Now that Laporte's here, Mangala's gone on loan to Everton. Just one training session and a few long passes is enough for Pep. He's delighted with their new signing's left foot: 'Laporte's fantastic. He strikes it beautifully – clean, long and precise. He'll be starting tomorrow. The moment Pep saw Laporte striking the ball he fell in love,' Estiarte tells me after training. The following day, without any more preparation or training, Laporte is indeed in the starting 11 when City beat West Brom 3–0. The Spain international performs brilliantly. De Bruyne scores City's 100th goal of the season and the win takes the team to 68 points. They're already 2 points ahead of the 66 they achieved last season. In just 25 games. And they're well on course to smash even more records.

Pep's men are on the receiving end of some pretty brutal treatment from the opposition: James McClean, Matt Phillips and Allan Nyom in particular indulge in outrageously aggressive tackles on Bruyne, Díaz and Walker but the referee just shows two yellow cards and does not even book one of the players, which acts as no kind of deterrent.

Beating Manchester United and Chelsea increases the points difference by 15 and 18 points respectively and the coaching team start the countdown: they only need eight more victories to guarantee winning the league. Torrent tells me: 'You should call your next book about Pep, "Learning and Perseverance".'

• • •

On 25 February 2018, at Wembley, Guardiola wins his first trophy in English football.

This is one of his 'lucky' stadiums. As a 20-year-old he played in the Barcelona side that won the 1992 European Cup final here and then, 19 years later, returned as Barça coach to brilliantly win the 2011 Champions League. This is the third final he's disputed in England's legendary stadium. City beat Arsène Wenger's Arsenal 3–0 and Pep's on cloud nine.

The team has played four games in February before lifting the trophy. On 3 February, at Burnley, another goal from a set piece causes Guardiola to congratulate Domènec Torrent publicly after Danilo tucks the ball away following a corner. Although Pep's men miss an enormous amount of chances, and only manage a draw at Turf Moor, they nonetheless produce extraordinary football, with Gündoğan in particular on terrific form. City dominate and play exceptionally, but have 20 close misses on goal. It's their finishing that remains a colossal problem to the extent that they even fail to score in front of an open goal. Burnley grab their unexpected equaliser late in the game, thereby robbing City of three deserved points.

Pep's still pretty upbeat post-match: 'We played really well. Perhaps other people don't agree because we only drew but almost everything was perfect. The build-up, our defending against long balls, winning second balls, our gutsy performance … we simply missed too many good chances …'

Behind closed doors though, their finishing is really bothering him. We chat at length about the game and the goals, and I tell him what a joy it is to watch this team play. He doesn't disagree: 'We're very, very happy. We're not good enough to win in Europe yet because of our problems with finishing. We need a lot of chances for every goal we get and in European football, you have to be much more decisive than that because your opponents will take every chance they get. But we play great football and we're all delighted with the way it's going.'

I point out how well they're bringing the ball out and suggest that perhaps fatigue is causing them to make mistakes in front of goal. Pep sees it very differently: 'We're definitely going to be eliminated from the Champions League. And there's nothing we can do about it! We know that we play spectacular football and that no one (and I do mean no one) plays as well as we do. But that's not enough. We don't beat defenders one-on-one so it's impossible for us to win European trophies … Messi, Luis Suárez, Cristiano, Neymar, Mbappé, they can get past anyone and they will, if you give them half a chance. We seem to need two-dozen chances to get even one goal.'

I tell him that this is bound to improve once his attacking players are a bit fresher. He's not convinced: 'You still need to be able to score goals no matter how tired you are … I'm not asking for another Messi or a wonder goal like Danilo scored … but if you make it into the opposition six-yard box alone in front of goal, you simply must score! And then you'll start winning things … Without that we have no chance of winning in Europe.'

The reader should understand that this is how Pep almost always is. He's not a natural optimist, quite the opposite. After a game, no matter how good the result, he'll focus on the negative rather than the positive. I try to end the conversation on a high note, reminding him about how well the youngsters are doing.

'They're a marvel. Bernardo, Foden, Brahim. And Zinchenko! He's breathed new life into the team, with all the problems we've had at the back. The kid's an absolute joy.'

Manel Estiarte, as perceptive as ever, makes a timely intervention: 'Look Pep, we had a fabulous game out there. I think that was just about the best game we've ever played. We brought the ball out magnificently. I've very rarely seen this kind of performance at the top level. Did we miss out on a few goals by a matter of centimetres? Yes we did. But don't let it throw you. We play magnificent football and we can't let that one detail bother us. We have to just keep doing what we're doing.'

Guardiola decides to give the whole squad and the technical staff four days off. 'I want everyone to take a break and forget about football for a while. They need to clear their minds and come back fresh and revitalised.'

Not only are his players physically and mentally exhausted, but half a dozen of them are injured: Stones, Delph, Gabriel Jesus, Sané, Foden and Mendy. David Silva, of course, is also still absent a lot, making constant visits to and from the clinic where his baby son is slowly improving. Pep hasn't even been able to fill his bench with substitutes for the Burnley game. None of the injuries have been caused by muscle problems. They're all joint injuries, the result of violent tackles or collisions during a game. Dr Edu Mauri is exhausted: 'We're doing everything humanly possible to get them back on their feet so that Pep has players available.'

I catch up with Xabier Mancisidor, the goalkeeping coach, as we're leaving Turf Moor and congratulate him on Ederson's fantastic interventions in the game. The keeper has performed exceptionally well and Mancisidor is delighted: 'He's brilliant and I'm certain that he's going to make even more progress. He'll be in the top five in the world soon. We're really happy with him – I think Pep is too!'

On the journey back to Manchester, Pep's not up for any more chat. He's retreated back into his internal world of match analysis. But Estiarte's happy to talk and he explains the priorities they've agreed for the rest of the season: 'The whole coaching team have discussed it and we're all clear. Our objective is the Premier League. All the rest is of secondary importance. It's going to be very hard to get far in the Champions League. We just have to get on with it and do our job. That's all. We need to knock Basel out and then take stock. It will depend on a lot of factors, particularly on how the draw goes, but we're not going to get all het up about whether we can win the Champions League or not. Our objective right now is to reach the quarter-finals. The smallest of details can determine the outcome of Cup competitions so we're concentrating on the Premier League. We want to win the league but we also want to do it in style by maintaining the dominance we've established thus far. We probably won't win as many games in a row again because so many of our rivals are fighting for survival, playing all-or-nothing football. Winning 18 games in a row has been amazing but we can't expect to do that or anything like it again. It's vital that we win the league, though. We want to establish Manchester City as one of the great champions of English football.'

Seven days later, City extend their lead over Manchester United to 16 points by beating Leicester 5–1. Their performance in the second half is especially impressive. Kun Agüero scores four times (the fourth a sensational effort from outside the area) and distinguishes himself in many other respects. It's not just that he's found the net in all of City's previous seven games: most importantly, he's become a team player. Par excellence. He floats across the pitch, moves in perfect harmony with the midfielders and is clearly fully on board with what Pep is asking of him. City's coach sums up the Argentinian's role: 'Basically we need Kun to score goals but we also need him to make our playing model work. He's becoming a key part of our play.'

Meanwhile Dr Mauri's hard work pays off: Foden and Stones are back to full fitness. Gündoğan, Bernardo Silva and De Bruyne are on fantastic form but, typically, Pep is quick to find fault: 'We weren't fast enough in the first half because we weren't in the right positions. We corrected that in the second half and dominated the game as a result.'

Their game in the second half is utterly majestic and I tell him so, but Pep is his usual self … 'If we want people to admire our game we need to lift trophies.'

The league title is within their grasp now, with just 27 games played. Then, on Sunday afternoon, Manchester United lose 1–0 to Newcastle and José Mourinho is quick to concede the league title to his city rivals … Domènec Torrent sends a WhatsApp with a picture of a dart board with an arrow right in the centre.

City hit the target with three of the first four chances they have against Basel in St Jakob-Park. It's the last round of the Champions League group stage and İlkay Gündoğan rises to the occasion, producing the kind of dazzling performance he was known for at Borussia Dortmund. The Citizens' faithful immediately come up with a new nickname. From now on he's 'Silky' Gündoğan. City have pulled off the biggest away victory of any English team in the Champions League. They've completely overpowered Basel and have achieved 74 per cent possession.

Dr Mauri has also come up trumps and Sané is back on his feet, although, as Estiarte explains, caution is advised. 'We've already got Stones and Foden back to full fitness. Sané wanted to rush his recovery a bit because he wanted to be back in the team for our Champions League games, but the doctor wasn't keen for him to come back until he'd completed all the necessary stages of his recuperation. In Sané's case it's more complicated because the kid goes at breakneck speed the minute he gets a clear field ahead of him. Giving him the all-clear before he's fully fit would be very risky. He's young and desperate to play but we've told him to wise up. He needs to take it slowly.'

Sané only plays the last half-hour against Basel, as does David Silva, for whom this is a 28th consecutive victory. Delph is due to be the next player back but Estiarte tells me that Gabriel Jesus has a way to go: 'He'll be ready to come back in the next ten days, just in time for the League Cup. But he won't be fit enough to be in the starting XI. He'll be fully fit by March. Mendy is also doing well but he won't be a big part of our plans because, by the time he's back, at the end of April, he still won't be fully match fit. Right now, it's not about getting the injured players back, but making sure that no one else gets injured.'

Four days later City are eliminated from the FA Cup by Wigan. It's all pretty surreal given that Pep's men achieve 82 per cent possession but fail to convert at least five good chances on goal. Delph also makes a disastrous mistake just before half-time and is sent off. Despite being down to ten men City continue to dominate and have 83 per cent possession in the second half. They play a 2–3–2–2 formation and then switch to a 2–2–2–3 with Danilo on the right wing. City make 845 passes, take 27 shots at goal and have 15 corners but Walker messes up badly by failing to get to the ball in time and giving Wigan hero Will Grigg, the chance to put the home side ahead. It's City's third defeat of the season and the third game in which they haven't managed to score.

The setback doesn't affect City's confidence in advance of the League Cup where they face Arsenal at Wembley on the last Sunday in February. Pep and 6,000 fans arrive wearing yellow ribbons on their lapels (in support of jailed pro-Catalan independence politicians) despite having been threatened with sanctions by the FA. Sterling has had muscle problems since the Basel game so Pep positions De Bruyne on the right wing in the by-now traditional 2–3–2–3.

The Belgian moves up and down the inside lines, leaving the outside to Walker, while Danilo at left-back, in what is probably his best performance of the season, sticks to the inside. Pep's players look nervous and stiff in the first half (the midfield diamond of Fernandinho, De Bruyne, Silva and Gündoğan isn't working well today), but Pep's men go on to have an excellent second half.

With Fernandinho injured, Gündoğan is the organising midfielder with back-up from De Bruyne. The team press Arsenal high, controlling the ball and attacking with such precision that Wenger's men are left exposed. Kompany defends brilliantly and makes sure that the Londoners have no real goal opportunities. Agüero opens the scoring, receiving an assist direct from Claudio Bravo, and then Kompany and Silva get one apiece, securing the trophy for City. It's the fifth time City have won the League Cup (1970, 1976, 2014, 2016, 2018). After eight weeks out, Gabriel Jesus plays a few minutes.

At last, 20 months after arriving in Manchester, Guardiola has won his first trophy in English football. It's his 22nd since becoming a coach. He doesn't go up to collect the cup with his players, however: 'I prefer watching it all from the pitch.'

There's very little time to celebrate and by 11pm they're already on the way home to Manchester. Monday is a day off, a chance to recuperate with only the substitutes attending training. They do drills to practise producing explosive bursts of speed. At this stage of the year it's vital that the players have sufficient recuperation time in order to withstand the pressures of the season. Everyone has Tuesday off and then it's training as usual on Wednesday. On Thursday the team heads back to London for a league match against Arsenal.

It's another victory for City at the Emirates, with the same score (0–3). Guardiola's 100th match in charge of City (66 victories, 21 draws, 13 defeats) is settled after 33 minutes via three fabulous goals: a superb slalom run from Sané, who dribbles past four opponents and then passes to Bernardo Silva, who curves the ball into the top corner; Sané then beats two Arsenal men, finds Agüero, who gives the assist to Silva who switches foot, finds the defender's blind spot and slams it home; City's third goal comes from a long sequence of one-touch passes by Agüero, De Bruyne and Walker. This time it's Sané who does the honours.

In the first half, the young German is involved in nine attacking sequences, beating his markers every time. He scores one, gives an assist and a 'pre-assist'. Over the weeks and months Sané has established himself as one of Pep's star players, just as the Catalan had predicted some 12 months ago. He is on exuberant form right now, an irresistible whirlwind of pace and energy that leaves his opponents dazed and stunned in his wake. The Gunners are powerless to stop him and, for the first time, Arsenal concede three goals at home in the first half of a game.

City have hit the target with all of their last six shots on goal against Wenger's team. But everything changes after the break and there's a distinct lack of competitive aggression in evidence once Pep's men troop out of the dressing room 3–0 up. Pep's furious: 'The start of the second half was horrific.'

Ederson stops Aubameyang's penalty. It's the 11th save made by a City keeper out of the last 10 spot kicks (not including penalty shoot-outs). The team has scored 82 goals in 28 league games, 2 more than in the whole of last season.

Seventy-two hours later, Guardiola's men clinch the league title. To everyone's surprise, Chelsea play a defensive game and park the bus. Coach Antonio Conte defends his tactics: 'Playing City is very difficult at the moment. They're super-talented and extremely strong. If you leave them space between lines, they'll put three or four goals past you.' City take full advantage of Chelsea's 5–4–1, a choice of formation that leaves Eden Hazard stranded in the centre circle. The Citizens make 902 accurate passes out of a total 975 attempted (93 per cent). And another record is shattered. Playing as a midfielder in Fernandinho's absence, 'Silky' Gündoğan makes 174 passes, thereby beating the current English record. For the first time since 2004, Chelsea don't get a single shot on goal. Pep is delighted: 'To prevent them putting a single shot on target means we played brilliantly. And against the current champions!' Pep has lots of praise for Agüero in particular: 'He's hungry. Over the last two months we've seen him transform into the best possible version of Kun.'

City go into their Champions League match against Basel on 7 March with the security of the massive lead they achieved in the first leg. The Swiss beat them 1–2. Just City's fourth defeat of the season and their first at home. Guardiola fields 'Zinchenko's Team' but his men look ungainly and slow. Stones, Yaya Touré – in his last few weeks as a City player – Foden and Zinchenko are all off form. Although they produce their usual number of passes (978, a record for the Champions League), they do so in the 'unimportant' zones of the pitch. After 36 consecutive games without a loss (29 victories and 7 draws), the defeat, and their performance, disappoint Pep, 'Our second half was very poor.'

It's Sunday, 11 March, and out on Training Pitch 1, something happens which could have dire consequences for the rest of City's season. Kun Agüero takes a bad knock to his right knee around the meniscus. Dr Mauri's prognosis isn't good and he can't promise that Kun will be back playing soon.

The following day, David Silva, aka 'The Magician', undeterred by Stoke's 5–4–1, scores twice, putting City 16 points ahead of Manchester United and 20 in front of Spurs. They've won a total of 26 league games. The other good news is that Sterling's back to top form. But Agüero's injury is weighing heavily on everyone's minds as Guardiola and his family head off to soak up the sun in Abu Dhabi at a warm-weather training camp for the team. As usual Pep wants to take full advantage of the rest days provided by the Premier League. (The Premier League calendar provides a total of 19 rest days between the first and the 30th league games.)

City put on another great exhibition of football on the last day of March, this time at Goodison Park. In beating Sam Allardyce's Everton 3–1 the Sky Blues add another feather to their cap: they're the third team in history (after Chelsea and Manchester United) to beat every single one of their Premier League opponents. It's Guardiola's 50th triumph in the Premier League (out of 69 games played). They've achieved 83 per cent possession, rising to 90 per cent for significant periods of the game. Silva and Sané in particular have played outstanding football today. Both players provide their 11th assist of the season. De Bruyne also gives an assist. It's his 15th of the season so far.

In preparation for their Champions League game against Liverpool, Guardiola is trying Laporte out at left-back – Delph's knee is still troubling him. He asks the Frenchman to combine with central defenders Otamendi and Kompany as a three when bringing the ball out but then move to 'open' left-back as soon as possession passes beyond the centre circle. Laporte is performing better and better every day, making key contributions whenever he plays. The team as a whole is also still smashing records. After 31 league games (27 wins, 3 draws and 1 defeat) City have now surpassed the number of victories achieved by Arsenal's 'Invincibles' in 2003–4.

ACT 5. SIX DARK DAYS AND LOTS OF RECORDS

Liverpool/Manchester/London, April–May 2018

The league title's almost within their grasp: so close they can almost taste it. Right now however, European football awaits: up next are none other than Jürgen Klopp's Liverpool in the Champions League quarter-finals. The Reds have been a thorn in Pep's side over two seasons and the stats speak for themselves: two defeats, a draw and just one victory – his worst results against any English club.

Back in Germany, Klopp's gegenpress had been the bane of Pep's life and he got to know it inside out, without managing to come up with an effective antidote. It's a counter-pressing strategy whereby Liverpool's 'wolf's mouth' 4–3–2–1 shape entices opponents into areas of the pitch where, if complacent, they are then devoured.

Once the ball carrier is in the centre of the structure Klopp's men flood in, trapping the opponents in a fatal embrace. The Reds' aggressive pressing means they regain possession just outside the opposition's area and the ball is theirs once more. If the opposition tries to avoid this trap altogether by moving down the wings, Klopp's men will launch an aggressive 'two-against-one' attack there. The gegenpress: simple but lethal. There's no shortage of advice and information as to how to neutralise Klopp's iconic tactic, and Pep's considered all of it. But Liverpool remain a very tough proposition.

Especially given the exceptional abilities of Klopp's 'wolves in sheep's cloth-ing' – gegenpress maestros like Salah, Firmino and Mané.

Guardiola left Germany placed just ahead of Klopp in the Bayern Munich/Borussia Dortmund contest: 4 wins, 1 draw and 3 defeats. But, here in England, Klopp has refined and perfected his methodology. Pep faces a gargantuan task.

The Catalan decides to approach the Anfield game with a new forma-tion – setting aside the 2–3–2–3. Agüero's injury is a big factor in his decision but not the main reason. There's psychology at play here too. Dome Torrent explained it to me years ago in Munich just after Bayern had drawn 0–0 at Shakhtar Donetsk. 'We haven't managed to control the Champions League games away from home. The 4–0 loss to Real Madrid in Munich did us damage and now we've gone to the other extreme.'

İlkay Gündoğan can be the man to give City greater control over the ball and frustrate Liverpool's suffocating counter-press. Or so Pep believes. Sadly, his midfield diamond formation (Fernandinho, De Bruyne, Silva and Gündoğan) is off form and it doesn't work. Three serious defensive errors later and City are out of contention. Salah scores in the 12th minute and sends a wave of panic through City's lines. Not for the first time, Pep's men seem totally unnerved and it takes a while for them to rally – twenty minutes to be precise – during which time both Oxlade-Chamberlain and Firmino score for the Reds. Elimination looks inevitable for the Citizens.

City dominate the second half – 71 per cent possession. But they fail to create any real danger for Liverpool, who revert to defensive mode and pack players into their area where they construct an impenetrable defensive wall. Gabriel Jesus scores with seven minutes left but what should have been a legitimate, potentially crucial, goal is given offside: Dejan Lovren's position as the Brazilian scores means it's a poor decision.

A few days later City take another body blow, this time at home in the Etihad. It's the Manchester derby.

Going in, City know that victory will effectively make them league cham-pions. Guardiola reverts back to the 2–3–2–3, although on this occasion Sterling is a false 9 positioned between Bernardo Silva and Sané; Gündoğan and David Silva are the attacking midfielders. Walker, De Bruyne, Gabriel Jesus and Agüero – with his torn meniscus – are all on the bench.

At the end of a storming first half City are 2–0 up despite Sterling missing two one-on-one chances with De Gea. The stats speak for themselves:
nine shots on goal for City, none for United. In truth, City should be 4–0
up by now but, frustratingly, Sterling keeps fluffing the many chances the
team creates. Pep's starting to despair of the young winger who's capable
of producing the most exquisite action one minute and then screwing up
the next. It's as if there are two, diametrically opposed Sterlings fighting for
supremacy. He's smashed his own personal goal record this season but he's
probably also outdone his previous stats in terms of missed sitters.

Despite this, Pep's men are still two ahead at half-time. The match looks
done and dusted. The Premier League is almost theirs. Until a 15-minute
collective lapse in concentration in the second half gives United the chance
they've been waiting for. Mourinho's Red Devils attack. At the final whistle,
United have won 3–2.

It's City's first league defeat at home this season and only the second time
since 2015 that a Guardiola team has conceded three goals in a defeat. This
is the most brutal disappointment – especially for diehard fans, who've come
here today to watch City clinch the title at home against their bitterest rivals.

Still worse, Sergio Agüero has suffered more, serious meniscus damage
thanks to Ashley Young's outrageous tackle. The Argentinian will need surgery
and his season is over. All the more galling given that no action is taken in
response to the blatant foul. No sanction for Young, no penalty for City.

City now face the second leg of the Champions League tie against
Liverpool minus one of their key players. It's a major blow.

The upcoming battle seems an almost impossible task. Guardiola's
going with an aggressive, high-risk strategy: a 2–1–4–3 formation. Central
defenders Otamendi and Laporte at the back, with Fernandinho just in
front; Walker, De Bruyne, David Silva and Sterling form the next line with
Bernardo Silva, Jesus and Sané up front.

It's the Brazilian who gets the opener for City just two minutes in and
Pep's men then take complete control of the game. There are four more
decisive moments in the first half: possible handballs from James Milner
and Andy Robertson, which referee Mateu Lahoz ignores, Bernardo Silva's
shot off the post and a Sané goal ruled offside despite Milner having played
the ball to the City winger. Four refereeing decisions, three of which are

completely wrong. The Spanish referee clamps down hard on the players' protests (and sends Pep off for complaining about Sané's goal being chalked off), but somehow fails to spot these infractions. Two penalties denied and an incorrectly disallowed goal are his tally of poor judgements from this game.

City's first-half dominance is absolute, and David Silva and Sané work in tandem to drive the ferocious attack up the left wing with the aim of giving Bernardo Silva spaces to finish chances down the right-hand side. Jesus dances round the visiting defenders while Sterling moves freely all across City's attacking zones, causing major headaches for Klopp's men. The build-up phase flows through De Bruyne and he combines with Fernandinho to move the ball forward. But the team are still struggling to convert chances. Then Guardiola is sent off at half-time. Another big setback for City no matter how imperiously they are playing in search of cutting their aggregate 3–1 deficit.

An hour into the game, Ederson dives at Mané's feet to try and block a Liverpool counterattack, the ball squirms loose, Salah finishes with a little lofted chip and City's fate is sealed. Liverpool are through and City won't be in the Champions League semi-finals. A miserable end to a very black week.

Just to tie a ribbon around things it's another Otamendi error in the 76th minute that gifts Firmino the winning goal. Forty-five minutes of audacious, high-risk football have come to naught for City. In the final analysis, Liverpool have defended better and finished more effectively over the 180 minutes. City have created more chances, for sure, but their own mistakes compounded by indefensible refereeing decisions have cost them. Although Guardiola's impressed by his players' competitive courage, he's deeply worried about defensive lapses in concentration.

I quiz him about what's causing these lapses and the flood of goals conceded in the Champions League.* Pep's response is brief but revealing: 'It's totally psychological.'

•   •   •

Four days later, City are back to their customary 2–3–2–3 at Wembley, temporarily home to Spurs while White Hart Lane is being rebuilt. High

---

* Meanwhile, Liverpool would go on to beat Roma in the semi-final, but lose 3–1 to Madrid in the Champions League final.

pressing, efficient recuperation of the ball and total domination are all very much in evidence but, after nine shots on goal, the visitors are only 2–1 up at half-time. It's not an accurate reflection of the way they're playing. Pep's men have totally bossed Spurs.

Making so little of City's utter domination of the game evokes the ghosts of recent weeks. Memories of the last few games are still raw and no one who's seen them can avoid wondering whether City can hold their ground against a second-half revival from Pochettino's team. Or will panic set in, as has happened before, and open the door for a Spurs comeback?

Guardiola's response is to substitute Sané for Otamendi so that he now has three central defenders (Otamendi–Kompany–Laporte) and switch to a 5–3–2 in the 64th minute, after Spurs dominate for a quarter of an hour. The change in formation stops the home side in their tracks and gives City several good chances, which Sterling and Jesus fail to convert until finally the Englishman tucks the ball away to give City a 3–1 advantage. Sterling's 17th Premier League goal (22 across all competitions), and a personal best tally. It's a real achievement for Sterling, who on average needs 3.5 shots for every goal scored, which is a better ratio than Liverpool's Salah has achieved this season (4 shots for every goal). A vast improvement on the winger's stats from last season (7.6 shots for every goal) but nobody on the hawkish staff is fooled. They are well aware that, although he scores a lot of goals, Sterling also continues to commit too many errors in front of goal, particularly if he has time to weigh up his options before making a decision about how to finish. When he thinks about what he's going to do he actually performs worse than when he has to make a split-second decision and act on pure instinct.

With 15 minutes left, Pep makes more changes in the hope of consolidating their advantage. His team shape is an impenetrable 5–4–1, meaning game over for Spurs, who haven't lost since December 2017 (14 games) or conceded three goals at home since March 2015.

In terms of legendary venues, so far this season City have triumphed at Stamford Bridge, Old Trafford, the Emirates and now at Wembley, England's most famous stadium, for a second time (following their League Cup win in February). They've beaten Chelsea, Arsenal and Tottenham home and away, defeating Manchester United and Liverpool once each. Their results against the five other 'greats' of the Premier League are impressive: 8 wins

out of a possible 10, 24 points out of a possible 30, 27 goals in favour and
11 against. A huge improvement on last season when they accumulated just
6 points out of 30.

By 10pm on this day, Saturday, 14 April, City aren't yet officially champions of the Premier League. That's tomorrow's big news. Just as Guardiola
is teeing off with Tommy Fleetwood (fourth place at the 2017 US Open), Jay
Rodriguez nods the ball into Manchester United's net at Old Trafford and
West Brom win.

Guardiola's City are champions of England.

Last week, 3,000 United fans raised the roof in the Etihad after their team
prevented City from winning their seventh league title on home ground. Now,
70,000 United fans are facing the awful truth. They've just handed City the
title on a plate. By losing in the Theatre of Broken Dreams – Old Trafford.

But Pep never rests on his laurels. There are five more league games to
play and he's already making plans. On 20 April, first thing in the morning,
he summons his squad to the room in Sportcity where they usually analyse
videos of their opponents. 'Lads, we've had an extraordinary season but
I know from my experience at Barça and Bayern how tempting it is to
relax after winning the league. And it's a horrible feeling losing the last few
games after winning the title.'

This time, the video isn't about their rivals' strengths and weaknesses.
Instead it shows three historical statistics relating to the league records
for total points, total wins and total number of goals scored. The holder
of all three high-water marks? It's Chelsea, although the stats are drawn
from three separate seasons under three different coaches: José Mourinho,
Antonio Conte and Carlo Ancelotti. There are other stats: number of away
wins, goal difference, the points difference from the league's runners-up and
so on. In total, there are ten separate categories but Pep wants to focus on
the first three: points, wins and goals.

'Now we have a chance to make history – if we manage to beat each of
these records we'll be remembered forever. And if we smash these records,
we'll automatically break others. So, lads … are you up for it?'

The league champions hammer Swansea on 22 April in a resplendent
Etihad Stadium. Another exhibition of phenomenal football, which culminates in five excellent goals scored by David Silva, Sterling, De Bruyne,

Bernardo Silva and Gabriel Jesus. As has so often been the case this season, Swansea huddle in a 5–4–1 and essentially gift possession to the home team. During the first 15 minutes, City make 174 passes to Swansea's 29, the equivalent of 90 per cent possession vs 10 per cent. The Citizens focus their attack on the left flank where Laporte, Delph, David Silva, Sterling and De Bruyne are posted today while Bernardo Silva and Danilo patrol the right. By the break, the team has beaten the record for the number of passes in the first half of a Premier League game: 582, with 93 per cent accuracy and 86 per cent possession. Twenty-five minutes before the end, Benjamin Mendy returns from a six-month absence. He's evidently nervous but it's great to have him back. Today Yaya Touré is approaching the end of his 'farewell tour'. City set a new record for the most passes in the history of English football: 942 accurate passes out of 1,015 attempted.

Amid the celebrations I chat to Estiarte about the season and what we both hope will be a multi-record-breaking finale. 'We're delighted. Winning the Premier League has been one of the most satisfying things we've achieved. We've played spectacular football – on a similar level to what we achieved at Barça and in our third year at Bayern. Now, all that's left to do is strive for more records and turn our minds to new signings. We definitely need one more attacking player. Pep's had his eye on Riyad Mahrez so we'll probably go for him. Some of the players have mentioned that Hazard is interested in coming here. But I'm not entirely sure I see that happening …'

Then Estiarte tells me about how far ahead the coach is already thinking. It's typical Pep: 'He's actually prepared the first team talk for next season. He'll say something like: "Lads, we really know each other now. We know each other's strengths and weaknesses and because there aren't going be any real novelties or surprises about how we work together or what I'll be demanding of you, it's even more vital to concentrate on maintaining our focus, stiffening our resolve and our determination to win. In other words, the drive must come from within." From now until the end of the season we need to push ourselves and work to achieve perfection in everything we do so that we retain the title.'

Listening to Estiarte it's clear that the coming season is going to be tough. There will be few reinforcements and lots of opponents who will definitely be out to 'get' City.

Sterling provides three assists at West Ham on 29 April, giving City the win. Pep's men have provided another football masterclass using their habitual 2–3–2–3. All of Pep's players are totally comfortable with this system. De Bruyne's cross is turned in for an own goal by his former Sky Blue teammate Pablo Zabaleta for 2–0 – it's also City's 100th league goal. They're the first team in English football to score over 100 goals in two different seasons, having notched up 102 in 2013–14. Deposed champions Chelsea hold the overall record with 103 goals. But that high mark suddenly looks very far from secure.

Guardiola gives Lukas Nmecha his Premier League debut, and Yaya Touré continues his series of 20-minute cameos during which he produces clever passes and draws opponents to him all the while reminding everyone what a great player he has been.

After 35 games and 30 victories (equalling Chelsea's all-time record), 15 of which have been away from home (equalling Chelsea in this respect too), City have 93 points. There are other impressive stats. In the rankings of total assists in the league, the first four places are occupied by City players: De Bruyne (16), Sané (15), David Silva (11) and Sterling (11). No club has ever had four of its players give more than ten assists in the same season. Until now. Sané (10 goals, 15 assists) and Sterling (18 and 11) are the only players in the Premier League to have reached double figures in both goals and assists, with David Silva not far behind (9 goals and 11 assists) despite the Spanish magician having played in just 29 games. City have also scored four or more goals in ten different league matches.

Huddersfield Town hold the league champions to a 0–0 draw in a game that's a bit like 90 minutes of repeatedly crashing into a brick wall. Then it's time to use the Brighton match at the Etihad to say goodbye for the season to the home faithful. City win 3–1. Bernardo Silva gets the second goal and brings City's Premier League goal total to 104. Another record smashed. And number three, courtesy of Fernandinho, is the 23rd goal of the season scored from a set piece. A huge total. This result adds to their points total record – 97 now – and the record for total wins (31). Pep's three milestone objectives have been achieved. The points difference between the new champions and their nearest rivals is colossal: Manchester United trail them by 20, Spurs by 23, Liverpool 25, Chelsea 27 and Arsenal 37.

But Pep *still* isn't completely satisfied: 'I'm delighted with all the records we've broken as a result of the great football we've played this year. But now I really want to make it to 100 points – that would make this league title absolutely perfect. But even if we manage that I still don't think we can yet claim to be up there with the greatest all-time English clubs. We need to win a few more league titles before we can make that sort of claim.

'If we want to be on a par with Ferguson's Man United or the Liverpool of the eighties we need to win again and again. In terms of records and statistics we're already the best ever but we need to be even better. I'm desperate for a holiday but I really want to reach a hundred points first.'

City's final game is in a sun-drenched Southampton on 13 May, the sixth anniversary of that epic Sergio Agüero goal that clinched the club's first Premier League title of the twenty-first century. And there's an echo of that moment today. To defeat QPR in extremis, and pip United to the title, Agüero produced the dramatic winner on exactly 93 minutes and 20 seconds. Today, just past the 93rd-minute mark, De Bruyne makes a 50m pass to Jesus, who controls it with his left foot and gently lobs it into the net with his right. City score their 100th goal of the season on the anniversary of the Kun moment and it's tucked away just 18 seconds short of the mythical 93:20. It's the apotheosis of a glorious campaign, shattering all available records and securing themselves an unrivalled place in the history of English football.

Four days later the club confirms they've renewed Pep's contract. He'd initially signed for three seasons (2016–19) but wants to stay in Manchester for another two – until 2021. It's been obvious from the beginning that he'd need more time to develop his playing model here and construct a legendary, unbeatable team.

100 POINTS AND MORE

Never before has a team dominated the Premier League the way City have and certainly not playing a style of football that is both beautiful to watch and ruthlessly effective. There's unanimity across the country: Guardiola's Manchester City have rightly earned their place among the greatest champions in English history. There may be troubles and challenges ahead but right now they look unstoppable. This group of supremely talented men are hungry for success yet humble enough to confront and correct the flaws that still undoubtedly exist. This is the Manchester City of the 100 points, the record-breaking 'Centurions', the Premier League's ultimate proponents of 'beautiful football'.

Look at any of their stats, from any angle, and City always lead the pack, but I want to highlight two stats that tell you all you need to know about the Citizens' juggernaut. Out of the total 3,420 minutes of league football in 2017–18 (in practice there were more than 3,600 minutes of competitive football once stoppage time was added in), Pep's team have only trailed an opponent in a game for 153 minutes, a tiny 4.47 per cent.

The second statistic is based on a more fanciful premise, but bear with me. It's a doozy. However absurd it sounds, if City had played all of their 19 home matches without a keeper and so every single one of their opponents' shots on target had gone in, City would still have won the league. In other words, if Pep had fielded just ten outfield players and conceded 39 goals more than they actually did, City would still have amassed 82 points, one more than second-place Manchester United. Absurd as it may be, this illustration goes a long way to convey the absolute dominance of the Centurions.

One phrase has been repeated over and over from October 2017 onwards: England has never witnessed this quality of football before.

Gary Lineker sums it up well:

City have had a phenomenal season not just in terms of their emphatic league triumph but in terms of the sheer joy their football brings. It's been a breath of fresh air: attacking, open, adventurous football played by players of real quality. Guardiola is great for English football. A lot of people said that he couldn't practice his kind of football in the Premier League and I'm delighted that he has imposed his style of play here and stuck to his own principles. He's not only demonstrated that you can win playing his style of football but that it's great to watch too.

Without a doubt, signing players like Ederson, Walker, Laporte and Bernardo Silva has been a crucial factor in City's success. And the willingness of Otamendi, Agüero, Fernandinho and Kompany to learn and implement the fundamentals of Pep's playing model has also been vital. As has the continued consolidation of players like Sané, Sterling and Laporte, who, although there is still a way to go, are learning to play 'the Pep way'. One player stands out, however: Kevin De Bruyne. Called upon to lead the team in David Silva's absences, the Belgian has undergone his own personal metamorphosis. Without him, City would not have achieved all that they have. His impact transcends that of any other single player.

City become Premier League champions with five matches left – a feat achieved by Manchester United in 1908 and 2001 and by Everton in 1985. Every other record has fallen: points, goals total, goals in favour or against, home wins, expected goals, possession, number of passes, number of accurate passes and consecutive wins.

For the Citizens faithful, though, the stats and numbers are just a postscript. It's the majestic displays of glorious football that will stay in their hearts. As the late, great Terry Venables put it, 'English football has witnessed the most significant of Guardiola's triumphs, which he has achieved playing a Catalan style of football: fluid, entertaining and trophy-winning.'

NEW RECORDS SET

- Greatest number of points in the history of England's top division: 100. Previous record: Liverpool, 98 points in 1978–9.
- Most wins: 32 out of 38 matches. Previous record: Spurs, 31 out of 42 games in 1960–1.
- Greatest number of points in the history of the Premier League: 100 points. Previous record: Chelsea, 95 points in 2004–5.
- Biggest lead over runners-up: 19 points. Previous record: Manchester United, 18 points in 1999–2000.
- Most victories in the Premier League: 32 out of 38 games. Previous record: Chelsea, 30 out of 38 in 2016–17.
- Consecutive victories in a season: 18 (26 August–27 December 2017). Previous record: Chelsea, 13 in 2016–17. (Arsenal, over two seasons, 14 victories in February–August 2002.)
- Most away victories: 16 out of a possible 19. Previous record: Chelsea, 15 out of 19 in 2004–5.
- Most points away from home: 50. Previous record: Chelsea, 48 in 2004–5.
- Highest number of goals scored: 106. Previous record: Chelsea, 103 in 2009–10.
- Biggest goal difference: +79 (106–27). Previous record: Chelsea, +71 in 2009–10.

- Total minutes spent trailing in a game: 153. Previous record: Arsenal, 170 in 1998–9.
- Highest rate of possession in the Premier League: 71.9 per cent. Previous record: Manchester City, 65 per cent in 2016–17.
- Highest possession in a single match: 82.9 per cent (22 April 2018 against Swansea). Previous record: Manchester City, 82.28 per cent (13 May 2012 against Queens Park Rangers).
- Most passes in the Premier League competition: 28,242. Previous record: Manchester City, 22,705 in 2016–17.
- Most passes in a single game: 942 (22 April 2018 against Swansea). Previous record: Manchester City, 905 (31 March 2018 against Everton).

THE FUNDAMENTALS OF HIS PLAYING MODEL

In his career trajectory from Barcelona to Manchester, via Munich, Guardiola has never changed the fundamental principles of his game. For him it's all about the ball. His teams take the initiative, and always want the ball. When they attack or defend, when they seek to disorganise their opponents, and in order to win.

Pep's mantra is: 'There is only one ball and it belongs to us! When we have it, we play it. We make passes and play our game. If we don't have it, then we get it back. It's our ball, so that when we lose it, it means that the opposition has stolen something that belongs to us and we have to get it back. We aren't stealing. We're merely recuperating what is ours.'

Winning is all about the ball. Defending is all about the ball. It's a playing model with a good rate of success but it's not the only model and offers no 'absolute truths' (as Domènec Torrent claims). It's a playing model he had to adapt to the German game with its philosophy of counterattacking down the inside. He's also had to develop and adapt certain parts of his model to the direct, attacking style of English football with its counterattacks on the outside.

As Juanma Lillo once explained: 'In England it's all about teams launching non-stop counterattacks against each other. It's a counterattacking style of football because in the past teams didn't aim to build sequences of passes. Players run up and down on the outside and the guys on the inside support the counterattacks.'*

---

* Martí Perarnau, *Pep Guardiola: The Evolution* (Arena Sport, 2016).

Pep dedicated his entire first season in Manchester to introducing City's squad to the fundamentals of his game while competing on all fronts and trying to absorb the idiosyncrasies of English football: constant back and forth counterattacking, 'second balls', playing long and high, ferocious tackling and the permissiveness of referees. One particular characteristic stood out for him: English clubs possess the kind of dogged fighting spirit that keeps them battling to the death, no matter how far they are trailing on the scoreboard. In other countries, a 2–0 lead is considered pretty much game over. In the Premier League, you don't give in until the final whistle. Ever. Pep learned this the hard way in his first season when even at 2–0 or 3–0 ahead he couldn't relax. One of his oft-repeated messages to his players has been the importance of breaking this psychological dynamic in order to break their opponents' resistance and avoid repeating the bad experiences of 2016–17. And they obviously listened. City won more than 17 games by a margin of three or more goals in Pep's second season, broken down as: five victories of five or more goals, five with a margin of four goals, seven with a margin of three, as well as another ten matches where (irrespective of winning margin) they scored three goals or more. Of the 57 official games City played, they failed to score in just 5. These figures are a direct result of what Guardiola asked of his players. It wasn't just about establishing their advantage in a game. It was about establishing as big an advantage as possible and psychologically destroying the other team.

There's no doubt that the execution of these fundamental principles has not been perfect. City's players still have to improve their collective organisation and psychological maturity. Their visits to Anfield alone tell us that there is still work to be done.

25 PER CENT MORE PASSES

Passing. One of the cornerstones of Pep's philosophy. And one of the areas City most improved from his first to his second season. 'You have to pass the ball. Pass, pass. And then pass again. Then an extra one and another one. Going for that extra pass will always help us achieve our objectives.'

For most of the season Manchester City have been a precision-passing machine: 265 shots on goal, 106 goals and 23 off the woodwork. Which means that 40 per cent of their shots have found the target and another 8.6 per cent have hit the posts. Taken as a percentage of City's total shots

(665), the accuracy rate is still phenomenal: 15.9 per cent have ended in a goal. They have, however, shown an even greater improvement in their passing. In 2016–17 the team made 597 passes per game with 86 per cent accuracy. Some distance away from Bayern's average under Guardiola: 726 passes per game, 87.9 per cent accuracy. These numbers changed radically in Pep's second season: 743 passes per game with 89 per cent accuracy. Just to put that figure in context, in one of Barça's greatest games under Pep – beating Alex Ferguson's Man United in the 2011 Champions League final – the Catalans produced 777 passes with 90 per cent accuracy.

The improvement in City's performance is breathtaking. To go from 597 to 743 means an average of 150 passes more per game, a whopping 24 per cent increase. And yet these are more or less the numbers Guardiola was aiming for. It's City's passing sequences that help them dominate their games.

The rankings by number of passes speak to the style of game preferred by each coach. The top three? City, of course, with 28,242 accumulated passes in league games; Arsenal, with 4,715 fewer; and, in third place, Mourinho's Manchester United with 8,179 fewer passes than City or, to put it another way, 215 fewer passes per match.

All of this was a gradual process. Let's review: West Brom, October 2017, City make 843 accurate passes; by March 2018, they produce 902 against Chelsea; and on 22 April of the same year, against Swansea, Pep's men set a new record of 942 accurate passes, becoming the first English team ever to exceed 1,000 passes in a single game (1,015 in total, 92.8 per cent accurate). Pretty impressive, although City still trail the 1,006 accurate passes (out of a total 1,078) achieved in 2014 against Hertha Berlin by Guardiola's Bayern Munich. And İlkay Gündoğan, no doubt proud of his record-breaking 174 accurate passes against Chelsea, may well be eyeing Xabi Alonso's numbers enviously. The Spaniard's top number is 196 passes made in a Bundesliga game. But let's not forget City's performance against Basel on 7 March 2018 in the game that put them through to the next round of the Champions League: 978 accurate passes.

By the end of his second season Guardiola has successfully inculcated his passing philosophy despite the frenetic pace of the English game. And that's not to say that City aren't up for some direct football. Quite the contrary – they relish fast, ferocious attacking, whether it's a long ball from the keeper to a forward (two goals scored this way) or the likes of Sané, Sterling, De

Bruyne and Gabriel Jesus sprinting up the pitch with the ball at their feet. The key thing for Pep this year has been his players wholehearted acceptance and application of this aspect of his philosophy.

But it's never passing for passing's sake. There is always, always a clear and defined purpose. This is a game of position and by building sequences of passes you generate positional, organisational and psychological advantages, all of which are impacted by the situation and context of the particular game. Let's say, for example, City are up against a risk-averse opponent. One of the 'park-the-bus' brigade. Pep's men will go into 'rondo' mode, calmly passing the ball to each other, forming triangles and teasing their opponents who, after a while, will stop pressing and end up bemused and defeated by every new repetition. Each repetition has a threefold effect on the opposition. The players closest to the action are trapped chasing a ball that moves at lightning speed between City's players; the rest of their team become frustrated and lose their organisation; and, eventually, the whole team are left dozy and directionless. Almost like a drug-induced stupor. To date, only Jürgen Klopp's electric Liverpool side has consistently managed to resist City's knockout drops.

City have used seven different methods of bringing the ball out. They've obtained the same number of points home and away (50) with exactly the same results: 16 wins, 2 draws and 1 defeat. They've made the defence-to-attack transition a fundamental part of their game. They've also scored 23 goals from set pieces: 16 corners (8 per cent of those taken), 7 free kicks (2 direct and 5 indirect) plus 6 penalties. Last season they got 15 goals (7+8). They've only conceded 4 times from set pieces: 2 corners (1.9 per cent of those taken), one of which was an own goal, plus 2 free kicks (1 direct and 1 indirect). Last season, City conceded 9 times from opponents' set plays.

THE CHALLENGES AHEAD

Pep and I chat about the season ahead. He's clear about his objectives and the challenges they'll face: 'We need to focus much more on domestic competitions rather than the Champions League. I want to win the league again. That's our main objective for next season.'

The last three Premier League champions – Chelsea, Leicester, Chelsea successively – not only failed to retain the title but didn't make it in to the top four the year after winning. This speaks volumes about how difficult the Premier League is and makes it clear why the campaign to retain the title is their top priority. Next season is going to be tight. The 'big five' will be looking to add reinforcements in an effort to stop the City juggernaut and the smaller clubs will no doubt keep parking the bus with renewed cunning and energy whenever City come to town. Pep is going to have to find creative ways to unblock the log jams that they'll encounter in the tightest of spaces.

What's Pep's message to his players? He's been quite clear: he wants the same level of ambition they showed this season. It's the only way they'll pull this off and it's non-negotiable. There are one or two other areas in need of improvement and Pep's to-do list reads something like this :

- Grow up and stop giving in to panic.
- Find the right way to deal with their nemesis, Liverpool.
- Access all that untapped potential in the shape of Ederson, Stones, Laporte, Walker, Mendy and Sané, and get the best out of each of them.
- Reboot the midfield with the two new signings (already agreed with management) of: a midfielder to replace Yaya Touré and a sixth striker (hopefully Mahrez).
- Run with the idea of using inverted wingers (thus far his wingers have performed best when they're playing on their favoured side).
- Bring Gabriel Jesus shooting ability along (an impressive 59 per cent of his shots have found the net but Pep still sees room for improvement).
- And, especially, try to improve Raheem Sterling's efficiency. He's made huge progress this season (he's achieved the same impressive numbers two seasons in a row and is the league's fifth best goalscorer) but there's still a lot of room for improvement.

Guardiola's only halfway through his Manchester City project. It's a work in progress, as İlkay Gündoğan, Pep's first signing in England, puts it: 'This is a journey and we've not got where we want to be yet. There's still a lot we need to do better.' Kevin De Bruyne, another iconic Guardiola-era player, sums up what the squad and the fans feel: 'People judge you on trophies and stats because they are the most important things. But statistics are just one part of the story. For me the real beauty lies in the journey, not the destination. Which is why I value what we've done this season.'

Pep's had ten seasons as a coach and almost never before has he been as content and fulfilled as he is in Manchester, where everything has come together for him: a board that's shown him unflinching support, players who are totally committed to his playing philosophy, a united and loyal staff, all pulling in the same direction, and a fanbase who love what he's doing so much that they sing songs about him: 'We've got Guardiola!'

Guardiola puts it this way: 'People say that we're successful because the club is rich. But that's not it. It's because of our passion, our hard-working dedicated staff and the fantastic infrastructure the club has created.' Until now it's been about the 'process'. But there's now another word on everyone's lips: 'legacy'.

Pep's happy in Manchester. Even the problems of his first season here couldn't dampen his spirits for long. Let's see what he can achieve if they have an even better third season. The sky's the limit ...

STATS 2017–18

	P	W	D	L	GF	GA
Premier League	38	32	4	2	106	27
Champions						
League Cup	6	4	2	0	11	5
Champions						
FA Cup	3	2	0	1	6	2
Fifth round						
Champions League	10	6	0	4	20	12
Quarter-finalist						
Total	57	44	6	7	143	46

- 77.2 per cent victories in matches all season
- 84.2 per cent wins from all Premier League matches
- 2.51 goal average per match scored in the entire season
- 2.79 goal average per match scored in the Premier League
- 0.81 goal average per match conceded in the entire season
- 0.71 goal average per match conceded in the Premier League
- 97 positive goal difference across the whole season
- 100 points in the Premier League
- 23 efforts off the post in the Premier League (4 De Bruyne and Sterling)
- 66.2 per cent possession in the entire season
- 71.9 per cent possession in the Premier League
- 83 per cent highest level of possession (vs Swansea, April 2018)
- 51 per cent lowest level of possession (vs Napoli, November 2017)
- 743 average number of passes per match
- 978 highest number of passes (vs FC Basel, March 2018)
- 89 per cent completed passes per match
- 17.5 shots at goal per match/7 on target
- 6.2 shots at goal conceded per game/2.2 on target
- 18 best run of consecutive wins in the Premier League
- 30 top goalscorer: Sergio Agüero (21 in the Premier League)
- 21 most assists: Kevin De Bruyne (16 in the Premier League)
- 52 most appearances: Kevin De Bruyne (37 in the Premier League)
- 0–6 biggest win (vs Watford)
- 4–3 biggest defeat (vs Liverpool)

Season 3: 2018–19

Chasing the Red Rabbit

On 14 July 2018, six City players (De Bruyne, Sterling, Delph, Stones and Walker) are still in St Petersburg in the final stages of the World Cup. In Manchester, pre-season training started a week ago but almost none of Pep's first team players are here. They're either representing their countries in Russia or on a well-earned summer break. So Pep's going to use this pared-down version of pre-season training to become better acquainted with the academy players.

He's facing the season without his right hand, Domènec Torrent, who has just been appointed as the coach of New York City, replacing Patrick Vieira, who's returning to France to coach OGC Nice. It's all happened very fast. Vieira announced his departure on 10 June and the following day Torrent accepted the New York club's offer. It's not the first offer he's received but this is the only one that really appeals. New York feels like a great place to restart his career as head coach after a decade as Pep's assistant.

Given the short notice, Domènec's had to come to Madrid to pick up a fast-tracked US visa and I've travelled with him to help with all the other last-minute arrangements. He packs his gigantic suitcase – purchased yesterday – and we head off to the airport mid-afternoon. He also has a suit-bag slung over his arm, too, and tells me with a wry grin, 'Pep told me he wants to see me on the bench wearing a suit – so that's what I'm going to do.'*

Torrent's already scheduled his first training session, twelve hours after he arrives in New York. He has no option – they're playing Toronto, current MLS champions, in the Yankee Stadium in two days' time. 'I've studied the way Toronto play and I'm not going to make a lot of changes in my team. I don't want to confuse them. I just want to make a couple of alterations to the way they press Giovinco and Bradley.'†

He's already signed a new striker, 19-year-old Argentinian Taty Castellanos, and over the next few weeks he will bring in the technical staff he needs: assistant coach Albert Puig, fitness trainers Francesc Cos and

---

* The suit doesn't last long in the suffocating heat of a New York summer and, after three matches, Dome dumps the jacket and dons a short-sleeved shirt for games.

† New York City beat the reigning champions 2–1 in their debut match.

Ismael Camenforte plus analyst Jordi Gris, whom he's pinched from City. Torrent's excited about working in a championship that's so different from European football and is determined to win some silverware.* 'I've got just one message for the players. I want to win the MLS. If we don't win it this year, then we'll do it next year. And we'll do it with the right attitude. No whining. No moaning. Thinking like champions.'†

Before we say our goodbyes, I ask Dome what he thinks of Mikel Arteta, his successor as Pep's principal assistant at City: 'Mikel will be brilliant. He's very talented and was the obvious choice. He was on the point of being appointed as coach of Arsenal so he's definitely good enough. He's going to be a big asset to Pep in terms of helping the players continue to understand and adapt to his playing style. We won the league in style and, right now, Pep's on cloud nine, but he needs to keep his feet on the ground. The man's a genius at what he does and works best when he feels that his players understand what he's asking of them and are confident and comfortable putting it into practice.'

One footnote to City's season has given Guardiola another boost. Former sports editor of the *Wall Street Journal*, Sam Walker, has just published a brilliant new book, *The Captain Class*, in which he lists the 16 best sports teams of all time and identifies the characteristics common to those who've managed them. The list includes world-beating teams like the New York Yankees (1949–53); the Magical Magyars of Ferenc Puskás and Nándor Hidegkuti; Bill Russell's Boston Celtics, who won 11 NBA titles in 13 years (1956–69); the Brazil of Pelé and Garrincha; the legendary Soviet Union ice hockey team the Red Army (1980–4); the Cuban women's volleyball team, Las Morenas del Caribe (The Caribbean Girls), who won eight consecutive world titles including at three Olympic Games, two World Championships and three World Cups between 1991 and 2000; the All Blacks led by David Kirk in 1988–90, when they became the first ever world champions, and

---

* The MLS is very different from what Torrent's used to. As well as natural grass pitches they also use artificial turf in certain stadiums and, at times, the packed football calendar will mean that the team have to make repeated exhausting and lengthy journeys. New York City's stadium isn't even a football stadium and its dimensions are absolutely tiny.

† Torrent's team were champions of the Eastern Conference in 2019 (64 points) and qualified for the CONCACAF Champions League for the first time.

the 2011–15 side captained by Richie McCaw which won two World Cups; five-time NBA champions the San Antonio Spurs, led by the magician Gregg Popovich; and France's Les Experts, who dominated world handball between 2008 and 2017; and, of course, the legendary 'Pep Team', the Barcelona side managed by none other than Pep Guardiola.

The seven characteristics identified by Walker are:

1. Extreme doggedness and focus in competition.
2. Aggressive play that tests the limits of the rules.
3. A willingness to do thankless tasks in the shadows.
4. A low-key, practical and democratic communication style.
5. Motivating others with passionate non-verbal displays.
6. Strong convictions and the courage to stand apart.
7. Ironclad emotional control.

Pep's face lights up when he sees his 'Pep Team' included in the ranks of the all-time greats but the moment triggers a recurring worry: 'They were the best. Nobody can create two masterpieces.'

I try to reassure him, offering the example of Edmund Hillary, who, after becoming the first man – along with Tenzing Norgay – to conquer Everest, the highest peak in the world, continued to set records by scaling the most difficult mountain ranges. Pep seems to like the analogy: 'You're right. That's definitely what we're aiming at. And with really good players we can produce awe-inspiring football again. It's just hard to keep believing when things are going wrong.'

• • •

They keep the pre-season tour short. A mixed bunch of players – mostly academy boys and those on the 'for sale or loan' list – head off to the US to play three games. In truth, it's more about ticking boxes than achieving anything of real value. As most of the first team are still on their post-World Cup summer break, only seven of their number are here: new signing Riyad Mahrez; Foden; Zinchenko; Laporte, who's still struggling with an injury and can hardly play; Sané, still stinging from being left out of Germany's World Cup squad; Claudio Bravo who, a few days from now, will tear his

Achilles tendon and be out for the rest of the season; and Bernardo Silva. The Portugal international has delighted everyone by cutting short his holiday to join them halfway through the tour. It's clear from the start that his second season is going to be very different from his first.

They play in a 4–3–3 against Borussia Dortmund, who win (0–1) thanks to a Mario Götze penalty. Pep switches to a 3–5–2 for the next two games. The lineup consists of academy players Cameron Humphreys and Eric García in central defence, accompanied by Jason Denayer; full-backs Luke Bolton and Zinchenko, although the Ukrainian switches to organising midfielder for the Liverpool game (a 1–2 defeat), replacing Douglas Luiz, who takes that position for the games against Dortmund and Bayern Munich (a 3–2 victory).

None of the games really matter but it's been important to make a start in advance of the new season in which Pep will be without Dome Torrent and working with his new assistant, Mikel Arteta. Riyad Mahrez is their one and only signing. But, given last year's net investment (signings minus transfers) of £226 million, Pep's had to take the club's circumspection with good grace. This season's bill will be £18 million net, which includes the cost of signing Mahrez minus the income from seven transfers. Disappointingly, Brahim Díaz will be among the players who leave. In January 2019, tired of Pep's 'easy does it' approach to his career progression, he decides to do a 'Jadon Sancho' and leaves City for pastures new.* In his case, to Real Madrid. Neither of the youngsters has shown the patience and forbearance of Phil Foden.

MONTH 2. AUGUST 2018

London/Manchester/Wolverhampton

On 5 August 2018, Pep wins his third title. It's the fourth time he's lifted a trophy at Wembley. The Community Shield may not be the most prestigious competition in the world but it means a lot. City have started the new season with the same winning mentality of last season.

---

* Real Madrid paid €17 million (£15 million) for Brahim Díaz in January 2019 and in September 2020 they loaned him out to AC Milan. The other six City players sold ahead of the 2018–19 season are Angus Gunn, Jason Denayer, Pablo Maffeo, Joe Hart, Bersant Celina and Olarenwaju Kayode.

City go into the game against Chelsea having had almost no pre-season training. The defending FA Cup champions have a new man in charge – Maurizio Sarri, who replaced Antonio Conte three weeks ago. It's a double coup for Chelsea since Sarri has brought Jorginho with him from Napoli. Pep himself has long admired the magnificent midfielder.*

Kyle Walker and John Stones have just come back after their post-World Cup summer holidays and their only preparation has been a couple of sessions of gentle stretching over the last two days. The coach has no problem with their late return: 'It was really important that they had a proper holiday. The seasons are very long and I'd rather that they get a good rest so that they're able to face what awaits us. We've focused on tactics with the lads who've just come back from the World Cup. We didn't want to put them through fitness preparation yet.'

It's stiflingly hot in London with the thermometer hitting 37 degrees. Today, Mendy starts for the first time in 11 months. He works with the other defenders to bring the ball out. It's textbook Pep – an unhurried, precise build-up from the defensive line through Stones and Fernandinho and then onto Foden and Mahrez, who are playing deep, and finally to Kun who puts City ahead.

The second goal is also straight from the Guardiola playbook. It comes from a brilliant counterattack launched by Gündoğan, with support from Mahrez and Bernardo Silva, and converted again by Agüero. It's all exactly what Pep wants to see for the rest of the season. One goal after a sequence of careful passes and another from an aggressive counter. City have 18 shots at goal (close to last season's average) against Chelsea's 5. It's the fifth time the club has won the Community Shield in its history (1938, 1968, 1972, 2012, 2018) and Pep's 25th trophy as coach.

Bernardo Silva has begun his second season hoping to emulate Leroy Sané, who started out shy and diffident in his first year but had become a star player by the end of the second. Silva moves up and down all the zones of the pitch as part of the 2–3–2–3 formation. He starts as an inside-left midfielder and then, after the break, is pinned to the right wing – Mahrez

---

* Jorginho was Pep's first choice to replace Yaya Touré but Sarri's appointment as Chelsea coach made the player's transfer to the London club inevitable and he signed for €60 million (£50 million). Manchester United have made a big signing: Brazilian midfielder Fred, for £47 million.

takes his place on the left. Seventy-five minutes in, he switches to inside-right midfielder and ends the game on the left wing. Just after the final whistle I get a text from Pep, 'Right now the team is Bernardo and ten others.'

Seven days later it's back to London to play Unai Emery's Arsenal in City's first league game as defending champions. Pep fields a 3–1–3–3 with three central defenders (Walker, Stones, Laporte), Fernandinho in the pivot position, and then a mixed line made up of Mahrez, Gündoğan and Mendy, plus three asymmetrical forwards: Agüero and Bernardo in central positions and Sterling on the left. Whenever they lose possession, the team falls back into a 4–4–2.

Sterling is on phenomenal form and scores the first after a horizontal slalom run which he maintains until he finds the gap through which he scores. This is only his third goal from outside the box. He's also a key part of the second goal. Cutting inside, he opens up the wing for a killer assist from Mendy, which Bernardo Silva finishes. Kevin De Bruyne comes on for the last 30 minutes. Three days later he damages his lateral knee ligament during a weight-training exercise and it looks like the man around whom the team's creativity revolves will be out for ten weeks.

On 19 August it's Huddersfield at the Etihad. The visitors are thumped 6–1 after what turns out to be one of the best games of the season. Pep's men are positioned in a 3–3–4, with Stones, Kompany and Laporte in central defence and a triangle of players (Fernandinho, Gündoğan and David Silva) in midfield. Bernardo Silva, Agüero, Gabriel Jesus and Mendy are in the attacking positions. But owning 77 per cent of possession means David Silva, too, sneaks into attack, leaving City 3–2–5.

The highlights of the game? Ederson's first assist of the season in a direct pass to Agüero; Kun's ninth Premier League hat-trick; a fighting-fit Mendy and his three assists; and Sané and Jesus's ferocious counterattack in the closing minutes of the match. City achieve double their usual shots at goal (32). Pep explains his use of two strikers to the press: 'Last year we suffered against teams who packed their defenders tightly at the back, so we decided to try playing with two central strikers.'

Later we chat about Agüero. 'His knee isn't hurting now that he's had the op. Dr Cugat has done a brilliant job. He's already on great form. It's not just the goals, he moves brilliantly and creates a lot of space. When he's on top form like this, Kun's one of the best in the world.'

August ends with a visit to the mythical Molineux Stadium where Wolves won promotion to the Premier League at the end of last season. City have won all their away games since 3 February 2018, when they drew against Burnley, but today marks the end of their winning run as Nuno Espírito Santo's team hold City to a 1–1.

Today Pep has gone for a 2–3–2–3, with Walker helping to bring the ball out as the third central defender, after which he moves up to the midfield with Fernandinho and Mendy. City dominate the game with 71 per cent possession, 664 passes (91 per cent are accurate) and 18 shots at goal, 3 of which hit the post. They only score once, however (Laporte's header from a free kick), after Willy Boly's 'handball goal' is allowed by the referee. It's not the referee's only bad decision, given that Rúben Neves's foul on David Silva is also ignored by the man in black. Two bad calls that clearly put City at a disadvantage. But Estiarte doesn't want to argue the point: 'We need to keep a cool head. We know that no one is going to do us any favours. So we have to do things even better. We have to improve.'

The technical team have already noticed a few flaws; the players were a bit imprecise in bringing the ball out, they didn't manage to cut off Wolves' counterattacks as soon as they lost the ball, some of the players aren't in great shape (Walker) and their passing in the opposition box was very inaccurate. Only 40 per cent of Sané's passing is on target in the 20 minutes he spends on the pitch, and it's clear that his surprise absence from the World Cup has hit his self-confidence hard.

MONTH 3. SEPTEMBER 2018

Manchester/Lyon/Cardiff/Oxford

Sané doesn't make the team sheet for the home game against Rafa Benítez's Newcastle at the start of September. Pep goes for a 2–3–1–4, with creative midfielder David Silva, who's given the freedom to roam, stationed just behind the four attacking players: Mahrez and Sterling on the wings and the Agüero/Jesus duo up front. City take 24 shots on goal but only win 2–1. It's par for the course – these days all their opponents lock down into defensive mode in the hope of avoiding a thrashing from the champions.

Guardiola isn't able to stick with this formation as the month progresses. Almost a year to the day (350 days exactly) since his ligament injury, Benjamin Mendy injures the fifth metatarsal of his foot while on international duty for France. His absence forces Pep to make immediate changes. He uses Fabian Delph as Mendy's replacement, scraps the creative midfielder plus four forwards combo, and puts Leroy Sané on the left wing and Sterling on the right. His left-back will now take on more midfield duties.

Although his players stick to the fundamental principles of Guardiola's philosophy, Pep's annoyed by the fact that several of them are not on top form and their passing is sloppy. Although they beat Fulham comfortably (3–0) in mid-September, the cracks begin to show four days later when City host Olympique Lyonnais at the Etihad.

It's the first game of the new Champions League campaign and the visitors aggressively press City as they bring the ball out, forcing errors. City miss the chance for an early goal. Laporte's header hits the post and Sterling fails to finish after City produce an extraordinary sequence of passes, which goes from the defensive line right up to Lyon's area. The visitors defend expertly and take full advantage of Fernandinho's multiple errors to go 0–2 ahead. Bernardo Silva does get one back but, otherwise, the team performs badly and City suffer their fourth consecutive loss in the Champions League, the first English team to lose so many games in a row in this competition.*

In Pep's 300th game with City he surprises everyone by putting Sergio Agüero on as a false 9 in the 2–3–2–3 formation that faces recently promoted Cardiff. Gündoğan plays a part in four of City's five goals (800 passes, 91 per cent accuracy, 79 per cent possession and 21 shots). With 15 minutes left Pep puts John Stones in as an organising midfielder for the second time this season. The young centre-back is good enough to step in for Fernandinho now and again, although he needs more experience before he can fully assume the role.

In fact, Pep starts Stones in central midfield against Oxford in their first League Cup tie. Eighteen-year-old Phil Foden produces his first goal for City, making him the club's first player born after 2000 to score in an

---

* Last season City were beaten by Basel in the return leg of the knockout round and then by Liverpool in both legs of the quarter-final.

official match. Foden drops to his knees and kisses the badge. The fans are delighted: '*He's one of our own.*' Fellow academy alumni Arijanet Muric and Brahim Díaz (shortly before his transfer) are also part of the team today but it's Foden who stands out as the academy star.

Pep sticks with the 2–3–2–3 formation for the 2–1 victory over Brighton at the end of September (900 passes, 80 per cent possession and 28 shots at goal). De Bruyne and Mendy are both missing but the team has moved up a gear since the Lyon disaster. Pep's pleased: 'We've not allowed our opponents a single shot on goal in the last few games. Every time we lose the ball we get it back immediately and stop them counterattacking. We're playing excellent positional football.'

MONTH 4. OCTOBER 2018

Sinsheim/Liverpool/Manchester/Donetsk/London

It's a tough calendar in October. Liverpool in the Premier League and then Spurs, plus two away games in the Champions League: Hoffenheim and Shakhtar Donetsk. These last two are must-win, given City's poor result against Lyon.

It takes Hoffenheim just 45 seconds to demolish City's carefully constructed defence. Pep's planned a 3–1–3–3 in the hope of stopping the preferred vertical, game-stretching style of Hoffenheim's brilliant coach Julian Nagelsmann. Central defenders Kompany, Otamendi and Laporte are the backline, Fernandinho's in the pivot position with three midfielders (Walker, Silva, Gündoğan) and three forwards (Sterling, Agüero, Sané).

Momentarily it feels like the Champions League is slipping through City's fingers but six minutes later David Silva flights an 'impossible' pass into open space, Sané provides the assist and Agüero scores. But they're not out of the woods yet and for the next hour the game's on a knife edge, with the German side packed in at the back and taking advantage of Fernandinho's slightest errors to steal the ball and launch aggressive counters.

Then Guardiola comes up with an unexpected solution. He puts Stones on for Otamendi but positions the defender as a double pivot alongside Fernandinho, moving Walker back to be the third centre-back. It works, effectively neutralising Hoffenheim's attacks, and City fly through the last half-hour, pulling off a 1–2 victory. The narrow margin doesn't do justice to the number of good chances City have generated. For the third time in four games Stones has pulled off his role in organising midfield. For Pep, the accuracy of the player's ball control and passing plus his tactical nous make him uniquely qualified to transition into a midfield role as required: 'You know how I feel. If I could I'd play with 11 midfielders, if the false 9 gives us superiority in the centre of the pitch, and if the full-backs can play as midfielders, why can't a centre-back play there too if he's got good ball control?'

• • •

Next stop Anfield. Pep goes for a 'Yugoslavia' game plan: our terminology for tactical discipline in defence, sharp, no-nonsense clearing of the ball when the opposition threatens, total concentration and tight marking. Mendy's still on the mend but fit enough to play up and down the left touchline, which relegates Sané to the bench. Pep fields a 3–3–3–1 with Walker, Stones and Laporte in central defence, Bernardo Silva, Fernandinho and Mendy play as deep midfielders with Mahrez, David Silva and Sterling ahead of them in attacking positions and Agüero up front as the lone striker.

As might have been expected, Liverpool dominate completely at first, leaving City – who switch to a 4–4–1–1 when they don't have the ball – a paltry 37 per cent of possession in the opening minutes of the game. The Reds apparent dominance is deceptive, though – they don't create any real chances and, 15 minutes in, City assume more control. Stones and Laporte are playing confident, decisive football today and Bernardo Silva is on top form as he relentlessly drives possession from the back right up to City's attacking line. It's another of Pep's ingenious innovations – the transformation of a pugnacious winger into a creative midfielder.

The first 15 minutes of the second half are a repeat of the first half's pattern. City don't feel under huge pressure and Mahrez is superb in his role, receiving the ball on one side and initiating the sequence of passes that allows his teammates to organise and create positional superiority. As per the coach's instructions they keep the pace slow and steady. For Pep, it's all about a patient build-up. And nerves of steel.

Minute 85. City are awarded a penalty, which Mahrez takes. And misses. The game ends 0–0. City drop two points but it's the first time since 1992 that they haven't conceded at Anfield. Stones has had a colossal game with 97.5 per cent passing accuracy. He's also won six out of the eight duels he's been involved in. Of the eight league games so far, this is the fifth in which City haven't conceded.

For the Burnley game on 20 October, just after the international break, Pep returns to the tried and tested 2–3–2–3. With both his right-backs injured, he repositions Stones again. Twenty-four shots later, City beat Burnley 5–0. The visitors haven't had a single chance. David Silva, Sané and Mendy combine brilliantly on the left flank, constantly passing the ball back and forth between positions on the outside and the inside. Mendy gives his fifth assist of the season (no. 1 in City's rankings) – impressive given the length of time he's been out. A guy who's now averaging six accurate crosses per match.

For the first time since 2011–12, three teams (City, Liverpool and Chelsea) are still unbeaten after the first nine league games. Only two points separate the top five (including Arsenal and Spurs).

• • •

'That was the best first half since I've been in charge here!' City have just defeated Shakhtar 3–0 in Kharkiv and Pep's thrilled by their performance. City now lead their group, the disastrous performance against Lyon completely forgotten. They're on fire in Kharkiv with 24 shots, many of which are close misses with two hitting the post. Including today's three, Pep has chalked up 50 Champions League goals in charge of City but the hyper-vigilant technical team are still worried about the ratio of chances finished. Planchart explains, 'You can't afford to miss so often in the Champions League. You can't afford any slip-ups if you want to win.'

City close a fruitful October by beating Tottenham at Wembley. This despite the lamentable condition of the pitch, turned into a potato patch by the three NFL matches played over the four previous days.* Not long after kick-off, Ederson lobs a long ball up the pitch to Sterling, who controls it, passes to

---

* New England Patriots vs Tampa Bay Buccaneers (25 October 2018), San Diego Chargers vs New Orleans Saints (26th), New York Giants vs Miami Dolphins (28th).

Mahrez and the Algerian winger scores. It's the only goal of the match and for the next 85 minutes Pochettino's men hardly get a sniff of the ball.

For City, it's the sixth Premier League match in a row without conceding and their seventh out of ten Premier League games so far. They've visited Arsenal, Liverpool and Tottenham – as well as Chelsea in the Community Shield – without a single loss. They've also conceded just three in ten games, the second best figure ever.*

Guardiola's got a lot on his mind, though. He's very pleased with the team's consistently excellent defensive play – they've faced an average of just 1.7 shots per game. However, their finishing is still poor: 38.6 per cent of their shots are on target but only one in ten results in a goal. As Estiarte says: 'We need more goals. We're not converting enough chances and too many results are tighter than they should be.' The good news is that City's intensive high pressing is paying dividends. No less than 19 per cent of their winning back possession happens when their opponent is still bringing the ball out in their own defensive third. Pep's men have clearly absorbed his message: 'The ball is mine and when the opponent has it, I'm not trying to steal it. I'm just getting back what is mine already.'

The seeds of an idea are growing in Pep's mind. Stones as the organising pivot in midfield? If he's proved that the full-back/creative midfielder idea can work, why not a centre-back/pivot? Pep files it away for future consideration.

MONTH 5. NOVEMBER 2018

Manchester/London/Lyon

City have six games in November. They win the first four, at the Etihad, scoring 17 and only conceding 2. Impressive.

De Bruyne makes a welcome return in the League Cup against Fulham on 1 November but doesn't last the full 90 minutes after suffering a knock to his injured knee. As we're going into the dressing room later, Estiarte tells me, 'Six weeks, minimum.' Planchart is even more pessimistic: 'We'll have to

---

* Chelsea conceded just two goals in the first ten league games of 2004–5.

do without Kevin for at least two months.' Brahim's two goals have knocked
Fulham out of the Cup but losing De Bruyne again, after ten long weeks
out, is a high price to pay. The best-performing player during last season's
historic triumphs will be out until Christmas. Pep will have to keep producing emergency solutions.

Three days later City smash Southampton 6–1 with both Silvas in
midfield. The scoreline reflects City's powerful attacking – they score four
in the first half, something they haven't achieved for a year – but it's also a
bit deceptive. Ederson has to save five shots from the visitors, an unusually
poor defensive performance given that City have only allowed their rivals a
total of 17 shots in their last ten league games. Pep isn't at all happy: 'We're
not stable enough in some areas of our game. That much was clear today.'

Pep's players give him no cause for complaint three days later when they
maul Shakhtar 6–0. It's the 13th time his City have scored five or more goals
and their best goal tally in the Champions League. Almost everything goes
well. They control the match, without any problems, and combine moments
of slow, patient passing with high-speed counterattacks, converting all of the
six big chances they get. Two games at an average of six goals each time. It's
the perfect way to prepare for the Manchester derby.

City are outstanding for the first 15 minutes against Mourinho's United.
They hold on to the ball, passing 107 times (82 per cent possession) against
United's 19. The combined efforts of the two Silvas produce the opening
goal and it's very clear that the players on the left flank are driving the attack.
Mendy, Laporte, David Silva, Sterling and Agüero make mincemeat of
United while Mahrez on the other side waits patiently to receive the ball and
go head-to-head with the keeper. City's third goal, scored by Gündoğan,
is the result of a ten-man masterpiece of teamwork. For 1 minute and 54
seconds the team passes the ball between themselves, hypnotising United
until their heads seem to nod and their eyes glaze over. Their sequence of
44 consecutive passes ends with Silky Gündoğan's gentle tap into the net.
They've just scored the 'perfect goal'. For Guardiola it's the stuff of dreams.

For the first time since 2011–12, three Premier League teams remain
undefeated after their first 12 games. Only four points separate City,
Liverpool and Chelsea, although Sarri's men drop back a few days later
when they lose to Spurs.

Through no fault of his own, Benjamin Mendy messes up Pep's plans. Again. Halfway through November he has to undergo surgery on his meniscus, which practically guarantees that he'll be out for the rest of the season. He's played 11 out of the 19 games so far and has been a crucial part of Pep's game plan. With Mendy in the lineup, Pep knows that his 2–3–2–3 will work. Getting to grips with his role in Pep's go-to formation has been challenging for the Frenchman, particularly since he missed most of last season when the team were consolidating their understanding and execution of Guardiola's tactical mantras. But Mendy has grown into the full-back/midfielder role. He may not make the right call every time but his physical and technical abilities have more than compensated for any lack of understanding. Despite being prone to drifting out of position, his impetuous, lightning-quick dribbles into the centre of the pitch are a joy to behold and usually leave slack-jawed, bewildered opponents in his wake. For the second year in a row, City will be without a specialist left-back and Pep will have to use players like Delph, Zinchenko, Danilo and Laporte.

City's 0–4 victory at West Ham is their sixth consecutive win in the capital and the third time in a row they've scored four or more against the Hammers in their manor. The game's put to bed in the first 30 minutes but both Bernardo Silva and Gündoğan pick up injuries. Pep now has two more key players (beyond De Bruyne and Mendy) out when they play Lyon in France. He plays Sterling in midfield but the England international fails to control the game, which turns into a complete nightmare for Pep. Every time Sterling loses the ball in the central zones, the French side launch a counterattack. City respond with counters of their own and the game ends 2–2.

The absence of a third midfielder to combine with Fernandinho and David Silva's passing sequences and calm the game down is the main Achilles heel. Agüero has scored today, for the sixth consecutive time in a European game away from home. After the game Pep, rather than being annoyed at the lack of control, is full of praise for the strength of character his men have shown. 'It takes guts to equalise from behind twice. For footballers there's always that doubt as to whether you can come back from behind but the lads showed that they've got the strength of character to do just that.'

FROM 3+2 TO 2+3, WALKER'S THE KEY

Kyle Walker is the key to the team transitioning from one playing model to another in one simple move. The 2+3 that Pep used before Mendy's injury has now become a 3+2 in which Walker drops back a few metres during the build-up phase, moving from a full-back/midfielder to the third centre-back.

In this model, Guardiola aims to reduce the high number of offensive movements Walker undertakes and have him focus on defending and bringing the ball out. The tactic depends on how many opposition forwards try to stop City building their game like this. It's common for teams to field two strikers and having Walker as the third centre-back gives City numerical superiority in the initial phase. Once the ball reaches the centre of the pitch, and depending on how the move is developing, Walker can opt to stay back alongside Stones and Laporte or move forward towards Fernandinho in the midfield. However, if their opponent presses with just one forward Pep will instruct Walker to move up beside Fernandinho and the team revert to a 2+3 for the build-up. Pep's therefore used the 2–3–2–3 to handsomely beat Rotherham, Burton and Burnley but against Chelsea (twice), Everton, Tottenham, Manchester United and Leicester he's reverted to the 3–2–2–3. Towards the end of the season having Zinchenko at left-back will make using one or other of these formations much more straightforward. Guardiola uses the 2+3 formation 24 times (12 of them before Mendy's injury) and the 3+2 on 26 occasions (25 of them are post Mendy's injury).

MONTH 6. DECEMBER 2018

Manchester/London/Leicester

Since coming to England, the month of December has always been challenging and difficult for Pep and he doesn't approach the end of the year lightly. The long, dark, rainy weeks of December 2016 saw his men lose to Chelsea, Leicester and Liverpool, and set the tone for the remainder of City's season. The end of 2017 was better and the Centurions suffered just one, unimportant, defeat in December, against Shakhtar. Then their draw at Selhurst Park on New Year's Eve brought the Citizens' 18-game winning streak to an end.

So Pep's a little apprehensive right now, not least because they're facing the hellish prospect of nine matches this December, one every three days. Everything goes swimmingly until 8 December. City have beaten Bournemouth (3–1)* and Watford (1–2), and are now sitting on 41 points out of a possible 45 with 13 wins and only 2 draws (with Wolves and Liverpool). They've played 14 consecutive away games without losing and have scored 28 goals in the last 7 games. Now they face Chelsea at Stamford Bridge, without both Agüero, injured abductor, and Zinchenko, who has a broken nose.

Maurizio Sarri's Chelsea is a million miles from Antonio Conte's Chelsea. Their stats speak for themselves. Against Newcastle they have 82 per cent possession and make 913 passes with 91 per cent accuracy. Their gifted new midfielder, Jorginho, has already surpassed Gündoğan's record, having completed 180 passes against West Ham. The team is obviously well on the way to implementing the basic playing philosophy that Sarri installed at Napoli so successfully. And nobody's forgotten what it cost City to best Napoli last season.

Agüero's injury means that Sterling's alone up front, although 20 minutes in he swaps with Mahrez on the right wing. Sané is on the left wing, in the absence of Mendy, who's been substituted by Delph at the back. City are excellent in the first half but the combination of a superb pass from David Luiz and a momentary lapse in Sané's man-marking allows N'Golo Kanté to score just before the break. One–nil up, Sarri's men reform into a highly effective, defensive 4–1–4–1 and City struggle to find a way through. They maintain possession and keep driving their attack forward without success. David Luiz scores again from a corner. It's City's first league defeat this season but Pep is upbeat post-match: 'We played much better than last year, although of course last year De Bruyne managed to score the winning goal!'

It's just one defeat but the team, en route back to Manchester, is down in the dumps. David Silva has injured his hamstring. Pep loses another key player.

Four days later, City dispatch Hoffenheim in the Champions League. Sané is in tremendous form and scores an exceptional goal from a *folha*

---

* On 1 December, Raheem Sterling becomes the first player to score against Bournemouth in six consecutive games.

seca free kick (a dipping, swerving shot, named after the Portuguese for 'dry leaf'). For the ninth time in ten Champions League competitions, Pep's teams win their group.

Seventy-two hours later they face Everton at home. The Toffees haven't lost at the Etihad since 2014. It's a cold, wet day and Estiarte's looking glum pre-match: 'This is a much harder game than it looks – there's a chance we could lose three vital points. Everton are very dangerous when they press and attack. I really hope they don't do that today.' The excellent Portuguese coach Marco Silva is in charge of the Toffees, who are currently seventh. Silva goes for a defensive 5–4–1, which actually plays in City's favour. Pep's fielding a 3–2–2–3 today and his men own the ball throughout the match. They win 3–1. But City have no time to catch their breath and it's off to Leicester in the League Cup, where the soggy pitch is slippery. Pep once again fields 'Zinchenko's Team' with youngsters Foden, Brahim and central defender Eric García, just 17, who combines well with the rest of the team and produces excellent football. Stones is in central midfield again. Pep's determined for Stones to learn the basics of the position. For the second consecutive year, same stadium and competition, Leicester and City draw 1–1 but City win the penalty shoot-out. A year ago it was Claudio Bravo who saved the day. And the penalties. This year it's Aro Muric who seals City's victory by blocking James Maddison and Çağlar Söyüncü's attempts.

With the Chelsea defeat behind them and Klopp's Liverpool, who haven't lost any of their 17 league games so far, just one point ahead, everything feels pretty positive as they head into the hectic festive football around Christmas. Before the month is out, though, Pep's hit by two unexpected setbacks.

It's 22 December and the game against a highly defensive Crystal Palace (4–5–1) at the Etihad looks straightforward. City start strongly, with periods of 80 per cent possession and a goal from Gündoğan in the first 30 minutes. Everything's going to plan until a mistake from Walker (1–1) followed by a poor clearance of Palace's corner and a quite brilliant shot from Townsend give the visitors the lead (2–1). In the second half, Walker, whose recklessness and dips in concentration occasionally ruin otherwise superb qualities, messes up again for a penalty and the Eagles go two up. Despite a last-minute all-guns-blazing City assault, they lose 2–3. It's just their second league defeat and the first time they've been defeated at the Etihad this season.

But it all happens again four days later.

It's Boxing Day in Leicester. A minute in, Bernardo Silva scores. So far so good. Then a massive error in central defence lets Marc Albrighton through. Leicester 1 City 1. De Bruyne and Bernardo are in midfield with Sterling and Sané on the wings, each playing on their favoured side. The four men combine to press Leicester back into their box but, today, it doesn't work. Then another poor clearance of a corner gives Leicester a chance and, for the second time in a row, City's opponents go ahead thanks to a goal scored from outside the box. Leicester win 2–1 and a disconsolate City troop out of the King Power Stadium knowing that Liverpool are now seven points ahead. City are on 44 points with Spurs on 45 and the Reds way out in front with 51.

In three of the last four games, City's opponents have converted their first shot on goal and it's clear from the glum expressions of the coaches and players, as they head home, that everyone's fearing the worst: City's fortunes are about to take a tumble.

They have one more game to face before the year ends: Southampton at St Mary's. Then with De Bruyne and Gündoğan both out injured, Liverpool come to the Etihad early in the New Year. The Reds have just crushed Unai Emery's Arsenal 5–1 and are no doubt feeling invincible as the year draws to a close.

It looks like the Southampton game is going to be a rerun of the Crystal Palace/Leicester playbook: David Silva scores nine minutes in but then a Zinchenko error nine minutes before the break lets the locals equalise. Today, however, City are playing from a different script and by half-time they're ahead 3–1. In the second half they then close things out – Saints don't have a single chance on goal.

The year 2018 ends with Liverpool surging ahead with that seven-point lead (54 vs 47). December has once again been unlucky for Pep and if Klopp's men manage to beat them at the Etihad on 3 January, Pep can kiss the league title goodbye.

MONTH 7. JANUARY 2019

Manchester/Newcastle

What's the difference between a champion and an 'also-ran'?

It's 11mm, of course. The difference between success and failure, between winning the title and going home with nothing. Today, 11mm will be all that stands between City and heart-wrenching defeat, between Liverpool and ultimate glory.

City–Liverpool. An all-or-nothing game. A final in all but name. If Klopp's men win, it's 'Sayonara City'. If Pep's men finish ahead, there's still hope in the title race …

The two great sides meet on 3 January 2019. Liverpool lead the Premier League with 54 points, 7 ahead of City, and it feels like the whole championship is already bathed in red. Klopp's men have become an unstoppable machine. They've pulled off 17 wins out of 20 league games, drawn away to Chelsea and Arsenal and at home against City. They've scored 48 times this season and only conceded 8, testimony to first-class defensive organisation and to Klopp's recent signings: keeper Alisson Becker, and player of the year, centre-back Virgil van Dijk. City have scored more goals over the 20 games (54) but they've also conceded more (16), as well as having lost three times during 'black December' (Chelsea, Crystal Palace and Leicester). They've also drawn two: Mahrez missed a penalty just before full-time against Liverpool and they were robbed in Wolverhampton when Willy Boly's handball goal was allowed.

It's a freezing cold day when Liverpool's team bus pulls into the Etihad Stadium but the cheerful faces of Klopp and his men belie the frosty temperatures. This seven-point advantage feels unassailable and they look pretty upbeat as they step down into enemy territory. Meanwhile, the mood in the home dressing room is sombre. For Pep and his men, today's game is crucial, particularly since Tottenham and Chelsea are snapping at their heels.

Guardiola's game plan has had to take account of Mendy's and De Bruyne's absences plus Walker's dip in form. Instead of the usual 3–2–2–3, he's gone for a more conservative 4–3–3 in the hope of avoiding losing the ball in danger zones. Danilo is at right-back, Laporte left-back, Stones and Kompany in central defence, then Fernandinho with the two Silvas either side of him in midfield. Sterling and Sané are on their favoured wings and Agüero will move positionally like a false 9. The defenders bring the ball out cautiously and both full-backs remain open and don't go deep, in contrast to Pep's usual instructions. Today, Bernardo Silva will be looking to receive the ball directly from his central defenders. Danilo and Laporte hardly venture over the central circle.

Despite all these precautions, City's passing is below par – 81 per cent on target, 10 points less than normal. Having anticipated Klopp springing his gegenpress trap in the centre of the pitch, Pep's instructed his men to move the ball up the wings, which they do, with support from Bernardo Silva and Fernandinho on the inside. Agüero drops deeper than usual to receive the ball and keep everything flowing.

Seventeen minutes in, the game erupts into action. It's the turning point of the season. Salah and Firmino combine beautifully, and the latter feeds the ball to Mané who runs into the box and shoots diagonally across goal. Fifty thousand City fans hold their breath for a fraction of a second as they watch the ball hit the post and land back at Mané's feet. Stones gets there first, though, and thumps the ball away, only to have it bounce off Ederson, who was also going for it. Their bad luck continues as the ball, rebounding for a second time, heads straight for the net. Stones, with Salah pressing at his heels, gets to it and thumps it away, not knowing whether or not it has gone in. After a few tense seconds, the referee confirms that the ball didn't fully cross the line.

This all-defining moment fell 11mm short.

Agüero produces a first-class performance in the testing false 9 role – a blur of constant movement, repeatedly dropping as far as the centre circle to pick up possession and give Bernardo Silva secure passing options into Liverpool's half. Forty minutes in, Kun scores his 250th goal for City after a fabulous counterattack from Sané and a clutch of failed attempts to clear by Liverpool followed by the killer assist from Bernardo Silva. Agüero has so little room for manoeuvre in the penalty box but he nevertheless spots a negligible space inside the post, which Alisson has left exposed. The Argentinian, upon whom every City fan dotes, launches the ball at goal. And somehow scores.

Agüero, Bernardo and Sané have maintained constant pressure on Liverpool's defenders and it's paid off but, gradually, Klopp's men reassert themselves as the second half develops and Firmino equalises. Seventeen minutes later, Fernandinho robs possession off a Liverpool build-up, Sterling launches a blistering counter, which is finished by Sané. It's victory for the Citizens, Liverpool's unbeaten run is over and it's the fourth time Sané has scored against the Reds in two and a half seasons.

Stones, Fernandinho, Danilo, Sané and Agüero have all been brilliant but Bernardo Silva stands out. The supremely gifted creative midfielder has turned into an enforcer and, here, robbed more balls than anyone else (ten in total, against Fernandinho's nine), and he's run his legs off – 13.7km: a Premier League record this season. His combination of innate talent and athletic ability is unstoppable. This is one of the players who most epitomises Guardiola's 'perfect footballer': players with prodigious talent and great tactical understanding as well as stamina and speed.

• • •

Having won the first 'match point' of the season and anticipating an easier run in the impending matches, Pep can breathe again. Indeed, the team storms through the next two assignments: Rotherham (7–0) in the FA Cup and Burton (9–0) in the League Cup, becoming the first English team since Leeds in 1967 to score seven or more goals in two consecutive matches.

In both ties Pep fields a more relaxed 2–3–2–3, although he reverts to a 3–2–2–3 for their league win against Wolves. City dominate to such an extent that Wolves don't manage a single shot on target, the first time this has happened to them in seven years. City also amasses hundreds of passes (869) and touches (1,050), and shoot at goal 22 times.

Six days later, with Gündoğan and De Bruyne back in harness for City's visit to Huddersfield, Pep uses a 2–3–5 in an attempt to break down the locals' ultra-defensive 4–5–1. Once again, he puts Sterling and Sané on the wing on their natural side. Danilo provides the opener, which is also City's 100th goal this season. The game plan is so successful that Pep repeats it for their 5–0 Cup win against Burnley.

They're almost through January, having conceded just once and scored 29. They're also through to the League Cup final at Wembley for the second year in a row. Then, on 29 January, they're off to St James's Park …

After just 25 seconds Sergio Agüero opens the scoring. He gets another just minutes later but it's disallowed – De Bruyne took the free kick before the referee's whistle. City dominate and accumulate good chances but, much like the Crystal Palace and Leicester games, Newcastle fight back. An unlucky rebound gives Newcastle parity, then a mistake by Fernandinho results in a penalty and gives the home side the win despite the fact that Rafa Benítez's men have only managed two shots on goal. For City, it feels like game over. Liverpool are still in pole position. Bruised and demoralised, Pep's men go home believing the title, their title, is now out of reach.

The next day, however, 30 January, Liverpool suffer a major setback at Anfield. Mané scores within three minutes but Leicester's Maguire duly equalises. What should have been Liverpool's comfortable seven-point cushion suddenly is 'only' five. WhatsApp groups all over Manchester start buzzing: 'All's not lost – we can still do it!' proclaim the messages.

Liverpool would appear to have resuscitated Manchester City's campaign to retain the league title.

MONTH 8. FEBRUARY 2019

Manchester/Liverpool/Gelsenkirchen/London

As they hit February Liverpool lead by five points. There are 14 matches left. Every single one is going to feel like a final. Pep believes City will have to win them all: 'Leagues are decided in the last ten matches. Liverpool will make very few mistakes – if we want to be champions we need 14 wins.' It's something that no English team has done in the final weeks of a season. (City won 18 in a row last season but those were in the first half of the season.) Liverpool are like a red rabbit haring towards the title but Pep's rifle is locked and loaded. And, boy, can this guy shoot.

City reaching the League Cup final unfortunately requires bringing forward their league match against Everton. They'll now squeeze the Toffees in on a rare free Wednesday night between two already brutal tests against Arsenal and Chelsea. This calendar alteration sparks a tense psychological game of cat and mouse between City and Liverpool – for the rest of the season the two teams are always at different stages of their individual league calendars. Sometimes Guardiola is one game ahead, sometimes it's Klopp.

City's long sprint to the final begins at home against Arsenal. Unai Emery plays a 4–4–2 with Alexandre Lacazette and Pierre-Emerick

Aubameyang up front, and Guardiola surprises everyone with a 4–1–2–3 in which Fernandinho is a central defender off the ball and the pivot midfielder when City have the ball. It's the same kind of transition Pep's used with his full-backs in the past. This time it's the centre-back who must switch into midfield. Full-backs Walker and Laporte stay wide and Otamendi partners Fernandinho in the backline. Gündoğan, De Bruyne and David Silva all move between the lines, which, with Fernandinho's specific, attacking brief, gives City numerical superiority in the centre of the pitch. Bernardo Silva and Sterling are inverted wingers today.

Agüero doesn't waste any time and scores 48 seconds into the game but Arsenal equalise ten minutes later from a corner. Now City begin to smash the Gunners hard; Gündoğan begins what will now become a personal weekly magic show and Agüero registers his tenth Premier League hat-trick. In the second half, City take 13 shots at goal and deny their opponents any of their own. It's total Sky Blue dominance. De Bruyne is struggling with cramp, though, and those two knee injuries he's suffered have clearly left him less than 100 per cent in terms of stamina and power.

The following day, Liverpool draw 1–1 at West Ham. More dropped points. The gap is narrowing.

City's visit to Goodison Park is high risk. Pep fields a 3–2–2–3 with Stones, Otamendi and Laporte in central defence and Walker supporting Fernandinho in the midfield. Everton press Fernandinho hard and succeed in short-circuiting the visitors' game plan. Until Pep comes up with the solution. Once again its name is John Stones. From the 25th minute the centre-back repeats the strategic role that Fernandinho played four days ago: the dual function midfielder/centre-back, depending on whether the team has the ball or not. It's a simple solution but it immediately deactivates Everton's strategy and City win the game (0–2) without their goalmouth being troubled. They've equalled Liverpool on 65 points but City have played a game extra. Still, the red rabbit is definitely in their sights ...

Chelsea's 10 February visit to the Etihad will surely go down in the annals of the Premier League. Their 6–0 defeat is the worst Chelsea has suffered in this competition (they lost 7–0 to Nottingham Forest in 1991, before the Premier League was established). Agüero gets his 11th hat-trick (equalling the number achieved by Alan Shearer). City play a 3–2–2–3 formation when they have the ball and switch to a 4–5–1 whenever they lose possession. The game is decided in the first 24 minutes – City score four in that time – and for the remainder of the game Chelsea have just one chance when Pedro goes head-to-head with Ederson. And loses.

The Citizens make quick work of the FA Cup fifth round against Newport (1–4) when they play the 2–3–2–3, which works so well against highly defensive teams. Four days later Pep uses a 3–2–2–3 against Schalke in Gelsenkirchen for the first leg of the Champions League knockout round.

Initially all goes well. Agüero scores the opener (now he's the first Premier League player to score in seven consecutive Champions League matches away from home). Then two penalties are awarded to the home side as a result of fouls by Otamendi and Fernandinho. By the time Otamendi is sent off after 67 minutes, City's domination is under serious threat.

Ironically, the resulting numerical inferiority seems to give City wings. They reorganise into a 4–4–1 and end up winning the game thanks to a fantastic direct Sané free kick and then another of those amazing assists launched up the pitch by Ederson, which Sterling converts.

On 24 February Pep is back in Wembley, his 'lucky' stadium, for the second time this season. It's Chelsea in the League Cup final (the two sides also met last July in the Community Shield). Thirty minutes before kick-off there's good news in the Citizen's dressing room. Liverpool have drawn 0–0 at Old Trafford. The Reds are now only one point ahead (66–65).

We all learn from our successes but perhaps it's our failures, large and small, that teach us the most. It's the wounds they leave that force us to reflect on exactly why we've failed. And that's precisely what Maurizio Sarri has done over the last two weeks.

The devastating 6–0 thrashing dealt out by City last time has caused the savvy Italian to bin his offensive game plan and he crowds his men into the box around Kepa. He's parked the 'Sarri bus'. City manage very few shots on goal as a result – just three, significantly fewer than their average. But Sarri's tactics mean Chelsea don't manage a single shot on target.

The Londoners block all potential passing lines and City struggle to find even the tiniest chink in their defensive wall. With Fernandinho and Laporte injured, it's not until extra-time that Pep's men create any real chances. A recalcitrant Kepa, who ended the final feeling nagging muscle problems, point-blank refuses his coach's order to come off and be replaced by penalty-saving specialist Willy Caballero.

The penalty shoot-out starts with Ederson stopping Jorginho's shot. Five penalties later Kepa blocks Sané's and then David Luiz hits the post. City win the final. It's the first trophy City have ever retained, also the sixth consecutive penalty shoot-out they've won. This is Kompany, Silva, Agüero and Fernandinho's fourth League Cup medal and the 11th final Pep's won out of the 12 he's disputed. It's his 26th title as a coach.

City have scored eight times against Chelsea this season so far, and conceded twice. They've won both trophies in play but Chelsea's strong defensive organisation has also stopped City scoring on two occasions.

After two and a half weeks with no Premier League action, City beat West Ham in Manchester. But with Łukasz Fabiański doing a superb job in goal, it's only 1–0.

The chase continues. And stays nip-and-tuck. Liverpool and City have played the same number of games and the Reds are only one point ahead (69–68).

MONTH 9. MARCH 2019

Bournemouth/Manchester/Swansea/London

Eddie Howe doesn't make things easy for City. Once again his game plan is extremely conservative – it's all about closing down any space City might exploit. Most of their opponents will do something similar from now until the end of the season to try and prevent this fearsome team tearing them apart. To a degree it works. Pep's men score less often. But still keep on winning.

Today Bournemouth have shut down into a tight 5–4–1 and City manage just one goal – from Mahrez – despite their clear domination (82 per cent possession, 811 passes, 735 of which are accurate, and 23 shots at goal). The home side don't manage a single shot at goal, even one that's wildly off target.

In their last five Premier League games City's opponents have only managed eight shots at goal. In total. Something which delights Pep: 'Today was one of our best games of the year. We didn't let them get a single shot in. I love that.'

The bruising match schedule is still depleting his squad, though. Stones injures his knee – he'll be out until April. De Bruyne has to come off because of a hamstring strain. He won't be back until the end of the month. Carles Planchart shares his concerns with me: 'The number of games we've had this week is totally crazy. Three games in six days and one of them went to extra-time. It's absolutely exhausting for everyone and we're picking up injuries because of it. But we're determined to fight on.'

It's Sunday, 3 March, and over at Goodison Park, Everton are hosting Liverpool in a game that could make all the difference to City's title challenge. The hard-fought derby ends in a no-score draw with each team managing just three shots on goal. Over at Pep's place everyone's celebrating. It feels like they've just played and won the game themselves. City are now league leaders, with 71 points against Liverpool's 70, on the same number of games. In under two months they've managed to accumulate eight points more than Klopp's Reds. Back at the start of the year, it looked like Liverpool had done enough to secure the title. Now Pep has turned the tables. Ever cautious, he's keeping a cool head: 'We're not taking anything for granted. There are nine games left. The title is still a world away and we have a lot still to do to be champions again.'

Fernandinho's absent for the whole of March. Gündoğan takes his place in organising midfield and immediately brings much greater fluidity to City's game. From now until the end of the season the German will be in the form of his life. Less strong defensively than Fernandinho, OK, but he directs the play beautifully and produces extraordinary assists, constantly catching his opponents unawares with his deft passing. Guardiola makes sure Silky always has a couple of steely bodyguards at his sides, constantly using the 2–3–2–3 formation, usually with Walker and Zinchenko (who's won the contest to be left-back ahead of Delph). Pep wants to protect this German talent.

The Silva 'twins' move like electrons against Watford (3–1), feeding Sterling, who scores a hat-trick in just 13 minutes. Then City host Schalke in a Champions League game. Pep's dealing with a vastly depleted squad – Kompany, Mendy, De Bruyne, Fernandinho and Stones are all injured and Otamendi is serving a ban. Laporte is back, having recovered from the injury he picked up playing Chelsea, and Danilo joins him in central defence. Pep's keen to protect Laporte, though, and takes him off 20 minutes from the end, leaving a backline made up of four full-backs: Delph on the right, Zinchenko on the left, and Walker and Danilo in the centre. Gündoğan is in superb form in midfield, hitting creative levels seldom seen in a pivot.

City hand Schalke a 7–0 drubbing. It's a new, if unenviable, Champions League record – Schalke become the German side who have conceded the highest number of goals in a Champions League match. City have destroyed them 10–2 over the two legs, the highest goal difference ever achieved by an English club in this competition and the biggest aggregate defeat of any German side. Leroy Sané produces three assists, equalling the record set by Franck Ribéry in 2012. It's the seventh time this season that the team has scored six or more goals and, for Pep, it's the ninth time he's qualified for the Champions League quarter-finals in ten seasons.

The Premier League has to alter the league calendar again to accommodate the FA Cup quarter-final ties, and from 16 March until the end of April Liverpool always play before City do. The two teams are neck and neck, although Pep still leads Klopp by one point at the end of March. The slightest misstep could tip the balance in the other team's favour, though, and everyone's nerves are shredded.

City beat Swansea in the Cup. Agüero's winning goal is actually offside and Pep is quick to acknowledge this after the game. Swansea go 2–0 ahead in the first half, scoring from a penalty awarded for a Delph foul and then from a stunning counterattack. But City are the dominant team throughout and in the second half they score three times. Bernardo Silva smashes home the first, then Agüero's penalty rebounds off Swansea keeper, Kristoffer Nordfeldt, into his own net and finally Kun produces the winner with a diving header.

It's the first time since Pep took over that they've managed to fight back from 2–0 down. City are through to the semis.

There's a brief pause for the international break and then it's back to the league campaign. Pep maintains the 2–3–2–3 with Gündoğan bringing his superb leadership qualities to bear. They go to Craven Cottage and produce both goals in a first 30 minutes of exceptional football. De Bruyne is back, playing in creative midfield, and Bernardo Silva is on the right wing. Fulham can't even manage a single shot on Ederson's goal. Pep, who's always considered defence as one of his strong points as a coach, is happy: 'A good defence is absolutely crucial. Everyone looks at the way we attack but the quality of our defensive organisation is actually the key.'

MONTH 10. APRIL 2019

Manchester/London/Burnley

Football can be fickle. One moment you're riding high, victory within your grasp, then, in an instant, the tables turn and all your hopes are dashed.

One minute, 7 seconds and 42 hundredths of a second are all that stand between Manchester City and the Champions League semi-finals. The time it takes for the cries of 'Goaaaaal!' to turn to heartbreak and desolation as the VAR decision comes in: 'Goal disallowed.'

Pep and Klopp are still neck and neck in the league. Both teams storm through the month of April, although Guardiola suffers a major setback against Cardiff when Zinchenko joins the ranks of City's walking wounded. The Ukrainian has developed a remarkable connection with David Silva, Sané and Sterling, adding fluidity to City's game. He's going to be badly missed for the three or so weeks it'll take to repair him. Mendy, who's still not fully fit, replaces him. But not for long. His knee problems will send him back to the medics soon – he's going to need arthroscopic surgery.

Cardiff (in a league fixture) and Brighton (in the Cup semi-finals) both go for a 4–5–1. City face solid defensive walls, which aim to starve them of passing lines on the inside and create opportunities for their opponents to rob the ball and counterattack. It's business as usual for City, however. They breeze through both games, although the goal difference isn't huge (2–0 and 1–0).

On 9 April the Citizens visit Pochettino's Spurs in a renovated White Hart Lane for the first leg of the Champions League semi-finals. Given City's extensive injury list – Bernardo Silva, Zinchenko and Mendy are out, and neither De Bruyne nor Stones are 100 per cent – Pep's had to restructure the team. Today's all about caution and control, and Pep's produced a similar game plan to the one he's used so successfully against Liverpool. He leaves Sané and De Bruyne on the bench, saving them for the crucial league game against Crystal Palace in five days' time. He's opted for a 3–3–2–2, the formation he often used before Mendy became so injury prone. His centre-backs are Walker, Otamendi and Laporte; Gündoğan, Fernandinho and Delph are in midfield while Mahrez and Silva move between the lines and Agüero and Sterling are up front, in asymmetrical positions.

Guardiola isn't looking for dramatic results. It's just about getting through this night unscathed. And they almost get away with it. Neither team takes a lot of risks – it's a contest of very few chances (City get just one shot on target and Spurs two). In the end, it's unforced errors that give the home team their 1–0 win. Twelve minutes in, Agüero misses a penalty. The moment has particular resonance for Pep. Back in the day, both Messi (for Barça) and Thomas Müller (for Bayern) missed penalties at similar stages of this Holy Grail competition, resulting in the elimination of their respective teams.* And, with 13 minutes left, Delph's over-confidence allows Son Heung-min to score the game's only goal. A bad result after a lacklustre game. Cautious, conservative football doesn't feel natural for Pep's City and they've paid the price. Although, had Agüero's penalty gone in, we'd all be feeling very differently …

On 14 April, City visit Selhurst Park. Pep has enormous respect for Roy Hodgson's Palace. And with good reason. Last season City only managed a nil–nil draw at Selhurst Park and in December the Eagles beat them at the Etihad. Fernandinho's still injured and Gündoğan takes his place. Mendy's also back but he's struggling. Ten minutes in, the Frenchman is gasping for breath and Pep instructs him to conserve his energy. He does what he can, and it's a heroic performance, but the effort of playing leaves him utterly exhausted. Three days later he'll be asked to go in again in the second leg of the Champions League semi-final at home to Spurs.

In the end, City win comfortably at Selhurst Park (1–3) with Sterling scoring twice and Gabriel Jesus providing the third. Palace's goal comes from a free kick, which owes as much to Ederson's poor organisation of City's defensive wall as anything else. It's a good result, though, and brings City's goal tally to 150. Leroy Sané, who's seemed below par all season, has done well too. He's now provided 17 assists this season.

· · ·

* On 24 April 2012, Messi's penalty hit the crossbar of Petr Cech's goal in the second leg of their Champions League semi-final against Chelsea and Barcelona were eliminated. On 3 May 2016, Müller also missed a penalty in the return leg of the Champions League semi-final against Atlético Madrid and were likewise eliminated.

Sometimes you win, sometimes you lose and sometimes you do both things at once.

On 17 April, City defeat Spurs 4–3 in an absolutely epic second leg of the Champions League semi-final, at the Etihad. It's not enough though. Thanks to UEFA's (now abandoned) 'away goals' rule, City are eliminated from the Champions League. Agüero's missed penalty in the first leg comes back to haunt them …

Both teams bring their A-games today and it's glorious to watch. Guardiola directs his disciples with even more frenetic energy than usual. He adapts the structure on the hoof, changing it according to which team is ahead. Whenever it looks like City are in danger of being eliminated he switches to an aggressive 2–3–5, reverting to a 4–2–3–1 if City are on top. Four minutes in, Sterling produces one of his signature changes of direction, from outside to in, and uses his right foot to bend a truly wonderful finish across Hugo Lloris and into the far corner of the net.

As is so often the case in this unpredictable sport, one of the team's special-ists messes up the very responsibilities in which he is a specialist. The team's most regular defender, someone Pep knows he can always rely on, the unbeat-able, unflappable Aymeric Laporte, makes two huge mistakes in less than three minutes, allowing Son to equalise and give Spurs the lead in Manchester.

City fight on and within one minute Bernardo Silva puts their second goal away. At the end of a mad, frenzied first half, it's City 2 Spurs 2. Sterling scores again in the second half, as does Agüero, and, at 4–2 after an hour, City have done enough to go through to the semi-final. Gündoğan in organising midfield combines brilliantly with De Bruyne and Bernardo who, as creative midfielders, are free to roam. Disastrously, in the 73rd minute, Llorente scores from a corner. It's now 4–3 on the night, 4–4 on aggregate, but, because of their away goals, Spurs are going to play Ajax for a place in the Madrid Champions League final.*

But there's an end scene, a bitter pay-off. The scoreboard clock shows 92.25 when Sterling produces the miracle goal City's fans have been praying for, but euphoria soon turns to bitter disappointment. The goal

---

* Fernando Llorente knocked the ball in off his right elbow but the Turkish referee Cüneyt Çakır still allowed the goal after consulting VAR. He wasn't shown the TV footage that clearly showed Llorente's infraction.

is disallowed. It takes VAR one minute and seven seconds to decide that Agüero was offside.

Devastation. The players shut themselves away in the dressing room for almost an hour, too dejected to move and completely inconsolable. Pep's in a state of shock. Not only is this the end of their European ambitions but a crushing blow to their morale. One which threatens to undermine their ongoing campaign for the trophies still in contention. From glory to desolation in little more than a minute.

Ironically enough, this despondent version of City must host Spurs again only three days later. Pep fields his favoured 3–2–2–3 but his men, still bruised from the last encounter, struggle to produce their usual effervescence. Strangely, Spurs too seem off form today. Although it's more likely to be the euphoria of winning that's affecting them. City are just one point ahead of Liverpool in the league so this game is crucial. They can't even afford the luxury of a draw. This is a test of character, resolve and will to win.

Pep has Foden in midfield today and the youngster repays the trust by scoring the only goal of the match after just four minutes. From then onwards, the match follows the identical, repetitive pattern: City flood forward and Spurs counterattack. De Bruyne, who's probably spent more time this season with medics and physios than on the pitch, suffers another muscular problem. It's almost too much to bear – yet another star player out through injury. Despite the victory, today has probably taken the greatest psychological toll of the season to date.

City still have a game in hand and the postponed match has been rescheduled for 24 April. Pep and his men don't even have to leave the city – it's the Manchester derby at Old Trafford. Perhaps a visit to their biggest rival will be just the thing to pull them out of the post-elimination doldrums?

The first half is a washout. The match is as tense as any final and City are a bundle of nerves, making so many mistakes that by half-time only a measly 85 per cent of their passes have reached their target. At the 50-minute mark, Fernandinho injures his knee – he'll be out for the rest of the season – and Sané comes on in his place. And immediately changes the whole game. The tempo and rhythm move up a gear, their heads go up and the monotony is broken. The German international flies up and down Old Trafford, his evident strutting confidence infecting the whole group. City awake.

Gündoğan's forced return to the centre of midfield also proves decisive. The whole dynamic of City's game changes and they begin to produce fast, precise and flowing football, resulting in a goal apiece from Bernardo Silva and Sané. Pep is now officially the first coach to have achieved three consecutive victories at Old Trafford, and David Silva the first player to win six in a row there. City are increasingly scoring more goals from counterattacks and the two from today's game give them an overall total of 157, a new record for goals scored by an English club (the previous record, 156, was set by Manuel Pellegrini's City in 2013–14).

After a miserable week, Pep leaves Old Trafford a happy man: 'This team has real strength of character. Getting knocked out of the Champions League was very, very tough and then, although we beat Tottenham, we didn't play well. But the lads pulled off a massive victory here today despite all the pressure. We've won three in a row at Old Trafford. That's a huge achievement and these players have my total admiration. Now I want them to disconnect, to not read the papers or watch TV. It's all about relaxing, eating, sleeping … and then we'll be ready for the four "finals" we've yet to play.'

This is a sentiment he feels intensely because the title race remains excruciatingly tight. Liverpool beat Fulham and Tottenham (2–1 each time) but City also chalk up another victory on the last Sunday of April, against Burnley. The 0–1 scoreline shows just how tight the margin is between success and failure. Agüero's shot crosses the goal line by just 29.51mm.

Tiny margins …

MONTH 11. MAY 2019

Manchester/Brighton/London

It's still too close to call as the end of the season approaches. Liverpool are in Newcastle for their penultimate league game and come very close to disaster. They go ahead twice, only to have Rafa Benítez's men equalise each time. In the end, an 86th-minute Divock Origi goal gives the Reds last-minute victory. Jürgen Klopp is still in with a chance and will no doubt be willing Leicester on in their game against City at the Etihad the following day. After a long, tortuous season (37 league games so far) Pep is facing his bête noire in City's last home game of the season.

At this stage of the season, Guardiola's not making a lot of changes. Essentially, the players currently in the best form are in the starting 11. Kompany has a guaranteed place in central defence alongside Laporte – leaving Stones and even Otamendi on the bench. Walker and Zinchenko are automatic picks at full-back, as are Gündoğan at pivot and David Silva in creative midfield. Bernardo Silva and Sterling remain as inverted wingers and Agüero, of course, is up front. With De Bruyne out, the only variable is who Pep picks to play in right midfield. Today it's the golden boy himself, Phil Foden.

Brendan Rodgers's game plan has been meticulously prepared. Leicester let City circulate the ball without interference until they get to the centre circle, where Jamie Vardy, Wilfred Ndidi and Youri Tielemans surround the ball carrier in order to rob possession. Maddison, whose superb passing skills have been the revelation of the season, then initiates the counterattack. If City manage to push through towards Kasper Schmeichel's penalty area then nine men work double-time to shut down any possible space.

The tension of today's game causes City to make a few careless mistakes but they also create several chances including an Agüero header that hits the post. Nothing bears fruit, though, and Guardiola sends Sané on for Foden in the 56th minute, thereby freeing Sterling up to move into attack on the inside, just behind Agüero. The game moves up a gear immediately and within minutes both sides launch dangerous attacks. Harry Maguire's counterattack culminates in a shot from Maddison, which is just wide of Ederson's goal, and then the action is at the other end of the pitch, where Agüero's point-blank shot is saved by Schmeichel. Pep watches the seconds tick by. They're in serious danger of letting Liverpool go ahead.

Then, something astonishing happens. City's captain scores. Seventy minutes in and all Pep's men, bar Ederson, are crowded around Leicester's penalty box. It's been more than five years since Kompany has taken a shot from outside the box.* And it's more than 12 since he's scored from

---

* The last time Kompany shot from outside the area was December 2013, in a Manchester City–Crystal Palace game.

that position.* But City's captain is undeterred. He's spotted space on the right-hand side that Leicester aren't covering. Agüero shouts, '*No, Vinnie, don't shoot!*' It's an instinctive response and a totally redundant request. Kun and everyone else (teammates and opponents alike) know *for sure* his captain won't take the shot. Maddison and Ndidi don't even trouble themselves trying to stop the big Belgian. City's captain is in range now, he gets ready, takes another couple of steps forward and blasts the ball into the top corner of Kasper Schmeichel's net from 30 yards out. Thundering, heat-seeking perfection – as if it were Kompany's speciality rather than a mind-boggling rarity.

And goal number 100 for City at home this season. Overall, their 900th goal at this stadium. Former Man City striker Kelechi Iheanacho gets a chance just before the final whistle but manages to mess it up completely. City win. The title is almost theirs again.

Players and staff sprint onto the pitch to celebrate. There will be great hilarity later as they relive the moment when several voices – including the coach's – joined Kun's: '*No, Vinnie, don't shoot!*'

Captain Kompany bids farewell to the Etihad. A fitting end to an incredible career. For the second year in a row, City have beaten all of the other 19 Premier League teams at least once, equalling the achievement of Preston North End in the nineteenth century.

On 12 May at four o'clock in the afternoon, another historic Premier League season draws to a close. Liverpool beat Wolverhampton 2–0 but Man City deliver a masterful 4–1 defeat of Brighton in the Amex Stadium. For the fifth consecutive season Sergio Agüero has scored 20 or more Premier League goals, matching Thierry Henry's record between 2001 and 2006.

Guardiola has anticipated a highly defensive game plan from Brighton and puts Sterling in the midfield on the right while Bernardo and Mahrez are on the wing. In an echo of some of their worst points of the season, Pep's men seem momentarily thrown when Glenn Murray puts the locals ahead after 26 minutes. But when Agüero slams in the equaliser 60 seconds later,

---

* Kompany scored the winning goal for Hamburger SV against MSV Duisburg on 28 October 2007.

equilibrium is restored. Within ten minutes, Laporte gets City's second and by the time Mahrez and Gündoğan have produced one each, the Citizens know the league title is theirs once more.

But the season isn't quite over. City go back to Wembley and beat Watford 6–0 in the FA Cup final. It's the sixth time they've won in the national stadium. Guardiola goes with the 3–2–2–3 he's used over the last few weeks: Bernardo Silva's in midfield on the right with Mahrez on the wing beside him. Gabriel Jesus is up front. Ederson saves a point-blank shot from Roberto Pereyra after a ferocious counterattack by Gerard Deulofeu and Watford seem to go to pieces. They only manage one more shot for the rest of the match while City produce 11 and convert 6 of them – 2 from fierce counterattacks. They've matched the record set in the 1903 final (Bury–Derby County).

It's their 15th consecutive victory (14 in the Premier League plus the Cup final). They've won four trophies and have only been eliminated from the Champions League because of that damn away-goals rule. Fifty victories in 61 matches (plus 2 more in which they won on penalties). They've scored 169 goals and conceded just 39. Pep has delivered the best performance of his ten years as a coach, having won 84 per cent of City's league games.

TWO GIANTS

The statistic that best sums up the colossal achievement of Man City in the Premier League this season is this: they've spent just 132 minutes out of a total 3,420 (3.8 per cent) trailing their opponents during open competition (153 minutes last season). Last year, six crucial, near last-minute goals, scored between the 82nd and the 97th minute, helped secure the league title and their historic 100 points. This season, their latest goal came in the 72nd minute (Sané's goal against Liverpool). In other words, this season City have needed 20 minutes less per match to win the league.

In contrast, Jürgen Klopp's extraordinary Champions League-winning (in Madrid, 1 June 2019) Liverpool side have spent 156 minutes out of a total 3,420 (3.8 per cent) trailing their opponents during open competition despite losing just one game (against City at the Etihad). They've also needed five near last-minute goals (against Chelsea, Everton, Fulham, Tottenham and Newcastle), scored between the 81st and the 96th minute.

Liverpool have produced the best performance ever of any second-placed side, achieving 97 points* and only just losing out to City, who won 18 of their 19 games in the second half of the season. When the two great sides faced each other on 3 January, the Premier League was already bathed in red and Liverpool had a seven-point advantage. Guardiola's men then went on to rack up 48 points out of a possible 51 over the next 17 league games, with the Reds getting just 43 over the same period.

Each of them scored 41 goals during this time but City conceded just 7, against Liverpool's 14. City became the first English team to win the last 14 games of the season (Arsenal's 'Invincibles' won 13) and also matched the previous season's tally of 32 victories (a record-breaking 18 at home and 14 away). In a repeat of 2008 and 2013, Liverpool were Premier League leaders at Christmas but slipped back in the new year and failed to win the title. The other big-hitters finished some distance behind City – Chelsea (26 points behind), Tottenham (28), Arsenal (29) and Manchester United (32).

This is the first time since 2009 that a club has retained the league title and Guardiola now ranks with Ferguson and Mourinho as one of just three coaches to do so. City have achieved 64 victories plus 6 draws and 6 losses from 76 games, and a total of 198 points over two seasons (84.21 per cent).[†] In the same period, they've scored 201 goals, conceded 50 and played 36 games in which they didn't concede.

This is the fourth Premier League title City have won this decade (2012, 2014, 2018 and 2019), and the third time their final game has been the decider. In 16 of their 38 league games City's opponents have only managed one shot on goal (Leicester, Crystal Palace and Manchester United are examples) and four opponents (Burnley, Cardiff, Fulham and Bournemouth) have failed to get even one effort on target. Ederson has conceded just 38 goals in 55 games and has given three assists: against Huddersfield (to Agüero for the first goal of their 6–1 victory), Tottenham (to Sterling for their 0–1 win) and in the Champions League against Schalke (to Sterling in the 89th minute for their 2–3 final score).

---

* Ninety-seven points would have been enough to win Liverpool the Premier League every season since its inception except in the years Guardiola's City won it.

† Guardiola amassed 198 points over his two consecutive Premier League-winning seasons. José Mourinho's tally was 186, and Sir Alex Ferguson's 177.

Pep's men have also achieved more than 75 per cent possession in all their matches in 2019 and achieved 82 per cent against Bournemouth in the Vitality Stadium when they made 811 passes with a 91 per cent success rate, took 14 corners and shot 23 times at goal. Bournemouth didn't manage any shots or a single corner. This was the game that encapsulated everything that makes City such an extraordinary side.

THE FOURMIDABLES

In his third season in charge of City, Pep has won all four English trophies. Something Sir Alex Ferguson believed wasn't possible. In August 2018, City won the Community Shield; in February 2019, the League Cup; and in May 2019 the Premier League and the FA Cup, rightly earning the sobriquet 'The Fourmidables'. As Alan Shearer puts it, 'I've played against great teams, invincible teams, but this Manchester City is the best in the Premier League's history.'

Individual players stand out. Some performances dipped in comparison to last season. Leroy Sané, for example, has given very mixed performances all season despite his moments of sheer brilliance and his third-place ranking behind Sterling and Agüero in terms of total number of goals and assists (16 and 17 respectively). Riyad Mahrez has also failed to come up to expectations, probably because he hasn't fully grasped the complexities of the Guardiola playing style and has therefore not adapted. Agüero and Laporte have both been outstanding but Bernardo Silva has undoubtedly been the best player of the season. The Portugal international has been City's most complete player and his superb tackling abilities combined with his physical stamina (he covered more than 13.7km in his games against Liverpool and Spurs) have made him the team's most impactful player.

Serious injuries have robbed the team of three key players this season. Kevin De Bruyne was only able to start 22 of City's 61 games as a result of the four injuries he incurred; Benjamin Mendy has mostly been out since November; and captain Vincent Kompany only returned to full match fitness on 14 April.

This season City have won 19 games by a difference of three or more goals (compared to last season's 17 times). Specifically the goal difference has been as follows:

- 9-goal advantage: 1 game
- 7-goal advantage: 2 games
- 6-goal advantage: 3 games
- 5-goal advantage: 5 games
- 4-goal advantage: 1 game
- 3-goal advantage: 7 games

The team has scored 15 out of 95 league goals from outside the area and a further 19 (11 per cent of their total tally) from counterattacks. The changes in pace and rhythm applied by Guardiola have meant that they have alternated between long periods of domination and much shorter periods when they've launched powerful counterattacks from their own half of the pitch.

The FA Cup final against Watford was a typical example of this strategy. After dominating for a significant period, using passing and triangulation to produce two goals, City retreated and scored two more through fast, aggressive counterattacks, followed by another phase of passing, which resulted in the final two goals.

City have increased their counterattacking and the total number of passes they achieve has therefore decreased from an average of 743 to 699. They are also scoring less often from set pieces. Last season, they scored 23 goals from set pieces (16 from corners and 7 from free kicks) while this season they've scored 18 (10+8). They've also increased the number of goals conceded from set pieces: 4 (2+2) last season and 9 this season (6+3).

Tactically speaking, Guardiola has made very few changes this season. If, at times, events beyond his control have forced him to adapt his playing model, the fundamentals of his game have always remained the same. As a coach, Pep has always looked to change and innovate but at the same time he also has an innate understanding of what his players need most: to be in an ecosystem where the fundamentals of their game remain constant and which allows them to achieve their full potential individually and collectively.

Throughout the season, various factors have compelled Pep to adapt. The high rate of injury, for example. Mendy's absences provoked a change in the playing model and Fernandinho's caused Pep to play with a 'delicate' midfielder like Gündoğan at pivot. De Bruyne's absences meant that Bernardo Silva moved from the wing to the centre of the park while Sané's inconsistent performances caused him to make more use of inverted wingers.

THE PARTY IN THE HILTON

Two hours after lifting the FA Cup, their fourth trophy of the season, the team head down Lakeside Way to the back door of the Hilton Hotel, just four minutes' walk from the statue of Bobby Moore that presides over the entrance to Wembley. The players have brought the trophy with them but they're all dead on their feet and there's very little chat as we all troop into the service lift that takes us from the garage to the room the club has booked for the party. The four trophies are then laid out so that friends and family as well as sponsors can take photos with them as they enjoy the champagne and canapés.

Spiritually, Pep's on cloud nine. Full of praise for his men – for the way they've played and for the fighting spirit they've shown. They've battled to the last breath for every single point and he couldn't be prouder. Standing in the centre of the room, Khaldoon Al Mubarak pays tribute to his coach and promises more success in the future. Pep's dad, Valenti Guardiola, is also here, totally thrilled that several fans have asked him for selfies.

The celebration doesn't last long. Just over an hour. Everyone's exhausted and they have a huge celebration on the streets of Manchester tomorrow. The challenges of the new season are just 70 days away and City will no doubt be facing opponents who are even more well-organised and aggressive than this year. Pep will once again turn his thoughts to the Champions League and to the ways in which the squad can continue to improve.

Now that English clubs have begun to dominate in Europe,* there will be no respite for the newly crowned king of English football.

---

* Liverpool beat Spurs 2–0 in the Champions League final and Chelsea beat Arsenal in the Europa League.

STATS 2018–19

	P	W	D	L	GF	GA
Community Shield	1	1	0	0	2	0
Champions						
Premier League	38	32	2	4	95	23
Champions						
FA Cup	6	6	0	0	26	3
Champions						
League Cup	6	4	2	0	16	1
Champions						
Champions League	10	7	1	2	30	12
Quarter-finalists						
Total	61	50	5	6	169	39

- 82 per cent victories in matches all season
- 84.2 per cent wins from all Premier League matches
- 2.77 goal average per match scored in the entire season
- 2.5 goal average per match scored in the Premier League
- 0.64 goal average per match conceded in the entire season
- 0.6 goal average per match conceded in the Premier League
- 130 positive goal difference across the whole season
- 98 points in the Premier League
- 21 efforts off the post in the Premier League (8 Agüero)
- 67.4 per cent possession in the entire season
- 67.9 per cent possession in the Premier League
- 82 per cent highest level of possession (vs Bournemouth, March 2019)
- 49.6 per cent lowest level of possession (vs Liverpool, January 2019)
- 699 average number of passes per match
- 872 highest number of passes (vs Wolverhampton, January 2019)
- 89 per cent completed passes per match
- 18 shots at goal per match/7 on target
- 6.2 shots at goal conceded per game/2.1 on target
- 14 best run of consecutive wins in the Premier League
- 32 top goalscorer: Sergio Agüero (21 in the Premier League)
- 17 most assists: Leroy Sané (10 in the Premier League)
- 55 most appearances: Ederson Moraes (38 in the Premier League)
- 9–0 biggest win (vs Burton Albion)
- 2–0 biggest defeat (vs Chelsea)

Season 4: 2019–20

Five Dinners and a Funeral

DINNER 1. AT PEP'S HOUSE: THE ARTISAN

Manchester, 18 August 2019

The whole of Manchester lies at his feet.

Literally and metaphorically.

Night is falling as Pep gazes down from the huge window of his 14th floor apartment and raises his glass in a toast to the city. To the left, the cathedral and the Irwell River, with its silent, sinuous curves. A little further away lie the National Football Museum and Deansgate, the main artery of the city, always bustling and noisy no matter the time. It's been another day of high winds, lashing rain and biting cold. Summer in Manchester.

Three years have passed since he arrived in the city, full of ambitious plans for the club Alex Ferguson called 'noisy neighbours'. In that time they've won seven trophies: two in his second season, four in the third and their seventh just two weeks ago (they beat Liverpool in the Community Shield). Right now, Pep's not thinking about trophies, though. It's the quality of City's play he's turning over in his mind. They didn't beat Spurs yesterday, in the second league game of the season, but 2–2 wasn't an accurate reflection of City's performance. They'd had 30 shots at goal, Spurs managing just 3 and producing a measly 5 passes in City's area against 52 for the Citizens. It is one of the frustrating paradoxes of football that total domination of a game doesn't necessarily guarantee you victory. Pep is a master craftsman, constantly driven to improve on his own achievements in the search for perfection.

'I'm really happy with yesterday's game. It was the best we've produced since I arrived. Now that we've worked together for three years we all know each other well and each of us understands exactly what he has to do. Our positional play is sensational. None of my teams have played as well as this since the Barça days. We totally dominated Tottenham yesterday and I reckon that even Spurs fans would accept that it could have been 7–2. If we can improve our finishing we'll have a brilliant season. And if we can correct some other details we'll also have a good chance in the Champions League.'

When I arrived earlier this evening, Pep was sitting on a kitchen stool hunched over his laptop, watching and rewatching videos of yesterday's game prepared for him by his assistants, analysing one player after another, and pleased with his conclusions: 'We had a great game. We attacked well and knew exactly what to do when we lost the ball. Having our full-backs positioned asymmetrically [Zinchenko inside and Walker outside] in the middle really helps our play. We've reached the stage where everyone knows exactly what they should be doing and our positional play improves the performance of every single one of them.'

But, long ago, Pep had learned from Johan Cruyff to always focus on the future, so that's what he's doing now, his eyes fixed on the red-brick warehouses of the Bridgewater Canal, just visible through the mist. 'Now that we've won the title twice in a row, what I really want to do is build my legacy. I want this team to be remembered for the brand of football we play, excellent football that's exciting to watch. That's what I want my legacy to be.'

If I had to define Guardiola in one phrase it would be 'a master craftsman of football'. The quest for perfection drives him as he seeks to create a style of play that both anticipates every possible variable and is also versatile enough to adapt and conquer the unexpected. It's about creating excellence. Achieving glory. Richard Sennett defines craftsmanship as the 'ability to do things well. It is an enduring, basic human impulse, the desire to do a job well for its own sake.'* Plato too talked about excellence when he said that the aspiration for quality will drive a craftsman to improve, to get better rather than simply 'get by'. This is exactly the kind of passion Guardiola feels for football.

All craftmanship is founded on skill developed to a high degree. Pep's particular talent is the art of analysing his opponents. He'll spend endless hours analysing the micro-actions of an opponent in order to identify the patterns of behaviour, interaction and positioning that might present a threat or an opportunity to his team. The following day he'll talk to Mahrez, Foden or De Bruyne and explain in detail the weaknesses in an opponent's defence or how they're likely to react to specific situations, how best to attack, exactly how De Bruyne should bluff so that Mahrez can exploit the merest defensive weakness. It's like a form of alchemy: Guardiola extracts the essence of the opposition's weaknesses or behaviour, distils it and then delivers it to his players in a small flask. As Messi put it, 'Pep tells you what's going to happen. And then it happens.'

---

*   Richard Sennett, *The Craftsman* (Anagrama, 2009), p. 20.

The craftsman often faces conflicting objective standards of excellence; the desire to do something well for its own sake can be impaired by the pressure of competition, frustration or obsession. 'We are more likely to fail as craftsmen due to our inability to organise obsession than because of our lack of ability' (Sennett). A tendency to obsess is another of Pep's characteristics and it's a quality that has caused him more than a few problems over the years. He's often accused (especially in England) of 'overthinking' his match preparation but Sennett argues that this kind of obsessive thinking is inevitable. Every great craftsman is obsessed with perfection: 'the desire for quality presents a motivational threat: the obsession with perfection seems a preparation for failure.'*

One of the characteristics of craftmanship is that you do things over and over again. As the celebrated architect Renzo Piano said: 'Circularity is a distinguishing feature of craftsmanship. You think and you do at the same time. You draw and you build. The drawing … is revised. You do it, you redo it and then you go back and do it again.'† Which is exactly what Pep does. He does something, then he redoes it, and then he goes back and does it again. Of course, on occasion, he thinks too much about something and it doesn't turn out well, but there is no doubt that his obsession for excellence has turned him into an exceptional craftsman.

Unfortunately, on this evening's evidence, Pep's talents don't extend to opening wine. As we chat, he's been struggling to uncork a bottle of wine gifted to him some months ago. It's a good one, a 1984 Château Clarke, Baron Edmond de Rothschild, Listrac-Médoc, but the cork is damaged and is proving difficult to get out. Joan Patsy, the director of football at the City Football Group's base in South America, politely suggests that he needs to be a bit more gentle with it but, instead, Pep adds even more pressure. The cork fragments and falls into the wine. Manel Estiarte and my wife, Loles, burst out laughing at the sight of Pep, enthusiastically assisted by Patsy, clumsily trying to save the situation by filtering the wine into a crystal decanter. There's worse to come though. Once it's decanted and poured, it's immediately clear that whoever gave him the bottle hadn't stored it properly. It's gone off. Completely

---

* Ibid., p. 21.
† Edward Robbins, *Why Architects Draw* (MIT Press, 1994), p. 126.

undrinkable. Pep's gutted but Patsy saves the day: 'I brought a lovely bottle of wine, although it's not as fancy as that one. Let's have mine.' He quickly opens the wine and finally we can all sit down to dinner, beautifully prepared by Fernando, the chef Pep hires whenever he has dinner guests.

Inevitably, the conversation is about the season that's just started. Liverpool will be the big rival in the Premier League – there was just one point's difference between the two sides last time out. But what about the Champions League? 'Details. Victory or defeat – it all comes down to details,' according to Estiarte. We all know that they'll need a bit of patience as far as the Champions League is concerned. With conspiratorial smiles Pep and Manel both suddenly switch to Italian. Apparently they're quoting a Chinese proverb about persistence requiring a lot of patience …* It's just as well that patience and tenacity are two of Pep's defining characteristics.

He's also supremely talented, of course – except perhaps when it comes to opening wine – and brings a unique mix of determination and eclecticism to his work. He's never satisfied, never totally happy with a performance, never complacent in victory. A man who lives fully in the present rather than clinging to past achievements, he's ferociously competitive and always, always wants to win. And, if he has to lose, he wants to do it on his own terms. You'll find that his most ardent disciples can be dogmatic and obdurate in their admiration but he himself avoids dogmatism at all costs. He's totally up front in press conferences (although obviously he'd never reveal his lineup in advance), except when the questions are ill-intentioned or likely to cause trouble. He'll also often publicly praise a player whom he has criticised in private or whom he is about to put on the bench. He always wants to produce entertaining football and genuinely cares about how people feel about the quality of play his team produces.

İlkay Gündoğan lives in the flat opposite Pep. Both luxury apartments are absolutely enormous with the same layout – a seemingly endless number of bedrooms leading off the long hallway plus fantastic views over the city. Many's the night Pep will sit and gaze down at Manchester, perhaps musing on how he can bring his craftsman's perfectionism to the business of football.

---

* The proverb has been attributed to Confucius: 'Sit by the riverbank and sooner or later you'll see your enemy's corpse go by.' Pep quotes it in Italian: 'Siediti lungo la riva del fiume e aspetta, prima o poi vedrai passare il cadavere del tuo nemico.'

Richard Sennett has explained that the secrets of great maestros like Antonio Stradivarius and Guarneri del Gesù died with them. Others have invested lots of time and money in trying to replicate the magnificent violins they created. All of it fruitless. Perhaps the knowledge and skill of a genuine craftsman is just too unique to be passed on to others. Pep understands that his is the work of a true craftsman and that the pitches of City's Sportcity are his workshop. But will he pass on the secrets of his own craft to the people who come after him? Will he find fitting successors to carry on his legacy, as he has done with Cruyff's? Benvenuto Cellini, the revered Renaissance sculptor, left a posthumous note that said, 'the secrets of my art will die with me.'* Let's hope Pep's secrets enjoy a different fate …

We end this dinner by turning to Sennett once more:

> The master craftsman was present for all stages of production. Thanks to Toby Faber's investigative work, we know that Stradivarius was involved in the most insignificant details of the process of producing his violins. Although he very rarely travelled, at home he was constantly moving, never focusing on just one thing at a time: his overwhelming and domineering personality meant that he was prone to fits of rage and he barked out instructions and exhortations without pause.[†]

Remind you of anyone?

DINNER AT PEP'S

MENU
- White 'Mongetes' beans with clams
- Fried egg with porcini mushrooms, potatoes and truffle
- Monkfish with langoustines
- Tarte Tatin with ice cream
- Mouton Cadet Pauillac, 2018 (red wine)

---

[*] *La vita di Benvenuto di Maestro Giovanni Cellini fiorentino, scritta per lui medesmo, in Firenze* (1728).

[†] Sennett, *Craftsman*, p. 97.

DINNER 2. TAST CATALÀ RESTAURANT: ON GOOD TERMS
Manchester, 23 October 2019

'How do you remain on good terms with a player who hasn't had a game for a month?'

Silence.

We're having dinner in the private dining room of Tast Català, in King Street, Manchester. The simple décor – pale blue walls, dark blue chairs and varnished wooden tables – is perfect for a pleasant, relaxed evening of good food and good company. The restaurant was opened last year (July 2018) by Spaniard Paco Pérez, a 5-star Michelin chef, with the aim of bringing the best of Catalan cuisine to the UK.

Tast, part-owned by Pep, Txiki and Ferran Soriano, has a private room on the third floor named after one of the most emblematic of Catalan customs. It's called the 'Enxaneta' – the name given to the kid who clambers up to the top of the human pyramids or *castells* (castles), which are constructed as part of traditional festivals all over Catalunya.

Still, no one responds to Pep's question.

He isn't really expecting an answer. He's simply thinking aloud. 'I'd pay a million quid to anyone who can show me how to pull that off … It's the holy grail of player management.' In one sentence he's summed up all the complexities and contradictions of football.

For Pep, matchday is the high point of the week but it also involves one of the most unpleasant parts of his job – leaving half a dozen of his best men on the bench or, even worse, in the stands. He always feels terrible for the guys he hasn't put on the team sheet, who won't get to play: 'It's the hardest thing about this job. I try to make sure that my decisions are always based on what's best for the particular match we're playing but, at the same time, I'm very conscious that those decisions mean some players don't get to do what they love, to play football and exercise their profession. Obviously that's just how it is and everyone knows that, but it's still very, very hard to leave out kids who give their heart and soul in training all week. Which is why I don't believe that they can genuinely think that much of me. It's impossible to think highly of someone who's essentially preventing you from doing the job you're paid to do.'

If you've ever wondered why Guardiola prefers to keep his squad numbers low, even when it seems to make no sense at all, then here's your answer. He'd rather have fewer players in his squad because that way he can reduce the likelihood of certain players almost never getting a game. With a smaller squad, normal player rotations mean that all his guys will get some playing time, although obviously he'd never base his choice of lineup on this. Fielding the 11 men most likely to win the match is always the priority.

It also explains a central part of how he decides whether to sign someone. 'The first thing I want to know is if he's a team player or not.' It's something that's been an important part of his philosophy for a long time. 'Any great team needs good substitutes to be successful so I'm always interested in a player's record when they've not been an automatic starter. I want an idea of how this guy behaves when things get tough. If I can see that he's been a good substitute then I'm definitely interested. If it's obvious that he's not responded well at the most difficult times of his career, then I'll probably not sign him.'

But there will always be players who end up playing less than they think they deserve. Take City's new captain, Fernandinho, for example. He made his first appearance five matches into the season and even then only because Laporte's knee cartilage injury had put him out for five months. And the teacher's pet, Phil Foden, has only been given 12 minutes during the club's first eight games this season.

Last night, City beat the Italian team Atalanta 5–1, but that scoreline is slightly deceptive. Sterling was unusually clinical and scored a hat-trick with Agüero adding two more. Gündoğan, who was obliged to play as the organising midfielder, and Foden were the two outstanding players of the match. The young Englishman, in particular, performed magnificently in attacking midfield and created four big goal chances until he got his second yellow and was sent off with eight minutes left.

The same Foden whom Pep has only included in his starting 11 once in the first 13 games of this season … 'Nobody believes in Foden more than I do. I was the one who brought him into the first team. Nobody thinks more of him than I do. Although I know he's getting a lot less playing time than he deserves.' Fitness coach Lorenzo Buenaventura shares one stat that brings the point home, 'Across this match Foden ran 1,600m at more than 22km an hour. Nobody produced more sprints than him even though he played ten minutes less than everyone else.'

The team's performance has been up and down since August. They beat Bournemouth and Brighton comfortably but then suffered a shock defeat in Norwich, followed by beating Shakhtar 3–0 in Kharkiv and Watford 8–0 at home, just four months after their 6–0 victory over the Hornets in the FA Cup final. Three more victories (Preston North End, Everton and Dinamo Zagreb) were then followed by a brutal defeat at home by Wolverhampton (0–2), giving Liverpool an eight-point advantage at the top of the league. Pep's worried. His men seem to have much less mental energy than they had in the two previous seasons.

In the Atalanta match, City's build-up play was unusual. The Italian team is known for its aggressive pressing so Guardiola picked his lineup accordingly: Walker and Mendy as full-backs, Rodri and Fernandinho in central defence and Gündoğan as the pivot.

The coach's objective is that City bring the ball out smoothly despite the high, aggressive press from their opponents and he's planned a 3+1+1 build-up with Walker, Fernandinho and Mendy as the line of three who begin driving the ball forward, with Rodri positioned a few metres in front of them outside the penalty area to provide a constant passing outlet to whoever has the ball. Gündoğan is then freed up to make space and receive possession further up the pitch. Rodri Hernández was City's biggest signing of 2018–19 and Pep maintains high hopes for him as an organising midfielder.*

These tactics against Atalanta mean Rodri playing the dual role of central defender/midfielder, which Pep used Stones to implement last season. He'd previously tried it with Sergio Busquets years before at Barcelona without great success. The Stones experiment worked better but has only been used in a few games.

Now, he's convinced that Rodri is the guy to pull it off. Unfortunately the plan goes awry because Walker and Mendy really struggle to make the right choices and, thus, to find the correct player to pass to in tight build-ups. Their

---

* City's other signing was João Cancelo, the Portuguese full-back they bought from Juventus in exchange for Danilo plus £27.4 million. The other main transfers were Vincent Kompany to Anderlecht, Fabian Delph to Everton and Douglas Luiz to Aston Villa.

incorrect solution is to repeatedly send it to Rodri by default – meaning that Atalanta are quick to mark him extremely tightly. This becomes self-defeating.

The basic concept is very good because it brings Rodri up almost as far as Gündoğan positionally and offers City a clear opportunity to have superiority of numbers in deep midfield, but the poor performance of his full-backs means that Pep decides to change to a 4+2 build-up after 20 frustrating minutes, with Rodri and De Bruyne both dropping back one position respectively.

Over dinner at Tast, Joan Patsy tells Pep that João Cancelo is the ideal man for this type of build-up play: 'we bring the ball out better when João is playing.'

Cancelo, the other big signing of the season, is talented and Pep particularly rates his creativity on the pitch, but he wants him to work on some defensive weaknesses he still exhibits. 'We've been working really hard with him for weeks. We've shown him videos so that he can see how he tends to turn and play the ball backwards when he's under pressure. We want him to see how he plays out from the back, how he marks …'

Manel Estiarte points out that this kind of training has had to be repeated over and over again. 'In the four years we've been here, we've had to keep practising bringing the ball out from the back with the midfielders every two weeks. Without fail. It's simply one of those things that they forget or become less precise at, if you don't keep practising it.'

Pep gives his views on last night's build-up: 'If the full-backs aren't making the right decisions, we won't be able to bring the ball out with three men like we tried to do last night, with Rodri positioned just in front of them. We would have to stick to a four-man build-up with the full-backs positioned higher up the touchlines or a three-man build-up with the pivot dropping back between the two central defenders. Everything depends on the precision of their passing.'

By midnight it's already time to head home. Early training tomorrow. As Loles and I stroll through King Street towards Deansgate, I recall Domènec Torrent talking about how much pressure Pep puts on his players. 'He stretches them to the maximum.'

It's true. Pep wants to test their limits until he can get the very best out of each one of them. With the obvious risk that either he, or they, can reach breaking point.

DINNER AT TAST CATALÀ

MENU (to share)
- Duck egg, baby squid, potatoes soufflé
- Scallop stew
- Butifarra (Catalan sausage) with white beans
- Catalan rice with socarrat*
- Wild seabass 'El Txiringuito, 1939'
- Light crunchy bread, tomato and extra virgin olive oil†
- Traditional pastry filled with custard and chocolate sauce
- Idus de Vall Llach 2015 (red wine)

DINNER 3. SALVI'S: THE ORCHESTRA

Manchester, 22 December 2019

We're back in Salvi's, the Italian trattoria in the Corn Exchange, run by Maurizio. There's a delicatessen on the ground floor just as you go in and a private dining area downstairs. One of Pep's favourite places to eat.

Today we're revisiting a topic of conversation we discussed in depth a couple of years ago: orchestra conducting. Back then, we delved into the contrasts between Herbert von Karajan and Leonard Bernstein in terms of their different styles – the wall and the bridge.

Today we talk about the legendary conductor Nikolaus Harnoncourt, whose book I've just finished reading. Harnoncourt, a Mozart expert, said that often the lack of passion felt by a musician is a response to the conductor's ego:

The typical orchestra musician is inevitably miserable, given the work that he does. There's not a single orchestral musician who has a vocation or great enthusiasm for the job he's chosen. One day he joins an orchestra. He's been listening to magnificent orchestral pieces for years and he says to himself, 'Fantastic! Now I'm going to be a part of this group.' But as soon as he starts he discovers what a terrible experience

---

* Socarrat is the well-done, caramelised layer that clings to the bottom of the pan after cooking rice in homemade broth and then finishing it in a charcoal oven.
† Prepared by grating the whole tomato over the bread, not with puréed tomato.

it is. The guy in front of him has a particular philosophy but it's absolutely incomprehensible. Or, even worse, he has no philosophy at all!*

Pep suddenly butts in: 'It's the shining eyes thing!' In fact, he's talking about
another great, charismatic conductor, Benjamin Zander, and the famous
quote from his TED talk:

> I had a realisation. The conductor of an orchestra doesn't make a
> sound … He depends, for his power, on his ability to make other people
> feel powerful … I realised my job was to awaken possibility in other
> people. And of course, I wanted to know whether I was doing that.
> How do you find out? You look at their eyes … If their eyes are shining,
> then you know you're doing it. If the eyes are not shining you get to ask
> a question: who am I being that my players' eyes are not shining?†

It's exactly what Pep would like to achieve: to make his players' eyes shine.
He has absolutely no time for Harnoncourt's views on the weaknesses and
faults of orchestra musicians:

> Indifference … I probably understand better than most that musicians
> become more and more jaundiced after years of directors demanding
> that they play with passion, but without they themselves contributing
> equivalent passion so that after years and years there's hardly a trace
> of receptivity from those orchestra players for even the most outstand-
> ing conductors.‡

Pep prefers a completely different concept that he picked up from the extraordinary Argentine volleyball coach Julio Velasco: 'Julio explained to me that
our job as coaches is to teach so that others can do. He says that having the
enthusiasm and ability to learn is also a talent. That learning is a skill in itself.'

* Nikolaus Harnoncourt, *Diálogos sobre Mozart* (Dialogues with Mozart) (Acantilado, 2016), p. 61.
† TED Talks are given by experts from a range of different fields who have ideas worth sharing. TED stands for Technology, Entertainment, Design.
‡ Harnoncourt, *Diálogos*, p. 41.

Pep's disappointed by the performance of some of his players this season. Liverpool are already 11 points ahead after 18 league games. It's not that City are playing badly, they've just lost the momentum and rhythm of previous seasons. They're still producing moments of sheer brilliance but not consistently enough. After a great start – they've already won the Community Shield – things have taken a downturn, particularly since Jürgen Klopp's Liverpool look invincible at the moment.

Since our dinner in Tast Català a couple of months ago, Pep's City have beaten Aston Villa, Southampton twice (Carabao Cup and league), Chelsea, Burnley, Dinamo Zagreb and Arsenal, playing high-quality, confident football. They've also drawn with Atalanta and Shakhtar and are at the top of their group in the Champions League, the 10th time Pep's achieved that out of 11 attempts. But they've also occasionally messed up, sometimes in a big way. Take their latest defeat at Anfield, for example, the last-minute draw at St James' Park or their defeat at home to United (1–2).

This is, so far, Guardiola's worst ever season as a coach: 12 wins, 2 draws and 4 defeats in 18 games. Thankfully though, we've something to celebrate this evening: yesterday's superb victory over Leicester at the King Power Stadium (1–3), Pep's 99th win in the Premier League. The three points weren't enough to knock Leicester off their second-place spot, however. They're ten points behind Liverpool and one in front of City.

By the time dessert arrives, we're already deep in a discussion of yesterday's game, which was a masterclass. It's really cheered Pep up after several weeks of inconsistent performances.

'Yesterday's game and the one against Spurs were our best of the season. We managed to achieve the most difficult thing in football – to play simply. They played a clean, simple game, without any complications. I need to convince them that that is the team we want to be. Whether we win or lose, we want to be that team that I watched in Leicester. We were incredible, on and off the ball. Pressing brilliantly, high up the pitch. I'm so proud of the players for believing in me.'

One of the challenges for any team is successfully and consistently sticking to the path laid down by their coach. Pep said the same thing years ago in Munich, 'a team's character is actually their coach's character.' Again, Harnoncourt has a lot to say about the challenges of people management:

It's impossible to teach someone how to deal with a large group of people. An orchestra is a group of very diverse people. Very often musicians only talk about music during their breaks because that's the only thing they have in common. And the conductor has to convey his own understanding of a piece to this hugely diverse group of people. It's this one thing that probably ends the careers of the majority of conductors who have come from a formal education.*

We have a good laugh at another quote from Harnoncourt's book, where he explains why conductors sweat so much and musicians don't.

It's about differences in temperament. A musician has, at most, one move-ment and then 16 pauses. Sometimes just reading the score makes me sweat. As I read the passages which I know will make me sweat for real later on. Music excites and moves me. I sweat because I'm so emotional.[†]

Pep tells me that a similar thing happens to him when he thinks about the upcoming game.

Joan Patsy then chimes in with a funny story about Winston Churchill.

Just after a desert battle, Churchill is visiting the New Zealand troops who, despite the heat, offer him some oyster soup. Sometime later General Montgomery, the tank commander, arrives. Unlike Churchill he turns down the offer of soup and stays outside the tent. The general has a strict rule about never fraternising with the lower ranks. Two different leadership styles. Churchill sits down with his subordinates in the desert heat to eat a bowl of soup. Montgomery stands outside eating a sandwich and drinking lemonade.[‡]

It's that same old question: Karajan or Bernstein, the wall or the bridge, Montgomery or Churchill?

---

* Ibid., pp. 60–1.

† Ibid., p. 64.

‡ You can read the whole anecdote in Winston Churchill's *The Second World War, Volume II* (Editorial La Esfera de los Libros, 2002), p. 275.

DINNER AT SALVI'S

MENU (to share)
- Focaccia with Italian cheese, rocket and cherry tomatoes
- Italian charcuterie
- Fried aubergines
- Seafood tagliatelle
- Macaroni with ragu
- Mushroom and truffle risotto
- Tiramisu with ice cream
- Cannonau Riserva (red wine)

DINNER 4. WING'S: DISRUPTION

Manchester, 8 January 2020

Bernardo Silva at Old Trafford, playing as a false 9.

Sublime.

Pep used the same strategy three years ago, during another freezing December, with Raheem Sterling in the false 9 position. It worked brilliantly – then and now. Pep's just achieved his fourth victory out of the five games they've played at Old Trafford. A huge 3–1 win in the League Cup semi-final first leg at the Theatre of Dreams.

We're having dinner at Wing's, the Chinese restaurant in Lincoln Square, and have opted for the tasting menu this evening. Pep's helping me to come up with an exact definition of the false 9. I'm writing a book about the tactical evolution of football from its origins and the development of the false 9 is the theme that ties the whole book together. Juanma Lillo and Paco Seirul·lo have lent their considerable knowledge and expertise to the project and, between the four of us, we've finally come up with a definition with which we're all happy.

The false 9 is a centre-forward who 'drops' deep down the pitch in order to achieve one or more of the following objectives: shake off the central defenders marking him; draw those defenders out of their zone of influence; create spaces for his teammates to penetrate; actively collaborate in the organisation of the attack; confuse and misdirect the opponent's defenders; create permanent superiority in the centre of the pitch, whether it be numerical, positional, qualitative or in momentum.

His mission, like all centre-forwards, is to score goals. He works to achieve the objectives mentioned above with that one fundamental priority still in mind. He might at times look a little clueless, wandering about like an absent-minded midfielder, but it's all part of the ruse, as he subtly bluffs and feints his way around the pitch. His focus, at all times, is the same: 'get a goal'. I'll say it again. The fundamental objective of everything he does is for his team to score.

The false 9 doesn't stick to a predetermined area of the pitch. His role is all about different tasks, spaces and objectives, and at first glance, much of what he does might seem contradictory. Moving down the pitch *away* from the box in order to score goals, for example. He is a central forward who doesn't stay in the area. You'll only see him in the box when he's scoring goals. All of which means that we have to see the false 9 as a strategy and a 'function' rather than an actual position.*

The first footballer to perform as a false 9 was the Uruguayan José Piendibene, way back in 1910. Since then there have been 50 or so players who have mastered the art – football legends like Matthias Sindelar, György Sárosi, Adolfo Pedernera and Nándor Hidegkuti, whose names are written in golden letters in the history books. Later, stars like Alfredo Di Stéfano and Gerd Müller (in the German national side) became full-time false 9s while others, like Bobby Charlton, Cruyff, Diego Maradona and Messi, dipped in and out of the role.

Pep reaches for the false 9 on special occasions, like he did with Messi in 2009 in that all-important 6–2 win against Real Madrid at the Bernabéu. He also used it in both of his Champions League final victories over Manchester United (2009 and 2011). Which is perhaps why he always tries to employ it at Old Trafford.

And it's paid off again. Big time. It takes about 30 minutes for Bernardo Silva to score the opening goal, give Mahrez the assist for the second and spearhead the counterattack that culminates in City's third goal of the night.

---

* Martí Perarnau, *La evolución táctica del fútbol, 1863–1945. Descifrando el código genético del fútbol de la mano del falso 9* (The Tactical Evolution of Football, 1863–1945: Using the False 9 to Decipher the Genetic Code of Football) (Córner, 2021), pp. 17–18.

For the first time in more than two decades, Manchester United head into their dressing room at half-time losing 3–0.

As we leave Old Trafford later, Bernardo tells me, 'I love playing as a false 9. Pep wanted an extra man in the centre of the pitch and I had a great time playing that dual role.'

Now, as the food arrives, Pep explains how he uses the false 9 (although he prefers the term 'false forward'): 'Using a false forward solves all your problems. It's not always necessary but I like to use it in really big games against teams who aren't going to limit themselves to defending the area. Teams that you know are going to man-mark you. For those matches I like my false forward to play in the centre of the pitch and, if it's someone who really knows how to play, like Bernardo does, I know he'll run rings around the opposition.'

But should we see Pep's particular use of the false 9 as a new invention or as an innovation? The two concepts are easily confused. Invention is the creation of something that previously didn't exist. Innovation is about using something which already exists in a new way. The fundamental tactical and technical aspects of football were all established prior to 1945, the product of the work and dedication of numerous players and coaches. Since then, there have been lots of innovations but no more inventions, and Pep has always seen himself as an innovator, not an inventor.

'We have to incorporate some of the improvements other, more advanced sports have made to their game. Football has a long way to go to reach the level of other disciplines, not in absolutely everything but definitely in some areas. There's huge room for improvement and innovation.'

Throughout his career Pep has learned from some of the brightest minds in football, although his greatest teacher was Johan Cruyff, whose own knowledge and expertise drew on the ancestral wisdom of the likes of Jack Reynolds and Jany van der Veen, as well as coaches like Vic Buckingham and Rinus Michels. All of them had witnessed, either directly or indirectly, the football played by superb teams in the 1950s, such as the Austrian Wünderteam and Hungary's Magical Magyars.

Cruyff took everything he'd learned and distilled it to produce a very specific playing style: positional play and the false 9 were crucial to that style. The Dutchman had himself been a false 9 in the national team and, sporadically, in Barcelona. Then, as coach, when he created the 'Dream Team' he used Michael Laudrup in the same role. Years later, his one-time protégé Pep Guardiola would ask Messi to perform the same function. Now, at City, Bernardo Silva has taken on the mantle.

Pep's now considering using it against Real Madrid in their Champions League knockout match at the end of February. 'When I got home last night from Old Trafford I watched the Spanish Super Cup. I wanted to see how Madrid are playing. And they're on top form. Absolutely superb. We've been bloody unlucky. I always seem to have to play them when they're at the top of their game. They're incredibly good. So I'm going to have to work out how we can do them damage. Even a little bit of damage would be good.'*

I then tell him something that very few people know: in the history of football, the three teams that have used the false 9 the most are Peñarol, from Montevideo, the Hungarian national team and his own Manchester City.†

Two weeks ago, City lost Mikel Arteta to Arsenal, where he's taken over from temporary coach Freddie Ljungberg, who'd stepped in when Unai Emery left. Pep had always known that Arteta was desperate to coach Arsenal and had no problem supporting his assistant in achieving his dream, although it's now left him shorthanded for the rest of the season. Rodolfo Borrell and Lorenzo Buenaventura will help out now that Arteta has gone.

City's league campaign isn't going smoothly. Their defeat by Wolves at Molineux (3–2) ten days ago was particularly galling. City were down to ten men after Ederson was sent off but the worst thing was the manner of their defeat.

After 48 minutes, City are leading 2–0, then a couple of bad mistakes, including a massive screw-up from Mendy, allow Wolves to equalise. Wanderers have no fewer than 21 shots at City's goal (the worst tally of the last four years), then, disastrously for City, they produce the winner in the dying minutes of the game.

---

* Real Madrid beat Valencia 3–1 in the Super Cup semi-final.
† Peñarol's false 9s were José Piendibene (1910), Luís Matoso Feitiço (1935), Pedro Lago (1936) and Sebastián Guzmán (1938). Those of the Hungarian national team were György Sárosi (1938), Péter Palotás (1950), Nándor Hidegkuti (1950), Ferenc Szusza (1951), Lájos Tichy (1955) and Ferenc Machos (1956). Manchester City's have been Fred Tilson (1931), Eric Brook (1936), Johnny Williamson (1953), Don Revie (1954), Raheem Sterling (2017), Sergio Agüero (2018), Bernardo Silva (2020), Phil Foden (2020), İlkay Gündoğan (2021) and Kevin De Bruyne (2021).

Liverpool are now 14 points ahead and well on their way to winning the title, which is why Pep is focusing on the cup competitions and is already also planning for the Real Madrid game just a day after taking a decisive step forward in the League Cup.

Pep's disappointed not to be able to fight for a third title but he still approaches everything with the same intensity, including our dinner conversation. 'Obviously football today isn't played the way it was in 2009. We coaches have changed. Klopp, Conte and I are all better at our jobs now because we've learned from experience. And teams that manage to hold on to their core group of players also improve because by playing together for four years the players learn and master so much more.

'I'm delighted that my team is so flexible. I want us to get to the stage where we can easily adapt our game according to whatever's happening at any given moment. I want us to play good positional football but at the same time defend brilliantly in our own half, if that's where the action is.'

That leads the conversation round to disruptive innovation, the idea of introducing ideas that lead to big modifications or even drastic change. Not just using a false 9 when the moment's right but questioning what a fullback or a winger is, or whether or not a central defender can also function as a midfielder.

'We can't stand still. It's not just about boosting the squad by bringing in some fresh blood every year, we have to add new elements to our game. Otherwise our opponents will catch on to all our tricks and tactics.'

Pep understands that you have to make changes when things are going well, not when they're going badly. In that respect, he resembles Steve Jobs, who didn't invent the mobile phone but was a born innovator who was never completely satisfied and always looked for new features to add to his products.*

The developments and progress made in football have always been the result of disruptive thinking, often introduced by people who have expanded their horizons by travelling or living abroad. It's come from the sharing and debating of ideas and knowledge, from the perennial law of action–reaction.

And from the ability to make footballers' eyes shine.

We finish dinner talking about chess, another game that has a lot in common with football. It too has different stages of play: the build-up stage,

---

* The engineer Martin Cooper invented the mobile phone in 1973.

the main game and the endgame. I point out that world-class chess players aren't satisfied with being the best. They want to be immortal.

Pep's slightly more pragmatic: 'Talking about immortality is a bit excessive. If people remember you for the beauty of your game, that's more important than all the trophies in the world. At the end of the day, trophies are just hunks of metal after all.'

DINNER AT WING'S

TASTING MENU (to share)
- Selection of dim sum
- Crispy duck
- Salt and pepper shrimp
- Steamed seabass with ginger, onion and soy sauce
- Fried rice
- Lamb with broccoli in a black bean sauce
- Cantonese-style beef fillet
- Seasonal fresh fruit
- Taittinger Brut Réserve Champagne

DINNER 5. EUROSTARS MADRID TOWER: THE IMPOSSIBLE

Madrid, 26 February 2020

It's tough at the top.

Pep's reflecting on four seasons spent in Manchester. The victories, defeats, the pain and the joy. The times he's been moved to tears and the moments he's savoured another victory with a celebratory cigar … He's been happy here. He's still happy but there's always that nagging thought at the back of his mind. Is it even possible to achieve something on the same level as his first year at Barça? Sometimes he thinks so. At others, he's sure it's an impossible dream. Ten years of the same internal debate.

The players troop into the basement floor of the Eurostars Madrid Tower Hotel, hungry, tired and ready to eat. As usual, City's chef, Jorge Gutiérrez, and his three assistants have carefully planned and prepared their post-match meal in line with the nutritional guidelines laid down by Tom

Parry. The choice of ingredients is designed to replenish the players' glyco-gen levels after a game – absolutely crucial for their muscle recovery. Jorge always tries to include a dish that's emblematic of wherever they are and tonight *jamón ibérico de bellota* (Iberian ham from acorn-fed pigs) is the star of the show. Perhaps almost as good as the pasta napolitana the chef laid on after that 2017 Napoli game when Sergio Agüero became the club's top goalscorer ever.

Pep's happy. They've just beaten Real Madrid at the Bernabéu. His sixth victory in the legendary stadium. An outstanding performance in which the home side were outmanoeuvred by Pep's tactics. With Bernardo Silva back as a false 9 he's done them precisely the 'damage' he'd planned over dinner in Wing's. He'd pulled Gündoğan back to play beside Rodri and had his wingers Mahrez and Gabriel Jesus stationed as wide as possible. His decision to do without a striker left Madrid's defenders completely thrown – confused as to whether they should move out of position or stick to their area.

When they have the ball, City play in a 4–2–2–2 formation. As before, Bernardo excels as the false 9 – De Bruyne's movement is also particularly bril-liant. When Sterling comes on for Bernardo (73rd minute), Pep modifies the structure. De Bruyne and Gündoğan become creative, attacking midfielders in front of Rodri and Gabriel Jesus moves up front as the sole striker.

It's one of those typical Champions League games where dominating the game doesn't necessarily put you ahead. Madrid control the first 30 minutes and then City dominate for a quarter of an hour. Madrid manage one on-target effort, a Karim Benzema header saved by Ederson, while Gabriel Jesus has two good chances, which Thibaut Courtois and Federico Valverde block.

In the second half, City take control and Mahrez misses a sitter, which Courtois easily saves. Pep's men are playing brilliantly until a succession of errors by Rodri, Otamendi and Walker give Isco his chance to put Madrid ahead.

Then, just as the Citizens begin to look shaky, Gabriel Jesus produces the equaliser followed by a De Bruyne penalty sent low to Courtois right and into the back of the net (all the more satisfying given that City have missed their last seven Premier League penalties). A magnificent counterattack just before full-time almost gives City their third of the night but Mahrez fails to score. It doesn't matter, though. They've beaten Madrid in the Bernabéu. It's a massive achievement.

The dining room's set up with tables for eight and a serving station in the centre. It's a calm, low-key setting: gentle lighting, brown walls, brown chairs, pristine white tablecloths and a beige carpet. The players are served first. It's essential to get the nutrients into them quickly to kickstart the recuperation process. All of them will need as much energy as possible: their third consecutive League Cup final is in three and a half days' time. The clock's ticking. They've already had their post-match smoothie in the dressing room – a mix of carbs, proteins and creatine. After dinner they'll have another one composed of 4 grams of tart cherry and 1 gram of curcumin. It's all part of the post-match R+S (replenishment and supplementation) plan.

Manel Estiarte usually has an early night on these occasions and tonight is no different. After a light omelette and a soft drink he's off to bed. Pep stays up to eat with his men and tucks into some *jamón ibérico* and a plate of pasta washed down with a nice glass of red. I remind him of the conversation we had three years ago in this hotel about whether it was possible for another team to play the way Barça did between 2008 and 2012.

It's 28 April 2016. In the wee small hours of the night of the Champions League semi-final, Bayern have just been knocked out by Atlético Madrid (1–0) and everyone's hurting. I'm heading up to bed in the same lift as Pep. It stops on the 23rd floor, the doors open and another intense debate begins.

Pep's adamant: 'No, I definitely won't be able to repeat that. It was like climbing Everest. I've done it. I've reached the summit and that's that. There's no taller peak … it's not possible to do it again.'

It sounds to me like he's giving up. Insisting that he can't build another magical team that consistently produces extraordinary football and wins trophy after trophy. A team that is so good it is immune to the vagaries of football. 'It's just not possible. That was the ultimate achievement. Unrepeatable.'

I try everything I can to change his mind, pointing out not for the first time that Edmund Hillary found other, new challenges after becoming the first man to conquer Everest with Norgay. He couldn't climb higher mountains but he could create new challenges for himself by making more difficult climbs, tackling peaks of 8000m, many of which were much more dangerous than Everest. I tell Pep that the difficulty of the route you take is much more important than the exact altitude of the mountain. But he's unconvinced. His face a blank mask.

Now, almost three years later, he's just beaten Real Madrid in their own backyard, he's won seven trophies with City and is about to go for number eight. There is no doubt that he has built an exceptional team in Manchester. I put the same question to him.

'I'm torn. On the one hand, it does feel like creating another team like that Barça side is impossible. As frustrating as that is. But on the other hand, I'm desperate to try and do it again and am sure that it's possible to get a different team to produce a similar level of football.'

Finally! He's coming round to the idea at last, my friends! He may not have admitted that it's possible but at least he's not arguing that it's impossible. That's been his great internal dilemma. Possible or impossible? It's the craftsman's endless search for perfection, his mission to achieve excellence in everything he does – with different groups of players and in different competitions. It's like a raging river within him that ebbs and flows. And as always, his gaze is firmly fixed on the future, as if he will, somehow, find the answer there.

It's late when we finish. Nearly three in the morning. And Pep's off to bed. I grab a minute with Txiki Begiristain. Pep's contract runs out in summer 2021 and I want to know if City have a replacement in mind. 'It's something I think about from time to time but it's not easy to come up with the right person. There are coaches whose style of football or methodology I admire. Guys who get great results. But it's very difficult to find someone who even gets close to Pep. We've still got another year so we've got a bit of time to keep thinking about it. The best thing would be to hold on to Pep. I'm well aware that that's a tough ask. By 2021 he'll have been here for five years and that's already much longer than he's spent at any other club, but it would definitely be the perfect solution. If we can persuade him to renew with us again. Let's see if we can pull it off …'

Whether or not Pep renews, there's no doubt that it will be very, very hard to replace him, whenever that may be. Pep's had the great good fortune to learn from true masters of the game. His mentor, Cruyff, schooled him in the fundamentals of his playing model and helped him develop his phenomenal intuition. But he had other great teachers: he learned much of his brilliant methodology from Louis van Gaal; his instinctive and intellectual understanding of the game from Juanma Lillo;

and his grasp of how to design and build the perfect ecosystem for players to thrive from Paco Seirul·lo.

And there have been many other teachers, within football and in other spheres from whom he's 'stolen' ideas on the way to becoming a master of his own craft. Engaged as he is in a constant search for absolute excellence, nagged by doubts and a perpetual sense of frustration, Pep Guardiola is still, without a doubt, the most influential coach of the twenty-first century. Always close to perfection but ... plagued by feelings of dissatisfaction and the eternal question: possible or impossible?

People who've read my previous books, *Pep Guardiola: The Evolution* and *Pep Confidential*, often ask me what Pep's really like. If, in private, he's the same guy we see in public settings. And I always tell them that he is. He's the same guy with the same strengths and flaws that we can all see. But this is my chance to refine that response a bit.

Pep's a good guy, a thoroughly decent person who really cares about his friends and is always concerned about their difficulties and problems. The type of guy who wants to help people in need even when he knows the problem's way beyond anything he can do. There are just too many people in need! In fact, and this is a secret so I hope he won't mind, on occasion he's suggested going to an African country where people are struggling to survive in order to help, telling me: 'But we'd have to do it in secret so no one finds out.' In the end, we haven't done it because I didn't want to make the journey but Pep's definitely keen. Don't get me wrong. I'm not talking about a male version of Mother Teresa. Neither am I trying to paint some idyllic picture of Pep. I'm just saying that he's a good guy who likes to help people if he can.

The following day we're at Atlético Madrid's Wanda Metropolitano Stadium where Txiki and Pep are reunited with Manuel 'Manolo' Sánchez, a former Atlético striker who is the protagonist of an anecdote Johan Cruyff was fond of telling. Sánchez, the top La Liga goalscorer in 1992 (27 in 36 games), was a centre-forward famous for his goalscoring, his speed and his ability to shake off opposition players. The story goes that Cruyff had repeatedly asked his full-back Albert 'Chapi' Ferrer or his centre-back Miguel Ángel Nadal to mark Manolo but he always managed to get away from them and create serious danger for Barcelona, until one day Cruyff decided to try a more drastic approach. In his pre-match team talk he told the players: 'Manolo is brilliant at getting away from us when we mark him. So let's not mark him! If we're not covering him, it won't be possible for him to get away from us!' The players were totally gobsmacked but they did what Cruyff had told them and didn't mark him. Manolo didn't score.

Pep, Txiki and Manolo all played in that game and the three of them hoot with laughter as they retell the story. Beside them, on one side of the pitch, there are a dozen or so bikes City's players have used to warm their muscles up before they do Lorenzo Buenaventura's gentle mobility exercises.

The team is in good shape despite having missed the boat in the Premier League. Liverpool are 22 points ahead of them, well on their way to beating the 100 points achieved by Pep's Centurions. So far this season, after 27 matches, Klopp's men have chalked up just one draw and no defeats.

But City have their sights set on the League Cup final at Wembley in three days' time.

Nineteen-year-old Phil Foden is the standout star of City's 2–1 victory over Aston Villa at Wembley on 1 March. Pep's gone for fresh legs and Walker, Rodri and Gündoğan are the only ones who also played in the Real Madrid game. City have now won their third straight League Cup trophy. It's the 6th domestic trophy and the 29th of Pep's career to date.*

With two domestic trophies in the bag, City refocus on their FA Cup campaign, defeating Sheffield Wednesday 1–0. Then the preparations for the Champions League return leg against Real Madrid at the Etihad.

Then, on 5 March, news breaks of the first UK death from COVID-19. Cases of the virus begin to multiply until, on 16 March, with 55 people dead and 1,500 sick, Boris Johnson issues the official government advice to avoid all non-essential contact. All football competitions are now suspended. Millions of people are now facing an invisible enemy that has spread to all corners of the world: the COVID-19 pandemic.

No more dinners with Pep for a long time to come.

---

* City won four domestic trophies last season and so far in 2019–20 have won the Community Shield and the League Cup.

DINNER IN THE EUROSTARS MADRID TOWER

BUFFET
- Iberian bellota ham with puffed rolls
- Salad of sprouts, goats cheese, orange vinaigrette and walnuts
- Bluefin tuna tartar with yuzu gel and wasabi mayonnaise
- Macaroni with chicken and cheese (Riyad Pasta)*
- Sushi
- Wild seabass with pepper sauce
- Grilled Iberian pork with sweet potato cream
- Fruit salad with sorbet
- Caramel brioche French toast with dulce de leche and apple
- Pago de los Capellanes (red wine)

A FUNERAL. THE SHERATON CASCAIS

Lisbon, 15 August 2020

It's midnight in the Sheraton Hotel in Cascais, just outside Lisbon. Khaldoon Al Mubarak puts his arm round Pep's shoulder and announces, 'You're the man, Pep, you're the man!' He wants everyone to hear how much he rates City's coach.

Pep just stares at him, glassy eyed. As if he hasn't heard.

He's just suffered the worst shock of his tenure.

Against all predictions, City have just been knocked out of the Champions League by Olympique Lyonnais, the last few rounds of the competition having been rescheduled by UEFA after an enforced break of three months due to the COVID pandemic. Now City are out of Europe.

Everyone's devastated.

These are tragic times. Around 15 million lives will be lost to COVID-related causes between 2020 and 2021. The problems and dramas of football seem insignificant compared to such tragedy and it's been tough for everyone in football to come back to work amid so much suffering and death. Clubs have tried to provide as much protection as possible for the players,

---

* 'Riyad Pasta' was named after Mahrez because he asked for it every day. It's pasta with chicken and cheese.

who are under constant scrutiny. All installations and equipment are cleaned constantly, the players are taking the correct precautions and receive regular check-ups. These are dark days for everyone. With no end in sight people have changed their habits and lifestyles, and have begun to re-evaluate their lives. Life seems more precious than ever, now that it seems so easy to lose.

Millions of people are also struggling with mental health problems. The world has been turned upside down in the space of a few weeks. Prisoners in our own homes, deprived of our liberty, everyone is exhausted and over-whelmed by the fear of catching the deadly virus. City's team manager, Marc Boixasa, sums up how we've all been feeling: 'Total mental exhaustion. Exhaustion and despair. The hope that things will get better and then the desolation of every new setback. Every time things seem to be getting better, there's so much hope but then within days we seem to be back where we started. So many months of restrictions. And then the sheer joy of being able to get back to some normality. I'll never forget the huge smile on Mahrez's face when he kicked the ball for the first time. It was one of the most beautiful smiles I've ever seen. Just because he was back at work and able to kick a ball again.'

Spectators are still banned from matches and some clubs are piping recorded crowd noises through loudspeakers – but it all feels a bit fake, like an episode of *The Truman Show*. Although there's no doubt that having to play with no fans in the stadium has an impact on the players.

Football restarts, behind closed doors, on 17 June. City play ten league games, win eight and lose two (against Chelsea and Southampton). But it all feels like a bit of an anticlimax, including their 4–0 victory over Liverpool. They finish 17 points behind Liverpool, who are champions with 99 points, one less than the record set by the Centurions. Klopp's men have won 32, drawn 3 and lost 3 against City's 26 victories, 3 draws and 9 defeats. City have scored more goals, though – 102 compared to Liverpool's 85. And have conceded 35 to Liverpool's 33. Frustratingly for Pep, who sees the league title as the priority, City have not been serious contenders for the title at any point this season.

On 26 July, after 434 games, 77 goals and 140 assists for City, the legendary David Silva bids farewell to the Etihad Stadium, pausing to applaud the empty stands. A week before, City had been beaten 2–0 at Wembley by Mikel Arteta's Arsenal in the FA Cup semi-final. It had been a disappointing game, particularly in view of the attitude some of the players had shown on the pitch and in the dressing room.

The result surprises everyone. City have beaten Arsenal 3–0 in both their league matches this season, before and during the pandemic, and Arteta is only at the start of rebuilding his team. City take 15 shots at goal against Arsenal's 4, and have 71 per cent possession, but two errors from Walker and Mendy give Aubameyang his chances, which he immediately converts. It's a bitter blow for Pep. Two weeks later Arsenal go on to beat Chelsea in the FA Cup final.

Back in Manchester, Pep has begun to really notice the massive hole left by Arteta. The Spaniard had established a strong connection with the players, almost one-on-one with each of them, and his knowledge of English football stadia, referees and other teams had been a huge help to Pep. Having coped without him for a few months, Pep decides that it's time to replace him and on 9 June his mentor, Juanma Lillo, joins City's technical team.

I chat to Pep by phone on the morning Juanma starts (for obvious reasons dinner isn't possible). 'I felt it was really important to bring Juanma in. I need intellectual challenge and Juanma will provide that. I thought about it over the last few months and I think it's definitely the right decision although not necessarily the easiest option from my point of view. A more conventional assistant would make my life easier but I think I need someone who's going to challenge me more. I think I can improve, do much more as a coach but, in order to do that, I need someone who's going to pressure me, who knows more than I do and who's willing to challenge me. Do you see what I mean?'

Obviously I completely understand what he means but he seems keen to explain it again: 'Juanma has so much expertise. He sees things in football that nobody else does. He has a lot of experience and will know exactly how to challenge me. It's very possible that we'll disagree regularly and even end up fighting. But he'll insist that I check everything I do every day and will question if it's the right thing to do. It's the intellectual challenge I need. I don't want people agreeing with me all the time. I want people around me who'll tell me that I should be doing things differently. And Juanma is perfect for that. I've thought about it long and hard at home. If I'd wanted to make things easy for myself I'd have picked someone else but I'm not here to take things easy. I'm here to work hard and keep getting better.

'I'm completely serious about needing intellectual challenge. I want to do everything better, be a better coach, take one more step on the ladder. And I really think that Juanma's the man to help me do that. It won't be easy but it's exactly what I need.'

Fifteen minutes later we end the call and I call Lillo to congratulate him. His response is exactly what I would have imagined, 'I'm the new boy, the last to come to class. I won't be rocking the boat.'

• • •

The month of August is reserved for Champions League matches. UEFA has put together a one-off tournament with eight teams. They all have to qualify first and City welcome Real Madrid to the Etihad on 7 August. Pep and Lillo have spent two weeks preparing for the game: the first week training the players for the match and the second week rehearsing the game with them. It pays off and City beat the visitors 2–1, the same result as at the Bernabéu almost six months ago.

Pep fields a 3–2–2–3 formation with Foden as false 9 and the team maintain sustained, aggressive pressing, which gives them the first goal eight minutes in. It's Sterling who puts the ball away, making it his 100th goal for City across all competitions. City continue to create chances but it's Benzema who gets the equaliser at the 30-minute mark. In the second half City look even more dangerous and Gabriel Jesus, who has moved up as lead striker, leaving Foden on the right wing, scores the winner. City have qualified for the tournament in Lisbon.

It's an outstanding victory against the kings of Europe and is the first time Zinedine Zidane has been eliminated from the Champions League. It is also Pep's fourth victory out of the five knockout ties he's coached against Madrid.*

Guardiola's only the third coach to have twice knocked Madrid out of the Champions League[†] and this is the 29th time he's won a knockout tie in the same competition. No other coach has performed so well. 'It was a

---

* Barcelona beat Real Madrid in the Champions League 2010–11, Spanish Super Cup 2011–12 and Copa del Rey 2011–12; he lost to them in the Copa 2010–11.
† Marcello Lippi did it in 1995–6 and 2002–3, and Ottmar Hitzfeld in 2000–1 and 2006–7.

mistake to trap Sterling and Gabriel Jesus inside on the right in the first half because we weren't able to find space. But then, with Sterling and Foden more open on the wings, we played much better.'

De Bruyne has set another record today, becoming the first player ever to create nine big chances in a Champions League match, and Gabriel Jesus has equalled Ruud van Nistelrooy's achievement as previously the only player to score in both the home and the away games of a knockout match against Real Madrid.

There are huge smiles on faces all over Manchester on 13 August, as City set off for Lisbon to face Lyon in the quarter-finals. Guardiola is taking nothing for granted, though. He knows this French side of old and is justifiably wary of their lethal counterattacking. They were impossible to beat last season in the group stage.

I chat to Lillo en route to Lisbon. 'Pep is very clear about the structure of the game. We've actually watched several of Sheffield United's games because they have a similar playing style to Lyon. Pep's convinced he's got the right strategy. We need four men behind the ball and six in front. That's the structure we're going to use because we don't want our defenders ending up two on two. Lyon are very dangerous in those situations.'

In the end, the game goes just the way Pep had hoped it wouldn't. He's made sure that Ederson is protected by three centre-backs (Fernandinho, Eric García and Laporte), bringing Walker and Cancelo up to the middle line and attacking via the inside with De Bruyne and Sterling either side of Gabriel Jesus. But his players don't establish a sufficiently fast tempo and they fail to mark the French midfielders closely enough. Twenty-three minutes in, Eric García clears a long ball only to Maxwel Cornet, who immediately scores and City now face an uphill struggle.

City maintain dominance but don't produce enough good chances. Pep brings Mahrez on for Fernandinho, who's looked sluggish in the first half, and he immediately changes the dynamic. Mahrez generates several dangerous moments until De Bruyne duly equalises. But ten minutes later, a poor pass from Laporte – barged over in a foul completely ignored by the referee – puts Lyon ahead, just three minutes after Gabriel Jesus has missed an open goal. Sterling then makes an even worse mistake five minutes before full-time when he fluffs a perfect Gabriel Jesus assist in front of an open goal.

It's a disaster for City. Converting what should have been an easy goal would more or less have guaranteed extra-time. Two minutes later it's Ederson's turn to mess up. Lyon 3, City 1.

A catastrophic end to a bumpy season. A huge disappointment. The Sheraton in Cascais, set in beautiful, leafy woodland, should be just the place to wind down and relax. But the post-match dinner takes on the dimensions of a Greek tragedy. It feels cataclysmic.

Nobody can eat a thing. All the hurt and disappointment of every previous elimination have combined in one massive blow. Pep's suffering. Everyone's suffering. All the pain of past Champions League defeats hits him again, right back to that 4–0 defeat of Bayern by Real Madrid. We've all been there. Having your ego bruised like that can really hurt. There is so much residual pain tonight in Lisbon …

Over dinner, Pep lets rip, 'We've still got so much work to do to up our game. That's four years in a row we've been knocked out in the quarter-finals.' (In his first year they were actually knocked out in the last 16.) Rodolfo Borrell seems to agree: 'If we keep losing in the quarter-finals then that must be the level we're at.'

But Txiki shakes his head. He doesn't agree. Neither does Lillo: 'That's not it. We're definitely good enough. The majority of our players are as good as or better than Leipzig's and they've made it to the semi-finals. We're definitely as good as or better than Lyon too. In fact, it's debatable whether any of the other semi-finalists are better than us …'

Both points of view duly aired, Pep still looks utterly crestfallen, afraid that his team will never improve. Upset at seeing his friend so down, Lillo tells him, 'There's definitely room for improvement.' The intellectual gauntlet has been thrown down.

Khaldoon gives a short but encouraging speech and then hugs Pep, massaging his shoulders in an attempt to cheer him up. 'You're the man, Pep, you're the man!'

But tonight, Pep's not listening … to anyone.

STATS 2019–20

	P	W	D	L	GF	GA
Community Shield	1	0	1	0	1	1
Champions						
Premier League	38	26	3	9	102	35
Second						
FA Cup	5	4	0	1	11	3
Semi-finalists						
League Cup	6	5	0	1	14	5
Champions						
Champions League	9	6	2	1	21	9
Quarter-finalists						
Total	59	41	6	12	149	53

- 69.5 per cent victories in matches all season
- 68.4 per cent wins from all Premier League matches
- 2.52 goal average per match scored in the entire season
- 2.68 goal average per match scored in the Premier League
- 0.89 goal average per match conceded in the entire season
- 0.92 goal average per match conceded in the Premier League
- 96 positive goal difference across the whole season
- 81 points in the Premier League (Liverpool, champions with 99 points)
- 27 efforts off the post in the Premier League (6 De Bruyne)
- 65.8 per cent possession in the entire season
- 66.2 per cent possession in the Premier League
- 81 per cent highest level of possession (vs Dinamo Zagreb, October 2019)
- 38 per cent lowest level of possession (vs. Wolverhampton, December 2019)
- 692 average number of passes per match
- 870 highest number of passes (vs Dinamo Zagreb, December 2019)
- 87.1 per cent completed passes per match
- 18.5 shots at goal per match/6.3 on target
- 7.1 shots at goal conceded per game/2.8 on target
- 5 best run of consecutive wins in the Premier League
- 31 top goalscorer: Raheem Sterling (16 in the Premier League)
- 22 most assists: Kevin De Bruyne (20 in the Premier League)
- 53 most appearances: Gabriel Jesus (Ederson, Rodri and De Bruyne, 35 in the Premier League)
- 8–0 biggest win (vs Watford)
- 2–0 biggest defeat (vs Wolverhampton, Tottenham, Manchester United and Arsenal)

Season 5: 2020–1

Sisyphus on Top of the World (the City of the Yugoslavs)

MOMENT 1. 'I STILL WANT TO DO GREAT THINGS'

Barcelona, 18 August 2020

It all starts with a WhatsApp sent by Sergio Agüero.

'Something big might be happening. Leo's just asked me how long Pep has left on his contract.'

Everyone back in Manchester is immediately buzzing but Pep himself doesn't see the message for several hours – he and most of the squad are on the way back from the defeat in Lisbon and none of them see it until they touch down in Manchester.

Pep's still reeling. Getting knocked out by Lyon feels like a punch in the gut. It's like losing to Monaco in the last 16 of the Champions League three years ago. Being eliminated by a weaker rival really, really hurts. OK, Lyon are a good side – they managed to draw with City in France and win at the Etihad last season but still …

City had been on a glorious Champions League run until yesterday. How else would you describe beating Zinedine Zidane's Real Madrid home and away (with a gap between the games due to COVID)? They'd arrived for the final rounds in Lisbon in good shape, with the whole squad available, except for Kun Agüero, who tore his meniscus at the end of June and couldn't play. The defeat has really knocked Pep for six. He, the players and most of the technical staff are totally destroyed. They already had a two-week break planned and, boy, do they need it. Time to relax, clear the head, chase the demons away …

Pep re-reads the text: Leo's asked when my contract expires … It's not clear what's behind Messi's question. Perhaps Barça's hoping to lure Agüero away from City so that the two friends can partner up? Pep decides not to waste any more time on it for now. His head's pounding and his body aches. He desperately needs some sleep.

Fifteen hours later he's back in the air. This time aboard the small private plane he uses for his trips to Barcelona. Juanma Lillo and Lorenzo Buenaventura are with him, en route to a well-earned break. As they touch down in Barcelona, Pep switches his phone back on. There's a message. Just five words: 'Hi Pep: how are you?'

* * *

It's 4pm on Monday, 17 August, and Pep's head is throbbing. Since football resumed, they've only won 10 out of their 14 matches, with the disastrous game against Liverpool plus their disappointing performance in the FA Cup. And, despite two magnificent victories against Real Madrid, in the Champions League they've been unceremoniously knocked out by Lyon. The lowest point of an utterly miserable season.

It's hit him hard. For the second consecutive year, marginal individual errors have cost them their Champions League campaign. His players are suffering too. Each of them dealing with it differently. There's a sense of stunned disbelief in the squad and some players are still angry: even furious. Others are just down in the dumps.

The blow is exacerbated by the fact that they worked so hard in preparation for the game. They'd practised the three-at-the-back formation over and again, and the players seemed comfortable with the game plan despite their usual resistance to making any structural changes. Guardiola chose the tactic in an effort to protect his defenders, prevent them having to go one-on-one with the dangerous French forwards. But, as almost always happens whenever he produces a relatively conservative game plan, it doesn't work.

Pep always gets better results when he takes the fight to his rival, like a nineteenth-century cavalry officer, lance at the ready, leading his men in a high-risk, full-frontal assault. Granted, the strategy didn't work out too well in the Charge of the Light Brigade, but that total fearlessness is what makes Pep the winner he is. However, no one is immune to worry and doubt, not even Pep Guardiola. Hence the 3–4–3 formation, designed to compensate for the fragility of his defensive line. And it looks like a perfectly good plan until three defensive errors, plus Sterling's unbelievable miss in front of an open goal, leave City crushed and beaten. Out of Europe. Again.

Now, in Barcelona, Pep's looking forward to two weeks of holiday before he returns to the grey skies of Manchester to start his fifth and final season with City. The good news is that the club have already signed winger Ferran Torres and defender Nathan Aké, and are on the point of signing one more central defender. He'll be returning to a greatly reinforced squad.

Unbeknown to Pep, Leo Messi is also struggling with a major headache of his own. For the past four days, he's been brooding over the 8–2 mauling handed out to Barcelona by Bayern Munich; 14 August 2020 is now seared into the memories of Barça fans everywhere. Shame. Humiliation. Their worst result in living memory. It's all too painful and Messi has come to a decision. It's time to take the initiative. He needs to move on. Perhaps Pep has a place in his squad for his former protégé …

In another part of Barcelona, Pep's still feeling the effects of his sore head when his phone buzzes.

They meet the next day. Twelve o'clock at Pep's place. It's actually the second time they've met like this. The last time was four years ago, in the summer of 2016 when Messi was facing a 21-month prison sentence for tax fraud and looking for a lifeline. A move to Manchester City seemed like a possible option. His dad, Jorge, contacted City's chief executive Ferran Soriano, who asked Pep to meet with the player. For the first time in years the two men met up in Barcelona, at Leo's house on that occasion. It was clear to Pep that Messi was serious about City potentially offering a practical solution to his problems but the coach didn't detect a whole lot of enthusiasm for the move. Sure enough, within days, the player had begun to change his mind and, as soon as his teammates began to return from their holidays, with close friends Luis Suárez and Jordi Alba among the first to get back, things began to look a lot less bleak. Suddenly Manchester lost its appeal and the whole thing came to nothing.

Four years on, the situation's very different. Messi's frustration with Barcelona has mounted with each Champions League elimination over the last few years. In 2017 they lost to Juventus (3–0), the following year it was Roma (3–0), then the disaster at Anfield against Liverpool (4–0) and, now, the humiliation of an 8–2 defeat by Bayern Munich. Messi, undoubtedly the best player of the last decade, if not the best ever, won the Champions League twice with Guardiola, but has only won it once in the nine years since then, his best years as a professional footballer. It's not a great tally for the most gifted footballer in the world. He's rapidly losing patience with his club.

Which is why he's here, sitting on Pep's huge sofa, ready to talk. 'Boss, I just want to go as far as I possibly can. I still want to do great things.' It's a statement of intent from the Argentine.

The pair of them are still talking six and a half hours later.

IT RAINS A LOT IN MANCHESTER

They've never had this kind of long, intense conversation before. Back at Barça, whenever they chatted it was always about the game, the tactics to be used or their next opponent. But they've both changed a lot since then. The quiet, reserved kid, who only seemed to come fully alive with a ball at his feet, is now a grown man. With a beard! This is an adult who knows what he wants and has carefully considered everything he's about to say. A professional, with an exhaustive knowledge of football, who speaks with precision and intelligence. Pep's heard how much Messi's changed but now he's witnessing it for himself. And today, it's Leo who does most of the talking.

Guardiola's different too, of course. Gone is that young, inexorable winner who seemed to possess some kind of magic aura. Pep's own beard is streaked with grey as he approaches his half-century. He's matured and grown too. He knows what it feels like to lose. No longer the victorious monarch, nowadays he's like the heir to the throne who has to fight for every laurel as if it was his last. He's had years of success and glory, won 29 trophies. Ahead of him lie more years of fighting for trophies and, hopefully, redemption on the European stage. Every line and wrinkle on Pep's face tells the story of all that he's experienced and suffered since he last saw Messi.

Neither of them mentions what's just happened in Lisbon. Pep has no interest in going over it again and Messi's certainly not here to talk about how it feels to be humiliated. He has a very specific purpose. Sick and tired of the way he's been treated over the last few years, and of the dishonesty and betrayal he feels he's had to put up with. He's ready to leave.

Pep can relate. He himself feels he had to put up with similar treatment as a player, meted out by then club president Josep Lluis Núñez, who had also seemed to take against Johan Cruyff and do everything he could to push the great Dutch coach out of the club. And so it goes on. Pep, as a new coach, had similar problems under president Sandro Rosell. Now the circle is closing: Cruyff, Guardiola and Messi, the holy trinity, seemingly object of the hate and scorn of three 'Nuñista' presidents, all of them part of the same clique of powerbrokers who have run FC Barcelona for four decades, bar the brief break between 2003 and 2010.

'Only the mediocre are truly loved by their countries,' wrote Nietzsche. In Johan Cruyff, Pep Guardiola and Leo Messi, the club had three of their brightest and most brilliant sons, all of them skewered on the lance of mediocrity.

So no, Pep doesn't need the details. He understands exactly what Messi's saying.

'You do know that it rains a lot in Manchester?'

Their cards on the table, everyone now understands what's at stake. Pep makes it clear that he'll be willing to extend his contract if the move goes through. Jorge Messi and Ferran Soriano will handle the negotiations. Messi still has a year left on his contract with Barça and has a rescission clause of €700 million (£600 million). Nobody thinks that will present insurmountable problems and the club surely owes Messi, not least for his refusal to speak publicly about the disgraceful treatment he feels he's endured.

Today, Pep discovers in Messi a man who is surprisingly well-informed about world football. It's obvious that he has superb football vision and a precise grasp of the concepts, tactical variants and innovations they chat about. They discuss Liverpool and Bayern, Antonio Conte and Thomas Tuchel, Kevin De Bruyne and Kalidou Koulibaly. Pep talks him through City's squad, their new signings and the defenders he's got his eye on. Leo has opinions on all of it. It's clear to Pep that Messi joining City will bring so much more than a reunion with his former star player.

It would mean an immediate, gigantic shot of adrenaline for the team – still struggling and in a state of shock after their Champions League elimination. For the last few days, it's all that Pep's been able to talk about: 'How on earth am I going to keep these players motivated now?' And his technical staff feel exactly the same way. After the Lisbon debacle the team will need more than new signings, some tactical innovations and a few motivational speeches. After four, hugely demanding, seasons the core group of players don't need speeches. They need to win.

Pep's first season in Manchester was tough but the next two were hugely successful, the lack of Champions League medals notwithstanding. His fourth season got off to a promising start but finished as grey and miserable as a winter's afternoon in Manchester. The fifth is set to be Pep's last and it begins in two weeks. For once, his players are as worried and uptight as their coach. Another year of ferocious battles, taking on the might of Liverpool and the rest of the Premier League plus competing in the increasingly competitive Champions League. Unless of course …

Lionel Messi could be the answer to all their problems, the missing link that turns everything around. It would be a great move for both the player and the coach. At six o'clock on that Tuesday evening in August, the idea of getting to work together again appeals to them both.

'We train hard in Manchester …'

'Doesn't bother me. I'm ready for hard work.'

'And I still give long tactical talks. Maybe you'll get bored …'

'I'll cope, I can cope with anything you throw at me.'

'Leo, we're both much older than we were. Maybe we won't get on now.'

'Pep, I just want the chance to do great things, to feel like I'm ready to smash it again.'*

At 6.30 they say goodbye with a warm hug. It's not going to be easy but if they pull this off, there's no knowing what they can achieve. Two years to smash every obstacle.

MOMENT 2. HIGH HOPES CRUSHED

Manchester, 3 September 2020

A text from Bernardo Silva arrives, 'Is it true about Messi?'

'How would you feel about him coming?'

'I'd run twice as much!'

Three days ago Messi sent a recorded delivery letter to Barcelona informing them that he intended to apply clause 3.1 in his contract thereby ending his contract on 3 August. His lawyers have advised him that this is perfectly legal given the changes made to the football calendar as a result of the pandemic. The season, which was due to end on 30 June, had been extended to 23 August.

In Manchester, the excitement's mounting at the prospect of Messi joining City's ranks. Manel Estiarte is already calmly analysing exactly what

---

* Messi uses a colloquial Argentinian expression, *romperla*, which literally means to 'smash it'.

Messi could bring to the team. His conclusion? 'We already have a very good team. With Leo, we'd have a brilliant one!'

Carles Planchart is equally thrilled: 'I'm so excited. I'd be over the moon if Leo joined us.'

Planchart's hit the nail on the head. It's that sense of excited anticipation that the team's been lacking of late. There's a general sense of complacency within the ranks. A combination of egos swollen by all their past successes plus the departure of Mikel Arteta has led to a definite, if subtle, dip in standards. And it's been noticed. One key player has been carrying extra weight since June and has been making lots of mistakes. Another, clearly carried away by an overweening sense of superiority, is refusing to accept correction or guidance, let alone demonstrating any willingness to autocorrect or push himself. One player in particular looked totally disinterested throughout the Arsenal FA Cup game, his careless mistakes a major factor in City's defeat. And nothing had changed in terms of his attitude and performance for the Lyon tie. The coaching team have always believed that success is only possible if the entire squad is pulling in the same direction, completely focused on their shared objectives. Any imbalance in the players' attitudes and efforts makes winning impossible. That's exactly when you start missing in front of an open goal or conceding unnecessarily silly errors.

Pep's worried. He knows that, without a major reboot, his team will inevitably slip into a downward spiral. Papering up the cracks won't do. This requires serious changes. And Messi's arrival could be just the catalyst they need. At the end of their short break, Pep and Lillo use the flight back to Manchester to draw up hypothetical plans. When the opposition have possession both of them see Leo stationed near the centre circle, forcing their opponents to play on the outside, where City will be more aggressive in recuperating the ball. When City have the ball, Messi will move up towards the box, bringing his teammates with him. For the time being, of course, it's nothing more than an intellectual exercise. Everything has to fall into place before they can start to plan for real.

Sure enough, Messi doesn't show up at Barcelona on 30 August for the post-summer COVID testing. But, unfortunately, it's also looking increasingly likely he won't be making an appearance in Manchester any time soon. Negotiations have tailed off. Then, on 3 September, Jorge Messi reaches an agreement with Barcelona. Eager to avoid getting into a protracted legal dispute with the club, Messi has decided to stay for one more year.

There will no reunion for Pep and Leo after all.

Messi still wants to do great things. He just won't be doing them at Manchester City.

MOMENT 3. DESPONDENCY

Manchester, 7 September 2020

The new season's about to start and things couldn't really be going any worse. It's bad enough that most of Pep's squad are away competing for their countries in the Nations League, and now he's just been informed that both Aymeric Laporte and Riyad Mahrez have tested positive for COVID and will be confined at home until 17 September at the earliest. It means that he won't be able to play them in City's first league game of the season, on the 21st against an always difficult Wolves at Molineux.

City's first training session of the new season takes place just 15 days after the end of the last one. Only seven members of the squad are here. The three goalkeepers, Ederson, Zack Steffen and Scott Carson, plus four defenders, Mendy, Fernandinho, Stones and Otamendi. Three youth players have also been told to attend. Juanma Lillo and Rodo Borrell run the session.

Pep's not here. He's holed up in his office. Utterly despondent. Hours and hours spent with Messi over the last two weeks, endless discussions about how they might use him at City, which position would suit him best and what kind of central defender would be a good fit. The discussions with his bosses at City, analysing exactly what impact Messi's arrival in the Premier League might have. All of it for nothing. Pep has been left high and dry, facing the season without the player he'd hoped would make his final year at City his crowning glory.

This time it's hit him really hard. They'd got so far down the road with this that it had begun to feel like a done deal. Particularly since the player himself had done all the running at the start. Pep knows that Barcelona is in serious financial difficulties and securing this wonderful asset might well be on the cards next season when Messi's out of contract. But by then Pep might be gone and the club will probably no longer be interested anyway. A year is a long time and, right now, Pep has zero desire to speculate about summer 2021.

His two-week break in Barcelona had gone by far too fast and now, with no Messi on the horizon, Pep can't summon up any enthusiasm for the coming season. Like Lillo, under COVID regulations, he'd had to self-isolate on his return from Barcelona and had spent the time brooding on what awaits them. Another year in a league famous for its physicality and intensity; Klopp's amazing Liverpool; a Manchester United that's performing better every day; a newly invigorated Chelsea with an array of superb new signings; and, looming above them all, the competition that's fast becoming Pep's personal bête noire, the Champions League.

Pep's feeling none of the usual pre-season excitement and has decided to sit training out. He has no interest in heading over to Training Pitch 1, where, just four weeks ago, he stood shouting instructions as they prepared for the Lyon game, full of high hopes and confidence. Now Lillo's and Borell's voices are the only sounds to be heard as they work with the few players who have made it back, while Pep's sits silently thinking dark, bitter thoughts.

And just as he's thinking that at least his day can't get any worse, another kick in the teeth. Around lunchtime the news breaks that Phil Foden, City's great hope for the future, has been kicked out of the England team for a serious breach of protocol. After making their England debuts, Foden and Mason Greenwood had sneaked two Icelandic girls into their room and have now been kicked out of Gareth Southgate's squad and sent home. On his arrival, a shamefaced Foden immediately issues a message apologising for his behaviour. And there's more bad news from the Nations League. Left-back Nathan Aké has picked up a muscle injury while playing for the Netherlands. *What next?* thinks Pep at the end of a brutal day. *What else can possibly go wrong now?*

The next day Pep and Lillo have a furious row in Pep's flat. It's nothing new. They often have vicious arguments and end up telling each other to go to hell. But it never lasts for long. Today's set-to is all about the best way to challenge oneself intellectually.

MOMENT 4. COACHING THE COACH

Manchester, 15 September 2020

Challenging yourself intellectually doesn't mean thinking profound thoughts. It's much more about working on your faults and maximising your talents. Pep wants Lillo to help him do this. He wants Lillo to be his coach, to push him to improve. Lillo believes that Pep will actually be a better coach if he calms down a bit and gives his players space for their natural abilities to flourish. He advocates less intervention.

'As coaches we often make the mistake of making training all about ourselves rather than the players. We have to provide the kind of training that leaves them going into the game as confident and secure as possible, not nervous or insecure. We generally talk more about tactics than we do about actually playing and the players also have a tendency do that. We forget that it's all about winning, whether we do that by following the coach's game plan or whether it's actually the decisions made by the players that bring that about.

'You see a lot of young coaches who believe in this idea of "interventionism". That's the side of things they want to develop. It's as if they believe that they must have a hand in everything that happens and they tell themselves: "If it weren't for me …" More experienced, wiser heads understand that a coach should always be in the background, not front and centre. The ultimate aim of the *magister* or true maestro is to blend into the background. Nowadays, there are too many teachers and too few maestros.'

The general atmosphere within the squad improves dramatically over the first week of training. Lillo picks up on it immediately: 'It's been great to see how hungry they still are. Not only that, but I can feel their excitement about the new season building every day. Right now, I'm very much closer to believing that we can win every trophy going.'

The first team play a training match against an academy 11 today and then everyone is invited to the club barbecue in Sportcity. Pep's smiling and happy again, as are the players, with Fernandinho and Walker taking it upon themselves to make sure they're all in the party spirit. Suddenly, everyone seems rejuvenated.

Lillo's taking his new role as Pep's 'personal coach' very seriously and has already made several recommendations. Top of the list? Shorter team talks and more restraint in terms of the amount of instructions he gives from the bench so that the players will be free to use their own initiative. 'We have to get to the stage where the players tell us what needs to be done, not the reverse. That's the best way to win. We don't want "obedient soldiers". We want guys with initiative, which means we have to loosen the leash and give them the space they need.

'Pep needs to avoid driving himself to the point of exhaustion when he prepares for games. If that process is the "be-all-and-end-all", then you become a slave to it. If he can change the way he prepares, it could reap dividends for him.'

MOMENT 5. USING A DOUBLE PIVOT

Wolverhampton, 21 September 2020

The difficulties of last season hang heavy on Pep.

City squandered too many points against much weaker teams whom they should have thrashed. They regularly failed to convert domination into big leads and then sometimes paid a high price by giving away points after opponents' sudden, sporadic attacks.

The same story time and again. City would need a dozen attempts to score one goal while the opposition managed to stick the ball past Ederson at the first attempt. The majority of their nine defeats and three draws last season followed this pattern and took a toll on the team psychologically. That frustration is a wound that is still festering as the new season starts.

Their first game is in a tough stadium against a team that has already caused Pep plenty of headaches. Wolves won both their games against City last season and it's the memory of those defeats that's uppermost in Pep's mind as he prepares for this next meeting. He goes with a double pivot, putting Fernandinho and Rodri in the middle of the pitch. It's a sign of the nerves City's coach is feeling at the start of his fifth season. He's used this formation before with these same players, or with Gündoğan partnering Rodri, but only as an occasional tactic specifically designed to defeat a particular opponent. This time, it's not about that. This time, it's much more to do with the fragility Pep perceives in his team.

At the moment, they feel debilitated: at the mercy of any opponent who can defend tightly and aggressively but can also counterattack with speed and precision. Everything they've gone through recently still feels very fresh. It hurts and it's having a profound effect. There's fear of repeating the same mistakes with the same painful results. Familiar demons returning to haunt them.

The use of a double pivot is anathema to Guardiola's purest ideology and he's only using it because he feels exposed and on the defensive. Gone is the brilliant, daring leader of men who won two titles in a row, and the astute, high-energy coach who picked up four trophies in one season. For the moment at least.

This Guardiola is wounded and tentative, having to cope with a dramatically reduced squad, a woeful lack of pre-season training and his team's fragility. Circumstances beyond his control are weighing down on him. There are seven absentees at the minute: Laporte and Gündoğan have COVID-19; Bernardo Silva and Zinchenko are out with muscular problems; Cancelo, a foot injury that has prevented him from training; Agüero is still recuperating from July's meniscus operation; and Eric García has needed 19 stitches for a head injury he received in training.

Pep knows that his men won't be able to produce their normal level of performance so he's had to reshape things and play a much more defensive game, copying the 'tortoise formation' used by Roman legions in siege situations.

He decides on a system of distribution that he thinks is most likely to stop Wolves' counterattacks. City bring the ball out in a 3+3, with Mendy moving up into the midfield beside the pivots. Once across the centre circle, they switch to 2–4–2–2, with Gabriel Jesus and Sterling leading the attack and the attacking midfielders behind them. The plan works like a dream. City dominate possession (67 per cent), boss the pitch, pepper Wolves' goalmouth with shots and win 3–1. For the tenth season in a row, City has won their first league game, something no other club has ever achieved.

Pep's had to battle the storms for too long. Time to batten down the hatches.

MOMENT 6. FUCKING THINGS UP

Manchester, 27 September 2020

Withdrawing Fernandinho is like pulling out the nuts and bolts holding the scaffolding together. Without him the entire edifice crumbles.

Pep, not for the first time, sees it differently. Forget the Brazilian's brilliant performance in their win over Wolves last week, this is now and something's changed. The Catalan's not happy with his captain. Even in the warm-up things don't feel right. One of Pep's staff pointedly demands of Fernandinho: 'Are you guys confident … or just complacent?'

From the bench, the staff detect an almost unheard-of and unpalatable apathy from their normally combative captain. In particular, they are all ticked off with the bland effort to finish a nicely delivered De Bruyne free-kick into the box. In any other circumstances they know 'which' Fernandinho they'd have seen … a fiery, energetic attacking of the ball, battering any defenders out of the way. Today? Badly timed jump, barely getting his head to the cross, letting Schmeichel completely off the hook.

For half an hour City have shredded Leicester. Mahrez sets the tempo, a right-footed missile sent into the top corner of the net after a City corner barely three minutes after the first whistle. It's the exquisite aperitif for a banquet of fluid, commanding football but, to Pep's perpetual frustration, Rodri shoots over, Sterling's apparently 'guaranteed' goal deflects away off Schmeichel's torso and then, the straw to break the camel's back, Fernandinho totally wastes that easy chance to nod home De Bruyne's silver service. City 'own' the ball, averaging 75 per cent possession, and only allow one Leicester counterattack, which Eric García mops up without breaking a sweat.

Everything is under control, until it isn't. Walker unnecessarily brings down Vardy and it's a penalty. Even though it's the first sign of life from the Foxes, there's the whiff of catastrophe in the air.

When City go in at half-time, ghosts of travesties past go with them. Total domination but hauled back to parity because of one mistake. It pisses Pep off.

As the second half starts, immediately City pepper Schmeichel's goal frame with efforts which either hit the post or threaten to. The pattern is identical and the coach has seen enough. Surprise ripples across the stadium when not only does he make a substitution earlier than usual, barely six minutes after the restart, but Liam Delap, author of a nice goal against Bournemouth a couple of days ago, comes on not for the tired-looking Foden – but for Fernandinho. Pep's essentially demolishing the 'construction' he's used with great success up until now, against Wolves for example, but, right now, it's 'captain off and no more double pivot in midfield'.

This is almost unprecedented for Guardiola, who wouldn't usually leave a player looking like he's been singled out in this way, least of all a loyal foot soldier like his captain. Nor, at first glance, can everyone understand the decision. City are playing well, they've generated two new chances and Vardy's managed just a single attacking run in 50 minutes. And a draw wouldn't be a disaster.

Delap for Fernandinho comes from a cocktail of built-up frustration, fury and impotence – the idea of playing well, completely dominating an opponent but suffering from the twin sin of not tucking them away and, then, going all wobbly at the knees after one lucky counterpunch to the jaw. Today has been salt in old, old wounds and Pep's had enough. He's got unmerited defeats in his mind and he's not having it – time for radical action. No matter the consequences.

The question hangs in the air, however: 'Given how City are actually playing, is this dismantling of a strong structure really the right thing to do?'

Within two minutes of the change, Leicester are knocking the ball about in a way they couldn't possibly have done when Fernandinho was on the pitch. He's not there to break moves up; Rodri's running around like a puppy after a tennis ball but he can't plug all the gaps – so Leicester, unable to believe their luck, have their tails up. Mendy, increasingly overwhelmed by the supply of balls Harvey Barnes is getting, loses a ball, which Vardy uses to showboat his superb technical skill and, suddenly, it's 2–1 Leicester.

City aren't controlling possession, the visitors know they need to make the most of their advantage – so they do. Barnes shoots, Ederson saves then García gives Leicester their second penalty in the match. Vardy's running and pressing seem to be driving him to distraction. The Foxes' legendary marksman hits a different part of the target from 12 yards, keeper's left, but it's in the net, City are in the doldrums and Leicester, almost unbelievably, lead 3–1.

The team who want to be champions again, having surrendered Blue Riband status to Liverpool last season, are reduced to a bag of nerves.

Everyone thinks they've seen this film before: wasted domination and a fortunate counterattack by a side that had been looking like victims. But, hold on, this is worse … much worse.

Rodri, not his fault, is overwhelmed. De Bruyne looks bewildered. Every attempted attack looks disorganised. Young Delap's header thumps the bar but nobody's fooled. Maddison adds a genuinely wonderful top-corner free kick to give Leicester a three-goal lead, having been 1–0 down. Aké does produce a powerful header from a corner to reduce the deficit but, just to cap the humiliation of an awful day at the office, there's yet another penalty, thanks to Mendy this time, and Tielemans gleefully crashes it past Ederson.

Losing 5–2 at home isn't simply catastrophic in its own right. It's historic. Not one of Guardiola's teams has ever conceded five times and, probably worst of all, this has been an crystal-clear exhibition of the same old, deeply annoying flaws, the same ones that made last season such a bitter experience – such a drop-off, in points and achievement, from the two title-winning seasons before it.

The dressing-room door remains closed for an almost unheard of half an hour. This is a moment to close ranks, to draw firm and important conclusions rather than waiting until a cold-blooded Monday autopsy. In due course a sombre Rodri sums things up: 'It feels like we are obliged to play brilliantly and beautifully all the time, to score three times in a ten-minute blitz …' His argument is philosophical, it's about the idea that things don't have to be like that – in fact, they shouldn't be. There's a firm belief, throughout staff and squad, that when City go 1–0 up, the team that has to go up a gear is the opposition. The team who's losing is the one that should suffer from nerves, the one that needs to produce something special, rather than continue the ultra-defensive tactics – or they'll lose.

Rodri's argument is that City need to learn to show patience, patience and still more patience as they pass opponents into submission once Guardiola's team has the lead. Right now, things are out of kilter: City chase more goals, get nervy if they don't score them and are far from cold-blooded, controlling or ruthless. Rodri's the voice, but the consensus is total – City have to get back to the 'take the ball, pass the ball' formula that has made them historically great.

Dressing-room issue airing is one thing but, naturally, there's a crisis analysis session afterwards between Pep, Estiarte and Lillo. The same themes as were aired in the dressing room dominate now. No one is suggesting an earthquake in terms of playing philosophy – far from it. City will always play to win, they'll try to dominate the rival, spend more time in the opposition half, keep the ball as far away from Ederson's goal as possible. Unchanging tenets. But the central recipe to avoid days like this is going to be about match tempo, about calm, patience and much-improved match management.

These were missing against Leicester. Nerves and overeagerness, where steely *savoir faire* is needed, will too regularly lead to dropped points and a frustrating inability to apply whichever kind of knockout blow it takes to finish off a rival. A tempest of goals and great football … or a lead that you then defend to the last thanks to a superior match mentality than is currently common for City.

Added to which is the fact that Pep really only has 13 fully fit first-team players at the moment. The overload of big games isn't a trickle, it's a torrent, and letting the ball do more of the work, dominating opponents via their passing skills, becomes all the more vital. The watchwords will be 'pass the opposition to death', circulate possession throughout the whole team, with both full-backs getting involved numerous times in the same sequence of moves, use the entirety of the pitch and find good positions high up in the opponents' defensive third. Staying calm in the face of nerves and nagging doubts has never been an easy challenge – but that's the task in hand right now.

MOMENT 7. INTENTIONS AND TEMPO

Manchester, 30 September 2020

Training now has two new elements. Small-sided games (usually seven-a-side) and rondos where there are no limits on the number of times each player can touch the ball (as opposed to the high pressure of one-touch rondos). The mini-matches (winner stays on) have the aim of simply reintro-ducing a certain instinctive, natural freedom to their game. Arguably, they've been saturated by repeated, highly technical exercises aimed at drumming in very specific tactical concepts.

Playing a couple of full-sided 'bounce' games in slightly smaller pitches every week should get City's players enjoying themselves again, thinking and playing with all the natural instincts that make them so special. It's something of a reset: get the mood right and things will, automatically, be healthier.

Making the rondos 'unlimited touches' has a more sophisticated tactical intention. When this lightning-fast drill is limited to either one or two touches, it's all about honing specific technical skills. Controlled, well-aimed first-time passes help the players elude their opponents' press in matches. Lateral vision, awareness and mental sharpness all get super-charged using this drill, which is so emblematic of Pep's Barcelona, Bayern and, now, City.

That said, when everything is done at such intense speed you simply cannot produce 100 per cent perfection and if their opponents press the first- or second-touch passes well enough, they often rob possession. In other words, playing that one-touch, two-touch football is thrilling and can be utterly devastating to their opponents … but it's high risk as well as high art.

When, for the moment, the rondos are suddenly freed-up for it to be cat-and-mouse rather than at ice-hockey speed, freedom of touches rather than everything on the volley, there'll be a distinct result. Circulation, among the circles of either six, eight or ten players, with one or two chasers in the middle, will be slower. But because the players in the circle can take more time on the ball they'll come up with tricks to stop the 'chasers' closing them down. The 'chaser' too has to be smarter, more calculating than when they're rushing in to block or rob a first-touch pass when the only question for the guy on the perimeter is, *Can I execute this more quickly and accurately than you can get over here to shut me down?* So what happens if the guy on the perimeter is allowed three touches? If he's permitted to put his foot on the ball and tempt the 'chaser' to come in and tackle him? This 'freedom' requires the passer to be more of a street-footballer, full of ingenuity and invention. It also makes it more fun. This is closer to how all of the players learned to play as kids and it's a smart move by the coaching staff.

In the months to come, this change in tempo and the alterations they've made in the way the team trains will really pay off in some of City's biggest games.

There's a final rationale behind making these two changes (small-sided matches and free-touches rondos) to training and it stems from some of Lillo's brainstorming: 'When we dissect sport, the battles aren't always about dominating space. They can also be about intentions and tempos.'

Football has evolved through three phases. First, it's all about what you do in the penalty boxes – that's where you score or avoid conceding goals. Then, the idea emerged that creating, finding or denying 'space' were the be-all-and-end-all of how to impose your play. And the third 'great idea' is that it's fundamentally all about the ball. That possession is what dominates all decision making.

The first era could be said to have emerged because of how the earliest rules of the sport were drawn up. The second was Herbert Chapman-inspired and the third flows from the genius of Johan Cruyff.

Now, 'intentions and tempo' are emerging as another concept around which new ideas and styles of play might develop.

MOMENT 8. SIGNING RÚBEN DIAS

Leeds, 3 October 2020

After six long, frustrating weeks of negotiations Txiki Begiristain manages to sign one of City's key defensive targets from his four-man shortlist: José María Giménez, Kalidou Koulibaly, Jules Koundé and Rúben Dias.

In truth, the first three are pretty much out of reach financially given the prices demanded by their clubs. So Begiristain has focused on Dias, who's decent on the ball, has a strong personality and boundless energy. The price is doable, not least because his €68 million (£62 million, rising to £65 million with add-ons) cost is offset by the sale, in return, of Otamendi to Benfica for €15 million, meaning that the net outlay is €43 million. The wholesale remodelling of the centre-halves is also given impetus by the €45 million (£41 million) purchase of Nathan Aké. (Up front, Ferran Torres joins for €23 million [£21 million] while Sané is sold to Bayern for €50 million [£46 million].)

The driving concept behind this deal is to add consistency at the back, something Pep feels has been lacking for some time. City are aiming to build a 'Yugoslavian defence'. The Yugoslavs, and then the independent nations that formed post-secession, stood out in all team sports for being defensively excellent. Defending was seen as an important discipline requiring courage, solidarity, effort and strength. Estiarte is not alone in feeling all this but he's a vocal disciple (and, as the greatest water polo player of all time, he's prone to including Hungarians in this admiration).

'Yugoslavian defending', as far as Pep's concerned, revolves around tough, pitiless, consistent attention to detail and pride in performance – no weaknesses, no gaps. Carles Puyol, his captain at Barcelona, was an example of this kind of defender. City has two central defenders who are skilled in bringing the ball out from the back, Laporte and Stones, but Pep thinks his back four needs a player for whom defending is an end in itself – someone who looks adversity in the eye and comes out counterpunching. This will now be Rúben Dias's task. A Portuguese man-of-war to make Manchester City a little bit more Yugoslavian. Forty-eight hours after he arrives in Manchester on 1 October, he's straight into battle – away to Leeds. It's a contest that evokes the past.

· · ·

6 November 2011, San Mamés, Bilbao, Spain.

Athletic Club de Bilbao and FC Barcelona do epic battle under a rainstorm of biblical proportions. The game ends in a 2–2 draw with Guardiola describing it as a 'homage to football' and 'one of the greatest games I've ever seen … a marvellous spectacle'.

That night, it was also Guardiola vs Bielsa as the heavens opened. The two men know each other well, and, when Pep decided to embark on his coaching career, he set off to Argentina to consult Marcelo Bielsa. Fifteen years later they've both ended up, albeit via vastly different routes, competing in the Premier League. Just by the by, it's only three months since Pep invited Bielsa to come to Manchester so that they could dine together at Tast Català, the restaurant in which he's a shareholder.

The Premier League season is still in its opening stanzas but Leeds already look attention-grabbing – especially after an exhibition of courageous football at Anfield, where they lost 4–3, and then successive wins against Fulham and away to Sheffield United.

Guardiola can't count on Cancelo, Zinchenko, Gündoğan, Agüero or Gabriel Jesus – they're all out. But Rúben will play as Laporte's new partner in central defence, and hopefully bring a degree of consistency.

Previewing the match, each coach reckons that this is going to be a breathless, end-to-end contest, which will revolve around a 'you attack me and then I'll attack you' spirit. City have a better 11 than Leeds, that's a fact, but Lillo points out: 'We'll need to outperform them to win.'

In the end, City don't impose their quality consistently over the 90 minutes and though the scoreline is 1–1 – two goals short of that epic clash in the Basque Country all those years ago – it's still a spectacle where there's no quarter asked or given.

City can boast 30 initial minutes of magnificence. Sterling waits barely two minutes to shoot but it goes over. De Bruyne senses that Leeds's keeper, Illan Meslier, is slightly out of position and tries to expose him but hits the post. Leeds avoid another 'must score' moment from the wonderful, on-form Belgian after ten minutes and then it's just a torrent: Dias heads just wide of the post; Torres sees a goalbound shot blocked and deflected; Ezgjan Alioski heads over when he should score after a mistake by Walker (only 13 minutes have passed in the match); Torres is again denied what looks a certain goal when Mateusz Klich gets in the way and then, hallelujah, Sterling puts City ahead in the 17th minute. Mendy wins it in midfield and puts his head down. On the run, he feeds Torres, who sends the ball out towards Sterling. The England international hasn't scored this season but he's about to, spectacularly so. He's sprinting and dribbling in one blur of action, evading Bielsa's men in the penalty area and then finishing with power and precision so that even Meslier's full dive can't stop the effort. It's a great goal.

City maintain their aggressive push. Laporte and Foden both have good chances to make it two, or even three–nil. They don't, however. And, 30 minutes in, everything changes. Mendy sparks Leeds's fightback with a horrible mistake and not one which is out of context across the breadth of his sometimes over-exuberant career. Luckily, Ederson digs the Frenchman out of trouble with a one-on-one save against Luke Ayling.

We're 40 minutes into the match and it's still pouring with rain when, out of the blue, Bielsa stomps out of his technical area and into City's zone, right past Guardiola, so that he can shake hands and say 'Hola amigo!' to Juanma Lillo, whom the Argentinian has failed to spot up until this point. Both teams are going at it hammer and tongs out on the pitch and Elland Road is a tumult of noise and energy, but Bielsa spends about a minute saying sorry to Lillo for seeming to ignore him up until now. Pep isn't often lost for words but, right now, he's torn between refocusing on the match and being amused by the demonstration of old-fashioned manners going on behind him.

Half-time comes and goes and so does City's pre-eminence. Leeds simply take over. They log 68 per cent possession for the first quarter of an hour, an ultra-rarity against Pep's City. It culminates in Rodrigo Moreno hitting Ederson's post and demonstrating that Leeds have claws as well as sudden control.

Within 30 seconds the claws draw blood. Admittedly in horrible conditions. A Leeds corner fools Ederson, his attempted punch is very poorly executed, the ball inadvertently rebounds off Mendy's back and drops to … Rodrigo. This time he simply says, 'Gracias,' and sends Elland Road into rhapsodies of delight with the easiest equaliser he'll ever score.

The match plays out full of risk, daring, back-and-forward attacks and counters. Both teams look close to scoring again. For City, Sterling, Fernandinho, Mahrez and De Bruyne have good chances. And it's only thanks to Ederson, Dias and the goalpost that Leeds's shots don't go in. Sterling and Patrick Bamford, for City and Leeds respectively, are both guilty of 'thinking too much' instead of finishing instinctively when they are through on goal.

Festival of football or not, City leave Leeds with a bad taste in their mouths. Not a new sensation by any means. Neutrals would say that to draw with a threatening, daring, creative rival when City are patently not at their most ruthless or consistent could be viewed as a respectable night's work. But it's anathema to Pep to have his team 14th with four out of a possible nine points on the board. They're suddenly eight behind the leaders – Carlo Ancelotti's impressive and ambitious Everton side. Elland Road leaves a patchy report card – 48 per cent possession (very disappointing), fewer passes than Leeds, only 82 per cent passing accuracy (again, deeply troubling) and, while they managed a high number of counterattacks (6), too few of them were really high-quality goal opportunities.

Pep's staff are, nevertheless, still optimistic: 'We only need to stay calm and patient because our ideas are right. We are there or thereabouts and what's lacking are the players. Things will pick up when we have a full complement again.' Somewhat against the grain, Pep's pretty upbeat too.

He reckons that, although it's a slow process, the team is en route to reaching ramming speed – occasional stumbles notwithstanding.

One of his inner sanctum tells me: 'We're in better shape than it might seem. Much. Some of the things which aren't being focused upon really couldn't be much better. Look at how well we beat Burnley! The key factor is that we aren't finishing ruthlessly. This leaves us fixated on how we are at the back, and alarmingly dependent on that factor, because if you're getting into goalscoring positions a couple of hundred times but don't score and the opposition gets to your area once and puts it away, then the damage is magnified hugely. Every error seems to be fatal.'

The very next day, Liverpool get smashed 7–2 at Villa, United lose 6–1 at home to Spurs and City's conquerors, Leicester, lose 3–0 at home to West Ham.

The lesson? Don't waste time on damaging self-flagellation. You never know what's just around the corner.

MOMENT 9. CANCELO: FREE ELECTRON

Manchester, 17 October 2020

The competitive restart after the international break brings news. Good and bad.

The bad news is that Kevin De Bruyne has returned injured but, on the plus side, Kun Agüero is back after four months' absence due to a torn meniscus. Two others also make their season debut: Bernardo Silva and João Cancelo.

Against Arsenal, Guardiola deploys a concept that will become the foundation of the season: a line of three defenders protected by a double-pivot partnership. One or other of the two full-backs, depending on the match circumstances, will be in that midfield partnership. It's a flexible structure: 3–2–2–3 when City bring the ball out. Match-by-match the structure will be finetuned until it becomes the preferred approach for City's players and coaches.

Today's three defenders are Walker, Rúben Dias and Aké. Rodri is accompanied for the first time by Cancelo in the new midfield role that Guardiola has planned for him and which will yield spectacular performances.

This is a dual concept. Cancelo has the rare ability to take on, and beat, opponents in risky areas and, simultaneously, draw opponents to him, thus freeing creative space for teammates. Gold dust for Guardiola.

Cancelo, with Rodri, is playing in what can be called a 'double pivot' but his actions, his abilities, the impact he can have all become, literally, of pivotal structural significance to the team's performance. Whether playing on the right side or on the left, the Portuguese has begun to emerge as key to how games take shape. Now, with this central and advanced position, his tactical self-confidence and high technical quality liberate the creative midfielders from the task of initiating attacks so that they can focus much more on actually organising those forward movements.

So … Cancelo's impact is now multi-dimensional. He 'pushes' the creative midfielder on his side of the pitch into advanced positions, turning whoever it is almost into a 'playmaker', which is directly influential on Gündoğan's increased scoring performance. Cancelo significantly helps Rodri in his defensive/organising midfield role, and gives one more passing line to the three defenders as they try to build from the back. But he *also* positions himself specifically to give numerical superiority in the centre of the pitch – a foundation of Pep's game – plus around the edge of the rival penalty area, meaning that City effectively always have at least four strikers: the two wingers, who in this way can play very open, the central striker and the creative midfielder who, thanks to Cancelo's daring, high positional play, converts into a playmaker around that centre-forward.

Cancelo and how he interprets his role as midfielder-full-back-creative attacker is the key to the eruption of irresistible, thrilling play that City are beginning to enjoy. Where has this metamorphosis come from? How did Cancelo go from being an apathetic and unreliable player to this abundant and decisive footballer?

The answer is … COVID-19. Before the pandemic, in March 2020, Cancelo wasn't happy in Manchester. He didn't understand the team's playing style, he couldn't do what Pep asked of him, he didn't defend intensely and he didn't contribute in attack. He wanted and expected to be a starter, but his performances were, at best, adequate, which increased his discomfort and his morose mood. By March 2020 – the Premier League stopped between 8 March and 17 June – the Portuguese had started 22 matches, a decent number, but his performances underwhelmed the coaching staff to the point that he was more 'out' of the side than in. Fate then intervened.

During lockdown, Cancelo's introspection finally helped him – with time to reflect on his footballing qualities, matching them to the 'learning' tasks in front of him, it drove an improvement in attitude, confidence and application. The Portuguese returned to City more or less a 'new' man. Those who saw him arrive smiling and happy at the first post-lockdown training session were instantly struck by the massive change in his demeanour. His work rate from then on matched his new perspective and, these days, he is an indisputably key piece in Guardiola's plans.

In the front three against Arsenal, Mahrez is pegged to the right wing, as will be the case almost all season, while Sterling and Agüero alternate as centre-forward and second striker, leaving Foden on the left wing, often needing to hurtle up and down, attacking and defending.

The 3–4–3 thrives on many nuances and details that Guardiola introduces or modifies in response to the successive changes Arteta makes to the organisation of his Arsenal side. He's built a team that aims to dominate possession but they're suffering today against this powerful City side.

Mahrez should score after 30 seconds, but the tantalising curve he puts on the ball only shaves Bernd Leno's far post. Midway through the first half Agüero, in one of his forays back into the central circle looking for good-quality possession, feeds off Mahrez, turns, sprints forward and lays it off to Foden, who shoots, right-footed. Leno saves … but only as far as the penalty spot and Sterling hammers the rebound home with his left foot.

Arsenal counterpunch three times, with two point-blank shots from Bukayo Saka and one from Aubameyang, all of which Ederson saves. Clear scoring opportunities for Mahrez and Foden are repelled by Leno, who's on magnificent form today.

The second half is less vibrant, with City dedicated to controlling the game and preventing the visitors from counterattacking. Arsenal look completely trapped in City's intricate web of passing sequences.

It's intriguing to see Ederson skipping the process of playing out from the back and evading the Gunner's press by sending several long balls to Mahrez. The effect? Arsenal have to retrench and increasingly drop their high press. The game ends 1–0.

We're halfway through October and City are still in 11th place, with just seven points, but Pep knows he's come up with a brilliant idea, which he can develop and perfect over the coming months. Three at the back and two in organising midfield with the emphasis on Cancelo, his radical free electron.

MOMENT 10. BUILDING FROM THE BACK VIA 3+2
Sheffield, 31 October 2020

Four games crammed into the last ten days of October allow the coach to make small adjustments to the structure of their game.

The infirmary is still full. Nathan Aké, with a groin problem, adds to the numerous absences and, since John Stones is looking a bit hesitant on the ball at the minute, the coach chooses Eric García to partner Dias in the centre of defence in City's first Champions League game this season. They are playing Porto at the Etihad.

Porto line up in a 5–3–2, turning the first half into a very slow, dull show, without anything approaching brilliance. City handle possession comfortably, but only really do so in their own half. Their 70 per cent possession is deceptive because they don't really penetrate the Portuguese armour and, in fact, are forced into committing nine fouls simply to cut off potential counterattacks from the visitors.

Rúben Dias, frustrated by the stalemate, risks a vertical pass but it's badly executed and contributes to Porto's opening goal, thanks to a sharp, daring invention by Luis Díaz, who dribbles past the entire local defence, wrongfooting them to conjure up the 1–0. Immediately, however, City counterattack and a Mahrez effort is steered at goal by Gündoğan but it smacks off the post. Drama follows drama as in the very next skirmish Pepe fouls Sterling. Penalty. Agüero shoots low to the right of goalkeeper Agustín Marchesín, who fingertips the effort but simply can't prevent the goal. The equaliser doesn't seem to inspire City to up their game and the next important moment comes when Porto almost make it 2–1 but Walker averts disaster just as the visitors are starting to celebrate what should be a goal.

The second half is very different. Porto are suddenly stymied and don't manage a single threat on goal. City, now much more aggressive in their attacking, accumulate good chances until Gündoğan's terrific free kick from the edge of the area brings the dividend. The ball flies into the top corner and Pep immediately breathes a sigh of relief. It's the first of the season for the small midfielder, who, in the coming months, will discover his previously hidden penchant for goalscoring.

The match has become rough and intense. And very aggressive. But a few minutes later Ferran Torres grabs the spotlight with a good dribble and a magnificent shot inside the penalty area to give City an insurmountable 3–1 lead. There are more chances – Mahrez forces a good save and Rodri hits the post. Then, in the 93rd minute, having only been on the pitch for eight minutes, Fernandinho suffers a severe groin injury, which will keep him out of action until the end of November.

One more casualty. The infirmary is still limping room only …

Seventy-two hours later, the team turns up at the London Stadium with the bare minimum bench resources and a very young Cole Palmer in the match squad. Pep's men appear to be on effervescent form at the start, but they create too few chances and, in fact, it's the Hammers who score with their first visit to Ederson's penalty box. Michail Antonio overpowers Rúben Dias and scores with an extraordinary overhead kick. Following the Porto error it's a second consecutive setback for the Portuguese defender.

West Ham are about to enjoy a good season, and will emerge as one of the most aggressive teams in the English competition, but that's not on display just yet and, after Antonio's goal, they close ranks in a rigid 5–4–1. David Moyes's team put huge effort into blocking all the inside passing lines, with the result that there's a flow of errors in passes initiated by Dias and Eric García. The absence of key players is being acutely felt by City. They're really missing Laporte, who can change the orientation of a game with his long, accurate passing, De Bruyne, who could help break the opponent's lines, and Gabriel Jesus, whose aggressive pressing of the back four would be a godsend today.

Agüero can't continue after the break, a victim of hamstring pain, something which is about to become a constant frustration for him. Foden's entry, however, palpably increases City's fizz and energy – a goal seems inevitable now. Cancelo makes the crucial incursion down the left flank and his service is controlled and finished off on the half-turn by Foden.

Coming away with a draw doesn't feel like a great result given that, with only eight points from five games, this has now become City's worst start since 2014. However, by the end of the season, City's coaching staff will look back on this as a good result and a significant turning point in their season.

The other plus point is the clear evidence that Cancelo is becoming a ubiquitous and influential presence in midfield. He will become the most essential components of the team this season.

There's no question though. City aren't in good shape. Too few wins, too few points, too few goals. Three straight Premier League matches scoring only once per game – it's unknown for such an offensive team. Moreover, Agüero's hamstring problem means their goal machine will be missing for several weeks, with De Bruyne's return to fitness representing the only counterbalance.

There's no respite, though, and three days later City visit Marseille's Stade Vélodrome, where they break the curse of never having won on French soil. They absolutely dominate an ultra-defensive Marseille, who only manage to shine at the start of the second half. Ferran Torres is playing at centre-forward tonight and demonstrates how comfortable he is in the position. Marseille are making a lot of errors and De Bruyne exploits this to create the opener for Torres, whose special ability inside the area makes him more effective there than in his usual position as a winger. His is City's 600th goal under Guardiola.

In the 75th minute, Foden's creative burst and cross is moved on by Sterling's header and finished off by Gündoğan. With each passing appearance, the German's efficacy as a creative, attacking midfielder is becoming more evident. He has a talent for arriving at exactly the right moment in the opposition's area to produce goals and assists. Finally, one of De Bruyne's trademark killer passes sets Sterling up to get the third. The Champions League charge is well on track.

This has been Guardiola's 106th game with City in which the team have scored three or more goals. A stellar record.

Next: Bramall Lane on a windy and cold midday, not a great setting in which to shine. Sheffield United present them with a five-man defence and an unshakeable determination to protect their young goalkeeper, Aaron Ramsdale. Three City players stand out, apparently undaunted by the solid defensive wall facing them. Sterling zooms up and down the left wing with the electricity of his best days, Walker imperiously patrols a stadium he knows well because he grew up in it, and Torres flits in and around United's area with the air of someone brimming with confidence.

Despite the number of injuries, this team is somehow gradually moving through the gears towards cruising speed. Can it be because they have De Bruyne back? Answers on a postcard.

But, once again, Cancelo emerges as the differential factor. Guardiola persists in his idea of generating a clean build-up using his 3+2 idea, three defenders plus two midfielders, a structure in which the Portuguese is fundamental due to his skill, speed and intelligence. Cancelo laps this up – not only does he facilitate the build-up, but his contribution to the attack is enormous. In the first half alone he creates five scoring chances.

City keep their opponents under constant siege for 45 minutes and create lots of very clear opportunities: a cross from Cancelo headed by Torres; a long shot from Rodri; a terrific pass from Sterling that Torres, at point-blank range, hits against the goalkeeper; a direct free kick from De Bruyne that brushes the post; a quick counterattack by Mahrez plus De Bruyne setting up Torres, who's goalbound effort is cleared by a defender ... It takes the prodigal son, Kyle Walker, to finalise a good Sterling–Cancelo–De Bruyne move. The burly defender's shot from outside the area is unstoppable, low and hard across United's goalkeeper and into the corner of the net: 0–1.

The second half is a repetition – irresistible force against an almost immovable object. The sun blinks out for a moment on the freezing day and Torres shoots, Ramsdale deflects, Mahrez shoots from a free kick, Ramsdale saves, De Bruyne's free kick hits the post ... Then, across three mad minutes, between the 66th and 70th, the Blades have three good chances to level but they miss one and Ederson blocks the other two.

City are fighting like crazy in difficult circumstances and are gradually beginning to see the light. But they're still very far from where they should be in the league table.

MOMENT 11. PEP RENEWS

Manchester, 20 January 2021

Eighty days later, City sit third in the Premier League, four points behind Manchester United and with a game in hand. Despite appearances, not the best scenario.

At the end of November, Pep Guardiola renewed his contract, which was due to expire the following summer. This extension is for two more years, until June 2023, as had been Txiki Begiristain's intention when I spoke to him months ago, when he said it would be the perfect outcome.

Instead of five years at City, Pep's now going to be here for seven: an inarguable indication that he feels comfortable, well supported and happy in his work. You need time to build a legacy of true quality and, until now, the Catalan has denied himself a lengthy stay at the clubs he's managed. At times, he's seemed like his own worst enemy. Acting too hastily and leaving too soon because of anxiety, anguish or in response to the stress and disappointments that come with the job. Or perhaps because of the successes? His first big coaching job, in charge of Barcelona, was the football equivalent of conquering Everest, and it's that metaphor he always uses whenever he expresses doubt about being able to improve on past achievements. But now he has given himself time. It's the best decision he's ever made: bucking the trends of a fast-paced society and giving himself the luxury of time.

Between November, December and most of January, the team play 19 games and only lose one, at Tottenham (2–0). They draw with Liverpool, Porto, Manchester United and West Bromwich Albion, winning the remaining 14 games, so they are third in the league. They are also finalists for the fourth time in the League Cup, paired with Borussia Mönchengladbach in the round of 16 in the Champions League and are at full tilt in the FA Cup. Not bad for a season that began with general dejection, abundant casualties and some very low-key performances.

Playing out in a 3+2 is now their go-to build-up. It's become as familiar and effective as the 4–4–2 shape with which they defend when they don't have the ball. These are structures that Pep has tinkered with and developed to give his players greater freedom to achieve their attacking potential.

Without Sané's blistering pace, City counterattack less effectively, but the other creative components look increasingly fluid and dangerous.

'Since the Newcastle game we've really started to play well,' Pep tells me, recalling the 2–0 win on Boxing Day. In fact, it's not fundamentally the goals or the results that keep him so encouraged, but the perception that the team is growing in the exact direction he intends. Building attacks from the backline with confidence and clarity, a 'free electron' as the team's second midfielder, a Yugoslav-style defensive attitude, players who feel they can take the initiative without waiting for instructions to be given to them from the touchline …

I'm not suggesting, of course, that they haven't had bumps along the way before getting to this point. Not so long ago Pep was in his office, surrounded by all his *consiglieri* facing a long, dark night of crisis talks …

MOMENT 12. ON A CRISIS FOOTING

One month earlier … Manchester, 15 December 2020

It's 2.15am on a cold, dark December morning. The lights in the Sportcity car park go on and the security guard stationed at the northern end of the complex makes a note in the logbook, 'The boss. Leaving for the night.'

The automatic gates slide open to let Guardiola and other members of the technical team leave. They've just come from Pep's office where they've been since 11.30pm, having watched the team produce a miserable 1–1 draw against West Brom. It looks like they've just kissed goodbye to any chance of regaining the title from Liverpool. They're now ninth after 13 games.

Pep's down in the dumps. Again. They've talked for almost three hours. About everything: the disastrous result; the performance of specific players and the group as a whole; their tactical moves … It's another kick in the teeth. Probably even worse than the Leicester screw-up in September, given the relative weakness of today's opponent.

Food has been laid on – pasta, Parmesan cheese, some cold cuts – but no one's really interested. There's an air of total despondency. Their hopes and plans for this season have just come crashing down. They're now on a crisis footing.

Estiarte's looking for the positives: 'This isn't the end. The league's got a long way to go. It's not a normal year and we're going to find that nothing's the way we expect it to be. Everyone's going to be losing points. Mark my words. We're not the only ones going through this. Liverpool are going to lose a lot of points too and I don't think anyone's going to get over 85 points in the league this season. I bet 80 points would do it this year. There's no way you're going to see anyone getting 100 points like the last three seasons. That's what we should be aiming for, 80 points, not 100. I think that will be more than enough. Then, if we get our heads down and fight for every point, we'll definitely be in with a chance.'*

Pep wants to focus on the lessons to be learned from today's game. He thinks his men became a bit disoriented. After hours of discussion they reach a consensus: it's back to basics. Wingers staying wide and open, one player as the pivot with Cancelo helping him on the inside, two creative midfielders who move between lines, either supporting the pivot or moving up into the opposition area. Agüero won't be back to full fitness any time soon so they'll put a midfielder in as lead striker, although he'll actually be acting as a false 9. And then? Passing, passing, passing. City will once again be all about passing the ball.

Which is where they've got to by 1am and everyone's feeling a bit better, particularly after Estiarte's comments. Pep's already thinking about those 80 points. If they can get back to consistently producing quality football, maybe they'll make the 80 points and be in contention for the title.

Then Lillo pipes up: 'I've no idea why you're all so worried. We're going to win everything this year. The league for sure and maybe even the Champions League.' He says it as if it's the most obvious thing in the world. He's not joking and he's definitely not just trying to cheer everyone up. He's completely serious. 'Look, we've got a team of superb players. They just need to reconnect with the game, to start feeling totally invested again. We need them relaxed and comfortable with what they're doing so that they go in to games feeling calm and confident, not tense and overwhelmed. If we're a bit more chilled, they will be too. If we manage that, we'll win at least two competitions, if not more.'

Total silence.

---

* Estiarte's predictions were spot-on. The 2020–1 title winner finished on 86 points, the runners-up on 74 and third place 69.

Each of them has his own opinion of what Lillo's just said but no one's going to openly contradict him. Some of them don't agree. He's exaggerating, building castles in the air, kidding himself. But others are immediately on side: City have everything they need to win trophies. They just have to impose a bit of calm so that the players go into games clear-headed and confident. As they head home for the night, those members of the coaching team are feeling much happier, convinced they've just heard Lillo make a 100 per cent accurate prediction. The rest, still unconvinced, are asking themselves, *Is he off his head?*

Pep calls the meeting to an end at 2.15 and drives home. Most of his staff do likewise. Lillo wanders off to spend the night in his bedroom at the training ground: room no. 30. He said what needed to be said.

Onwards and upwards.

MOMENT 13. VICTORY AT ANFIELD

Liverpool, 7 February 2021

Pep's delighted with their resounding victory over Liverpool although the 4–1 would have been even sweeter in a packed stadium. 'Next time we win at Anfield, let's hope we can do it with the stadium full of supporters.' Liverpool haven't managed the eviscerating, high-speed demolition they usually dish out and, in the first 20 minutes, City take control of the game.

Pep has favoured a cautious approach today. This is one opponent with whom you don't take any chances. City bring the ball out in a 3+3 with Stones–Dias–Zinchenko in central defence and Cancelo–Rodrigo–Silva in behind the Reds' attacking/pressing line. Cancelo's positioning has thrown Mané, who doesn't know whether to station himself near the centre circle to mark him or stick to his wing duties. If he stays close to Cancelo, it allows Stones to combine with Mahrez on the right wing. If he doesn't mark him, it leaves Cancelo free to receive Rúben Dias's passes. Klopp's spotted the problem, though, and moves Andy Robertson up the field. It does the trick and, 20 minutes in, Liverpool begin to assert themselves.

Now, City begin to look a bit ineffectual. The idea behind the 4–3–3 is that they have lots of players on the inside to attack Liverpool's central zone, but, when they have the ball, they're failing to find the right combinations. The fact that Sterling and Mahrez are 'tucked in', as per Pep's instructions, also signifies that any decent diagonal ball in behind them risks releasing one of Liverpool's rampaging full-backs, although their crosses into the box will still encounter the solid wall named Stones–Dias.

Around 38 minutes in, Fabinho fouls Sterling and Gündoğan takes the penalty. The ball sails over the crossbar. It's the third penalty City have missed against Liverpool out of the last four they've taken.*

City haven't had a single shot at goal in the first half. Liverpool have had two: Ederson manages to save Firmino's shot and Mané's header is too high. At half-time the technical team discuss how to change the structure of the team and stop the advance of Klopp's full-backs. Pep, Lillo and Borrell consider a 4–5–1 but in the end opt for a 4–4–2. Without the ball, Foden and Bernard Silva will be up front. And Sterling and Mahrez will now move back beside Rodri and Gündoğan.

They make the changes in the second half and things click. They block Liverpool's attack and start to dominate the game without exposing themselves to any more threat. Gündoğan scores the opener following clever overload down Trent Alexander-Arnold's wing – the England international has looked hassled and harried the entire game. Then, Rúben Dias, who seems below par today, makes an uncharacteristic error by failing to clear a long ball from Liverpool's central defence. Penalty to Liverpool. Salah equalises.

Pep puts Gabriel Jesus on and everything changes. His aggressive pressing combined with Silva's and Foden's efforts forces Alisson, Fabinho and Georginio Wijnaldum into mistakes, which give City three more goals in just ten minutes (from the 73rd to the 83rd). Gündoğan gets his ninth goal of the season and Sterling his hundredth since Pep took over. He's the third player to have scored 100 goals under Guardiola (Messi 211, Agüero 120).

It's Pep's first victory at Anfield. City haven't won here since 2003. They now have ten points more than the Reds, having played one game less. It's also the first time since 1937 that the Citizens have scored four at Anfield. This is City's 14th consecutive victory across all competitions and their 10th win in a

---

* Mahrez missed at Anfield on 7 October 2018; De Bruyne scored at the Etihad on 2 July 2020 and missed at home on 8 November 2020.

row in the league. All of which adds to the record they broke just a few days ago when they became the first English side to win all nine of their games in January.

Whenever the team pull off a big win Pep likes to point out the areas in which his players can improve. Today, Phil Foden's under the spotlight. 'Phil didn't press well in the first half. Sometimes, when I put him in midfield, he seems not to fully understand what I expect of him. He's going to need to work on that.'

MOMENT 14. 'KÜNDOĞAN'
Manchester, 13 February 2021

City haven't played six consecutive matches at home without conceding since 1902. Today they beat Mourinho's Spurs, who were the last team to defeat Pep, three months ago. Back then, at the end of November, Spurs were at the top of the league with an eight-point advantage over the Citizens, who were 13th – closer to the relegation zone than to the top of the board.

City have made some radical changes and improved dramatically in the weeks and months since that miserable night in London. They've upped the quality and complexity of their game, in terms of defensive strength and scoring efficiency. And they're on a winning streak. Today makes it 16 consecutive victories across all competitions and their 11th consecutive league win. They now have a comfortable lead in the title race and are 14 points ahead of Spurs. In three months, they've accumulated 22 points more than the north London side.

The performances of one player in particular stand out: İlkay Gündoğan, City's new, improved unstoppable goal machine. Pep's not surprised: 'I said he'd make a good false 9 and people laughed. Today he got us the penalty and scored two goals. He was our best player in January and is well on his way to repeating that in February.'

Pep's not the only one who's noticed. Gündoğan is the Premier League's player of the month for February, the first City player to win that award twice in a row. For his own achievement of six wins in six games, Pep is February's Premier League coach of the month, having received the same honour in January.

The team has established a consistent style of play. They alternate between a 3+2 and a 2+3 in bringing the ball out, defend in a 4–4–2 or 4–3–3 and attack highly defensive teams with an aggressive 2–3–5 with Bernardo Silva and Gündoğan using the channels between the full-backs and central defenders. Sometimes, like today, playing two inverted wingers, Foden (on the right) and Sterling (on the left), hampers the fluidity of their attack because, as they move inwards onto their stronger foot they inevitably draw defenders to them and lose any chance to take a shot at goal. Today marks Foden's 50th Premier League victory out of 59 games, equalling Aymeric Laporte's record.

City are awarded a penalty and Rodri takes it. Given their poor record in this area, none of his teammates are demanding the ball from him. Pep's well aware that penalty taking has become something of a bête noire for his men: 'We need to give this some thought. I really admire Rodri's courage even though his penalty wasn't the best …' Indeed, Lloris comes very close to stopping the low shot from the Spanish midfielder, who chooses not to follow the advice Ederson tried to give him via Bernardo Silva: 'Goalies tend to know the weaknesses of their counterparts and Ederson passed on one of Lloris's weak points but I preferred not to follow his advice and just did my own thing.'

The ball hits the back of the net and Pep makes the most of their solid advantage by changing his wingers' positions. They swap sides, thereby doing away with the bottleneck that keeps building up in the opposition's area. City's dominance also means that Sterling is no longer fixed in one position and can move creatively around Spurs' penalty box. Which is exactly how their next goal arrives. Sterling dribbles across the attacking line, moving from right to left, passing to Foden who filters the ball into the box so that Gündoğan can toe-poke in off his left foot.

Then, 15 minutes later, as Spurs increase their high pressing, Ederson and Gündoğan produce a little magic of their own. While all his centrebacks are being blocked by Spurs' pressing, Ederson calmly makes a long, box-to-box pass, thumping the ball 80m up the pitch to Gündoğan, who, despite Davinson Sánchez breathing down his neck, controls it exquisitely, produces a couple of dribbles and then deftly cuts the ball across Lloris as the French keeper bursts out of his goal towards him. A technical masterpiece.

It's Gündoğan's 11th league goal of the season (13 across all competitions) and his 9th across the 9 matches they've played so far this year. Minutes later, because of some groin pain, he asks to be subbed off. It's one of the things Guardiola really appreciates about these players: their willingness to own up to any pain or discomfort that might develop into a more serious injury. He's always insisted that his players be honest about even the slightest signs of muscle problems or fatigue. Professional footballers have a tendency to play down injuries for fear of losing their place in the team and Pep has put a lot of effort into persuading them that it's better to stop and sit out the next few days in order to recuperate from pain or fatigue. It's much better to take a short rest, even if that means missing a couple of matches, than risk a long, serious injury. He's always rewarded players who have been honest with him and does his best to ensure they don't lose their place in the team. Which is why he's so full of praise for Gündoğan: 'He's been very smart. He preferred not to take any chances and risk a more serious injury.'

On the subject of injuries, Sergio Agüero deserves a mention. He hasn't featured in the starting 11 for four months, since West Ham on 24 October. On the plus side, his absence has allowed Gabriel Jesus to flourish – he's now the only player to have scored in the Premier League, the Champions League, the FA Cup and the League Cup in 2018–19, 2019–20 and 2020–1. And Jesus isn't the only alternative at Pep's disposal. So far, he's used Foden, Bernardo Silva, De Bruyne, Mahrez and Ferran Torres up front either as lone strikers, or in a fusion of the striker, playmaker and the false 9, with the aim of achieving superiority in the middle of the field.

Gündoğan definitely emerges as the star of today's spectacular performance and has earned a new nickname. Step forward 'Kündoğan'.

This is the 118th match under Pep (44 per cent of the 269 games managed by the Catalan) in which City have scored three or more goals. An incredible achievement.

MOMENT 15. SIXTEEN POINTS IN TEN DAYS

Manchester, 18 February 2021

It's 9am and Txiki Begiristain is sitting down to his usual breakfast: *pan con tomate* with sliced ham. The director of football has breakfast every morning with Guardiola and Estiarte in the canteen on the first floor of the first team's building. They tend to grab the table nearest Estiarte's office and then get down to addressing the big issues of the day.

The working hours of Pep's staff vary enormously – their timetables as different as the menus prepared by chef Jorge. Lillo, for example, gets up at 5.30 and is at Sportcity by 6am. He always carries a crate of bottled water up to his office, which is next to Pep's, and dumps it on a low shelf so that it's available for everyone to help themselves. A bit like a water carrier for a professional cycling team. Then he makes a cup of maté (a type of herbal tea) for himself, something he'll do throughout the day. Lillo's office will eventually become the central nervous system of the coaching team. Mainly because they all love him so much – he's like everyone's dad – and also because his endless supplies of water keep them all hydrated.

Next to arrive is the goalkeeping coach, Xabier Mancisidor. He's a quiet guy who likes to keep a low profile but is hugely respected and valued by the rest of the team. He doesn't say much but, when he does offer his opinion, it always makes sense. Estiarte is another early bird, unlike Pep, who only comes in at the crack of dawn if there's a specific reason to do so. On those occasions he likes to tell everyone, 'I did a Lillo today.'

The team got back to Manchester at 1am after yesterday's win at Goodison Park so today they've scheduled their breakfast meeting a bit later. Lillo's up with the sparrows as usual, though. He slept at Sportcity last night and has been up for hours drinking maté in his office, working on various ideas for training sessions.

Yesterday's game against Everton, originally scheduled for 28 December, was postponed after several players tested positive for coronavirus.*

In the eight subsequent weeks City have hit fantastic form, winning every match, while Everton have struggled to maintain any kind of consistency. They've had some huge successes: a 3–3 draw at Old Trafford, victories at Leeds and Wolves, plus an FA Cup win against Spurs. But they've also lost at home to West Ham, Newcastle and Fulham. There's no doubt Carlo Ancelotti and his men come into today's game against league leaders Manchester City with some trepidation.

---

* Walker and Jesus fell ill on 23 December and five days later Ederson, García, Torres, Tommy Doyle and Cole Palmer were also diagnosed with COVID-19, followed by Agüero on 8 January.

And all their worst fears are realised. City are sensational. Despite the absence of their star player, İlkay Gündoğan, Pep's men hardly put a foot wrong. His three centre-backs (Walker, Dias and Laporte) are positioned wide across the pitch with Cancelo moving from the left to support Rodri in the build-up. As usual, Rúben Dias's leadership skills come to the fore and the hierarchy within City's defensive line is clear. Dias has already played a vital role in John Stones's impressive comeback and he's also managed to impose some control over Walker, who is prone to accelerating moves too soon and is now more considered and calm on the pitch. Having spotted Laporte's occasional lapses in concentration, Dias has also taken steps to ensure that everyone understands the need for maximum focus, regardless of how naturally talented they believe themselves to be. Dias, as the undisputed leader of City's defence, demands nothing less than total concentration. From the first to the final whistle.

The main idea behind positioning the three centre-backs in such an 'open' formation is so that they cover the width of the pitch. Pep has refined this approach in other games and in training sessions. It helps his defenders dilute and disperse the efforts of the opposition forwards and it opens up central passing lines so that they can more easily feed the ball to City's midfielders in the build-up. Once the action moves to the opponent's half, Cancelo joins Bernardo Silva and Foden in organising the attack, thereby achieving the superiority across the zones that Pep is always looking for. Cancelo positions himself next to Rodri, which then allows the creative midfielders freedom to join them 'inside' or move up towards the forwards. In essence, the formation when City are playing through the midfield is a 3–4–3 with built-in flexibility. Cancelo's role as second pivot or 'false interior' is fundamental to the team's strategy. His ability to fulfil this triple function (he reverts to the role of full-back if City need to defend in numbers) is essential for the creative midfielders to 'break' lines towards the opposing goal in the knowledge that they are totally protected in behind. Then the team moves into their usual formation, a 3–2–2–3 with Mahrez and Sterling pinned to the touchlines on their wings.

It's this strategy that helps City demolish Everton, who barely manage to complete 150 passes in the first half and 156 in the second. The Citizens' total dominance results in countless incursions into Everton's penalty box, most of which, unfortunately, they don't convert. Foden finally takes advantage of a succession of rebounds, following a corner, to score the opener but Everton equalise five minutes later when Mahrez and Walker fail to coordinate effectively to stop Richarlison scoring.

Guardiola uses the half-time break to make adjustments and asks Bernardo Silva to move closer to Mahrez on the right wing. He also instructs everyone to focus more on passing. Post-match he insists: 'Sometimes we're in too much of a rush! Especially when we are close to finalising a move and scoring. Look at our second goal. The situation wasn't clear so they made a few more extra passes. That was perfect.'

As a result, in the second half, City make even more passes: 414 compared to 339 in the first half. The aim is to establish clear lines of players in each zone, which then allow them to easily identify and feed the 'third man'. Bernardo Silva, Mahrez and Gabriel Jesus, in particular, produce a masterclass of clean, accurate passing, which leads to City's second and third goals and effectively finishes Everton off.

It's the first time since 1981 that City have beaten Liverpool and Everton, one immediately after the other, in their own stadiums. And Pep's men are still breaking records. Seventeen victories across all competitions, 12 in the Premier League and the 10th win this year. Something no other club has ever achieved.* Bernardo Silva in particular has played an absolute blinder today, achieving 94 per cent accuracy in the 61 passes he's made. 'Everything he does, he does brilliantly,' Pep tells me. 'Bernardo the Unstoppable is back!' Behind him, Rodri has also been fantastic, proving how far he's come from the hesitant performances he produced last year.

Now they have a couple of days training and then two important away games. First of all, it's Arsenal, then they face Borussia Mönchengladbach in Budapest. Any match in London can bring surprising complications. For example, making the journey from Stamford Bridge to Luton Airport can easily take an hour and a half. Which often sparks the argument: 'Why not simply continue and make the entire return trip to Manchester by bus?' Pep's doggedly against it. More than three hours stuck in a bus

---

* Bolton Wanderers in 1909 and Manchester United in 2009 won nine games in a row at the start of the year.

would risk his players' muscles stiffening up and could easily result in more serious injuries.

The Catalan has never forgotten the journey from hell they experienced in his first season with City. They'd just played their 3pm kick-off against Crystal Palace at Selhurst Park and were heading to Biggin Hill Airport late in the afternoon. Halfway there, the team manager, Marc Boixasa, gets a call from the pilot. There's a fault in the aeroplane and it won't be fixed before 9pm, which is when the airport closes. They're going to have to catch a train. The frantic race is now on to get to Euston Station for the last Manchester-bound train of the day. But this is London. With depressing inevitability, they hit a horrendous traffic jam and get to the station with just ten minutes to spare, not nearly enough time to unload all the equipment required for a group of 70 players and staff. They try, but fail, to persuade the Virgin train conductor to open the doors and let them board, and the entire party is left on the platform watching the last train home pull out of the station. There's nothing else for it. They're all going to have to stay the night in a hotel.

Pep learned a hard lesson that day back in November 2016 and these days he always approaches their London fixtures with extreme caution. Leaving nothing to chance, he checks and rechecks the travel plans and accommodation that Boixasa has arranged. In particular, he wants to know well in advance where they'll be staying and likes to give his own feedback on any hotel the team visit. He was particularly delighted when, on one visit to Watford, he discovered that they'd booked Sopwell House, the hotel Barcelona used in 2011 when they beat Manchester United in the Champions League. Great place. Great memories.

But the London trip is still two days away and right now he's focused on the breakfast meeting. As the coffee is served, Pep, Estiarte and Begiristain all have their eyes fixed on the canteen's television screens. They're showing the league table: City are top on 56 points with United and Leicester their closest rivals on 46. Txiki breaks the silence: 'Remember when we hadn't even made it into the top half? If we'd lost that game at Anfield ten days ago, right now Liverpool would be 4 points behind us. Now we're 16 ahead of them. In just ten days …'

The conversation moves on. Txiki and Pep evaluate the various candidates to replace Sergio Agüero next season. Leo Messi's name doesn't come up …

MOMENT 16. AN ARMOURED CAR

Budapest, 24 February 2021

It takes three attempts and less than a minute for Sterling to turn the game in London.

Minute 40. Sterling's in position, a couple of metres from Arsenal's goal. He takes the shot. And misses. He tries again. Another miss. Thirty-five seconds later Mahrez gently flicks the ball in his direction. Sterling goes for the header, sending the ball straight into the back of the net. City 1 Arsenal 0. The only goal of the match.

It's taken less than a minute to finish the Londoners off.

Pep's using a 3–2–2–3 again today. His central defenders (Stones–Dias–Zinchenko) are very open again, positioned across the entire width of the pitch in order to stretch the press of their opponent's attacking line. In front of them, Fernandinho and Cancelo will complete the build-up, thereby liberating De Bruyne, Gündoğan and Bernardo Silva to move freely around the pitch. Mahrez and Sterling are once again pinned to the wings with the aim of dividing Arsenal's defensive line. Pep hasn't included an outright striker today. He wants to achieve superiority in the centre of the pitch and there are up to five of his players there at any one time. This strategy leaves Arsenal's centre-backs with nothing to do.

Mikel Arteta has instructed his men to mark City's midfielders one-on-one during the construction phase. Saka sticks to Cancelo, and Martin Ødegaard to Fernandinho, so that Pep's three centre-backs are forced to bring the ball out without their help. They have two options. Aim directly for the opposition box or risk passing through balls all the way to Bernardo Silva or De Bruyne.

Arteta's got it spot-on. He understands City's game inside out and knows exactly how to mess with the Citizens' build-up. It works beautifully and his team begin to dominate half an hour in. He's been particularly prescient in instructing left-back Kieran Tierney to attack Cancelo and the two players are often left one vs one as Arsenal attack. The weakness of City's 4–3–3 defensive formation also lets Granit Xhaka turn easily on the ball and organise the Gunners' attack.

At half-time Pep alters how they press. Silva and Mahrez must now relentlessly close down Arsenal's keeper, Leno, and Cancelo must press Tierney as high up the pitch as possible. The Gunners don't manage a single shot at goal in the entire second half. Pep's particularly pleased with Fernandinho, 'My God, did you see Fernandinho? What a game he had.' Rúben Dias's leadership skills are once again in evidence today. In the 65th minute a poor header from Stones puts the ball out of play. Then, when Stones, playing his 100th game under Pep, redeems himself within seconds, Dias trots over to give him a congratulatory slap on the back. Shrewd leadership.

There are more records today: 18 consecutive victories across all competitions, 11 wins away from home, a stat which equals their achievements in May–November 2017. It's also their eighth victory in a row over Arsenal in the Premier League. They've accumulated 33 points since the turn of the year, more than Tottenham, Liverpool and Arsenal combined (31). For the 23rd time in 38 games this season, City haven't conceded. They achieved the same number last season too, over 59 games. In the 25 league games they've played, their opponents have managed a total of just 55 shots at Ederson's goal.

Pep's men are still feeling pretty pleased with themselves when, several hours later, they land in Budapest for the Borussia Mönchengladbach tie. They've been forced to play the game here because Germany's current COVID regulations prevent the English team entering the country.

Here, in the Puskás Arena, João Cancelo looks for all the world like a budding Philipp Lahm. Maybe he's even an upgrade in one or two areas. The Portuguese has superb technical ability and a natural attacking spirit. The accuracy of his passing is becoming legendary and he's also highly effective in front of goal. But he differs from the great German captain in several respects. His vision of the game is less panoramic, he doesn't defend with the same tenacity and tends to take too many risks in terms of control and passing. It's that same tendency to take risks that often finds him moving out of position. He definitely has a way to go before true overall comparisons can be drawn with Lahm but Cancelo obviously believes he can get there.

Today, City play with a level of harmony that we haven't really seen before and it feels like we may well be witnessing Pep's greatest creation to date. Back at Barcelona, Guardiola based his positional play on the unique abilities of Xavi, Busquets, Iniesta and Messi to coordinate their moves with unmatched precision and elegance. Their quality took that Barcelona side right to the top of world football.

At Bayern he got close to repeating the same phenomenon, although without bringing everything to full fruition, with players whose ability sets were opposed to the style of play he wanted to achieve. There, he based almost everything on Bayern's exceptional wingers, their dribbling and the team's finishing power.

Then, here in Manchester, he moulded and shaped the 100-point Centurions, blending David Silva's control with Sané's pace and Agüero's ability to score from any angle. He's also transformed De Bruyne into the superb playmaker he has become. Today, his men switch easily between tough physicality and smooth, rhythmic football, alternating between blistering speed and calm, measured control. If the Centurions were a convertible sports car tearing up the motorway, his 'Yugoslavs' are an armoured car demolishing everything in its wake. If Barça danced to the sound of violins and Bayern to the rhythm of trombones, then City have the entire orchestra behind them, producing exquisite music with aplomb and style.

It's Cancelo who leads the symphony today, moving backwards and forwards while his teammates instinctively organise themselves around him. They've shed the precise, almost mathematical organisation that Guardiola imposed in his first few years. Under Lillo's influence, Guardiola has loosened his Germanic tendency to direct and control, and is now allowing a level of anarchic creativity, which has benefited their game both in terms of the amount of freedom his players have as well as their performances. Pep's team is less of an automaton these days. Having cast aside some of the more robotic tendencies, the group has become 'humanised' – which will inevitably result in the occasional mistake, but will also take them to greater heights.

Cancelo is undoubtedly City's star performer today: 118 touches on the ball, 91 per cent passing accuracy, 7 duels won, 100 per cent accuracy in long passes, 8 interventions in the penalty box, 1 assist and 1 pre-assist. He's striking all the right notes.

City maintain the 3–2–2–3 as they bring the ball out, moving to a 3–3–4 for the attack. Without the ball, they press using two different approaches: for high pressing, it's a 4–2–4, but in the centre of the pitch it's a 4–3–3. The symphony is close to perfection and it's just their finishing that needs finetuning. The frustration is already showing on the faces of Pep and his assistants. 'We need a bloody goal!'

Gabriel Jesus is a powerhouse: he presses harder than anyone else and reads the game brilliantly, knowing exactly where and when to attack his opponents. He's happy to drop deeper to the centre of pitch to support his teammates, controls the ball superbly and interprets the third-man run in a way that few forwards are capable of. But he's too hesitant in front of goal. He's scored a lot (77 plus 33 assists in 178 games) but his strengths definitely lie in his contribution to the team effort rather than his finishing. Like Sterling, Jesus is more effective in front of goal when he has no time to consider different options. No time to let the nerves get to him. Fifty-three minutes in, he has a golden opportunity. He's alone in the box but instead of taking the shot, he hesitates, looking for the best angle, waiting for the perfect moment, the best way to beat the keeper … and, in the seconds it takes for him to settle on the best option, a German defender is on him and his chance is lost. But look at what happens 11 minutes later. With several German defenders bearing down on him, he calmly receives Silva's header and, with the sole of his boot, taps the ball home for City's second goal, leaving the Gladbach keeper slack-jawed and helpless. For this particular Brazilian, less thinking means more goals.

Cancelo is decisive to both this and Bernardo Silva's earlier goal. On both occasions he twists on the right-hand side of the box, cuts a chip away from the Gladbach line of defenders and finds Silva, who's in the form of his life today. The Portuguese then produces two superb headers, the first straight into the back of the net and the second to Jesus for the goal. Silva is daring, explosive, aggressive and tireless. So fundamental that Pep is considering ways of keeping him in the team even after De Bruyne's return. The Portuguese has played a part in eight of the goals (three goals and five assists) scored over the last ten games.

Guardiola has just clinched his 28th victory in the Champions League knockout rounds, edging ahead of Alex Ferguson, José Mourinho and Carlo Ancelotti. The team has already secured 19 consecutive victories, 12 away from home, another English record. They've played four Champions League games in a row away from home without conceding a single goal. Only Manchester United have ever done this before (2010–11).

Armed to the teeth and ready for battle, the 'Yugoslavs' tank division rolls on. They're taking no prisoners.

MOMENT 17. RODRI: OMNIPRESENT AND OMNIPOTENT

Manchester, 2 March 2021

Neither West Ham nor Wolverhampton manage to slow down the relentless 'Yugoslav' progress.

'That was one of those victories that spurs you on and replenishes your energy,' comments Lillo as he leaves the Etihad dressing room after a tough game against West Ham (2–1). We may have just witnessed City's worst performance in the last three months. No other team has succeeded in scoring at the Etihad since 15 December last year when West Brom managed to hold City to a draw. Now, after 629 minutes without conceding, City gift the goal to the visitors. Agüero loses the ball in the centre of the pitch and Ferran Torres fails to mark the tireless Czech full-back Vladimír Coufal, all of which leads to Michail Antonio's brilliant goal.

City are using their customary formations today: 3–2–2–3 when they bring the ball out; 4–3–3 without the ball, alternating with a 4–2–4; and 3–2–2–3 when in full attack mode high up the pitch, which occasionally switches to a 3–3–4. But their usual fluid play is notable for its absence. A few players are definitely off form, most notably Agüero, Torres and De Bruyne, and the aggressive combination of Tomáš Souček and Declan Rice has effectively neutralised Fernandinho, who is also lacking his usual panache. This is their 18th game in two months and everyone's tired. Physically and mentally. Eighteen games in eight weeks is hugely demanding and it's only the stoic commitment of the whole team that is pushing them through.

Central defenders Rúben Dias and John Stones produce the goals in this, their 20th victory in a row. Both men score off the 'second ball' from corners. For a while now, Pep has been happy for his men not to worry too much about the first ball from set pieces and to focus more on the follow-up. Which is why the defenders stay in their opponents' area even when it looks like the set piece is going nowhere. And from today's evidence, that's exactly the right thing to do. In the lead-up to the first, De Bruyne sends a powerful 'banana'-shaped cross flying into West Ham's area. Stones misses it but Dias gets his head to the ball in time and sends it into the goal to open the scoring. Then, 68 minutes in, Mahrez filters a low pass to the penalty spot where

Stones produces an Agüero-esque finish. (Laporte will do something similar in three days' time but his goal will be disallowed by VAR.)

So City's winning streak continues, despite today's game being scheduled for midday. Pep hates kicking off at this time of day, when the pitch is half in the shade. They've pulled off eight victories in eight games this February, six of which have been away from home. A phenomenal achievement.

This is Guardiola's 200th victory with City, out of a total of 273 games, now that the International Football Association Board has declared that those games won through penalty shoot-outs count as draws. It's also his 500th win at the elite level: 179 with Barcelona, 121 with Bayern and now 200 with City; 500 victories out of 681 games. Incredible.

SIMPLICITY WINS THE DAY

'Rodri's at the top of his game. It's like he's omnipresent and omnipotent. He's the player of reference in the middle of the pitch and he's getting better at everything he does. I watch how he plays defensively and he's like a professional fencer who is able to switch instantaneously to the *en garde* position. Bit by bit, he's learned how to anticipate defensively to the point that he's on the verge of greatness.' (Just to clarify, Lillo is using terminology which refers to the kind of parrying techniques used in fencing to avoid an attack from an opponent and in this instance is drawing a comparison with Rodri's defensive moves.)

Lillo has actually been heavily involved in Rodri's ongoing improvement. When he joined City he was already an excellent footballer, blessed with a fantastic physique, but he initially struggled to adapt to Guardiola's game. Used to moving around every area of the pitch, he'd find himself regularly out of position. Like the Forrest Gump of Manchester he ran further and longer than anyone else on the pitch, chasing every ball, mowing his opponents down in the process and, usually, ending up way out of position. Pep, who'd signed him for his excellent potential to play as a positional pivot in midfield, had begun to tear his hair out. Rodri seemed incapable of resisting the impulse to keep running all over the pitch.

This is why Lillo and Pablo Barquero, the player's agent, intervened in the hope of getting him to direct his energies more judiciously. Day after day, the two men worked with Rodri to help him deconstruct everything he'd learned so far in his career and instil in him an understanding of what Pep needs from a pivot in his positional play. Almost immediately, Pep noticed a difference. Rodri was running less and seemed to be playing more intel-ligently, sticking to the theoretical circle in which he was expected to move. Praise began to pour in for a player who had been very harshly criticised in his first season. Nowadays, Rodri wins the ball back more than anyone else in the Premier League and initiates more attacks that lead to shots at goal than any other player. All the patience and hard work have paid off. Rodri is now spectacular in midfield.

•   •   •

For the first 15 minutes City have 86 per cent possession and Wolves barely get a sniff of the ball. Then, an own goal from Leander Dendoncker puts City ahead. No real blame for the poor Belgian, Mahrez's pass was three-quarters of the goal already and if Dendoncker had left it then Sterling would have scored anyway.

Pep reckons this has been one of City's best games this year: 'We played very well. Apart from those five panicky minutes after Wolves scored when we attacked impetuously.' He's been asking his men to 'attack with calm and defend with fury', and Lillo also keeps repeating that the key to any game lies in the rhythm you maintain and your intentions. Pep: 'We need to stick to the process when we attack. More passing, then even more passing. All of it done calmly.'

Rushing into the next move is counterproductive. It creates a false sense of positive momentum and actually leads to mistakes and missed opportu-nities. All of which are borne out when, after the equaliser, Rodri, whose performance is otherwise stellar, rushes things and commits errors. The whole team is desperate to continue their winning streak but his mistakes are careless and give Wolves an opening in which they manage to create two of the few chances they get during the entire game. It's enough to unsettle Pep's men, who struggle to regain the fluid, effective attacking and domina-tion they've achieved over the previous 60 minutes. VAR, which disallows Laporte's goal, and Rui Patrício, who repels shot after shot, ensure that the scoreline doesn't change. With 20 minutes left, Guardiola has a word with Rodri and manages to calm him down. The rudderless boat rights itself and they regain their rhythm and direction.

City dominate from now on, pressing into Wolves' box and eventually producing an avalanche of goals in the last 13 minutes of the game. Clearly, maintaining their rhythm has been the single most important factor in City's victory today. Establishing the right tempo has allowed them to amass passes and corral their opponents in certain areas so that they can finish them off in other parts of the pitch; 41 per cent of the action has taken place in or around Wolves' box, with the visitors taking just one shot on goal. On only the eighth occasion ever in the Premier League, all four of City's goals have been scored without the benefit of an assist. Impressive stats and more records: 21 victories in a row, 15 of which were league games, 28 games unbeaten and 19 straight league games in which they have never gone behind, a record previously held by Arsenal (1998–9).

More importantly, ever since Pep decided to establish a measure of calm in the group, they've gone from strength to strength, proving that they have the energy and unity to keep achieving at this extraordinary rate. Even his rough diamonds are beginning to sparkle. Laporte seems to be back on form, Walker's now playing with greater calm and control, and Gabriel Jesus is a torrent of power and pressing. Only De Bruyne is still not firing on all cylinders. Mahrez's contribution has been sublime. He's definitely at the peak of his powers and Pep's impressed: 'Mahrez is a man who dances with the ball. He never loses it and always comes up with that extra pass. He pulls opponents towards him then passes behind them, crosses terrifically and produces the cleanest of shots. I know what he's capable of, which is why I push him so hard.'

Rodri has developed into the team's quarterback and can be guilty of misdirecting his generosity of spirit and commitment to the team. He's always believed that he contributes the most when he does a lot of running, which usually happens towards the end of each half. He moves up the pitch and he's off, running. But this instinct is exactly what causes him to lose position. Now, he's well on the way to addressing this 'flaw' and learning to moderate his runs.

The 3–2–2–3 formation is extremely adaptable and allows for so many variations that Pep sends up his thanks to Herbert Chapman every night. The following day, both Manchester United and Leicester draw their games, stretching City's lead to 14 and 15 points respectively. Guardiola's third league title win in four years is beginning to take shape and one message is whispered throughout Sportcity: 'We've got this half-won!'

MOMENT 18. BERNARDO IS THE GLUE

Manchester, 7 March 2021

Although Pep was already convinced of Bernardo Silva's importance to the team, today has made it even more apparent. Deciding on the starting 11 has been tougher than usual. De Bruyne desperately needs the playing time as part of his ongoing recuperation but can Pep really do without the man that binds the whole team together?

He's decided to keep Gabriel Jesus as his striker given his excellent performances of late, which have combined passing precision with skilled finishing. So, two good reasons to leave Silva's name off the team sheet.

Later, of course, after being badly beaten by United, the coach will regret this decision. At the time, it seemed like the right call but, in retrospect, the Portuguese is badly missed. They've fallen apart without the man his assistants call 'the glue that binds the whole team together'.

Despite the 2–0 defeat, City have actually performed well today. It's just that United have been better: producing thrilling, effective football and making full use of every opportunity that's come their way. They've brought City's 21-game winning streak to an abrupt halt.

Within the first minute, United put the ball out of play. In a déjà vu of last week against West Ham, the throw-in is directed to City's centre-forward in the middle of the pitch. Today it's Gabriel Jesus who fails to control it. Then, just like last week, the opposition take possession and instantly build towards the opening goal. Furious about his mistake, Jesus chases back, starts to press Martial in City's box, despite him being surrounded by four defenders, and ends up barging the French striker over. The resulting penalty is a kick in the guts for Pep's men, who've looked all over the place in the last ten minutes. They've made it far too easy for United to score and the deficit could have been greater.

They pull themselves together and normal service resumes. United have fielded a particularly challenging formation today. It's a 4–2–3–1 with Fred tight on De Bruyne and Scott McTominay marking Gündoğan. United's double pivots have been able to maintain some distance from each other thanks to Bruno Fernandes and Marcus Rashford, who are doing a stand-up job of neutralising Cancelo's unpredictable and lightning-fast incursions into the centre of the pitch – Pep's secret weapon over the last few months. Luke Shaw's energy and aggression, as he gets in behind the Portuguese full-back, are also causing City problems. But they still produce lots of impressive football, mainly thanks to the skills of their passing triangle on the left: Zinchenko, Gündoğan and Sterling.

In the second half, Gabriel Jesus, who's not having the best of games, sends a glorious pass to Rodri, who hits the crossbar. This is the moment when Shaw takes advantage of Cancelo mistiming his forward press to drive the ball into space behind him and register the Reds' second goal. City keep up the pressure but, despite their 23 shots at goal, fail to turn the game. United's defenders block most of them. Both Sterling and Jesus have had off-days and haven't converted their goal chances. As expected, Kevin De Bruyne is still struggling with match fitness. But Pep has to keep giving him game time. It's the only way any player gets back to full fitness.

The Reds' win gives Ole Gunnar Solskjær his fourth victory over Guardiola and makes him the first United coach ever to have won his first three derbies away to City. City's 21-match winning streak is curtailed, as is their run of 28 consecutive games without conceding more than one goal. Pep's worrying takeaway from today's match is the continued poor performances of Sterling and Gabriel Jesus in front of goal. It's also becoming clear that his team are at their best when they have five men in the centre of the pitch: a full-back, an organising midfielder, two creative midfielders and another man in the false 9 role. Silva is the undisputed master of the false 9 and he's been sorely missed today. What's more, United have produced the perfect antidote to Cancelo, Pep's free electron/full-back/midfielder. Pep's been here before, watching one of his most brilliant tactics being effectively neutralised by a canny opponent. It's back to the drawing board.

Their best performances of January and February have all involved Silva in a key role connecting and harmonising their play, regardless of the position he's officially occupying. Creative midfielder, winger, false 9 … Silva weaves intricate patterns across the pitch and then, like Odysseus' Penelope, unravels those same patterns. No one else even comes close. If De Bruyne is City's 'hammer', never happier than when he's demolishing walls, then Silva has become the thread that weaves their most intricate tapestry. The glue that binds the team together.

MOMENT 19. EGO
Manchester, 10 March 2021

Pep and Raheem Sterling are having words in Pep's office.

Then Sterling's heading out the door with Pep shouting after him, demanding that the player come back. He isn't finished yet.

No one else has witnessed their argument at first hand and Pep's not sharing: 'It was a private conversation between me and the player.' But they've all heard the raised voices and later will piece together what's just happened.

Sterling's dropped. He'll be on the bench tonight against Southampton. Everyone's taken aback. Guardiola makes a point of never justifying his choice of lineup. To anyone. And now he's done just that with Sterling. Today's run-in has been on the cards for a couple of weeks now, ever since Sterling demanded an explanation for his absence from a particular team sheet. Now, Pep's decided to spell out exactly why the Englishman won't be starting this evening: the team's finishing isn't good enough and, after spending several weeks tinkering with his attacking line, this is his solution.

None of which has gone down well with Sterling, who's stormed out of the office twice, only to be called back in again. Then, after several more furious exchanges, a clearly livid Sterling exits, leaving Pep sitting alone in his office. With the lights out. Simmering with rage.

There's nothing outrageous about Pep's decision; it's the kind of call coaches have to make all the time. But Sterling doesn't see it that way. The player seems to consider himself a guaranteed starter, in a league above any of the other forwards, and, so I'm told, has also objected to the way Pep's been talking up De Bruyne and Silva. He feels his own performances merit a similar level of appreciation from the boss.

The bust-up has affected the whole team and Captain Fernandinho is quick to intervene in the hope of calming things down. With limited success.

Pre-match, Pep's still furious and his distraction is obvious as he delivers a rambling team talk and sends his men out to face Southampton. It's deeply unsettling for everyone. Sterling's in attendance but spends the entire game on the bench. Mid-afternoon, the game kicks off on a pitch that is in shameful condition. If the Citizens are looking forward to redeeming what's been a horrible day so far, then the first ten minutes come as a shock. City are dismal and look totally outdone by a Southampton side who are playing out of their skins, retaining most of the possession (69 per cent) during those opening ten minutes. They ruthlessly shut down all passing lanes on the inside, block all the attempts of City's centre-backs to bring the ball out and press City's lines to the point of suffocation.

Fortunately, at least one of Pep's men has kept his head. Zinchenko assesses the situation calmly. It's clear that the visitors' tactics won't allow him to 'do a Cancelo' – he won't be able to execute his unique function of full-back/organising midfielder as Pep has planned. Time for some drastic action. He's going to rip up the boss's game plan, move wide and play as an open full-back. It changes everything. Four minutes later, Rúben Dias, who's anticipated one of his sprints, sends him a long diagonal ball. Zinchenko controls, moves further up the pitch and passes back to Foden, who slams it at goal. Southampton keeper Alex McCarthy does OK. He punches it out, but De Bruyne (alternating false 9 with Silva) is ready for it. He puts it away. Zinchenko deserves all the credit for this goal, his split-second decision to move to the outside has confused and confounded Southampton's defenders.

Seconds later, Laporte fouls Jannik Vestergaard. It's the second penalty they've given away in three days and it leads to the worst period of play they've had for a while. Southampton have three shots on goal (Nathan Redmond, James Ward-Prowse and Ché Adams) but City are having one of those moments only the biggest teams seem to be gifted. Just as they're playing their worst football, the goals start to come.

The first was Zinchenko-inspired and now it's the forwards who create City's second goal of the day. Their aggressive pressing results in Mahrez robbing the ball and scoring from outside the box. The third goal comes right at the end of added time, just before the break. De Bruyne hangs on to the ball as Mahrez arrives in the area. Mahrez then dribbles round three defenders, shoots with his right and hits the post. Gündoğan is there to intercept the ricochet and it's he who sends it into the back of the net. His tenth league goal. Interestingly, none of the goals have required 'assists'. Added to the four goals against Wolves, City have now scored seven goals without any assists, a feat possibly unique in the history of football.

Despite the scoreline, Pep's not impressed with their first half so he makes modifications during half-time. De Bruyne is positioned on the right in the midfield while Foden becomes the striker, Silva moves to the left wing and Zinchenko moves inside. It transforms City's game and they dominate (91 per cent possession between minutes 46 and 52). It's a glorious performance and Mahrez scores the fourth after a strong push from City's attacking line, a ball robbed by Fernandinho and a cut-back from Foden. Mahrez turns and dribbles forward, expertly evading the five defenders, and scores.

Silva helps Southampton claw one back after messing up a backwards pass but City maintain their rhythm and De Bruyne scores their fifth just before the hour mark. The last 30 minutes aren't quite as impressive. Pep uses them to give Torres, Agüero and Mendy some playing time. He's conscious that he needs them all back to match fitness for the tough final sprint to the end of the season. Winning the title this year has begun to look realistic.

But the Sterling/Guardiola situation has left a bad taste in everyone's mouth. Fernandinho and Walker are keen to get things back on an even keel. Both men have come a long way over the last five years and appreciate what they've achieved under Pep's direction but they also prefer a happy, harmonious dressing room. Sterling, though, isn't in the squad for City's next game, at Craven Cottage. Pep's clearly taking a strong stand. Without Sterling, the Citizens beat Fulham 3–0, giving them a 17-point advantage over United with just eight games to play. Happily, Sergio Agüero, who's been out for 417 days, scores.

MOMENT 20. HARICOT BEANS

Budapest, 16 March 2021

They're in Budapest for the second leg of their Champions League tie with Borussia Mönchengladbach. After eighteen minutes, it's all over, bar the shouting. In that short space of time, City's lead from the home tie is doubled and the Germans are going out. They start off well enough, aggressively pressing City's defenders in a bid to shut down their carefully choreographed build-up. And it works. For all of three minutes.

It's business as usual for the Citizens. Three centre-backs plus Cancelo moving up beside the pivot with the two creative midfielders free to roam. But Gladbach come out with all guns blazing and the German forwards initially do a brilliant job of messing up and slowing down the Citizens' build-up. It's time for Pep's men to show just what they're made of. Can they keep their cool, work together and outsmart the opposition? Course they can.

For me, the moment calls to mind the 'haricot beans principle', one of the many theories with which Pep likes to inculcate his players. It goes like this:

> Sometimes you get games in which you realise from the start – six or seven minutes in – that it's not working. Everything's going wrong. Whenever that happens I always think of Charly Rexach's "haricot beans" theory. If you throw them, dry and uncooked, onto a plate they land in a pile. One on top of the other. But if you gently shake the plate a bit, each bean will eventually fall into place on the plate. And that's how football works, it's a brilliant analogy. You're watching the game and you can immediately see that there's one player not doing what he's supposed to be doing, but you say to yourself, "Stay cool. Give them time and they'll fall into place." So, one minute everything seems to be going wrong, they've not managed a single clean pass, they're not winning the ball back … nothing. Then, all of a sudden, they rob the ball, pass it, then over and over again, and again. And just like that, all the beans have fallen into place – and we're back.

That's exactly what happens today in the Puskás Arena, where both legs of this tie have been played. Gladbach press aggressively and even manage a good shot at goal from outside the area. But there's a flaw in their plan and Pep's men have spotted it. Yes, the Germans are closing City's centre-backs down and are also doing a great job of nullifying Rodri and Cancelo in the middle, but none of them are thinking about what's happening on the wings. Gündoğan and De Bruyne see it immediately, of course, and they both move outside, positioning themselves behind the German forwards, who are pressing enthusiastically. City's central defenders spot what their teammates are doing and start to redirect the ball towards whichever of the two creative midfielders is left unmarked. Silva, Pep's false 'any position on the pitch', drops into the middle to contribute to the passing combinations and give City the numerical superiority Pep insists on to disrupt the opponents and win games.

The first goal goes in, De Bruyne's left-footed drive into the top corner from outside the box, then Foden, taking a leaf out of Silva's book, manages to distract and confuse Gladbach to let Gündoğan score number two (his 15th goal of the season). The second goal pretty much decides the game, which then starts to look more like a training exercise, a great opportunity to put De Bruyne through his paces, than a crucial Champions League game. He's now just about back to full match fitness since his injury on 20 January. Pep, with one eye on the rest of the season and the many trophies still up for grabs, gives his bench some playing time. After a three-game hiatus, Sterling comes on but is way below par. Losing what he considered was his rightful place in the team has obviously knocked him for six. Agüero's 15 minutes are another disappointment. Nobody passes him the ball. And poor old Mahrez manages to mess up no fewer than five great chances.

Today City have become the third side in Champions League history to play seven consecutive games without conceding – equalling AC Milan in 2005 but still some way off Arsenal's record of ten in a row. Effectively, City have played 11 hours and 31 minutes without conceding. This is also the 26th match this season in which they haven't conceded, just 7 off the club's own record, and their 24th victory out of the last 25 games. For the 8th season in a row they're about to reach the 100-goals mark across all competitions.

Pep's happy, 'We're playing well again. Everyone is in exactly the right place.'

I point out that their best performances happen when they have five players in the midfield.

'That's definitely true. When we have a lot of men on the inside we not only avoid counterattacks but we create chances. It's all the passing we do. Passing, passing, passing … and then the chances come.'

But you need very, very smart players to produce football like this. 'When Gladbach shut us down on the inside, we looked for Foden and Mahrez on the outside. Then, when they attacked on the outside, we redirected all our efforts to the inside. It's all down to having skilled, highly intelligent players who keep passing, rarely lose the ball and know exactly the right moment to strike. We defend with the ball at our feet. It's also great that we've not had a lot of injuries lately. It's allowed me to rotate the players – five or six per game. It's vital to ensure that we have fresh legs and, just as importantly, clear heads going forward.'

It looks like he's finally put the Sterling incident behind him. Let's hope so.

MOMENT 21. FERNANDINHO'S MASTERCLASS
Liverpool, 20 March 2021

There will always be players who seem to stand out more than others. The guys with that special something that grabs our attention and won't let go: Phil Foden's intuitive attacking skills; Riyad Mahrez's intelligence and superb control; Rúben Dias's superhuman powers of concentration; Gündoğan's nose for a goal; and Kevin De Bruyne's extraordinary abilities and sheer ebullience.

But look beyond the spotlight, to the swamplands where snakes and dragons lurk, in the dangerous midfield, and you'll see one guy stepping lightly around those hungry predators, twirling past opponents in an endless, elegant dance. Fernando Luiz Rosa. Or Fernandinho to you and me. But even the best dancers need a day off and Pep tries to restrict the Brazilian's match appearances to every ten days.

Today, he's centre stage again, at Goodison Park, giving yet another masterclass. He sets the rhythm of play, slowing down Everton's counterattacking, redirecting play when necessary, pushing forward, robbing ball after vital ball, neutralising threats at source, using his body, his legs … his elbow if needs be. This is Fernandinho at his peak, the master of his craft in all its complexity. His performance is breathtaking. A living, breathing monument to the art of the pivot.

The scoreline's a repeat of Tuesday's result against Gladbach and, as in Budapest, it's Gündoğan and De Bruyne who score. That's where the comparison ends, though, and their performance today is a vast improvement on the Champions League game – it needs to be as Everton are a much more demanding opponent. As usual, Pep has changed half the team. Standard practice, and a golden rule, at this stage of a long, bruising season. They've played 23 games since 3 January. That's 23 in 11 weeks. With no rest periods, no space for training, no time to catch their breath. How do you cope with all that and still keep producing brilliant football? Player rotation, of course. They need time to recuperate physically and mentally, recover their energy and get in a few good training sessions, confident that Pep has someone else lined up for the next game. Which is why every team sheet from now on contains five, six or even seven names that didn't figure last time out. Inevitably, constant change affects the dynamic of their play and the trick is to minimise the impact. There are bound to be differences depending on who's playing. Football is a game of relationships, after all, and if you change the main characters, what they produce will inevitably vary. What Pep has managed to do, though, is ensure that these variants don't affect the outcome. Their game may change in some details. The quality of their performance does not.

Zinchenko brings qualities Cancelo doesn't have; Silva doesn't interpret the role of creative midfielder in the same way as De Bruyne; and Fernandinho is a very different kind of pivot from Rodri. None of which matters today at Goodison.

Ancelotti's game plan focuses on shutting down the passing lines in the centre of the pitch at the expense of marking the wings. This results in a sluggish first half. City have no problem bringing the ball out but then fail to penetrate Everton's defensive work in the middle of the pitch. Gündoğan, who's being closely marked, is struggling to advance through the spaces even when Sterling moves into position behind Gabriel Jesus and Zinchenko stations himself on the left wing. Walker and Laporte are also taking too many risks, which isn't helping City's ability to penetrate. Everton are dug deep into their fortified positions – it's going to take patience to chip away at their defences. The home side have very few chances, though. One shot at goal, which goes high, and another attempt in the second half, punched away by City's keeper, Zack Steffen. Everton are at their most dangerous when it comes to set pieces, which is when the strength and skill of Ancelotti's men really comes into play. Nevertheless, none of those moments bring goals. The home side begins to wilt as the game proceeds. They achieve just 25 per cent possession and fail to put together even four consecutive passes. Their defences already feel like they'll be breached even before Mahrez and De Bruyne leave the bench and join the fray.

Laporte spots the point of weakness in Everton's defence and makes three aborted attempts to push through. Then, fourth time lucky, he catches the Toffees' defenders unawares and pushes forward to combine with De Bruyne, who is then knocked off his feet, but Laporte takes advantage of the confusion with a right-footed shot that rebounds off the crossbar to where Gündoğan (who else?) is waiting. The German nods the chance into the net – goal 16 of the season for him. Shortly afterwards, Rodri, with his first touch of the game, gives a gorgeous pass to De Bruyne and the Belgian scores City's second.

Game over. City are off to Wembley to face Tuchel's Chelsea in the semi-final. This is their third consecutive FA Cup semi, the same record number set by the club back in the 1930s.

Today, Pep's men have smashed the English record for the most consecutive away wins: 14 since they beat Southampton 1–0 on 19 December. The previous record, also set by City, was 13 consecutive victories achieved by Joe Royle's side in January–September 1999. This is also the 17th game in a row without a loss away from home. Their last defeat was against Spurs in London on 21 November.

Fernandinho has given another bravura performance today and, as the team leave the dressing room, Lillo pulls him to one side: 'Dinho, do me a favour. Don't ever retire. Please!'

MOMENT 22. NO. 9 IN NO MAN'S LAND

Manchester, 29 March 2021

Pep and the rest of his technical team get the COVID-19 AstraZeneca jab first thing on the morning of the Everton game on 20 March. Then, immediately after the game, the exodus begins. Most of the squad are off to play for their national teams in an endurance test of three games over ten days.

Pep seizes the chance to take a much-needed break in anticipation of the last ten weeks of the season. Lillo is left in charge and he runs training sessions for the eight squad members still in Manchester (Ederson, Carson, Laporte, Aké, Mendy, Fernandinho, Agüero and Gabriel Jesus). Lorenzo Buenaventura is also still hard at work with these players. He's focusing on strength-building work. For Lillo, though, the priority is to establish an atmosphere of calm confidence. He knows how vital these squad members are going to be in the final sprint.

Pep's first job on his return is to speak to Agüero. They won't be renewing the Argentine's contract next season. Agüero accepts the news without complaint. He knew this was coming. And there's absolutely no suggestion that he'll take his foot off the pedal, quite the opposite. Kun is superb at training on Tuesday, aggressively chasing the ball and then producing confident, accurate football whenever he has it. The technical staff are stunned by his performance, maybe his best training session in years, and even Txiki pops down to have a look. A good training session obviously isn't the same as performing well in the heat of competition, however. Agüero unquestionably remains a superb footballer but he's also definitely suffered something of a decline over the last 18 months as a cruel result of successive injuries.

The names of potential replacements are being kept under wraps by City's management team. As we know, talks with Messi fell through in September and since then his name hasn't come up again. In fact, the two names that are the focus of Pep's breakfast meetings with Estiarte and Txiki are the same ones as last summer: Harry Kane and Erling Haaland. Negotiations have not yet begun but they have a good idea of the exorbitant fee Dortmund and Haaland's eccentric agent, Mino Raiola, will demand for him. Inevitably, the rumour mill is in overdrive so Pep tells the press on 2 April that City will probably not look for a replacement for Agüero. He attributes this decision to the financial crisis facing football as a result of the pandemic but everyone's aware of the subtext, 'Stop speculating about Haaland or anyone else coming to City.'

Pep's pretty sure his team will play better without an outright central striker – as Barça did in 2009. Back then he told me: 'I sometimes think that, when I'm analysing an opponent and watching one of their games on my laptop, I see every single player apart from the no. 9. As if, for me, he doesn't actually exist. I see him as a player who doesn't do all that much! The keeper tends to do more: he brings the ball out; copes with the other team's high press; gives us a moment to catch our breath when we need it; decides where we're going to start the build-up, from the right or left or down the middle …

'I'm not talking about Leo because he's a unique kind of no. 9 but, in general, the job of a no. 9 is to find space and then put the ball into the back of the net. And that's it. The team crosses him the ball in front of goal and he tucks it away. I've never thought about this before but at Barça we're always talking about methodology and processes and maybe we forget about something as simple and basic as shooting. Shooting at goal, then, shoot and shoot again …

'It's weird but I guess it's the position to which I've paid the least attention – but it's arguably the most difficult and crucial for the team. I'm so focused on the game, on the "how", the process, that I sometimes forget that it's about putting the ball in the back of the net …'

But a lot has changed since 2009, back when Messi was just embarking on his new role as a false 9. Since then, Guardiola has had great results with supremely talented strikers like Robert Lewandowski and Agüero, and has focused his energy on perfecting the whole group's game as well as improving their finishing. He hasn't focused on the no. 9 position for years. Building City's play and achieving superiority across all zones in order to unravel, and then destroy, their opponent has become Pep's overriding objective. Scoring is the end result of everything that's gone before. First, you dominate, disorganise and confuse your opponent. Then you finish them off with a goal, but only once you've left them crushed and defeated because of how you use the ball and create space. City have had some of their best games playing without a centre-forward, flooding the midfield and defeating their opponents that way before finishing off with a goal. It's what Pep's Barça did and, increasingly, it's what has happened at City this year. They play better with three centre-backs, five in the midfield and two wingers than they do when they go for a more traditional formation, with a striker at the top. And it's not that Pep just replaces the striker with a false 9. Increasingly, City are playing with no one in central attack. For Pep, this zone is becoming more and more of a no man's zone, although undoubtedly he'd also love to have a good replacement for Kun Agüero. It's always good to have a superb goalscorer in your side.

MOMENT 23. MUHAMMAD DE BRUYNE

Leicester, 3 April 2021

City arrive in Leicester ready to redeem themselves after their disastrous home defeat (City 2–5 Leicester) last time against the Foxes. Brendan Rodgers's team are having a brilliant season – currently in third place. Pep can't afford to take any chances so he repeats the same midfield partnership of Fernandinho and Rodri as he did at home against Leicester but he's done away with the double pivot. Today, Fernandinho will be his sole organising midfielder, leaving Rodri and De Bruyne to roam, create and attack. The Belgian is now fully recovered from his injury. He's ready to fly.

At this stage of the season, match preparation is all about fresh legs and Pep's priority is to play the guys who stayed in Manchester during the two-week international break. That way, those who've just come back from a brutally intense couple of weeks get to rest and recover while the men who stayed behind and worked hard at training get their moment to shine.

Leicester are a tough proposition, no doubt, but Pep's not going to risk pushing his top players who've been away on international duty. So, he plans his lineup around those who are much more rested and then factors in how many minutes each of the internationals had with their countries in order to make up the rest of the team. With one exception. He knows he has to pick centre-back Rúben Dias instead of Nathan Aké today in order to avoid ending up with two left-footed defenders bringing the ball out, something they've never practised in training.

'I decided to play all the guys who stayed in Manchester except for Nathan and then looked at the international players who weren't used in the third game for their countries. Most of them had to play all three games over ten days and have done a hell of a lot of travelling too. Fresh legs. That's always been our priority and it remains so now!'

So, that's the order of the day: fresh legs and clear heads. Now, all they have to do is stop Jamie Vardy being fed the ball on the run, or pick up possession and then pick up speed.

The game plan that Pep has selected is all about the high press and cutting Leicester's attacks off at their origins. City alternate between a 4–3–3 and a 4–2–4. Gabriel Jesus, Agüero, De Bruyne and Mahrez are relentless, harrying the home side so that they barely have any time on the ball. Certainly no comfortable time. On the few occasions they manage to feed their creative forces, Ayoze Pérez and Tielemans, Rodri or Fernandinho are on them, ready to short-circuit their drive up the pitch – which the two of them achieve with consummate ease, such that Leicester really struggle to get the ball across the centre line and even when they do, they're immediately faced with the unbreachable defensive wall of Dias and Laporte. Essentially, Pep's planned a series of obstacles, designed to block and neutralise Leicester's rare talent for producing short but precise passing combinations that become lethal counterattacks. Between the 20th and 25th minute, City manage an astounding 96 per cent possession. Another all-time Premier League record. They've established superiority in every zone of the pitch and achieved total dominance.

Having successfully cut Vardy off completely, City now need a goal. They've had lots of chances but Rodri, Jesus and Mahrez have all seen their shots blocked by the excellent Schmeichel and De Bruyne's free kick hits the crossbar. In the midfield Fernandinho and Rodri continue to calmly pass the ball at their own tempo. Experience has taught them that, with patience and perseverance, the results will definitely arrive. Pep's planned his typical asymmetrical attack. Mahrez is positioned, open on the right wing, in front of the five defenders; Mendy's closer to the midfield, ready to run into space down the left; and Kun Agüero and Gabriel Jesus are up front leading the press on Leicester's defenders. And De Bruyne, who has complete freedom to move across the whole pitch, does the rest. The Belgian is on fire today. He robs possession from the opposition – at one stage he steals the ball four times, one after the other. And his passing is out of this world. He feeds his teammates constantly, robbing the ball an impressive 14 times in 88 minutes. De Bruyne exploits opportunities that nobody else can even see or imagine.

Unsurprisingly, the Belgian is involved in the first goal, sending an exquisite pass to Mahrez, who shoots. Schmeichel parries it out but Rodri gets to the rebound in time to send the ball to the surprise scorer of the night. Benjamin Mendy controls and finishes with his weaker foot – the right. It's more a pass into the net than a shot. Pep's bet that Mendy can attack down the left and arrive unmarked and unnoticed has paid off big time. City do what they do best. They create glorious passing sequences, win the ball back quickly whenever they lose it and attack relentlessly. But Leicester are not about to throw in the towel just yet. They open up, looking for the equal-iser, ready to fight tooth and nail for every ball and achieving 71 per cent possession between the 60th and the 65th minute. But it comes at a cost. De Bruyne is now even more of a threat. He's not being well marked because of Leicester's all-in attacking and knows that he can rely on Rodri to back him up. The two work brilliantly in tandem and, instead of Rodri being anchored next to Fernandinho, Pep tells them to swap from left to right and vice versa at three key moments. The coach's instructions depend on whether Rodgers's team are attacking or defending more on one particular flank or the other.

The clinching goal, for 2–0, comes from a throw-in in City's half. Walker to Mahrez, who's right in the centre of the pitch. The winger feeds De Bruyne who sets up Jesus with a made-to-measure assist into the path of the Brazilian. This is the kind of action from Pep's favoured pupil that can't be fully reflected in pure stats. It's the kind of match-killing moment upon which empires are built. The ball splits three Leicester defenders, it's perfectly weighted and the timing is Swiss-watch perfect. Jesus computes that the best way to score is a one–two wall pass with Sterling. The Englishman draws Schmeichel and two defenders, tees up the Brazilian and that's the game in the bag.

City's performance today has been a masterclass of precision football. They've faced down a formidable rival at their own ground and simply haven't allowed Leicester to play their game. City have now won 15 in a row away from home and produced their 28th clean sheet of the season (out of 47 matches). They've been the 'Yugoslav' City without the ball and a charging herd of buffalo with it.

As Ali would have said: 'Float like a butterfly, sting like a bee!'

This is the Manchester City of Muhammad De Bruyne.

MOMENT 24. KEEP CALM AND CARRY ON

Manchester, 6 April 2021

'The title's almost in the bag. We're nearly there, so it's vital not to put ourselves under extra pressure for the Borussia Dortmund game. One game at a time. We play to win the first one, and then we do the same for the second one. It's that simple. Play to win and not think about anything else. Let's see if we can do a bit better this year and finally get to the semi-finals.'

It's the morning after the Leicester game and Pep seems pretty chilled. For the fourth year in a row City have made it through to the quarter-finals of the Champions League. Crucially, of course, they've haven't made it past this stage on the three previous occasions, losing first to Liverpool, then Spurs and, last year, to Lyon. This year they're going up against Borussia Dortmund, who've come ready for battle, bringing with them their deadliest weapon: Erling Haaland.

Pep's tried to keep everyone calm in the three days prior to the game. The tactics are important, of course, but going into the game with the right mental attitude much more so. He knows that nerves can get to even the most experienced players like Gündoğan, Fernandinho and Silva, and that, no matter how ambitious and determined guys like Rodri, De Bruyne and Stones are, not even they are immune to big match jitters.

There's no doubt Rúben Dias's arrival has imposed a strong sense of leadership on City's defence but the team has yet to prove once and for all that they are capable of playing with the level of calm confidence essential at this level of elite football. And of becoming immune to fear of failing. Pre-match, the word 'calm' is also never far from Rodri's lips. The message is clear. Don't think about the future, focus on the present moment and play with calm. But things never seem to turn out the way you expect them to.

City get their win. They beat Dortmund 2–1 at home at the Etihad. But it's a dreadful performance, partly because of Dortmund's first-class organisation but mostly because of the nerves that seem to paralyse half a dozen of Pep's men, thus destroying the fluidity and harmony of their game. So many of their fundamental principles are momentarily forgotten.

Pep's gone about preparing for today's game much as he would for any other tie, carefully avoiding any reference to the importance of the Champions League or to their quarter-final hoodoo. He doesn't even call his players in for an early morning training session to practise set pieces, allowing them to come in at 6pm, just three hours before kick-off.

Determined to avoid creating any extra pressure for his players he's sticking rigidly to their basic game plan. This is not the day for innovations or change. He's also picked the guys who are in the best shape and has lined them up in the positions they're most comfortable with. He knows that, in previous years, he's been guilty of overthinking the really important games and has ended up hindering rather than helping his men. So today he's not going to change a thing. He fields the most obvious lineup and treats the tie like it's just another game. No special demands. No extra pressure.

So, a super-chilled Guardiola. But his players? Not so much.

Dortmund come out with their heads up, ready for the fight. Unusually for the Etihad, the pitch is a bit of a mess today. As are the home team. Stiff and sluggish, Pep's men show none of the energy, aggression and daring-do we're so used to. Their passing is slow and tentative, as if they're terrified that even the smallest mistake will bring disaster down upon them. The bad memories of Monaco, Liverpool, Tottenham and Lyon that still haunt them, albeit at a subconscious level, seem to overshadow every pass and affect their control. This isn't City, it's a ghost team.

The Germans ruthlessly cut the connections between Rodri and Cancelo and the two roaming midfielders, De Bruyne and Gündoğan, which leaves Pep's men flustered and dithering between just passing the ball among their own defenders or trying to make a pass to their wingers, who themselves are being closely marked. The fear of losing the ball, exposing themselves to a counterattack and giving the formidable Haaland his chance seems to paralyse the home side. They're unrecognisable out there today. Diffident and ill-at-ease … scared to take a risk.

Unsurprisingly, Dortmund create the first big chance. Seven minutes in, Jude Bellingham sends a beautiful shot straight to City's goal. Fortunately, Ederson gets to it in time. And then, against all the odds, a tiny miracle. The Germans make a massive mistake. Emre Can badly fluffs a pass, which Mahrez intercepts in the middle of the pitch. He passes to De Bruyne, who's already sprinting forward in a thunderous counterattack which uses four of the vertical attacking channels. Foden's on the left, ready to receive it, and he sends a tight pass to Mahrez on the other wing. He can't take the shot so he controls the ball and sends it straight to De Bruyne in the middle of the penalty area. The Belgian slams it home. Unbelievably, despite their desultory performance so far, City are ahead.

Somewhat counterintuitively, the goal makes City's players even more risk averse. *Why take any risks when you're ahead and halfway to a win?* seems to be their subconscious logic. The first half ends with City having taken a grand total of two shots on goal, against Dortmund's one. Champions League football, but full of fear.

When the action kicks off in the second half, Dortmund immediately look much more aggressive and City even more spooked than before. Aware of how uptight his men are, Pep changes the structure to make them feel more 'protected'. He needs them to relax into the game. Cancelo's now at left-back but in defensive mode while Gündoğan moves back in line with Rodri to help him bring the ball out. Two minutes in, Mahmoud Dahoud sends a long pass into space and Haaland, who's started the race second-best position-ally, easily beats Dias to the ball and out-muscles him. The big Norwegian smashes it right on target but Ederson pushes the shot away (Haaland will end the game without a goal, his fifth game in a row in which he's failed to score). It's another close shave for City, who respond by redoubling their precautionary efforts to the extent that some players look absolutely frozen out there. It's an extraordinary demonstration of the power of the mind.

We're then treated to a long sequence of pointless passing. City's strategy is now all about killing the game and holding on for dear life. But there are four rebels in the ranks. Stones moves into super-defender mode, Walker decides to start attacking deep, De Bruyne toils away, desperately looking for the second goal, and Foden produces a recital of dummies, flicks, dribbles and all-in creativity, which fails to produce a goal because of teammates' inability to finish. Everything else is quite anodyne but from time to time a spark of brilliance gives City another chance. A total of six in fact, all of which are badly squandered. But then, just as it looks like a second goal might be on the cards, Bam! – Dortmund equalise. There's a moment of confusion and disorganisation in the centre of the pitch and Dahoud sparks a perfect 'third-man run'. He passes to Haaland who sends it to Marco Reus as he runs into City's box, having shaken Walker off. The German captain tucks away his 18th Champions League goal, setting a new record for his club and beating Lewandowski's tally by one.

It's the first goal conceded by City in the Champions League since 21 October, when Luis Díaz scored for Porto. Thirteen hours and eight minutes of play without conceding a single goal. And now it's happened at the worst possible moment. All their fears have been realised. It's another kick in the gut, possibly heralding another early exit from the European stage.

But then, somehow, everything changes. Suddenly, City are back. And not like a boxer scrambling up from the canvas battered and bruised, this is City the Brave, throwing themselves back into the fray with pluck and determination. De Bruyne and Foden lead the charge, furiously driving the action forward until the 90th minute when De Bruyne sends a left-outstep 'banana pass' to Gündoğan, who controls it and lays it back for Foden to score the winner.

City 2 Dortmund 1. A big advantage to take to the second leg. Despite all the nerves, they've pulled it off and the semi-final's firmly back in their sights.

'We'll go to Germany to win,' Pep tells me after the game. 'Not just to defend. But we'll have to adjust the way we press, our build-up, what we do off the ball …' It's likely to take more than some adjustments, though. Maybe a complete overhaul? And he's not mentioned the real problem: the old wounds that still fester. He needs to find a way to get his players relaxed and confident again, help them shake off their jitters and the memories of past mistakes that clearly haunt them still.

MOMENT 25. FOUR SCENARIOS
Manchester, 7 April 2021

It's 1am and the light in Pep's office is still on. The coach and his assistants are discussing the best tactics for the return leg against Dortmund at Signal Iduna Park. He knows it well, having produced some stunning performances there and having also been roundly beaten. Next Wednesday, they'll be looking for one of those epic wins, although a draw would do them. All eyes are on the prize – getting through to the semi-final and taking their rightful place among the greats of European football. Pep achieved it four times with Barça and three with Bayern. He's yet to reach that level with City.

With his customary calm assurance Manel Estiarte goes over the four possible scenarios they'd predicted for the first leg: pull off a resounding victory, scrape a win, lose, or lose by such a huge margin that any kind of comeback in the second leg would need a miracle. They've come away with the second best option and that's OK. They should be reasonably satisfied and resist obsessing about the negatives. 'Our main objective right now is getting the players confident and relaxed again.'

Pep agrees. He'd put a lot of effort into making things as stress-free as possible for his players in the run-up to the game. He wanted them unburdened by the memories of past defeats. But it's clear it didn't work. He's had to watch his brilliant, mature players, who have just produced an extraordinary season, crippled by anxiety – guys like Dias, Cancelo, Rodri, Gündoğan and Silva, five of his best this year, playing like shadows of themselves, beaten by tension and stress rather than anything their opponent produced. If anything, today was a demonstration of the importance of the psychological side of football. An athlete's mind can be his worst enemy or his best friend – behaviours, habits, intentions and emotions all have a huge impact on the outcome of a game. It's mental calm that brings victory and glory.

They all agree. The priority now is to get the players feeling relaxed about the return match in Dortmund. They need to loosen up, shake off the fear of making mistakes and play with confidence and audacity. Obviously, though, they'll still have to bear in mind where not to take risks. It's about finding the right balance. That's the answer and the challenge. The yin and the yang of football. Be audacious and bold, passionate, aggressive. Fight to win. But at the same time, go easy, step lightly, proceed with caution. 'Get the balance right,' advise Manel Estiarte and Juanma Lillo, the two most laidback members of the coaching team. The right balance. Audacity and caution.

A couple of hours ago, down in the dressing room, Captain Fernandinho was thinking along exactly the same lines and already planning how to turn things around before the return leg. He's going to be key in the coming week as they start the work to get the team into the right mental headspace. De Bruyne has also realised that they need a psychological boost and, the day after the first-leg match, makes a big show of the fact that he's renewed until 2025. He's all-in, backing City with total faith. And he wants his teammates to really feel that impact. By now, Pep has considered all the possible variants for the game and decides to go with the same lineup, although he might swap Bernardo Silva for Gabriel Jesus. He has blind faith in all his guys.

Minutes later, over at the north end of Sportcity, the nightwatchman opens his logbook again: '1:30. The boss. Heading home.'

MOMENT 26. A HICCUP

Manchester, 11 April 2021

Estiarte tells me again, 'Juanma has really helped Pep relax. He's basically the coach's personal coach. And he's also helped knit the whole coaching team closer together.' The two men have a lot in common – both of them are given to calm introspection and lots of 'alone time'. Like a couple of hermits.

Lillo tells me he's reading Michel de Montaigne's sixteenth-century *Essays*. Again. It's one of the books he likes to keep on his bedside table in room no. 30 of Sportcity, where he's spending the night before travelling to Dortmund. 'I've read it over and over. It's vital reading.'

Manchester United have just taken three points off City's Premier League lead. But neither that, nor the fact that City lost to Marcelo Bielsa's Leeds at the Etihad yesterday, is cause for concern to Lillo: 'It doesn't bother me that United keep winning. Not at all. I don't want our guys falling into the trap of thinking that we've got 11 first-choice players and the rest are the back-ups who'll play the league games so that the "important" players can get a rest! I want them all to feel that the title belongs to *all* of us and that every single game has to be played with identical determination. I always think that it's better to win the title as late in the season as possible. It helps maintain that hunger.' A somewhat unusual view for someone working in elite-level football but, thinking about it, it actually makes good sense.

Pep was planning to start Agüero yesterday, for a second consecutive match, in the hope of pushing him towards full match fitness after nine months of repeated setbacks: torn meniscus, several different muscular injuries, COVID-19, another slew of muscle strains … but, just as he looked fully fit and ready to score lots of goals again … another injury. It now looks unlikely, if not impossible, for Kun to play any part in the team's final sprint of the season. Which has put paid to Pep's plan to reserve all his top players for Wednesday's crucial game in Dortmund. He needed to replace Agüero and Laporte for the Leeds game. He uses Gabriel Jesus, whom he'd hoped to rest until Wednesday, instead of Agüero and Nathan Aké replaces Laporte. Aké hasn't started a game for ages, almost 100 days, ever since a serious muscle injury at the end of December. This will be his tenth game with City and only his seventh in the league. Disappointing for someone signed as an alternative to Laporte but who, so far, hasn't had a chance to prove himself.

All of which leaves Walker, Dias, Rodri, De Bruyne, Gündoğan, Mahrez and Foden on the bench. Pep wants to spare them suffering the perpetual end-to-end transitional football Leeds bring. Endless running up and down the pitch. Torture. He wants his top men mentally and physically fresh for Dortmund. Of that 'top' group only Cancelo, Stones and Gabriel Jesus plus Ederson start against Leeds – an important test because a win would bring the title ever closer. But, right now, the Champions League is the priority. No question about it.

Unfortunately, City suffer one of their rare off-days. Leeds have just two shots on goal the entire game. Both of which go in. City dominate completely and take 26 shots. None of which trouble the back of the net. Once again, a couple of defensive errors are to blame for this, their third home defeat this season. A new record for Pep's career. In all the wrong ways.

And they actually have a good game. Mendy is back as left-back after his impressive performance in Leicester. Zinchenko is on the left in midfield, where he also does a bang-up job. Fernandinho's looking completely confident in his role as an organising midfielder, ably supported by Cancelo beside him and Bernardo Silva a few metres in front. The game starts with lots of chasing up and down the pitch but, after 15 minutes, City secure possession and begin to control the pace and tempo.

Fernandinho repeatedly attacks the central spaces Leeds have left exposed with Jesus and Sterling taking turns to move down to the central circle to receive the ball with their backs to goal and make third-man runs. It's not exactly fast and furious, nor do City create a multitude of chances, but they dominate Leeds completely despite the fact that Sterling isn't on top form. Silva's also looking a bit fragile out there, now that he's no longer considered a first-choice starter by the coach.

Forty-two minutes in, Cancelo makes a careless mistake, letting the ball run away from him rather than clearing it. It's not the first time he's looked a little over-confident in the last few weeks, a consequence perhaps of the starring role he played in the team's successes in January and February, which seems to have gone to his head. Cancelo's mistake leads directly to the visitors' first goal, knocked in off the post by Stuart Dallas. Minutes later,

Leeds's central defender Liam Cooper is sent off for a poor tackle on Gabriel Jesus. It'll prove to be the turning point of the whole game.

In the lead and one man down, Leeds go into defensive mode in the second half. With an impressive and apparently effortless ease Marcelo Bielsa's men seem to have transformed into a completely different team as they trot back out after the break. Instead of throwing themselves back into constant transitions and chasing the ball all over the pitch, they hunker down like a besieged army taking refuge behind fortress walls.

Guardiola responds by moving Mendy to the left wing where he can link up on the inside with Sterling and Jesus. Gündoğan – in his 200th game for City – comes on for Aké, giving Pep an extra man in midfield. City then proceed to dominate the rest of the game. A fearless Stones, apparently impervious to any sense of threat, repeatedly drives the ball forward, right up to the edge of Leeds's area, with each of his incursions opening up another chink in their armour. Today, he embodies the dual defender-midfielder role Pep envisioned for him back in 2018. City produce 23 shots at goal, although not all of them are accurate and most are blocked by the visitors, who defend with guts and determination. With 15 minutes left, Silva receives a nice pass from Fernandinho and gives it to Ferran Torres, who gets the equaliser. The young Spaniard is once again performing well in the box but not outside it. With victory in sight, the team redouble their efforts but are immediately hit by a lethal Raphinha counterattack, which Ederson just manages to block.

Fernandinho, who is superb as a single organising midfielder when he has his back covered, struggles to cope alone in open spaces when faced by the kind of electric bursts of speed typical of most forwards. Then, just before the final whistle, as though the fates are anxious to remind City that they're human after all, with all the faults and frailties that entails, the match produces a killer blow. Leeds attack at lightning speed, cleverly nipping in behind Stones and Fernandinho, and Dallas beats Ederson as he comes out to try and close him down. The whole thing evokes dreadful memories of last season when City lost innumerable points through a mix of slack defending and clumsy attacks. The defeat doesn't really matter in practical terms but a dark cloud begins to gather over the Etihad on Saturday night. It's only too easy to be wise after the event but football is a strange game and sometimes there's just no explanation for the outcome of a match. No matter what anyone tells you.

At the end of the day, this has done nothing to harm City's title aspirations and we'll all look back on the defeat as a little hiccup in what has been a glorious campaign.

The main objective has been achieved. They'll have fresh legs in Dortmund on Wednesday.

MOMENT 27. VIDEO SUNDAY

Manchester, 11 April 2021

Pep's decided to cancel Sunday's training session. He still wants his men rested, physically and mentally, for the big games. They'll start again on Monday. He spends the day at home, watching Borussia Dortmund videos and making notes. The Leeds defeat, just 18 hours before, completely forgotten. Now all his focus is on their German rivals.

Over in Sportcity, Lillo gets to spend his morning reading Montaigne's *Essays* but his mind is on the Dortmund game too, so the two men exchange messages throughout the day. One of the things on Pep's mind is how to press the Germans as they bring the ball out. Disrupting Mats Hummels, Can and Dahoud's passing combinations is going to be crucial. If they do that, they'll have Dortmund on the back foot. They toss various solutions around. The key's going to be short-circuiting Dortmund in their own half. They're much more dangerous on the inside. Blocking the central zones will force them wide and give City the advantage.

And so they go on, weighing different tactics and discussing plans, while the players enjoy their day off – although, for many of them, it's not as restful as it might be. Losing to Leeds still hurts. One player's even complained to the coaching staff about Pep's decision to keep so many top players on the bench. The explanation for that decision is simple, of course. He couldn't risk someone like De Bruyne getting injured. He needs his stars full of beans, not knackered after too many games. OK, they lost the game, but that was a small price to pay. They're still well ahead in the league and Pep has no regrets about leaving those seven men out. He fielded the strongest team he could against Leeds … just not his top 11. As Lillo pointed out: 'I wish we had the luxury of being eight points ahead with 18 games to play every year …'

Another player was unhappy with the way Pep kept pressurising him during the game. Pep's definitely become more relaxed and less interventionist over the last few months, particularly since Lillo's arrival. These days he gives far fewer instructions from the touchline and allows his men greater freedom in a game. He wants them to make their own decisions, to be confident enough to take the initiative. And it's paid off. Both players and coach have been much calmer of late. Yesterday, however, he felt the need to intervene. His players were struggling to find a way around the defensive wall Bielsa had constructed so he got involved, pointing and waving, shouting instructions and giving the odd kick up the backside when necessary. Post-match there had been some griping from one particular player but his teammates were quick to defend the coach. He'd been absolutely right to intervene. So, as Sunday morning dawns, more than a few of Pep's men are still sore about the defeat but nothing more serious than that.

The sun shines down on Sportcity as the players arrive for Monday's training session. Laporte's back, fit and well, but Agüero's still injured. Everyone's relaxed and smiling as the ball flies up and down Training Pitch 1 at the City Academy. Pep has Wednesday's game plan ready. They'll play in a 3–2–2–3, pressing the Germans hard as they bring the ball out in the hope of forcing them wide. They're going there to win and the stated aim is to score at least twice, just to be safe. Only a couple of decisions remain: Cancelo or Zinchenko at left-back? Gabriel Jesus as a striker or Bernardo Silva as a false 9?

He'll make those calls after watching how they do in training.

MOMENT 28. AND FINALLY …
Dortmund, 14 April 2021

The Radisson Blu in Dortmund is a pleasant, functional hotel although not particularly luxurious. About six minutes from the Signal Iduna Park as the crow flies, it's much slower-going on matchdays. There's not enough turning space in front of the hotel for the squad bus so it parks some metres away, waiting for the team to board. Then they're off, weaving through the match-day traffic, past the stadium and then crossing over Autobahn 54 until they get to Schwimmweg, where they drive through the tunnel that takes them into the bowels of the magical Signal Iduna. On foot, the journey takes 15 minutes, and the Dortmund fans who've been drinking since mid-afternoon in the hotel's lobby, singing songs and draped in the yellow and black of their team, will make their way to the ground at around 8pm. For security reasons they have to be in the stadium 40 minutes before kick-off.

Last night, Pep was pretty relaxed when we spoke: 'It's going to be fine. We'll do everything we need to do … and more. It's all about what happens out there on the pitch tomorrow. As always.' Not the most profound obser-vation, but you can't expect the man to come up with a philosophical treatise the night before one of the biggest games of the year.

As the Dortmund fans gather in bars, Pep gathers his men and announces the team. Just one change from the first leg. Zinchenko's in and Cancelo, whose performance has dipped slightly in his last couple of games, is out. Silva will play instead of Gabriel Jesus although it's De Bruyne who'll be their false 9 today. Pep reckons that his unique way of pressing defenders might give City an edge. As always, he keeps the team talk brief. The play-ers have to listen to 60 of these talks every season, year in, year out, and you can't blame them for becoming immune to them and losing concen-tration. Pep understands and goes for maximum brevity. The shorter, the better. So, not much chat then. But he does have a video for them to watch, of Scott Carson, City's third goalkeeper. He's not travelled to Dortmund today, ceding his place to James Trafford, who, at just 18, is the youngest player in City's youth team. Carson is a battle-hardened veteran who won the Champions League with Liverpool in 2005 but hasn't played a single minute for City since he signed in August 2019. Down to earth with a great sense of humour, he's adored by his teammates, who see him as a kind of surrogate big brother. His storytelling is also legendary and many's the time he's had the entire dressing room helpless with laughter with one his anec-dotes – about the day of his presentation as a new City player, for example, when most of the younger players thought the club was playing a prank. How could this old guy (he was 35!) with his greying beard, his lined face and croaky voice be a footballer? Overweight and slow, surely this was the new kitman having a laugh? The incredulity quickly changed to genuine affection for City's 'big brother' – even Pep has an enormous soft spot for the keeper despite the fact that he's regularly late for training. 'Why are you always late, Scott?' the coach once asked in exasperation. 'Well, I live in Derby, boss, and I get the train. It takes me more than two hours to get here in the morning.' Pep was speechless. A professional footballer coming to work by train! Four-and-a-half hours of daily commuting? Unbelievable.* Carson's recorded a typically jokey message for his teammates today but he finishes by telling them to relax, go out and play their game with confidence.

It's chilly for April. But only the visitors look frozen out there on the pitch. Frozen with fear.

Dortmund haven't made it to the Champions League semi-finals since 2013 and, given their poor Bundesliga campaign this season, nobody expected them to get this far. With nothing to lose and everything to gain, they've come out to enjoy the game. This is their big chance, and they're relishing it. For City, this game is of monumental importance. It's their chance to take their rightful place among the top four in Europe, and a decisive moment in the history of the club. But it's recent history that's weighing them down tonight, the memories of past defeats and the fear of failing once more …

Everyone in the technical team – Guardiola, Estiarte, Lillo, Buenaventura, Mancisidor and Borrell – has spent the last ten days trying to get the players to relax, to shrug off any lingering memories of past European debacles. All of them have scrupulously avoided anything that might pile the pressure on. No epic speeches, no calls for heroism, no demands, no stress … Never before have a group of Guardiola players been handled with kid gloves like this before a match. The coach has stuck faithfully to the deal he struck with Lillo. No lectures, no last-minute instructions and definitely none of his usual gesticulating. It's all about being relaxed and calm.

Nevertheless, the difference between the two sides' states of mind is evident from the start. Pep's men look jumpy, their nerves becoming all

---

* Carson's morning commute meant that he had to change at Sheffield and take the TransPennine Express to Manchester Piccadilly, where he'd catch the Metrolink to Velopark. From there it was a ten-minute walk to the City Academy. The journey took two-and-a-quarter hours, although at times there would be delays and he'd be late for training.

the more apparent as Zinchenko messes up three passes in a row. Then, 15 minutes in, a hammer blow. Hummels sends a long ball to Haaland, who's shaken off Stones and is running inside the penalty box. He passes to Dahoud, whose shot rebounds off Dias and lands at Bellingham's feet. The English international sends it into the top corner of Ederson's goal. It hits City like a bucket of cold water on an already freezing Dortmund night. Pep collapses back onto the bench, his glacial expression a mixture of fury and misery, while, beside him, Lillo leaps to his feet to try and lift the players' spirits. Out on the pitch, Dias is also desperately trying to rally his troops, as several heads have gone down.

Lillo's reaction is typical of him, in the sense that he always does the opposite of everyone else. After a goal, everyone else in the dugout will be on their feet, hugging each other in celebration, while Lillo doesn't move, just sits impassively on the bench. That rarest of things, a football coach who doesn't celebrate goals. But if they concede a goal, it's a different story. Lillo will rush to the side of the pitch, shouting words of encouragement. Sure enough, right now, he's there on the touchline, screaming like a man possessed while Pep sits rigid in his seat, momentarily, turned to stone.

Dortmund are now ahead on away goals. It's the moment of truth for City. With another 75 minutes remaining they need to put up or shut up. How much do they really want this? Are they even up to it? All of Europe is waiting and watching. Are Manchester City a serious contender for European glory or merely an also-ran. This isn't about tactics and strategy. It's not even about football. Right here, right now, the question is whether they have the mental toughness to turn this game around.

In that moment, the dynamic shifts. Suddenly, City are the ones with nothing to lose and Dortmund are under pressure to hold on to their advantage. For Pep and his men, it's a game-changer. City's lines advance by 20m and their forwards, with De Bruyne at the head, begin to press the German defenders. Ten minutes later, the Belgian's already deep in Marwin Hitz's area when he steals the ball and shoots. It hits the crossbar but leaves no one in any doubt. Notice has been served. The boys in blue are back. Their heads go up, the football flows and City are in control. Total domination: 18 duels won (Dortmund win 7); 45 balls stolen (36 for their hosts); and 11 corners (2 for the men in black and yellow). City's defenders, led by the outstanding

Stones–Dias partnership, are on fire and, for the rest of the game, Erling Haaland doesn't get a sniff of the ball anywhere close to Ederson.

Guardiola's always seen something of Gerard Piqué in Stones. Mental resilience, great vision, superb ball control, and the aggression and toughness required to win one-to-one tussles. But he's not quite there yet. Back in 2017, Pep told me: 'John has everything it takes to be an absolute phenomenon. But to get him there I'll need to pair him with the right player. A warrior, someone with the same character and spirit as Carles Puyol.' This is where Rúben Dias comes in. Together, they're Pep's new Piqué and Puyol. The ace defender and his 'tough as old boots' wing man. Over both ties, the duo have allowed Haaland just four incursions into their area, three in the home leg and one tonight. By taking out Dortmund's biggest gun, they effectively disable the German attack and Dortmund only manage one more effort on target – a Hummels header that goes over.

Going one–nil down seems to have given City wings and they begin to hit their rhythm. İlkay Gündoğan, who still looks a bit tense, will tell me later what was going on in their heads: 'For the first 15 minutes we were terrified of losing our advantage. Then, at 1–0, we felt suddenly liberated.' Gündoğan takes a bit longer to settle down but has an outstanding second half when he's positioned close to Rodri and sets the rhythm of their game, dominates the ball and becomes the link that connects the rest of the team. Today, he's shown us both sides of an athlete's psyche: choked at the start, unfettered and electric in the second half.

They get two great chances before the break thanks to Mahrez but neither comes to anything. At half-time they head into the dressing room, still one–nil down but by no means out. There's a real sense that they're on the point of breaking down the German side's resistance. 'Lads, we just need one goal,' Pep tells them. 'Even if they score again, we just need one. Go out there and get me that goal!'

Dortmund retreat further and further back into their area. They struggle to get beyond the centre of the pitch and only a few long balls reach Haaland, who comes off worse in every single clash with Stones or Dias. Marco Reus has moved to the right wing to help defend against the Foden–Gündoğan–Zinchenko triangle, who use long passing sequences to draw their opponents towards them and away from other areas of the pitch where

City can attack. Eventually, the visitors get their chance. The action starts down the left-hand flank. Zinchenko has a close miss with an on-target shot, then he's back on the attack, combining with Foden who goes for a cross that bounces off Emre Can's head and onto his outstretched hand. VAR confirms the handball and Mahrez takes City's penalty. Looking on, many of us are willing De Bruyne to take the shot. Mahrez has had a bad run of late – 14 Champions League matches without a goal. Later, the Algerian international tells me that, after practice on Tuesday, everyone knew he would take it. And tonight, he's golden. The ball sails into the goal, mid-height on the left-hand side, just out of reach of Hitz's lunge. The yellow wall is down. It's enough to put City through. The ball is now in Dortmund's court.

What happens next is almost incomprehensible. Dortmund continue to hunker down in defensive mode and the Gündoğan–Rodri–Silva passing extravaganza continues. The three control the rhythm of the game as the defenders resist all Dortmund's attempts to push forward and De Bruyne dances rings around them. City dominate completely, repelling all comers and managing three counterattacks. Rodri's header from a free kick hits the crossbar and De Bruyne produces a superb low shot, which Hitz blocks. Another goal is coming. From a corner, Mahrez plays it short to Silva, who feeds it to Foden on the left-hand edge of the box. The idea is that Foden draws opposition players towards him, so that he can cross to his own centre-backs to head in a goal. But the Germans fail to take the bait and Foden has spotted that Haaland is partially blocking the keeper's line of sight. Instinctively, he goes for goal. The ball thuds in off the post. City are through. Dortmund are defeated.

A jubilant Foden, Stockport's answer to Andrès Iniesta, gallops straight over to Pep to celebrate. The two have an extraordinary bond. Foden sees Pep as his mentor, and for Guardiola the youngster has always been the jewel in City's crown. He spotted his potential way back: 'Remember his name: Phil Foden' (2016); 'Foden's a genius. He's going to be a star … One of the best young players I've ever seen' (2017).

The team have two more good chances in the last 15 minutes but Silva and Mahrez manage to mess up the first and Sterling, still not at his best, wastes the second. Needless to say, City are now completely relaxed and are hitting the same kind of numbers as the first leg: the same level of possession and clean passes, and a slightly higher number of shots on target. The score is also identical. This is now their 16th away win in a row and Guardiola's 100th away victory since the summer of 2016. They've won 100 out of the 142 games they've played, drawn 18 and lost 24, with 313 goals in favour and 120 against. So far, they haven't lost a single Champions League game this season: 9 wins and 1 draw. They've scored 21 goals and have only conceded 3, with Ederson's goal untroubled in 7 of their 10 games. For the second time in the club's history they're through to the semi-finals, where this year they'll play Paris Saint-Germain, last year's runners-up. It's the eighth time Pep has contested a Champions League semi-final and will be the biggest challenge of their season.

Tonight, Pep's men have shown that they have the mental resilience to fight back. In Manchester, they came back after Reus's goal and here, tonight, they also rallied after a nervous start and the shock of Bellingham's goal. Finally they can put to rest all the disasters of the past few years and move on.

Several hours later, Pep's enjoying a glass of champagne in the Radisson Blu and I remind him what he said to me four years ago after their defeat by Monaco: 'I've not managed to give them the kind of character they need for the big events. They don't believe in themselves. It's like they're scared of playing.' Now Pep smiles, 'It just shows you … character's much more important than stats.'

MOMENT 29. GUNDO'S ANNOYED

London, 17 April 2021

City choose to confront Chelsea in the semi-final of the FA Cup at Wembley with just three outright first-choice starters: Rúben Dias, Rodri and Kevin De Bruyne. After the stress of the Dortmund game, Pep wants to give his top players a break. Their loss to Leeds last Saturday has also left them needing to win in Birmingham at Aston Villa on Wednesday to secure their place at the top of the league. So, the starting 11, which in normal circumstances would be full of his top men, consists mainly of subs today. Pep doesn't like making such a clear distinction between the substitutes and the regulars.

It's much better to field a mix of players. But today he's had no choice. Unfortunately, the substitutes are well aware that they're back-up players.

Pep wants to limit Chelsea's very vertical attacking, which has become one of the team's signatures under Tuchel. So he's instructed his men to establish a slow rhythm of play. Fernandinho and Rodri are in the middle of the pitch with De Bruyne – who is playing today despite looking utterly exhausted at the end of the Dortmund game. The Belgian will try to slow the game as well as hopefully produce a couple of his magnificent assists. But Chelsea are fine with the slower pace and have no difficulty pressing City as they bring the ball out. It's not a 3+2 defence today, with Cancelo moved up towards the pivot, but a 2+3 with Dias and Laporte in the backline and Cancelo, Fernandinho and Rodri in front of them. It doesn't work. Chelsea's forwards press aggressively and prevent City circulating the ball well. Pep's men look overwhelmed and lost.

Tuchel's come up with exactly the right structure: two centre-backs and two wing-backs allow Ben Chilwell to stick to Cancelo like a limpet, blocking City's route in this zone. City barely get 35 per cent of the ball in the first ten minutes. But by minute 25 they've rallied somewhat and De Bruyne is finally managing to set the rhythm of game. Most of the play remains outside of the boxes, though, and City manage just one shot on goal. Chelsea don't have a single chance. Each team has effectively neutralised the other's attacks and both seem to believe that one goal will be enough to decide the match. Then, 48 minutes in, De Bruyne turns his ankle chasing a loose ball and has to come off. Losing the Belgian at this stage of the season is disastrous for City. His absence will make absolutely everything harder. Foden replaces De Bruyne and is on his usual electric form but, in the end, it's Chelsea who exploit a double error from the Cityzens to seal the game. Chilwell takes advantage of Cancelo's overly ambitious burst forward – the same kind of pressing that cost them United's second goal at the Etihad – to find Jorginho. He then sends it to Mason Mount, who catches City's entire backline napping. Zack Steffen then messes up big time. He fails to intercept the ball and is caught way out of his goal as Timo Werner calmly sets up Hakim Ziyech, who takes advantage of the open goal. The brutal error costs City dearly. Within minutes Ziyech, left unmarked by Dias in front of goal, has another shot. This time Steffen's more than up to the task and makes a brilliant save.

In the last 30 minutes City lack edge in attack while Chelsea defend brilliantly. It's again obvious that winger Ferran Torres doesn't cope well in tight spaces. He's much more effective in the penalty area. Sterling's performance is even more disappointing. He's way below par today, although that may be because he's suffering emotionally. Rúben Dias, with a header that goes high, and Rodri with another header after a corner, make valiant efforts to turn the tide in City's favour, with no success. For the second year in a row, City are beaten by a London club in the semi-finals of the FA Cup. It's been a sluggish game with only three shots on goal apiece and distinctly below-par football. Pep's men have played better than they did last year against Arsenal but it's still a huge disappointment. City's subs have shown exactly why they are second-choice players but Pep's also worried that making such a clear division between the two levels is going to be problematic as they go into the final sprint. He's going to have to come up with something.

Since their defeat against United on 7 March, when it was clear that Solskjær had found the perfect way to neutralise Cancelo's double function of full-back/pivot, Guardiola's asked the Portuguese to play as a straightforward full-back: on the right against Fulham, on the left against Dortmund and on the right against Leeds. In each case, except for the first half of their home game against Dortmund, Pep had asked him to cover the wings and stay away from the spaces inside. Unfortunately, the change has led to a dramatic dip in the player's performance with a knock-on effect for the team, who have lost the superiority in the middle of the pitch that was so successful for them in January and February. It looks like a major tactical problem for Pep to sort out.

There's more trouble brewing, though. And, this time, it's not tactical. After coming off the pitch at the end of today's game, one of the players is on his mobile phone, laughing and joking. It infuriates Gündoğan, who makes his feelings felt. Loudly. Captain Fernandinho steps in and calms things down but later Lillo and Pep will tell both him and Gündoğan that they're going to have to sort it out among themselves. Gündoğan isn't a captain who's been chosen by the squad but he's a level-headed guy who sees this as an opportunity to get everyone together to agree their priorities and objectives, and Fernandinho's more than happy to organise it. He doesn't know if it's ego or a lack of a sense of responsibility that's led to this situation but, as captain, he understands the importance of nipping these problems in the bud.

Lillo puts it like this: 'Right now everyone has to think about his own ego in order for all of us to benefit. Towards the end of the season, players can lose a bit of focus. Those who want to renew are thinking about that, the guys who are looking to leave are considering their next move, etc. But they actually need to be looking at things differently. So, take the guy who's leaving, who hasn't had a game all year and is looking for more money or greater status elsewhere. It's far better for him if he's coming from a side that's won the title. Those that know they're staying would obviously prefer us to be champions and those who aren't sure yet, well, it will probably be easier to renew if we've just finished a title-winning season. So, essentially, for reasons of "altruistic self-interest" the better we do, the better for everyone concerned. Nobody benefits from the team losing although some wouldn't agree with me. And no one loses when the team wins.'

Gündoğan has his head screwed on. He wasn't really angry about someone being on the phone or having a laugh after a defeat. What has pissed him off is the disinterested way some of his teammates approached the game. As if it had no real importance to their own careers. The difference between the regular starters and those who spend much of their time on the bench is very stark. But all of them have earned the place Pep has assigned them through their performances. The team has always been a meritocracy and Pep has given everyone the chance to prove himself in this final sprint for the title. But it's left the dressing room divided into two separate blocks and several players are clearly demotivated, demoralised or simply just disgruntled. And this means that guys like Sterling, who are currently struggling with a serious dip in form, can't find their way out of their own personal crisis. It's a problem Pep's going to have to address if they have any chance of winning the three remaining trophies that are still to play for.

There's some good news on Monday, though. Having undergone an MRI on Sunday morning, De Bruyne's been told that he hasn't broken any bones in his foot after all. It's just a bit of bruising and he'll be fit for the League Cup final next Sunday against Spurs, who have just sacked their coach, José Mourinho.

The other big news, on Monday, 19 April, is the proposed European Super League. Some of the biggest clubs in Europe are looking for greater financial returns on their contributions to European football and have put forward a proposal to UEFA. Unfortunately, the specific demands made by Florentino Pérez (Real Madrid), Andrea Agnelli (Juventus) and the Glazers (Manchester United) are absolutely outrageous and immediately cause furore among the supporters of various English clubs. Manchester City and Chelsea fans take the strongest and most vocal stand, immediately calling for their clubs to condemn the proposal. Patrick Bamford, James Milner and Jürgen Klopp also make their objections clear after the Leeds–Liverpool game. Midday on Tuesday, Pep adds his own voice to the growing opposition to creating a restricted competition. He believes that it would be unfair in sporting terms to have a 'closed' (by invitation) competition. He also expresses his unhappiness with the lack of information that has so far been made available. City post his comments on Twitter and several of the players retweet them. Then Fernandinho, De Bruyne, Walker and Sterling meet with Ferran Soriano on Zoom, leaving him in no doubt as to their level of disgust with the idea. They're also not happy that they had to hear about it from the press. By late afternoon, the club's directors are convinced that some speedy back-pedalling is required and they duly make an announcement. The rest of England do likewise. The Super League is over before it's even begun.

MOMENT 30. TOO MANY GAMES, NOT ENOUGH TRAINING

Birmingham, 21 April 2021

They're playing on instinct, all their energies focused on the next match. Having to play every three days is exhausting and leaves them no time to review the fundamentals of their game beyond the odd correction in rare training sessions or via videos. Compete–recuperate–rest–compete. An endless cycle that leaves the players to draw on subconscious recall of the things they learned back when there was space and time for proper training.

Pep is painfully conscious of the toll this is taking: 'These lads are about to finish a really hard season, then they have six days' rest before they're off to play for their national sides. And during the season we've had no time to do proper training. All I can do is show them videos to refresh their ideas about what they need to do. We didn't even have a proper pre-season to go over the basic principles. Ten, 11 months of competition, 100 press conferences, 3 games a week ... It's too much. I've never experienced a season like it. We started late and we're finishing early but we have the same number of competitions and matches and the same pressure from the club and our supporters to win, win, win. I'm not complaining. It's fantastic that we've made it to the FA Cup final and are going to Paris for the Champions League semi-final. I'm immensely proud of my players and grateful for everything they do and everything we've achieved. They love their football and they love to play but this work rate leads to a lot of injuries. UEFA are well aware of the toll it takes but they don't care. It's honestly too much, week after week, without even a minute to draw breath ... we're bound to have more injuries.'

My previous books detailed the approach Pep takes to training and he still uses the same methodology today. Training sessions aim to get the players in the best possible shape for the next game. City play two or three games per week across the entire season so there are lots of maintenance sessions, which focus on protecting the players' joints, their leg muscles and the lumbar–pelvic area. The regulars will have a light recuperation session the day after a game but the subs or the guys who played less than 60 minutes will do a complete training session, which usually includes specific drills aiming to build reactive and explosive speed and power plus general endurance. There are also times, particularly after a lot of travelling, when Pep foregoes a day of training to give the whole squad a day off. It's a vital part of reducing the mental fatigue professional footballers suffer, even though this cuts away still more precious time for teaching, learning, remedying, updating.

Time pressures mean that they have to keep match preparation to a minimum. There's really only time to practise how Pep wants them to bring the ball out in the upcoming game. The starting point is always the basic 3+2 structure and then they add the variants Pep's come up with depending on who they're playing. Having the same basic structure to build on means that Pep can cover everything he needs to in the limited time available. For him, getting the build-up stage right is of fundamental importance.

He's had to accept, however, that, beyond practising the precise way he wants them to bring the ball out, it's impossible to go over the fundamental principles of their game during normal training sessions. There just isn't the time and any extra work would put too much pressure on a group of players who are already under intense stress. He just has to trust in their natural talent plus their ability to retain and apply the things he's already taught them. It's been impossible to practise many of Pep's fundamental concepts, like drawing opponents to you by driving with the ball or disorganising the other team by building passing sequences while, in another area of the pitch, your forward is waiting to decide what happens next. All of it has had to be put on the back burner this season. So he's come up with his own terms for describing the concepts, like calling the Zinchenko–Gündoğan–Foden triangle down the left flank the 'juntarrivales', his decoy players, who draw their opponents towards them in order to free up other teammates. Pep's always said: 'If you keep practising a certain move, you never forget it.' But this year they've had to retain all the fundamentals of their game without any chance to practise. Which is why we've seen confident, assured performances from City that nonetheless have lacked the brilliance of previous years. Everyone knows that, next season, they'll need to dedicate much more time to drilling the basics. It's just hard to see where they'll find the time. Training sessions have prioritised specific areas this year. The players have worked hard on physical conditioning, in particular injury prevention and strength building using small weights. They've also dedicated a lot of time to going over how they bring the ball out for each game … plus finishing.

Nicolas Jover is the set-piece coordinator. This is an area they've also spent time on, either out on the pitch or via video training. There have been huge improvements in this aspect of their game. The team has scored 19 goals from set pieces (12 from corners and 7 from free kicks, many of the goals coming from the second ball). They've also only conceded 3 from corners. Their results from penalties are less good. They've scored 6 but conceded 7.

Pep himself is still taking a more minimalist approach to coaching and his previously long, wordy, intense team talks are now much shorter and more succinct. This is probably the area where he's made most personal changes. Instead of bombarding his men with every last detail about the opposition and running through every possible response, he now keeps it brief, much to his players' relief. 'Pep the minimalist! Who'd have thought it.'

To learn more about the value of acquired knowledge and the role played by the subconscious mind, I talked with Gil Sousa, a young Portuguese football coach who undoubtedly has a brilliant future ahead of him. He's written a book, *Decidir como um treinador* (Decide like a Coach), and much of what he says can be directly applied to what City are going through now.*

> The most neglected aspect of training is the players' subconscious, emotional state. We develop the training routines but we need to place much more importance on the players' subconscious thought processes. If we think of the cycle of football like the cycle of life, you have a good experience, then life becomes a bit harder and then you have another good experience and so on … Our training should focus on somatic moments in order to rid the players of the memories of bad experiences. It's vital to avoid the mistake of talking about *automatismos* [automatic decisions and actions], we should be talking about dominating the game.

· · ·

There's no time to enjoy a 'somatic moment' during City's visit to Villa Park, however. The hosts defend in a tight 5–4–1, hunkered down near Emiliano Martínez's goal, under siege from a relentless, dominant opponent (City achieve 82 per cent possession). On the left, the Zinchenko–Gündoğan–Foden triangle creates long passing sequences. Not only do they never lose the ball but they draw Villa's defenders towards them in order to stretch their defensive line and allow Mahrez and Silva to look for space to drive forward unimpeded down the other flank towards Villa's goal. Meanwhile, Pep's 'decoy men' just keep passing in their triangle. The so-called 'juntarrivales' is proving its worth as a top-drawer weapon in Pep's tactical armoury. Villa press aggressively as City bring the ball out from the back. Ederson's spotted that Zinchenko is unmarked, on the far side of the centre circle. He thumps one of his long, killer passes to the Ukrainian who cuts the ball back to meet Foden's forward

---

* Given the brilliance of Gil Sousa's thinking, the Portuguese Football Federation decided to publish *Decidir como um treinador* in 2018. The book's subtitle is 'Science and practice in football and in life: Do we act because we think or do we think because we act?'

charge. The Stockport Iniesta immediately crosses to the opposite wing where Mahrez controls it and gives it to Silva, who moves into the box and sends it straight to Foden's feet. The youngster puts the ball into the back of the net (his 14th goal of the season). Villa 1 City 1. It's taken nine touches from one goalmouth to another. An incredible example of the skill, savvy and sheer dynamism of Pep's men. They're electric out there. Villa's fortress continues to crumble. City drive forward inexorably until, taking their seventh corner, Silva sends a perfect high ball to Rodri who heads it in. Martínez has no time to react. City have absolute control. It's going to be plain sailing.

Then, just before the break, Stones is sent off. A red card for his hard, although unintentional, tackle on Jacob Ramsey. Pep's furious at what he thinks is a massive overreaction by the referee but his assistants put him straight. Stones deserved the red. After the break, Laporte comes on for Gabriel Jesus, who's clearly not happy. The Brazilian thinks they still need him out there, given his superb pressing of rival defenders, but Pep sees the Foden–Mahrez partnership as their best bet for making it through the next 45 minutes with just ten men. He stays with his backline of four centre-backs and has a line of five players with Foden 'floating', moving up and down and across the pitch. Aston Villa are now holding on to the ball for longer periods but City are still able to keep robbing it back to attack. Pep's trio on the left wing aggressively maintain the pressure and the Cityzens continue to dominate. Foden is on superb form and is rewarded when his marker, Matty Cash, receives two yellows in the space of three minutes. Red card. Villa are also down to ten men. Now, for the last 30 minutes, City shut the game down. Overall, they pass the ball more than 800 times, denying the home side any chance to counterattack. The 'Yugoslavs' at the height of their power, opting for control rather than feats of daring do. They have three more chances but are obviously more focused on maintaining their advantage rather than increasing it.

Foden's been sublime today. He's already exceeded anything we could have imagined back when he was a wide-eyed newbie. Silva, Zinchenko, Gündoğan and Rodri have also played brilliantly. It's all looking good for the sprint to the finishing line. The victory means the title's nearly in the bag. City just need three more wins. They've now won 17 away from home, 10 of which were league games. (City achieved 11 in a row in May–December 2017.)

Pep's third title in five years is in sight.

MOMENT 31. FOUR IN A ROW

London, 25 April 2021

'There's absolutely no complacency in the team. Everyone is completely focused all the time. We're not taking any of our games lightly, regardless of who we're playing.'

Pep's asked Brian Kidd to take the press conference after City's League Cup victory, their fourth in a row. From his days in the youth categories as a striker to training City's young hopefuls and third assistant coach since 2011, Kidd's become something of an institution at City and a huge support to first Roberto Mancini, then Pellegrini and now Guardiola. His in-depth knowledge of the club has been invaluable in helping the successive coaches connect with City's history and culture. Kidd's now planning to retire and is keen to deliver one clear message before he goes. Nobody at Manchester City is complacent.

Son Heung-min has collapsed on the pitch at Wembley, his eyes welling up. Nearby, Harry Kane and Hugo Lloris, his captain, are trying to console each other. Tottenham have just lost another trophy. Harry Kane, an exceptional player and proficient striker, hasn't won a single trophy to show for his ten years at Spurs.

Two days later, Kane puts things in motion. He's leaving. He'd already had contact with City a year ago, but the whole Messi drama put paid to that. Now the only thing that seems to be standing in the way of a move to Manchester is the issue of whether Erling Haaland is still an option or not. City won't know the answer to that for a couple of weeks. After the Super League fiasco things have changed on the European stage. It was clear that Florentino Pérez wanted to increase Madrid's earnings so that they could buy Haaland and/or Mbappé. Now, it's anyone's guess as to which other European clubs are going to be interested in the player and City's directors aren't at all sure they want to get involved in haggling in an over-inflated auction.

Harry Kane would be a superb option and City's directors have Pep's full agreement in reaching out to the player. Stories begin to leak to the London press: Harry's sick of his team's lack of competitiveness; he wants trophies and he's not going to get them playing for Spurs; he's telling them it's time for the club to agree a reasonable price so that he can move on.

Over in Paris, Txiki Begiristain is delighted with the various messages he's getting on his mobile. Spurs are undoubtedly going to demand an exorbitant price. But Harry's worth it.

Four thousand fans have been allowed into Wembley this evening. Two thousand from each club. It's a small step back to normality but a huge one in terms of the difference it makes to the atmosphere of the game. It's like a tiny window has opened in the claustrophobic world of COVID-19. Football suddenly feels different.

City haven't lost a single League Cup game since 26 October 2016, when United beat them 1–0 at Old Trafford: 19 victories in a row and now their fourth consecutive final. And in Guardiola's favourite arena, 'his' Wembley where he won his first European Cup, as a player, in 1992 and where he's now won numerous trophies as a coach: the Champions League 2011, the FA Cup of 2019, the 2018, 2019 and 2020 League Cups … Yes, Wembley is definitely Pep's playground.

And his men prove it once again. From kick-off to the final whistle, with De Bruyne back and fully fit, the team are phenomenal. It's probably their best first half of the entire season. Only Lloris's brilliance and the superb defensive play of Eric Dier and Toby Alderweireld prevent Spurs from taking an absolute thrashing. Even the prediction of 3.6 vs 0.06 expected goals doesn't reflect the spectacular football we're watching today and you'd have to go very far back indeed to find a Cup final where one side has dominated so completely.

Sterling is back on form, at least as far as his attitude is concerned – he's still making some of the same blunders than have kept him on the bench over the last few weeks. Mahrez is outstanding, though. Bullish and aggressive, he fizzes with energy while Foden revels in his false-forward role, weaving connective threads between one flank and the other, controlling the tempo and rhythm of their game, and anticipating exactly what the team needs at every moment. But it's the silent heroes of City's defensive lines who really excel today. Walker, Dias and Laporte combine beautifully, anticipating Spurs' every move and preventing them from making their signature sudden runs into open space, usually Tottenham's biggest threat. Cancelo, in particular, has a sublime game. Back in his full-back/attacking-midfielder role he's not only pitch-perfect in defence, but fearsome when he switches to offensive mode. Tottenham manage one shot at Zack Steffen's goal, which he flicks away with ease. Twenty-one shots at goal for City eventually produce the breakthrough, just when they least expect it. De Bruyne takes a wide free kick, almost from the corner spot, and Laporte, who has had no problem getting away from Moussa Sissoko's sloppy marking, runs forward and heads it into the net to win the game. It's his eighth goal for City, all of them scored away from home. Many of them crucial.

On the way to this victory Pep's men have faced down some of the biggest clubs in English football in their rivals' own backyards: Arsenal, Manchester United and, now, Tottenham at Wembley. Now, with their fourth League Cup trophy in a row they've matched Liverpool's achievements in the same competition in 1981–4. It's also the eighth League Cup they've won, which again puts them in joint-first place with Liverpool,* and Fernandinho and Agüero have each accumulated six League Cups, the highest number of any individual player. Pep's also just won his ninth trophy with City, which, considering the club has won 27 in its entire history, means that he's been responsible for one-third of their silverware. Today's win also marks his 31st trophy as a coach.†

MOMENT 32. 'GO OUT AND ENJOY IT'

Parίs, 28 April 2021

Today, the real magic happens in the dressing room.

It's the second leg of the Champions League semi-final. And City are losing. Down 1–0 to Paris Saint-Germain in the Parc des Princes … their first-half performance an anaemic facsimile of the football we've come to love. At half-time, Pep joins his men in the visitors' dressing room. He's going to have one more go at fixing this, get them to relax and just play their game. It's now or never.

He's spent weeks trying to get them to this point. Working closely with his loyal *consiglieri*, Manel Estiarte and Juan Manuel Lillo, Pep has transformed how he interacts with his players. No more flailing arms on the

---

* They won in 1970, 1976, 2014, 2016, 2018, 2019, 2020 and 2021.

† Guardiola won a trophy with Barça B (the third division), 14 with Barça, 7 with Bayern and now 9 with City.

touchline or picking up on every error or making constant demands. And much, much less pressure. Don't get me wrong. This is still Pep Guardiola. As perfectionist, demanding and determined to win as ever. A man who never, ever gives up. But right now, the pressure valve needs to be released a little and that's what he's tried to do.

European football is something of a thorn in Pep's side. Take Bayern's 4–0 defeat to Real Madrid in 2014, when, against his (and Philipp Lahm's) better judgement, his team played the kind of football his attacking players (Thomas Müller and Bastian Schweinsteiger, for example) favoured rather than his own brand of play. Then, the following year, the German champions were thrashed again. This time 3–0 by Barça at the Camp Nou. Despite struggling with injury problems, his men almost pulled off an epic comeback in their 3–2 victory in the return leg. Close, but no cigar. Again. Then, in his third year in Germany, despite having prepared the team for Atlético Madrid to come out firing with both barrels, Pep was forced to watch helplessly as the home side scored in the first 15 minutes. Despite one of Bayern's most dynamic Champions League performances in the return leg, the Germans went out on away goals.

More recently of course, City have had various foul-ups of their own: losing out to Monaco and Spurs because of the away-goal rule; his men going to pieces for a full 15 minutes at Anfield; the defensive blunders against Lyon; Laporte, his best defender, making tiny errors; Sterling missing in front of an open goal against Lyon; Agüero's botched penalty against Spurs; Llorente scoring with his arm … the list goes on. But Pep has moved on from the memories of past mistakes. Nowadays he's less driven by ego, willing to keep his instructions and his team talks short and to the point. He's a changed man, this Pep the minimalist. And his men appreciate him for it. The years have rubbed some of the sharper edges off that young, fearless, brilliant guy who led Barça to glorious victory. Guardiola is now more mature, calmer and much less histrionic, more willing to listen to advice and more realistic in terms of the demands he makes of himself and others. It occurs to me, as I watch him pick up his phone and calmly answer a few texts just four hours before kick-off (something that would have been unimaginable a few years ago), that, in fact, he's become much more *Cruyffista* than ever before.

With Dortmund defeated and the curse of the quarter-finals finally broken, Manchester City have made it to Paris and the semi-final of the Champions League. Although he's always been a superb tactician, with an astounding ability to anticipate exactly what's going to happen in a game, Pep has, of late, begun to prioritise what Seirul·lo calls the 'emotional/ volitional side of man management', the socio-affective structures that impact us all. There are more important things than the team's formation, the 3–2–2–3 or the 2–3–2–3. And any competition involves much more than tactics and counter-tactics. Over the years, Pep has come to recognise that the emotional connections and interactions between his players, plus the psychological wellbeing of individuals and the group, must form the basis of any successful campaign. Emotional wellbeing can make the difference between resounding success or total failure. He's experienced it at first hand over so many years that he now dedicates as much attention and energy to this as he's ever done to tactical analysis. This is why he's found himself constantly quoting his mentor, the great Johan Cruyff, throughout the week prior to today's game. He quoted Cruyff in the press conference yesterday – one of his best ever – during which he treated the gathered media to a profound discourse on human behaviour in the context of elite football. And he'll do it again. In the half-time break, with the team trailing and his men drowning.

·   ·   ·

There's just been one question mark over today's lineup and, in the end, Pep's chosen João Cancelo at left-back. The Portuguese international had a great game against Spurs and should be more than capable of marking PSG's great 'connector', Argentine Ángel Di María.

City stride out into the Parc des Princes knowing exactly what they have to do. It's all pretty straightforward. Shut down the spaces. Don't let PSG counterattack. Total focus. Control every pass. Don't lose the ball. Message received. Loud and clear. They just take it too far. Focus and control become hypervigilance and extreme caution. And that leads to mistakes. Their passing is off. Just by a fraction, but, at this level, that's all it takes. They're not producing their long passing sequences and there's little sign of the lightning-fast connections between players that we're used to.

They're struggling to impose their usual, high-tempo rhythm on the game. Excessive caution is effectively short-circuiting them.

The team's had almost no preparation for today's game. It's been a busy week. Sunday, win the League Cup at Wembley. Check. Day off on Monday. Check. Tuesday, head to Paris for the Champions League semi-final. Check. They have done a bit of training on defensive and offensive set pieces though, but that's exactly where they mess up now. PSG have just taken their third corner when their captain, Marquinhos, manages to shake off Gündoğan and Rodri. Dias and Stones then find themselves totally blocked by Leandro Paredes and Marco Verratti. The Parisians go ahead. Fifty minutes later, City will also produce a goal from their third corner. So the set-piece training pays off in the end. But there's a lot more action before that happens.

PSG take control from the second minute of the game when Rodri loses the ball, allowing Mbappé to counterattack and set Neymar up. His weak shot doesn't go in but there's more to come. Ten minutes later, after PSG's first corner, the Brazilian has another shot. Ederson manages to block it but can't do anything about Marquinhos's header three minutes later. By now, PSG are completely in charge – on the pitch and on the scoreboard. Neymar moves back almost as far as the centre circle to direct operations, causing Pep's men to go into panic mode. The guy's unstoppable. Even when they do manage to take the ball from Neymar, Di María is always ready and waiting, with back-up from Alessandro Florenzi. All City's channels of connection are cut off. They try to strengthen their build-up by switching their usual 3+2 to a 3+3 as they bring the ball out, with Rodri, Gündoğan and Cancelo in the second line, but this means they have one less man up front to face seven French defenders. Only a long-distance cross puts PSG under pressure, courtesy of a Cruyff-style back-post flying volley … but they're not producing enough volume to create their usual quality of chances. Suddenly, it feels like Pep's players are carrying the weight of the world, and all their previous defeats, on their shoulders. Neymar and Di María are bossing the game and another goal for the French feels imminent. Pep looks on, determined to trust his players and stay calm. And things pick up in the closing eight minutes of the first half. Silva, De Bruyne and Foden begin to press more effectively; Silva steals the ball and passes to Foden, who slams it straight at goal from the penalty spot – but too straight. Keylor Navas reacts in time but it's a good try. City are still in the game.

Half-time. City's players sit in absolute silence as Pep quickly goes over a few small changes he wants to make to their distribution on the pitch, their pressing and the direction they're moving in. But he needs to address the elephant in the room: how they're all feeling, and this is definitely not a 'whiteboard moment'. As Lillo always says, 'The whiteboard is a screen behind which players and coaches hide. Its use contributes to one of the great curses of our times: the need to offload responsibility to other people.' Years later, Marc Boixasa still gets emotional whenever he recalls what Pep said to his men that day. 'It was magical. We all thought he was going to stick to tactics but he gave this really heartfelt talk about how great each of the players were and he told them that all they had to do was go out and "be themselves".'

> You're all brilliant. Much better than them. Just relax and play your game. Don't worry about the results or the consequences. That's my job. You're footballers. Go out and play football, enjoy yourselves like you did when you were little kids and weren't afraid of anything. Leave the stress and the worries here in the dressing room and then shut the door on all of it. The anxiety, the press, social media, what everyone's going to say, the consequences … Leave it all here and just go out and have some fun. Just like you did back when you were kids. Enjoy yourselves.

It's exactly what they need to hear. Manchester City emerge from the dressing room utterly transformed. The boss is taking all responsibility for what happens next and all they have to do is play their game. They organise themselves according to Pep's instructions. He hasn't made many changes but every last one of them proves to be decisive in the second half. When he has the ball, Foden moves away from the left wing and drives through the central lines of attack, dragging Florenzi with him while De Bruyne 'pins' PSG's two centre-backs. Foden's position on the outside is then occupied, albeit slightly deeper, by Cancelo, who thus takes Di María with him, effectively breaking the Argentine's connection with the deadly Neymar–Mbappé partnership. Consequently, Mbappé will only lead one more serious attack on City's goal for the entire second half, which ends in him sending the ball across Ederson's goalmouth with no one there to convert the chance. Cancelo's position high up the pitch and Foden moving more centrally leave space for Gündoğan to stitch all the important elements together. He connects 26 times with Rodri, 11 with Foden, 13 with Cancelo and 9 times with Zinchenko.

City are now controlling the ball with precision and speed, passing to the dominant foot of each of their teammates. The momentum drives them on, their passing becoming faster and faster as they advance deep into PSG's territory. Gündoğan, backed up by Rodri, weaves in and out, while Dias covers Mbappé's every move and Walker sticks close to Neymar. They'll chase them all over the pitch if they have to. Stones is then free to 'sweep' behind the centre-backs. By now, City are monopolising the ball high up the pitch. And even when they don't have the ball, Pep's men still look the dominant side. They move into a 4–4–2 and press the French team on the right. De Bruyne drives Marquinhos to the PSG right, where Foden is controlling Florenzi and Cancelo has Di María's number. In the centre, Silva, who has the stamina of three guys today, manages to mark Paredes while also causing Presnel Kimpembe problems and Gündoğan doesn't let Idrissa Gueye out of his sight. Mahrez and Walker lie in wait on City's right, like hunting dogs with their first scent of blood. City's distribution means that, as PSG bring the ball out, Marquinhos is forced to either pass to a teammate who's being closely marked by a City player or thump a long ball up the pitch, where City will intercept it.

The stats give us some idea of the huge transformation that's taken place since the first half. City's first-half possession was 53 per cent, it's now 61 per cent. Pep's men rob 45 balls against PSG's 31, and the French side only manage 170 clean passes in the second half, 80 less than the first half. Their rate of accuracy also drops from 90 per cent to 85 per cent. In contrast, City increase their total passes from 304 to 351, maintaining a 92 to 93 per cent accuracy rate. The Cityzens make 12 incursions into the French penalty box while the home side manage the equivalent just once in the whole of the second half, and fail to produce a single shot on Ederson's goal.

Pep decides to bring Cancelo off. They have PSG on the ropes now and the last thing he wants is one of his men to be sent off. He can't risk Cancelo adding another yellow to the one the referee's already shown him. So, Zinchenko comes on and becomes the third corner of the lethally effective Gündoğan–Foden–Zinchenko triangle. Now City get lucky. The first goal comes from a corner forced by Walker. City produce a series of short passes across the whole breadth of the box, from the right wing to the left, where De Bruyne whips in a curving cross looking, speculatively, for Dias's header or Stones's shot at goal. But neither of his teammates reach the ball in time. The ball twists in the air one last time and the bounce takes it straight into the far panel of the net while Navas looks on in despair. A beautiful fluke. But a fluke nonetheless. Then, just seven minutes later, Gueye fouls De Bruyne outside the box. Mahrez steps up to take the free kick and sends it straight through PSG's wall, in between Paredes and Kimpembe and into the Parisians' net. City 2 PSG 1.

This is their 50th victory out of the 90 Champions League games they've played so far and their 18th win away from home. It's their 10th victory in this season's competition and the best semi-final result Pep has achieved in Europe since beating Real Madrid 2–0 in the Bernabéu in 2011. They've still a way to go though, so City's celebrations are subdued. Pep's impressed: 'I'm happy that the players didn't overdo it in the dressing room, it was very low-key. Happy, but without needing to shout it from the rooftops. All of us know that anything could still happen in the return leg.'

Both De Bruyne and Mahrez have played superbly today. Their stats are surprising. Unusually for him, De Bruyne, with four, is the player who has committed the most fouls, and Mahrez, with seven, has robbed the ball from PSG more than any of his teammates. Gündoğan and Silva have also impressed in their roles but the standout, if low-key, stars today have been the two centre-backs, Stones and Dias, who have prevented Mbappé from getting even a single shot on goal, the first time this has happened in the Frenchman's undoubtedly illustrious career. He's not alone in this, of course. Both Erling Haaland and Harry Kane know at first hand what it's like to come off worse against City's formidable backline.

This is a huge moment for City. They've stuck to all the basic principles of their game and they've come through the mental and psychological barriers. They're well on their way to taking their rightful place among the greats of European football.

Pep got it absolutely right today: 'Sometimes you need to relax and just be yourself. I just want one thing in the return leg. That we go out there and just be ourselves. Nothing more than that.'

MOMENT 33. 'FERNANDINHO – YOU'RE IN'

Paris, 29 April 2021

Before the return leg against PSG, City face Crystal Palace at Selhurst Park so they take the chance to do a training session in Paris the morning after the semi-final first leg. Captain Fernandinho has been chatting with the coaching staff and agrees that those who didn't play against PSG, or Borussia Dortmund, should start a match that will take them ever closer to the title. It's something that's been on his mind since the defeat to Chelsea in the FA Cup semi-final, when Gündoğan was furious at what he saw as the passivity of some of his teammates that day and first raised the issue with the Brazilian. Gündoğan knows instinctively that it's a bad idea to create a huge separation between starters and substitutes, not because he doesn't believe in the importance of lining up the best and fittest team you have but because the attitude of the guys who don't get to play can bring down the whole group. As it did against Chelsea. The two men have agreed that they need to shake things up a bit, not to point fingers but to ensure that everyone is pulling in the same direction. It's time for some of their teammates to come off the subs bench, literally and figuratively. Over the next few days, the pair work with the technical team to address the issue, with Fernandinho initiating lots of conversations and Gündoğan doing his best to bring the other players around to their ideas. In the end, consensus is reached: 'It's in all our interests that this final sprint goes well and we all need to make sure that we keep winning … Nobody wins when the team loses and nobody loses when the team wins.'

It's a turning point. They've made it clear that they don't expect to see anyone play like he's just there to make up the numbers or turning up to training with a face like a wet weekend, playing the victim card. No more moaning and groaning about a lack of playing time. Gündoğan's and Fernandinho's instincts have been spot-on, and there's a completely different atmosphere at training the morning after the PSG match. They have their usual laughs but there's a real sense that everyone is taking this seriously, working hard and competing aggressively. Just ten men train fully at the Paris FC facilities – those who'll play at Palace on Saturday. This is the group who'll hopefully take City one step closer to the title. The important thing, though, is that everyone's heading back to Manchester fully committed to the team's success.

On Thursday evening, back in Manchester, Pep's still trying to find a way to field a strong starting 11 while saving his key men for the PSG return. His main problem will be ensuring that they bring the ball out well, despite playing with three left-footed centre-backs.

In the end, they produce a solid, if unremarkable, performance at Selhurst Park, winning comfortably by sticking to their fundamentals. It's the City of the Yugoslavs again: defenders are completely focused and keep mistakes to an absolute minimum; their teammates in the centre of the pitch play with intelligence and consistency, setting and maintaining the rhythm; and the forwards work together to create the fluid attacking moves. There's no star striker today but everyone is contributing up front. This is the way they've won game after game since the end of 2020 when the City juggernaut became unstoppable. It's not the brilliance we witnessed from 2017 to 2019 nor is it a perfect rendition of Pep's signature 'positional play'. Their counterattacking isn't up to normal standards, partly because they're still missing Leroy Sané's long legs and speed, and partly because of Sterling's dip in form. They also no longer have a worker ant like David Silva, who is able to pull together all the disparate parts of the team with the patience of a craftsman. But City have developed other strengths. A defensive line that has increased their levels of concentration and minimised their errors; midfielders who understand that their job is to set the speed and rhythm of the game and weave an unbreakable web of connections with the rest of the team, and players up front who know that arriving in the box just at the right moment is the way to win matches. This 2020–1 Manchester City may not be the most spectacular of the Guardiola era but it is undoubtedly the most compact, cohesive and versatile of his five seasons at the club. The City of the Yugoslavs.

So, just 60 hours after their Paris triumph, City's players line up in south London. Ederson, Cancelo and Rodri start but the rest of the team from Paris get to sit this one out. Pep wants them rested and sharp for their next European test – finishing PSG off. He's come up with an unusual spine: two left-footed centre-backs (Aké and Laporte), two in the midfield (Fernandinho and Rodri) plus two strikers (Agüero and Gabriel Jesus). In truth, it's a bit of a juggling act to ensure the ball circulates fluidly. Fernandinho drops off to the right touchline to help Aké and Laporte bring the ball out, while Cancelo, Mendy and Agüero move closer to Rodri in the second line. Agüero, who's positioned behind Gabriel Jesus, is absolutely key to their efforts today. He anticipates his teammates' moves, protects the ball when necessary and distributes it beautifully. Having to spend most of the time outside the box, his natural habitat, has clearly done nothing to blunt the Argentine's killer instinct and outstanding skill. It is, nonetheless, a huge challenge for Pep's players to produce fast, fluid football within this unusual formation and the game drags a little. Palace don't help matters by huddling down into a defensive block while they wait for a chance to counterattack. They produce a beautiful sequence of passes in the first half and Christian Benteke gets a shot at goal, which Ederson saves superbly. Jesus has a goal disallowed for what's a clear offside – Sterling and Agüero both have a couple of unsuccessful chances.

Things pick up in the second half. Torres has a good chance and then City produce two goals in quick succession to win the game. The first one is an Agüero special. Mendy sends him the gentlest of passes, which he controls and then converts into the kind of screamer for which he's famous. Then, just 80 seconds later, Ferran Torres gets to the ball as it rebounds from an Agüero–Jesus combination and scores from outside the area with his left foot. It's goal number 700 for City since Pep took over (out of 288 games). Liverpool have scored 543 in the same period, Manchester United, 512.

Fernandinho is outstanding today, consistently beating the colossal Benteke in their one-on-one duels and giving a passing recital plus a demonstration of perfect positional play. Watching him, Pep decides to make Fernandinho his organising midfielder for the PSG game, so he replaces him with Zinchenko as a precaution. Tomorrow he'll confirm this decision. Fernandinho will be in the starting 11 for the semi-final second leg. Rodri is out.

It's clear that Sterling is desperate to score today, hoping perhaps to redeem himself after so many weeks of poor performances. But it's not to be. His first left-footed shot hits the post and he converts neither an Agüero-inspired counterattack nor, finally, a brilliant pass from Zinchenko, which again bounces off the post.

Just as he did last Sunday, Pep makes a point of praising Sterling post-match, highlighting how good his attitude has been. It's something Pep always does when he feels that one of his important players has lost a bit of confidence. Unfortunately for the player, being publicly praised by the boss usually means just one thing. You'll be on the bench for the next game.

Their victory in London leaves them just one good result away from winning the title. They're 13 points ahead of United, although their city rivals have a game in hand after their meeting with Liverpool was postponed because of a pitch invasion by the Old Trafford fans protesting against the club's owners. But City return to Manchester feeling like Champions. They've now won 11 Premier league games away from home – matching the records set by Chelsea in 2008 and City in 2017 – and 19 across all competitions, another English record.

Pep's happy to share with me what he sees as the secret of their success: 'Our success this season is definitely down to the strength of character of our players. And one other thing: our determination never to think beyond the next game.'

MOMENT 34. 'WE'RE GOING TO CRUSH IT'

Manchester, 4 May 2021

Just five words.

Pep has a couple of hours off after lunch and spends them responding to a few text messages he's not yet got around to answering. It's as good a way as any to relieve the tension that starts to build on the eve of a big game. He has a while before he has to get the players together for a bite to eat and a brief team talk – with almost no tactical instructions! They don't need speeches or tactics. They all know what they have to do and exactly what's riding on the semi-final against PSG. No inspirational speeches required. No extra pressure either. And Pep's actually feeling quite relaxed. Or as much as it's possible to be when you're the coach of an elite team about to go into a high-stake, high-stress Champions League semi-final decider. So, he's focusing on the text messages that have been coming in since the first leg: congratulations for the victory in Paris and best wishes for tonight's game. His response to almost all of them is short and sweet, 'We're going to crush it.'

Meanwhile, dark clouds are forming outside. The skies open and the rain begins to lash down on Manchester. Snow is just around the corner.

He's given them just one instruction. 'Take no risks.' And it feels all the more important now, as the snow begins to blanket the ground.

It's something he and Domènec Torrent used to tell players: 'In the Champions League, never take unnecessary risks.' The risks they took in the second half of the Paris game paid off. They just need to hold on to their advantage so … 'Take no risks!' Which translates into a 4–4–2 formation with De Bruyne and Silva up front. Their job will be to try and drive their opponents down the inside channels, where City's indomitable trio, Stones–Dias–Fernandinho, will be waiting to pounce. Mbappé's out through injury and Pep's hoping to force the Parisians into the middle of the pitch where they'll have to finish their attacking runs with crosses from the wings, which is what City feel at their strongest in dealing with. His men will be taking extra care with their passing, particularly given the thick layer of snow that is now covering the pitch.

It's no surprise then when PSG come out all guns blazing while City play it safe. Pep's filled the centre of the pitch, ensuring that his men have all the intermediate spaces covered while retaining the flow and movement of their game. He's changed the initial build-up phase from his usual 3–2–2–3. Today, his men are distributed in a 2–4–4 to bring the ball out, then a 4–2–4 for the construction phase and, finally, they switch to an attacking 3–4–3. Whenever they lose the ball, they reform into a 4–4–2, although De Bruyne and Silva don't press particularly hard at the start, thereby letting the French play their game. The Parisians are ably led today by the diminutive but super-talented Marco Verratti, who sets and controls the rhythm of their game. But City's pressing begins to force them into the centre of the pitch and starves them of space to run into – the PSG trademark. The French, who have beaten Barça at the Camp Nou and Bayern at the Allianz Arena, are forced to pass the ball long into City's box. Seven minutes in, the referee blows his whistle and awards a penalty against Zinchenko. His decision is immediately rescinded, however, on VAR advice. The Ukrainian didn't use his arm – the ball bounced off his back.

City are taking no risks. They're also dragging PSG into dangerous areas and stretching their lines, and that's exactly how they get the first goal. City have a free kick in the visitors' half, which Fernandinho takes short to Gündoğan, who passes to Zinchenko on the left. The Ukrainian is forced back by a tightly packed PSG defensive line. The centre-backs drive the action towards the right-hand side, where Walker meets the same wall of PSG men and makes the same choice as Zinchenko: move back towards Ederson. PSG sniff opportunity with Neymar, Mauro Icardi and Di María leading the charge. They clearly feel that the exchange of passes between Gündoğan and Ederson has made City vulnerable. However, City's passing choices, and particularly that apparently inspiration-free Ederson and Gündoğan interplay, with the ball going back and forward between them, stretch PSG's resources vertically – magnetically drawing them up towards City's backline.

Pochettino's four centre-backs move up the pitch to the centre circle; their three strikers are now on the edge of City's area and their midfielders are split up across the pitch, marking De Bruyne, Fernandinho and Silva closely. Now the French team are stretched vertically and from side to side; they're tactically 'open' and potentially overstretched. Ederson, so exceptional with the ball at his feet, fixes his panoramic vision on the opposition goalmouth. He has two teammates free – the full-backs. Walker's on the right, halfway up the pitch, behind Mahrez, and he's totally unmarked, But, on the left, Zinchenko's in an even better position. He's on the halfway line, and Florenzi, who's been dragged out of position by Bernardo, is some distance away. With his body already half-turned towards the opposition goal, Zinchenko is Ederson's best bet. The big Brazilian thumps the ball long, 60m up the pitch, where the Ukrainian full-back has already attacked PSG's exposed spaces. Marquinhos is after him immediately but Zinchenko holds possession intelligently and calmly times his pass with De Bruyne's arrival, while Foden draws Kimpembe away from the Belgian's zone of influence.

De Bruyne, who's shaken off Verratti and Ander Herrera, takes a superb shot, which would have gone in but for Florenzi's outstretched right boot. The ball ricochets and lands in front of Mahrez, who tucks it way. All 11 of City's men have played a part in the last 42 seconds, which saw their 15-pass sequence stretch PSG way out of position and Ederson demonstrate his amazing ability to find exactly where to put the ball so as to exploit City's numerical superiority. It's how they've strived to play all season: lots of passing sequences, magnetically drawing opponents where you want them; calm, patient play that aims to establish superiority in unexpected areas plus solid, efficient finishing.

Going ahead does nothing to change Pep's strategy. If anything, in fact, he becomes even more cautious, oscillating between a 2–4–4 and a 4–4–2. Above all, he doesn't want to stretch City's lines too much. Despite these tactics, PSG have a couple of good chances: Marquinhos's header hits the crossbar and Di María takes advantage of a serious error from Silva but, somehow, he fails to score despite the open goal. City continue to control the pace of the game, maintaining a slow, steady rhythm during the last 30 minutes of the first half, and PSG's attacks also gradually decrease both in speed and frequency. The Parisians have had more possession (56 per cent) and have tried to play daring, aggressive football but, so far, have utterly failed to disrupt City's rhythm.

After the break, Pep decides to shake things up a bit, just as he did in Paris a week ago. The ground staff have done a great job of clearing the snow and now De Bruyne, Bernardo, Foden and Mahrez lead the Cityzens in a high-pressing attack, with support from Fernandinho, whose relentless recuperation of the ball is exceptional. Foden has a shot on goal saved by PSG's Costa Rican keeper and then Neymar gets on the end of a long diagonal ball in City's area. No dice though. Zinchenko blocks it – earning a celebratory hug from his fellow defenders. It's still pouring with rain as Zinchenko initiates a counterattack. De Bruyne and Foden build it down the left until the Stockport Iniesta sets up Mahrez, who's unmarked having left PSG's Abdou Diallo far behind, for 2–0. Midway through City's counterattack, Neymar had decided to mark De Bruyne instead of Mahrez. A fatal error, which has essentially left City's winger alone in the PSG penalty area. His goal effectively ends the contest. Almost before it all sinks in Di María is sent off for fouling Fernandinho. Now, all City have to do is keep their cool for the last 20 minutes – which is more challenging than you might think, particularly for Zinchenko, who almost loses it but calms down after a severe ticking off from Fernandinho. The captain, who turns 36 today, is taking his *in loco parentis* duties very seriously indeed.

City create four more presentable chances and a Foden shot almost goes in but just clips the post. They don't really need it, though, and, as the final whistle blows, City are through to the final of the Champions League for the first time in their history. There's a muted celebration on the pitch followed by a bit more revelry in the dressing room. Nothing excessive though. The really big test is still to come.

Manchester City become the ninth English club to reach the European Cup final and the first to do it after winning 11 games in the competition (plus 1 draw, against Porto). This is their seventh consecutive victory and their eighth clean sheet. They've scored 25 and, as a result of superb defending, conceded just 4.*

The centre-backs have been key to City's defensive prowess, although, as Mahrez is quick to point out, 'every single one of us has to defend!' The Algerian has been City's star attacker: an assist against Gladbach, an assist and a goal against Dortmund and three goals against PSG.

It's worth highlighting the three factors that have played such a crucial role in City's success in this competition. The first relates to psychology. Pep asked his men to keep calm and they supported each other in doing just that, with Stones telling his teammates yesterday, 'we just need to be ourselves.' Dias is also conscious of the importance of having a strong mental attitude as a group: 'When the chips are down that's when we really show what we're made of!'

The second factor is the 'magnetic attraction', which City's players use to draw opponents in a specific direction and which has worked so well even against an elite side like PSG. We saw it in the build-up to City's first goal and the Zinchenko–Gündoğan–Foden trio used it to stunning effect throughout the game, maintaining passing sequences that drew their opponents to them, thereby gifting their teammates advantage in other zones.†

The third thing I'd like to highlight is Guardiola's strategy: play with audacity in the away game and conserve your advantage in the return leg. Brilliant.

Right now, though, even the two most serious and abstemious members of the coaching team are ready to relax and enjoy the (muted) celebrations. I catch Estiarte and Lillo chuckling quietly together. 'Who'd have thought it? The more Yugoslavian we are, the better things go. The more sober we are on the pitch the more the champagne flows off it!'

---

* They conceded against Porto, one in each game against Borussia Dortmund and one in Paris.
† Seventeen passes from Zinchenko to Gündoğan and 15 to Foden; 14 each from Gündoğan and Foden to Zinchenko.

THE PORTUGUESE WALL

Sooner or later Rúben Dias is going to find himself slipping on the captain's armband – inevitably his teammates will want him as a captain and already, despite being so young (he's still only 23), Dias's charisma, leadership skills and total focus make him a natural. A player who combines strong intuitive qualities with an irresistible physical exuberance, he demands nothing but the best from himself and his teammates. Whether he's chasing his opponents all over the pitch or throwing himself into a high-risk tackle, it's Dias who has lit the fire in the belly of City's defence this season. He's the defensive virtuoso for whom Pep's been looking for a long time. There have been other contenders for the role: Vincent Kompany, who was sadly too injury-prone, and later, John Stones and Aymeric Laporte, neither of whom quite made the grade. Now, with Dias at the helm, Pep's managed to create the defensive organisation of his dreams, a replica of his Barcelona backline. Dias has a similar style to Carles Puyol. Stones is the man who brings the ball out with precision and ruthless efficiency (as does Laporte, despite his intermittent concentration), just as Gerard Piqué did in the Barça glory days. Walker provides the strength, speed and sheer physical force of an Eric Abidal while Cancelo and Zinchenko complete the picture with creativity and audacity. Guardiola's tried repeatedly to recreate that Barcelona defence – albeit with different kinds of players and in totally different circumstances. In Manchester he's done it, and City have made it to the Champions League final thanks largely to their defenders.

It's the factor that meant that PSG's last shot on target in the tie occurred in the 28th minute of the first leg (although Marquinhos's header hit the bar in the 15th minute of the second leg).

Haaland, Mbappé, Neymar, Kane ... the list of elite players brought low by City's defenders just keeps growing. None of them has managed to score or get a shot on target in the last four weeks, with Pep's men blocking 27.3 per cent of the shots taken by opponents. As Walker puts it: 'when we block a shot at goal, it's like we've just scored a goal,' and none of these interventions was more spectacular than Dias stopping Ander Herrera's dangerous shot by sticking his head in the way. And Dias's brilliance isn't restricted to beating opponents, blocking their shots on goal and creating an impenetrable defensive wall. In his last seven Champions League games he hasn't dropped below 91 per cent in terms of accurate passes.*

It's fitting that he should have the last word: 'Football changes fast and you have to stay prepared.'

MOMENT 35. CHELSEA ARE FAVOURITES

Manchester, 5 May 2021

Only some guilty-looking grey clouds remain as evidence that it was snowing in Manchester last night as morning sunshine lands fondly on City's Academy. Pep has his squad divided into four groups. Those who started yesterday don't do much more than jog around the pitch, stretch and unwind after the PSG battle.

Xabi Mancisidor has all three keepers, Ederson, Steffen and Carson, under his orders on the Trautmann pitch (named after the mighty German keeper who was City's biggest hero between 1949 and 1964). There are ten kids from the youth ranks practising a rondo – guys like Delap, Doyle, Palmer and Lukas Nmecha have been called up to put some pressure on those who are likely to play on Saturday against Chelsea.

Speaking of whom, nine first-team squad members train under the watchful eyes of Lorenzo Buenaventura. Three of them had fleeting moments against PSG: Agüero, Jesus and Sterling. The other six are Cancelo, Laporte, Aké, Mendy, Rodri and Ferran Torres. Fifteen minutes into it Pep's explaining his vision to the rest of the staff: 'On Saturday it'll be these nine who'll play, plus Ederson and Rúben.' Typically for the City coach, he's put a lot of strategic thinking into his statement. Chelsea play their Champions League semi-final second leg tonight and, if they make the final, then Pep wants to play Tuchel's Blues in a completely different manner for Saturday's league game. He plans to change 90 per cent of the team that knocked PSG out. It'll feel odd, but that's not the point – this is potentially a cold war of bluff and double-bluff. 'Look, if we line up this way, so out of character,

---

* Dias's stats in terms of accurate passes are 96.4 per cent against Porto; 98.4 per cent and 94.1 per cent against Borussia Mönchengladbach; 94.3 per cent and 95.2 per cent against Borussia Dortmund; and 94.8 per cent and 90.3 per cent against PSG.

and we win then we win hugely ... but if we lose we lose very little!' The whole concept is to deny hard information to Chelsea's German coach and his players. The more you play one another they more you learn about one another. It's inescapable. Well, almost ... Study tapes all you want, work on strategic ideas, break the opposition down ... absolutely nothing compares to the mental muscle-memory of actually playing a tough rival repeatedly.

But a strategic gamble like this has tactical implications. Pep doesn't want to play with two left-footed centre-halves so he adds Dias to the schematic – it'll be three central defenders plus two wing-backs. And given that there'll be two central strikers and two wingers, it means there'll only be one genuine midfielder. Meaning that Sterling and Ferran must alternate in dropping back to become the attacking, creative midfielder. An atypical set-up, but it's governed by what type of players there are in the nine he's chosen to start for strategic reasons.

Three days after this mid-morning conversation under the pallid east Manchester sunshine, City lose the match 2–1 – albeit that a weak, missed penalty from Kun before half-time would have changed the vista of the contest. Losing to Chelsea is painful ... but dropping three points makes no real difference to the title chase and Pep's made sure that nothing about the defeat or performance has direct relevance to what will be, it's now confirmed, a City vs Chelsea Champions League final. Maybe it allows the media to tag the Londoners as 'favourites' but ... so what?

In the end, Pep decided to play Chelsea ... 'like Chelsea'. For three reasons.

First, it's tactical. He's interested in facing Chelsea with a 'mirror image' of themselves – using his own players as he guesses Tuchel will use his. The second is about group management. Despite the fact that Pep has already more or less decided on the 11 he'll use in the final, he's absolutely committed to the idea that every single one of his players gets a chance to compete for a place in that team right until the last moment. He even takes the step of making it public: 'I've not decided who'll start against Chelsea in the final – any player in the squad can still earn himself a place in the 11.' Something for the fans and media to dissect but what he's really doing is telling his players that whoever wants to start in Istanbul, or wherever this match is eventually sited, needs to fight hard to win his place over the next three weeks. Which, again, is why, although Chelsea keep half the team that has won them their semi-final against Real Madrid, Pep makes nine changes and, as planned, maintains only Ederson and Dias from the PSG win. The third reason is his determination to throw Tuchel off the scent – to keep his ideas and lineup for the final completely under wraps and not easy for the German coach to anticipate.

The match is evocative of the FA Cup semi-final. Two big beasts circling one another – it's slow and dull. Plenty of those who're involved have a lot at stake but, still, this never fizzes and crackles like the truly big 'all-in' matches always do. Rodri's pretty exposed in midfield so the City centre-halves spend a lot of time shuffling the ball between themselves, waiting for openings, and Pep's team, much more often than usual, are left looking for a quick, vertical movement of the ball to get in behind the backs of Chelsea's defence. Chelsea have more variety in their midfield-creative areas but neither team really dominates play. Then, out of the blue, there are two big moments just as half-time is looming. Dias plays it long, aiming at a Jesus run, and Christensen, who badly damages his left hamstring in the action, fails to cut it off properly. The Brazilian feeds Kun, who should score but instead doesn't finish instinctively with his left, fails to control with his right and, when the chance seems as if it'll be criminally squandered, Sterling nips in and slots the ball home. One–nil after a whole lot of nothing.

Then the entire afternoon pivots. Cancelo and Ferran combine, Jesus is about to add the second but Billy Gilmour bowls him over and it's a penalty. Agüero chooses risk over bankability and tries a 'Panenka' chipped penalty but forgets to add any chutzpah to the effort – Édouard Mendy looks both grateful and a little underwhelmed as he easily clutches the penalty to his chest. Kun is Kun, but this is a blunder. Four penalties missed this season, five the season before … no team's ever missed four or more in two consecutive Premier League seasons. Another record but both unwelcome and embarrassing.

The second half is more of the same until Ziyech presses Rodri towards the touchline, César Azpilicueta robs his international teammate and, thus, catches City badly out of shape tactically. The Spanish full-back plays a one–two with Christian Pulisic, cuts an assist back to Ziyech and it's 1–1. These momentary glitches from Rodri are what kept him out of the second leg against Paris and, now, might rob him of starting the final. Chelsea feed off the goal and Guardiola reacts with three changes – Gündoğan and Foden are on, adding instant impact, while Zinchenko for Benjamin Mendy means that Reece James, who's been toying with the French full-back, doesn't have it easy all of a sudden. Then, in added time Chelsea seal the game. Werner sprints in behind Laporte, and neither Aké nor Rodri can react in time to prevent him putting the winner on a plate for Marcos Alonso.

City have only lost five games all season, four of which have been at home! The last two consecutively were both 2–1 defeats with both away-team winners coming in the 92nd minute. Worse, it's Pep's second loss to Tuchel in a short space of time and everyone's crowing about how Chelsea are now Champions League favourites for sure.

Amidst the wound-licking is the realisation that, for the first time all season, City have six free days.

Time to start the process of resting up, recovering, getting their heads straight … but also time to win the Premier League, get business done and turn all their attention to the Istanbul final.

MOMENT 36. WHAT IF CARSON PLAYS?

Manchester, 11 May 2021

There's a variety of pizzas, mostly cheese and ham but bacon and salami and vegetarian, too. It's all been hastily thrown together by team manager Marc Boixasa. The minute his mobile started to explode with messages, he knew what kind of celebration this was going to be and, now, almost every City employee is gathered at the Academy training ground. The clarion call has gone out: Leicester have just beaten United at Old Trafford. City are champions!

As per Pep's instructions, all rules – particularly those relating to nutrition – are forgotten for the night. Anything goes right now. Tonight, everyone will drink and dance the night away as if there's no tomorrow – all the fiesta-goers already decked out in a specially made title-winning memorial T-shirt. It immediately morphs into a celebration of every single squad member who's been part of putting City on top of the pile again. One after the other, they get the spotlight, the applause, the adoration. It's noisy, feels like it will never end. Not so the pizzas. Boixasa's ordered 50. Which are gone in 15 minutes! The fiesta, like the team, takes shape at Pep's tempo – he's unleashed the inner party boy. Dancing, drinking, singing, all the while accompanied by a beautiful big cigar (it's a Partagás No. 4, his absolute favourite).

It's five months since the team was lying 12th in the table. Almost nobody gave them any chance of winning the title again. There was, however, a hardcore of faithful disciples – two in number. Manel Estiarte and Juanma Lillo. Day after day they preached. They promised that what felt like a gale in their faces was not the relevant factor – this group could, and would, be champions again. Their calculations were that the point gap, back then, wasn't the key factor. They argued that the Premier League would need something like 80+ points to win it – and that City could get there. Lillo insisted that the team was in good shape and really only needed calm, serene conditions to start to perform sufficiently well. As it turns out, they were both spot-on, and it'd be hard to argue that anyone's happier than the two of them tonight. Maybe that's where the extra, surprising, boldness comes from when Estiarte suggests that, perhaps, Scott Carson should be in goal when City play their first match as new champions – against Newcastle? Unusually, there's immediate and complete agreement across the technical staff – Carson starts.

Three days later the fanciful proposition is made fact. St James' Park, Newcastle, is where Carson, a year and a half after signing for City, makes his debut.

It's a week since the Magpies smashed Leicester, thanks to their lethal counterattacking. Steve Bruce's team needed a good result to avoid relegation and if they could tear a counterattacking specialist like Leicester apart – a side that would imminently beat Chelsea to win the FA Cup – then their transitional attacking pace is to be taken very seriously.

That's what the incoming champions now face and nobody could claim that pre-match preparations have been up to Pep's usual rigorous standards. After the Chelsea defeat they'd had two days off and then the improvised party once the title was confirmed … well, it was a mega-fiesta. Wednesday's training was not much more than shaking off the post-party excesses. So, only by Thursday is any proper Newcastle preparation undertaken. The decision is that this 11 will be a 'mixed' one: first-team stalwarts plus squad men.

Newcastle's match strategy is as expected. They 'gift' possession to City in the hope of sucking them in and then counterattacking on the gallop. Thus, City have the ball for 82 per cent of the match (the second highest figure after the 83 per cent achieved against Swansea in April 2018). There are even periods when City 'own' possession with 96 per cent. Remarkable.

For the opening 20 minutes City are sleek and quick with Cancelo and Sterling in their pomp down the left – but Newcastle score first. Walker breaks up their counter but at the cost of a corner. When it's taken, Aké drops his concentration, loses Emil Krafth and the centre-half heads home. Ten minutes later, from a free kick, Jonjo Shelvey thumps an effort off the City crossbar.

But then City bounce off the ropes. They attack down the left, Rodri gives Cancelo a cut-back and the Portuguese shoots off the outside of his boot such that the ball deflects in off a Newcastle man. And then, almost instantly, Gündoğan's free kick finds a spectacular finish when Torres, his back to goal, levitates and backheels the ball in past Martin Dúbravka. This, however, is proving to be a Premier League all-time epic and Newcastle not only draw even but lead in relatively short order. Aké fouls Joelinton and the Brazilian slots the penalty. Bruce's team have taken aim at the champions' goal twice, scored twice and poor old Scott Carson, on his 'big day', hasn't had a sniff of a chance to save either. Half an hour left and it's 2–2.

During the break Pep changes things – Jesus to the right wing and Ferran at centre-forward against the home side's three-man backline. Before that can bear fruit it's 3–2 to the Geordies. Penalty again – not a great moment for Walker. Joe Willock takes the spot kick, Carson shows he's not just here for show and saves well … but it's one of those days when, of course, Willock edges ahead of Eric García and slots home the rebound.

Now it's personal, now the Champions feel slighted. They erupt.

Jesus blitzes down the right, crosses in a fiery one and Ferran slots home left-footed from inside the six-yard area. It's a fabulous, Agüero-esque goal and Ferran repeats the trick within moments – a gymnastic flick when Cancelo's shot comes back off Dúbravka's post. These are signature penalty-box goals from young Ferran Torres. Fourteen starts this season, seven goals, two assists. He's the youngest player to hit a hat-trick for a Pep team (21 years old and 75 days, ahead of 22 years and 200 days by a certain Leo Messi).

All in all, it means that the Sky Blues have celebrated their new status with a victory, which breaks a record dating back to 1888. This squad now has 23 matches unbeaten away from home in England's top league (21 wins, 2 draws) – the 4–3 St James' blitz also means that City have 20 straight wins away from home in all competitions and 12 on the bounce in the league. Record after record.

The iconic image, however, is human, not statistical. Carson is deluged by embraces, congratulations, slaps on the back – this, his first Premier League match in ten years, has been a fantastic debut, a brilliant demonstration of competitive authority. And he's celebrated it with his boots on.*

'Yeah, I did think that Premier League football had left me behind forever – but I never gave up, and now I've had this fantastic new opportunity,' Carson admits. Ederson, who's not even been in the squad today, Xabier Mancisidor, the keeper-coach, subs and starters, all hustle to their much-loved if 'elderly' reserve keeper who's had his day in the spotlight. Carson has celebrated his 146th Premier League match by setting a new personal best – 90 per cent accuracy in his passing.

●   ●   ●

There's a fortnight until the Champions League final, which has been moved from Istanbul to Porto because of the complicated medical and social situation the pandemic has left in Turkey. There had been no way that the 12,000 fans scheduled to travel with City and Chelsea would have been allowed past Turkey's borders. So, UEFA has taken the decision to move everything to Portugal.

Two weeks of preparation left: the top priority is that De Bruyne switches off mentally and rests his aching right leg, which has been carrying damaged hamstring tendons and a wobbly ankle for most of the calendar year. The Belgian magician was far from full fitness for the semi-finals and now the staff have designed a ten-day recovery programme aimed at regenerating his most powerful leg muscles, his foot and his ankle so that he's in the best possible shape for the final.

The Newcastle match wasn't just a homage to big Scott – it had been an opportunity to rest several first-choice starters. Most of whom now have

---

* His last Premier League match was in 2011 for West Brom.

a full week where the objective is regeneration … shedding niggly injury problems, disconnecting mentally from the domestic campaign and building strength and resistance for what lies ahead.

Eric García played his last City game at St James' and he's now off to FC Barcelona. Ferran Torres seems to have seized that same match to underline his case for starting against Chelsea.

It's back to business now. The title-fiesta and the epic in Newcastle have given them a huge boost. But Pep and his men now face a crucial and tense season climax.

MOMENT 37. THE DYNAMIC OF THE UNEXPECTED
Manchester, 16 May 2021

You plan, you prepare, and then football laughs in your face.

Dante Panzeri, Argentinian intellectual and journalist, came up with an unbeatable phrase for this cruel phenomenon: 'Football, the dynamic of the unexpected.'

All your schemes, all your preparation – tipped over and scattered on the floor by something out of the blue.

We're in Pep's office at the training ground. Subject? How to win the Champions League final against Tuchel's Chelsea. Present? Pep, Juanma and Manel. So, everyone who played against PSG is now back in as good a shape as feasible at this stage of the season, physically and mentally recharged. Some have needed physical work to get back to top power. Others, like De Bruyne, have needed overworked muscles and tendons to be rested and regenerated. Kyle Walker's the only 'guaranteed' starter who's got a problem – he's twisted his ankle at home, playing with his kids.

Pep's instinct and experience are telling him to use the same 11 who played against PSG in the semi-final second leg. Nevertheless, the Catalan has too much experience not to expect the unexpected. Maybe someone injures himself in training or there's a player who, completely unexpectedly, begins to rip it up in training, forcing a last-minute reassessment of who's starting.

Premier League matches against Brighton and Everton remain. Title in the bag or not, the only way Pep knows to keep the squad in tight, aggressive, competitive sharpness is to play these two flat-out – no matter the temptation to wrap key footballers in cotton wool. Anyone spotted 'reserving' his energy will be in grave danger of being dropped for the showpiece final. These two league matches will be used to provide testing-ground opportunities for Cancelo, Rodri and Torres. Can they do enough to start in Porto? Agüero is still feeling abductor pain and can't play against Brighton – but the aim is that he gets his chance versus Everton.

Two days later, the unexpected happens ten minutes into the match at the Amex. Cancelo is sent off. Despite his magnificent performance against Newcastle at left-back, the red card might well have just cost him his place in the final. It now looks like Zinchenko will be in the starting 11 instead. Cancelo leaves the pitch quite evidently pissed off at what's happened – and what the consequences might be. Almost immediately Torres also loses a huge chance to persuade Pep that he should start in the final. The lovely hat-trick in Newcastle has vaulted him over Jesus today and Pep's planned to use the game to judge his play, his goalscoring and his sharpness. In brutal terms, it will be Ferran Torres or Bernardo Silva competing for one place in the biggest match in City's entire history. But Cancelo's red card automatically means someone has to stand down so that Eric García can come on – the hapless victim is Torres.

Rodri also fails to pass his audition to nudge the phenomenal Fernandinho out of the starting 11 in two weeks' time. He's magnificent, he's had a top season, he's the team's most natural pivot, but, particularly in recent weeks, he's looked just a little hesitant. Everyone, from Pep to Fernandinho, Lillo to Estiarte, wants him to make that final step. Everyone wants to help the imposing Spaniard evolve and get past the occasional insecurities he's shown in the toughest moments. Until the semi-finals he was first-choice organising midfielder. No doubt. But nerves in Paris led to Fernandinho replacing him for the return leg and that has knocked his self-confidence. It was Rodri's error that left Ziyech free to score the equaliser at the Etihad a couple of weeks ago. Pep kept him in the centre of midfield at Newcastle, and today in Brighton, but a new error seals his fate. Foden's just put City 0–2 up when Rodri turns to slide a pass back to Stones but mishits it, feeding Leandro Trossard in a gross error; Brighton not only score but begin what will be their victorious fightback. Rodri's face is a picture. And not a pretty one. He's grabbed his shorts, hoisting them up; his face is twisted in disgust and he's roaring up to the sky in fury and pain.

The Spaniard can already intuit that this might cost him a place in the final. He's right, too.

This is the hill upon which their away-win run will perish. Twenty-three victories since losing at Spurs in November last year is an incredible record. Six months of 21 wins, 2 draws, 53 scored and only 12 conceded – literally colossal.

City leave Brighton with a sour taste in their mouths and equally sour mentalities. Three players in particular, Cancelo, Torres and Rodri, trudge out of the Amex convinced that a golden opportunity has just slipped agonisingly through their fingers. Whether it's their own fault or Panzeri's 'dynamic of the unexpected' at work matters not a jot.

MOMENT 38. GOODBYE, KUN

Manchester, 23 May 2021

Agüero pulls the trigger twice and Everton's net billows – both times.

Football truly writes the best scripts. We're celebrating a prodigious decade during which Sergio 'Kun' Agüero has debuted and then departed the stage, with two almost identical flourishes. From 15 August 2011, when he came on against Swansea and scored two in the last half-hour of City's 4–0 victory, to today, 23 May 2021, when he's come on with 30 minutes left and scored twice to seal a 5–0 win over Everton. The alpha and omega of a brilliant career in light blue. Kun says 'Adiós!' to Manchester precisely as he said 'Hola!' – hitting the net for City.

On the day, Everton still have a last-gasp chance to qualify for Europe but City aren't having any of it.

Pep's 11 is going to be as near as dammit his starting lineup for the Champions League showpiece. Standard backline, De Bruyne and Foden as attacking midfielders, Mahrez and Sterling wide. It's the template for Istanbul with Fernandinho his pivot today, even though Pep's considering using Gündoğan there against Chelsea. Jesus is the centre-forward this afternoon – although Bernardo Silva might well take that slot in the Champions League match.

Pep's team play this season-ender with the same verve and mentality that, since Christmas, have made them virtually unstoppable. It's a three-man play-out-from-the-back, Walker plus the two centre-halves, making it a

3+2 when they combine with Fernandinho and Zinchenko. This structure is tried and tested, particularly effective when the opponent presses with two forwards and two midfielders or a striker plus three midfielders. It usually works, pretty much like clockwork, but today it's the interventions of De Bruyne and Foden that really elevate City's play. The young Englishman and the Belgian genius are working their routine up to be red-hot against Chelsea, and Everton pay the price. For just under an hour the two of them lay waste to Everton's midfield and Ancelotti's men just can't cope. From the very start, De Bruyne sets up Gabriel Jesus but Jordan Pickford makes a big stop. Then, six minutes later, a combination between Jesus, Foden and Mahrez returns the favour to De Bruyne, who thrashes home his 14th goal from outside the box for City. Since September 2015 in the Premier League only Harry Kane has scored more (19) from outside the penalty area. Almost instantly Fernandinho wins the ball back in the middle of the pitch and it's Gabriel Jesus (with his 50th league goal) who benefits to make it 2–0. Fernandinho wrenches the ball off Ancelotti's side and sets up Foden for City's third – the party is rocking.

This is when it becomes Agüero time, just 30 minutes before the final whistle. Again, it's Fernandinho who's the architect, ruthlessly turning over Everton's ball and becoming 'best supporting actor' as Kun says goodbye to fans who absolutely worship the ground upon which he walks. He scores. His first is finished off the outside of his right foot after a couple of neat feints. A virtuoso finish, which sparks delirium around the stadium. Never mind the final for the moment … THIS is a finale! Kun's still thirsty, though, and he heads home a divine Fernandinho cross about which De Bruyne himself would have been blushing with pride. Last day in Kun's Kingdom and, in 28 minutes, he's taken 22 touches, made 15 passes and broken the goalscoring record for one player with the same club in the Premier League.*

His statistics are dazzlingly good but nothing can eclipse the memory of the most explosive and volcanic goal in City's history: his 93:20 winner against QPR that won them the title, and left United broken-hearted in the last seconds of the 2012 season. Kun says goodbye after 260 goals in 390 matches, City's record scorer. He's won 14 trophies. With Pep alone, he's scored 124 times and lifted 9 trophies, 3 of which were league titles.

---

* Wayne Rooney scored 183 league goals with Manchester United.

The two men had a bumpy start and then hit a critical moment where mutual understanding was in short supply, but Kun stepped up, took on board Guardiola's arguments and demands, and the rest is history … Pep sheds a rare tear: 'Kun has been someone really special for me.'

City's history will always shine with the memory of Sergio Agüero – *adiós* Kun.

MOMENT 39. FILL THEIR HEADS OR KEEP THEIR MINDS FRESH?

Manchester, 24 May 2021

It's Monday, 24 May, and it really feels as if half the world is here to listen to Guardiola and Gündoğan answer questions. It's the Champions League final 'Media Day' and City's idea has been to get it over and done with as soon as possible. The Everton win was only yesterday and it's like there are still echoes of the title celebrations, and the 'Goodbye, Kun' game which rocked the Etihad. Those who played against the Toffees are doing the traditional, ultra-lite, recuperation session. The others, including Agüero and Rodri, are training far more intensely.

Tuesday will be a highly prized day off. The Academy will only host two more training sessions before the final because Friday's workout will be in Porto. Guardiola and Lillo are still doing some of their figuring out – testing and pressing each other for conclusions. For example, how much detail do the players genuinely need in terms of pre-match Chelsea analysis? What, precisely, remains to be underlined for a group of players who already know Tuchel's side pretty well?

Lillo's reading Montaigne assiduously again. He's a guy who doesn't drink alcohol, doesn't smoke, isn't on social media and doesn't bother reading the press (digital or print). He wouldn't know how Twitter works, what it's for, and doesn't want to either. Whatever's written about him, he's got no interest, even more so when he's told that an article is full of praise for him. You'll not see him in too many group photos and, when celebrations are at their most effusive, he'll try and edge to a peaceful place on the sidelines. On Sunday evening, as thousands of City fans roared their joy, two of Pep's players had to seek him out in a wee corner of the stadium and firmly ask him to come and join in the group celebrations because, in everyone else's eyes, he deserved to. He acceded, but as a spectator, not a main participant.

Post-match, home or away, he'll stay overnight in his Academy quarters – spartan and simple in room no. 30. Even then he'll often not sleep – tension isn't a good bedfellow.

Lillo hasn't got to know the city very well. He'll bounce between his flat and Pep's (about a minute apart), or from home to the supermarket and back. Honestly, that's about it. Between January and April he's had offers: a national team across the Atlantic, a Mexican club and a European national team. All a polite 'no thank you'.

He's rereading Montaigne (when is he not?) and today he's reproduced a critical section and left it on Pep's desk. It has impacted Juanma sufficiently to pass it on to the boss: 'We work only to fill our memory but leave consciousness and understanding empty.' It does cause Guardiola to stop and reflect. 'Fill their heads or keep their minds fresh?' The answer is obvious. Minds don't require to be full, but they must be fresh!

The other question of the day is about how City will structure their midfield against Chelsea. Rodri's name is on the wane – nagging gaps in his concentration and intensity in recent weeks. That'll cost you in any week of a Guardiola season. So … Fernandinho or Gündoğan? City's captain can be counted on for power, aggression and ball-winning. The German makes City's play fluid and when he's the organising midfielder, he almost always brings a wonderful kind of harmony to the play of those around him.

There might be a tipping factor. If Gündoğan is the pivot, then Foden can be used as an attacking interior midfielder rather than pegged out wide left. That, hypothetically, means Foden playing much more in the precise areas where City want him to be on the ball. This is a big debate and the two of them chew it over and over until a plan is set. It'll be Gündoğan as the organising pivot … both for the unifying, harmonising effect he has on midfield and because of where that will allow Guardiola to deploy the Stockport Iniesta.

'If we can have Phil on the ball every 30 seconds then more things will happen – good things.'

MOMENT 40. SISYPHUS AGAIN

Porto, 29 May 2021

Possibly the most important moment of the final comes off rather than on the pitch. Until Thursday things are going swimmingly – everyone's in the zone mentally. The mood is fabulous. Pep sets the tone – he's laidback, transmitting confidence and security. Training has increasingly been marked by bouncy attitudes, smiles and an overall feeling that things are going to be just fine.

Everyone's passed their COVID tests, on Wednesday and then again on Thursday morning. Then, en route to the airport, Juanma Lillo doesn't feel well. Sore throat, aching head and a tight chest. He's definitely got a respiratory problem. By the time they're all in the Porto Palácio Hotel, near to where the River Douro pours into the Atlantic, Dr Mauri is already very tempted to send City's assistant coach home to Manchester.

Lillo's not well and his temperature's up to 38. Still, Pep's very keen that, even if Juanma needs to remain confined to his room, he stays.

Friday evening means the last training session before the date with destiny and the atmosphere is a bit … 'off'. This session is different from the last few – quieter. No jokes and smiles and confident banter. The faces look wholly different from the last 48 hours in Manchester. There's tension gnawing at them, but something else is there too.

Two of the players quietly tell their captain that they've guessed the lineup … and they have doubts about it. Fernandinho, with typical tact and care, tells Pep that there's disquiet, rather than dissension, in the ranks.

Guardiola's no fool: he tells his captain that he'll go over it all in his mind again, that he'll even use Lillo as a sounding board, and get back to him. The two old friends genuinely do just that but believe that their original conclusions were well worked out, that they were sound. They still feel that the plan works because Gündoğan brings important positive benefit for the midfield composition as well as fluidity. Having him there, rather than Fernandinho, allows Foden to be used nearer to Chelsea's penalty area. Both coaches understand why there are concerns – the night before a big final is when the mind over-analyses, when doubts sneak in. But Guardiola and Lillo conclude that just because a couple of their soldiers are a bit uptight, that doesn't mean the battle plan is wrong. Sticking to brave principles has paid off far more often than not. The generals aren't spooked – but it has genuinely made them go over their ideas microscopically. No bad thing.

So, the lineup that City present to the UEFA match officials on the Saturday evening in the build-up to kick-off will be very much altered, in names and in strategy, to that used in almost all of the recent City–Chelsea battles. With respect to the FA Cup semi-final, City only repeat Dias, De Bruyne and Sterling. Nor will it look anything like Guardiola's 3–1–2–4 at the Etihad, in their May Premier League home defeat, from which the only guys who repeat are Ederson, Dias and Sterling. And the 3–1 January win at Stamford Bridge where Pep unveiled his 'Yugoslav' philosophy? Nah, this is a wholly different concept tonight.

The plan is daring but still absolutely in line with Pep's basic principles despite the fact that neither Rodri nor Fernandinho will start at pivot. Instead, City unite their best four outright footballers in midfield – Gündoğan, Bernardo Silva, De Bruyne and Foden – with the occasional support of Zinchenko moving forward from left-back. The 'Yugoslav' backline of Walker, Stones and Dias isn't a surprise to anyone nor are the wide men – Mahrez and Sterling.

Daring, brave, coherent, risky – call it what you want. All those adjectives have been in Pep's and Juanma's minds this week. If it flops, the criticism will be ferocious. They know that. The topic of 'to pivot or not to pivot' has dominated the pre-match analysis and, now that it's confirmed Rodri and Fernandinho won't start, the critics are licking their lips in anticipation. In fact, the condemnation starts before the match does: general feedback from the fans and media is that this is an error, that City need an organising pivot, so that Gündoğan can play as an attacking midfielder where Foden is, and Foden can play wide left.

Lillo's still sick with a high temperature. He's tested negative for COVID, again, but he's feeling really poorly as he joins the expedition to the stadium. Pep's been mulling over not giving a big set-piece tactical briefing in the hours before kick-off. He likes to keep his players' minds fresh, rather than filling them with more detail. But he can really feel the tension among the squad and, in fact, there's been a brief raised-voice moment between a staff member and a player not long ago. Pep makes the decision – better to speak and make it crystal clear to everyone that *all* the responsibility for what's been chosen, for how they are going into battle, rests on him.

And him alone.

The plan doesn't work.

And not because of Gündoğan either. I've now rewatched the game twice and Gündo really doesn't commit a single appreciable error. There's nothing about Kai Havertz's 42nd-minute winner that is attributable to Gündoğan's presence or the absence of either Rodri or Fernandinho. The winner comes from something that has become central to Chelsea's identity under Tuchel. An idea Pep knows and likes too. Chelsea draw opponents to the right-hand side so that, like lightning, they can switch play to an unguarded left channel and then feed off the disorganisation and consequent errors their opponent makes. As a tactic it's risky and tough to pull off with clinical efficacy but, tonight of all nights, Chelsea do just that.

Tuchel's team lure Sterling, Foden, De Bruyne and Silva to the right, then use Édouard Mendy to feed Ben Chilwell at left-back. This is when the consequences of seeding the disorganisation that leads to spontaneous decision-making can yield benefits. Walker's been marking Mason Mount, but he chooses to push aggressively at Chilwell – failing to snuff out Chelsea's well-oiled tactic. Stones sees that Walker has left Mount, moves out of the defensive line to try and close down his England teammate – decisions, decisions. So when Mount turns he spots that Werner has drawn Dias out of position, too far to City's right, and only Zinchenko can now hope to thwart Mount setting up Havertz one-vs-one against Ederson. But there's a chasm of space between the Portuguese and the Ukrainian and, sod's law, Mount's pass is exquisite. Chelsea manage to make every moving piece clinical and City are always a beat too late. Havertz grabs his moment. And if the finish looks a little inelegant, a toe-poke that bounces back to him to finish into an empty net when Ederson's dive nearly saves the day, it's cruelly effective. From the moment Walker chooses to abandon his set task and anticipate what he sees happening, Chelsea march through every City crack. It's evocative of the goal conceded to United when Cancelo's precipitated choice to push into a unilateral press caused a chain reaction and cost them dearly. In context, Gündoğan simply isn't a factor – nor, realistically, would Fernandinho or Rodri have been. This wasn't a goal that came because City did or didn't have a dedicated pivot.

Just as in the other two slow, dull recent contests with Chelsea, Tuchel's team is perfectly happy with this match tempo and City fail to turn their possession domination into cutting-edge chances that will change the scoreline. It's an affliction that worsens after Antonio Rüdiger smashes into De Bruyne and the Belgian suffers fractures to his nose and eye socket. He's carted off directly to hospital and spends several hours there. In the cold light of day, the move doesn't look completely unintentional. Watch the replays – Rüdiger loses focus on the pass De Bruyne has released to Mahrez and connects with the Belgian with the full force of his huge frame. It's the German's right shoulder that causes the double fracture and removes De Bruyne from any further participation. No doubt, Rüdiger's intention wasn't to injure De Bruyne, but he's made a mess of his face all right.

Chelsea defend like Fort Knox – using their three terrific centre-backs, Azpilicueta, Thiago Silva and Rüdiger, with supplementary preventative work from their defensive pivots, Jorginho and Kanté. They're impenetrable.

Chelsea have a couple of efforts on target, City just the one. But, frankly, either team could have scored more than the solitary goal the match produces. The excellent Azpilicueta stops Gündoğan making it 1–1 with what should be a tap-in and Pulisic wastes a one-vs-one with Ederson. A mention in the dispatches for an off-target effort from Mahrez, whose 96th-minute volley shaves paint off the crossbar as it goes over.

Chelsea are European champions. Not City.

Results talk and defeat leaves Pep 'in the wrong'. It's a human tendency, however misleading, for those who want to attribute blame, or even praise, to use the final result as 'binding' evidence. You win and you were right all along. You lose: 'tough luck sucker'. This has almost always been our Machiavellian, and stupid, reasoning. And it's just not like that. It is neither true that victory proves that you were right, nor correct that defeat means you had it wrong all the time. It's about cause and effect. We look for motives for what happens – it's written into the human psyche. But to answer the 'why' using only the final result simply ignores that, often, you can win or lose because of reasons that we don't and will never fully understand.

Anyway, be that as it may, this loss is attributed as 'factually' down to the use of Gündoğan instead of a traditional organising pivot. The public and the media have 'spoken' and there's no possible way to refute something that is now engraved, like graffiti, in football history (even though there's no way to prove this permanently engraved conclusion either).

I was there, and I've watched the game back twice. There's no way that the 1–0 loss can be attributed to where Gündoğan played, or who was benched ... although it's also true that the German's role that night failed to unleash the positive impact that Guardiola and Lillo had planned.

Them's the breaks.

If Guardiola erred, then, in my humble opinion, it was adjusting a beautiful, muscular system that was functioning really well, just at a crucial moment. Using Gündoğan as a pivot, instead of the specialists, had no negative impact on the match or how it played out but perhaps it impacted a little on the mood and confidence of City's troops. A couple voiced their concerns and others showed a trace of insecurity and uncertainty – the enemies of victory in the face of a tense winner-takes-all encounter. City were restless that night, there was anxiety and there were minute indecisions.

They've had a formidable trajectory to the final this season: 11 wins, 1 draw and just a single defeat. But the sorest defeat of all. To score 25 times, concede only 5, but still lose, seems counterintuitive. But that's football. Most of the play during City's 12 UCL matches has been thrilling, entertaining, clever, effective. Then, on the only 'mistakes-prohibited' day – disaster.

The 'Yugoslav' season thus concludes with a bitter taste in the mouth. But you never win unless you choose your methods and stay convinced by them. This time, for once, there were a couple of unconvinced components and a tough mission thus became impossible.

Guardiola's masterpiece at City remains incomplete. Just as it did at Bayern. But the City project, for now, is still under construction. Lessons continue to be learned and ideas continue to evolve. This reverse, however sore, will help. The coach is now under contract until the end of the 2022–3 season, meaning that there's still time to assess, review and retouch the plans and ensure that the cathedral is eventually built. Some of history's most illustrious artists have left their greatest works unfinished – Schubert's Eighth Symphony, Mozart's *Requiem*, Raphael's *Transfiguration* ... but within Pep Guardiola beats the heart of both an artisan obsessed with the slightest of details and a warrior, endlessly driven to compete and win. There's simply no room for another incomplete work of art. It has to happen, however it can be achieved, no matter the test. Like Sisyphus, condemned by the mythical Greek gods to keep rolling that massive boulder up a hill, only to see it crash down to earth again, the fates have left Guardiola's project staring up at a long, upwards climb. Let's go, Sisyphus ...

STATS 2020–1

	P	W	D	L	GF	GA
Premier League Champions	38	27	5	6	83	32
League Cup Champions	5	5	0	0	12	2
FA Cup Semi-finalists	5	4	0	1	11	3
Champions League Runners-up	13	11	1	1	25	5
Total	61	47	6	8	131	42

- 77 per cent victories in matches all season
- 71 per cent wins from all Premier League matches
- 2.14 goal average per match scored in the entire season
- 2.18 goal average per match scored in the Premier League
- 0.68 goal average per match conceded in the entire season
- 0.84 goal average per match conceded in the Premier League
- 89 positive goal difference across the whole season
- 86 points in the Premier League
- 20 efforts off the post in the Premier League (4 De Bruyne and Sterling)
- 63.2 per cent possession in the entire season
- 63.5 per cent possession in the Premier League
- 83 per cent highest level of possession (vs Newcastle, May 2021)
- 37 per cent lowest level of possession (vs Brighton, May 2021)
- 675 average number of passes per match
- 925 highest number of passes (vs Newcastle, May 2021)
- 88 per cent completed passes per match
- 15 shots at goal per match/5.6 on target
- 6.9 shots at goal conceded per game/2.1 on target
- 15 best run of consecutive wins in the Premier League
- 17 top goalscorer: İlkay Gündoğan (13 in the Premier League)
- 18 most assists: Kevin De Bruyne (12 in the Premier League)
- 53 most appearances: Rodri (Ederson 36 in the Premier League)
- 5–0 biggest win (vs Burnley, West Bromwich Albion and Everton)
- 5–2 biggest defeat (vs Leicester)

Season 6: 2021–2

5 Minutes and 36 Seconds

1. CITIZEN KANE

'There's only one person in the world who's going to decide what I do and that's me.' Harry Kane feels exactly the same way as Charles Foster Kane, Orson Welles's emblematic title character in *Citizen Kane*. The player has made it clear to his agent (his brother, Charlie Kane) that he isn't prepared to stick with Spurs, who have just finished seventh in the league, 24 points behind City. He's under contract until 2024 but hopes that the chairman, Daniel Levy, will be willing to at least negotiate with City.

Kane goes in to the talks with his club, feeling like the master of his own destiny. Five minutes later he's disabused of any such notion. Levy's not even prepared to discuss it. There will be no talks with City, and Spurs' star striker is going nowhere. End of.

Some dreams just aren't meant to be. As Emily Monroe Norton Kane, Charles Foster Kane's first wife, says to her husband, 'There seems to be only one decision you can make, Charles. I'd say it had been made for you.'

Sorry, Harry. It's out of your hands. You're stuck, for the time being, playing for a team that won't win any silverware again this season.

2. HUNDREDTHS OF A SECOND

It feels as if last season's just finished and already the new one's begun. Rodri's certainly playing like no time at all has passed. And not in a good way. He's making exactly the same kinds of errors he was committing at the end of last season. He's come on for Gündoğan towards the end of the Community Shield final at Wembley. Leicester have been attacking brilliantly today, particularly in the first half, but going in to the second half Pep's changed the way City are bringing the ball out, going for four against four instead of three on three.

City have thrown themselves into the game, but so far haven't managed to score. Rodri passes the ball backwards, unexpectedly, catching teammate Nathan Aké unaware and the Dutchman gives away a penalty. Zack Steffen has already made two huge, goal-preventing saves but not from the spot kick, which gives Leicester the trophy – all because of Rodri's decision-making. It's not the first time he's let himself down like this, making backwards passes that aren't a disaster in their own right but which end up costing City goals.

Looking on, Pep and his assistants immediately see that a lot of work will be required to sort out the young Spanish midfielder. He's an extraordinary player, hugely talented and with so much more to give. But he needs to be calmer out there: run a bit less; pass the ball better; be confident without getting cocky. It's a tough balance to achieve but should be a piece of cake for a guy who's so committed to becoming a better player. Rodri's position in midfield is the most high risk there is but he's making mistakes precisely because he's taking too many of the wrong risks.

Apparently, Spurs don't need Harry Kane to beat City. Now his transfer to City isn't going to happen, Kane's decided to make his desire to leave public. And he's not playing. But even without such a key player, the Londoners have no trouble securing their fourth consecutive victory over Pep's men, handing the Cityzens their first defeat in the inaugural game of the season since 2011. Eleven years ago it was also Spurs who defeated City in their first game of the season and history repeats itself today.

Son shoots from distance and Rúben Dias looks as if he's going to block it, leaving Ederson confused and unable to get to it in time. A hundredth of a second is all it takes for Dias to hesitate, 'will-I-won't-I' style, leaving the ball to sail into the back of City's net and seal the Londoners' 1–0 victory: City's third defeat in a row, having also lost the finals of the Champions League and the Community Shield. A miserable start.

3. ONE YEAR

Now that Agüero has signed for Barcelona and Gabriel Jesus has been reassigned to the right wing, City no longer have a pure centre-forward. Pep really rates Jesus. The player has a brilliant vision of the game, is technically superb, passes exquisitely, and brings energy and dynamism to City's play. Pep's sure he's going to thrive on the right.

Just last week, Jesus provided two excellent assists against Norwich and today, against Arsenal, gives Gündoğan the first goal then scores one of the five goals they produce in their demolition of Arteta's team. This is their third consecutive 5–0 victory at the Etihad, including their win against Everton last season plus the Norwich game seven days ago. Since Pep arrived in England there have been 50 league matches in which five or more goals have been scored – half of them have been City victories.

There's a lot of excellent football on display today: brilliant man-marking; superb technical control from Jack Grealish, City's signing of the season, as expensive as he is impressive; the rhythm imposed by Silva, Gündoğan and Jesus … but none of it manages to eclipse the magic produced by Rodri 50 minutes in. The Spaniard takes aim from 25m and curls a sweet drive from outside to in, bending the ball around Arsenal's defenders and putting it perfectly inside Leno's left post.

It's a beauty. Not only haven't we seen Rodri pull off a goal like this before, worthy of the great Toni Kroos himself, but it's clear that we can expect many more nights of spectacular football from him. The brilliant but impulsive midfielder is gradually maturing into a player with the discipline to hold his position and consider his next move, rather than speed off up the pitch as soon as he gets the ball.

In the space of just a year, this high-energy, big, strong defender has transformed into a midfielder with 360-degree panoramic vision, who's in total control of the rhythm and intentions of City's game and who's capable of producing a 'hole in one' golf swing in the heat and chaos of battle when he takes aim and shoots.

4. KEEP MOVING FORWARD TOGETHER

'Nobody likes to find fault when we win but that means that nobody really reflects properly on our victories,' comments Lillo. 'Our 6–3 against Leipzig in the Champions League was incredible but I'm actually prouder of our 0–0 against Southampton. There are some games that tell you a lot more than massive victories and that game was one of those.'

Ralph Hasenhüttl's Southampton press City high up the pitch, effectively trapping Walker and Cancelo and snapping constantly at Fernandinho's heels. They've hurt City's ability to play out. With City's organising midfielder covered and their full-backs thwarted at every turn, it's been impossible for the Cityzens' centre-backs to get the ball to the attacking midfielders. Southampton have turned the centre of the pitch into a minefield.

Even the considerable talents and hard work of Grealish and Jesus on the outside haven't managed to produce a lot of chances. Southampton's box has been busier than Oxford Street in rush hour. City's midfielders achieve just 86.9 per cent accuracy in their passing, 5 percentage points less than their average. It's been six months since City last failed to score at home and Pep puts the blame firmly on their failure to bring the ball out as intended.

'During our build-up we move the ball from our defenders to our midfielders and then on to the wingers. We have to move forward together and coordinate our movements to do this, and we didn't manage that today. The players weren't mentally fresh and failed to construct our normal build-up. We didn't end up with a draw because we didn't have a striker but because our process wasn't good and we didn't send good balls to the guys in front.

'Moving forward together' is one of the fundamental parts of Pep's game. As Lillo puts it, 'It's about travelling together, not just in the same train but in the same carriage. If everyone travels solo, the train will never get to its destination.'

Hasenhüttl, less given to using metaphor to explain his ideas than Pep and Lillo, presents his strategy in typically blunt terms: 'Pep always wants to play football but, if we play a perfect 4–2–2–2, we can put a stop to that.'

5. ZERO POINT SOMETHING

Pep prefers to share some of his proudest moments with just his closest friends. Today, he tells a few of us, 'We just prevented the European champions getting a single shot on goal!'

Indeed, City are the first team to have stopped Thomas Tuchel's Chelsea from shooting on goal. The Blues are top of the league after five games in which they've conceded a single goal and scored a dozen. So, Pep's justifiably proud to have taken three points from Chelsea at Stamford Bridge. Not only has he beaten his nemesis, but he's prevented the home side from playing the superb football they're capable of. As well as Jesus's goal, City have had three other good chances today, either saved by keeper, Édouard Mendy, or, in one case, kicked off the line by Thiago Silva.

It's Pep's 221st triumph with City. The spine of the team is hitting a Herculean consistency of selection and performance – Rúben Dias at the base through Rodri, Cancelo and Bernardo Silva up the middle. His men have 'moved forward together' today and are looking more and more like the City of the Yugoslavs. They've only conceded one goal in six league games and their defensive line is close to unbreachable, as evidenced by Chelsea having just one vague chance today (Mateo Kovačić's shot, blocked by Dias).

On the flight back to Manchester, Juanma Lillo has a thought: 'We need to become a "zero point something" team. What I mean is that we need to concede on average less than one goal per league game. It doesn't matter what the "something" is, but if we keep our average below a goal per game, we'll be champions again!'

6. 2.92 SECONDS

It's a wide free kick. Always dangerous when Liverpool have the ball. Jordan Henderson feints that he's going to cross but, instead, slips it to Salah who's unmarked and who puts the ball into the area off his left foot so that it swings in with exactly the opposite curve on it than City's defenders are expecting. Bernardo Silva doesn't get to the Egyptian to block him in time and, now, the penalty area is like vegetable soup. There are even more Cityzen defenders than Liverpool attackers crammed into the small space. Walker, Dias and Rodri make it a three vs two – touch-tight with Van Dijk and Mané. Two metres away, Laporte's watching Joël Matip with Cancelo on Firmino. Three metres the other way, it's Gabriel Jesus's job to mark his fellow Brazilian – Fabinho. The clock shows there are four minutes left of this heavyweight slugfest in which City and Liverpool have gone at one another – each seeking to land a knockout blow on the other's jaw. Two behemoth sides have gone hard at it … all-in, nothing in reserve.

It might be an exaggeration to say that City are four minutes away from achieving 'Mission Impossible' by taking a point at Anfield but, so far, only leaders Chelsea have managed this. Four more minutes to ensure that the top of the table stays well within their reach – in fact, four short minutes to get what the Sky Blues actually deserve. They've gone toe-to-toe with Klopp's side (Rodri, Foden and Silva the standouts) and matched them big chance for big chance. Twice behind, twice pegging Liverpool back.

But, let's return to Henderson's simple little trick of pretending to do one thing but actually opting to do the unexpected. Now, with so many players in the box there's a sea of heads, necks craned upwards to find the flight of the ball. Ederson leaps for the cross but doesn't get a firm hand on it. Salah's ball drops at Fabinho's right foot and suddenly everyone notices that the Liverpool midfielder has given Jesus the slip.

Not by much … but enough.

Fabinho takes a deft touch, lets the ball settle and starts to pull the trigger. This is a nailed-on goal and vast red swathes are bubbling up in cele-bration while the Mancunian minority watch with jaws slack in anticipation of the pain and humiliation that is about to hit them. Fabinho will score and Liverpool will be four points clear at the top. City, condemned to chase the 'little red rabbit' after just seven matches of the new season! No one really has time to calculate that Rodri's exactly 5m from the unfolding disaster but, while Fabinho's getting ready to burst the net, the Spaniard simply erupts. His long, powerful strides take him to where he can throw one leg out and, somehow, the Brazilian's shot cannons into Rodri's diving block.

It shouldn't have been possible, but it's happened.

This thunderous moment, just like Stones produced back in January 2019, is the kind of thing that wins a title when the final accounting will be done in several months' time. Yeah, yeah, it sounds odd to tag Rodri's remarkable mini-miracle like that in October but in due course everyone will see that this was a moment to tip the balance of who will win the Premier League. It's that simple.

From the instant Salah crosses until Rodri blocks, it feels like three or four minutes have dragged by in slow motion. But it has, in fact, been just 2.92 seconds. From Fabinho striking the ball until it spiralling away from goal off Rodri it's been 80 milliseconds.

A lightning-fast, league-winning moment.

7. A FALSE 9

Sometimes Foden plays centre-forward, sometimes he's the chosen false 9. It depends. Today's destruction of Brighton has been conducted from the latter, 'conceptual' position. He's been aided by a monumental Silva and, to a lesser extent, by Grealish. The instinctive English wide man keeps letting us glimpse his ability but he's obscuring it with a demonstration of precisely how difficult it is to adapt to Guardiola's playing style.

Foden, on the other hand, has the kind of inherent brilliance you can't go shopping for. Pep explains: 'There are footballers who play in a certain position and there are others who "play football". Phil is one of that privileged latter group. If I use him deeper in the set-up, then he's dangerous because he's still young, still blessed with huge energy, meaning he's actually capable of initiating a move and being on the finishing end of it too. All that's really left for him to do is to refine his decision-making in front of goal.'

If Pep uses Foden as a false 9, Gündoğan can then play much deeper, nearer Rodri at pivot, meaning that Cancelo and Silva can exploit their enhanced freedom to link with Foden or feed the wingers. That four-man midfield dragnet (Rodri, Gündoğan, Cancelo, Silva) makes City look and feel unbeatable – not necessarily because of superiority of numbers but superiority of talent.

Between Silva and Foden there's an ocean of energy – the Englishman is very, very fast and his elder teammate seems to be able to go on and on without flagging. Unleash them and City can play vertically, up and down, with most opponents unable to keep pace, never mind thwart them. Brighton's tactic to try and repel the onslaught works … once we've reached the second half and they're already losing 3–0. The seasiders try a 'diamond'-shaped midfield right in the middle of the pitch and City set to working it out – even though they're already done and dusted as far as the points go. The solution's not too orthodox for a Guardiola team – they go 4–4–2, cede Brighton more possession but then hit back with lightning-fast counters. The eventual 4–1 win has Foden's magnificence stamped all over it.

Oh, we do like to be beside the seaside …

8. SNARED

Between 2017 and 2021, City have effectively owned the League Cup. Four straight wins. Sometimes, though, October is cold and cheerless for a reason. This time, it's because the holders go out at the first time of asking, beaten by West Ham after a decent if not stellar City performance.

It finishes 0–0 in east London and the Hammers win the spot-kick shoot-out. Another anomaly – City have won four of these 12 yards contests in the last four seasons. Not tonight though. Foden misses the goal frame (left) meaning that a 5–3 win for the Irons deprives City of a shot at five titles in a row. It would have been the competition's outright record dominance – but that's gone now.

Fifteen matches into the season, City are totally comfortable in the 4–4–2 when they don't have possession. Furthest up the pitch in this defensive organisation is the central striker plus one or other of the attacking midfielders (as appropriate) – behind them are the organising pivot, the other attacking midfielder and two 'wingers'/wide midfielders.

Pep has used this concept in the past, but really only when the qualities of their opponents demanded this kind of approach. Right now, this far into the season, it's quite clear that City are very strong defensively when they use this shape. They've only conceded four times in nine matches, a superb achievement, particularly when you consider that Liverpool, Spurs, Arsenal and Chelsea are included in those nine. Pep's players feel totally secure playing like this, but neither their confidence nor their impressive track record prevents what happens three days later against Crystal Palace. The Sky Blues go head over heels in a banana-skin pratfall. At home.

Five minutes in and the visitors 'seek-and-destroy' squad have snared Laporte. Between them, Conor Gallagher and Wilfried Zaha, force the Spanish central defender into their well-worked trap – Gallagher plundering with Zaha profiting. The winger rubs salt in the wound by shooting hard and low, diagonally, across Ederson – an unfeasibly left-footed finish. But it goes in.

Five matches without conceding – five minutes in and 0–1 down. The first visitor goal the Etihad's suffered this season. Laporte has many virtues – the best long pass in the Premier League, he's got panoramic vision, which helps him bring the ball out brilliantly. But he's got in a muddle again. And will repeat the misstep in the second half when a tug at Zaha brings a red card. Guardiola's deeply concerned about how his most 'complete' defender is playing after an afternoon of errors.

First home defeat since May. Not cool.

9. EIGHTY-SIX SECONDS

It's not the longest sequence of passes strung together since Pep took over. That was against West Brom in September 2017. The Baggies chased shadows while Pep's lads knocked the ball between them 52 times without West Brom getting a sniff of possession. Oh, and Leroy Sané ended the move with a goal, too.* Today? This is about half the fun, 26 passes, but it's a goal to City all the same.

Man United's Maguire and Shaw freeze when Silva nips in behind their backs and the two England defenders waste time in a 'how did that happen?' glance. David De Gea's expression says, 'Oh come *on*, lads!' Bruno Fernandes is grumbling at his teammates; meanwhile Victor Lindelöf, McTominay, Fred and Aaron Wan-Bissaka are looking anywhere rather than straight at the ruins of their team's defending.

United are being taken to the cleaners in the so-called Theatre of Dreams. Derby day in Manchester finally has its lifeblood again – Old Trafford can let fans in once more, now that pandemic restrictions have been eased. It's precisely 20 months since the last derby was played in front of a crowd of seething, baying fans and the home side are playing calamitously. City fly out of the traps with two defenders plus three midfielders (2+3 when playing out), all in good form – Stones and Dias with Walker, Rodri and Cancelo. Their two wingers (Jesus and Foden), playing open on their naturally better foot, cause huge problems for United's five-man defence and, in the middle, there's relative freedom for De Bruyne, Gündoğan and Silva.

---

* It was a League Cup match against WBA on 22 September 2017 when City set their passing record. Every single one of their 11 players was on the ball at least twice during the move, and those 52 passes that ended in Sané's goal ate up 2.27 minutes.

City's grasp of positional play delights their coach with special mentions in dispatches to Silva, who ghosts in and out of the false 9 position, and the 'free electron' Cancelo. The Portuguese, so central to unlocking City's magic right now, adds to the three assists he provided in Bruges the other night with two more against City's city rivals. Five in a week – hats off to João.

The lead takes six minutes to achieve. Cancelo's cross and Bailly's uncoordinated own goal. Between the 28th and 34th minutes, De Gea saves blushes and what look like being four stick-on goals. This is a hurricane in sky blue. Total City domination, which might have ended in a record win but for this high-performance Spanish keeper – which explains his horrified expression, and the desolation of teammates all around him, when Silva materialises in behind United's heavily populated defensive line to make it 2–0 just before the break.

Silva's moment follows 86 seconds of City smarts. Cristiano Ronaldo is trying to counterattack but wastes his pass. This is no longer the majestic goal-scoring colossus of years gone by. Far from that version, if truth be told. He offered himself to City last summer but Pep wasn't interested. There's no question at all that Guardiola respects his immense ability to finish chances as well as his superb physical condition but how could this type of player fit into the precision machine the Catalan has painstakingly and strategically built at City? Thanks but no thanks, Cristiano. Not even after City's attempt to sign Harry Kane and buy an outright centre-forward ended in failure.

Anyway, it's CR7's poor pass that gives Stones the ball and he starts the passing party. Every City player, from Ederson to Foden, receives and distributes possession in this move. The first 16 passes are in City's half and it's obvious from the way United are haring after the ball, or at least huffing and puffing not to be pulled into bad areas, that this is precisely what City's coach wants to see. It all leaves Cancelo with time and space on the ball to move over the halfway line. The next nine passes, until the Portuguese gets the ball back on the left, fizz between City's attacking midfielders and forwards so that United are twisting and turning and wondering where the swinging left-hook will come from. It's Cancelo who obliges. City have a five vs eight situation, no numerical superiority, but positionally, and in terms of confidence, they ooze superiority. Even though his pass must thread through Lindelöf, McTominay, Maguire and Shaw, not one of them is given a chance to intercept the fiendish assist. De Gea thinks his far post is protected, and it probably should be, but we're long past that. Silva appears like an apparition and City, thanks to a subtle, minutely accurate finish, are two up. It's 'eye of the needle' stuff. De Gea issues Iberian curses; his shame-faced teammates look away.

Eighty-six seconds, 26 passes and a magical winner, which leaves the second half not so much a test as a stroll in the park as City play keep-ball. Foden sums it up afterwards: 'I'd say we produced the match of our lives!'

For City: 14 good goal chances and 262 of their overall 818 passes in the final third of the pitch defended by United. In the second half, Ederson didn't have to save a single shot. City's 753 completed passes is an all-time English record – and, folks, that's away to Manchester United! This exhibition of cold-blooded winning mentality and steely control means nobody even questions the fact that Pep's starting 11 all play 90+ minutes.

His cool retort: 'If it ain't broke, why fix it?'

10. A HISTORIC HOUR

Pep has enjoyed his eight days off holidaying in Dubai – sun, golf, family.

Manchester greets him with rain. Of course it does. This is our chance to dodge the bad weather and chat about how football has evolved. We get an hour – a very rare oasis of time to talk and exchange views. After again discussing the origins of the false 9 concept, we then agree that, in 1920, a Hungarian called Gyula Mándi developed the type of build-up from the back to which Pep is so devoted. And then we dissect the Cambridge 2–3–5 formation, which gradually evolved into the WM idea (3–2–2–3) with its Italian cousin (2–3–2–3) – all from many decades ago but all consistently employed by Pep at City in recent years. The legendary genius Herbert Chapman features a lot in our conversation. He was evangelical, from as early as 1907, about the free spaces that exist, or can be generated, behind an opponent's defence. Chapman experimented with a complex playing model that dropped the organising midfielder into a pattern with the centre-backs, moved the full-backs inside and started working on the benefits of inverted wingers (a right-footer down the left and vice versa).

Our conclusion is that, by 1945, all the really fundamental tactical ideas in football had been created and what has followed are innovations, reinventions, adaptations and the application of all those original ideas, but in a modern context that is profoundly different.

Juanma Lillo's influence comes up too. Pep sums up his great friend in just a few words: 'It takes Juanma two seconds to see things that most others either take hours to realise or perhaps never come to grips with. I can't describe how much he's helped me. Not just for the fact that he's the glue which unifies us across the entire tactical staff or that he possesses a superb vision of football in motion, but in that he hugely helps me stay calm, to add serenity to how I watch and think about football. That's priceless. Juanma never has a bad word to say about anyone and he'll somehow find the positive in literally any situation! The players just adore him.'

An hour of pure football conversation leads us to define a coach as someone who needs to inseminate good ideas and concepts and spread knowledge. The coach's life is nomadic. Like the wind that spreads seeds across the ground, although it will never see them flower and grow fully.

11. A CLONING FACTORY

The fact that De Bruyne has COVID means a Premier League starting debut for young Cole Palmer. This guy is an extraordinary prospect. Truly. It's a year since he started in the first team and, although his appearances have been relatively fleeting since then, Palmer has already scored in the Champions League and the League Cup.

An Academy boy, he's left-footed, just like Foden, and, like the Stockport Iniesta, is at ease playing on either side of the pitch – left going outside, right coming in. If Foden is Pep's 'Golden Boy', then Palmer has that status with Juanma Lillo, who's keeping a close eye on this fabulous prospect to see how he applies his formidable talents.

Everton are at the Etihad and Palmer's not just in the 11, he's at false 9 because Silva will fill De Bruyne's position. It's a big deal for the kid but he looks assured and creates good goal chances for Gündoğan and Bernardo Silva. It's beginning to look like he's played this role all his life but, honestly, that's not the case. Good shooting, split-second anticipation of when a teammate's made a shrewd movement off a marker – his performance is so impressive that Martin Tyler, Sky's veteran commentator, announces that City's Academy must be some kind of 'cloning-system'.

Three minutes before the end, Pep withdraws the star of the show and it's another Academy kid – James McAtee – who uses the following five minutes (including added time) to demonstrate that he too is a player of real quality. It's scandalous that City can debut one superb home-bred kid and then simply replace him with another. Gary Neville picks up the theme on comms: 'It's like they're clones of each another … ! They keep coming … it's like David Silva has rejoined City!'

Lillo adores seeing this kind of talent emerge: 'McAtee is a fine player and Cole is exceptional. Two top talents.'

My estimate is that McAtee will find it harder to carve out a space in this team because his speciality is playing as an inside-forward – an area where he's going to bump into De Bruyne, Bernardo Silva, Gündoğan and Foden, of course. Palmer, on the other hand, can play wide, inside and even at false 9, as he's proven today. More capability. More options. Perhaps most tantalisingly, Cole Palmer's got this priceless, innate understanding of what tempo is appropriate for each moment of a match – from first gear, through acceleration, into sixth. If you want to make a comparison, Foden's always in fourth gear. Or fifth, or sixth. He's sensational, no question, but not prone to subtlety – he wants things happening … and now! Foden's a rock-solid character – extroverted, confident, full of laughter, unlike Palmer, who's maybe a little reserved, capable of giving the false impression that he's not that sympathetic a guy, but body language can be deceptive. There's no question that being outgoing and popular can get you places more quickly.

There are details to pick out from the 3–0 win here. Sterling and Foden play as natural wingers, and that helps cope with the park-the-bus mentality Rafa Benítez inflicts on the match. Their width leaves little channels of space to exploit in the inside-forward areas – dream-ticket stuff for Gündoğan, Bernardo and Palmer himself.

Rodri scores a top-corner 'worldie' – his fourth Premier League goal from outside the box. This is becoming an important tactical solution for Pep's team. The Spaniard is working very hard indeed, and making no fuss about it, in order to upgrade his concentration and calm decision-making during big matches, and he's getting good, practical help from Pep's staff to achieve this slight but vital upgrade. Part of it has to do with understanding the tempo of a match and avoiding the temptation to go careering after the ball or into space when it seems there's an opening. Intelligence over impulse. He has the character of a mustang and conquering breeding like that is not an easy process but Pep's sure he will end up an absolutely majestic organising midfielder/pivot.

There's one delicious moment in this big win. It's not a skill that many can dominate and is generally the trademark of players from Spain, Portugal or Brazil (in Portuguese the trick is called a *trivela*, which surprisingly derives from the word for 'ordinary'). The trick is to give the ball an exaggerated curved trajectory off the outside of the toe of your boot – essentially just making contact with the outside three toes of whichever foot. Cancelo's *trivela* comes because he pops up miles from his nominal 'full-back' position and the ball swerves in that banana shape so that Sterling, equally impressively, can flick his ankle and connect beautifully with the ball to score a gorgeous goal. Some guy, Sterling – he makes the impossible possible and the simple look brutally hard!

Cancelo's technique evokes Ricardo Quaresma, Luka Modrić and, further back, Franz Beckenbauer, Kazimierz Deyna and Henryk Kasperczak or the mighty Hungarian Tibor Nyilasi. All maestros of the three-toed *trivela* technique. Lillo has a view on the *trivela* too, 'that speciality "three-toed" pass, like other flourishes of technique, is in danger of becoming extinct because football is no longer run by "street" players and it's a factory run by coaches who too often want to stamp out the risky but beautiful things in exchange for regulation and obedience.'

Cancelo struck a blow against the risk-averse mob today. And no one who witnessed it could fail to feel that surge of joy which daring invention brings.

12. FIFTEEN MINUTES

The Etihad groundsmen need to take a bow. Or be awarded medals. It takes them 15 minutes exactly to shift the layer of snow that has draped itself over the pitch in the first half of City's West Ham game. From falling flakes to an outright arctic blizzard – suddenly the match is in jeopardy. When the ball rolls from a pass it's leaving a deep channel behind it. Things are bad. City have smacked it about 367 times between them already in the first half – trying to warm the frozen spectators with the fury of their play. It's 93 per cent possession, as if the Academy whiteboards have been laid flat to play on. City hit the post twice.

Gündoğan finally makes it 1–0 thanks to mopping up a Mahrez chance on goal; it comes immediately before the ref's whistle and everyone sprints inside to thaw their extremities. This is when the City sherpas spring into action. Stars of the afternoon. They've got equipment but it's all manual – the things you'd used to scrape your driveway. Suddenly we can see green, there are ski-slopes of snow driven up to just behind the touchlines. If there's ice, it's smashed. These hard-working, often 'invisible' guys have done such a sweat-drenched pile of work that it's as if there's no trace of the preceding storm. The players, almost all gloved, trot out a little unwillingly, yearning for the warmth of the dressing room and another cup of tea, but they're amazed to find a lovely green bowling lawn to greet them. The little army of snow-removers have, as economist Joseph Schumpeter, said: 'destroyed in order to allow creativity'.

No longer snowed-in, City pick their rhythm up again, and while there's a blizzard of good chances it's only with a minute left that Fernandinho puts things to bed. Just as well, too, because cold, tired and two–nil up, City snooze and Manuel Lanzini gets one back for the Hammers. Good volley it is, too.

This is the same scoreline as a couple of days ago when the 2–1 win over PSG guaranteed group leadership in the Champions League, for the fifth straight season, as they go into the draw for the knockout stages. That night City were tight as a drum, properly squeezing a world-class trio of Messi–Neymar–Mbappé so far out of their comfort zone that the Paris forwards only managed one nice combination move – albeit that it produced PSG's goal. Across more than 180 minutes of the home and away meetings with PSG, City only allowed 5 shots from PSG (who scored 3 times) and City forced 34 shots – 13 of which were on target. Low return and only two goals from them.

As one of the staff mutters to me: 'We're like a great choir, the songs are soaring – maybe the best music we've made in the last five years – but we lack a soloist.'

They need a ruthless goalscorer. That same old refrain again.

13. STUPIDITY

What the hell was going through Kyle Walker's head before he acted so stupidly?

Tonight's red card in Leipzig might well be the daftest thing the English full-back, capable of such stirring cavalry charges forward but also of sudden losses of control, has done since joining City. This aberration stands out because not only is it unnecessary … it's completely absurd.

It's been a run-of-the-mill match in Germany; City have already won the group and are in the Champions League last 16. Job done. Nevertheless, Pep's stuck to his bible – the 11 are pretty formidable. No messing about. He's so, so averse to dropping his guard, or letting anyone else on City's payroll even think that way, that he's picked De Bruyne, Gündoğan, Stones and Mahrez. Any of whom could have been rested. Predictably, Leipzig are still digesting the bile of losing the first match 6–3 and they're up for it – still more so given the fact that, arithmetically, while they can't still join City in going through, third place will get them into the Europa League. They want a win. Badly.

Two defensive errors allow Leipzig to score twice but Mahrez gets one back with a header 15 minutes before the end. That's a scoreline more or less in line with how the game's played out even though Walker and Grealish might easily have scored and Foden hit the post. With ten minutes left, Walker, out on his touchline, boots André Silva from behind. It's a nonsensical action. Silva was going nowhere, offering no threat, and losing 2–1 wasn't a colossal deal because there wasn't really anything other than pride at stake. But for Walker, a pumping like this is the same as losing a Champions League final, and he's overcome with fury. Red card? All day long.

Guardiola's view on the idiocy can be judged by the harsh language he uses as he bawls at his player. Judging from Walker's body language, he's gritting his teeth, trying not to react and confront his coach. Self-restraint, but 60 seconds too late.

UEFA understandably decides this is a three-match ban offence and City appeal (albeit Guardiola isn't in favour of appealing something he thinks is fully justified). Appeal denied.

So ... City are without their first-choice right-back throughout the first knockout round and then, hypothetically, the first leg of the quarter-final. Pep's fury brews for a long time – Walker can judge this from the fact that he doesn't play a single minute of City's next six consecutive matches. Message received?

Guardiola nails his feelings to the mast when Sporting Lisbon come to Manchester for the first match of the knockouts in March 2022. 'Kyle deserves the three-game ban. When a player does something *that* stupid it's a three-game punishment. Sorry! I'm still angry with him, really angry. And Kyle knows that.'

14. FIVE TOUCHES

Tuesday, 14 December, and there's a very special match at the Etihad. Not just because of the scoreline, but for the statistics, the records and because of the on-pitch mentality and actions. Details: City beat Leeds 7–0 – historically, the visitors' biggest defeat.*

This is the sixth time that Guardiola's City have scored seven or more in a match (equalling City's all-time record set by the teams of Wilf Wild [1932–46] and Peter Hodge [1926–32]). And it's the first time in City's history that six different players score for them in the same match (Foden, Grealish, De Bruyne, Mahrez, Stones and Aké). The magnificent seventh means that Pep's players have scored 506 goals since he took over, the fastest any coach has broken the 500 mark.†

Now – attitudes. Right from the start there's a huge alteration in what you'd normally see from a City team. Players perform with positional abandon

---

* In 1934, Leeds lost 1–8 against Stoke City in an old Division One match.
† It's taken Guardiola 207 matches in charge of City for his team to notch 506 goals. That's 2.4 per game. Klopp, 234 matches, Sir Alex Ferguson, 265.

and some of them drive or dribble with the ball instead of pass-pass-pass. This is a huge cultural change for Guardiola's City, explained by the fact that the match strategy is man-to-man marking across the pitch. Bielsa's players chase after City shadows but never once manage to cut out a pass or rob possession without a foul. Watching this is startling – it's like City have shed one personality and adopted a completely different one. The final score says it all. The same Leeds who, under Bielsa, have perpetually been a pain in the backside are left shredded. The radical City change of tactics has worked.

I'm keen to understand the strategy in detail but Carles Planchert's first answer is cryptic: 'All the players have played their roles nicely today.'

Yeah, fine … but today's script is radically different from almost anything that City have shown since the big boss took over. Time to go direct to source.

Pep: 'Juanma won this match – he persuaded me that we give the men freedom against Leeds. The match should belong to the players, not the coaches, so we told them that the brakes were off but that they had to come up with the game plan and then execute it well.'

Rituals changed in order to facilitate this cultural leap.

Pre-match prep is very different – a few video images of Leeds in action but no specific recommendations about what they do well or how to damage them. A 180-degree change. There's no match-morning 'activation' training session, although they do have a mid-morning tactical briefing on matchday.

Pep emphasises three fundamental things: first, that the team need to achieve a certain distal spread, like points of a compass … open positioning so that they can cut off Leeds's ability to support one another. The points of that compass should be Ederson, very advanced even for a sweeper-keeper; Foden, dropping almost to the pivot position; with Mahrez and Grealish east and west. Second, Stones and Zinchenko, positioned wide, and Rodri and Silva, on the inside, occupy positions where City can 'hide' possession and take a breather – change the match tempo if they choose. Third, and most importantly according to their coach, City have to play with a minimum of five touches each time they're on the ball. Five! A fundamental ripping up of everything Pep Guardiola's ever learned as a player or taught as a coach.

This is how he explains it to pretty shocked troops: 'I forbid you to pass the ball until you've had five, five minimum, touches in possession!'

His theory is based on how Leeds are programmed to play. Specifically, their man-to-man marking. If City stick to their general trademark of one-touch/two-touch football, then each Leeds player will fast-press his direct opponent, generating not only a sequence of pressure but a tempo in which errors of passing or control are more likely or even inevitable. But if footballers of the quality City can deploy are told by their coach that they can take time on the ball, then the Leeds players are going to be confused, made to doubt their actions and, likely, thrown off their game completely.

Lillo breaks it down for me: 'We asked the players to receive, turn, survey, hide the ball, take little touches, five, six, seven of them, as many as they want, and circulate with intelligence and accuracy so that Leeds literally had no chance of pressing, causing errors or intercepting.'

Estiarte butts in, 'How weird does it look, when you see City players holding the ball like that?!'

The idea was: confuse Leeds, get them chasing shadows, then get them doubting themselves, profit from the confusion and drive at them. De Bruyne and Foden turn out to be key – full of little dummy movements which confuse Leeds still further. De Bruyne against Adam Forshaw and Foden against Diego Llorente move to their marker, again and again, then immediately sprint off somewhere else, buying metres of freedom each time they do. So City's usual tactic of creating a 'free man' is augmented to regularly having two or even three free men simultaneously.

Lillo, again: 'Another key concept is that, if you rob the ball, you don't stop to wonder "what now?" … you drive or dribble with it. Immediately. Vertically if possible. The reason being that Leeds's system, their Bielsa philosophy, is so firmly embedded that, because they are man-marking really tightly and every Leeds guy has his City rival drummed into his mind, they won't come off marking duty in order to help a teammate … even though we are driving the ball forward and attacking that space aggressively.'

It's a radical departure, and 180-degrees different from how City face Manchester United. Then it's one-touch/two-touch with speed of thought and action in order to crack United's defensive block open. The message from the coaching staff is: 'We pass right to a teammates' boot – anyone who puts a pass into space, rather than right to the next guy's stronger foot, gets subbed immediately!'

15. THIRTY-SIX WINS

Since the Premier League was born, Boxing Day football averages three goals per match.

City's meeting with Leicester makes it look like the two of them have prearranged to combine to smash this stat.

It's 26 December 2021. City 6 Leicester 3, with Guardiola's side already 4–0 up by half-time, during which time they've hit 93 per cent possession. Then, after the break, the home team doze off somewhat – conceding three in 11 minutes.

Happily enough, they react immediately – snooze over – with Laporte and Sterling adding a couple to seal City's festive cheer. It's a huge score-line, and means ten scored in the last two matches, although Pep wasn't impressed by their 4–0 away win to Newcastle a few days ago: 'one of the worst matches of our season – my players really lost focus.'

The year-end contest comes at Brentford's Community Stadium, 1–0 (Foden), which tots up City's 36th Premier League win, and their 53rd in all competitions, in the last 365 days. Another English record.*

Winning in London is the tenth straight Premier League victory – the fourth time City have racked up a run that impressive since Pep took over. The team is now nine points ahead of Liverpool as 2021 becomes 2022. Equally impressive is the fact that, as December dawned, City were a point behind Chelsea. Seven straight wins and the advantage hasn't just switched hands – the Sky Blues are now eight points ahead of the London Blues. Did Pep always enjoy Christmas football? No way. Does he right now? You bet.

16. MINUTE 92.28

This is an Alfred Hitchcock script.

Picture a stadium, chock-full: it's midday on 1 January and there are many in the crowd who'd admit they're still in their Hogmanay outfits

---

* City: 44 league matches in 2021, 36 wins, 2 draws, 6 defeats, 113 scored, 32 conceded. The goals scored is an all-time record, beating the 102 in 2017, the 99 from 2018 and 95 in 2019 – all by City. Gündoğan (15) and Sterling (13) are the principal scorers.

and have arrived at the Emirates in north London straight from all-night partying. There are faces that show the festivities' toll, 'Happy New Year!' greetings abound and there's a general air that might lead you to believe this is an outdoor rave – not a big football match.

Maybe not the ideal ambience for a titanic battle, but that's what's on the cards. City are away to Arsenal today and everyone involved knows that both teams will go flat out – it's like an end-of-season winner-takes-all battle. Colossal competitive aggression. From coaches to players – no question. Arteta's Arsenal have developed a new toughness, they don't wilt – they rise to big occasions. Pep's City are implacable – to win the title they need to come out on top of every meeting of this stature, to draw blood and then go in for the kill when their opponents stagger.

Then Hitchcock ratchets up the tension. The crowd have caught the atmosphere, they know this is a 'no quarter asked' contest, and both the ref and VAR somehow miss an Arsenal penalty when Ederson tumbles Ødegaard. Drama.

Arteta's strikers work like Trojans to try and muck up City's build-up, and the result is that Pep's team drop their passing accuracy to 88 per cent. Arsenal have periods of 75 per cent possession. This is unheard of!

Saka puts the Gunners 1–0 up with a lovely goal, Gabriel Martinelli thumps two shots just narrowly wide of the City posts and then VAR chooses to intervene when Xhaka tugs Silva back in the area. Mahrez elegantly tucks it to the left of Ramsdale despite the fact that, as the penalty's being argued about, Gabriel's had a good go at stamping all over the penalty spot to chop it up in an attempt to spoil the Algerian's chances of scoring. The Brazilian defender is booked for his attempted malfeasance. Remarkably, all this is just a teaser for the drama that is about to ensue.

The remarkable Rodri block on Fabinho in front of an open goal at Anfield, Stones's league-saving clearance in 2019 and Walker's scissor-kick, which saved City in the 93rd minute of the Community Shield that same year – remember those? Today's hero is Nathan Aké.

It's been 1–1 for just over 60 seconds when Aymeric Laporte wins a duel and heads back in the direction of his keeper without realising that Ederson's moved out of his normal positioning. The defender's innocently intended header looks like it's irreversibly looping over City's last man and into the net for a hugely embarrassing own goal.

Pep's roaring 'Ayme, Ayme, Ayme!' … as if his player could really hear the recriminations against a background of throbbing crowd noise with the home supporters begging the ball to roll over the line. But into the breach appears a curly mop of black hair and then an outstretched Dutch leg. Aké's miracle clearance scoops the ball away from the net – salvation by millimetres, not centimetres.

Madness follows miracle. The clearance lands right at the feet of Gabriel Martinelli, who only needs a simple, calm finish to score despite Aké's efforts – but the Brazilian stabs at it and, somehow, hits the post. Within a minute Arsenal's Gabriel smashes his City namesake (Magalhães thudding into Jesus) and is sent off for seeing his second yellow card.

The match changes hue and Arsenal's threat drops. But their energy and commitment, even with ten men, doesn't. The fact that this brutal battle is City's third match in just six days looks like it's taking a toll – they seem flat and affected by the fact that Foden, Zinchenko and Stones are absent due to being COVID positive. Never underestimate this group of players, though. A little bit of De Bruyne magic turns Laporte into an attacking threat and, ultimately, it's Rodri who stabs home from close range for a 2–1 lead. It's the winner and everyone knows it because the Emirates clock is showing 92.28.

The Hitchcock drama is over and has led to City's 11th straight Premier League win. It's turning into a bad habit, this tendency to make the final seconds of any big match their killing zone. Remember when Agüero won the title in minute 93.20? Or Gabriel Jesus making City the Centurions in minute 93.02? Maybe Rodri scoring in minute 92.28 will end up being just as crucial but, one thing's for sure, nobody will ever forget the magical moment when Nathan Aké appeared from nowhere to stop Arsenal going 2–1 up.

17. TWENTY-ONE INFECTED

More names on the sick list. Guardiola, Lillo, Fernandinho, Sterling and Grealish are COVID positive, meaning that recent weeks have seen 21 City staff and players receiving the same bad news. There's hardly a single player who's dodged this bullet.

Rodolfo Borrell takes charge when City go to the County Ground and he's leading a skeleton crew. Basically, anyone who's not an invalid. There's also a healthy dose of kids who'll be involved against Swindon in the FA Cup third round. One name will emerge from the mini-crisis: Cole Palmer. He's still 19 but he possesses as much maturity as he does quality. It's his assist which lets Silva put City 1–0 up and Palmer will score to make it 4–1 too. More than the hard stats, though, his display underlines that this is a golden pupil from the City Academy. He's now scored in the Champions League, the League Cup and the FA Cup – despite the fact that he's only played 90 minutes on one occasion (13 appearances in total). Usually, he's used like an inside-forward/attacking midfielder but he's often featured as the false 9. Today, Palmer's outside right – and he's gobbled up the opportunity. He's going to be a smashing footballer. Just one question remains: is he capable of the same stubborn patience Foden has had to show in order to develop at the pace Guardiola dictates? Let's hope so.

18. TWENTY-ONE GOALS

Today makes it five goals De Bruyne has scored against his ex-club, Chelsea. They squandered his brilliance in 2014, thinking that the Belgian wasn't at their level. Six years later he's, unquestionably, the Premier League's defining footballer. City started December a point behind Tuchel's team and are now 13 ahead. Embarrassing for the Blues. Chelsea are still formidable – they're reigning European champions after all – but City have twice beaten them 1–0 in this current title chase. Guardiola's chuffed: '180 Premier League minutes against Chelsea and we've only allowed them one shot on goal!'

They're aiming at Lillo's formula: 'allow zero point something in the goals-against column'. Against Chelsea they're achieving zero point zero. The wider context is that Ederson, right now, is keeping a clean sheet every other match (166 Premier matches and 83 without conceding).

Pep's almost as fixated by another tendency – the duels. 'Having this type of control against such a fantastic team is super-difficult but we showed lots of patience and we kept on winning our duels.' Laporte has won 100 per cent of his aerial duels, so has Stones. Nine between them.

Chelsea's attitude has been to defend, hard, in a low block and then counterattack via lightning transitions. It hasn't really functioned because City's forwards have worked their socks off and shown real football intelligence to disrupt Tuchel's idea of how to play the ball out. They've heaped lots of pressure on Chelsea's Basque keeper, Kepa, so that he's only completed 50 per cent of his passes – and not a single one of the long balls he's attempted.

This makes 12 straight wins for City in their title charge and De Bruyne's now scored 21 goals from outside the box. Nobody has a bigger total than that since 2015. Not bad for someone Chelsea got rid of because they didn't know how to handle him.

19. 500 POINTS

Guardiola's blind faith in Bernardo Silva is so obvious it doesn't really need describing. A number will do: Silva's just racked up 22 consecutive Premier League starts.

In the opening 20 minutes, City have 81 per cent possession but between minutes 50 and 60 that goes up – the visitors have their foot on Southampton's throat. The Saints are tough to beat at home and Kyle Walker-Peters has put them one–nil up after a long counterattack move sparked when Sterling lost possession.

City dominate, hit the post twice, shoot at Forster's goal 20 times, equalise thanks to a Laporte header and get within touching distance of a thousand passes. But their winning streak is going to hit the buffers on the south coast. Twelve and over. But Pep's euphoric about the draw: 'We played spectacularly!'

Just one of them today but this makes 500 points in the Premier league after the Catalan's 213th match in charge – quite something. De Bruyne's reached 80 goal-assists to equal Beckham's Premier League total … but a booming 68 matches more quickly than the legendary Englishman. That's properly remarkable. In comparison, Mourinho needed 231 Premier matches to hit 500 points, Klopp, 236, Ferguson, 242, and Wenger, 249.

20. THE CONTROLLER

Riyad Mahrez has scored eight goals in the last seven matches. There have been four penalties in that total – three put to the keeper's left but, today, he's sent one to the right of Brentford's David Raya. City have a player here who's always available. He's got a remarkably injury-free record for the club – five days for a twisted ankle in August 2018, three in January 2020 when he took a kick and a couple of weeks off for COVID nine months later.

Coming to the end of his fourth season as a Cityzen, Mahrez has missed a total of 8 days injured and 15 days ill. That's so unusual that Guardiola's dark humour with the winger is always: 'Look at your legs – you've got no muscles! There's nothing there to injure … !'

Another central element to this happy phenomenon is that Mahrez loves his football just as much as he did as a kid – he simply wants to play all the time. The more the better. The downside is that guys like him are bound to take it personally when they don't get a game. In the team? Happy as a sandboy and it really shows. He radiates contentment and confidence. The flipside is that he can also behave like a big kid when Guardiola, for whatever reason, doesn't select him. Remember the guy who 'owned' the game when you were kids because he was the only one who had a proper football? That's Mahrez. And if he's not picked for the team, it's like some-one's stolen his ball.

His passion for the game goes some way to explaining his superb control. The Algerian is one of those players who actually love being on the ball, and we've watched countless times as he's turned the ugliest pass into something useful or even beautiful.

In my time, I've witnessed Rivelino, Pelé, Cruyff, Zidane, Iniesta and Messi show off their control of the ball, and Mahrez is undoubtedly part of that tribe. In fact, if anything, he has a greater tolerance for, and capacity to, receive poor distribution and convert it into something usable. Whether it's shot at him like a cannon or dropping out of the sky, come rain or shine, a good playing surface or a muddy pitch … it makes no difference. He's a man with the capacity and mentality to make the ball obey him in any circum-stances. At times, it's like watching an altogether different sport from the one the majority of players engage in.

Mahrez gets the first today – but this is a day when defenders will be the chief protagonists. 'João [Cancelo] was our best winger today whether he was dribbling or shooting,' Pep says post-match. Cancelo's played as a 'false full-back' and his thrilling, daring interpretation of the role has produced four delicious dribbles, two shots on goal, three sweetly delivered long passes, four big tackles and ten duels won. Omnipresent, brilliant.

Stones is up there on the pantheon too. Nominally right-back, he's moved into midfield and operated like a pivot, as an attacking midfielder and as a second striker. It's been an outstanding exhibition. One day in the future, perhaps those outside the club will give him the recognition he most certainly deserves.

City's 60 points from 24 matches is their second best return at this stage (fewer than the 65 they achieved to became the Centurions and ahead of the 57 in season 2011–12).

Carles Planchart has started the countdown to glory: 'Fourteen matches to go and counting.' And Pep adds: 'Over the next couple of months we'll be competing against ourselves.'

These days, Pep is much more willing to open up, so I'm going to succumb to the temptation of reproducing everything he said, before the Norwich away match, about the constant pressure and the expectation to win trophies.

'When you take over a team with the most incredible football talents around you, with a very special staff and you win everything in your first season … don't get me wrong for a second. This wasn't about "me" – there were so many talented and important people involved in that treble. Then we went on to win all six trophies available to us and, in the blink of an eye, everyone seems to think that every season's got to be the same. It reaches a stage that, because you win trophies year after year, if you qualify for a Champions League semi-final and then lose, it's suddenly "a disaster" of a season! A "disaster" when you've won the League and the Cup! That really impacted me both when I was there and from a distance. Perhaps now people will realise how successful all those seasons really were? A good few years ago, Manchester United controlled the Premier League like nobody had ever done before. Could anyone have imagined, then, that they could go six, seven or more years without winning the title? Was that even conceivable? No, I don't think so, but it's happened. And if it happened to that version of United then it can happen to us starting from tomorrow. Not next season ... tomorrow!

'Football is brutally difficult and so unpredictable. We are human beings and we're imperfect, fallible. So, less than perfect things can happen. What's vital is how you behave and think and what you work for. You have to look "inwards" and decide what it is you want and how to behave in order to achieve it. I've made this point an infinite number of times to my players: "Our biggest rival is ourselves." That's who we're really playing against.

'With all due respect to our rivals, they're not our biggest opponents ... we're competing with ourselves. That's the objective. If, on the day, our rival is better than us, then you have to just accept that. Next day, you dust your-self down, you improve and you beat them next time up. Our real, baseline competition is to be the best version of ourselves every single day – training and competing in matches. Or striving to achieve that, at least. Every great side is like that – no question. There will always be rivals in their path but that's not what's super-important – the key is how demanding we are with ourselves, how relentless. Our standards.

'Are we playing a side which defends deep and in numbers and who doesn't care about attacking so that it's hard to open them up? Like Brentford the other day ... ? OK, fine, that's our job. You're playing Fulham, a team with a wholly different philosophy, who want to compete for the ball with you and who are flying in the Championship – right, fine, bring it on.

'The big question is: "What shape are we in ... how demanding have we been with ourselves day in day out?" Without exception, this has been my mentality since the first day I became a coach. And here I've pushed for everyone to focus inwardly – from the first day I joined. There are no excuses here, none. They don't exist. If you start moaning, there's no place for you here. Errors are part of the process, we are human and we will make mistakes. That can happen. But effort and the constant intention to improve are non-negotiables. And our attitude when we lose is to behave as if it was our own fault. Refereeing decisions to blame? Just more excuses. The answer is to play better. Work harder. Run more. Be driven by the desire to improve. If that's how we live every week, then not only our fans, but we ourselves, will have nothing to reproach ourselves for.'

21. TWELVE POINTS

By Saturday, 12 February, City have a 12-point advantage over Liverpool – but it's a bit of a mirage because Klopp's men have played two fewer matches.

Ten opening minutes where City have 83 per cent possession are enough for them to boss the match at Norwich, where Sterling produces a hat-trick.

But Guardiola's not fooled easily. Whatever the table says right now, Liverpool should be considered to be only six points behind and, with the Champions League knockout stages about to hove into view, any distraction, any trip up, can be seriously bad news.

Happily for him, this 4–0 away win in Norwich is followed by an absolutely spectacular 5–0 thrashing of Sporting Lisbon, where Silva really lets rip. One of his great games. It's not irrelevant that Mr Silva is a Benfica fanatic so facing Sporting at the José Alvalade Stadium is a massive stimulus for him. He's more determined than ever to take control and punish City's opponents. He scores twice, sees a third disallowed, gives Sterling a goal-assist and it's such a memorable night that Pep says: 'Bernardo doesn't just "play", he understands football. He interprets and anticipates every move in a way that very few anywhere in the world can match.'

Last year, I wrote about Silva being a tailor, a weaver. The attacking midfielders under Pep fall into two very different categories: those who stitch things together and those who try to smash opponents. Gündoğan and Silva come from the first group. Their specialist role is to thread all their teammates together into a cohesive whole. To make the whole greater than the sum of the parts. They pass, pass and pass again and again with the knowledge that every movement of the ball from teammate to teammate is like a form of communication about threats and opportunities. They knit movements together, shifting City men to one zone of the pitch, herding opponents to another – pass, think, move, stitch, knit, create.

The match-breakers, in the other group, need to add the finish to the tailormade moves. They take the elegant and make it threatening or deadly. De Bruyne and Foden are the ones who get involved to culminate, rather than create. They are the 'individuals within the collective'. Free spirits, among the very few who are allowed to seek anarchy, to shrug off the orthodoxies Pep and his staff spend so long establishing so that their 'irreverence' can unlock blockages.

City going 4–0 up by half-time is the biggest lead in the first period in a Champions League knockout and the final 5–0 scoreline is the 43rd time Pep's City have scored five or more in a match. That's 13 per cent of the matches of which he's been in charge. It's also the 14th time this season City have scored four or more and they've become the quickest team to reach 200 goals in the Champions League (97 matches). Despite virtually being in the quarter-finals after the first leg, Pep chooses to demonstrate what seems to some like his state of permanent dissatisfaction.

'The players know me well enough – they know I'm going to tell them we need to do better. One or two were below their best level today. We lost some possession, which we should never have done. Easy passes misplaced. OK, we were properly clinical in our finishing but I saw errors in the build-up and that's something I want improved immediately. There's a simple rule I won't ever let them forget – when you have the ball, don't lose it!'

22. A MOMENT OF DOUBT

The 53,201 fans leave the Etihad totally convinced of one thing – if City had bought Harry Kane, they'd be invincible. Kane's scored twice today and toppled Pep's team, who, despite showing lots of creative brilliance, have also demonstrated rare defensive fragility. Walker hasn't pressed well and has looked clumsy on the ball. Cancelo – super in attack, superseded in defence. Laporte – playing the ball out nicely but playing with fire when defending close to his area. Even big Rúben Dias, the chief of the 'Yugoslav' defenders, has had a bad day at the office and has failed to repel Kane and Co.

The 2–3 defeat looks very sloppy – an afternoon of City men caught between action and inaction. To press or not to press – that was the question, which was answered far too late. A total of three goals conceded over their last seven matches and, now, three conceded in this one bad performance today. Including the first one after just four minutes – Dejan Kulusevski doing the damage.

Remember the goal conceded last season in the Champions League final against Chelsea and the one at Old Trafford? The Swede's goal is similar. This time, Walker doesn't rush to press but, instead, starts and then hesitates, stuck in no man's land. Kane takes full advantage, feeds his partner-in-crime, Son, and the South Korean puts the goal on a plate for Kulusevski. Pep hates his pre-match 'script' being ripped up – but most especially he hates it when it happens after just a handful of minutes.

Gündoğan, Cancelo and Foden take the initiative and the German hits the post before hitting the net. Kane has enough of the parity after an hour and snaffles an opportunity when Dias fails to clear. Spurs' record scorer gallops between Laporte and Cancelo before leaving Ederson helpless. He very nearly produces the identical trick four minutes later but is thwarted by the big Brazilian, who's fuming that his defence has gone walkabout.

Antonio Conte's teams are always muscular, quick and pretty unpleasant to face. They love you to advance your lines, to attack them, and then they wrap you up in their defensive schemes, trapping players in the wrong places before smashing forward at speed. When it clicks, it's devastating. Two–one down isn't a brutal scoreline but it's costing City the world to get an equaliser precisely because of how Spurs compete and how comfortable they are playing this way.

After Gündoğan sees Lloris make a superb save so that the ball hits the post, Cancelo and Mahrez come close, and Kane has a goal ruled off by VAR. It's also the VAR system that grants City a 92nd-minute penalty, which Mahrez thrashes home extravagantly to Lloris's left. It sneaks in under the crossbar.

Now, what's the golden rule when you equalise in a brutally hard game like this and there are only three minutes of added time left? Well, there are, of course, a lot of differing points of view. City choose the daring one – flat-out looking for a late-late winner. And, for that reason, they lose.

Walker, again, misjudges when to feed De Bruyne and the possession turnover leads to Kulusevski crossing brilliantly for Kane to pop up between Dias and Walker and head the winner home powerfully. Poor strategic decision, poor execution, poor result-control and, ultimately, poor defending against a guy who needs no second invitation to ruin everyone's afternoon.

Guardiola's super pissed off with Walker because it's one thing to chase a dramatic winner – fine. But it's quite another to do so with blood rushing through the veins and not quite reaching the brain. This tendency is probably the only major defect from which Walker suffers. But his coach is fuming and, although there's very little time left, the match is still in play at 2–3 down so the recipient of Pep's vitriol is poor old Rodolfo Borrell, simply because the Catalan is sitting right next to Guardiola. It looks, to the uninitiated, that Borrell's getting it in the neck, but every last ounce of it is meant for Walker. Right at the heart of the fury is the fact that Liverpool, a couple of hours earlier, have beaten Norwich and are now three points behind City. There's zero margin for error. As ever, Lillo's point of view is slightly unorthodox: 'A team with such good habits, such self-belief as ours isn't going to be derailed just because of an "accident" like this one today.' And then, with one of his cheeky grins, he adds, 'We're already champions anyway because we only lose once every 15 matches and there are only 13 to play – as long as we stick to that average, the title's ours.'*

By the end of the season, of course, Lillo will be proven right in his Mystic Meg prediction – in their last 12 matches City don't lose once: 9 wins, 3 draws.

23. THE ARM

Jordan Pickford isn't a giant (he's 1.87m/6ft 1in tall) but he's genuinely blessed with sensationally quick reactions. Which is why he can produce so many improbable saves.

He does exactly this at the end of February against City. The first half against Everton isn't great – the Toffees press brilliantly and asphyxiate City's game. But, after the break, with Foden and Sterling playing as 'open' wingers, each going outside on their stronger foot, City rain shot upon shot on Pickford's goal. The keeper blocks at least five that otherwise would have been goals. Shots from Foden, Stones, De Bruyne, Silva and then Foden again are all knocked away by the England keeper with the cat-like reflexes.

---

* City have only lost three Premier League matches this season. The opening day against Spurs (1–0) in August last year, against Palace (0–2) in late October, and today in the 26th match (2–3).

Not until there are only nine minutes left do City turn superiority into an advantage. Michael Keane messes up and that substitutes for a moment of brilliance from the champions elect. The game swivels. Keane's clumsiness means that Foden can slot home from about a metre away from the goal-line and City have won. Well, they assume they've won, but there's a sting in the tail.

With four minutes left, Rodri, without intending to, helps the ball away from danger with his arm. It's in the penalty area and, while City are clamouring that Everton were offside anyway, VAR ponderously reviews the action for what seems like an eternity. The Spaniard has tried to chest the ball down, it hits his arm, albeit potentially above the infamous T-shirt line, and in due course neither the onfield ref nor his video assistants give Everton their spot-kick. It's an error – no way around that fact. But no matter how strongly the Liverpudlian team protests, it's done and dusted. Fortune has favoured City.

It's a massive twist in the title race, honestly, because if the league leaders had drawn at Goodison, then it would have been a glorious opportunity, all of a sudden, for Liverpool.

It's also true that only four weeks ago at Southampton, City didn't get a clearcut penalty for a foul by Mohammed Salisu on De Bruyne – maybe the age-old saying about things evening out across a campaign is true after all?

Neither of these were the first nor will they be the last VAR errors, and the way Liverpool feel today is how City felt in dropping two points against the Saints back in January. Swings and roundabouts.

24. THE DEMOLITION

Football is a continuous tale of the unexpected. Jam-packed with uncertainty and the inexplicable. Like life, I guess. Try and apply 'reason' to football and you'll drive yourself nuts.

It's the Manchester derby and, 35 minutes in, a fan at the Etihad has a medical emergency so the referee, Michael Oliver, stops the game to ensure that proper treatment can be administered. The pause is about three minutes long. Nothing, right? But Guardiola pounces on the chance to get access to his players in order to correct how they're constructing their build-up from the back. City lead 2–1 but they're suffering as a result of United's well-applied pressing. Pogba is aggressive in how he's applying this tactic and it's troubling the Catalan coach.

United are using a 4+2 scheme to press City's build-up and they're doing so very high up the pitch. It's so threatening that City have modified their habitual 3+2 build-up shape and converted to 3+3 and, even then, they're not gaining the 'superiority' needed to punch through United's oppressive red blanket.

City use Stones and Laporte, with Ederson between them, as their first line of build-up. The second line in what is now a 3+3 comprises Walker, Rodri and Cancelo – the former and latter very wide and open to stretch the territory that United need to press. But City are only managing to break through when Silva and/or Foden drop really deep to help galvanise the play, to win extra space and to create superiority. De Bruyne's brace of goals comes from the same production line – a nice pattern of passing down the left, followed by Silva and Foden penetrating into good areas to set up the Belgian maestro. Jadon Sancho, ex-City, then puts a blot on the jotter of that fine first half-hour as he slams home a goal for the Reds.

While the medics attend the stricken supporter, Pep stamps his authority all over the problem. He calls Ederson, Laporte, Rodri and Cancelo over so that he can issue his instructions. The idea is to take advantage of what Pogba's doing and turn a United strength to City's advantage. Typical Guardiola. There's a space in behind United's big French rampager and, while his men aren't finding it right now, it's glaringly obvious to City's coach that this is what they need to do to turn the game in their favour.

Ederson is told not to advance so much, to be the key 'support' to the two centre-halves – but deeper by a few metres than he has been. More of a mini-triangle shape than a straight line. Rodri is told to go markedly wider on the right, almost like a 'false' full-back, and Stones must play further left of the central position he's been in. Laporte has to mimic Rodri's position on the left so that, however hard he runs, however well he anticipates, it will be impossible for Pogba to cover all the ground and, if he tries to, it'll be to his and his team's detriment.

Pep orders Silva to try and cat-burgle that space in behind Pogba's bullish pressing and to wait there for his teammates to find him. This effectively makes the Portuguese the pivot (with Rodri splayed out right) and so Grealish moves 'inside' by a few metres to help Silva and to give him a quick passing channel.

Immediately when the match restarts it's clear that City, via Silva, now have oodles of space and superiority. It's fiesta time again. At half-time Mahrez admits, 'I only touched the ball four times in the first half-hour!'

Sixty per cent of City's attacks have come down the left, 21 per cent down the middle and 18 per cent in Mahrez's area. The staff tell him: 'Be patient, be calm. Things are changing. We've had the spare man down the left and that's the only reason you've not seen the ball. But when it comes this half you'll be in space and it's going to be your job to finish moves and score.'

Post-match, the Algerian, having seen the ball 36 times and scored twice, tells me, 'I listened, I concentrated and I trusted that the ball would start reaching me. I heard the message that I had to "make the difference" and I think I did.'

The second half is a massacre. That old City adage of 'find the feet, not space, with the ball' bears fruit again. City don't let United compete and produce 404 passes, about four times the number United manage, achieving 94 per cent accuracy (the Reds hit just 80 per cent). The combination of both factors means that United don't manage a single counterattack in the second 45 minutes.

The last half-hour should go down in Manchester derby history: quality, accuracy, confidence and domination. De Bruyne crowns himself king of positional football and United simply chase shadows.

Between minutes 80 and 90, when Mahrez tucks away their fourth, City make 120 passes and shoot at goal six times while United manage a measly 16 passes and would need binoculars to see Ederson's goalmouth. The last quarter of the game is dominated by 92 per cent home-team possession – 365 City passes in United's half (141 for the Reds). Silva, just like the derby last November, when he powered through 12.5km at Old Trafford, is the player who's covered the most ground – 12.8km this time. Of the 15 highest marks for ground covered this season, Silva has 11.

While the laurel wreaths and plaudits go to De Bruyne, Mahrez, Foden and Silva, Stones has had a glorious game too. He's won 88 per cent of his aerial duels across the season and has had 91 per cent passing accuracy across the last few months. He's in the best form of his life. Nobody else has ever hit these combined numbers in the Premier League. Stones ability to play in, and dominate, four or five different positions is something Guardiola really values.

This is the 50th time since he took over that Pep's City have scored four or more.* And, on this occasion at least, he allows himself to purr with satisfaction: 'If that second half display isn't one of the absolute best that my team's produced, then I don't know what else we have to do … ! I'm extremely demanding but I know my players' outer limits and we performed at our top level in the second half, in terms of effort and everything else. And we did it against United!'

25. DEFENSIVE INJURIES

From March until the end of the season, Guardiola endures nightmare after nightmare with regards to his defensive lineup. First, Rúben Dias suffers a nasty injury in the FA Cup tie against Peterborough and he's out until the end of April. Then, just when the big, imposing Portuguese is back to take control of how City defend, Stones is struck down by another muscle tear. It's a big loss – Stones is vital at the back but can double- or triple-up in a number of different positions. Indeed, the England international won't be involved again until, as a bit of an emergency option, he's bandaged up and pushed out in the last match of the season on 22 May.

In the midst of all this, Walker is debilitated by a badly twisted ankle, which does such damage that it means he's likely to be out for the rest of the season. He fights back to make a seven-minute cameo against Real Madrid to try and contain Vinicius but suffers further damage to the same ligament. Then, rubbing salt in the wound, Aké suffers an almost identical injury and that's him out of the last stretch of games.

So, the City defence, for some considerable time, the last three months in fact, will be Cancelo, Laporte plus support from Zinchenko and

---

* In the same timeframe, Liverpool have managed this 41 times, Spurs 29, Chelsea 23, Arsenal 22 and United 20.

SEASON 6: 2021–2   375

Fernandinho – with the odd cameos from the injured guys as and when they are intermittently fit.

For a team that had adopted Pep's 'Yugoslav' philosophy, and which was thriving in that state of mind, it's horrible to be stripped of so much experience, talent, muscularity and pace. With or without an old-fashioned no. 9 up front, City will score goals. But their competitive status in this vital phase of all competitions owes much to how robust they are at the back.

Without the mainstay men, they've lost much of their strength and power.

26. TWENTY-EIGHT STARTS

Having put on a five-star display in the derby, it's on to the straightforward business of putting Sporting out of their misery.

Pep takes the opportunity to play some of the youngsters: C.J. Egan-Riley starting at full-back, James McAtee and Luke Mbete making their debuts in the Champions League and even Scott Carson taking over from Ederson for 20 minutes. Nil–nil is a big change from the first-leg thrashing but it does the job – shake hands and move on. It's Atlético Madrid in the quarter-final now – a thorny prospect.

The next 0–0 is one with very different characteristics and leaves a nasty aftertaste. It's Palace again, this time at Selhurst Park, and the draw means Liverpool have nudged closer (70 points plays 69) with eight games left until the end of the Premier League season. It's the same old story: City trample all over Palace in every metric except for goals. The one that really counts. Pep's side comes as close as two efforts off the woodwork but Patrick Vieira's team defend for their lives and look like they're loving every second. One of Guardiola's assistants hits the nail on the head: 'it's like they bricked up the entire Palace goalmouth!'

The next few days are even worse: Liverpool win 2–0 at Arsenal and Guardiola, Estiarte, Buenaventura and even Dr Mauri are all struck down by COVID.

Bernardo Silva's been in the starting 11 for the last 28 consecutive matches, something which is wholly out of character for Pep's entire coaching career. With the exception of his keepers, there are very, very few who've been given this much of a 'you're the main man' label by Guardiola. And it makes no difference which position the Portuguese is asked to play, this stat, on its own, tells a huge story about his importance and reliability. Pep loves this guy.

27. THE DENTIST

It's sometimes said in jest but a tie against this Atlético Madrid team can be about as much fun as an emergency dentist appointment. One without anaesthetic. You'll come out alive, probably … but there'll be pain.

Patience is going to be a vital ingredient.

No matter what kind of shape they are in when you play them, it's inevitable that Atleti will play like a python, trying to squeeze the life out of you. They are as accessible as a wall you can't scale without crampons and as annoying as the neighbour who insists on mowing the lawn at 7am on a sleepy Sunday morning.

First leg, first half and it's 74 per cent possession for the home side – but zero shots on goal. Nobody in the City dressing room is shocked by that. Pep and Rodri, who was a *Colchonero* (a mattress maker, the nickname, owing to the club's red-and-white striped shirts, for someone who plays for Atleti) in a previous life, have spent time warning the rest of the team what this is going to feel like.

City are even more dominant in the second half and they create three good chances. But it's still 0–0 when Foden comes on and, with his first few touches, gifts De Bruyne an easy goal – the only one of the match, indeed of the entire 180 minutes. Foden very nearly repeats the trick a few seconds later but the score doesn't alter, despite the fact that City win the ball back 37 times from Atleti and take a total of 15 shots at goal. Foden's goal is the only one of the match, indeed of the entire 180 minutes.

It means that, in seven days' time, there'll be only the minimum lead to defend in Madrid.

The second leg is much more combative – Atleti rob the ball 50 times from City, who do the same to Diego Simeone's team 40 times. The ball doesn't really have a single dominant master this time. The *Colchoneros* have 14 shots but only put three on target. City have ten, with only one fully on target and another off a post.

The first half feels relatively calm and City look as if they're cruising through to the last four. But that changes, radically, after the break. Atleti finally decide to go 'all in' and attack. It's aggressive, it's dangerous and suddenly the tie is in the balance. There's no Walker, but City still need to adopt their 'Yugoslav' personality and Stones saves a sure goal in the dying seconds with one of those monumental goal-line blocks. It's a defensive moment but it feels, to everyone in blue, like it has the worth of an actual goal scored in their favour. The clock ticks on and Ederson needs to make two huge saves in the 97th and the 101st minutes – but, eventually, the drilling stops, the filling is replaced, the pain is over and the dentist allows the patient to get out of the chair.

For the second consecutive year, City are in the final four of the Champions League.

It's been painful but, what a joy to have got there.

28. HANGING BY A THREAD

In between Atleti behaving like a pain in the neck, there's a lot of Liverpool time. The league and the FA Cup are both at stake, across 11 short days. On 10 April there are 90 utterly frantic minutes at the Etihad – it's a normal league match but played with all the intensity and ferocity of an all-time great final, another enthralling episode in the long-running Guardiola–Klopp drama.

City play vertical football and impose high levels of control. Liverpool, as ever, are 100mph in their intensity and speed of action. In the stands, the fans are transfixed and find themselves without time to draw breath and assimilate what's happening between the flood of good chances, good passes, good tackles – really good entertainment.

Sterling fails to score, one vs one, in the fourth minute but, less than 60 seconds later, De Bruyne scores thanks to a bit of mischief from Silva – the ball goes in off Matip. Within just eight minutes Diogo Jota makes it 1–1 thanks to a nice team move and the chances just come in rat-tat-tat, staccato fashion. De Bruyne's passing, timing and use of space are a marvel to behold, but Salah is working with exceptional intelligence and skill to make sure that Liverpool match the home side, blow for blow. Cancelo's cross lets Gabriel Jesus put City 2–1 up but that's only a provocation for Sadio Mané to make it 2–2.

The first ten minutes of the second half are owned by Liverpool – the remainder of this titanic battle are City's. Four times it seems that City have broken Liverpool. Four times they're denied: Van Dijk somehow stops Jesus from converting when it looks like a certain goal; VAR rules out a Sterling 'goal'; Jesus, again, can't quite finish a gilt-edged chance; and then Mahrez hits the post from a free kick. Each team is loyal to its well-constructed identity. City defends 'with the ball' and Liverpool defend with their players. City's final 'must score' moment of the afternoon is created by De Bruyne's brilliance but it's Mahrez who takes the shot. It's perfectly acceptable but Matip just manages to deflect his effort wide.

The 2–2 draw leaves the entire title chase hanging by a thread. City stay just one point ahead (74 vs 73) and we're down to seven nail-biting matches left.

Six days later and, this time, it really is 'all or nothing' because the two teams have to do it all again at Wembley in the FA Cup semi-final. Pep's team, indeed his entire squad, are completely knackered after the Atlético experience. Not so their opponents. Liverpool beat Benfica in the first leg of their Champions League quarter-final and Klopp was therefore able to rotate his team in the second leg. It's a big advantage.

Pep's lost Walker, Dias and De Bruyne to injury and he judges that Rodri and Mahrez are dead on their feet. He's therefore forced to field a very 'mixed' 11. Silva has been asked to step into De Bruyne's shoes for this game, but he's evidently suffering and Liverpool smell blood. They smash through City in the first half, play with mean-eyed ruthlessness and go 3–0 up.

Steffen, in goal today, has a nightmare for the 2–0 goal – a bit of Rip Van Winkle with Mané bursting through. That's not good for team morale and the US keeper also doesn't do brilliantly when Liverpool get their third. Those errors aside, Steffen actually shows a lot of character under the Liverpool bombardment. He's a good keeper, suffering from the misfortune of perpetually having to wait in line behind Ederson.

Kudos to City for a muscular reaction in the second half where, barring miracles, Liverpool aren't going to surrender their lead. Grealish starts the fightback with a goal and Gabriel Jesus has a good chance but loses his one vs one with Alisson. It's a critical moment and there's a feeling that, had it gone in, his goal would have changed the entire momentum of the game. In the end, it's Silva who gets City's second, making it 3–2. It's just come too late. The FA Cup semi-final has been the 'end of journey' for City for three straight seasons now.

A few weeks later, Klopp's team will convert this fine win into an FA Cup final victory – defeating Chelsea in a penalty shoot-out. That's two knockout trophies for Liverpool this season and only City can stop them making it a domestic treble. It's been a brutal campaign, mentally and physically, and Pep knows that all his principal players are either injured or barely clinging on. For their part, his men can see that the boss is reaching the outer limits of his energy, patience and inspiration.

29. ANKLES

Kyle Walker's left ankle gave up the ghost quite some weeks ago. Aké (injured against Brighton) has followed him into the dry-dock for exactly the same problem. Then Stones's hamstring twangs and De Bruyne limps out of the Etihad with his ankle puffed up the size of a tennis ball.

Six days ahead of Real Madrid coming to the Etihad in the Champions League semi-final first leg, the situation is so dire that Dr Ramon Cugat, the legendary specialist in football injuries (usually via surgery), is asked to fly over to Manchester to take a microscopic look at all the injured guys – in the hope-against-hope that he has some kind of magical solution. But medicine is categorically not based on magic and those who've suffered bad injuries will not be fit for the first match against Madrid. Perhaps not even the return leg.

In the run-up to the Madrid game, City have dealt easily with Brighton and Watford. De Bruyne is also back and Stones is filling in at right-back.

30. NINETY-THREE SECONDS

De Bruyne's goal after just 93 seconds goes directly into the record books as the fastest in the history of a UEFA semi-final. City are a hurricane – Madrid are being tossed about helplessly and this is a display of power that is awesome to watch. Hellish to play against. Nine minutes after 1–0, Jesus spins Alaba in a move that any classic no. 9 would be proud of and makes it 2–0. For a while, it looks like the most unlikely surprise might come to pass – City not only finishing the tie in Manchester, but doing so before half-time.

With two goals already in the bank, the hurricane continues to blow straight at Courtois goal. Mahrez, with Foden free, fails to pass, shoots instead and doesn't score. Three minutes later, some brilliant City play lets De Bruyne feed Foden, whose shot hits the post. And, within 120 seconds, Zinchenko's shot kisses the Madrid woodwork – it's still 2–0, but it could easily have been 4–0 and it feels like it might even have been more.

Football has its own secret codicils, though; everyone knows they exist but nobody knows why they work the way they do. Rule one is: take your chances or suffer the consequences. Tonight, it doesn't feel feasible that City's profligacy will present them with a bill to pay. But, rules are rules.

About 100 seconds after City have tapped Madrid's jaw instead of landing a big right hook, Benzema scores a beauty after a couple of rebounds have favoured Los Blancos. Suddenly, being within one, instead of trailing by four, gives Madrid wings. Stones has to go off and the temperature alters – noticeably. Still, City erupt again after the break – Mahrez hits the post, Dani Carvajal somehow blocks Foden scoring the rebound, and then Fernandinho becomes the main protagonist. For good and bad. On for Stones, he shows his appetite for the big moment by crossing for Foden to head home. But, without pause for celebration or assimilation, City concede again – Fernandinho doesn't come close to containing his compatriot, Vinicius, and Madrid's Brazilian makes it 3–2 City. Guardiola's team just can't shake Los Blancos off but the scoreline totally contradicts the pattern of the match so far.

In their post-game analysis the following day, the technical team will debate whether Fernandinho should have just accepted the risk of barging Vinicius over but, after watching the video, nobody's even sure that it would have been physically possible. Vinicius got his shot off like an absolute rocket. It's caught the rest of City's defence out of position – Dias too high up and Laporte in two minds as to whether his job is to move towards Vinicius or cover Benzema. In rare, crucial moments like this, the absence of Walker and Stones is deeply felt. A football team is like one of those iconic Antoni Gaudí mosaics, known as *trencadís* in Catalan. The pieces are lovely in their own right and a few of them are interchangeable, but when too many are absent or the key ones are missing, all harmony disappears and it becomes clear that the arresting beauty is a product of the unity of the whole. All the pieces have to be in the right place for it to work.* Walker may have his off-moments but his extraordinary talent plus his ability to complement those around him means that he multiplies everyone else's contributions. His style of play, his mentality, is all about ensuring that the whole is greater than the sum of its parts.

The next 30 minutes somehow manages to repeat the astonishment factor of the first hour. It's one of those nights. Laporte squanders a chance but Silva isn't so wasteful – he scores a beauty. Mahrez and Modrić both shave the post at either end but, no matter how glorious all this has been, it ends badly for City. Laporte is penalised for a totally involuntary handball and Benzema slams the ball home to make it 4–3.

Guardiola puts on a brave face: 'We could easily have won this 6–3 or 7–3 – but it is what it is.' There's a tight look of barely contained disappointment written all over his face. It's a presage of what, incredibly, will be worse to come.

31. THE COFFIN

Guardiola has plenty of personal experience of what lies in store now but it's taken suffering through a brutal night in Manchester for his players to learn. You can only be sure that you've killed Real Madrid off when there's a stake through their heart and the coffin's sealed by a hundred silver nails.

---

* Gaudí's mosaics were made of little pieces of ceramic, ivory or glass in a massive variety of shapes and sizes, and this abstract design is an identifiable mark of Catalan modernism, of which Gaudí was in the vanguard.

Even then, you can't be absolutely sure. To finish Los Blancos off, particularly in Europe, you have to kill them three times.

City have another 88 minutes of domination when they play Madrid in the Santiago Bernabéu Stadium – an awesome arena, which City's dominant performance shocks into silence. The first half feels like business as usual for Pep's men, who play as if they know all Madrid's foibles. It looks like an uneven battle. Ancelotti's team don't have a shot on goal. At the other end, Courtois has had to be standout brilliant to prevent Silva and Foden making City's advantage two or even three goals.

As the second half begins, Madrid wake up. Right from kick-off they spark a move which Carles Planchart predicted in the previous few days' video briefings. Modrić to Casemiro, who gives it back to the Croat. It's dispatched to Kroos, who hits one of his quarterback passes diagonally to Carvajal, who centres on the half volley. Benzema and Vinicius are queuing up to score. The Brazilian takes the shot, which goes wide, but it's a shot across City's bows.

Then, with 18 minutes left, Walker has to sit down on the Bernabéu pitch – he can't go on. His season is now definitively over. Even to perform today, half-lame, has been a colossal effort and shows precisely what the team means to him. In short order, De Bruyne, utterly exhausted, is taken off and replaced by Gündoğan, which is the signal for City to, apparently, put the tie to bed and qualify for another Champions League final.

Already 3–2 up on aggregate, and with time running out, Mahrez scores. The Bernabéu is suddenly completely silent. City have a two-goal advantage, Madrid still haven't got a shot on target tonight, and Guardiola's team are the ones who are creating the big chances – underlined by Courtois's superb save from Cancelo. Then Grealish streaks past Éder Militão down the left and sends a diagonal shot across Courtois – it looks to all the world like it's going in. But even when Mendy gets a touch to it, and it rebounds to Foden, City can't tuck Madrid away. As ever, even on a nonsensical night like this, there's a bill to pay.

Once again, with the clock ticking determinedly towards home and victory for Guardiola's team, Grealish gets past Militão and Carvajal to shoot for the far corner but Courtois's outstretched boot somehow tips the ball millimetres wide. It's jaw-dropping stuff. Less than a minute and the

English winger has nearly scored twice and Madrid seem to be clinging on by their fingertips. There must be a killer blow coming.

Almost inconceivably, some Madrid fans are beginning to leave the stadium. Estiarte has moved to the dugout to sit next to Guardiola because we're into the last five minutes. He recalls: 'You can't begin to imagine the deathly silence in the Bernabéu. It was honestly funereal. Normally they're the "12th man" but nobody was getting behind the team, nobody believed any more. Ancelotti was standing there, arms folded, chewing his gum … looking like he was just waiting for our second goal.'

Then the madness begins.

Cancelo loses Benzema for a split-second, the Frenchman glances a header onwards from Eduardo Camavinga's cross and Rodrygo makes it 1–1. It's minute 89.21, that's Madrid's first on-target effort of the night and City are still ahead on aggregate. A draw feels ugly to the dominant side – but it'll do. They'll still be in the final if they can just shut up shop. Any jittery City fans will be cursing the fact that Stones and Walker are absent and still more so when, a minute and a half later, jack-in-the-box Rodrygo pops up to make it 3–3 on aggregate – partly thanks to the fact that City have stopped 'owning' possession. The impossible has come to pass. Now the stadium's a tempest. Which becomes an indescribable racket when Dias gives away a penalty and Benzema does what he did in the first leg and tucks it past Ederson.

City's players now know that if you don't kill Madrid off with 1,000 per cent certainty, then that's as good as reviving them yourself. Nobody in the City camp sleeps a wink tonight. Not even Estiarte, who's been through everything in his sporting career. The club's decided that the post-match dinner at the Ritz Mandarin is now open to family and friends – the players are on their knees and need any type of consolation that's on offer.

Their second consecutive Champions League final was in their grasp but it's slipped through their fingers. This is easily the bitterest blow they've had and now the fear is that the hangover might rip through their chances of beating Liverpool to the league title. In fact, Liverpool have eased into the Paris Champions League final themselves. Pep's morale is in his boots tonight. We leave him well alone.

32. THREE POINTS

The horror of the Bernabéu is only 72 hours in the past and the players are still picking away at their mental scars. They all have their personal images – Courtois saving from Foden, Fernandinho missing an extra-time chance which would have squared up the aggregate … Their mental circuit boards are still burned out and it's a brutal task to somehow wrest everyone's minds back to Premier League duty.

There are four matches left, every second of them will count and City really aren't in shape. Real Madrid have inflicted seven shades of pain on them. Liverpool are breathing down their necks and everyone at City can feel that hot, sticky sensation. It's not pleasant. Rodri: 'We are in the midst of a big war – a mental battle.'

Wednesday night was the massacre; Thursday, if anything, felt worse – ghosts, sore bodies, guilt, embarrassment and that ache of *we should have done it … how the hell did we lose … ?*

For once, it's a wholly unified mood – from their experienced, battle-scarred coach through the captain, Fernandinho, to the kitmen and even young Egan-Riley. Everyone's in a daze. Rodri: 'You wait eight months for this big moment, then in the dying seconds, it all disintegrates – it's really, really hard to digest.'

So, the 5–0 win over Newcastle is the performance of true champions. The team has fallen down a well but then they've formed a chain and helped each other out of danger. That's how Grealish sees it at least, 'We've shown such incredible personality to pull one another out of the depression of losing.'

Liverpool draw at home to Spurs and, suddenly, City have a three-point gap at the top. If they can win their next three matches they'll be champions again. But their defenders keep falling like flies – today its Dias and his thigh is the problem. When you lose three 'Yugoslavs' in Walker, Stones and Dias then your defensive spine will suffer. No question.*

---

* Losing their best defenders means that, above and beyond the five goals scored by Real Madrid, City will concede another five in the final three Premier League matches.

33. DOWN THE LEFT

Crossing with his left, shooting off his left foot, dribbling the keeper with his left.

Right from when he was a little kid, De Bruyne learned the value of strengthening his left foot – not just to impose himself on matches but to enhance his career. He's dedicated hour after hour to refining his first touch, his passing and his shooting with what was, originally, his weaker foot. Today, the benefits couldn't be clearer – he's not only scored a hat-trick but every one of the goals has come from his left boot. Then he puts a ribbon on it by adding the fourth, this time off his right foot. He's even hit the post with a left-footed drive. It's only taken 24 minutes for him to get the hat-trick, making it the third fastest in Premier League history ... behind Dwight Yorke's 22-minute display and the 16-minute extravaganza by Sadio Mané in 2015. It all adds up to a 5–1 win against Wolves at Molineux and, while sticking the three points on top of their existing total is vital, it might eventually also become significant that City's goal-difference advantage over Liverpool has gone up to seven.

Pep's mental calculator now tells him that one more win plus a draw probably wins City the Premier League. Today's has been a huge victory but it's come at a price ... again. Laporte's suffered a knee injury, Fernandinho's hamstring has tightened up and Aké's ankle is in a bad way. Constructing a decent defensive line in the next two matches is going to be very complicated indeed.

I notice that they've repeated the 'kick-off sent back to Ederson' move which they also used against Madrid at the Etihad. It clearly wasn't a one-off and seems to be a new tactic, now that it's been repeated against Wolves. Something to note down and ask Pep about ...

34. THE PENALTY

Fernandinho and Laporte start on Sunday against West Ham because there's no other alternative. Aké's on the bench even though there's no danger of him playing because his ankle's in pieces! The physios have worked day and night to patch Fernandinho up and to squeeze that hamstring overload out of his right leg. Laporte's a different story – it's a huge risk for him, personally, to agree to play today. The Spain international knows his knee is in bad shape – he's limping and he's in pain.

As soon as the season's finished he's going to have surgery and that means that he'll be out until next October. Even if Laporte is occasionally singled out for Pep's ire because of mini-errors, this is an exemplary display of not only professionalism but self-sacrifice. Self-interest subjugated … 'the team comes first.' This will make it three games during which his knee's been agony but he's a fighter.

The London Stadium gives us a sense of déjà vu. City own 86 per cent of possession, shoot at goal 13 times, shave the post 3 or 4 times, pass the ball 4 times more than West Ham and so much more accurately. But, by half-time, it's David Moyes's team who lead 2–0. They've punted the ball long a few times and, twice, Jarrod Bowen has sprung the trap and galloped into the space behind City's backline. It's raining, City look anodyne, they're losing and this is not great at all.

But the déjà vu works both ways – somehow the champions produce a thunderous second half, out of nothing, and the 2–2 draw is practically worth the title. Grealish starts it off with a volley, which thuds home with a little glance off Craig Dawson. There are 40 minutes left in which to carve out a draw and Guardiola's on the sidelines repeatedly demanding calm, patience and cool heads. Chances come and go but Fabiański and West Ham's defensive unit keep thwarting City. Eventually, a Mahrez wide free kick is headed into his own goal by Vladimír Coufal: City were heading over the precipice but now, suddenly, the vista is beautiful. The 79 per cent possession they use to scrabble a point is the second-biggest domination of the ball all season.

Five minutes from the end, they have the whole world in their hands. Dawson trips Gabriel Jesus and it's a VAR-awarded penalty. Mahrez has been Man of the Match this afternoon and now he can wrap up the title (as good as, if not arithmetically) if he scores the winner. He's seven for seven on penalties so far this season (four in the league) but even before the Algerian runs up to strike it everyone on the City staff is aware that Fabiański is something of a penalty-save specialist. He strikes it mid-height to the keeper's left but Fabiański guesses correctly, launches himself and produces a big save. A draw will have to do.

This is their final league away match of the season. They've played 19, gaining a total of 46 points – just four under the record set in the Centurions' title win. They've only lost once in those 19 – the first away game at Spurs. Two days later, Liverpool win at Southampton. It's all down to the final day. It's still a one-point margin – City ahead of the Reds, meaning that all Guardiola's side has to do is match whatever result Liverpool produce. This is going to be an anxious week during which the medics and physios will work flat-out to patch up Laporte and Fernandinho. They're working hard on Stones too – just in case. We're in the endgame – no effort is to be spared with the finishing tape in touching distance.

35. FIVE MINUTES AND 36 SECONDS

You can win a league in five minutes. Five mad, impossible, illogical, absurd minutes.

There are precisely 57km between the pitches at Anfield and the Etihad. Today, the kick-off times are identical – it's winner takes all and there's no advantage to be offered up to either of the two behemoths who are scrapping it out. De Bruyne wants to contribute to the pre-match talk: 'Lads … no errors today, no red cards!'

Wolves go 1–0 up at Anfield after only 3 minutes – Mané equalises 20 minutes later. City are stuck at 0–0 against Villa until the right-back, Matty Cash, nips in behind Cancelo and scores the goal that chills the Etihad stadium.

Right now, we're in the red zone – disaster threatens. Red for danger, red for Liverpool. Red mist for Pep. Because this would count as one of the worst 45 minutes of the Cityzens' season. There are nerves and lots of mistakes. Easy passes missed, Stones looking ragged, Cancelo all over the place, Fernandinho slow, Mahrez, Jesus and Foden a little imprecise … even De Bruyne fluffs a couple of counterattacks. There's a state of high nervous tension and it's turned Guardiola's team into a pale shadow of themselves. Five minutes before the break, Pep tells Zinchenko to warm up. The dressing room is funereal at half-time. The Ukrainian has been told he's coming on for Fernandinho. But if you judge by the body language and the facial expressions then there's not a huge level of belief right now. Those who are expecting a big tempestuous row from Guardiola are pleasantly surprised – it's quite the opposite. With three minutes left before the buzzer goes to send the players back out to the tunnel, their Catalan boss gets them in a huddle. His tone is calm, his words are smoothly delivered – there's no anger, no reproaches. Not even close to a shouting match. Later on, dust settled, he'll admit: 'I spoke to them like that because I'm learning patience – I'm not as fractious as I was.' He's not quite whispering, but not far off. 'We are definitely going to do this – OK lads? I know it's impossible not to think of the consequences of not pulling this off – that's completely normal. But we have to be positive right to the final seconds. It's not over till we say it is. We only need one goal and, as soon as we get that, we'll settle, we'll have momentum and we'll score the second – I know it. When they scored we got mad – we dropped right back. It feels like we're verging on a defeat but I'm certain we're going to win. I know precisely how you all feel – I feel the vertigo effects of pressure. It's all normal. But we wouldn't be in this situation, on the verge of being champions, if we hadn't been the best team in England all season. I know we'll go out there and play to win but I want it established in all our minds before we do. That's where the challenge lies – in the mind. We'll go out, believing, we'll play aggressively – Alex [Zinchenko] is super-fast, he'll get up and down, he'll facilitate quick changes of direction with possession. Try to put the ball up the inside channels of space. I just want you to show your quality … OK? Let's go!'

Once they're out there, City are a bit better. Zinchenko creates space but neither Mahrez nor Jesus finish their chances and Villa, via Ollie Watkins, hit the post. Over at Anfield, Liverpool see a goal ruled out for offside. Pep puts Sterling on for Mahrez and, eventually, Gündoğan for Silva. It coincides with a moment that looks likely to finish the title race off. Villa punt a goal kick long, Watkins knocks it onwards and ex-Liverpool midfielder Philippe Coutinho makes it 2–0. Anfield erupts at the news, while the Etihad is a deflated, stunned mass of disbelief. With 11 minutes of the season left, Liverpool are champions. It's a little kink in the narrative that this is, of course, a Villa side leading 2–0 under the coaching of Liverpool legend Steven Gerrard.

City haven't fought back from a 0–2 deficit since February 2005 when they did so to beat Norwich 3–2. Not a good stat in this particular situation. De Bruyne will reveal afterwards that: 'I only worried that we might not win the title for about ten seconds after they scored again.' The Belgian spends those ten seconds retying his laces. Then he stands up and demands the ball. He combines with Jesus and Sterling in a move that ends with the ball delivered perfectly for Gündoğan to smash home a header. We've hit minute 75.10. Gündoğan dives into the bottom of the net to collect the ball, runs back to the centre circle and places it there for Villa to restart. They do so by minute 76.03. Zinchenko wins it back quickly and in the immediate ebb and flow it ends up as a City corner. Minute 76.50. Stones gets on the end of it but Robin Olsen saves.

Gündoğan regains the ball in the middle of the pitch and feeds De Bruyne, who moves it out to Zinchenko. He bursts into the box and cuts the ball back for Rodri. The Spaniard's shot is powerful, elegant – his trademark execution with his instep. From 25m out, the ball clips off the inside of the post and we're now at 2–2.

Minute 77.43. There have been a grand total of 133 seconds between each of City's goals hitting the net. This time, it's Gabi Jesus who races into Villa's net, grabs the ball and sprints off to the centre circle again. Villa kick off. It's minute 78.53. Once again, it's the Ukrainian substitute who wins possession back only for Rodri to shoot high and wide. Clock reads: 79.21.

Olsen takes his goal kick long again and Cancelo gobbles up possession. He pings the ball directly to Jesus, who's intercepted by Tyrone Mings, but De Bruyne is sharp on his toes and he nicks the ball. The Belgian magician powers forward and cracks in a low, powerful diagonal centre, which is perfect for Gündoğan to make it 3–2. Minute 80.46. City have won the title.

Anyone who was there will tell you that the wave of joy and relief, the dawning celebration, the euphoria … all of it was intoxicating beyond belief. The whole business took precisely 5 minutes and 36 seconds. Eternally burned into the club's consciousness.

From the Gündoğan moment until the final whistle there's not any real football played. City simply try to contain their emotions, try not to get carried away by the manic euphoria raining down at them from the Etihad stands. Grealish has to go to the dressing room to throw up – that's what nerves can do. Walker's stomping around the quiet corridors inside the stadium, tense and anxious because he's got no way of helping his team-mates, and celebrates the third goal by running madly up and down. On his injured ankle. Pep's yelling unintelligible instructions from the touchline and Dias is entreating the fans to sing louder.

Pep's onfield players try to take the ball into the corners in an attempt to kill the game. Liverpool have scored twice in the space of five minutes – great minds think alike. But poor old Salah celebrates them with the look of someone who thinks he's just won the title. Liverpool's fans disabuse him of the false notion and take the wind from his sails.

As the Etihad match winds down, the party starts too early, fans on the pitch because they think the whistle's gone. As Walker says later: 'I've never seen anything like that in all my life.'

It takes me two whole days to get to speak to Pep. He's been party-ing, and deservedly so. When we meet up he's empty, partied out. But very happy indeed.

'This has been a complete rollercoaster of emotions and thank heavens it's ended well. We really need a break from all this now. Because, however we feel now, we need to come back and do the same all over again – but with more effort and more success next season.'

Nobody really sums up the secret of City's success better than Scott Carson, who tells me: 'We just really, really hate losing!'

STATS 2021–2

	P	W	D	L	GF	GA
Community Shield	1	0	0	1	0	1
Runners-up						
Premier League	38	29	6	3	99	26
Champions						
League Cup	2	1	1	0	6	1
Fourth round						
FA Cup	5	4	0	1	16	6
Semi-finalists						
Champions League	12	7	2	3	29	16
Semi-finalists						
Total	58	41	9	8	150	50

- 70.7 per cent victories in matches all season
- 76.3 per cent wins from all Premier League matches
- 2.58 goal average per match scored in the entire season
- 2.60 goal average per match in the Premier League
- 0.86 goal average per match conceded in the entire season
- 0.68 goal average per match conceded in the Premier League
- 100 positive goal difference across the whole season
- 93 points in the Premier League
- 24 efforts off the post in the Premier League (4 Foden and De Bruyne)
- 66.1 per cent possession in the entire season
- 67.9 per cent possession in the Premier League
- 81 per cent highest level of possession (vs Arsenal, August 2021)
- 49 per cent lowest level of possession (vs Liverpool, April 2022)
- 687 average number of passes per match
- 861 highest number of passes (vs Everton, November 2021)
- 90 per cent completed passes per match
- 18.1 shots at goal per match/6.2 on target
- 6.8 shots at goal conceded per game/2.5 on target
- 12 best run of consecutive wins in the Premier League
- 24 top goalscorer: Riyad Mahrez (De Bruyne, 15)
- 14 most assists: Kevin De Bruyne (Jesus, 8)
- 52 most appearances: João Cancelo (Ederson, 37 in the Premier League)
- 7–0 biggest win (vs Leeds United)
- 2–0 biggest defeat (vs PSG and Crystal Palace)

Season 7: 2022–3

Moving On

SCENE 1. 'DON'T WORRY, WE'RE GOING TO WIN EVERYTHING'

Manchester, 24 June 2022

Monday, 20 June, and Juanma Lillo's in Doha, being presented as the new coach of Al-Sadd. He heads back to Manchester the following day to clear the flat in which he's lived for the last two years and pack up his belongings. In due course, on the 24th, he's come to Sportcity for the final time, to collect the rest of his personal possessions and say *adiós*!

He leaves a message on the whiteboard for Pep, Txiki and the rest of the staff: 'I'm not really leaving you. I'm still available for anything you need. And, don't worry, we're going to win everything this season: the title, the Champions League. Everything. For sure. And I'll be with you all the way, giving you any help I can, willing you on. I'll always be there when you need me.'

SCENE 2. 'WE'RE GOING TO MISS LILLO'

Pescara, 30 June 2022

Manel Estiarte's on holiday in Italy, indulging in one of his favourite vices: toasting himself, hatless, under a baking sun on a beach in Pescara. Smooth, golden sand, the calm, warm water of the Adriatic, a wonderful restaurant close at hand and an endless expanse of beach, neatly lined, in typical Italian style, with row upon row of blue sun loungers.

He's sitting astride his lounger, close to the water's edge with his phone at his ear. We're chatting about the coming season: 'We'll really miss Juanma. He had such a calming influence on us all and he's been a huge help to Pep. Not just in terms of tactical planning but helping him to relax and chill out. Juanma's so laidback, never up or down too dramatically. He doesn't get carried away when we win and he's never thrown by defeat either. Somehow, he managed to imbue all of us with that same sense of serenity. His relationship with Fernandinho also really helped him transmit this laid-back approach to the players. It's the way he lives his life – day in, day out.'

Pep's promoted Enzo Maresca to the senior technical team this season. Maresca played for WBA, Juventus, Fiorentina and Sevilla, and has coached City's U-20s to victory in the Premier League 2.

Estiarte: 'Maresca's going to be a good addition … although this will be his first experience of coaching at the top level. Pep really rates him and has always said that Enzo's got what it takes. He understands exactly what we're all about and knows our game inside out. He'll prove to be an excellent new resource.'

All good things must come to an end, of course, and summer's almost over for the reigning Premier League champions.

Txiki Begiristain's had a busy summer pushing through a number of profitable deals: four new players have been signed, another four have left City and there's been a good deal of movement within City's youth team too.

Estiarte explains: 'We're still in June, there are two months before the transfer window closes but Txiki's already made a lot of very interesting deals. We've got Haaland, Julián Álvarez, Kalvin Phillips and Stefan Ortega coming in to replace Gabriel Jesus, Sterling, Fernandinho and Zack Steffen – new faces and new energy. Some of them might struggle to adapt initially, but hopefully all of them are arriving ready and willing to learn – precisely the shot in the arm Pep needs to keep progressing and improving.

'We've added goalscorers, something we've sorely lacked on previous big occasions. Now, all being well, we're adding a prolific supply of "killer-goals" to all the team's other qualities. As you know, I'm not a natural optimist, but even I can see that we've built a very, very good side. We just need to sort out what to do about the left-back position if Zinchenko leaves.'

Pep hasn't yet extended his contract but he dropped enough subtle hints at the end of last season to have made me think he'll renew. Estiarte won't be drawn on the subject: 'I've no idea whether he's going to renew for a couple of years or not. I don't think he's decided yet. It isn't something to which he's giving much thought at the moment. It'll depend on a lot of factors: what happens next season, his relationship with the players, what his family think about having to go on making so many personal sacrifices … Things can go unexpectedly wrong in life and it's too early for him to anticipate what might happen. He'll probably put off even thinking about it until after Christmas, although I'm certain the board will put a lot of effort into persuading Pep to stay. I'm not going to speculate at this point.'

Estiarte's happy enough to answer my next question, though. My view is that Pep's currently creating a more important legacy with City than he did at Barcelona or Bayern. This is his best project yet. Does his *consiglieri* agree?

'I don't know whether this is his best-ever work ... but, probably! The Barça years were more successful, certainly – six trophies in one year is unbeatable. But he's achieving unbelievable things with City. Our team's outstanding and, although we have very few "world number ones" in the team, we consistently and repeatedly produce exceptional football. Yes, I think maybe I'd agree that City's going to turn out to be Pep's greatest-ever coaching achievement.'

It's been several weeks since City dramatically won the title on the last day of the season after making an astonishing comeback against Aston Villa. It's also just a few weeks since they were so painfully defeated by Real Madrid in the Champions League.

'We were all completely gutted after losing to Madrid. Nobody had expected it – I still can't get it out of my head! I always go down to the dugout around ten minutes before the end of the games and, that night, we were winning – two goals ahead ... at the Bernabéu! The whole stadium was in complete, stunned silence. We had Madrid on the ropes. They were going out. And then Grealish had those two chances that we were sure were going to go in, and either of which would have killed the tie stone-dead. Because of two defensive miracles neither chance went in but, even then, there wasn't even a hint of a fightback.

'I remember Ancelotti standing there with his arms crossed, his face totally ashen. It was the 87th minute and the mighty Bernabéu felt like being in a graveyard. Afterwards, people went on about us lacking character and experience but they were wrong! We've shown that we've got what it takes plenty of times. Look at our last league game! We were playing really badly – the worst match of Pep's entire time in Manchester! But we conjured up the energy and strength of character to score three goals in five minutes and then we shut the game down by showing both character and experience and keeping the ball hidden away near the corner for what felt like quarter of an hour!

'So why couldn't we manage to do that in those last three minutes in the Bernabéu? Probably because we all thought it wasn't necessary! Madrid were "dead". It never crossed our minds that we might need to smuggle the ball away to the corner flag to waste time! They were out. And then everything changed ... It was horrendous losing like that. We were all knocked for six. I've really no idea how we managed to regroup and go on to retain our Premier League title.'

Following their disaster in Madrid, City then had to face the might of Liverpool.

'The last few weeks of the season were so tough. Probably our hardest-ever. Two Champions League knockout ties, one after the other, against the big Madrid teams – each of whom is a brutal opponent in their own unique way. Then, being turfed out of the semi-final like that at the Bernabéu left us on our knees. We were staring right down the barrel: having to win all our remaining league games, knowing that Liverpool would exploit the smallest slip-up. That final sprint for the title ended up feeling like another miracle – but in reverse compared to the Bernabéu! I'll tell you: Pep was down but not out.

'Somehow he managed to pick himself up and get us back in the fight. He was true to his word and got the team as far as that final day when we saw the same kind of ludicrous thing happen again … although this time the comeback was in our favour!

'Those memories from the Villa game! Everyone totally wiped out mentally and physically … the stench of defeat in the air. We concede two goals and are playing like amateurs … And then, the final apotheosis, three goals in a row – one after another. A miracle – in our favour! One, two, three. It was very, very tough. One of the toughest league finals ever.'

Our trip down memory lane has to finish there, though. It's lunchtime. There are some lovely smells coming from that wonderful seafront restaurant … calling to Estiarte.

SCENE 3. NUMBER 9

Barcelona, 4 July 2022

Summer's over for City's coaching team. They're back in Manchester and Carles Planchart is pleased with the new faces in the squad: 'Bringing new people in always revitalises a team. Just like any other area of life. A football team has to be evolving and renewing all the time and our four or five new players, each with his own particular skills, will help us take a big step forward. It's a process we do very well as a club. Every year, one of our veterans will take on the role of instilling a level of calm and patience in the dressing room. Zabaleta, Kompany, Silva, Agüero, Fernandinho … our golden generation of players have done a superb job – showing leadership and sharing their experience within the squad and then passing the baton on with grace and elegance. Now the great Fernandinho has gone, let's see who's going to step up and take on the captaincy. It's up to the players to decide and I hope they pick the right guy.'*

Haaland and Álvarez have both been signed, above any other component of their play, for their goalscoring skills. Having gone for so long without a traditional no. 9, City suddenly have two players in this role. Planchart: 'It's brilliant. We've scored loads over the last few years but we've let ourselves down in that crucial area at certain decisive moments. Haaland and Julián Álvarez bring specialisms that we didn't have enough of.

'So, with them, plus Kalvin Phillips, a new keeper and left-back, we'll be able to compete for everything again this season. That's always our principal objective. Winning is the result of the hard work we do across all the competitions, which is why I talk about competing for everything rather than winning everything.'

And will Grealish play more of a role? 'I think he's going to have a breakthrough season. He went from being the standout star player in one team to becoming "just one of the squad" at City. I'm convinced Jack's accepted this now, which will help him start to make a real difference.

'I agree with Manel that we're really going to miss Lillo. He brought such harmony to the coaching team. Not only dd he manage to keep Pep calm in moments of high tension but he was the glue that kept the whole coaching team together. Juanma's such a self-effacing guy. He much prefers a low profile, to stay in the background, and he always plays down his own skills and contribution. He's a great person to be around. Without trying to, Juanma's presence forces everyone else to be bit less full of themselves. This guy's the second coach with an absolute wealth of experience and he's constantly making jokes at his own expense, so what makes you think you've

---

* Several weeks later the squad elect Ilkay Gündoğan as their new captain; De Bruyne, Walker and Rodri, in that order, will deputise for the German in his absence.

got the right to strut about like the cock of the walk? Anyone who's too full of themselves ends up looking like a bit of an idiot in Lillo's presence. He kept everyone's feet on the ground and we're going to miss him.'

Losing to Madrid like that in the Champions League semi-final is still tormenting Planchart: 'That match will stay with me forever. It was a much worse experience than when our Bayern lost 4–0 to Madrid. Everyone's lost 4–0 at some time or other. But what happened in the Bernabéu semi-final defies explanation. It doesn't matter that it was Madrid … it was the third time they'd pulled something like that off in a matter of weeks!'

How? 'Weird things happen in football and that match was one of them, as was us scoring three goals in five minutes to win the title in the worst game we've ever produced since arriving in Manchester. I've no idea why these things happen. Nobody does. Things happen the way they happen and you just have to accept that. Sometimes you get lucky, other times, not so much … I can still see Grealish's two massive goal chances in less than a minute in the Bernabéu, neither of which went in … And don't forget that damn first leg in Manchester which should have finished at least 6–2 to us. Which would have given us an unassailable lead!! If only …'

SCENE 4. 'WE ASK A LOT OF OUR FULL-BACKS'
London, 7 August 2022

Mahrez has been lethargic and slow all week in training so Pep's left him on the bench and put Foden on the right wing, where he has a good game despite his lack of experience in the role. John Stones isn't in the starting 11 either for their first league game of the season. He's missed two training sessions this week because of a court case. Bernardo Silva doesn't start either. Despite the rumours that it's some kind of retaliation for the fact that his talks with Barcelona appear to be accelerating, Pep's decision is based purely on the fact that Gündoğan will use the spaces behind West Ham's pivots more effectively.

Pre-match, Pep's in the dressing room with his men, reminding them of how important it is to win the one-vs-one duels. He's not forgotten João Cancelo's poor performance against Mohamed Salah in last Saturday's

Community Shield final (Liverpool 3 City 1). Cancelo came off worse in almost every single duel and this apparent weakness in his best full-back is worrying. It's also not the first time he's noticed it. Technically, Cancelo is absolutely exceptional, no question. In a class of his own and capable of doing anything you ask of him. It's just that he has a worrying tendency to disconnect at key moments, as he did in Madrid, in the Champions League semi-final, where his failure to respect their defensive line contributed to Madrid's first goal. Pep's determined to avoid the same thing happening today against West Ham, who have repeatedly demonstrated their ability to take advantage of the slightest opening to launch one of their blistering counterattacks, usually led by the formidable trio of Bowen, Pablo Fornals and Michail Antonio.

West Ham press in a 3+1 formation while City bring the ball out in a 2+3 made up of two centre-backs (Dias and Aké) and three defensive midfielders (Walker and Cancelo with Rodri). When executed correctly, the 2+3 allows them to continuously triangulate their passing, which effectively neutralises the opponent's press. After a succession of passes it's then very easy to move the ball up the pitch via their wingers or their organising midfielders on the inside.

Pep began using the 2+3 at Bayern and he's perfected it with City, modifying his approach depending on how their opponent presses. If they use a 3+1, Pep sticks to the 2+3. If the other team opts for a 2+3, City switch to 3+2. Sometimes he'll use a different structure altogether, like the one he uses against Liverpool. The Reds press with a 3+3 so City reorganise into a 4+2 or even a 4+3 when necessary.

One coach who has used the 2+3 build-up to great effect is the Italian Roberto De Zerbi (Sassuolo, Shakhtar, Brighton), to the extent that it's now widely referred to as 'De Zerbi's box'. His teams try to draw the opponent's press into a 'box' of his own players and 'isolate' them there so that the ball can then be released at huge speed via wide positions.

Guardiola uses his inside full-backs to help construct a defensive wall of five men in the centre of the pitch with each of them required to win their one-to-one duels. He calls this technique *gestión de los descolgados* or 'freeing-up your teammates'. If the five at the back win their duels, the five guys in front can attack with freedom.

Today, Dias wins all his clashes with Antonio, as does Aké. Both players have terrific defensive skills and relentlessly cut off any attempt by the Hammers to counterattack. Aké, who's a fine defender, is looking very confident and comfortable, as if he were already an established regular. But the team's still missing Laporte's presence, notably his long passing and his precision in bringing out the ball. Aké has other impressive talents to offer the team but is clearly much more comfortable when he can pass an easy ball to a teammate and retreat back to his original position. He's risk-averse. Not the identity Guardiola requires when constructing from the back under pressure.

Pep's used inside full-backs since his first City league game, at home, on 13 August 2016 against Sunderland (2–1), when Sagna and Clichy were positioned on either side of Fernandinho. He's always said: 'We demand a lot from our full-backs: we ask them to be midfielders and to defend at the same time without losing concentration for a second. It's asking an awful lot.' Which is why he keeps reminding Cancelo of the need for 100 per cent concentration.

Today, Erling Haaland is the second City player to score twice on his Premier League debut. (The other player to have done this? Kun Agüero, of course.) City pull off an easy win (2–0) by stopping the locals from counterattacking. With 76 per cent possession, Pep's men produce 831 passes, 93 per cent of which are accurate. West Ham aren't given the slightest chance.

None of which qualifies this as an extraordinary performance by the Sky Blues and it's already clear that it's going to be challenging for Haaland to adapt to the team and vice versa. Using the false 9 position over the last couple of seasons has allowed City to build patterns of play that won't be possible now that the big Norwegian is up front. It's going to take a bit of time to create new movements and passing ideas. For now, though, they've pulled off a satisfactory victory by controlling their opponents and winning their individual duels. According to Estiarte, one player has truly stood out today: 'Walker was so good with his feet today. We were all knocked out!'

News arrives that Liverpool have only managed a draw at Fulham (2–2), which resurrects an old joke from 2018 when Pep won his first Premier League. Back then, one of the club physios took to announcing, 'We're halfway to the title!' after every win. Today it almost sounds even funnier, given that there are 37 more matches to be played before the end of a long, taxing season.

The following day, Michail Antonio, West Ham's centre-forward, chats to Newcastle striker Callum Wilson on their excellent BBC podcast, *The Footballer's Football*, and comes up with a perfect definition of how City play.

> Their system is liquid. You can't stop it. When I say to you, it's like they're rotating everywhere. Cancelo's popping up in midfield. Kyle Walker playing midfield. Then Grealish would be outside, then Bernardo would be inside him. So the full-backs can't come and mark and get tight. It was a masterclass, it was a masterclass. And do you know what? It's just one of those things where you've just got to put your hands up and say: they were incredible. I think I touched the ball seven times. So they quite literally had a lot of possession. The fact was that we couldn't even get close to them, we'd try to press them and they would surround us. It was a masterclass and that's exactly what our coach said at the end. Look, they were on fire and we just have to accept it.

No prizes for guessing which other team was once described as playing 'liquid football' – FC Barcelona under Pep Guardiola.

SCENE 5. 'JULIÁN IS BRILLIANT'
Manchester, 8 August 2022

Bernardo Silva's just finished training. He heads straight over to Lorenzo Buenaventura and Xabi Mancisidor: 'Julián is brilliant. Brilliant. This kid's going to be a phenomenon.' It's the highest of praise coming from another footballer.

Álvarez has started well. He scored the team's first official goal of the season against Liverpool in the Community Shield and has been outstanding in every training session. With a Gabriel Jesus-like energy when he presses and superb technical precision in his passing and finishing, he's impressing more all the time. He also seems to be overcoming his crippling shyness.

The Argentinian arrived at City a month ago and was presented at the same time as Haaland and Ortega, although the Norwegian naturally garnered most of the attention. Álvarez was originally spotted by Joan Patsy, the Catalan director of football for City's South American arm. Patsy pestered Pep and Txiki for months but they waited until the situation with Haaland was resolved before signing the youngster in January of this year. In the closing months of 2022, it wasn't clear whether or not Jesus and Sterling would continue with City, therefore nobody could say for sure whether or not there'd be space for another striker. But Patsy had been like a stuck record, insisting that Txiki should sign the youngster for City. He knew that Julián had all the potential to become a great player. Having debuted for River Plate, under the terrific Marcelo Gallardo, in October 2018, he'd scored 53 and given 31 assists in 120 games. He'd also already played nine times for Argentina and Patsy was determined that City's directors would sign him, especially when teams like Barcelona had begun to show interest. Juanma Lillo, who'd followed the youngster's progress closely, was Patsy's main ally at the Manchester end and was happy to lobby his bosses on the player's behalf. The deal was agreed in December 2022 and the contract signed in January, with an unusual clause that allowed River Plate to hold on to him until July, at which time he moved to the City Group.

Now, after just four weeks of training, everyone's impressed and, in many cases, astonished at the player's abilities while Pep is delighted to have such a superb back-up to Haaland in the squad. Or maybe they'd do well in a double-striker partnership? They're already establishing a strong connection on the pitch and Pep's rubbing his hands together in anticipation of everything the pair can achieve. As for Bernardo Silva ... he's blown away: 'This guy's amazing!'

SCENE 6. FODEN, THE NEW BERNARDO SILVA?

Manchester, 9 August 2022

The players have a rest today but the coaching team are at work – meeting with Txiki Begiristain so that he can run through his progress with regards to new signings. On Sunday, during a television interview, Pep pointed out that City have the smallest squad in the whole of the Premier League: only 17 outfield players.

It's also the smallest squad he's had in his 14 years as a coach: six defenders (two full-backs and four central defenders); six midfielders (including Cole Palmer) and five forwards. They need a new left-back too but, having seen Chelsea pay more than €70 million (£62 million) for Marc Cucurella, Txiki and Guardiola agree that they'll go for someone low cost. Which is why they've picked Sergio Gómez, the super-talented and versatile Catalan, who's cut his teeth under Vincent Kompany at Anderlecht and comes highly recommended. He's still lacking experience at the elite level, though, and the initial intention was to loan him out to Girona but, given the restricted squad numbers this season, they're going to have to keep him in Manchester.

The big question mark hangs over Bernardo Silva. Is he staying or is he moving to Barcelona? The press is already claiming that it's a done deal but Txiki is absolutely clear with Pep and his staff – nothing has been agreed as yet and, in any case, he'll only let him go for €100 million (£85 million). It's unlikely that Barcelona can come up with that amount unless of course they manage to sell Frenkie de Jong to Chelsea for the €80 million they're looking for … Nobody at City wants to see Silva go. He's an exceptional player who has performed at a level far beyond what anyone anticipated.

'He'd be a terrible loss,' is the general consensus, although everyone knows exactly who'll step into his boots if he does go: 'Foden, of course!' Foden, the 100mph player who's not yet learned to add a calm, tempo-reducing vision to his game? In fact, there are actually plenty of reasons why City think Foden could be the perfect replacement. Back in October 2016, Pep hadn't drawn up specific plans for Foden beyond knowing that he'd chanced upon an exceptionally gifted young footballer who was worth considering as a potential replacement for David Silva, by then a veteran of 30. David Silva, the little Spanish magician, was the conductor who set the team's rhythm of play, who decided when City slowed things down, hit the accelerator, played vertically or shuffled possession horizontally. Possessing an extraordinary vision plus superb technical skills, Silva was the cornerstone of the team and, before Pep's arrival, both Mancini and Pellegrini had constructed their playing strategy around him. But, time and tide wait for no man and, sooner or later, age was going to catch up with the diminutive Canarian maestro: a replacement was going to have to be found. As soon as Phil Foden, Jadon Sancho and Brahim Díaz began to train with the first team, a newly appointed Pep Guardiola immediately spotted the latent talent of the Stockport Iniesta. Was this the new David Silva? He seemed to have it all: exceptional technical skill; great vision; a wonderful left foot and the ability to control the ball in any circumstances and under intense pressure. Perfect … except for one tiny hitch. The lad was only 16 and a long way yet from even dreaming of stepping into the Spaniard's shoes. A temporary solution would have to be found until Foden was completely ready for greatness.

Step forward the 'other' Silva. One small consolation for Pep on the night City were knocked out of the Champions League by Monaco was watching Bernardo Silva's mesmerising performance for the French side and deciding, there and then, that City had to have him. Back in the summer of 2017, Bernardo Mota Veiga de Carvalho e Silva was 22, six years older than Phil Foden and eight younger than David Silva. Halfway between the two, the perfect link between the old timer and the raw young kid. He was as near as dammit a perfect clone of David Silva. Everyone at City was convinced. No question. The Portuguese had everything needed to be the Spaniard's successor. Down-to-earth and easy going by nature, both Silvas had the temperament to coexist happily despite having to compete for the same place in the team. Pep would be able to alternate their appearances while the pair would join ranks to mentor young Foden. Spend €50 million (£43 million) to guarantee that the Silva magic would continue long in to the future? Cheap at the price.

And so it came to pass. Both players were a crucial part of the 100 points season delivered by Pep's Centurions. The Spanish magician steered the team to thrilling victory while his new 'assistant' increasingly made his own exceptional presence felt with every appearance. Teammates like Sané, Sterling or De Bruyne possessed, and deployed, the acceleration and verticality that are always vital but the Silvas were the orchestra conductors. Their artistry on the pitch was duly enhanced by the judicious use of Foden, aged just 17 years and 177 days when he made his league debut, one of the youngest players to do so.

'But, what of İlkay Gündoğan?' I hear you say. Pep certainly imagined the multi-faceted German as a good alternative to David Silva in the centre of the pitch, whether as a playmaker against specific opponents or, as he proved in 2020–1, as 'Kündoğan', the man whose speed and athleticism meant that he would arrive in the box at exactly the right moment and who, in Agüero's absence, became City's top goalscorer. But the über-talented, tireless German was plagued by injury problems and, in the summer of 2017, was still recuperating from potentially career-ending issues: serious cruciate ligament damage and persistent back pain. No doubt, Gündoğan had been created in the image of the perfect Guardiola player, par excellence, but at that stage, there was no way of knowing whether he'd make it back to full fitness or not, and signing Bernardo Silva was a must.

In October 2017, Guardiola was at home watching England vs Spain in the U-17 World Cup final and mentally filing away the names of several Spanish players (Eric García, Ferran Torres and Sergio Gómez, the last of whom put Spain ahead by two goals in the first half an hour). But his eye was also drawn to one of City's own, a certain young Englishman with a masterful ability to penetrate tight spaces without losing the ball plus a prodigious talent for goalscoring (Foden contributed two to England's 5–2 victory and became the standout star of the competition). Steve Cooper, the U-17s coach, was playing him on the right wing, opting to use him on the outside from where he could launch lethal attacks, moving diagonally on the inside into the Spanish area. *Instead of looking for a David Silva replacement, maybe we've had the answer under our noses all the time,* mused the Catalan. *This lad looks like he could be outrageously good up front.*

Now, five years on, Foden has indeed become an exceptional goalscorer for City where, by now, it's De Bruyne, Haaland and Foden bringing the acceleration and verticality with Bernardo Silva, Rodri, Gündoğan and Grealish setting the tempo and rhythm.

Foden is still learning how to control the tempo of a game, how to impose thoughtful, calm decision-making in the most frenetic of moments. By nature he's a one-dimensional player who zeros in on the opposition goal and heads straight for it as fast as he possibly can. Like a cavalryman charging towards the Russian lines, chest bared and lance at the ready, Foden's impetuousness and utter fearlessness have become legendary, and his prodigious goalscoring has brought many a great rival to their knees. For all his swashbuckling performances, though, he still needs to develop David Silva's uncanny ability to slow down and even freeze time. Silva understood instinctively when to stop, when to attack, when to retreat and when to accelerate, just as his namesake, Bernardo, does. Despite being mentored by two of the greatest playmakers, Foden has taken time in learning how to apply the brakes. He breaks with the ball, dribbles past player after player and heads straight for the goal to score or provide the assist. If he hits a roadblock, he'll pass back to a teammate and keep on moving, ready to receive the ball again and repeat his forward momentum. Sometimes, it's possible to decipher the messages his teammates are sending him. Guys like Gündoğan, Cancelo and Julián Álvarez, on the few occasions the two have played together, will send him short passes back and forward on the left wing as if they're saying, 'Calm down, slow down, work with us, help us disorganise the other team, try passing the ball, there's no hurry …' And Foden can do it. He'll start off as the third point of City's decoy triangle whose entire objective is to force opposition players to abandon their positions. He receives the ball from Gündoğan, sends a gentle touch back and looks perfectly happy to go on passing patiently back and forth. He knows the score. He's got it. But then, suddenly, the scent of blood! He catches sight of the goalmouth in the distance and he's away, at the gallop, just one thing on his mind. If his run produces a goal, that's great, everyone's happy. But the fact remains, Foden still hasn't learned the crucial lesson. If David Silva catches a City game from time to time, he must end up pulling his hair out in frustration. His protégé still hasn't understood the fundamental importance of controlling the rhythm and tempo at every stage of a game.

Foden was earmarked first as David Silva the magician's successor and he's still on course to take on the mantle from Bernardo Silva when he moves on. But he's not quite there yet. Whenever the subject comes up, Pep insists that, with a bit more maturity, it will come, and I'm sure we'll be seeing much more of Foden in that midfield role. It has yet to be seen, of course, how well he'll do.

Phil Foden, the man with just one speed: fast and furious.

SCENE 7. LESSONS WITH PEP

Manchester, 14 August 2022

Pep's fury with Walker hasn't completely ebbed away. It dates right back to December 2021 when the defender was sent off in the Champions League game in Leipzig, leaving the team exposed in the next few games of the competition. At the time, the coach didn't even try to hide his disgust at Walker's stupidity and he hasn't let him forget it since, continuing to reprimand him in public from time to time. As recently as March, the coach declared: 'I'm still furious with him. He totally deserved the three-match ban. If you're going to be that stupid, you have to be prepared for the consequences.' It gets to Walker every time and, understandably, hasn't helped his performance on the pitch. The player's even confided in a few of his teammates, Fernandinho, Stones and Dias, about his discomfort ... but nothing that he does has managed to soften Pep's opinion.

The coach is (and was) convinced that losing such a key player badly affected the team's cohesion and harmony and, in the subsequent games, would loudly express this belief at key moments, like when Vinicius Junior managed to give Fernandinho the slip in the first leg of the semi-finals. Without Kyle Walker, City struggled and, so far, Pep hasn't forgotten or forgiven.

During the summer, Walker's had plenty of time to think about his career. At 32, he's already won plenty of silverware and is still a fantastic player with a lot to offer. Blessed with an incredible physique and great athleticism, he attacks like a winger, defends like a Cossack and is able to cover immense distances as he runs up and down the wing. A defender who throws himself into City's attack, knowing that his speed and acceleration will get him back to his defensive position in time to stop a sudden counterattack in its tracks. His impressive physique has been fundamental to much of his success but his physicality has also landed him more than once in very hot water. Like a steam train crushing everything in its wake, he's prone to making clumsy, unnecessary errors, fouling opponents and ending up being shown a red card. At his age, he can't realistically expect to have many years left at the elite level of professional football. Perhaps now would be a good time to work on his technical skills, in case his physical strength begins to wane, or even just as a self-improvement exercise. Walker's surrounded by footballers with superb technical abilities: De Bruyne, Foden, Grealish, Mahrez, Gündoğan, Silva ... and even defenders like the extraordinary Cancelo, Stones, whose ball control is second to none, and Laporte, with his amazing diagonal passing. So, as soon as pre-season training starts, Walker begins to work on this side of things, focusing on controlling the ball better in the practice rondos and trying to make his passing more precise and effective where, in the past, he'd have got by on his sheer physical abilities alone.

City play their first league match of the season away to West Ham in the London Stadium. Pep has both his full-backs position themselves in the middle of the pitch, beside Rodri in a tight but risky defensive shape. It means that Cancelo and Walker will have to be completely focused on producing precise, clean passes. An ideal scenario for Cancelo, who has freedom to move with Aké protecting his back and several teammates in front ready to receive his passes. For Walker, it all feels much more risky. He's played as an inside full-back many times before, of course he has, but never under such scrutiny, with the boss's baleful gaze fixed upon him. And only him. Or so it feels. He knows he's going to have to play out of his skin today. And so he does; 99 touches and 88 passes, 93.2 per cent of which find their target. He loses the ball just once.

At the end of the game, Walker's on cloud nine. Maybe he's not produced *exceptional* football but he feels vindicated. His newfound focus on developing his technique has already given his game added depths. Then a message pops up on his phone. It's footage from Pep's press conference: 'Kyle Walker had a particularly good game today. He was incredible and I'd like to congratulate him. All my players deserve praise for today but especially Kyle.' One hyper-vigilant fan even comments pithily on the club's Twitter feed: 'Looks like Pep's finally forgiven you for getting sent off, then!' And they're right. It's taken nine long months but finally Pep Guardiola has forgiven Kyle Walker for being sent off in Leipzig.

There's the usual post-match recuperation session on Monday, a day off on Tuesday and then the squad's back for normal training on Wednesday. The session lasts two hours and, at the end, everyone heads off to shower. Everyone, that is, except Walker, who's stayed on with one of the assistants to practise shooting at goal. Pep spots him and saunters over: 'Perfecting your technique Kyle?'

For the next hour Pep works with the big defender. Correcting and instructing: how to position his body in different areas of the pitch; how to control the ball better with the inside of the foot; the best way to control the tension you put into a pass depending on who's receiving it, where you are on the pitch and what else is happening; how to receive the ball with one leg outstretched and then pass with the other foot … they go over and over everything until he's got it right. Who'd have thought it? Kyle Walker getting one-to-one lessons from Pep Guardiola on a dreary Manchester afternoon.

There's another tough training session on Thursday, which focuses on shooting at goal, something Pep has prioritised for a number of years now. Bournemouth are likely to play a highly defensive game on Saturday so there are no startling tactical moves to impart to the players. They'll use a bog-standard 2–3–5 or a 2–2–6, and will go all-out to attack and deny Bournemouth the chance to counter. For City it's going to be about clean passing and good finishing.

Walker stays back after training again today, working with an assistant as he did yesterday. He's got his eyes peeled, though, just in case Pep fancies sticking around too. Sure enough, within minutes the coach has joined him and the two men do another hour of intensive training. Passing, controlling the ball, how to position your body, control with one foot, pass with the other, produce the right touch regardless of what position you're in or the circumstances … now Walker feels like the class favourite as members of the technical team trot over to have a look at this spontaneous football clinic being delivered by the boss.

City use an asymmetrical attack against Bournemouth. Mahrez is stationed outside on the right flank while De Bruyne is inside. On the left, Foden focuses on moving up through the inside and Cancelo sticks to the wings while Gündoğan moves with complete freedom, almost playing the role of second striker, beside Haaland. Pep has Rodri and Walker act as the pivots who will support the whole structure. Rodri supports the attack down the left-hand side while Walker focuses on the right. They'll form the baseline of umpteen triangular passing movements with any of the six City men ahead of them. The difference between the two being that, because of Walker's exceptional power and pace, Pep has assigned him the right and centre of the midfield organisation. Rodri needs to cover much less territory. The important thing is not necessarily how much ground they cover; as always, it's about establishing superiority across all zones and, today, in allocating the crucial pivot role to Walker, Pep has given him specific responsibility for deci-sion-making and controlling the game. Walker gives a superb performance, although his contribution goes largely unnoticed due to the glorious football being produced by several of his teammates. De Bruyne curves in a *trivela* with his outstep, and nutmegs an opponent for the assist to Foden. Cancelo creates all sorts of mischief over on the wing and Aké acts like a one-man defensive wall, repelling all Bournemouth's attempts at a counterattack.

Amidst all that shining talent, most people won't have picked up on Walker's contribution but he actually produces one of his best-ever performances for the team: 80 passes, 93.8 per cent accurately completed, he's 'pivoted' like a pro, launched ferocious attacks up the right, defended with precision and expertise, and also provided Gündoğan with the beautiful pass that led to the first goal.

During their 'tutorials' last week, Pep explained that passing is a way of communicating. You send a subtle, softer pass to tell your teammate he should take, turn and drive or dribble the ball forward, but you send a strong, precise pass if you can see he should combine with someone else with a one-touch/half-touch layoff. Today, Walker sent a fast, low pass to Gündoğan, who understood the message immediately, combined with Haaland and, two seconds later, the ball was in the back of the net. It's a few minutes later that De Bruyne produces that glorious *trivela* goal off the three smallest toes of his outstep after he's already beaten one opponent with a lovely dummy during a lightning counterattack. In the immediate aftermath, Pep walks over to Walker on the touchline and tells him with a huge grin: 'We'll have to work on *that* move next!' Walker's roar of laughter tells us all we need to know. Red card forgotten – reconciliation complete.

SCENE 8. EDDIE HOWE BEATS THE BOX

Newcastle, 21 August 2022

Eddie Howe is, along with Graham Potter, one of the most promising English coaches around. He did an excellent job at Bournemouth and, despite taking over a horrible situation at Newcastle, is making great changes there too. And he shows us all just what he's made of today, when Manchester City come visiting and he successfully deactivates the 'De Zerbi box' Pep plans to make use of this season.

Even going ahead doesn't help City establish their usual domination over today's game at St James' Park. There are two reasons for this – one City's fault, the other down to Newcastle and Howe.

First, City. For some time now, Pep has allowed City to increase the priority given to vertical play. He's perpetually used his team's horizontal lines to amass huge passing sequences that disorganise, tire and draw opponents out of position. They then push up the pitch vertically to attack: a winger penetrates the opposition's area, an organising midfielder makes his perfectly timed arrival in the box, the striker makes his final sprint towards goal …

In the past, Pep had Barça, Bayern and City playing a combination of horizontal and vertical football but, for the last couple of years, City have become more and more comfortable focusing on vertical play. Last season, they played entire matches with very few horizontal passing sequences at all – far less of performing compactly and shifting their opponent perpetually from one side to another. The decision for this alteration is largely based on the reality of the type of players City possess. De Bruyne and Foden are at their happiest haring towards the goal with the ball at their feet, and Cancelo and Walker are also very comfortable driving the attack vertically up the pitch. It's also proved to be a hugely successful strategy. Today, with Haaland up front, we're seeing a much more equal balance between horizontal and vertical play than the 70/30 per cent division they've chosen in the past. (These are my stats, not official ones.)

City open the scoring four minutes in. Playing vertically. Gündoğan sends a long diagonal pass to Bernardo Silva on the right wing. Silva then takes full advantage of Walker, De Bruyne and Haaland drawing all the attention of the Newcastle defenders as they gallop into the box. He passes back to Gündoğan, who's now perfectly placed, on the penalty spot. The German can't miss. And he doesn't: 1–0 City. Pep's men create three more excellent chances over the next ten minutes but Nick Pope, Newcastle's superb new keeper, stops De Bruyne's and Foden's shots and Haaland messes up his attempt to convert a pass from Gündoğan, which should, in itself, have constituted half a goal, it was that exquisite. So far, so good. Things are going much as Pep anticipated and it looks like this will continue to be a full-on, fast-paced match, with City bossing the entire game. But they are losing the habit of keeping the ball, splaying it from side to side, making opposing players dizzy and tired. That's one key way to control a match if the scoreboard, because of profligacy, isn't doing that for you. Eddie Howe, seeing how the land lies, has other ideas …

Newcastle's coach has prepared for this game with his usual intelligence and flair. He reckons he knows exactly how to deal with Guardiola's tactics and has just the kind of players he needs to deliver his lethal counter move. The Magpies have survived City's 15-minute avalanche of fast, attacking football; now it's time to dig in and disrupt their visitors' build-up. Howe's three midfielders Willock, Bruno Guimarães and Joelinton attach themselves to Pep's middle three (Walker, Rodri, Cancelo) and effectively shut them down, while Callum Wilson moves between Stones and Aké, short-circuiting their attempts to bring the ball out. Meanwhile, Newcastle's wingers, Allan Saint-Maximin and Miguel Almirón, are stationed high up the pitch, well into City's area, shutting down space and making it difficult for City to pass to their own wingers, Silva and Foden. All City's lines are blocked and Pep's version of the De Zerbi box', which worked so well against West Ham in their first game, has been completely neutralised. Not for the first time either. According to Juanma Lillo, the same tactic lasted three games last season. They'd used it against Leicester, Tottenham and Norwich, but by the time they faced Arsenal in their next game, the jig was up. The Gunners used one-to-one man-marking to great effect, meaning that they and all of City's other opponents were on to the new strategy and Pep was forced to change tactics.

Back then, the tactic was relatively novel. In football, you never know if a tactical idea is going to capture people's imagination and media attention, or if it's going to pass unnoticed. At this stage last year, City were using a 2+3 build-up with their full-backs stationed in the middle of the pitch, but garnered next to no media attention for it. Today, however, everyone and his dog seems to think that this has been an extraordinary move on Pep's part. Of course, bringing the ball out like this has its pros and its cons …

Nathan Aké's groin strain (subbed off after 21 minutes) bears some of the responsibility for City's problems today. There's no doubt that Howe's men do extremely well in disrupting City's build-up, and without left-footed Aké there to consistently feed the ball to Foden up the left wing, Pep has been forced to forego this vital advantage and introduce Rúben Dias in place of the Dutchman, leaving City a little more blocked at the back. Their end-of-game stats will show that just 86 per cent of City's passes are clean, meaning that Newcastle successfully rob an awful lot of the ball, which they then send straight to the wing for their ace dribbler, the super-fast Frenchman, Saint-Maximin. To add to City's woes, Walker's central position, plus his duties tight-marking Joelinton, prevent him from using his pace to constantly defend against Newcastle's counterattacking, meaning that Stones is on his own at times, outnumbered by the men in black and white, which leaves the rest of City's defence totally disorganised as they improvise cover to compensate for their numerical inferiority.

For a good ten minutes, Newcastle completely outmanoeuvre City. The Citizens lose ball after ball, allowing the locals to find Saint-Maximin, who's waiting in space, ready to sprint forward with no real opposition in front of him, while Walker, Stones, Dias, Cancelo and Rodri, caught on the hop, desperately thunder back towards City's goal in pursuit of their Tyneside opponents. Pep's men lose control of the ball and the space to the extent that, at times, they manage only 6 per cent possession (minutes 23 to 28). It's no surprise then, when Newcastle equalise and then go 2–1 ahead as a result of a phenomenal counterattack from Saint-Maximin, which is finished by Wilson on the inside. Indeed, at this point, City should probably consider themselves lucky that their hosts haven't converted more of their numerous chances. It's becoming more and more obvious that Walker's tight position, which serves him well whenever he has the ball, is actually preventing him from defending effectively against Saint-Maximin, who's maintaining a lot of space between himself and City's big defender. Walker's fast but even he can't cover the distance required every time Newcastle rob the ball.

Sure enough, during the break, Pep decides to change to a 3+2 build-up. But the contumacious Catalan doesn't move Walker. It's Cancelo who goes wide on the left flank and Walker stays in his central, organising position, miles away from the man he has to stop in a counterattack. Yet it works. City begin to dominate. Having done away with the 'De Zerbi box', City, in the shape of Rúben Dias, now find space on the inside. Dias feeds Haaland, who's on the edge of the box. The Norwegian takes the shot but Pope knocks it onto the post. It's clicking – Pep's adjustment seems to be working until, suddenly, Saint-Maximin launches another lightning-fast counterattack and is fouled by Stones just outside the box. Newcastle's free-kick maestro, Kieran Trippier, steps up and sends the ball straight into the top corner of Ederson's net. It's 3–1 to the Magpies.

But, wait, it's not over yet.

Pep's half-time tinkering really has done the trick after all. Now that they're back to a 3+2 build-up, City rediscover their chutzpah and score two goals in short order. First, Rodri gives the assist for Haaland to score into an open goal, and then De Bruyne, from outside the box, produces a Roy of the Rovers special, sending the ball straight through the legs of a Newcastle man 7m in front of him and to the penalty spot, where Silva's arriving. The Portuguese scores. Newcastle 3–3 City.

Everyone's expecting City to strike again, to take adversity and respell it as 'victory' – but that idea's dashed by Pope's absolutely fantastic one-vs-one save against the onrushing Haaland. It's the crowning glory of the keeper's first-class overall performance.

We can draw several conclusions from today's game: Eddie Howe is an exceptional coach with an excellent team capable of giving their opponents a run for their money, especially at home; the 'De Zerbi box' is of limited use against an opponent like Newcastle and particularly if City are playing without a left-footed central defender; and vertical attacking is one of City's key strengths thanks to the lethal strike force of De Bruyne, Foden and Haaland, but cannot be their only strategy if the aim is to dominate rather than just match their opponents blow for blow.

Juanma Lillo used to say, 'The quicker the ball goes, the quicker it comes back,' and Silva, who's decided to stay in Manchester for another year, also believes that this was one of the things that went wrong today in Newcastle: 'Out on the pitch it felt like we wanted to start attacking too quickly. And when we start off like that, going on the attack so quickly, it's actually better for our opponents than it is for us.'

Guardiola, who's absolutely exhausted after such a full-on game, shares his own takeaway: 'We had a chat at half-time. It's important to go through this kind of thing. That way, we find out what we're really made of as a team. Ever since that Aston Villa game [the final game of last season] I've known that we're capable of anything … But we have to be able to finish if we're going to play so vertically. If we don't finish well, our opponents will eat us alive …'

Over in Doha, Lillo's also been watching the game. He's as reassuring as ever: 'The first thing you have to acknowledge is that coming away from

St James' Park with one point is a good result. Nobody has realised yet just how well Newcastle's going to do this season. They are a brilliant side so getting a point there is very good.'

Lillo calls bringing the ball out using the 'De Zerbi box' 'a game of provocation' because the idea is to provoke the opponent to move out of position so that you can bring it out easily. 'You want them to come inside so that we can pass to the outside and avoid having to go through all those opponents, so that our winger gets the ball high up the pitch. Although, in practice, the winger always ends up dropping back to receive it and it's therefore better that you use inverted wingers who can play the ball inside rather than outside.'

His other name for this style of build-up is 'a game of attraction' because, 'we're simply trying to distract and attract our opponents so that we can pass to the wingers. As Pep says, whenever he's talking about Kyle, we should really call the full-backs who are positioned inside "midfielders" so that today, for example, Walker, Rodri and Cancelo all played as organising midfielders.'

This 'football of attraction' has two downsides. The first is that if the wingers have to drop far down the pitch to receive the ball you're gifting away the positional and strategic advantage you've been striving for and, second, if your opponents don't take the bait, it's hard to make any progress. Lillo agrees, to an extent: 'When you have to pass long to your wingers, they usually have to come deep to receive the ball, which is self-defeating … and it's why, after trying it out last season, Pep decided to abandon playing this way. In any case, the reason why City's opponents rarely counterattack successfully is nothing to do with "the box", it's because we're so good with the ball. If you never mess up your passes, they never get the chance to counterattack. It's not about formations, it's about being accurate and effective. If you put two slow, sloppy full-backs on the inside, they'll mess up their passing and you'll be slaughtered. But when you've got players with the kind of talent City have, guys who are so accurate that they can consistently pass the ball within half a millimetre of where their opponents can't reach it, then you can use this strategy all you like. The other problem is I'm trying to pull you into the "box" and if you fall for it, your line of three and your striker will be pulled out of position so that City end up with a five against four or a six against four. And then Gündoğan arrives to take a shot. But if you don't fall for it, and only one or two men are attracted into the "box" and you're neither too closed nor too open, you'll always be able to find one of your own men unmarked further up the pitch when you rob the ball. And if it's someone like Saint-Maximin, who's sensational whether he's playing on the inside or the outside, is a superb dribbler and operates brilliantly at any speed, then we've got a problem. That's the key point.

Look at it this way, if five City players have the ball in a 15 x 15 box and our opponents don't go in to try and rob it, then sure, five of our players have the ball, but they're not going anywhere with it. But if four of them come in to take the ball, effectively our "game of provocation" has worked, we pull them out of position, pass the ball outside and then we're way up the pitch, almost outside their box. But if they don't fall for it, what can we do? If we try to move forward and the opponent robs the ball there's big threat because they've still got support on the outside, they're the ones having a run at our goal. But, as I said, City has excellent players who have fantastic ball control and they can avoid these situations.'

In all likelihood, today's game has probably marked the end of Pep's use of the 'box' this season, as the Norwich game did last season. Football has always been about adapting your tactics to the reality of the situation. It's a battle of ideas, a game where every action has a reaction. Lillo's third law of motion, perhaps?

SCENE 9. 'WITH THE RIGHT RHYTHM WE'RE UNSTOPPABLE!'
Wolverhampton, 17 September 2022

Three days ago, a delighted Guardiola left the Etihad after a late comeback win against Borussia Dortmund, telling anyone who would listen: 'When we get our rhythm right, we're unstoppable!'

This evening, he's grim-faced as he leaves Molineux. They've actually beaten the always bullish and combative Wolverhampton 3–0 (Grealish, Haaland, Foden), even though the ball hasn't exactly flown across the short, dry grass – a poor pitch for Pep's brand of football. But neither did City establish a sufficiently good rhythm, which irritates Pep, whose maxim in this respect has always been: 'In sport, battles aren't just fought over space, they are also about ideas and rhythm.'

City, to paraphrase the great Louis van Gaal, lack rhythm. They don't seem capable of finding the necessary tempo for every moment of a game. Sometimes they're too slow, others too fast and for Pep, it's just not good enough. And it's not that his players aren't willing to improve this aspect of their game. It's just that, like everyone, they have their ups and downs, and will therefore sometimes miss a beat. At the start of September, when City were preparing for Aston Villa (3 September), they'd just pulled off four successful comebacks in six league games. In fact, they'd become so adept at overturning opponents' leads that everyone in the dressing room was joking about being the 'English Real Madrid'. But of course, to have made a comeback in so many matches, they must have made a significant number of errors in the first place …

Under Pep, City have always been an aggressive, attacking side, more than capable of producing amazing turnarounds in matches where a late goal defies the odds; Gabriel Jesus against Southampton, which gave the Centurions their 100 points, and Sterling's goal in another Southampton tussle are just two of the many fightbacks they've produced. Ironically, of course, the most seismic comeback of Pep's time at City was produced by Real Madrid in the Champions League semi-final. Just a few weeks after that bitter experience, City had to mount their own comeback to keep their title hopes alive, after going behind 2–0 away to West Ham. Seven days later, they secured the Premier League title after a dreadful performance, which they somehow managed to turn into a historic fightback against Aston Villa from 2–0 down. So far this season, they've managed to draw with Newcastle after going 3–1 down as well as turn a first-half 2–0 against Crystal Palace into a 4–2 victory (Haaland hat-trick).

And so, on 3 September, they go into the Villa Park game having made comebacks in four of their six previous league games. This time, they open the scoring and an excellent De Bruyne–Haaland combination keeps City ahead until the 70th minute when Leon Bailey equalises. Villa successfully close down the space on the inside throughout the match and maintain their near unbreachable defensive wall right until the final whistle, apparently impervious to City's 13 shots on target, one of which hits the crossbar, their 754 passes and their domination of the ball (73 per cent possession). The 1–1 draw means that Pep's men leave Birmingham having won just one of their last five away games. Pep's particularly unhappy with his team's defending: 'we made far too many mistakes.'

Their away form picks up in Seville, in their first game of the Champions League group stage, where City impose the biggest ever European home defeat suffered by the Spaniards (4–0). Haaland gets two of City's goals, giving him a total of 12 in his eight City games. The Norwegian scored 11 of those with his first touch. He's also set the record for the player who has made it to 25 Champions League goals in the fewest number of games (20), and is only the fourth person to score in his Champions League debut with three different clubs: Salzburg, Borussia Dortmund and City. (The others are Fernando Morientes, Javier Saviola and Zlatan Ibrahimović.) Not only that, but Haaland is also the first City player to score in his Premier League and Champions League debuts for the club. Thus far in his career, the Norwegian has scored with 137 of the 201 shots he's put on target.

But today, despite their resounding win, Pep's pissed off again: 'We attacked too fast in the first half because we were too quick to go looking for Haaland. Erling's presence seems to make the rest of them rush to get the ball to him. We need to time our attacks better, slow things down a little – be smarter. But in the second half at least we managed to establish a better rhythm.'

A week later, when Borussia Dortmund visit the Etihad, City's 'rhythm' problems are again apparent. The Germans imitate Aston Villa and close down all City's internal lines. Once again, Mahrez, Grealish and De Bruyne try in vain to deconstruct a solid impregnable defensive wall and then, at the start of the second half, Bellingham and Reus combine splendidly for the Englishman to put the Germans ahead. 'We played at the wrong rhythm for 60 minutes,' is Pep's furious conclusion at the end of a game in which he's shown his displeasure by making three major changes simultaneously: Álvarez, Silva and Foden on for Mahrez, Gündoğan and Grealish. The three new players bring a shot of adrenaline to City's attack and they launch another comeback. Stones scores with a powerful shot from outside the area, reminiscent of the legendary Vincent Kompany against Leicester, then Haaland receives a beautiful ball from Cancelo with the outside of his foot and tucks it away in an imitation of Johan Cruyff's magnificent 1974 goal against Atlético Madrid. Two extraordinary goals in 30 minutes. More than enough evidence, if needed, that City have everything it takes to fight back in tough situations: the ability and the self-belief. What Manel Estiarte calls *la voglia di vencer*, 'the desire to win'. Hunger and bad-assed defiance.

Silva gives an explosive performance in his 30 minutes, switching fluidly and easily from second pivot beside Rodri, to playmaker, to winger … the master of the ball no matter where he plays. Estiarte is stunned: 'Bernardo, with Foden and Julián – they changed the game. They're a step ahead of everyone else.' For Pep, it's still all about the rhythm: 'When we get our rhythm right, we're unstoppable!'

Later, some of the technical staff share an interesting fact. Whenever City are losing, they try to turn it around by holding on to the ball in order to create chances, and on these occasions they usually achieve more than 90 per cent possession.

SCENE 10. THE TERMINATOR

Manchester, 2 October 2022

The late Ferenc Puskás, a truly exceptional footballer, liked to tell stories of his playing days. He had one particular favourite …

As the referee blows his whistle to mark the end of the fifth European Cup final, Puskás picks up the football. He's scored four of Real Madrid's seven and, as such, should get to keep the ball. But there's a problem. It's May 1960, an era in which only one football is used in any single match and his teammate, the legendary, and famously self-important, Alfredo Di Stéfano scored the other three. The irascible Argentinian is also expecting to go home with the best memento from today's glorious 7–3 victory over Eintracht Frankfurt. So it's the ball he's after too … regardless of the fact that he's scored one fewer than Puskás. Which is when the canny Hungarian gets a brainwave. With a warm smile he suggests they present the ball to Erwin Stein, who's scored two of Eintracht's three goals today: 'We put seven past them, Alfredo,' he tells his haughty teammate, 'the least we can do is give him a consolation prize.' The imperious Di Stéfano reluctantly agrees and, in due course, the ball is handed over, a small consolation for the wretched German. And a fight avoided by Puskás.

Puskás always got an enormous kick out of recounting how he managed to avoid the inevitable, damaging, showdown with Di Stéfano, who, he remembers, considered himself to be the centre of the universe, head and shoulders above everyone else … even a football genius like the magical Puskás.

Fast forward to the Manchester derby, 2 October 2022, and these days there are plenty of footballs to go around. Just as well, given that Haaland and Foden each score three: the first time a Manchester derby has seen a hat-trick for 50 years (scored by the late Francis Lee in 1970). Haaland and Foden both go home tonight with a ball under their arm but there's no consolation prize for United, who trudge off having suffered a 6–3 hammering, which could have been so much worse but for the dip in City's rhythm after an outstanding first half and a 4–0 lead.

Even for their high standards, City are on fire today. They tear United apart in the first half, shooting 15 times, with 7 on target, 4 goals and 1 effort off the post. Gündoğan reigns supreme across the centre of the pitch in Rodri's injury absence. The German international effortlessly sets the pace for the team, ably assisted by Silva and backed up by a superb defensive line in which both Manuel Akanji (the Swiss centre-back who has just arrived from Dortmund for only £15 million) and Aké star. Grealish's doggedly aggressive attacking combines brilliantly with the indomitable De Bruyne–Haaland–Foden trio as the home supporters roar their approval, blown away by this exhibition of breathtaking football and gloating over every last second of the hated United being demolished.

The second half allows United some breathing space simply because City take their foot off the pedal and errors begin to creep in, such that they finish with the previously unheard of midfield partnership of Bernardo Silva and Sergio Gómez. Haaland and Foden nevertheless manage to complete their respective hat-tricks. As ever, Pep's not afraid to put a bit of a damper on things and, post-match, is quick to highlight the team's second-half dip: 'We don't do the simple things well. We need to improve how we manage the easy stuff.'

Haaland has played 11 games for City. Today's hat-trick is actually his third and brings his total goal tally for the Citizens to 17: 1.5 goals per game, or 1 every 58 minutes. He's scored three hat-tricks in eight Premier matches, matching the total number of hat-tricks scored by the likes of Cristiano

Ronaldo, Drogba, Solskjær, Lukaku, Son, Emmanuel Adebayor and Vardy over their entire careers in England. Michael Owen took 48 games to score three hat-tricks and Ruud van Nistelrooy 59.

So what, exactly, is Haaland's secret? Let's ask the experts …

For Pep: 'Erling's main quality, as well as his precision shooting, is his speed.' Lorenzo Buenaventura reckons that 'It's his sheer speed that gives him a vital tenth of a second advantage over opposition defenders and allows him the time and space to take his shots.' According to Estiarte: 'He has the ability and the speed to avoid being caught offside,' and for Lillo, 'His main strength is his intelligence.' And they're all right. Haaland is the 'Terminator', a precision-guided missile with the talent, intelligence, natural athleticism and ambition necessary to make him the ruthless scorer he's become. His joining City has ensured that the Etihad's stands are full to bursting for every game these days and that matchday tickets are nigh-on impossible to get hold of. No City fan worth their salt is willing to forego the chance to witness the incredible feats of City's star striker, who bagged his first hat-trick on 27 August (a 4–2 comeback against Crystal Palace), his second on 31 August (6–0 against Nottingham Forest) and his third, today, in the Manchester derby.

Just a few weeks ago, coach Aldo Sainati described Pep and Haaland as 'the fusion of fire and ice'. Unbelievably, this fusion has yet to reach its apotheosis. Pep would like Haaland to intervene more in the team's play rather than simply waiting for the ball so that he can score. He wants him to join his teammates in circulating the ball … without sacrificing any of his goalscoring prowess. Haaland will never be a Leo Messi or a Harry Kane, but he's well on the way to becoming City's most voracious predator ever.

Of one thing there's no doubt: finding the right fusion between such fire and ice will take a bit of time.

SCENE 11. THIS IS ANFIELD

Liverpool, 16 October 2022

João Cancelo makes a rare mistake, which results in Liverpool's 1–0 victory over City at Anfield.

Foden's already had a goal disallowed after Haaland's 'foul' on Fabinho. There's a general feeling in City's dugout that this kind of mild transgression would not normally be considered serious but on this occasion, after due consultation with VAR, the referee decides to deny City their goal. Pep opts to bite his tongue on this occasion. He's used to City coming off worse whenever there's a particularly controversial decision. But I get a furious text from one of his assistants: 'What the ref's just done is absolutely inexcusable. This is Anfield!'

It's City's first away defeat since 15 August 2021 (1–0 at Spurs). They've had a very good October so far. After wiping the floor with United, they beat Copenhagen in the Champions League (5–0) and then Southampton in the league (4–0), with Haaland adding three more goals to his already impressive tally. Their return leg against Copenhagen resulted in a goalless draw, which, although far from a good result, wasn't a disgrace given that Sergio Gómez was sent off after 30 minutes, forcing his teammates to 'shut down' the game in order to earn the point needed to pretty much guarantee progress to the next round.

Anfield is very different. City know that the first 15 minutes of each half against Liverpool are absolutely vital and that they must do everything they can to prevent Klopp's men using the sheer electric energy of their style, and the crowd, to dominate. Pep therefore makes sure that his men keep a tight grip on the game at the start of each half. The first is pretty anodyne, with lots of passing but very few chances. In possession, City play three central defenders (Akanji, Dias and Aké), with Cancelo on the right touch-line and Foden in an attacking position on the left. They use their customary 3–2–2–3 when they bring out the ball, a 3–2–5 in attack and a 4–4–2 when they lose the ball, with Cancelo moving to right-back and Aké to left-back. Pep knows that his strategy of one-to-one marking when the Reds bring the ball out takes huge amounts of stamina and energy, and therefore changes his distribution in midfield 30 minutes in: Gündoğan moves back to support Rodri while Silva moves up next to De Bruyne to lend his considerable energies to their press. City's game lacks fluidity in the first half but, given the quality of their opponent, Pep's prepared to let this go. He doesn't mention it at half-time but he does remind his men: 'Make sure you have maximum control in the first ten minutes. They always come out like gangbusters.'

And he's not wrong.

Mo Salah launches a lethal counterattack and Ederson makes an extraordinary save. Then, as if in direct defiance of Pep's instructions, the game explodes into a fast and furious back-and-forth, with each side creating lots of threat. Ten minutes after the break, Foden scores. It's disallowed. Diogo Jota messes up a good one-to-one with Ederson. Then, it's back to the other end of the pitch where Haaland launches a screamer, which is saved by Alisson, before Silva and Salah both fail to finish their respective counterattacks. City continue to man-mark their opponents, their pressing is excellent overall, but not even they are able to stop every single long ball thumped up the pitch by Robertson and Harvey Elliott towards the Reds' super-talented strikers, who are engaging in hand-to-hand battle with City's three centre-backs. Cancelo's mistake happens just 15 minutes before the end. De Bruyne botches a free kick, allowing Alisson to collect and then quickly send the ball long. In the subsequent tussle for possession, the Portuguese messes up and effectively gifts the ball on a silver platter to Liverpool's beloved Egyptian. Salah puts it away. City have played well but the result is a real blow. They're now four points behind Arsenal, current league leaders. It's not a huge difference but they can't afford to pass up any more opportunities to keep pace with Arteta's side.

On the journey back to Manchester, Pep really looks worried. Using Cancelo as a full-back/winger didn't work – he didn't manage to attack effectively, nor did he connect with De Bruyne as intended. The team played well enough, the poor refereeing decision notwithstanding, but, right at this moment, Pep would prefer 'that they'd played less well and won!' He's troubled by the number of individual duels his men lost and reminds me that: 'Whether you play well or badly depends on whether or not you win your duels.' He's also clear that they've just faced a particularly tough opponent: 'Liverpool also played well. Each of us has their own style. We take more risks than them but, each to his own.' He's not saying anything yet but Cancelo is genuinely worrying him. Kyle Walker has just undergone vital surgery on his groin after injuring himself in the derby and will be out for the rest of the year, and Pep's worried that, in the meantime, Cancelo's not going to last.

SCENE 12. 'THE NEW LAHM'

Manchester, 2 November 2022

Carles Planchart's excited. Normally a man of few words, the serious Catalan is positively buzzing: 'I think we might have found the new Lahm.' He's referring to Rico Lewis, the 17-year-old who's just made his Champions League debut in City's 3–1 victory against Sevilla. And, to the immense delight of fellow Academy alumni, Foden and Palmer, he scored.

Lewis lines up as a right-back but then immediately moves beside Gündoğan, Pep's organising midfielder today, to complete the three-man intermediate wall with Sergio Gómez. Intelligent on the ball, the youngster combines well with Gündoğan and the two roaming midfielders, who, today, are his best mates, Palmer and Foden. Working with Mahrez and Julián Álvarez, the youngster makes several incursions into Sevilla's area until, 51 minutes in, he receives a perfectly measured assist from Álvarez, which he slams into the back of the net. There's general jubilation on the pitch – City's senior players are genuinely delighted that this talented, ambitious kid has become the youngest starting debutant to score in the Champions League. Just 17 years and 346 days old, he's six days younger than Karim Benzema was in 2005 when he set the previous record for Lyon against Rosenborg.

Pep has used Lewis in a few games already and put him in the starting 11 for their friendly against Barcelona in the Camp Nou in August, a game organised as a fundraiser for Juan Carlos Unzué to support him in his battle with ALS (amyotrophic lateral sclerosis). But this has been the first 'serious' game he's started (City came into today's game knowing they had already qualified for the last 16). Until now, he's been just another of the kids who'd made brief appearances pre-World Cup when the squad was struggling with injury problems. Today, he's been a starter, he's had a brilliant game and he's scored. As he leaves the pitch five minutes before the end, suffering from cramp, the Etihad erupts in an ovation to City's young hero.

But none of that has contributed to the chief analyst's sudden ebullience. Planchart's watched Lewis, day in, day out on the training pitch, and he's spotted an uncanny resemblance with that German great: 'He possesses a lot of Lahm's qualities. He's not tall or strong, and nor is he particularly fast, but he has the kind of brain that processes what he sees on the pitch very quickly indeed. He's talented and intelligent with a good touch and he seems to understand instinctively where his teammate will need him next. I watch him every day and it's unmistakeable. I see so much of Philipp in him. Only time will tell, but I think we've definitely got a "new Lahm" on our hands.'

SCENE 13. TERRA INCOGNITA
Manchester, 31 December 2022

The Qatar World Cup has been moved to the middle of the season but it's as yet unclear exactly what impact this will have on domestic football. Players are saturated, already competing to their maximum, so just how are they going to cope with this? And exactly how will it affect the calendar of league and cup competitions in Europe? This, without a doubt, is terra incognita – unknown territory. Nothing like this has ever happened before – club seasons split in two with a World Cup right in the middle of Europe's winter. Coaches, fitness coaches, indeed, anyone responsible for how elite players perform are facing a mammoth challenge – and with no previous data to help understand it.

And it's not just post-World Cup that's a conundrum. How should coaches, players, physios and fitness staff work and behave in the build-up to the Qatar competition? Most of the top players on this continent will play 60 matches and upwards, so won't the extra stress of a midwinter World Cup hugely increase the likelihood of injuries? And what can coaches expect from their international players once they return and are thrown right back into club competitions? Everything's in doubt: their level of performance, their stamina, how much rest they'll need, how much the rate of injury will increase …

City hope that the way they organise training might, just might, reduce the impact. Lorenzo Buenaventura uses 'micro-cycles' in his physical preparation, focusing solely on how best to prepare the players for the next game or two and never thinking mid-term – let alone long term. It's for this reason that he's still moderately optimistic about how much impact the timing of the World Cup will have on City's top players – notwithstanding that they'll obviously need more rest periods at different times than in previous years. The baseline is to treat these next ten months as completely atypical – as if there were two different seasons rather than one divided in half. In psychological terms, they'll have to approach it as if they're competing for two different league titles – pre-World Cup and post-World Cup.

The three weeks immediately prior to the shutdown for Qatar 2022 are nothing less than a frenzy of competitive action for City – seven matches, just one defeat. During this time you can sense, in training and in matches, that everyone's taking maximum precautions. Nobody can bear the idea of getting injured now and missing a World Cup. The end of October brings a win over the delightful Brighton side De Zerbi's constructing and there's another victory over an increasingly pallid Leicester and a draw against Dortmund. The win over the Seagulls means City have achieved 10 straight home victories in which they've scored 3 or more: 10 wins, 43 scored, only 10 conceded. The Etihad has become an invincible fortress. Which is not to say Brighton are mere cannon fodder. They go for man-to-man marking and, after only six minutes, Pep needs to move Silva back, next to Rodri, so that Haaland can have a little pocket of space to work in. 'We understood beforehand that this would be a very demanding match in tactical terms, which means that our players did really well to win,' is Planchart's post-match verdict.

The Citizens produce a solid performance against Dortmund in the Champions League. Both Haaland and Cancelo register feverish temperatures and only last until half-time, but City still come away with a result that guarantees them winning Group G. Coming into the game, Dortmund need a win but a point almost certainly will put them through too – meaning that they mount a massive defensive exercise based around Hummels, who's in imperious form. Nil–nil by the final whistle in what could actually have been a victory for City, given that Mahrez misses a penalty with 30 minutes left. It's the second consecutive miss in European competition and, in fact, they've only scored 70 per cent of their penalties (57 of 82), which is the worst rate of any of the top English sides. It's as yet unclear if that stat's a mere irritant or a big problem.

Next up, that defeat of Leicester – more proof that the aggressive, dangerous team of recent years is vastly diminished. Leicester are flirting with the relegation zone and are increasingly resorting to mass-defending.

Some might call Brendan Rodgers's formation a 4–5–1 but, in practice, it's actually a 5–5–0 – wholly dedicated to asphyxiating City's creativity. But Guardiola's daring 2–2–6 keeps threatening the Foxes. There's total control of the ball and only one attacking team on the pitch but, eventually, De Bruyne converts a superb direct free kick to give the Citizens the win. Everything else today has been a process of creative ideas and ingenious moves crashing up against a dull, resolute, defensive wall of home players.

The Champions League group stage concludes with Sevilla at the Etihad. Rico Lewis becomes the fifth youngest English player to start a Champions League match* and brings all of his innate Philipp Lahm flair to the game. His goal also earns him the record of 'youngest debut scorer' in UEFA football.† Tonight's result means that City are unbeaten in Group G and Sevilla no doubt leave thinking, *Ninety minutes in the Etihad are very, very long.* (Italian teams infamously say the same thing about the Bernabéu: 'Novanta minuti son molto longo en el Bernabéu.')

November brings Fulham and some agonising moments. It's not as if Guardiola's ever felt relaxed about playing Marco Silva's teams, but Cancelo getting sent off rips up his pre-match strategy. Playing with ten men from the 26th minute means battling uphill into a ferocious headwind. We've been here before – watching a Guardiola team go a man down and facing an opponent who just wants to rob the ball and break, not dominate. Fulham score the spot kick that results from Cancelo's red card, to make it 1–1, after Álvarez's early opener but, then, only shoot on target once more for the rest of the match. Because Rodri, Stones and Akanji put so much effort and skill into protecting them defensively, De Bruyne, Gündoğan and Silva construct, attack and behave as if this were still 11 vs 11. City pass and pass, open Fulham up and get shots on target, which only yield two disallowed goals. At least until minute 95, in added time, when they win a penalty. 'That was one of the tensest moments of my life,' Haaland admits afterwards. The Norwegian, now recovered from a minor injury, plays the last 30 minutes

---

* The other four were Jack Wilshere, Josh McEachran, Phil Foden and Jude Bellingham.
† Phil Foden scored his first Champions League goal when he was 18 years and 288 days old; Cole Palmer achieved it at 19 years and 166 days, Rico Lewis at 17 years and 346 days.

and, as he takes the crucial shot from 12 yards, looks as though he's gasping for breath. Sweating, tense, his mouth opening and closing, he shoots low and hard to the keeper's left. Leno gets close but … not close enough.

The players celebrate as if this were a title-winning moment, rather than the 13th match of the league season. The crowd is euphoric, the players are embracing and celebrating wildly but it's clear that no one's more relieved or excited than the boss. Guardiola's body language never deceives. And tonight, as he salutes the adoring fans, he's clearly proud of his team, proud of the fact that their intensity of work over the previous weeks has brought such a big dividend. He tells me later: 'Moments like that, in the context of what had been happening, give meaning to how hard we all work. To see the fans' happy faces, and then, just wandering around the pitch to thank the crowd – all of that was so emotional. If you spend seven years in one place there will always be doubts about whether you're doing the right thing. You go through hundreds of training sessions, matches and there's so, so much travelling … Then something like this happens and you're just so proud of everyone involved but also of the direction we've taken and how hard we've worked to get here.'

If you are predisposed to be looking for hints, and like reading body language, then Pep's beaming face and his energetic gestures to fans and players alike would tell you that this is a man who's seriously considering staying to create more history in Manchester.

Chelsea's League Cup trip to the Etihad is one that confirms Stefan Ortega as a keeper of colossal talent and character. Pep's chosen to mix the 11 – old hands and newbies. So Rodri, Gündoğan, Mahrez and Grealish work alongside Lewis, Gómez, Álvarez and Ortega. There's no argument that City don't dominate the match, nor that they fail to produce lots of tasty goal chances, but the truth remains that their hero on the night is this German back-up keeper who produces five superb stops in order to prevent Graham Potter's team deservedly scoring. Mahrez and Álvarez win it for City, Grealish looks lively up front and Lewis has a tough evening – losing nine duels but working like a Trojan to turn things his way. A kid with real competitive character.

It's only against Brentford, during this whirlwind of matches, that City walk away disappointed and empty-handed. The Bees' star striker, Ivan

Toney, is a handful for Ederson from start to finish and the Englishman scores twice in their 2–1 win. No excuses, but this is the last match before the World Cup break and it's clearer than ever where the players' minds are focused. Pep's used his best-available team – no prevarication about protecting players he's about to lose for a month or more. Brentford use a high, athletic press and City don't play out well. When, eventually, they do begin to construct from the back, Brentford consolidate in a 5–3–2, making themselves very compact, and resort to letting keeper David Raya punt long balls to Toney. Pep: 'We didn't press them well up front because they didn't let us. They were happy to hit the ball long from Raya and ask us to compete for headers and "second balls" – Toney won every knockdown, I think, and gave possession to Brentford's midfield off them.'

A side issue is the fact that Pep has harsh words for his team at half-time. Today's been off kilter and City's demanding boss genuinely isn't impressed with the level of enthusiasm and positivity his players are giving him out there. Are their minds somewhere else? He thinks so. It's a big, forceful ticking off for his men – without much noticeable effect in the second half. City don't attack well, they rush things and the passing accuracy is only 84 per cent – way, way too low. By the end, it's the better team who's won. When the whistle goes, it's World Cup time and, frustratingly, Arsenal have a five-point advantage at the top of the table (37 vs 32), despite the explosive impact of Haaland's performance since he arrived: 18 goals and 3 assists in only 13 matches. A goal contribution every 58 minutes.

TWO MORE YEARS WITH PEP

There are still six months left on the boss's contract when he decides that he's going to renew until June 2025. A few things have to fall into place before he signs on the dotted line, however. The first is a superb renewal offer from City. The second, his need to be sure of his own and his family's continuing enthusiasm for the project. And he also needs to be certain that, beyond having a terrific squad, every single person, from the canteen staff all the way up to the owners, are pulling in the same direction, to know that everyone is committed and unified in the belief that City are on the right path. He wants a club-wide unity of purpose – something he's never found elsewhere.

Combine all three of these and, suddenly, it's far easier for Pep to accept a contract extension. Money's not an obstacle – club and coach are quickly in harmony on that. The family discussion's much more crucial. Two initial years living as a family unit in Manchester have, in due course, splintered into three different locations for work-related reasons. Cristina went home to Barcelona in 2019 to take personal charge of her family business – the Serra Claret clothes shops – and young Valentina also opted to finish her schooling in the Catalan capital. Maria, their elder daughter, has completed her studies and established herself in London, and Pep and Màrius are now going to be in Manchester longer than was planned. The family make a point of getting together for home games but the next day, Cristina, Valentina and Maria will head off to their respective homes. Away games in London also present another regular opportunity for the family to reunite and there are often European matches where all five of them can enjoy some family time. Three or four times a year, usually during the international breaks, the Guardiola family also take a brief holiday together. But none of this negates the reality that they've now lived 'apart' for over three years. Which is why Pep wants it to be a decision for his wife and three kids as to whether he renews with City or not. On this occasion, they are unanimous – Pep stays and they can all, happily, put up with this slightly fractured but successful lifestyle where they're always travelling in order to be together.

So, on 23 November, a delighted Pep announces that he's staying: 'I couldn't be anywhere better than this. Over the last seven years we've had bad moments and the City organisation has always, always supported me. Starting with Khaldoon, but also including Ferran Soriano, Txiki of course, and Omar Berrada – everyone close to me has supported me. Without exception. If we've won a few trophies in that time you can explain it, above all, by the fact that the club has consistently given me total support.' He also takes time to remember his 'professor', his maestro: 'I honestly think Johan [Cruyff] would have told me to extend this contract by a couple of years – in fact I'm sure of it. Txiki and I, spiritually, are his kids.'

· · ·

While the World Cup is being played in Qatar, I get in touch with Roman Fedotov, a Vancouver-based football analyst who's written interestingly about the changes the Premier League has undergone in the last ten years.

Fedotov's study shows that over that decade 'direct' football has dropped from 45 per cent (in 2013) to 41 per cent. Crosses from the wing into the box have dropped from 23 per cent to 18.5 per cent, and shots at goal have diminished from 14 per match to 12.7. Shots are also more often taken from a position closer to goal in the modern game (shots from distance have dropped from 47 per cent to 35 per cent in these ten years). The number of times that possession is robbed by a high press around the opposition penalty box has gone up from 3 times per match to 4.5 – a 150 per cent increase. Overall, Fedotov's study evidences a pretty radical change in ideas and practices among Premier League teams over the last ten years. All of the trends demonstrated are in line with how Guardiola sees and teaches football. It's impossible to assign specific amounts of credit to the influence of any single coach but it's inarguable that the arrival in England of coaches like Klopp, Tuchel, Bielsa, Pochettino, Unai Emery, Arteta and De Zerbi have contributed hugely to the changes. And, within this cadre of philosophical evangelicals, the fact that Guardiola has had a significant impact is equally obvious.

'ARSENAL, WE HAVE TO HUNT THEM'

It's three days before Christmas by the time Premier League football returns to the Etihad. City have had to watch 16 of the first team competing for their nations in Qatar, meaning that, when full-time training recommences in Abu Dhabi on 5 December, there are only seven squad members on duty: Haaland, Mahrez, Lewis, Palmer, Gómez plus the keepers Ortega and Carson. The natural solution is to fill the gaps with promising youngsters from the Academy. Which is what Pep does.

The League Cup last-16 tie with Liverpool is fixed for 22 December, meaning that some of those who've been eliminated early from the World Cup can probably join those who've been training flat-out with City for the last couple of weeks. The bench will be Carson plus the English and Portuguese players, with the exception of Dias, who's got a lengthy injury problem, and Kalvin Phillips, who only played 40 minutes for his country in Qatar and has returned to City overweight. It brings a public reproach from Guardiola and a lot of media coverage. Liverpool are obviously struggling under all the same burdens, meaning that their team at the Etihad is a hybrid too – not that they lose their aggressive playing identity. It's another brilliant and enjoyable chapter in these clubs' modern rivalry, with City taking the initiative and Liverpool defending deep and breaking. Haaland, Mahrez and Aké score the home team's goals while Fábio Carvalho and Salah notch for the Reds. It means that City are in the quarter-finals, having knocked out the two teams who were the most recent finalists of this competition – Chelsea and, now, Liverpool.

City face Klopp's team with a daringly high defensive line – 58m from their goalmouth. Akanji and Laporte roam around like wild beasts, Lewis plays as if he were a battle-hardened veteran. His performance is sensational and there's no way, if you're encountering him for the first time in this match, that you would believe he's only 18. His performance is textbook – helping an equally terrific Rodri to thrive in the organising midfielder role. Not for the first time there's talk, among Pep's staff, that this guy has the 'potential to develop into a new Philipp Lahm'.

Pep's public verdict is, 'Cole [Palmer] and Rico performed incredibly well and they're going to be hugely important to this club over the coming ten years or so … Rico is such an intelligent player and humble when it comes to the hard-working part.'

Not only does Lewis shine in the full-back/inside-midfielder role but he also presses brilliantly and contributes hugely to City's overall control. City press in a 3–4–1–2 formation – Haaland and Mahrez attack the Liverpool backline, De Bruyne sits on their pivot (Stefan Bajcetic), Rodri attempts to stifle Thiago Alcântara, while Palmer goes up against the Reds' hugely experienced right-back, James Milner. As soon as Lewis sees that Liverpool are circulating from the back, he knows that they'll try to escape City's press down the left. He then sprints like a madman, haring off from midfield towards Robertson and trying to cut his line of pass down Liverpool's left.

At the other end, City take the high-risk option of going three vs three against Liverpool's strikers: Akanji on Carvalho, Laporte against Darwin Núñez and Aké closing down Salah. If Lewis's mad, athletic harrying of Robertson pays off then, grand, City win possession. If not, however, and Liverpool move possession to their right, then Lewis will sprint back defensively, take Carvalho off Akanji's hands, allowing the Swiss player to press Núñez, and Laporte will become the free man supporting his defensive colleagues. High risk, high stakes but, by definition, potentially high rewards. Lewis shows in every movement, every reaction, that he fundamentally understands his role and how to execute it in terms of positioning and timing. He's an athlete, physically strong, with massive stamina and today's display confirms his value to the team. If this guy can play the full-back/inside-midfielder role to such perfection, it will help them achieve numerical superiority in the centre of the pitch *and* Pep can ask him to jump a position and press the opponent's back four. To achieve all this, Lewis has to show intelligence and discipline plus athletic power and swift reflexes.

Guardiola also gives De Bruyne a mention: 'Kevin is a legend at this club.' Like Gündoğan, eliminated early from the World Cup, De Bruyne plays like a world champion tonight. Sensational pass after sensational pass to the point that the DAZN match analyst Nacho González uses a phrase that should be in big letters on the side of the Academy walls: 'Kevin De Bruyne was born in Belgium but his real nationality is a Manchester Citizen.'

The following week, City beat Leeds 1–3 at Elland Road and Lewis, Rodri and De Bruyne shine again. It's a nasty, windy afternoon and the pitch is terrible but City tuck the test away comfortably thanks to a brace from Haaland, who has now broken the record for the fastest player ever to score 20 Premier League goals (14 matches). That's half what it took Alan Shearer. When Pep decides to give Lewis and Grealish a rest, with 20 minutes left, City lose a bit of control in the match. Both of them have become key players for City. Lewis, especially in partnership with Rodri, plays a vital role in the initiation and continuity of attacking moves, and his presence on the pitch goes a long way to ensuring that City control possession. And Grealish? Well, alongside his other talents he's become fully aware that he's the team's 'rest station'. The first season for a new striker in one of Pep's sides is almost always tough. At City this was true for Sané, Bernardo Silva and Mahrez. Moderate first seasons, followed by exponential growth and importance. This is also the case for Grealish – particularly after returning from the World Cup. The penny has dropped as to what Pep wants from him in each action. His defensive work is now fantastic and he's one of, if not the best 'protecter of the ball' in Pep's squad. Which is why, now, City giving Grealish the ball means that, if they need or want it, the rest of the players can take a little breather – either to gather strength or, more likely, to gather their wits and press the mental reset button. Even if it's a fleeting thing, Grealish becomes a rest station for City's players. On top of this, the technically excellent Englishman is attacking better with each match he plays.

After the game today, Erling Haaland decides to use his social media profile to publish the words: 'Arsenal, we have to hunt them.' It's a declaration of intent.

The last day of the year brings one of 'those' matches for City. Nothing wrong with the quality of play but a result that sticks in the craw. Sixteen shots at goal, one off the post, 663 passes, 90 per cent accuracy and a total of 75 per cent possession – but a draw with Everton, who score with their only effort on target.

The year 2022 finishes with Arsenal, who have just beaten Brighton 4–2 on the south coast, seven points ahead of City after 16 league matches. It's a big advantage, which leaves Guardiola and his players without the option of even a small slip-up. Pep knows that the next few months will almost certainly bring unlikely and unexpected events as a result of the midseason World Cup. 'We're not even halfway through the Premier League and from now on, a lot of teams will be experiencing things they can't anticipate,' is his official verdict.

We're in terra incognita.

SCENE 14. THE FULL-BACKS AND THE OCEAN
London, 5 January 2023

Think for a moment of the power and reach of the Gulf Stream moving deep in the ocean basin. Then, imagine the Atlantic Ocean, at times calm and serene, other times tossing and rolling with enormous waves. For me, football's like an ocean. It's those powerful currents deep beneath the surface that provide the momentum and direction, but it's the surface movement that catches most of our attention.

Five months ago, in August 2022, Kyle Walker blew us all away with his incredible performances as a 'false full-back'. He'd begin his move from the right-hand side, join Rodri near the centre circle, dribble round opponents to get into the opposition area and then send precise, expertly timed vertical passes into the box, with the kind of calm deliberation nobody ever expected from this big, tough defender. It's obvious how much he's benefited from his one-to-one sessions with Pep and has taken a huge leap forward. Despite that, of course, the rest of us have continued to refer to him as a full-back.

Just three months ago, in October 2022, João Cancelo also took our breath away with his own take on the 'false full-back' position. He moved in from the left-hand side to join Rodri in the middle of the pitch, circulating the ball until he'd made it into the opposition's half, penetrating defensive lines through the inside, the outside or anywhere he could find a gap. He'd give curling assists with the outside of his foot or score the goal himself using his left or his right leg. He had become like a whirlwind, sweeping all before him. Yet, still we continued to refer to him as a full-back.

Now, in January 2023, Rico Lewis, aged just 18, trots on to the pitch at Stamford Bridge in the second half of a crucial Premier League game and immediately begins to work his magic, transforming the whole dynamic and inspiring his teammates to greater feats of excellence. Moving in from the right, he joins Rodri and moves the ball forward into the opposition's area. He then establishes himself in the 'Lahm position' and begins to direct the whole game. Only three months ago he was a raw kid, just out of the Academy. Now he's the player Pep relies on to shake the team up and win decisive games.

Three different false full-backs. This is a tactic first discovered by Pep years ago whereby he moved his full-backs away from the outside and had them play on the inside, as extra protection for his organising midfielders and as generators of the game. 'We can't go on seeing full-backs as the guys who defend the line and occasionally make attacking runs up the flanks. What I want are midfielders who play in the full-back position. That way, I can play true midfielders who might impose less "control" but who are better in front of goal, better at causing havoc. And they'll know that their backs are always covered.'

Pep developed this idea shortly after taking over at Bayern Munich. After suffering a series off crushing counterattacks in their Bundesliga matches, Pep spent several days at home coming up with a way to neutralise them. And on Sunday, 14 September 2013, he was ready to present his idea to his closest advisers; his eldest children, Maria and Màrius, who loved the idea. As did his players. Under the new plan, his full-backs, Rafinha and Alaba, would move up to midfield, close beside their organising midfielder, none other than Philipp Lahm. The three players would then form a central defensive wall, located in or around the centre circle, designed to short-circuit the opposition's counterattacks. The team used the new tactic for the first time three days later when Bayern beat CSKA Moscow in the Champions League. Rafinha and Alaba executed their new roles with intelligence and flair, prompting German sports writer Ronald Reng to comment,

> They were at the top of their game … they were passing so fast and with such fluidity that … they reminded me of Barcelona in 2009 but with the added ingredient of Bayern's speed. From that day onwards we've watched them become the kind of team we've never seen in Germany before.*

Pep would later laughingly confess to me that this had been his 'main tactical innovation' and it's worth just reminding ourselves of the difference between innovation and invention. An invention is the creation of something new, it's the action or effect of creating a work of art. Innovation, on the other hand, consists of modifying something that already exists. Everything in football was invented before 1945, as I explain in my book *La evolución táctica del fútbol* (The Tactical Evolution of Football), which focuses on the era when football was invented, between 1863 and 1945. During this period everything about the sport was invented: the main technical movements, the strategies, the ways of playing and the fundamental tactics. So how should we interpret the changes that were made after 1945? Everything that happened post-1945 was a type of innovation: the Cambridge pyramid, the WM formation invented by Chapman, the Italian method, the Austrian Wünderteam, the 'Máquina' of River Plate … all of them decided to use established resources in new and different ways. Which is why Pep is always so careful to describe his tactics, like the introduction of his false full-backs, as 'innovations'. He has never claimed to have invented anything.†

In fact, the first person to implement the idea of putting full-backs on the inside was Herbert Chapman, in 1925, in response to a suggestion from

---

* Perarnau, *La evolución táctica del fútbol.*
† Martí Perarnau, *Pep Confidential* (Arena Sport, 2014).

Arsenal's captain, Charles Buchan. The new tactic would drastically transform the traditional pyramid formation that every team tended to use. The pyramid was a 2–3–5, with two central defenders, three midfielders and five forwards. A half-back and two wing-halves made up the central line. These players had tended to have very specific profiles ever since the scholars of the University of Cambridge designed the playing model and created the post of midfielder in 1882. By designing the organising midfielder (pivot) as the principal hinge of their play, the wing-halves moved to the outside of the pitch without abandoning these zones, and ran up and down without stopping. They collaborated with the advance of the ball via triangulation if the team played a Scottish style of football or they simply moved up via the flanks. If the opponent counterattacked, the wing-half always marked the closest rival winger and would pursue him right to the end of the pitch as he tried to advance. This endless repetition demanded huge stamina from the wing-halves, given that they were in constant motion, running up and down the flanks of the pitch, although always within the area they'd been assigned.*

Chapman and Buchan redesigned the structure of teams. They moved the organising midfielder back, making him a third central defender and enabling the other centre-backs to open themselves up on the flanks so that the third player could fit in. To compensate, they then moved the two wing-halves 'inside', close to one another. Up front, they maintained the three forwards (two wingers and a striker) but moved the inside-forwards (nowadays known as double pivots) back so that they would form a central square with the wing-halves. This construction of Chapman's would later be referred to as the WM.

For Herbert Chapman, full-backs had essentially ceased to exist. The opposition wingers' penetration was covered by the central defenders and, when Arsenal attacked, the wingers controlled the flanks of the pitch. The old wing-halves, or full-backs of the pyramid, had become pure midfielders. Guardiola's 2013 version was slightly different from Chapman's. His full-backs also moved inside but he had them stay there acting as bodyguards for the organising midfielder who remained the pivot axis of the team. Chapman's 3+2 became Pep's 2+3.

---

* Perarnau, *Pep Guardiola: The Evolution.*

In fact, Pep has drawn much of his inspiration for this tactical innovation from the great Johan Cruyff, who also used full-backs as inside midfielders, although only sporadically. One such occasion was when Barcelona played Deportivo La Coruña in the Spanish league in 1993–4. The two great sides would finish joint-top of the league with 56 points apiece, although Barcelona would be crowned champions on goal difference. On 26 February 1994, Cruyff lined Albert Ferrer and Sergi Barjuán up as inside full-backs while a certain Pep Guardiola was the organising midfielder. Barcelona won 3–0 that day – a victory that would prove a decisive part of their eventual title win. So, Pep knows from direct experience how important it is to have two back-up players close by, although, in reality, Cruyff never used the tactic on a consistent basis.

• • •

It's interesting that Pep leaves Lewis on the bench at the start of this key game against Chelsea, despite having used him as a starter in the last five games. The youngster has consistently produced superlative performances but Pep reckons that he needs to give Walker and Cancelo some playing time, despite the difficulties each of them face.

Walker has had a bad run of injuries of late. His size and strength means that he possesses huge reserves of power and speed but these same advantages mean that he's prone to joint problems. He was out at the end of last season and was badly missed, particularly against Real Madrid, and, no sooner had he returned in August, he was injured again against Aston Villa. He fought back to fitness and had returned to full strength by 2 October for the derby match but had to be taken off after 40 minutes after a bad fall caused a groin injury that would require surgery four days later. Having recuperated sufficiently for the World Cup, Walker returned to Manchester, only to have an old injury begin to bother him again and he was unable to train until 3 January. With almost no preparation he's thrown himself into the game at Stamford Bridge but looks hesitant and makes several mistakes. A clear indication that perhaps he's come back too soon.

Cancelo is facing different challenges. He's the kind of player who excels when his confidence is high, as we saw over the last two seasons. During that time his performances have become increasingly impressive and in September and October he had several outstanding games. However, being sent off against Fulham after gifting a penalty hit him very hard. His performance immediately slipped and his confidence was desperately low as the World Cup started. He began the competition as a guaranteed starter for Portugal but his inconsistent performances landed him on the bench before too long. He returned to Manchester with his tail between his legs; he played 20 minutes against Leeds on 28 December but his discomfort was still very clear. Today, Pep's put him on the right wing in a similar position to the one he played in their defeat by Liverpool at Anfield last October. It's a position that takes him out of the zones he's most comfortable in and it's obvious that he's struggling.

On paper at least, Pep's plan is designed to thwart Chelsea's playing style. He has a defensive line of Walker, Stones and Aké, which means they can initiate play in the midfield alongside Rodri and Silva. Ahead of them, Gündoğan and De Bruyne are ready to send the ball to their forwards, Cancelo, Haaland and Foden. Whenever their opponents have the ball, Rodri retreats to the backline and Gündoğan occupies his place so that City can defend in a 4–4–2. The plan doesn't really translate to the pitch, though. On the wing, Cancelo is trapped between Cucurella and the touchline. Over on the other side, Foden's poor form is preventing him from beating Azpilicueta and, if I'm honest, he doesn't seem to be making that much of an effort to do so. Haaland doesn't get a sniff of the ball until 20 minutes in and can barely move because of the pressure from their opponents' centre-backs, so the ball is passed backwards and forwards between the five men at the back. It's a fiasco and City don't even manage a shot on goal until 32 minutes in, when Gündoğan makes a half-hearted attempt. This is the latest they've delivered their first shot on goal in the last four years. To make matters worse, the central corridor is without the usual protection provided by Rodri and the two false full-backs, leaving a gap through which Kovačić and Havertz make repeated runs, while Pep's men pursue them like headless chickens. A good shot from Carney Chukwuemeka thankfully hits the post.

Over in the dugout Pep, Rodo Borrell and Enzo Maresca have got their heads together. They need a different strategy. Right now, Walker and Cancelo are only managing 85 per cent accuracy, 5 points less than the team's average.

After the break, Lewis comes on for Walker and Akanji for Cancelo, and everything falls back into place. Rodri's king of the centre circle and Lewis changes the rhythm on the right while Gündoğan controls the left flank.

De Bruyne is now free to move wherever he wants, although he also has to drop to the right, given the lack of a pure winger. Seven minutes later, City have already established 86 per cent average possession. Aké's header hits the post, Haaland shoots wide and De Bruyne's shot is saved brilliantly by Kepa. Clearly, by returning everyone to his 'proper' place Pep has changed everything. Already, the team looks comfortable and productive.

Mahrez and Grealish, both of whom started the last two games, come on at 60 minutes. They were roundly criticised after the draw against Everton, when people accused them of being too conservative, but Pep has blind trust in their technical qualities and in their ability to control the ball, even if it involves them taking fewer risks than their teammates. Three minutes after coming on, Grealish takes advantage of a Gündoğan–De Bruyne sequence to send a curving pass beyond the defenders to Mahrez, who slots it home. It's a good goal, assisted in this case by Kepa's sudden state of paralysis, which gives them the result they need to reduce the points difference with Arsenal to five. City will be masters of their own destiny once more.

Several key players are still feeling the effects of the World Cup, notably Silva, Cancelo, Foden and Walker. On the plus side, Stones is better than ever and is even outplaying the superb Akanji and Aké at the minute. Lewis, Grealish and Mahrez are also on top form, and Haaland and Gündoğan near as dammit. It's going to be a team effort to get back to the City that we know, as Carles Planchart tells me as we leave Stamford Bridge: 'It's up to all the rest of us to support the guys who are a bit below par so that they recuperate fully.'

For Pep, tonight, it's all about the Rico effect: 'Rico Lewis makes his teammates play better. He changed the game. He's our mini Philipp Lahm.'

So, the false-full-backs: from Walker to Cancelo to Lewis … Waves ebbing and flowing on the ocean's surface or Guardiola's Gulf Stream?

You decide.

SCENE 15. YOU GO, KYLE!

Manchester, 8 January 2023

Pep's gobsmacked.

His eyes fill with tears, as he covers his face with his hands.

It reminds me a bit of that night in Munich many years ago when Lewandowski scored five goals in nine minutes against Wolfsburg, one of Bayern's toughest, meanest Bundesliga opponents at the time.

Out there, Kyle Walker has just changed the entire game. He's dribbled round defenders like the next Andrès Iniesta or Zinedine Zidane, then sent a perfectly timed Bernd Schuster-/Toni Kroos-like long ball so that Foden can score City's third goal. Pep's still not looking when the ball hits the back of the net.

They've played 37 minutes of this FA Cup game against Chelsea. It's the second time the two sides have met in just 68 hours and Pep's decided to go 'old school'. They bring the ball out in a 3+2 and switch to a 2+3 as they attack. Walker, Akanji and Laporte are the first line of the build-up with Sergio Gómez and Rodri in midfield. Chelsea's Havertz, Mount and Ziyech combine to press City hard, sticking close to each other for maximum impact. Nine minutes in, Pep seeks an antidote: Silva moves back to pair up with Rodri while Walker and Gómez move wide.

City have moved to a 2+4 formation. They're now in full-on attack mode, unleashing havoc as they drive down the wings. Chelsea don't stand a chance. Mahrez expertly converts a free kick, then Álvarez's penalty hits the back of the net, narrowly evading Kepa's outstretched hand. A noble effort by the talented Basque keeper but it's City's day – the ball belongs to them. Chelsea stick the 'out to lunch' notice up and sit back, looking totally dejected and losing ball after ball to City's ruthless pressing. As Carles Planchart tells me later: 'The lads ran their legs off but, even more importantly, they used that running to put pressure man-to-man on our opponents. That made all the difference.'

Mahrez is outstanding and directs Pep's strategy of luring Chelsea's defenders into the Citizens' cul-de-sac with intelligence and flair. He's got plenty of back-up of course – Álvarez, Foden, Palmer, Bernardo, Rodri and Walker are all on top, high-energy form. Time and again they trap Chelsea close to the left-hand corner and then take the ball off them. Seven Citizens make quick work of the eight Chelsea players valiantly trying to bring the ball out. On the few occasions they do manage to escape City's press, Graham Potter's men then have to face the combined might of Akanji and Laporte, who are stationed high up the pitch, about 58.5m away from their goal, ready and more than able to rob the Blues of the slightest of chances. In the first half alone, City short-circuit Chelsea's build-up 15 times. On eight of those occasions, the Blues don't make it past the centre circle.

Just past the half-hour mark, Bashir Humphreys, under pressure from Álvarez, sends the ball into space – just 'getting rid'. Rodri picks it up and immediately wants to let the team shift, positionally, into attack mode. Everyone quickly readjusts. Walker and Silva slow down their passing tempo so that Akanji and Laporte have time to retreat into City's backline. Within seconds the team has reformed into a 2+4 and Ortega starts to bring the ball out. It's Walker who receives it but he's being pinned on the wing by Lewis Hall. He can't pass back, Kovačić is blocking his path to Akanji, and he can't pass forward, there's nobody free and in position. Three feet behind him, Pep crosses his arms – no way out of this.

But Walker has other ideas. Having received the ball on his right foot, he moves it to his left, feints, goes back to his right, shakes Hall off and makes his break. He gets just yards up the pitch. Now, he's in even more trouble. Half of Chelsea's entire team descend upon him, sharks going in for the kill. Call it survival instinct or gut reaction, it's certainly not a conscious decision, but in that moment the big defender instinctively understands something … *If they're all coming for me, then that means someone else must be free* … He looks up, spots Sergio Gómez on the opposite wing, and thumps the ball 60m up the pitch. Pep buries his face in his hands: 'What have you just produced, Kyle?!'

Gómez feeds Rodri and receives again from the pivot's backheel. Gómez nips round Jorginho and Gallagher, and passes to Palmer, who calmly sends it back to Rodri. By this time, there are nine Londoners around the Spaniard, all of them having belted across the pitch away from Walker. Once again, it's instinctive: Rodri knows that Mahrez will now be free on the other wing. There's always someone free on the wing in Pep Guardiola's City. Twenty metres away, Walker's gesticulating furiously, telling him exactly where to aim the ball. But Rodri doesn't even need to look. He thumps the ball high. Time seems to stand still … And then nine Chelsea players burst into life. They hare back across to the other side of the pitch. Three 180-degree mass sprints in the space of a few short seconds. Walker's already running, speeding up the pitch into the 'no. 10 space'. He sends a deadly 'no-look' pass to

Foden, who, somehow, defying the laws of biomechanics completely, twists his hip and his ankle and sends the ball into Chelsea's net. It's the fifth season in a row he's scored in an FA Cup tie. A competition record.

This goal's a work of art. I'd call it exceptional but for the fact that it's fairly typical of the quality of football we've become used to from City. In the space of 1 minute and 2 seconds, every single City player except Álvarez has been directly involved – a total of 53 touches – and Chelsea haven't got a single boot on the ball. Everything about this goal has the Guardiola brand stamped all over it: a slow, controlled build-up within an established structure; technical brilliance, from someone not known for his technical wizardry; repeated use of the attraction–liberation principle (drawing your opponent in one direction in order to free up other zones); control and variation of the rhythm of play; establishing superiority in space; moving up the pitch through free space; the winger, open on the flank, waiting to receive the ball; the low, hard cut-back once in the Chelsea penalty box ...

After a superb start to the season, Kyle Walker has struggled with repeated injuries, meaning that he's only played 11 of the last 34 games. Despite this, his hard work has turned him into a superb inside midfielder/full-back without losing any of his physical strength. Before the World Cup he'd committed to putting in the extra work to become a better player: 'I'd like to start giving more assists, get further up the pitch and get balls into the box more. Up till now my role has been more to do with controlling transitions rather than providing assists. We're very lucky to have so many players who give a lot of assists without me having to get involved so high up the pitch. But if could add that to my repertoire ...' Which is why he did so much individual extra work on developing his technical understanding and abilities: when to stay in position to defend against the opponent's transition, when to move up and get involved in the attack. Today, Walker's demonstrated his newfound vision and technical nous: outstanding dribbling; a sensational long pass; high-speed penetration, timed to perfection; and a precisely judged assist.

Pep's delighted with today's performance. Doubly so. Not only have they thrashed Chelsea 4–0 but he's just watched Walker demonstrate how far he's come since they had those one-to-one sessions together.

You go, Kyle!

SCENE 16. BREAKING UP

Southampton, 11 January 2023

The devil is in the details and, sometimes, there's a mere hair's breadth between offering constructive advice and piling on the criticism.

St Mary's Stadium lies on the River Itchen, just a few miles from the English Channel. The humidity of the coastal climate makes it tough to maintain the pitch in good condition and today it's in a terrible mess – bumpy, rough and slippery. But that's not what's bothering the Cityzens. This is the quarter-final of the League Cup, and their worst performance since Pep took over. It's not just that they end up losing 2–0, these things happen, it's the way they've played. Pep's men sleepwalk through the game, as if unable to summon up any real desire to win, and produce none of their usual attacking threat.

Judging on today's performance they don't have a hope in hell of winning the title. Sergio Gómez struggles in defence. Kalvin Phillips looks like a baby deer surrounded by hungry lions and fails to demonstrate any of the impressive qualities he displayed with Leeds. Cole Palmer still seems unclear as to whether he should be following his own instincts or actually doing what he's been told to do. And as for the 'stars', the guys who, three months ago, were guaranteed regulars …

Foden is a shadow of the magnificent player we know him to be, as if participating in the World Cup has stripped him of all the ability he ever had. Cancelo is also light years away from the guy who used to direct and control the rhythm of play with such flair. De Bruyne, Haaland, Akanji, Aké and Rodri come on in the second half, and run Southampton off their feet, but even their contributions can't shake their own side from its stupor.

For the second consecutive season, City are eliminated from the competition that, between 2017 and 2020, seemed made for them alone. With today's result, City have lost 55 of the 380 matches they've played in the last seven seasons. That's just 14.47 per cent but it's their worse showing yet. There have been other massive disappointments, of course: losing 4–2 to Leicester and 4–0 to Everton in Pep's first year; the panic they experienced at Anfield; losing to Monaco, Tottenham and Lyon in the Champions League … but in all of those games, his men fought until the final whistle with every ounce of energy and determination. They hadn't always played brilliantly but their will to win was never in doubt. Here today, though, it's a different story. There's no ambition, no cohesion, no sign of City's fighting spirit, no sign of their game. They've not had a single shot on goal, only the third time this has happened since Pep took over.*

Another bleak stat from today's debacle? It's Pep's 100th defeat as a coach, 100 losses in 800 games (12 per cent). Although losing the game isn't a disaster in itself, it serves to highlight everything that's wrong in the team right now. Everyone's pissed off, some more angry at themselves than each other, although that's not necessarily how they express it. The team has reached an unprecedented crisis point: a mix of irritation, apathy, confusion and egotism. Almost like they're going through a messy break-up.

Pep lets rip in the dressing room. He's as furious as he's ever been and he doesn't hold back. This has been building for weeks. Retaining the title for the third year will be a colossal task, particularly with Mikel Arteta's Arsenal in the ascendancy, not to mention Pep's determination to make it to the Champions League final again. He's totally disgusted with the state some of his players are in after the World Cup and the way they've tackled the second part of the season. And he's made it clear how unhappy he is, calling out players whose body language he considers less than ideal. Today he tells them, 'When you don't bother to prepare properly for this kind of game, you come to every duel a second late and you end up not scoring goals.'

And the world is watching. When Cancelo is booked for taking a foul throw, the cameras turn to City's dugout, where Pep and Maresca seem to be having an angry exchange about the player ...

Two days later, the press is full of the news that several European clubs are interested in signing Cancelo. It surprises no one. He's had a bad run of late: his poor man-marking of Salah, which resulted in Liverpool's win, and his foul on Harry Wilson in the Fulham game. Since then, his form has become progressively worse and none of the technical team have been able to turn things around. The Portuguese is clearly struggling emotionally. A sensitive soul who can become overwhelmed by too much criticism and

---

* It occurred on 26 October 2016 against Manchester United (1–0), another League Cup game, and on 4 April 2018 against Liverpool (3–0) in the Champions League.

correction, he doesn't cope well when relations become tense, and just one look at his face tells you he's close to breaking point. His performances, which had already begun to dip before the World Cup, continued to deteriorate during the competition and he's continued his downward trajectory since coming back to Manchester. It's been a dramatic slump, made all the worse by the player's refusal to accept that he's playing badly coupled with his determination to blame everyone else. Pep opted not to use him in the last game of 2022, against Everton, and Cancelo stormed into the dressing room, post-match, absolute furious that Pep hadn't given him a single minute of playing time. Six days later, at Stamford Bridge, he made it into the starting 11, on the right wing, but was taken off for Akanji at half-time. More rage and resentment. Today, against Southampton, his indignation and displeasure are evident in the apathetic way he moves across the pitch. In Cancelo's mind, he's lost his rightful place in the team and he's not happy. Neither is Pep.

We all make mistakes. Pep understands that. But, in his view, many of the tactical and technical errors he's seeing are the result of apathy and a lack of commitment. They're clearly tired of winning so much, which is, he tells them, the greatest sin any player can commit. With every day that passes, the Catalan's getting angrier and angrier with those players he considers unwilling to give their all in training or in games. He's also becoming more and more aggressively vocal about his feelings and it's creating a barrier between the coach and some his players. Evoking orchestra–conductor analogies again, Pep was the Karajan of football, then he understood the benefits of becoming more of a Bernstein. At the moment, it feels like we're watching his metamorphosis back into Karajan, complete with that wall elevated between him, the maestro, and his players, the orchestra. Not good.

Gündoğan has been close to Pep from day one and, post-match, he has a warning for the team. If you were unaware of the context, it would seem way out of character for the German: 'I just hope we can look back in a few weeks' time and be able to take something positive from this game. We don't deserve a better result. We didn't perform like the City everyone knows – in attack or defence. We weren't aggressive or consistent enough and we didn't win enough duels. We messed up a lot of easy passes, we failed to establish our rhythm and we didn't create enough chances. It's obvious to me that something's lacking, something's not working. We've lost our spark: our performance, our hunger and our ambition just aren't what they have been in the last few years. I just hope that this is the wake-up call we need.'

Two days later, Pep tells me, 'All I can do is tell them the truth, when things are going well and when things are going badly. I'm the only person who tells it like it is. That's what I'm here for, to hold a mirror up to each of my players. There's nothing else I can do. I've done similar things in the past and I've started to do it here recently, and I'll keep doing it. Day in, day out. I've been doing it all this week. Sometimes I don't even have to say anything. One look at my face is enough. They're maybe not used to this kind of treatment because they're all surrounded by people endlessly telling them how wonderful they are. I'm the only person in their lives who gives it to them straight.'

His message is crystal clear: 'If you still want to win, give yourselves a shake. Drop the attitude, stop moping, put your backs into it and get with the programme. Being a big name with a few trophies under your belt … doesn't matter a damn.' It's the right message for the players. But it's also a message Pep needs to hear himself and, with Lillo gone, there's no one willing or able to challenge him on his own behaviour.

Perhaps he needs to have a look in the mirror too …

The great Argentine volleyball coach Julio Velasco coined the phrase 'the theory of excuses' to refer to the period in which a failing team begins to look for excuses to justify their poor performance. He also argues that, if the same team refuses to make excuses, then it's possible to become successful again. This depends on every component part 'accepting the challenge. If that doesn't happen, it won't work. Depression will set in. You have to create this sense of rising to the challenge. You adapt to the circumstances. You don't make excuses. You adapt.'*

Pep, who's a good friend of Velasco's, wants his men to apply this theory: 'Blaming their experiences on the World Cup isn't acceptable. Every club in the country had players there. All great clubs play 10 or 15 games more than everyone else. Perhaps you think that's unfair and maybe it is. We have to play more games than other teams. But if you don't like it, you're welcome to leave. Go and play for a team that has one game a week. If we were

---

* Isaac Lluch interview with Julio Velasco, *The Tactical Room*, no. 65 (June 2020).

capable of winning before, we're capable now. The World Cup? Keep your excuses for your free time. Don't make them here.'

Nowadays, analysts talk endlessly about tactics but what's actually happening at City just now is all about feelings and relationships. A football team is a living, breathing thing and its health is predicated on the quality of the interactions of all its component parts. Positivity contributes and increases the group's performance and negativity destroys it. We've already lived through Pep and Sterling's messy break-up: two long years of division and disagreement, which benefited nobody. Hopefully this crisis won't get to that stage but the barrier that's forming is clear to everyone. And, in particular, Pep's relationship with Cancelo is clearly foundering.

For Pep, it's up to the players responsible to sort themselves out. For their part, his players desperately need the coach to pull himself out of his bad mood and give them a chance. It's the fine distinction between advising and criticising. Their results this year will depend on how well they resolve the current conflict.

Are they going to break-up or make-up?

SCENE 17. TAKING A SWING
Manchester, 19 January 2023

So far in his coaching career, Pep Guardiola has held almost 1,600 press conferences. I've seen almost all of them: many during the Barcelona days, all of them at Bayern and almost every one he's done at City. Two stand out. The first took place on 26 April 2011 in the Bernabéu, the day before the tumultuous, hard-fought Champions League semi-final against Mourinho's Real Madrid, when Pep referred to the Portuguese coach as 'the fucking boss, the fucking chief'. The second has just happened. Here, in the bowels of the Etihad, Pep Guardiola has finally cracked. As his fist slams down on the table it's very clear how much he'd love to take a swing at his players, the board, City's supporters …

He's had enough.

Enough of the kid gloves, enough of the happy-flowers team, enough of 99 per cent effort. It's either 100 per cent from everyone or it's *adiós*.

He doesn't have to threaten to leave. His message is clear. It's a cry from the heart but it's also a declaration of war. On apathy and complacency. He's demanding a radical change in attitude. Otherwise this is the end of the project. And the end of the Guardiola era in Manchester. It's as simple as that. Either we're in this together, all the way, or I'm off. *Gracias* and goodbye.

Pep's chosen today, after City have just pulled off an incredible victory, to make his feelings felt. He could have said all this last Sunday but City had just been beaten 2–1 at Old Trafford after a flagrantly offside goal from Marcus Rashford had been allowed by the referee. Had the Catalan spoken up then, he'd have been accused of sour grapes – Pep finding something to moan about out of pique at his team's defeat. Never mind the fact that the referee had messed up big time. He'd had to hold his tongue. Until now. (Three weeks after this press conference, the director of English referees, Howard Webb, will publicly acknowledge that the goal should have been disallowed. But that doesn't give City the points they were robbed of back again.)

There's stunned silence in the Etihad dressing room. It's half-time and Spurs have just scored two goals in quick succession. Everyone's numb with shock – Guardiola, his players, the fans … They've actually played pretty well and have managed to keep Tottenham's major weapon, their ferocious counterattacking, under control. But Antonio Conte's men are also on form today and have successfully shut down the space that Gündoğan and Álvarez need to make their runs. They've also made sure Grealish and Mahrez are double-marked every time they try to move up the pitch. The combination of Højbjerg's aggression, Rodrigo Bentancur's smarts and Kulusevski's technical skills is proving too much for City even though the voracious Harry Kane keeps finding himself shackled by the assiduous marking of Manuel Akanji.

They're using a typical Guardiola game plan: three centre-backs (Stones, Akanji, Aké), two in the midfield (Rodri and Lewis), who ensure that City's attack moves fluidly up the pitch to where the five forwards are waiting; Grealish and Mahrez are on the outside today, Gündoğan and Álvarez inside, and Haaland is up front. Conte's come up with the perfect antidote, though, and his five defenders repeatedly block City's attack.

As ever, it's a mistake that breaks the stalemate. Ederson passes a sloppy ball in Rodri's direction. It's a gift for Kulusevski, who intercepts and slams it away. City's players run round like headless chickens for a couple of minutes, trying but failing to get the ball off Spurs, who, unsurprisingly, follow up with their second goal of the day. Emerson Royal scores it after City lose a succession of duels across the pitch. Two minutes and eight seconds after their first one.

Guardiola's stunned, totally appalled at what he's seeing and his mood isn't helped when, minutes later in the dressing room, he's informed, incorrectly, that the home support were booing his players as they trooped off the pitch. (A few City fans were booing but it was aimed at referee Simon Hooper, who had ignored Tottenham's repeated fouling of Lewis, including one clash in which Højbjerg stamped on the youngster's ankle and his leg.) But more than anything he's furious with his men: the number of duels lost; the general panic after the first goal; their failure to react to Tottenham's dirty tackles on Lewis plus the ponderous way they've played … it's all too much. He's not even going to bother telling them how to sort this. His men sit, speechless, in their customary semi-circle, looking utterly dejected and waiting for the mother of all tongue lashings. And they're not disappointed. Pep lets them have it. They're complacent and self-satisfied, carried away by their own greatness. They've lost their hunger and their edge … He knows they're not even aware how complacent they've become. It's a cycle we often see in sport. You make it to the top and then you start to settle, you begin to tread water and your performance slips. But, if you want to be a world-class competitor, there's only one way to get to the top and stay there. You must never, ever settle, never stop pushing yourself. Take your foot off the pedal for a second and the rot sets in. Which is exactly what's happened here. All their success has swollen one too many heads and several of the men sitting in front of him, right now, are coasting. And that's what costs you the millimetre of space you need to win a duel, or block a goal, or score a goal. That's all it takes. A little less effort, a millimetre of space, and before you know it, you're crashing down the table. Without even knowing why …

It's up to them now. Pep doesn't make even the tiniest of adjustments to his game plan. There are no instructions. Nobody's going to be warming up for the second half (and bear in mind, he has De Bruyne, Bernardo, Cancelo, Walker and Foden all on the bench). No changes, no reinforcements today.

Get the hell out there and sort it out yourselves.

Pep turns on his heel and leaves the dressing room.

The second half kicks off and everything suddenly feels very different. City's defenders are now winning all their duels, and Rico Lewis gives us two for the price of one in his dual role of inside full-back à la Philipp Lahm (facilitating the build-up as far as the centre circle) and attacking midfielder in the image of a traditional no. 10. Fifty-four passes, 96 per cent on target. He's spectacular as he breezes up the pitch, completely unperturbed by the wolves in the white shirts snapping at his heels. In front of him, Grealish and Mahrez have also hit their stride, remorselessly attacking from the outside in order to lure their opponents, each Spurs full-back given a personal praetorian guard ready to do or die. So, with wingers helping defenders, Emerson and Kulusevski block Grealish, and, on the other flank, Ivan Perišić and Son go up against Mahrez. City's objective is now to draw the opposition in one direction, so that there's always one of their own unmarked. Today it's Rodri and he's off like a rocket, forming a horizontal line of attack with Grealish and Mahrez. The three of them are about to turn this whole game on its head.

City are now effectively attacking with six men while Spurs still have just five in defence. It's Pep's numerical superiority in action. Lewis pelts up the pitch; he passes to Mahrez, who sends the ball to Álvarez. The youngster takes the shot. And scores. Two minutes later, Haaland gets the equaliser. City again construct a six vs five attack, although this time they progress horizontally. Mahrez pulls two of the Londoners towards him, leaving Rodri free to send the gentlest of chips to Mahrez, who nods down for Haaland. Two goals, 2 minutes and 9 seconds apart. But City aren't finished. This time it's Grealish who drags his opponents towards him before passing quickly to Rodri. The Spaniard's internal compass is, as ever, pointing due north, and he drives across the pitch so that Mahrez, who beats Perišić to the ball, can dribble inside and shoot off his right: 3–2 to the Cityzens. The home fans roar their approval while, down on the pitch, it's delighted hugs and pats on the back all round. But wait, Tottenham are on the move again. It's one of their glorious counters. A killer assist, Kulusevski to Perišić, 4m away from goal and the ball's heading straight into City's net …

Or is it?

It's another miraculous, championship-saving moment. Like Stones against Liverpool (2018–19) or Aké against Arsenal (2021–2), Lewis sticks his leg out and blocks what was definitely going to be the equalising goal. The Etihad explodes with rapturous applause for their young hero. The battle rages on until, in the dying minutes, Ederson gets the chance to redeem himself with a killer long pass to Mahrez. Clément Lenglet misjudges controlling a ball dropping out of the sky with his thigh, facilitates the Algerian and the second half's best player lobs Lloris for 4–2. Game over.

They've pulled off another epic comeback. The fifth time in a row that the team has fought back from two goals behind in a Premier League game (three victories and one draw). It's also the first time Conte's Tottenham has conceded four goals in the space of 45 minutes. Apart from their head-less-chicken moment in the first half, City have played impressively. We've seen good, solid defending from the three centre-backs and exceptional foot-ball from Rodri and Lewis. Gündo has played with his usual intelligence and flair while Álvarez has been a ball of electric energy and speed. Grealish is back on killer form. And Mahrez, a whirlwind of power and skill, has prob-ably just given his best-ever performance in the Premier League.

So, as the Etihad rejoices and City's players trot off the pitch, delighted with the result, what of Pep? He doesn't mince his words:

I don't recognise my team, they [previously] had the passion and the desire to compete. We are far, far away from the team we had in previous seasons. Do you think this comeback will happen every time? It won't. Today we were lucky. But we're nowhere near being able to compete at the highest level. I'm saying this today when we played good and we won, but, sooner or later, if we don't change, we'll end up winning noth-ing. We were lacking in passion! We have an opponent in Arsenal who have the fire. Two decades without winning the Premier League. They bite and snap at us, they fight to the death in every duel, for every ball.

We are very far away way from what we were, from a lot of things. No passion, no fire, no desire to win. If we don't change, sooner or later we're going to drop points.

I'm just explaining the reality, everything is so comfortable here … but opponents don't wait. If we want to win something or compete … but with the non-stop moaning, there's no chance we'll win anything.'

Not even tonight's standout hero, Mahrez, escapes the coach's sarcasm:

> Riyad Mahrez, what a player. Before the World Cup, he behaved as
> though this was a holiday camp. Now, finally, he's got the message, 'Duh!'
>
> My players want to do well. They work hard at training and they
> want this. But there's just something, something in the atmosphere,
> that's difficult to describe. Thousands of details we're getting wrong
> and that makes all the difference. And it's not just one player, it's all of
> them. And Arsenal's doing everything right, which is why they deserve
> to be leaders. What have they got? Two decades without winning the
> title. That's why they bite. We've won four titles in five years and now
> we're comfortable. It's a human tendency, when you've won so much
> … But I won't accept it.
>
> We're a happy flowers team, all nice and good. Everyone's so
> comfortable here, the players, the fans … but I don't want us to be
> happy flowers, I want to beat Arsenal. And if we play like today, Arsenal
> will destroy us.

Despite his scathing criticism of the team, Pep does have words of praise for
three players: 'We need the passion of Julián, Rico and Nathan. We need it.
They fight every duel, they fight for every ball as if it's the last thing they'll ever
do, it's all about attitude. Without that kind of passion we'll never get anywhere.'*
The Catalan saves his thoughts on City's supporters and the directors of
the club for last. Neither group come out of smelling of roses:

> I'm in the stadium and all I can hear are the Spurs fans. [Our team]
> lacked balls, passion, fire, hunger from the first minute but so did our
> fans who were silent for 45 minutes. I want the old fans back! Our
> travelling support are absolutely brilliant, but I also want our fans in
> the Etihad supporting us, pushing us, demanding more, making some
> noise. They should be screaming, "Come on lads! We know how good
> you are, show us what you're made of." You can't wait till we're losing

---

* Rico Lewis tells me later, 'I never think about whether I'm going to get a game or
not. For me, every time I'm picked to play, it's like a gift.'

2–0 to react. We were lucky today and we've made a few good come-backs of late but nine out of ten times you're not going to come back …

His final pointed words are for the directors: 'And I expect a reaction from all levels of the club, not just the players.'

Today's outburst has been a calculated risk on Pep's part. He's been thinking about it for weeks if not months, as he's grown ever-more frus-trated, repeating instructions and demanding better performances. He's watched them make error after absurd error, mistakes that cost them goals and points, knowing that it's not because of a lack of talent or tactical and technical deficiencies. It's about complacency. Most of all he's furious that the team as a group tolerate these errors without a murmur.

Pep wants to win, to win with passion, total commitment and obsessive dedication. Anyone who's unwilling to give 100 per cent, to go all in without lowering the pressure for one second … they may as well go now.

It's now or never. You're either with me or you're against me. He's fired his last shot tonight. Pep's always said that he'll go as soon as he sees the fire go out of his players' eyes. Well, it's the moment of truth – are they at the beginning of the end, or the end of their complacency? Only time will tell …

Meanwhile, as Spurs leave the stadium, we're all wondering if Pep had another, more subtle purpose for tonight's harangue. Mind games anyone?

SCENE 18. 'ARSENAL WILL TRIP UP'

Manchester, 22 January 2023

It's teatime in Manchester.

Down in London, Arsenal have just beaten Manchester United 3–2, giving the Gunners back their five-point lead (although they've played one game less). Midway through the game at the Emirates, with the match tied, their lead had dropped to three points, but neither that nor the eventual result has had any impact on Pep and his assistants up north. They know that they have to win 15 games to retain the title. With 18 left to play, there are 54 points up for grabs. But they're going to need to have a hell of a final sprint to their campaign.

They've done it before of course. Back in 2017–18, when they netted 18 consecutive league victories on their way to becoming the Centurions. In 2018–19, they won 14 games at the end of the season and beat the mighty Liverpool, who had been seven points ahead in January, to the title. And in 2020–1, they pulled off 15 wins in a row. If they manage to repeat the feat this year, they have a good chance of being champions again, although it's going to be a challenge. Arsenal have an incredible squad of players – young, hungry, aggressive, attacking, goalscoring – led by Zinchenko, who's in the form of his life.

In Manchester the view is: 'We just need to think about our own performance, about winning. Arsenal are bound to trip up eventually. We essentially have 18 finals ahead of us. And we need to win them all.'

They've started well: 3–0 against Wolves with a hat-trick from Erling Haaland, his fourth in the 19 league games they've played so far this season (his others were against Crystal Palace, Nottingham Forest and Manchester United). The Norwegian has scored 25 in the Premier League (18 at home). Which would have won him the Premier League's Golden Boot in any of the previous four seasons in which no individual player managed more than 23 goals. And, given that we're only halfway through the season, it means that he's scored a goal every 62 minutes in the league, which is pretty impressive. Ruud van Nistelrooy needed 65 games to score four hat-tricks; Luis Suárez, 81 games; and Alan Shearer, 86. For his 31 total (25 Premier League, 5 Champions League, 1 League Cup) he's taken 40 shots at goal, with 2 hitting the post. Perhaps the most startling statistic of all is that Haaland has actually missed 14 good chances. Which means that there's room for improvement.

Today, Pep's fielded the same team that pulled off the comeback against Spurs, except for two changes. De Bruyne is in for Álvarez and Laporte instead of Aké. Pep's been clear about this: 'Only those who deserve a place will get a place in the 11. Regardless of who it is!' There are definitely some disappointed faces sitting in the stands, although Foden's isn't one of them. He's only out because of a problem with his foot.

Today, Pep's players give him much more of what he wants to see: patience, mobility; a superlative Gündoğan appearing suddenly in free space; and the magnificent Rodri coordinating all their actions. Grealish and Mahrez are the living, breathing embodiments of the City brand and it's their efforts that make the first two goals. They stay wide, taking on defenders in one-vs-one duels so that they can then create chances in the box; if that's not possible because they're facing two markers (usually a winger and a full-back), they draw them out of position and then pass back to a teammate who will then move into the danger zone.

'We did almost everything well today,' Carles Planchart tells me. 'You can see how solid the team is. We've had a lot of good games lately but today we were really aggressive and that makes all the difference. They look good.'

There are other positive signs: the players all rounded on the referee after a bad tackle by a Wolves player and the fans have also been much more vocal today, their chants and songs giving City's players the impetus they need. Pep's tongue-lashing clearly hit home.

John Stones tells me: 'There were really mixed emotions after the Spurs game but we've put it right today. We know when we're not performing well. Pep let us have it at half-time and he was quite right. So we forced ourselves to have a bit more patience today, not to get frustrated when things didn't go our way. We set a very high bar in previous seasons and we're all now pulling together to get back to that level.'

Stones, in fact, is one of the players who is giving Pep the kind of performance he wants from everyone. A versatile, cool-headed footballer, he's one of Pep's 'triple-position' players and switches deftly between central defender, full-back and midfielder, depending on what is required at any given moment. Great ball control, technical ability, speed in transitions … Stones is the complete package.

The main takeaway tonight?

Pep's message is loud and clear: 'No one, except Rodri and Haaland, is guaranteed a place. I need to see you fighting for every ball in every single training session.' Johan Cruyff used to talk about the 'sacred cows' of any football team, the best, most experienced players. He liked to give those guys a bit of a wake-up call from time to time so that they didn't get too complacent. And Pep's taking a leaf out of the Dutch master's notebook. He's making sure his own sacred cows understand, once and for all, that nothing – not their big names, not their past achievements, not their seniority – guarantees them a place in Pep Guardiola's team.

One big fallout from this situation? Cancelo is seriously miffed and is making his feelings felt – very loud and very clear – in the dressing room, in the tunnel and on the phone to his agent, Jorge Mendes, 'Get me out of here!'

Pep just shrugs, 'Ah well, that's what great substitutes are for …'

SCENE 19. 'ARSENAL ARE GOING TO STUMBLE'

Madrid, 25 January 2023

'Arsenal will slip up. They're a fantastic side and Mikel is a superb coach but City have more experience in the final sprint towards the end of the season and that'll stand us in good stead.' Domènec Torrent's loyalties are, perhaps, somewhat divided. After his stints in charge of New York City, Flamengo and Galatasaray he's between jobs at the moment and has plenty of time to keep up to date with all things City. Pep's right-hand man from as far back as his Barcelona era, Domènec stayed in close contact with Pep when he left for New York and Dome sees as many Premier League games as he can.

But he's also a huge Arteta fan.

The pair of them teamed up in the summer of 2016, when Arteta, not long retired from playing, was offered a golden opportunity to join Guardiola's coaching team and grabbed it with both hands. Dome immediately took the shy, reserved newbie under his wing and made a point of going out of his way to ensure that Pep understood which brilliant ideas had come from the young Spaniard. Back then, Arteta was too shy and self-effacing to claim credit for his own contributions. The bond that was forged back then is as strong as ever and Dome has been blown away by what Arteta has done at Arsenal.

'He's doing fantastic work. And it's not just Mikel. The whole club is pulling together. They've had the good sense to let him make the decisions. He got rid of the players he didn't rate and has brought in lots of young talent. The club will obviously want results and there is bound to be a lot of pressure, but they've done him proud.

'City are still performing brilliantly. There was that short dip but they've got over that and are going to have a magnificent end to the season. It's obvious how much Haaland has changed their game. We don't see as many long passing sequences because Kevin always looks for Haaland. It means they don't so often establish superiority of numbers in any zone but if you look at the stats – Kevin's given 11 assists and Erling's scored 25 goals – it's worth the sacrifice. It may be that the team game is slightly less brilliant than it was last season but our new playing style might just end up being the thing that makes the difference in the Champions League. For years people have said that City need a really good striker if they're going to win in Europe. Well, now they've got him.

'Arsenal have an exceptional team. You don't get to 50 points at this stage of the season without being outstanding but City have much more experience of those last four months, which can be so tough. And Pep is Pep. He's the best there's ever been. I back Pep to win the final sprint.'

· · ·

Two days after my dinner with Dome in Madrid, Arsenal come to the Etihad in the FA Cup. Arteta's plan is to use man-to-man marking to corral City's key players and his men will be ready to take advantage of the slightest error from the home side. Of course, goalkeeper Stefan Ortega isn't being marked and not only does he make superb saves for Takehiro Tomiyasu and Trossard's shots, he distributes the ball like a perfect evangelical disciple. Haaland doesn't get to any of his long passes but Walker beats Zinchenko to them all, thereby winning a huge positional advantage for his team, which eventually bears fruit. Aké, who's defended like a tiger against Saka today, adds the breakthrough, just as he did last month in the League Cup against Liverpool.

Post-match, Pep is on chatty form – he heaps praise on the Dutchman and manages to stick the knife into a certain very disgruntled Portuguese. 'Everyone in the dressing room is over the moon for Aké. Or maybe everyone, bar one.' He's referring of course to João Cancelo, whose deal with Bayern Munich is agreed 48 hours later.

Breaking up. Not so hard to do after all.

Inevitably, the press want to know who his new left-back is going to be. Pep, straight-faced, muses aloud, 'Well … there are a few options: Aké, Laporte, Rico Lewis … and someone else who'd be brilliant there. I'll let you know …'

All heads turn to Phil Foden. As he knew they would. But it's a double-bluff. Pep knows exactly who it's going to be and it isn't the Englishman. It's another Portuguese. Watch this space …

SCENE 20. FIGHTING DEMONS
London, 5 February 2023

Arsenal take a tumble. City follow suit. Yesterday, after Arsenal's defeat in Liverpool, the title was within City's grasp. Today, frustratingly, they've just lost that advantage.

It's a bloody weekend all round for the big hitters of the Premier League. On Friday, Chelsea host Fulham at Stamford Bridge and just manage a draw despite their stellar lineup, which includes 'new' signings Enzo Fernández and Mykhailo Mudryk, both of whom cost a pretty penny in the summer. Then, Arsenal are overpowered by Everton, led by one of the few Premier League practitioners of good old-fashioned direct English football, Sean Dyche. Liverpool are up next for the slaughter. And it's a bloodbath, smashed 3–0 by Wolves. Even Eddie Howe's Newcastle only manage a draw at home to West Ham. So far, this weekend, only Manchester United have avoided the ill wind that seems to be wreaking havoc up and down the country.

Now, it's City's turn. It's not a meeting anyone's particularly looking forward to. Spurs away – City have lost all four of their last visits to the Tottenham Hotspur Stadium, failing to score a single goal in any of them, against Tottenham's six. Rodrigo Hernández proves it in the 14th minute, when he makes a mistake that allows the winning goal for Spurs and Harry Kane's number 267 in the white shirt, a record for the London club, one more than the legendary Jimmy Greaves.

Rico Lewis is in Cancelo's position today, alongside Rodri and in front of Walker, Akanji and Aké. They bring the ball out in a 3+2, sending it to Silva, who's stationed behind City's attacking line of Mahrez, Álvarez, Haaland and Grealish, who manages to keep slipping away from his marker to receive the ball. In order to slot Álvarez in, Pep has gone for Silva, who he

thinks will control the game better than De Bruyne in this particular formation. As ever, and especially since Haaland's arrival, he's looking for that
perfect balance between good control and full-on attack. It's a solid performance – not extraordinary – but full of energy and forward momentum. For
14 minutes, Spurs don't get anywhere near City's area. But then Rodri has
an idea. And, as it turns out, it's not a good one.

Instead of returning the ball to Ederson, he sends a risky pass in Lewis's
direction. The youngster is on the edge of the box, with Højbjerg bearing
down on him, and doesn't get to the ball. Harry Kane swoops in: 1–0 to the
Londoners. It's a similar error to the one Ederson committed against Spurs
two weeks ago. The kind of mistake that, in all honesty, is inevitable when
you play such daring, proactive football. But here, in north London, it feels
like so much more than that to Rodri.

The legendary Mexican diver Jonathan Paredes once said, 'In every
sportsman's brain rages an eternal battle with himself.' Right now, all
Rodri's hidden demons seem to be rising up to drag him down. He's assailed
by the same doubts he struggled with in his first season in Manchester, and
this time Fernandinho and Lillo aren't here to reassure him.* The human
brain is like a gigantic battleground, dark and murky, at times frighteningly
unfamiliar and disconcerting. Unfortunately for Rodri, football is played
in the brain. This is a man who has been Pep's most consistent player this
season (and last). Focused, determined, precise, at times exceptional, he's a
very, very good footballer whose been the mainstay of the team since 2021.
Rodri is that rarest of things: a guaranteed starter in a Pep Guardiola side.
But this one error knocks him for six, psychologically. Suddenly he looks like
he's never kicked a ball in his life before. He's all over the place, nervous and
hesitant, his passing erratic and clumsy. Back to his 2019 version.

And, of course, that knocks the rest of the team off balance too. De Bruyne
and Gündoğan come on but neither their efforts nor Mahrez's shot off the
crossbar do the trick. This is more than a problem of how to balance control
vs attack, this is a major psychological issue. Negative emotions crowding out
everything else with each new error, made manifest in the body language of
the whole team: wide-eyed stares, hunched shoulders, shaking heads …

---

* Isaac Lluch interview with Jonathan Paredes, *The Tactical Room*, no. 30 (April 2017).

The brain is the single most important muscle any sportsman or woman possesses. And City desperately need to sort this problem out. Guardiola leaping up and down on the touchline, as if he's a player himself, isn't helping. In truth, at some level, he probably understands that he's actually part of the problem. At the end of the day, any team is nothing more than a reflection of their coach. It's a battle every sportsperson has to fight. A battle with their own psychological demons. And, right now, City and Pep are losing the battle.

SCENE 21. 'NOW, MORE THAN EVER, I WANT TO STAY'
Manchester, 10 February 2023

Pep's had a hectic day. He spent the morning with Estiarte, getting ready for the lunchtime press conference before leading training and, since then, has been preparing for the game against Unai Emery's Aston Villa, who came very close to destroying City's title aspirations last season.

Last Monday, with no warning, the Premier League published a list of 115 charges against Manchester City, accusing them of having broken the financial fair play rules since as far back as 2009. The club's management immediately defended themselves, insisting that all their accounting practices were in order and that the accusations were totally unfounded. Shortly afterwards, it emerged that several of the charges were based on incorrect information.

Guardiola is the first staff member to find himself in front of the press. After consulting Estiarte he's decided on the approach he's going to take. One option was to simply point out the bleeding obvious; as coach, he has nothing to do with the financial management of the club and, in any case, the charges relate to a period of time before he was even considering coming to Manchester. But this is Pep Guardiola. Not a man to back down in the face of unjustified accusations. His sense of loyalty, to the club, the directors and the fans, is too strong. So, he goes on the attack.

I would say we are lucky we live in a marvellous country where everyone is innocent until proven guilty. We didn't have this opportunity because we are already sentenced.

When you read the articles you'll see that we are already being condemned. What has happened after Monday is the same as happened with UEFA. We were condemned. We have just a charge. With the accusation from UEFA, the club proved we were completely innocent, why should we now be condemned?

Nineteen teams of the Premier League are accusing us without the chance to defend. Ask the CEOs of those other clubs. Ask Daniel Levy. They want us out of the Premier League. But they've created a precedent and they should be careful in future. Many clubs have made insinuations and there are a lot of clubs who could be accused like we have been.

I haven't forgotten the nine clubs who wrote to the CAS [Court of Arbitration for Sport] demanding that they put us out of the Champions League. I haven't forgotten: Burnley, Wolverhampton, Leicester, Newcastle, Tottenham, Arsenal, Manchester United, Liverpool and Chelsea. I haven't forgotten that they wanted us put out of the Champions League so they could take our place, the place we've won on the grass. Julius Caesar said there are no enemies or friends, just interests.

What will happen if we are proven innocent? You are questioning like we have been punished. Just in case we are not innocent, we will accept the punishment. If we are guilty and they send us to a lower category, whatever, there won't be a problem. We'll call Paul Dickov and Mike Summerbee, and we'll move up again with the players that we have already.* But what will happen if we are innocent? How will they compensate us for the damage they've done to us? Condemned before guilt is proved.

I'm not moving out of this seat. I promise you. Now, more than ever, I want to stay here. I've had doubts in the past because it's many years in the Premier League, seven years, but now, I have no doubts at all: I'm going to stay right here. Look at what happened with UEFA. It's the same thing. Why shouldn't I trust my people? If it's a choice between people outside the club, and my people, I'm going to back my people.

---

* Mike Summerbee (b. 1942) was a legendary Manchester City striker, a contemporary and friend of George Best. He played 357 games for City, scoring 47. These days he's a club ambassador and a close friend of Guardiola's. Paul Dickov (b. 1972) played 174 games for City, scoring 35 goals. Today, he's a football analyst.

This is Pep in his purest state. No fear, total, categorical loyalty to his people, ready to step up and take responsibility and very happy to get right in your face. At the end of the day, any legal process takes time and he'll be long gone when this situation is finally resolved. But sitting back and just taking it is not an option. They're being attacked on all sides and Pep Guardiola is up front, exposed, leading the fight back, flying the flag for City. Behind him are thousands of fans who recognise their own fury and passion in this man. His words send a bolt of electricity through Citizens everywhere. Manchester City against the world.

He hits one wrong note though: 'I don't know if we are responsible for Steven Gerrard slipping at Anfield.' In 2014, Gerrard's slip against Chelsea had a major impact on City winning the title. It's a totally inappropriate comparison and, within days, Pep will contact Gerrard to apologise privately for 'my unnecessary and stupid comments' and then publicly withdraw the comments. A passionate man who, at times, goes too far, Pep's also big enough to acknowledge his mistake and make amends: 'I am ashamed of myself for what I said because he doesn't deserve it. I truly believe my comments about defending my club, but I didn't represent my club well putting his name in these stupid comments.'

Towards the end of what's been a brutal day, I manage to catch up with him. I'm curious to know why he decided to defend the club like this, instead of leaving it to the directors. He's done similar things in the past, at Barcelona and at Bayern, so I'm not wholly surprised by his response: 'I did it because I wanted to defend the things I love and the people who have shown me such affection and support. It's as simple as that.'

• • •

On Sunday, Pep's treated to a huge ovation from City's fans who get behind the team like never before, cheering them on to a comfortable victory with three goals in the first half (Rodri, Gündoğan and Mahrez). An enormous banner stretches across the terraces. 'Fight to the end'. Unsurprisingly, the Premier League anthem is greeted with boos and catcalls. It's a war cry. Total unity in the face of enemy fire.

When City don't have the ball, Bernardo Silva plays at left-back today. When Cancelo was let go, everything pointed to Silva stepping into his shoes. A player with huge tactical intelligence, he's the most versatile member of the squad: he's already played in every position except in goal. And today he doesn't disappoint. When he has the ball, he slots in as a second holding midfielder, working with Rodri to repel the visitors' press, although Villa's sole goal comes from a loose ball Silva can't get to. Without the ball, he defends like a full-back, although he tucks in alongside central defence to protect Laporte when the Spaniard joins City's attack force as the sixth forward (3–1–6 attacking formation against Aston Villa's 6–2–2). It's a bravura performance. Silva demonstrates yet again how brilliant he is in the heat of the action and the extent to which his performance dips whenever his allocated role keeps him at a distance from where play is developing. He has the kind of versatility and tactical flexibility that is going to be a godsend for the team in the coming weeks.

He'll often jokingly refer to himself as an attacking defender or a defending attacker, and they're actually pretty good descriptions of the role he plays. Post-match he tells me, 'It was challenging but fun. I love a tough opponent and always try to help the team as much as possible. I had to really focus on what I was doing, occupying the spaces and defending well. I didn't want to make any mistakes.'

Pep's been considering going back to playing with four in midfield (Rodri, De Bruyne, Gündoğan and Silva), which would give him an extra man in that area. His three forwards are untouchable so it would mean losing a defender, meaning that the fourth midfielder has to be capable of defending when necessary. Now, after much debate, Pep confirms that he's putting Silva in Cancelo's position. He may not be totally familiar with the full-back position but he's such an intuitive, natural footballer that he should take to it like a duck to water.

Arsenal have just lost two points at home against Brentford (1–1), which cuts their lead down to three. The two mighty sides will face each other on Wednesday, and Pep and his players are fully prepared. Everyone's wide awake and ready for the fight.

SCENE 22. ARSENAL SCREW UP

London, 15 February 2023

'Are you really going to put Bernardo Silva in left-back against Arsenal? Against a winger like Saka?'

'Definitely. Just wait and see. I don't see my players as defenders or attackers. All I see are footballers who can play in different positions at different times.'

Silva isn't quite so gung-ho: 'I'm not going to lie to you. It's very tough. When you play in those positions you have to start thinking like a defender and you can lose your attacking edge and momentarily forget everything you can do with the ball.'

After 101 days at the top of the table, Arsenal slip behind Manchester City, whose victory today puts them in pole position. Since January, Pep's men have won five out of the seven games they've played and lost two: 15 points. Arteta's lot have only won two out of six, drawing two and losing the other two, although their game against Everton is still outstanding and, theoretically, a win could put them back at the top spot. But, whatever way you spin it, it's not looking good for the Gunners. Having started the year seven points ahead of City, they've effectively squandered their lead. It's a screw-up.

Pep's anticipating that Zinchenko and Ødegaard will be on the inside as they bring the ball out and, just two days ago, he decided to change the structure of his own team without the ball. Since 2020 they've always used a 4–4–2 with a forward and an attacking midfielder up front and the wingers, in line with the other midfielder and Rodri, open on the flanks ready to block the advance of their opponent's full-backs. But Pep knows how dangerous Zinchenko and Ødegaard can be. Both are highly creative players who tend to position themselves around the centre circle where they can organise and direct the Gunners advance.

In his revised plan, Pep's tasked Mahrez and Grealish, his wingers, with the job of neutralising the two Arsenal players while De Bruyne and Gündoğan are sent to the wings. The team tried it out at yesterday's training – it's all the preparation time they have. Pep knows that they can expect the Londoners to dominate much of the game, so he's put Silva at left-back and the formidable Aké and Dias in central defence.

Usually, for 'easier' games, the ones City are likely to dominate, he'll use the defenders with the best ball control, a Lewis or a Laporte, for example. But for a game against a team like Arsenal, you need your big guns: Walker, Dias or Aké. The same applies to other zones too. You're more likely to see Silva and Gündoğan in the midfield if high levels of control and stability are required, but for speed and ferocious attacking you can't beat De Bruyne and Foden. It's all about matching the players with the right skillsets with each of the different opponents they play. It's not easy to find exactly the right balance, though, which is why Pep rarely ends up repeating the same lineup. At Bayern he played 100 games in a row without repeating a single lineup and he's taken the same approach at City. Your best 11's never your 11 best players, it's the lineup that is the most likely to beat the opponent you're facing.

Which is all great in theory.

Now, 20 minutes into the game, Eddie Nketiah has just wasted a brilliant pass from Zinchenko in front of goal and Pep turns to Rodolfo Borrell, 'This is shit. I've totally fucked up. It's not working.' And he's right. De Bruyne and Gündoğan look totally lost in this new structure where they're getting much less time on the ball. Arteta's outsmarted Pep by putting Zinchenko outside and asking Martinelli to generate play from the inside. City are struggling to shut down the central areas of the pitch and their 4–3–2–1 is pulled to pieces by Arteta's ruthlessly efficient strike force. Every time the Gunners make it past City's first line of defence, the Cityzens reform into a 4–1–4–1 in an effort to protect their area. But Pep's players aren't coping well with the new structure – they're struggling to put together even two passes in a row, let alone move up the pitch to launch their own attack. Pep will later tell his assistants, 'We ended up thumping long balls up the pitch. It was dreadful. Kicking the ball long is fine as long as you're doing it for a good reason but desperately thumping it just to get it away is another thing entirely.' But Ederson isn't prone to launching wild balls into nowhere and he, at least, continues to send long, accurate passes up the pitch. Tomiyasu is first to one such pass and, despite Grealish's hard pressing, he calmly passes back to his keeper to restart play. Minutes later, William Saliba intercepts another Ederson ball. The Frenchman heads it to Tomiyasu, whose backwards pass is slightly too short. De Bruyne is on it immediately and sends the ball soaring over Ramsdale's head. City go ahead. Not long after the break Rodri heads a chance against the Arsenal crossbar.

Towards the end of the first half, Xhaka breaks through City's lines to send a vertical pass to Nketiah and the move ends up in a penalty awarded against Ederson. It looks like the right decision by the referee but nobody in the dugout has missed the irony: just three days ago, the same thing happened in the Etihad, when Emiliano Martínez crashed into Haaland. On that occasion the foul was awarded against Haaland. These kinds of inconsistencies are not only extremely galling for the teams affected, who could be forgiven for feeling that there's a level of bias at play, but give an insight into the very real problems with Premier League refereeing, both on the pitch and behind the VAR screens. At half-time everyone in the dressing room is pissed off ... Pep decides to admit his mistake: 'Lads, I messed up. It was a terrible idea, let's get back to basics: without the ball, a 4–4–2, Riyad and Jack open on the wing, Kevin up front and Gündo beside Rodri.

'I know they're a tough team to play because they're very, very good and their man-marking is extraordinary. You're under a lot of pressure out there but I know you can handle it. You're very, very good as well. I want you to forget about pressing. Relax, pass the ball to each other and don't look for space so early, that's the quickest way to lose the ball. Stick close to each other, the closer you are, the easier you'll find each other. You can still send the ball long, but don't just smash it up the pitch with no specific intention.'

Pep now instructs Dias to mark Ødegaard, despite the fact that he has to cross half the pitch to do so, which will allow Aké to help Silva shut down Bukayo Saka. Rodri is given the job of sticking with the free-moving Martinelli, who, first half, kept getting in behind City. The changes transform the game and City's performance. But Pep has one more trick up his sleeve. At minute 61 he makes an unexpected switch: Akanji comes on for Mahrez, a central defender for a winger. It looks like a purely defensive move but turns out to be the turning point of the match, and perhaps the rest of City's league campaign.

Aké's now at left-back, with Silva moved to the right wing. They're now in a 4–3–3 formation for the build-up (instead of a 3–2–5), which gives them superiority as they bring the ball out. They outmanoeuvre their markers with sequences of short passes, combined with long balls sent towards

Arsenal's defensive line with the aim of winning all the 'second ball' challenges. Arteta looks on as Grealish beats Tomiyasu to the ball time and again, apparently unable to come up with a countermove to Pep's changes. Eventually, in the dying minutes of the game, he substitutes the Japanese player for Ben White. But it's too little too late.

Silva, back in the more familiar terrain of the right wing, goes on the rampage, aggressively pressing Arteta's men whenever they have the ball. It's like a homage to Jürgen Klopp's counter-press and Pep will later rave about his performance today: 'He's a diamond. Left-back or right wing, Bernardo always plays well, whatever his position, He's the complete footballer.'

But it probably wouldn't have been possible without Erling Haaland, a prodigiously talented goalscorer with the energy of ten men. *Homo haalandensis*, a new, more evolved species of the centre-forward. A beast of a man who hacks his way through lines of central defenders as if they're nothing more than bamboo canes ready to be snapped. His speed, the power of his sprints, his aggression and electric energy mean that Haaland is always running on the highest possible voltage. And today he's especially motivated. And very, very aggressive.

Arsenal's defenders are still putting up a good fight but even with the technical brilliance of Zinchenko, Xhaka and Martinelli, they're on a hiding to nothing. Silva, De Bruyne, Rodri and Walker overwhelm them, making it impossible for Arteta's men to hold on to the ball. Grealish and Haaland both find the net, in the 72nd and 82nd minutes respectively. It's a resounding win for the Citizens and puts them on top, at least for the time being.

It's Pep's seventh consecutive victory against the Gunners since 2020. City have had just 36 per cent possession today, their lowest percentage ever in a Premier League game and the second lowest across all competitions since Pep took over.* They've managed just 301 passes, compared to Arsenal's 522, roughly half their average, and only 72 per cent have found their target (20 per cent less than usual). Arteta's men have completed 20 sequences of 10 or more passes; City just 7.

---

* Against Barcelona they achieved 34.6 per cent in a 2016 Champions League game.

SCENE 23. MATCH POINT

Nottingham, 18 February 2023

The title race is as tight as ever and today there's high drama in Birmingham, where Villa host Arsenal and, two hours later, in Nottingham, where Forest and Man City go head to head. I'm reminded of the final scene in Woody Allen's film *Match Point* when the ball hits the top of the tennis net, wavers, swivels and hovers in the air for a fraction of a second before dropping down on one side.

Aston Villa go ahead twice, but Arteta's men, who are on splendid form, manage to equalise both times. Towards the end of the game, the Villans have another great chance but the ball hits Ramsdale's crossbar and it looks like they're going to have to settle for the draw. Then, unbelievably, 93 minutes in, Jorginho takes a shot from distance that hits the crossbar, bounces off Martínez's head and drops into the goal: 2–3 to Arsenal. Two of the Gunners seem offside and obscuring the goalkeeper's line of sight, but VAR remains silent. Then, in the final minute of the game, Martínez goes upfield for a Villa corner and Martinelli puts the ball into an empty net for Arsenal's fourth goal. It's a last-minute but well-deserved victory for the Gunners.

Meanwhile, all Pep's players can do is watch as the ball hits the back of the net: Forest have scored. City have dominated the entire game, at times achieving as high as 85 per cent and 91 per cent of possession. Silva's stationed at left-back today, although Pep's given him carte blanche to move wherever he wants on the pitch. He and the rest of the team have over-whelmed the locals with their interminable passing sequences and City have more or less set up camp in Forest's area to rain shot after shot down on Keylor Navas, who's had his best game of the season today.

City produce an incredible game – confident, precise and high-speed passing, fast, effective transitions and lots of chances on goal. But at half-time they're still just one goal ahead, scored by Silva from outside the area.

They continue to have numerous chances in the second half: Foden, Haaland, Rodri, Laporte, Grealish, Gündoğan … they all have a go but, somehow, the ball just doesn't go in. Only De Bruyne is looking a little off his game today. Then, just five minutes before the end, Forest penetrate City's area for the first time all game, and score. Forest 1 City 1.

It's the fourth game in a row in which City's opponent has converted their first chance. The Citizens have played brilliantly today but the result's a real blow and the tension's high in the dressing room post-match. Some old wounds are obviously still very raw …

SCENE 24. THREE OUT OF THREE, PLEASE

Manchester, 18 March 2023

After the missed opportunity in Nottingham there's an unremitting run of demanding matches. It starts with the draw in Leipzig – City establish control during the first 45 minutes, but then cling on for dear life in the second half. Next up, the Vitality Stadium: Rico Lewis's performance is the cherry on the cake of a 4–1 at Bournemouth who, *a priori*, look more testing than they prove to be in practice. The FA Cup means a visit to Ashton Gate and Bristol City, who're dispatched 3–0. Then, back home to the Etihad after five straight away matches in 13 days. It's the hard-running Newcastle who're visiting Manchester but are sent away with a 2–0 defeat in which Foden is flying. He equals his all-time season record of nine goals while Ederson's success in keeping the Magpies out means that he's reached 100 clean sheets since joining City (208 appearances). Arsenal, in the background, keep playing 'get out of jail free' cards with those goals in minutes 93 and 98 to beat Villa 4–2 and a similar late winner for 3–2 at home to Bournemouth – hats off to Reiss Nelson in the 97th minute. Without these Houdini acts Arsenal would, hypothetically, only hold a one-point advantage over City but their completely indomitable spirit and refusal to know when they're beaten means that the *actual* lead is five.

This is the moment Guardiola chooses to pronounce: 'Our next three matches will define our entire season. If we win them, we'll be alive in all three competitions – if we lose them then, frankly, it's all over.' He's drawing on 15 years of coaching experience and understands that both medium- and long-term planning in football can be a foolish waste of time and energy. You focus on the day to day – nothing more ambitious. In his mind it's crystal clear – City must win every remaining Premier League match. It's that simple. Forest was their last slip-up and there's no room, at all, for another. Winning 12 out of 12 includes beating Arsenal in London – and then hoping, praying, for Arteta's guys to stumble elsewhere. That's the only way City can retain the title. Which is why he's put such emphasis on his team's next three performances: the league match because it's a must-win, the FA Cup and Champions League because they're now knockout matches – winner takes all.

STEP ONE

The first test is passed, but not without a lot of effort. It's Palace in south London and everyone knows what to expect. The Eagles go 4–5–1 in shape, no surprise there, and dig in deep – 'Beat us if you can …' For long spells, it looks a futile and impotent effort – and, all the while, Ederson looks on, frustrated, with no work to do. Palace's end of the pitch is a frenzied mass of bodies, action, invention and intensity. Efforts at goal by Haaland, Grealish, Rodri, Foden and Álvarez fail to break the deadlock for one reason or another. Only when Palace temporarily try to draw breath and, simultaneously, drop their guard, can City break them down. Gündoğan receives a quickly taken short corner from Silva, heads goalwards and is tipped over – penalty! Meat and drink to Haaland. The final score is 1–0 and, for the first time this season, City have four straight Premier League wins. Arguably, the star of the show is Rodri – another demarcation of the fact that he's emerged as a smart, reliable, creative and powerful organising midfielder/pivot.

Leipzig can be a bitter pill and, in the build-up, Pep's tried hard to avoid focusing on how important the game is and, instead, to identify the German team's weaknesses. Reaching the quarter-finals, for what would be the sixth straight season, would be a big boost for City's momentum and confidence – but Guardiola keeps telling them: 'Treat it as just another match, heads down, hard work, do what we do best.' Two days before the match, City's coach has already decided how he wants to play Leipzig – and it's a departure from his usual approach. The away leg showed him Leipzig's strengths and, in particular, the left-sided connection between Joško Gvardiol, David Raum and Timo Werner. So, he's going to ask Silva to play as an offensive right-winger with particular responsibility for disrupting the connection between those three players. They can't be allowed to play out down their left with any kind of ease or efficiency.

Lillo is, as ever, Pep's sounding board on how to play this opponent. Instead of the good old days when they were around one desk in either man's Academy office, this is a FaceTime chat. Pep tells him: 'Three at the back [Akanji, Dias, Aké], three in the middle [Rodri, Gündoğan, De Bruyne], three forwards [Silva, Haaland, Grealish] and one in behind them aimed at winning us numerical superiority in the creative zone [Mahrez].' A big part of their chat is about the disadvantages of playing without a dedicated right-back and what advantages Mahrez's position can be expected to produce. For this match, Pep's modelled the Algerian's role on how he'd occasionally play Robben in his final season at Bayern. Mahrez actually played a very similar 'inside-forward' role against Leipzig before, leaving the wing-play to Walker. This will be a repeat, to an extent, but with Silva testing Leipzig on City's right, the Germans' left. The Portuguese will play 'open' and wide.

The tactical discussion lasts the same length as the match – 90 minutes. Geographically, they are far apart but, as the discussion shows, they've rarely been so in tune. They analyse how City dismantled Leipzig last season (6–2 in Manchester and 2–1 away). Were there weaknesses identified then that persist today? Pep's point of view is that he's not too worried if this match is much more 'back-and-forth' with fast transitions – something he firmly wanted to avoid in the first match three weeks earlier. This is an all-in night and, therefore, Pep's obsession with control levels out a little. Even more importantly, De Bruyne is back and ready to start.

Bravery is the watchword. Pep will sacrifice a little bit of control for what he hopes will be *blitzkrieg* damage to the visitors' game. Silva's work will be at the heart of this strategy: 'When he has the ball, his role is to find us numerical superiority with his movement and timing around the middle/creative areas. Without the ball, he's got to smash up their pretty play down their left.' The two Spaniards say goodnight around midnight. Forty-eight hours until kick-off but the plans are already set.

By now, you'll not be surprised that Pep tosses and turns all night, going over and over the strategy in his mind. All through Monday's training session, the subject is still percolating as he probes and checks for weaknesses. Eventually, he realises what's been nagging at his subconscious: the Silva circuit-breaker concept is good, but the absence of a right-back might, given Leipzig's power down their left, draw too much risk to the covering work which Akanji, Rodri and even Silva will need to do. Is the plan too risky? This is how he externalises the debate: 'Maybe I'm leaving the players too exposed? Am I substituting uncertainty where there should be security?' He's chewing on how to modify the plan, not thinking of abandoning it. Silva will maintain his dual role but he'll take Mahrez out of the 11 so that a more organising, more positional full-back/midfielder can be included. This might help Silva win superiority and bring strength in defending. Who then? Stones, of course.

There are other candidates: Lewis and Walker are obvious possibilities. The younger guy is profiling as precisely the kind of footballer who can play that full-back/organising midfielder role while Walker has played like this for Pep before and would be a good choice to try and asphyxiate Werner. However, it has come to light that Walker's behaviour wasn't A+ standard on the players' free weekend after the Newcastle win and he's back in the dog house with Pep. By midnight on Monday into Tuesday, Pep's finalised his game plan: 'I've decided that my original strategy might have unbalanced the team and disconcerted the players. Bernardo stays in position and has the same tasks … but Stones comes in to add security and organisation in his own double role on the right.' In Pep's mind, Stones will cover Werner, link well with Rodri, cover Silva down the City right and add just a little bit more liberty for the Portuguese to take risks and do damage to Leipzig.

Mahrez out, Stones in. Final answer.

STEP TWO

In the end, it's Erling Haaland's night. The Norwegian is dazzling: 30 touches of the ball, 16 passes, 8 shots on target and he's scored 5 (4 coming after corners).

In his career, he's played 25 Champions League matches and, thus far, scored 25 goals – 10 of which were for City this season.* Tonight, he's equalled the record of scoring five times in a Champions League match – held by Leo Messi and Luiz Adriano.† His thrilling night might easily have

---

* Leo Messi required 52 matches to score 33 in the Champions League.
† On 7 March 2012, Messi scored five when Pep's Barcelona knocked out Bayer Leverkusen (7–1) in the last 16. Luiz Adriano, the Shakhtar Donetsk striker, put five past BATE Borisov on 21 October 2014 in a 7–0 group-stage win.

been still more startling but for the fact that Janis Blaswich, Leipzig's keeper, has made three good saves from on-target efforts.

Haaland starts the demolition with an opening penalty. None of the Citizens have a mind to argue, but, in truth, it's the merest brush of a Leipzig defender's arm that buys the spot kick. It's another example of the ridiculous refereeing and VAR decisions that are so often given, particularly when you consider that, on the away leg, a different Leipzig defender, Benjamin Henrichs, used his hands to block Rodri's shot without any of the refereeing fraternity, on or off the pitch, seeming to notice! Refereeing decisions shouldn't feel like a lottery – but, increasingly, they do.

Anyway, Haaland's goal makes it 100 per cent success in his last six penalties. Eighteen seconds after the restart, Haaland presses Blaswich but the keeper kicks clear, Akanji knocks the ball to De Bruyne and the Belgian hits the bar. Who's free and waiting? Haaland of course – 2–0. In the course of half a minute Leipzig's chances are up in smoke. City's bogeyman continues to torment the visitors, with his fifth hat-trick for the team, when a Grealish corner is headed on goal by Dias. Blaswich and the post prevent it going in but Haaland applies the *coup de grâce*. A move between Ederson, Silva, De Bruyne, Haaland and Grealish lets Gündoğan score the fourth; Haaland makes it 5–0 off a Silva corner and, although Blaswich saves a good shot, the ball seems magnetically drawn to City's centre-forward tonight and he gets his fifth for 6–0. Leipzig's quality and their first-leg performance bear zero relation to the fact that, with time nearly up, De Bruyne makes it 7–0. A ludicrous, but delightful, scoreline. Still, though, Guardiola's teams have managed this four times at this stage of the Champions League: Barcelona 7–1 Bayer Leverkusen on 7 March 2012; Bayern Munich 7–0 Shakhtar Donetsk on 11 March 2015; and Manchester City 7–0 Schalke 04 on 12 March 2019.

The architects of today's startling demolition are Stones and Silva. The former is key to how beautifully and intelligently City bring the ball out from the back (using a 3+2 combination). Leipzig, as anticipated, shape up as a 4–2–2–2, giving City's three defensive players the space to play out without much difficulty. Rodri and Stones have been able to feed City's creative and attacking players with almost unheard-of ease. Maybe Lewis has 'better feet' than Stones … maybe. But the England international has passed well, found space, is daring and has Werner in his back pocket – just as Guardiola hoped.

For his part, Silva does a superb job of preventing Gvardiol connecting with Raum and his shrewd, sharp pressure on Blaswich forces errors from the keeper in his passing out. 'Silva is a smart, intuitive footballer. Somehow he can make three opponents feel that they are all being pressed at the same time. I've never seen anyone achieve anything similar,' Pep comments.

The night's garlands, glory and game ball all go to Haaland, but the technical staff reserve special, quiet praise for Stones and Silva. Guardiola will draw conclusions from tonight – winning the Champions League, in his mind, might well revolve around how brilliantly his wide men can press the opposition.

STEP THREE

Vincent Kompany has catalysed Burnley since taking over and they're en route back to the Premier league. They racked up special numbers in winning the Championship and, after a short, impressive spell in charge at Anderlecht, Kompany's transformed the unimpressive Burnley side he inherited. Nowadays, they're voraciously hungry, play great football and win games. They've won 24 of their 37 Championship matches so far – losing just twice, and now, halfway through March, they just need 8 out of the remaining 27 points in order to be arithmetically guaranteed promotion to the Premier League.* Right at the heart of this impressive stamping of his Belgian identity on ultra-British Burnley is a radical change in playing style. The last club to abandon the direct English football that was first played in 1863, the Clarets were warriors, old-English style, afraid of nothing, aggressive – but ignoring the tide of change lapping at their feet.

The FA Cup tie in the Etihad pits Pep up against his old on-pitch leader. Burnley are bold. Admirably so. Their idea is to mark City man-to-man, like Arsenal did in January (FA Cup, fourth round). But City clearly learned their lesson against Arsenal and use Ortega as the 'free' man with the aim of breaking Burnley's tight marking. The keeper sets the tempo, slows Burnley down and distributes the ball with good vision and accuracy. Their patience pays off and City bring Haaland into play to apply the jack-hammer blows

---

* On 7 April, seven days before the end of the season, Burnley secure enough points for promotion.

that smash Kompany's Championship leaders. The first goal is an Ortega–Haaland–Álvarez–Haaland combination 30 minutes in. City take the lead. Three minutes later, the Norwegian makes it two after De Bruyne and Foden take him to the trough to feed again. Then, his sixth City hat-trick comes with 30 minutes left. It's Haaland's eighth goal in the last 124 competitive minutes played. City show Burnley no mercy and, by the time it's all over, Álvarez (two) and Cole Palmer have made it 6–0, and City are in their sixth straight FA Cup semi-final, where they'll play Sheffield United at Wembley. Guardiola's team have knocked out Chelsea (4–0), Arsenal (1–0), Bristol City (0–3) and now Burnley (6–0) – 14 scored and none conceded.

'All' Pep asked his squad to do was to reach April having won three crucial matches so that they're still alive in the three tournaments, with a chance at the treble. It's still going to be tough to win one of them, never mind all three, but the key thing is that City are in the hunt. Arsenal have an eight-point cushion at the top of the title chase but they've played an extra match.

The Champions League last eight means a meeting with Pep's former employer, Bayern, and the FA Cup is a capricious beast. But City are in good nick and the tempo and the attitude bear no resemblance to earlier in the year when City looked pallid and out of sorts, post-World Cup. Today's their fifth clean sheet, their sixth straight win and they've now scored 1,200 goals at the Etihad. What Pep's happiest about is that his players are reaching ramming speed at the decisive part of the season.

To my eyes, three things stand out. Minor details perhaps. Others may not value their importance, but I'd like to put them on record here. The first is City's kick-off. No longer played from the striker back to a midfielder (usually Rodri), now it's sometimes played by Haaland straight back to the keeper. In the three matches where this has happened (Newcastle, Leipzig and Burnley) City's keeper has waited until his teammates have advanced several metres and then he's played it long, diagonally to one of the wings, looking for City's wide man to bring it down or, at worst, for the opposition to have a throw in but to restart play from very deep in their own half. There were a couple of examples of this last season – but very rare. Now it's becoming an established tactic.

Next: the use of the 'inside' attacking midfielders. Today, about 25 minutes into the first half is an example. De Bruyne starts in his favoured area, on the right, with Álvarez in the 'Gündoğan' zone on the inside left. But neither of them is connecting well with the organising midfielders or with the wingers thanks to the efficacy of Burnley's man-to-man marking, so Pep orders them to switch zones and it's like the sun coming out after a storm. Álvarez links up smoothly with Haaland down the right – *viz* the first goal – and De Bruyne pulls all the play together down the left so that City look slicker and smarter. He's the bridge that allows Lewis and Foden to link up. Álvarez and De Bruyne stay in their reallocated zones for the rest of the match.

The third micro-detail comes around the 65th minute when Akanji replaces Dias. Instead of playing to the right of the centre-backs, Akanji plays left and moves Laporte right so that City play the last half-hour with two of their central defenders on their 'unnatural'/weaker foot. Things become clear when Pep puts Sergio Gómez on at left-back instead of Rico Lewis. Gómez is different from Lewis in that he's left-footed. With Laporte at right centre-back his passes to Gómez meant that the younger Spaniard receives possession with his body shape already moving towards the opponents' goal. It's a micro-detail and it gains City milliseconds of an advantage.

So, a hat-trick of objectives reached and the team are still alive in the big three competitions. Hitting the short-term objectives, this time at least, means dinner out. MUSU Restaurant – full tasting menu. The big wish now is that nobody returns from the international break with injuries or problems. The final sprint to the tape has begun.

SCENE 25. STONES, THE CORNERSTONE

Manchester, 1 April 2023

Màrius keeps his dad up to date on the latest tweet from Opta as Pep drives them home from the Etihad: 'Look what it says about Stones: his passing accuracy is 93.3 per cent, that means he's completed 1,213 of the 1,300 passes he's made all season.'

Pep just smiles. He knew it would be something like that, 'Yeah, John's a star.'

He's certainly been fundamental in City's demolition of Liverpool today. This was one of the Premier League's standout exhibitions so far, not simply for passing accuracy but, still more significantly, Stones's influence on the entire match. In his role as inside midfielder/full-back, Stones moves up the inside, close to Rodri but deeper, the two players coordinating in the build-up to effectively thwart Liverpool's press.

The inside-midfielder/full-back position has become fundamental to Pep's playing model and he's already tried out several players in the role, with varying success – Zabaleta, Clichy, Danilo, Fernandinho, Delph, Zinchenko, Cancelo, Lewis and Walker. Stones's abilities make him a natural and today he's led the team to glory (4–1), moving across the pitch, on the inside and the outside, defending one minute and attacking the next. Watching him, a few members of the technical team tell me: 'Now we can definitely compete for everything.'

Pep gives much of the credit to Lewis: 'It's really thanks to Rico. The kid was the one who lit the way for us. I've used an inside midfielder/full-back for years so the players were all familiar with it but then Rico gave an absolute masterclass in how to execute it properly. He added so much fluidity to our game. It was just the jumpstart we needed at the time. Obviously, he doesn't have the experience of a player like Kyle but it was Rico who showed us all just what can be achieved in that position. And now John is doing the same thing.

'I know I'm like a stuck record on this point, but tactics aren't telephone numbers. Tactics are the way the players interpret an idea, their understanding of what they should be doing every minute of the game. They teach me, not the other way around. I can instruct and advise, and obviously I come up with the game plan, but they're the ones who implement it. And that's how the tactics take shape, from within them, as a result of their natural instincts and abilities and what they do on the pitch. And that's what Rico did, at a time when our game had become sluggish and slow.'

Post-match, something else has occurred to Pep: Haaland's injured so they played without him today, and they were outstanding, playing the same kind of brilliant football they produced last season when, in the absence of a striker, they were forced to use a false 9, which in turn gave them superiority in the middle of the pitch. Without Haaland, Álvarez has doubled up as a striker/attacking midfielder against Liverpool and the combination of his apparently boundless energy, plus Stones's and Rodri's phenomenal performances, has simply been too much for Klopp's men today. City have given the Reds more than one thrashing in the past (5–0 in 2017 and 4–0 in 2020) but they've never before managed to establish the level of total dominance we've seen today. Liverpool's 31.9 per cent possession is the lowest number in Klopp's entire eight seasons in England.

Klopp, undoubtedly one of the best coaches of the last 20 years, has hit a bit of a slump of late, just as he did with Borussia Dortmund in 2014. In fact, his trajectory with Liverpool has been surprisingly similar to his experience in the Bundesliga, where he coached for seven years. After two mediocre initial seasons, Klopp took Dortmund to win the Bundesliga two years in a row, won the German Cup and made it to the final of the 2013 Champions League, when only the phenomenal performance of Manuel Neuer and a last-minute goal from Robben succeeded in depriving Klopp of the ultimate European prize. Dortmund were holding their own in second place in the Bundesliga when Pep's Bayern Munich hit the accelerator and, by 2015, Klopp's team had dropped to seventh place, 33 points behind Bayern. And it wasn't just a question of the Bavarians' superior spending power. Bayern spent €53.4 million net compared to Dortmund's €44.15 million over the same three-year period. Just €9 million more. Now, after eight years, Klopp's Liverpool seem to be following a similar trajectory. A bumpy first three years (eighth, fourth and fourth) followed by four years of intense rivalry with City (second, champions, third, second), culminating in Liverpool's superb 2019 Champions League victory. Right now, though, the Reds are sitting 21 points behind City and 29 away from Arsenal. And, again, it's not about money. Just look at the recent spend of each of the top English clubs: Liverpool, £252.6 million, City, £224.74 million, Arsenal £549.61 million, Manchester United £611.40 million and Chelsea £850.39 million. So, differences in spending power aren't enough on their own to explain Liverpool's changing fortunes. There's no doubt, of course, that, with a coach as talented as Jürgen Klopp, Liverpool will soon be back as strong and aggressive as ever.

• • •

City give a bravura performance today. It's as if they've finetuned every aspect of their game in order to be on the best possible form at this decisive moment of the season. The backline of defenders gives the team confidence and a deep sense of security: Dias and Aké are currently on excellent form and, along with Akanji, they occupy the whole width of the pitch, bringing the ball out with precision and care, and defending well in open space. Rodri and Stones are flawless too, moving up and down with perfect timing and effectively constructing a wall in the central zones. In front of them, De Bruyne and Gündoğan work their usual magic and, up front, the three forwards are spectacular: Mahrez's dribbling and control of the ball; Álvarez's lethal abilities in front of goal and his intuitive positional play, which is fundamental to City's numerical superiority in key areas. The kind of skills, in fact, that you'd expect to find in someone like Bernardo Silva rather than a striker. Grealish has given another standout performance. He's improving with every game, adapting to City's style of play, winning the ball, controlling the tempo and creating real danger in the opposition box.

City are temporarily without not just Haaland (groin strain) but Foden (appendicitis) and Silva (food poisoning). Haaland and Silva should be back for City's next encounter, with the mighty Bayern, as well as their upcoming game against league leaders Arsenal. Pep and his men know that they have to win every single league and FA Cup game from now on (ten and two respectively). They've got two very tough weeks ahead of them and Guardiola knows that they need Haaland back, come what may. But how best to fit Álvarez in close to the Norwegian without disturbing the balance of their 3–2–2–3? Perhaps in a De Bruyne-type role? Pep makes a mental note: 'tomorrow – have a word with Gündo and Grealish …'

SCENE 26. 'WE CAN WIN THE LEAGUE ON SUNDAY'

Manchester, 9 April 2023

At times, Manel Estiarte seems to possess the gift of second sight. He's just finished his breakfast in Sportcity and has been joined by Pep, Txiki and Joan Patsy. After beating Liverpool, the players have had three days off but Pep and the rest of the coaching team are still hard at work. So far, this morning, they've discussed Bayern, Tuchel, Nagelsmann, Sané, Mané and Serge Gnabry. It's Bayern all the way until Estiarte's had enough: 'That's enough about Bayern, what about Southampton? You haven't forgotten that we could win the league on Sunday?' Txiki sees his point immediately. 'You know, Manel's absolutely right.'

Estiarte's obviously crunched the numbers: 'If we beat Southampton and they [Arsenal] draw with Liverpool, the title will be ours to lose.' None of them really needed it spelled out but just hearing Estiarte say it seems to make it real, somehow.

Three days later Pep plays his top 11 at St Mary's. A 3+2 build-up, with Stones, the interior full-back, working with Rodri to allow the three centre-backs (Akanji, Dias and Aké) to spread wide across the pitch. De Bruyne and Gündoğan have total freedom of movement behind Southampton's midfielders to move the ball up the pitch and connect with City's forwards, Grealish, Haaland and Mahrez. Despite a highly organised local defence, City go ahead 44 minutes in as a result of a brilliant combination between De Bruyne and Haaland, and score again in the second half, after sterling work from Grealish, Gündoğan and De Bruyne. It's De Bruyne's 100th assist in the Premier League. He's the fifth player to achieve this and has done it in fewer matches than anyone else. He's only taken 237 games to get there (Cesc Fàbregas took 293 and Ryan Giggs, 367). Haaland has now scored 30 goals in 27 games, and, again, he's done it in the shortest time (Andy Cole took 32 games). This is City's fifth league victory in a row, something that hasn't happened since May 2022. It's their eighth win across all competitions. More importantly, of course, City have achieved exactly what Estiarte has laid out.

• • •

Twenty-four hours later, Pep's perched on his kitchen stool, watching Bayern's last few games on his laptop: beating Borussia Dortmund, losing to Freiburg in the German Cup and beating them yesterday in a Bundesliga game. Bayern's coach Thomas Tuchel's used three different lineups and three different game plans, although he doesn't alter the team's structure too much from game to game. Pep's pretty sure that the German coach will use a 3–2–4–1 when he comes to the Etihad. He's already decided to field more or less the same team he used against Southampton, although is yet to work out who he's putting on the right. Stones or Walker? Silva or Mahrez? Today he's inclining towards Stones and Silva, which would be the same lineup that smashed Leipzig in the round of 16. As he works, he's got one eye on the television, keen to see if Jon Rahm manages to reduce Brooks Koepka's two-stroke advantage today, the fourth day of the Masters. Rahm's attempted comeback really resonates with him. The Catalan's in the middle of a major comeback against a talented opponent too.

Pep's avoided watching the Liverpool–Arsenal game today but, inevitably, someone gets in touch with the great news. It's Spanish doctor Edu Mauri and his message is just four words: 'It's in the bag.' Liverpool have fought back from 0–2 and the game ends on a draw. Just as Estiarte predicted, City have now reduced the distance between themselves and Arsenal to six points. Moreover, City have a game in hand and the two sides are due to play each other at the Etihad.

Dr Mauri has taken to sending his signature 'It's in the bag' message whenever City pull off an important result or when Liverpool or United have a major slip-up. It's now become something of a standing joke and one of the club physios announced 'It's in the bag' back in August last year when, in the first league game of the season, City beat West Ham, United lost to Brighton and Liverpool lost to Fulham. Now, in April, the good doctor's prediction has a much greater likelihood of being fulfilled, so Estiarte texts him back a cheeky, 'Looks like you might be right. There's a first time for everything, I suppose …'

Back at the Masters, Rahm catches up with Koepka at the fourth hole then goes ahead at the sixth before soundly beating the American. But Pep's no longer thinking about the golf or the title. Right now, it's all about Bayern. The passing line between Benjamin Pavard and Dayot Upamecano could be vulnerable to attack. Tomorrow, he must have a word with Gündoğan and Grealish …

SCENE 27. 'I'M FINISHED'

Munich, 19 April 2023

'I'm totally exhausted – I've burned out all my adrenaline. Honestly, I'm done in … there's nothing left. I need to sleep!'

It's 1am – two full hours since the Bayern match has finished.

The City squad and officials have made it back to the Mandarin Oriental in Neuturmstrasse – an insignificant little backstreet in Munich, a stone's throw from Marienplatz.

When the draw was made, pitting together two of the big favourites (notwithstanding Real Madrid), literally nobody could have imagined that the knockout tie would end with such a big difference in the scoreline. It looked nip-and-tuck as to who would qualify and, really, there wasn't enough in the play across 180 minutes to come close to explaining a scoreline like 4–1.

En route to the hotel from the Allianz Arena after the second leg I make sure to have a chat with Estiarte but he's finding it hard to explain things. Still shocked.

'There were moments during the match when we were fearful – for reasons you'll understand. If you arrive here in Munich carrying a 0–0 or a 1–1 from the first leg then, psychologically, you're fully aware that anything can happen. But when you've established a 3–0 lead from the match in Manchester the only thing that you cannot permit, under any circumstances, is that they fight back and overturn that kind of lead. Which left us with the feeling that, in every attack, Bayern might score and, with even a single goal back, they could erupt, carry their baying crowd with them and a historic comeback might suddenly be on the table. Anything like that, even a sniff of it, couldn't be permitted to happen – imagine the brutal impact that would have had. For that reason, I've just been through 90 very anxious minutes – or, at least, 70, until Haaland scored.'

The kind of mental anguish that Estiarte's put himself through has had a big physical impact on him. 'I'm in pieces. I'm going to bed!'

Estiarte's got a routine on nights like this – and he never varies. Off to his room, he orders a two-egg omelette from room service, pours a glass of mineral water, and into the Land of Nod.

Pep's knackered too. But his remedy is the opposite of his friend's. After a big night of stress, he feels a pressing need to have a late dinner with friends and some of the technical staff. He takes the opportunity to talk about what's just happened, think up new ideas, let the debate develop, wash it all down with a couple of glasses of Cava or Champagne – it'll be a late night. For sure. This is his chosen method of processing the stress, calming down and then, eventually, thinking about a couple of hours of rest. It's no different today. Estiarte's long gone but Pep's holding court. A couple of slices of *jamón*, a mouthful of pasta. These are the moments when he's at his most loquacious and clear-cut in his arguments – open to proper discussions so long as the game's been favourable. We seize the moment to try and get him to break down this strange knockout tie for us.

'First thing to admit is that we weren't better than Bayern. Let's not try and kid each other just because of the scoreline. I just don't believe we were better than them. In fact, I was really impressed by Bayern. We took our chances but we didn't outplay them. The main thing I've complained about in years gone by happened in reverse here – we weren't the superior team but we were really strong in both boxes. We defended superbly and it was a joy to watch how intelligently we attacked. End of story.'

Bernardo Silva told me something similar a week ago, after the first leg: 'We weren't better than them, but we did everything really well. Ederson made big saves, the defenders patrolled Bayern's strikers and the strikers tucked it away whenever they had a good chance.'

In Munich, in the Mandarin Oriental, we start by looking in the rearview mirror and dissecting the Manchester leg. That was the night when Pep surprised everyone by how he used Stones – no longer the hybrid of full-back/creative midfielder but, instead, a central defender/pivot.

'It was a nuance of a change in our 3+2 structure. John's such a good footballer and we reckoned that if he starts as a central defender there's a very short sprint of a few metres in order to reposition himself as the midfield pivot and support Rodri. If we use him as a full-back then he's got to do much more running, in a diagonal direction, to successfully move into the pivot position – and then the reverse again if he's got to sprint back and defend as a wide full-back. If you're up against guys with huge speed, like Sané or Coman, then even a tenth of a second where you hand them an advantage can be a disaster. Akanji's very good at man-marking and that finalised the decision. Akanji as a man-marking full-back and John as a centre-back/pivot depending on the phase of play-out – defender without the ball, organising midfielder when we are in possession.'

WHEN IS A 3+2 NOT A 3+2?

Let's pause now and look in detail at the 3+2 structure and how City use it because not all of Pep's 3+2s are the same. He places huge importance on the structure of his defensive and midfield players when trying to build the play from the back. But he also understands the absolute overwhelming importance of his players, even when operating within a detailed tactical structure, feeling that they can go with the flow of a particular situation and that his team, full of super-talented footballers, can let some of their natural instincts come into play when they're trying to apply his concepts. Equilibrium, in other words. Structure and strategy are important, but the players' minds and intelligence are crucial. Once that's established, let's look at the basic cornerstone of 'the build-up'.

The fundamental objective is to create superiority and use it perfectly in order to beat the opposition's press and, thus, bring the ball into their half in the right way, at the right moment, with the City players properly positioned. Naturally, how the opponent presses will hugely influence which structure, which idea, is applied to try and play out. Pep will usually employ five of his players in the build-up, not including the keeper who'll adopt a more, or less, proactive role in adding to the play-out structure depending on what the opposition's doing. Within the five, the structure will either be 3+2 or 2+3 and how that is formed will then influence how the creative/attacking five are structured – often 2+3. Since he took over, Pep's used both the 3+2 and 2+3 regularly with the success or failure of his choice largely depending on the opponent's press. Quite often, Pep will have to improvise on the fly and add a sixth man (a creative midfielder) to ensure that the quality of City's game in this crucial phase is matching his demands. Effectively, this tactic is to ensure that there's a free man and that City always have superiority of numbers in the build-up – especially if the opposition, like Liverpool for example, press with five men.

Across this book we've witnessed Pep using footballers like Zabaleta, Clichy, Sagna and Fernandinho in this complicated role of full-back/midfielder and then that evolving through Delph, Danilo, Zinchenko and Cancelo to the current ones – Walker, Lewis and Gómez. But the reality of life in the Premier league has influenced Pep's ideas given that the style and philosophy of counterattacking in England's top league contrast so much from the Bundesliga. It's a warning that Juanma Lillo gave right at the start of this project: 'The counterattacking concept in England is hugely different to what we've been through in Germany. Here, it usually means that there will be a player left high up the pitch for the long ball, they'll try to use the third-man run and to open up the wing channel. Often the big breakaways come down the wing, with one player supporting them inside. So, Pep's obliged to stick to core values like the high press and his hybrid concept of the inside full-back, who plays much deeper infield to try and counter the rival team's attackers.'*

The reality of how most English teams like to mount their counters has influenced how Pep asks his team to build from the back and where, precisely, he asks his full-backs to play. Across seven seasons he's really alternated between 3+2, 2+3 and even 3+3, depending on the opposition. This season has added more clarity to his ideas. He began it with 2+3 in standard fashion – trying to use the 'De Zerbi box', pushing Walker and Cancelo tight to Rodri, but that idea was torn apart at Newcastle and Pep reverted to 3+2.

Pre-World Cup 2022, he always had a player at full-back with a proven ability to play inside. So … the first line, the '3', would generally be Walker or Stones at right full-back plus a couple of central defenders – with the nominal left-back in this situation moving up, closer to Rodri, and forming the '2'. If Lewis was at right-back, and the objective was for him to keep moving up close to Rodri, then Aké would be the third centre-back with orders to also play left full-back. In other words, the coach is looking for functional balance – always having three defenders (usually centre-backs) plus a full-back who has a double function as organising midfielder alongside the actual pivot. However, after the World Cup, there was something of a crisis in how City were playing and how they were equipped to play. There was the loss of the 'subs-team' at Southampton, the sudden absence of Cancelo, the slow physical recuperation of Dias – all, in combination, leading to a profound alteration in ideas, especially as the really big matches came around. So, from the Palace match on 11 March, the backline was, for five out of six games, excluding Burnley in the Cup, Stones–Akanji–Dias–Aké. In those five matches, Stones is the one who's a full-back/pivot alongside Rodri and, in fact, demonstrates fantastic innate understanding of the Spaniard's movement and play. When City are without possession Stones's position becomes full-back – once they are back in charge of the ball, and building up, he needs to become that second pivot.

Then, from the home match against Bayern, Pep rejigs his thinking yet again. Meaning that, when City aren't in possession, Stones becomes the right-sided centre-back and it's Akanji who's tasked with playing wide

---

* Perarnau, *Pep Guardiola: The Evolution.*

left defender. In this scheme, Pep's using four natural defenders, like he did when he was in charge at Bayern and used four full-backs across the backline (Lahm–Joshua Kimmich–Alaba–Bernat) in five straight matches – three of which were vital to the Champions League challenge Bayern were mounting in February and March of Pep's last season there (2016). Back then, it was in response to his regular central defenders being injured but in Manchester, by now, he's using a back four because of tactical convictions – performance levels, and the 'feeling' between the four of them. These, it so happens, are guys he can ask, tactically, to double-up their functions so that one or other of them also plays in midfield in the same match as being a full-back or centre-back – but they're also four guys who love defending their penalty area, four colossal defenders with a 'Yugoslav' point of view.

All of which, I hope, helps clarify that one 3+2 isn't automatically the same as another identically numbered system of build-up.

• • •

Now, back to the Mandarin Oriental – Pep's enjoying the fact that the fantastic Japanese chef Nobu Matsuhisa has made a very rare exception and kept his kitchen open very late.

The City coach goes back to the huge value he places on multi-functional footballers like Stones. Someone Pep considers like a human Swiss watch – blessed with the tools for every occasion: full-back, centre-half, pivot … a rare combination. 'Where we used John positionally in the Etihad leg helped hugely because, automatically, Rodri was able to play just that little bit further forward.' It's how the crucial Rodri goal arrived in that first leg. Dias had just produced a brilliant block on what looked like a goal from Jamal Musiala, but then Rodri's ability to prowl a little further forward put him in position for another of his goalbound, thunderous strikes.

Pep: 'This is key, you know how much I love to work hard on our defensive line. Right now we've got exceptional guys defending for us – spectacular footballers. Ederson did his job, especially from Sané, but the defenders are literally spectacular. They win all their duels.'

This return to 'Yugoslav defence' ideals could easily be the key to the remainder of this promising season. In the first leg against Bayern, the team allowed the Germans four shots on target in just seven minutes (45–52) which, admittedly, Ederson saved with total confidence and ease. From that point onwards, City altered how they pressed Bayern and that put out the fire.

'At half-time we took the decision,' Guardiola continues. 'They were constantly smashing through the middle of our team. Without the ball, we were pressing in a 4–4–2 but we weren't closing Bayern down well enough and Musiala or Gnabry were dropping back to pick up the ball, to add superiority, and they were just ripping us open down the middle. So we changed to a 4–2–4 from the 55th minute. Instead of pressing their centre-halves via Haaland and De Bruyne, we did it with our wingers. But my players, and I, had to all show huge courage in order to make this effective.'

It was the same shape and strategy that City had used to thrash another German team, Leipzig, 7–0. Grealish stopped pressing his man, Pavard, and moved inside one to Upamecano, at right centre-back for Bayern. Silva copied him at the other side of the pitch – nominally leaving 'free' the Olympically fast Alphonso Davies and changing the press to Matthijs de Ligt. It was a huge, huge risk because these two excellent Bayern full-backs suddenly had no 'true' marker in front of them, meaning that any single attack from them would have been very dangerous. Meanwhile, Haaland and De Bruyne dropped their positions to join Kimmich–Leon Goretzka/Rodri–Gündoğan. The numerical alteration now meant that Rodri–Gündoğan could make minor adjustments and, at the same time, shut-off the central channels through which Musiala and Gnabry kept on bursting. Bayern suddenly lost their powerful grip on attacking inside and didn't manage to attack effectively down the outside. The new pressing idea had clicked and was functioning brilliantly.

'Pressing like that takes a lot of guts. We can talk about it in cold, clear tactical terms but it's actually to do with emotions. Do you, really, have the courage to press aggressively knowing that you're abandoning the press on someone who can, then, go whizzing past your shoulder down the wing? And, above all, do you have the guys to do that? We had Grealish, who's a monster in terms of how well and how quickly he understands the nuances of football ideas and who's got pistons for legs. And we have Bernardo Silva, who's the best in the world for ideas like this. The only guy I've ever seen who can give two or three opposing players the clear impression that all of them are being marked by him. That's magical.'

The culmination of all this is that City can overload their own pressing and damage Bayern's weakest area – the Upamecano zone. Precisely what Pep had visualised and planned for a few days ago.

'We were lucky that Upamecano's mind was playing with him in a negative way. When Álvarez came on, he immediately added a big plus in terms of energy. In theory he's a striker but when you've got Haaland in such sublime form, Julián can help us hugely by performing as a hybrid attacking midfielder/attacker. Like an old-school no. 10 but moved slightly off the centre and playing marginally to one side or the other.'

That's twice now that Pep's zeroed in on 'emotions' – but for different reasons. Here's the moment to quote Rodri, immediately after the first leg: 'We didn't rush things as we sometimes did in the past. We took advantage of the moments that our form and pressure presented us. You can't always achieve 80 per cent possession but today we showed huge patience whenever we didn't have the ball.'

Pep likes hearing this. 'Rodri's right. In some matches, any setback could throw us. Being "stable" in my definition is defending well whether something bad's happened or not. If it has, then you just get right back on the horse and defend as if nothing's changed. Then build 20 consecutive passes out from the back – build with calm. "Stable", in our terms, means having the midfielder's mentality of showing for the ball, taking it and starting/continuing a pattern of 50 passes to keep possession and to put the match to bed. Especially if you're in the position we were – 3–0 up at home to Bayern. If you don't quite have the killer touch that's going to put the opponent away, then it's "make the best of the first leg lead, wait for the second leg and then calmly, coldly pass them to death." Emotional intelligence and control matter very much.'

It's now almost 3am in Munich. Pep's still chatting with his brother Pere, Txiki, Joan Patsy, Rodolfo Borrell, Enzo Maresca and Carles Planchart, all of them resisting the temptation to head off to bed. The players, in contrast, went up to their rooms a while ago – so dead on their feet after the physical effort of the game that they've hardly celebrated reaching the Champions League semi-finals. Most of them have been content to sample the set menu from the chef, pat one another on the back, put out a little bit of social media content and then go off to sleep. Legs full of lead.

Last Saturday, against Leicester, Pep had used the central core of the team because it was crucial to get three league points, although Walker, Laporte and Mahrez had fresher legs than the rest. Fortunately, City had thundered ahead, 3–0 up after just 24 minutes, meaning that the full gamut of changes could be applied in the second half, something which brought two consequences. The first, good. Stones, Haaland, Grealish and De Bruyne, who'd started, could get a rest. Less good? The second half became a nervy affair. Leicester responded, scored and began to threaten that they were capable of equalising. The 3–1 final score was City's tenth straight win; given that, the following day, Arsenal tripped up at West Ham (2–2), the gap at the top has reduced to only four points in the Gunners' favour (74 vs 70) but with City still holding a game in hand. Things are moving City's way but Pep knows his team is seriously losing energy and stamina – exhaustion is a real risk. Which is why Silva's comments are so reassuring: 'The bottom line is that this is precisely what we wanted when we were kids – to be able to play day after day, hour after hour, with nobody telling us to stop! Now it's only every three days – we're doing what we love.'

Back in Munich, it's been a tiring, if profitable, excursion. The stadium was absolutely freezing – cold enough to cause you physical pain. I recall this sensation from when Pep was Bayern boss and it's weird to have it again now that he's the victorious visitor.

'Our first half press didn't really work all that well,' Guardiola admits. He wanted to use the same 4–2–4 that defused Bayern in the first leg with the City wingers attacking the spaces of the Bayern defenders ... with the slight nuance that, in the right situations, the press can alter to 4–3–3. Bayern, naturally enough, have studied what happened and are twice shy – Pavard and Coman, having been bitten, are much more sprightly, tactically, and their work means that the press isn't effective and Guardiola needs to make half-time adjustments. Effectively, it's back to 4–4–2 when they don't have the ball – just a change back to how they began the first leg. Grealish hands responsibility for Upamecano to Haaland and drops deeper to ensure that Pavard is blocked off. The English winger is absolutely excellent, creating, attacking and restarting the play intelligently when Bayern are robbed of the ball.

'I think they dominated the play but we were dominant in the two boxes,' Pep concludes.

Planchart, who, when younger, was a central defender, says, 'It's true, I suffer badly when the other team has us surrounded in our own penalty box!'

Everything this evening has been a function of the situation – 3–0 up and determined to hold that advantage. City wanted to snuff Bayern's explosive tendencies out and did so. Three players in particular have taken a lot of satisfaction from today's game at the Allianz – the three ex-Dortmund men who suffered at the hands of Bayern while playing in the Bundesliga (Gündoğan, Haaland and Akanji). It's not that they're *totally* driven by that – except perhaps Haaland, who celebrates his 22nd goal of the season with some gestures towards the main stand. Perhaps linked to something said when he missed a penalty – the third of his career in 33 spot kicks taken so far.* A brilliant Ederson night again – nine big saves across the two matches. And the four-man defence, so unusual for Guardiola's City, was a veritable wall. It's fun to watch them celebrate every block, every tackle, every winning header as if it were a trophy in itself. Even Haaland runs back to high-five Dias for one particularly impressive, providential block. They've known, and demonstrated, that success comes from stingy defending. Bayern raised eyebrows by playing Cancelo, not Davies, at left-back. Without Davies, they were robbed of that frightening pace which makes him so special. Overall, there's not really been a spark of a big Bayern comeback – the thing Estiarte feared and that Pep knew was a possibility. Sané's counterattacking was the worst threat – he shot close a couple of times. Their equaliser came late when a penalty was duly awarded for a foul which few noticed. Kimmich had run to take the corner while VAR was reviewing the action. Only Mané, close up to the action, bothered to demand it.

The worst news of the night is that Aké seems to have a minor tear in his hamstring. Dr Mauri initially allays fears and suggests that it's not a terrible problem. Maybe two weeks out. So, if the recuperation goes well, the Dutchman can be ready for the semi-final against Real Madrid. It's Pep's tenth Premier League semi-final, the all-time record for the competition, and City's third in a row.† Pep's also struck another record here – quickest coach to 100 UCL wins. He's needed 158 matches. This is also his 400th

---

* He hit the post against Union Berlin, Augsburg's keeper saved one and this penalty thumped off the Bayern crossbar.

† Ancelotti, 9 Champions League semi-finals; Mourinho 8; Ferguson 7.

match in charge of Manchester City – the 800th of his entire career.* These records really aren't a big thing for him. His mind is on something else. 'It's Madrid … again.'

It feels like vengeance is near. From the three tournament favourites we are down to two and they're going to face each other now.

'I feel like I've aged ten years in knocking out Bayern and now it's Madrid waiting for us … !'

Short sleep, early start, back to business. Last night, the subs who didn't play did an on-pitch set of sprints and now they work out in a gym that City has rented. Those who played are set stretching exercises but it's light work. A bit of static bicycle and some time in the pool. Eventually, at 6pm local time, the flight gets back to Manchester. Grealish stays late at City's Academy for extra recuperation. The following morning's training will still be short and sweet – 20 minutes but at a good tempo. They're fatigued and the FA Cup semi-final is near.

As Planchart says with an ironic smile: 'Don't worry, there's only 13 "finals" left!'

SCENE 28. SPRING FEVER

London, 22 April 2023

We're well into April and, all over Manchester, roses are gently blooming while noses begin to run. Hay-fever season is upon us.

Over in Sportcity, Pep's players are dealing with an altogether different seasonal ailment, which robs them of their mental energy: cognitive fatigue.

You might think that this kind of fatigue is a natural phenomenon but it's not. It's the result of City's collective ambition to compete for as many trophies as possible. For the last five years, they've started April still well in contention to win the league, the FA Cup and the Champions League, which

---

* Coaching Barcelona B, Barcelona, Bayern and City, Guardiola has reached 850 games: 618 wins (72.7 per cent), 130 draws, 102 defeats; 2,101 goals scored (2.47 average), 662 conceded (0.78); 32 trophies. At Manchester City, by the end of the 2023–4 season he had 472 matches, 434 wins, 66 draws, 63 defeats, 1,164 scored, 390 conceded, 1,164 goals scored, GD +774, 17 trophies, 72.67% win rate.

inevitably means a punishing schedule of games. April is, in other words, an endless round of play–recuperate–train–play–recuperate–train–play … Wednesday? It must be the Champions League. Saturday? A league match. Wednesday? Another Champions league game … week in, week out. The byproduct? Tired legs, stiff muscles, woolly heads. And, at this stage, every single match is a gruelling test, regardless of the level of competition or the relative status of their opponent. An objectively 'weaker' team that City face might be fighting for their lives and desperately need the points, or it may simply be that, because they've played fewer games across the season, they have fresher legs.

Take the FA Cup. Worldwide pandemics aside, the semi-finals always take place midway through April at Wembley and City have made it to this stage for the last five years. Back in 2019, they beat Brighton (1–0) just a few days before facing Spurs in the quarter-finals of the Champions League. They went on to win the FA Cup, beating Watford (6–0) in May, and ended the season having won all four domestic titles. As a result of the pandemic, the 2020 semi-final was delayed until mid-July when Pep's men were defeated by Arsenal (0–2) just before entering the final phase of the Champions League. The following year, the April semi against Chelsea ended in another defeat for City (0–1), just a few days after they'd eliminated Borussia Dortmund from the Champions League and just before their next European tie with Paris Saint-Germain, while also deep into the final sprint to the title. Last year's FA Cup semi-final against Liverpool (City 2 Liverpool 3) was, of course, sandwiched between Champions League games against Atlético Madrid and Real Madrid, and in the heat of their epic league title battle with the Reds, which, as we know, would go to the final minute of the last game of the season. This competitive drive, the ruthless determination to win every trophy, is part and parcel of elite-level football.

Of course it is. But whether the team emerge victorious or battered, bloody and beaten, by this stage of the year, there's always, always a bill to pay: utter exhaustion, both mentally and physically. Mental, or cognitive, fatigue is tough to deal with. You'll feel a bit dopey, the cogs are still turning, but much, much more slowly. And, if you're a sportsperson, you're likely to be dealing with other symptoms too: a general sense of physical fatigue; leaden limbs and a dramatic drop in the mental and physical energy that is so vital in any competitive sport. Juanma Lillo was the first football person I heard refer to this phenomenon, many years ago, and I take the chance to ask him about cognitive fatigue a couple of hours before City face Sheffield United at Wembley.

'Everything starts to slow down, life loses its spark and seems bleaker. Everything is slower, mentally and physically. And, as a result, decision-making becomes much more difficult. It's hard to convince players that this is a real phenomenon because, nowadays, footballers, regardless of whether they actually enjoy playing or not, always want to be *seen* playing, because: "I only exist if people see me play!"

'When exactly does cognitive fatigue set in? Well, it tends to start precisely because the player isn't acknowledging just how knackered they are. And it will show immediately in a slowing down of their reactions on the pitch. For example, if the coach can see that a particular player is exhausted and talks to the guy about it, the player then immediately knows that he won't be picked for such and such a game, which of course will allow him to rest and recuperate some energy. But it also means that people won't see him playing that day, which goes right to the heart of his whole purpose as a footballer and makes him deeply uneasy. And that's why so many players prefer to keep on playing, even though they've temporarily lost their edge in terms of speed of decision-making and reaction time.'

There are exceptions, of course. Bernardo Silva, for example, fronted up weeks ago to Pep about his level of exhaustion, knowing that the coach wouldn't automatically drop him as a result. But Pep knows that not all his players are going to be so forthcoming, so he makes a point of talking about it so that they can acknowledge it and he can take countermeasures. Which is why, on Thursday morning, after knocking Bayern out of the Champions League, they're to be found messing about in a Munich swimming pool (reserved for City's use only) before heading home in the afternoon. The game has left everyone utterly depleted, such that, last night, there was no enthusiasm at all for post-match celebrations.

Pep's told a few of the regulars, including Rodri, Stones and De Bruyne, 'Rest up, eat well, get lots of sleep and don't think about anything else.' No prizes for guessing who's on the bench for Saturday, then. It's all part of the culture Pep and Estiarte have established at City over the years and is based on the kind of strict care protocols Olympic athletes adhere to. Pep under-stands that, at this point in the season, the main problem is mental fatigue but that this in itself can lead to a sense of physical exhaustion, so Friday training will be 20 minutes of gentle exercises to stretch tight, weary muscles and relax overloaded brains.

• • •

As the plane touches down in London, there's an unexpected pick-me-up. Bottom of the table Southampton have held Arsenal to a 3–3 draw. The shark smells blood …

Pep's starting 11 at Wembley is a mixed bag. He lines up just five of his starters from Munich: Akanji, Silva, Gündoğan, Haaland and Grealish, although only the last two play in the same positions as Wednesday. The other three have been asked to do different jobs today. Pep's betting that a change of position will, indeed, be as good as a rest. Sheffield bring their A-game, presenting City with a muscular 5–4–1, but the Blades are fighting a losing battle and Mahrez becomes the first player ever to score a hat-trick in a Wembley semi-final. The Citizens are through to their seventh FA Cup final, which, on 3 June, will be Pep's second, after their victory in 2019. City will have got there having played Chelsea, Arsenal, Bristol City, Burnley and Sheffield – 17 goals scored, zero conceded. They're the first team to have reached the final without conceding since Everton won the FA Cup in 1965.

It's April in Manchester. The flowers are blooming, the birds are singing and the Citizens, battered, bone weary but just as bloody-minded as ever, march on.

SCENE 29. THE SHARK IS CIRCLING
Manchester, 6 May 2023

Ding Liren looks up, startled, and straight into the eyes of Ian Nepomniachtchi. The Chinese grandmaster can't believe what's just happened. It's the 12th game of the Chess World Championship. Nepomniachtchi is playing black and he's up 6–5. The Russian is dominating, and with apparent ease. If he wins, as looks pretty likely, then he'll be pronounced world champion, succeeding Magnus Carlsen. Nepomniachtchi is really dominant on the current board – Ding is teetering on the edge of disaster. Both are pressed for time to make their remaining moves and all the predictions are that Ding has no real chance of resisting Nepo's attack, but, then, on the 27th move, the Chinese player turns the tables. His boldness gives him the advantage, which he, unfortunately, squanders over the next few moves. Once again, Ding finds himself on the edge of the abyss. Then, on move 34, Nepo makes a fatal mistake and destroys his entire advantage. As soon as Nepo moves his pawn to f5, Ding Liren looks at him perplexed, astonished, because he simply cannot understand why his rival has wasted his advantage in this way. This time, Ding doesn't let go of his prey, he launches his attack, masterfully deploying his remaining pieces and, four moves later, achieves victory, equalises the overall score and focuses on completing a winning comeback that, just four days ago, was deemed impossible.

GET THE BALL LONG

Around the same time, but a world away from Ding's surprising win, Pep Guardiola's explaining the match plan to his players. Today, it's Arsenal at the Etihad. A proper showdown. Arteta's team is here to protect a five-point lead (75 vs 70) but City still have two games in hand. If the Citizens win both of those (West Ham and Brighton) they'll leapfrog to the top but, to do that, they must at least get a draw today. The strategy's based on their last two games against Arsenal in January and February. City won both of those but it was a grim experience dealing with the limpet-like man-to-man marking/pressing that Arteta's Arsenal have perfected.

For the Cup tie (1–0 win in Manchester), Haaland had no joy in trying to bring down and control any of the long balls that Ortega or the defenders fizzed up to him – the marking and the pressing was too tight, too physical. For the Premier League match (3–1 win in London), it was more of the same but Pep made some adjustments to how his men were playing when City didn't have the ball – better positioning, better pressing – and, after half-time, everything went much more smoothly.

By analysing those two experiences, Pep's come up with his match strategy for this last meeting of the season. It's a five-point plan:

- Ederson must slow the tempo when necessary. Stones and Dias are principally responsible for starting the playing out while Rodri and Gündoğan choose which area of the pitch the build-up is aimed at and how fast it should be.
- When pressed, City's players must circulate the ball, pass, pass, pass, suppress their own impatience and try to force Arsenal into reacting and making their own rash errors of enthusiasm.
- The midfield will operate with the sense of playing a 'double 6' not a 'double 8'.
- City's pressing will not be a 'blanket' consistent press. Instead it will be very selective and specifically aimed at certain pre-selected Arsenal players.
- The two City men who are generally liberated from all other duties, except for creating danger and, hopefully, scoring, are Haaland and De Bruyne.

It's a simple enough plan, drawn from long experience. But let's look at it in more detail.

1. TIME ON THE BALL AND PLAYING OUT FROM THE BACK

Today, Pep wants Ederson, more than anyone else in the team, to take time on the ball. He's given total liberty to take as much time as he wants before making a pass to beat the press or before hitting 'Go!' on building the play out from the back. Pep wants to provoke Arsenal into impatience. Into moving further and further forward so that they start to leave more space at the back – little chinks of room where Haaland and De Bruyne can do damage. Once City's forwards are two vs two, instead of being swamped, City can release the verticality in their play. In his team talk, Pep explains that this part of the plan, if well-executed, is the key to winning the match: taking time on the ball, provoking Arsenal into missteps and, then, getting the ball long quickly when the opening arrives. You'll hear Ederson referred to as a 'keeper who's good with his feet' but that doesn't really do justice to the role he plays. Any top keeper must have quick reactions, and, of course, the ability to save shots and take crosses, but, nowadays, goalkeepers who aren't also very good with their feet are in the minority and are far less likely to survive at the elite level. For Pep, all of the above is the bare minimum. He needs more from his keeper. He wants someone who understands the strategy of the game, who has terrific vision and is happy playing bold, daring football. A guy who instinctively understands and is committed to being part of an 11-man system – not the 11th player in a 10+1 group. In fact, Guardiola's brand of football has its bedrock in how the keeper analyses and understands the build-up. Taking the right decisions, using the right timing, sending the ball off in the right direction, a 'Guardiola-keeper' needs to be a complete footballer, not just an excellent specialist. Today, Ederson needs to demonstrate that more than ever.

The building-play-from-the-back ideal, under Guardiola, has a lot in common with chess openings. Everything needs to be millimetrically perfect – studied in minute detail and brilliantly prepared. By now, City have about ten distinct manners of 'playing out' codified and written into their circuit boards. But today it's a special hybrid prepared specifically to unpick Arsenal. The build-up, if looked at numerically, is structured 1+2+4+1+3. It's a 'game of provocation' – tempt Arsenal to do something that, deep down, they know they shouldn't but can't resist. Draw them forward, direct them inside, then accelerate the circulation wide and vertically so that City are attacking, eventually, against Arsenal men who thought they had superiority of numbers but, suddenly, don't.

2. 'PASS THEM TO DEATH'

When pressed, pass and pass and pass … Simple in phrasing, simple in concept and, hopefully, execution – but totally fundamental. Accumulating big numbers of the right passes can produce sensational results. As Paco Seirul·lo says: 'repeatedly passing, if done well, is the essence of football. Passing well, cleverly and repeatedly damages your opponent. They get bored and they make misjudgements or downright errors.' If a couple of players are passing the ball backwards and forwards, it generates a psychological reaction in opponents and causes frustration. The opposition loses patience and intervenes, errors of judgement are made and, hopefully, blocked passing channels open up and asphyxiating pressure suddenly dissipates.

3. THE DOUBLE 6

For the purposes of risk management, Pep's opted for a 'double 6' tactic instead of his much more usual 'double 8'. We already know that he likes his three main midfielders to create an inverted triangle (1+2), which is formed of the pivot/organising midfielder at the base and the two creative midfielders diagonally right and left a few metres ahead of him. Today it's a 2+1 structure, which is less risky but also less likely to generate creative opportunities. In practice, it means putting Gündoğan back in line with Rodri with the only 'between the lines' attacking midfielder becoming De Bruyne, who has a supernatural instinct for where and when to drift into spaces between the opponent's defensive midfielders. When the ball reaches the Belgian he's going to have to take responsibility for turning good possession into serious goal threat.

4. SELECTIVE PRESSING

This is a tactic specifically developed for today's game. Haaland and De Bruyne focus on Rob Holding, Aaron Ramsdale and Gabriel Magalhães, leaving Silva and Grealish to target the full-backs. Pep knows that the Arsenal build-up is intended to culminate in Zinchenko making the key forward pass to one of the Gunners' central attackers so that they can receive, recycle and turn, allowing their midfielders to take over the attack. The Catalan reckons he's come up with the perfect antidote. Rúben Dias is tasked with harassing Ødegaard – going tight on him and, if necessary, following him all the way up to the Arsenal box. Stones will do the same with Gabriel Jesus. If either Arsenal man drops deep, then Stones and Dias must follow them – relentlessly. The orders are to screw up their possession, and prevent them turning and finding time to give fluidity to Arsenal's passing. Similarly, as soon as Zinchenko pushes forward to try and organise his team's play, Rodri will be on top of him, although if, at that moment, the Spaniard's too tied up marking Xhaka, then Gündoğan will press the Ukrainian instead. The aim of these three simple moves is that the Gunners are frustrated, pressed and harassed as Arteta's meticulously planned build-up is torn to shreds by the Citizens.

5. TWO FREE RADICALS

The security blanket of the 'double 6' idea leaves De Bruyne with a pretty basic task – ensuring that he tricks and evades Thomas Partey and Xhaka. He and Haaland need to have reduced the battle up front to a state of readiness to act decisively when City's pressing and play-out have turned it into a two vs two against the Arsenal defenders. The last two matches have shown that City have an advantage when it does go to two vs two but this time Pep's wish is to specifically engineer this happening – not to simply hope that the pattern of the game produces it from time to time.

•   •   •

Having a plan is one thing, of course. Executing it is something else entirely. In practice, things start perfectly. Just over a minute after kick-off, Dias and Gündoğan follow orders and pass the ball backwards and forwards repeatedly until Ødegaard, already sucked in by frustration and an overdose of adrenaline, slightly drops his concentration and, in attacking the ball, gifts Gündoğan a chink of space allowing Grealish and De Bruyne to come close to an opening goal. It's City's first warning of things to come …

The build-up, however, isn't working as it was designed to. The 1+2+4+1+3 formation means that Ederson, Stones and Dias are the ones who structure and control how things begin. The second line, moving up, is Walker and Akanji, pegged to their respective touchlines, with Rodri and Gündoğan playing tight together in the middle as the aforementioned 'double 6' wall. Up front, De Bruyne should be in the no. 10 space, wherever there's a gap between the Arsenal backline and their midfield. The furthest forward City men are Grealish, Haaland and Silva, who need to tie Arsenal's back division up, to worry them, distract them and, generally, prevent them pushing forward and giving Arsenal's press more numbers and more efficacy. The simple fact is that, for whatever reason, Ederson doesn't take his time on the ball and hits a pass precipitately towards Stones, who's near the byline. Just like he did a week ago in the Allianz Arena when Stones's immediate long ball was controlled by Haaland, interchanged with De Bruyne and, ultimately, ended with the Norwegian scoring against Bayern. Stones tries it again and Haaland shows equally deft control, feeds De Bruyne and the Belgian bursts off on one of his 'I know exactly what I'm doing' charges. The shot that tops off his charging run is quite something – it swirls and curls and the trajectory means that Ramsdale is never going to get near it. The shot makes the net bulge, just inside the far post, so that, after only six minutes, City have an advantage which, in itself, might prove crucial to the title.

Guardiola, naturally, celebrates seeing the ball hit Arsenal's net but, immediately, turns and gives Ederson a big row for ripping the game strategy to shreds. It's a fierce ticking off, but brief, expressed in a roar of 'From him to you, from you to him, then to him again and keep that going!' It's all interspersed with a fair few strong curses too. The Brazilian tries to explain himself but Pep's not listening. All he wants is for Ederson to take his time on the ball, not to rush things, provoke Arsenal into pressing too high, and then to allow Rodri or Gündoğan to decide when to accelerate and go vertical. For this goal, Ederson's done exactly the reverse of what Guardiola asked of him, but the fierce, short roar from the boss means that the keeper will now revert to textbook for the rest of the match.

There's a bit of the old 'monkey see, monkey do' aphorism happening, though. Fifteen minutes into the match, Stones tries to replicate the move that brought De Bruyne his goal but it puts Haaland in a disadvantageous position and doesn't work. Another ticking off. This time for Stones. The coach wants Stones to follow the plan, to take it slower and give it back to Ederson if the build-up isn't properly developed yet. The coach's interventions have the desired effect and from now on his players stick to the plan.

Around their own area, Arsenal are suffocating under Rodri's pressure on Zinchenko, which is really messing up their game, while over at Ederson's goal, a sense of calm has been established, which conditions everything the Citizens do. The Gunners might have more possession but it's sterile possession, almost all of it in their own half, where they look a bit trapped.

City apply two diametrically opposed rhythms of play: they carry out the build-up with a restrained, slow, 'siesta time' tempo and then switch to a devastating, high-speed vertical attack to finish. Just look what happens between minutes 28.08 and 30.15. Ederson starts with the ball at his feet, looking like he has no intention of moving it. His defenders are open, the full-backs even more so, and Rodri and Gündoğan remain outside the area, endlessly scanning behind. It's desperately confusing and frustrating for Jesus and Ødegaard, who don't know whether to go or wait. Gündoğan is calling the shots, dictating who gets the ball and when, voice raised, arms constantly in motion pointing to where he wants the play orientated and, occasionally, giving one teammate or another the thumbs-up for a well-placed, well-timed pass. Gündo is much more static so that Rodri can stay mobile and draw opposing players to his movements but also be the moving piece in the triangulation that ensures that City will always seem to have numerical superiority. Two minutes of this can feel like hours to the Arsenal players and fans – they are being denied the rhythm and impact they wanted to have in this match. As a result of Pep's strategy now being applied with diligence and discipline, City have four huge scoring opportunities, which either Ramsdale or White manage to prevent going in.

Stones changes that pattern in the 46th minute, heading past Ramsdale from a wide De Bruyne free kick, and his goal closes off a first half that, after Pep's initial interventions, has brought a huge yield from the work put into preparing the game plan. In behind the Arsenal organising midfielders, the Haaland–De Bruyne partnership is creating gleeful havoc and, whenever it's two vs two, they turn into snarling, hungry predators. The Norwegian gives the best performance of his City career – goal or no goal. It's the Norway–Belgium accord that fosters the goal for 3–0 not too long after the restart, when they combine to steal possession from Ødegaard, Haaland's international teammate. That's game, set, match for City despite there still being half an hour left on the clock.

Whether by fluke or design, Haaland happens to have untied his pony-tailed hair when he storms in to add City's fourth in added time – a Foden assist now that he's back following appendix surgery. For 'Big Erl' it's his 33rd Premier League goal, one ahead of the previous competition record set by Salah across a 38-match season. The Norwegian has turned in a colossal performance today, demonstrating how much he's continuing to improve in his ball control, lay-offs and passing. His partner in crime, De Bruyne, finishes his afternoon with acute discomfort in his hamstrings – but the two of them can be ultra-satisfied with their part in dismantling Arsenal. City still need to deal with their outstanding matches but this will be, in Guardiola's view, a definitive blow in the title-race fightback. It's the Catalan's 13th win over Arsenal since coming to the Premier league – plus 1 draw – in 14 matches.

Grealish has also been in notably good, explosive form – attacking, press-ing, defending. He's become a full-on team player. The backline has gone all 'Yugoslav' again, with Akanji at left-back doing a fine job of thwarting Saka's efforts. Centre-backs Stones and Dias have also been excellent, and

Walker is fully back to his old form, focused, fierce and absolutely unbeatable. Akanji's the seventh left-back Guardiola's used this season following Cancelo, Gómez, Aké, Laporte, Lewis and Silva.

Guardiola's delighted: 'The defence, look at them! That's the area of the team where we've improved most since February.' The 'happy flowers' have now become hardy perennials who respond as a unit if someone goes after one of them.

In December, Haaland used his social media to say: 'Arsenal, we have to hunt them!' Tonight he's even more concise: 'Hunting.' The blue shark's circling, about to go in for the kill …

'RODRI IS EXHAUSTED'

The first thing Lorenzo Buenaventura says to Pep when they reach the Craven Cottage dressing room is that their pivot is exhausted. Everyone on the staff has already intuited that the Spaniard is going to be the next problem to resolve. More pressing even than the fact that De Bruyne and his hamstrings are at war with one another. The fact is that Rodri doesn't have a proper deputy at City – not like for like. Ortega can stand in for Ederson, Álvarez is a terrific striker, and we could go on, one for one, until we get to Rodri. Since Fernandinho left, Rodri's the only player without a same-quality understudy. Kalvin Phillips has always looked like he has the potential but his performance is still way off Rodri's. Guardiola played this position, brilliantly, when he was a key part of Barcelona's 'Dream Team' and, possibly for that reason, he's ultra-demanding of whoever fills that role under his command: Yaya Touré, Sergio Busquets, Philipp Lahm, Xabi Alonso, Fernandinho, Gündoğan and, now, Rodri. One thing is very clear: Phillips's current level doesn't satisfy the Catalan. It may be down to the typical 'settling-in' problems or, perhaps, the England midfielder possesses other qualities than the ones City's coach, and his team, really need right now.

Whatever the reason, Phillips isn't a candidate to stand in for Rodri any time soon – which doesn't remove the hard fact that, in terms of physical overload, the Spaniard is on his knees. This season he's already played 3,836 minutes – 2,269 of which have come since he got back from the Qatar World Cup (where he played another 180 minutes for Spain). Of his 47 appearances for City, 45 have been in the starting 11 and, if things go as planned, he's likely to end the season having played 4,500 minutes – a huge jump on the already impactful 3,928 of the previous season.* In recent matches it's been very obvious how much he's struggling, particularly towards the end of games. It was tough for him to make it to the end of the contest in Munich and still more so at home to Arsenal. All this, despite being rested for the whole of the FA Cup semi-final against Sheffield United. Today, he's clearly had a hard time against Fulham.

Pep comes into the dressing room after receiving a lengthy ovation from the fans. He's keen to solve the 'Rodri problem' as soon as possible.

'Rodri has reached the outside limits of what he's got left to give and we can't afford to lose him,' Planchart tells him. 'We'll have to invent or manufacture a way to give him some "oxygen" – we'll need to manage the next two home matches really well so that he's in as good condition as possible to face Madrid in the semi-final.'

'OK, let's see what we can manufacture,' agrees Pep.

Sunday's match with Fulham has been complicated. The Craven Cottage men are happy to gift City the ball – Pep can have all the possession he likes, he's welcome to it. Haaland puts them 1–0 up and, for a while, the visitors are on easy street. It's the Norwegian's 34th Premier League goal of the season, equalling the previous record. Guardiola's made up for the absence of De Bruyne by using Álvarez, which means that Gündoğan drops to play alongside Rodri and the Argentinian is like a free-ranging no. 10 liberated from all duties except scoring, assisting and pressing the Fulham defence when they have the ball. It's an interesting task for him because Álvarez isn't a midfielder at all, he's a centre-forward who's in the process of learning and adapting his game so that he can play either role without losing any of his scoring threat. Ten minutes before the break, he whips in a shot which makes it 2–1 to City, Carlos Vinicius having already equalised for Fulham. That, by the way, will be the home team's only shot on target all game.

The Craven Cottage pitch is poor – long grass, which has been left to sprout, a very dry surface which ensures that the ball doesn't fizz around. As a result, City only achieve 86 per cent accuracy in their passing. Overall, it's

---

* The final hard total, in fact, is that Rodri plays 4,465 minutes (excluding added time, which probably totals another 300+ minutes) across 56 matches.

an uncomfortable 90 minutes and the win can be filed in the folder: 'Getting the Job Done'. Coincidentally, the scorers, this time, are the same as in the win at the Etihad back in November: a Haaland penalty plus a goal from Álvarez. That match also lasted 98 minutes and Fulham made things just as tough as they have today.

So, three more points and top of the table. Arsenal have been league leaders for 274 days, City 14, but they've hit the top spot just at the vital time. There are six matches left and the next two will be the most decisive. Win them and it's very nearly 'job done'.

The journey back to Manchester passes by unnoticed for Guardiola – his mind is wholly engaged in the Rodri problem. The player needs whatever the staff can do for him, and while Pep is thinking about giving him a rest against West Ham and trying Gündoğan at pivot, the German's nearly as exhausted …

•   •   •

The following day, Monday, 1 May, Pep takes a little bit of personal time out of his schedule to catch up on Ding and his world title victory. This hasn't been just any old win – this was an epic 'comeback' from just about the most testing chess situation imaginable. When Ding Liren found himself on the edge of the abyss he dug deep into his reserves of character, and then produced a high-risk move that turned things around and made him world champion. The Chinese grandmaster will, from this moment, become another source of inspiration in City's colossally difficult sprint to the final of the treble tournaments – league, FA Cup, Champions League. Interviewed by the highly renowned journalist Leontxo García, China's new world champion explains how he coped with the suffocating pressure just when it looked like he was going to be wiped out by Ian Nepomniachtchi: 'I brought to mind something from the writing of Albert Camus: "If you can't win … you *must* resist."'

An aficionado of chess and its myriad strategies, Pep has a favourite phrase from grandmaster Rudolf Spielmann: 'You play the opening like a book, the middle-game like a magician and the end-game like a machine.' The translation of this idea to football, or Guardiola's at least, is simple. You play the build-up from memory, show creativity in the middle and are implacable when it comes to finishing. Spielmann, a brilliant Austrian grandmaster, was capable of twice beating the legendary José Raúl Capablanca and he stood out for his diabolically difficult playing style, a mixture of sacrificial moves, brilliant strategy and beautiful ideas – he became known as 'The Master of Attack'.

Pep feels in harmony with Ding Liren and with Jon Rahm at the Masters – City too are in the midst of a draining, daring but potentially wonderful comeback.

DAY OF RECORDS

Tuesday, 2 May: Arsenal take Chelsea to the cleaners (3–1). The Gunners shine but the Blues are well off their game – they're closer to the drop zone than they are the UEFA positions. Arteta's put his team back on top of the table even if that only lasts 24 hours before City put three unanswered goals past West Ham.

In the end, Rodri starts. It's Gündoğan who rests – De Bruyne isn't fit to play yet. Aké is back, though, and is at left-back. Ortega is in goal, so I ask Pep if Ederson has a problem. He tells me: 'Nothing, no. We just wanted to get Ortega game time before the FA Cup final because he's starting then too.' Álvarez is again on the right side of attacking midfield but he's asked to alternate between no. 10 and second striker too. It's something that I recall watching Pep getting Robben to do at Bayern – although not that often. Back then, Guardiola used to tell me: 'I want my best dribbler inside, not wide, so that he can run with the ball and trick defenders without any limits, like there are when a winger plays on the touchline – when a dribbler plays inside it means that as soon as he's produced his special stuff he's closer to shooting on goal.' In the Bayern days, Robben's interminable injuries meant he couldn't play this role too often but when this experiment functioned it really stuck in Pep's mind and he noted it away for future use. Like today. Álvarez can dribble, he's got a fabulous shot and this position allows him, and Haaland, to coexist harmoniously in the same 11.

The Hammers are missing key players and they really throw up a defensive wall (5–3–2), to which City reply with a 3–2–5, leading to the home side having 80 per cent possession. West Ham are so defensive, so little interested in taking the game to City, that Stones often ends up in the no. 10 position. For 45 minutes it looks like football is going to smile on David Moyes because, when everyone traipses back to the dressing room, it's still 0–0. The deadlock doesn't last long, though – Mahrez's wide free kick is nodded home by Aké, after which Haaland smashes the goal record held by Alan Shearer and Andy Cole. The Norwegian has scored 35 goals, 23 with his left foot, 6 with his right and another 6 from headers. He's scored once every 4 shots and after, on average, every 21 touches on the ball. He's already well within the top 50 scorers in City's entire history. And he's still in his first year as a Citizen. Near the end, it's Foden who scores the third, which also constitutes the 1,000th goal of the Guardiola era. If Pep could have, hypothetically, chosen one of his squad to score that historic number he'd have been in no doubt: 'Remember his name: Phil Foden.'

At the manager's insistence, every staff member and the entire squad form a guard of honour to celebrate Haaland's extraordinary record. It's a tradition from the Barcelona training ground, and whoever's being 'celebrated' will be slapped around the back of the head and neck by those lining up to 'honour' him. When the Norwegian is jogging through his guard of honour it's Pep who hands out the most energetic clap on the back of his head. He's totally exuberant today.

GÜNDO THE PASSMASTER

Pep is furious.

'Erling, never again, never! YOU have to take the penalty – YOU are the penalty taker!'

He's not only pissed off with Haaland, but Gündoğan too. 'Fucking hell, Gündo …! You're the captain … stop messing about!'

Once the blazing row is finished there's hugs, and peace instantly breaks out.

Deep down, Pep already knows full well that this was an act of kindness, of team bonding. Haaland's a really good lad, biggest heart you could wish for, and he wanted Gündoğan to get his first hat-trick rather than adding a goal to his own record. Later, the Catalan coach will praise Haaland's instincts, his wish to show generosity to Gündoğan – but right now, the reprimands are serious. Gündoğan's deputising for Rodri, who is finally getting that much-needed rest, and he's played really well. A hat-trick would have been wonderful but he's hit the post and Pep's indignant about the whole affair. It's the 83rd minute and City should be way in front, but the penalty miss followed by a rare mistake by Akanji mean that the scoreboard against Leeds reads 2–1 instead of a comfortable 3 or 4–0. In context, no wonder Pep's temporarily furious.

Nobody reading this should be surprised, by now, but Pep's quick to anger at these all-or-nothing moments. He's very English in the sense of that old aphorism: 'The English bring the values of good sportsmanship to their wars and a warlike spirit to their sport.' In crucial competition moments Pep goes into 'warrior mode' with no time for team-bonding generosity like we saw from Haaland to Gündo. Underneath it all, he values Haaland's team spirit and underlying decency, especially in someone who should be driven by the selfish need to keep on scoring. But Pep's in implacable 'nothing must interfere' mode, hence the crude words and the explosive fury he's directed at his star striker and his team captain.

In these all-or-nothing weeks, there are two sides to Pep's character – calm and agitated. Right now he's calm again, because he's convinced that the team is prepared, united and ready to meet the enormous final tests ahead. But, at the same time, he's irritable and won't let a single detail escape his critical eye if it threatens to dent any of his intricate plans. The smallest misstep can be treated like a disaster if you judge by his reaction. So, everyone knows that at any point in a day you can get serene, happy Pep or quixotic, irritable, snappy Guardiola. It's just how he is.

Leeds come to town looking like they're aware that they have one chance to escape intact and that's to defend for their lives – every man strung out across the back. Their relatively new coach is the veteran Sam Allardyce, and he surprises no one by using a 5–4–1 in a bid to contain Haaland. Pep's chosen a 3–2–5 structure, and Gündoğan and Lewis 'direct' the team from the centre of the pitch – it's a terrific, intoxicating display from these guys, total magic.* Within half an hour Gündoğan has tucked away a couple of goals – in identical style. Left-sided build-up from Mahrez, with Álvarez and Lewis driving into the Leeds area and drawing the midfielders back with them, leaving Gündo free to strike from the edge of the box. The Álvarez–

---

* Gündoğan: 182 passes, 170 accurately (93.4 per cent). Leeds United in total make 120 accurate passes, 50 fewer than City's captain.

Lewis movement has left him unattended on the edge and that's enough for him. First one in next to the right post, second one almost in off the left stanchion. Very evocative of a year ago when his brace helped City fight back and win the title on the last day in dramatic circumstances.

The missed penalty and the visitors' single goal are two of the very few low points of today's game. The other one is the fact that Nathan Aké appears to have fallen victim to his muscular problem again … 'Nathan says he's fine, that it's only tiredness … but we'll see …' is the coaching staff's verdict. A few key players have had a brief break today. Stones, Dias, Grealish, Bernardo and Rodri have either sat out the win or played a dozen minutes.* One oddity is that Haaland has had six efforts on target and hit the post twice but hasn't scored.

Suddenly, having played the same number of matches as Arsenal, Pep's team has a four-point advantage (82–78) and they seem to have sent a daunting, Dantesque message to the Gunners: 'Lasciate ogni speranza …' (Abandon all hope …).† They've maintained 82 per cent possession today, playing gorgeous football, and have made almost no missteps, apart from the penalty incident. Their confidence is at an all-time high, as if everything is coming together just when they need to be on the best form of their lives.

SCENE 30. KEVIN THE RED
Madrid, 9 May 2023

Kevin's face has turned an interesting shade of crimson, which goes well with his shirt. He's clearly feeling the effects of having just run 11.41km in the asphyxiating Madrid sun.

Red hair and pale skin … not ideal in this climate.

On the plus side, he and the rest of the team have acquitted themselves well against the kings of Europe, in the Bernabéu. It's been an energy-

---

* Silva's 300th City match, Rodri's 200th.

† The following day, Arsenal become the second team to defeat Newcastle at St James' Park this season. They win 2–0, the same as Liverpool did, and cut the gap behind City to one point. The Gunners have three to play, City four. But, implacably, like machines, City's endgame looks like it's ready to checkmate everyone else.

sapping, punishing 90 minutes but Pep's reasonably confident about the return leg, although there's no complacency: 'All we have to do is win 1–0 at home and we'll be in the final – although that return leg will be like a final in itself.'

And, thankfully, the temperature will be just a touch milder in Manchester. Interestingly, De Bruyne's cheeks are likely to be burning just as fiercely in the Etihad, which is exactly how the technical staff like it: 'It's always a good sign when Kevin turns red. Means something special is going to happen!'

It's all about eumelanin. Redheads have a series of genetic characteristics, which include a mutation of the gene responsible for regulating the skin's pigmentation. As a result, they possess less eumelanin than non-redheads and their skin tends to be pale and freckly. They also don't do well in the sun or very cold temperatures. It's not all bad news, though: redheads tend to have higher pain thresholds and their systems synthesise greater quantities of vitamin D, all of which is a bonus for bone density and strength. You'll often see De Bruyne red in the face if he's had to run a lot or it's very sunny. The process is called vasodilation, which is basically a rush of blood to the face, and it's De Bruyne's body's way of capturing more oxygen for his muscles and lowering his internal body temperature. By redistributing the heat to the skin, the body prevents him succumbing to heat stroke.

He's played 90 minutes tonight with his face this colour and, although he's not had an outstanding game, he's done his bit. Three good shots at goal, the third of which hits the net. Courtois can do nothing about it and it's now 1–1 (Vinicius scored in the first half). City have stuck to three of Pep's fundamental principles today: defend by controlling the ball; operate as a compact unit when you don't have the ball; and don't let anything throw your confidence and belief.

DEFEND WITH THE BALL

One of the key ways to minimise Real Madrid's lethal counterattacks is by building sequences of passes, as Pep tells me two days before the game: 'On Tuesday we'll use the ball to defend, just as we always do.'

By the end of today's game, City have made 566 passes, 90 per cent of them on target, and have had 56 per cent possession. A much better performance than last year's defeat (488 passes, 85 and 52 per cent respectively).

Madrid have also improved on last year: 449 passes and 87 per cent accuracy compared to last year's 453 and 83 per cent.

But it just takes a single error for Real Madrid to demonstrate their quality. Rodri presses Modrić a little too hesitantly and Madrid's phenomenal Ballon d'Or-winning Croat takes full advantage. With the lightest of touches, he changes direction and sends the ball to Camavinga, who's accelerating at ramming speed and gives Vinicius the assist for an amazing goal.

It's one of the few errors Pep's midfielders make today. Rodri's only messed up 4 out of his 85 attempted passes and Gündoğan has put 59 of his 64 passes to the feet of a teammate. Silva's ratio is unusually poor: 62 attempted passes but only 54 of them accurate. De Bruyne has an even lower rate of accuracy (81 per cent) but he's positioned much closer to Madrid's goal and therefore has to operate in much tighter, more dangerous space than his teammates.

'Defend with the ball and minimise risks' has been Pep's maxim whenever his teams (Barcelona, Bayern and, now, City) play a first leg away from home.* He also tends not to make substitutions if the team's control of the ball is good – something we saw in the Leipzig and Bayern games at the Etihad, where only De Bruyne was subbed because of injury. The logic behind his policy of *inmovilismo* (immobilism) is that his players on the bench are the men he uses to change the dynamic of a game (Foden, Álvarez, Mahrez), and that's precisely what he doesn't want! 'I considered making changes but in the end I decided against it because if I put one of my vertical players on, it might have made our opponents play more vertically too. And I didn't want that.'

CONTROL WITHOUT THE BALL

Today, Real Madrid have only had two chances, apart from Vinicius's goal, which came close to being damaging: Benzema's shot – which was probably offside anyway – and Aurélien Tchouaméni's attempt, both of which are swiftly dealt with by Ederson. Their eight other shots are all blocked by outfield players who, as instructed, are defending as a compact unit. In total,

---

* City's results from their previous five Champions League away games this season: 0–0 FC Copenhagen; 0–0 Borussia Dortmund; 1–1 RB Leipzig; 1–1 Bayern Munich; and 1–1 Real Madrid.

Madrid have 13 chances: Vinicius's goal, 2 close attempts saved by Ederson, 2 off-target shots and those 8 attempts blocked by City's defenders. These numbers are similar to last year's: 11 in the Etihad (5 on goal) and 12 in the Bernabéu (3 on goal), although their accuracy was much higher a year ago: 3 goals in the first leg and 2 in the return leg.* One possible conclusion is that City's level of match control when they don't have the ball has significantly improved since last year. They've definitely managed to reduce both the number of Madrid's transitions that break through City's lines and the number of clean shots on goal. On the other hand, City have also had fewer good chances compared to last season, when they took 16 shots (6 on goal) in the Etihad and 12 (9 on goal) in the Bernabéu for a combined total of 5 goals. Today they've taken 10 shots, 6 of them on goal.

After the break, Ancelotti pinches one of Pep's go-to moves: he moves Camavinga to the inside full-back position, emulating Pep's tactic of placing a defender beside Rodri (it's Stones today, in his new role of midfielder/centre-back). Camavinga's new position makes things very difficult for City and Madrid now have vastly increased numerical superiority when they bring the ball out. City's possession drops from 68 per cent to 46 per cent and the number of passes they attempt from 346 to 220. In contrast, Madrid's passing increases from 168 in the first half to 287 now. It's a similar story with shots on goal. Six for City before the break, just four afterward. One shot for Los Blancos in the first half and 12 in the second. Certainly, a pretty radical difference between the two halves and although it can't all be attributed to Camavinga's change of position, there's no doubt it's a big contributing factor.

The Bernabéu is a hellish stadium to visit, striking fear into the heart of any opponent unlucky enough to be drawn against Los Blancos in the Champions League. And it's a cycle of positive reinforcement for Ancelotti's men. The more intimidating the stadium's reputation, the better his team plays. And the more European trophies they win, the more intimidating the stadium becomes. And so, the mythology grows along with their trophy count. Last year's extraordinary comeback verged on the miraculous and only served to amplify their mythical status. That night, almost 12 months ago to the day, City battled not just one of the greatest clubs in Europe but

---

* The stats for the return leg of last year's semi-final don't include extra-time.

their own psychological fears and doubts. And now, here they are again, the same opposition, the same setting, the same atmosphere ... It would be impossible for the players not to be affected. Of today's lineup only Haaland and Akanji didn't play here last time around. And this is precisely where Pep's players do so well tonight. None of this fazes them. They go behind in the Bernabéu, at a moment in the game where they're actually the dominant team, to a Madrid on blistering form and they comfortably hold their nerve. No panic, no flashbacks to past catastrophes, no headless chicken routine ...

Madrid have lost just two of their last ten knockout matches in the Bernabéu. City won here in February 2020, just before the pandemic and, last year, Chelsea managed to beat Los Blancos in a victory that, ultimately, proved wholly Pyrrhic.*

Today's draw against the reigning European champions in Spain's capital is a notable achievement – that's definitely how everyone's feeling in the dressing room post-match. Last year, at the Etihad, it was the Citizens ruing their 4–3 victory while the Madridistas were euphoric – correctly it would prove. Tonight, the tables are turned, although that's not necessarily what the press are reporting.

City have executed Pep's game plan pretty well, although the emphasis on control has made it difficult to create good chances on goal, with Haaland suffocated by a superbly organised Madrid defence. In fact, neither team have managed to generate terrific danger in their opponent's area and both goals are shots from distance – as were all the shots saved by Courtois and Ederson.

In the return leg, City will have to play a similar game to the one they've produced tonight. As Lillo tells me after the game: 'Pep and I were talking about this and we agree that we'll have to play "two" games at home. One against Madrid, one "against" our own fans. Madrid will also play "two" games at the Etihad but they love doing that. Let's see whether we can't make them more uncomfortable than they expect when they come to Manchester.'

---

* Real Madrid's results from their last ten Champions League knockout games at home: 2019–20, lost to Manchester City (1–2); 2020–1, won against Atalanta (3–1) and Liverpool (3–1), drew against Chelsea (1–1); 2021–2, won against PSG (3–1), lost to Chelsea (2–3), won against City (3–1); 2022–3, won against Liverpool (1–0) and Chelsea (2–0), drew against City (1–1).

The key point here is Lillo's idea that 'Not for a moment can we be suckered into playing the second match at the helter-skelter tempo our fans will demand and would love to see. If we go hell-for-leather then we aren't thinking, our strategy can go by the board and Madrid will play *their* second game by encouraging our crowd to get all het up and, then, Madrid's experienced hard-nosed players will try to pick off our errors.

'When you're up against a team as good as Madrid, who have such an extraordinary group of players, their sheer speed of play can kill you dead. Which is why we'll have to play a similar game to today's. Pep will just change a couple of things so that we're more effective circulating the ball on the inside.'

The beautifully restored Villa Magna Hotel hosts the Citizens' post-match dinner. Everyone's in good spirits although it's a relaxed, low-key affair rather than a massive celebration. The food is delicious, and the players get stuck in, showing none of the complete exhaustion they were feeling after eliminating Bayern. De Bruyne's complexion is back to normal, almost as white as the Dsquared2 shirts all the players are wearing.

The team flies back to Manchester mid-morning on Wednesday under strict instructions from the boss not to set foot in Sportcity until Friday (unless they have to come in for physio). They need to switch off, spend time with their families. And Pep? He's already in Barcelona, having flown direct from Madrid on Wednesday morning for a couple of well-earned days with Cristina.

So, on Thursday morning, Estiarte and I have Sportcity more or less to ourselves. It's a good chance to catch up. 'We're exactly where we wanted to be in May, still in contention for everything. We're pleased with our progress, but we're also absolutely knackered. It's been very stressful. We've played a final every three days for the last three months. Without a break. One after the other. The Champions League, the Premier League, the FA Cup … we've had to keep going and keep winning. And we've got more massive games ahead against important rivals: Arsenal, Chelsea, Liverpool, Manchester United … and the biggest of them all, Real Madrid.'

I ask him about the problems City had getting the ball to Haaland in Tuesday's game. 'Madrid had two men on him all the time and that made things so much harder for him but all strikers face that at some point in their careers. You go to a legendary stadium like the Bernabéu and you're completely disabled by the other side's defenders. It's a tough thing to go through but you just have to suck it up. I think he'll actually feel a bit more liberated now and play even better. Anyway, look at the season he's had. It's very, very difficult to perform so well in your first year under Pep. The vast majority take a year to adapt. Look at Bernardo, Sané, Rodri, Mahrez, Grealish … they all needed a year to understand and adapt to our game before really taking off in their second year. Haaland has needed to go through that same process but he's having an outstanding year so far.'

Estiarte, himself an exceptional goalscorer in his career as the world's best water polo player, points out another vital contribution Haaland's making to the team: 'The atmosphere in the dressing room is sensational at the moment and a lot of that is down to Haaland. I've never seen anything like it. You have this amazing goalscorer but without a trace of the usual egotism – just as happy for his teammates to score five goals as he is when he gets them himself. He's so laidback. Look what he did when we got the penalty the other day. He gave the ball to Gündoğan so he could get a hat-trick. That's a hugely generous and noble thing for a player to do and it's not the norm in elite sport. He's also set up a WhatsApp group with the other players and some of the stuff they post is absolutely hilarious. It has all contributed to creating a brilliant atmosphere in the dressing room.

'We've got four and a half weeks left, at the most, and our next three games are going to be key. If we win them, the title's more or less in the bag and we'll also be in both cup finals. Ten days and three games. Pep's bound to make changes for the Everton game. It's going to be a real challenge because they'll be fighting for their lives but if we beat them and then beat Chelsea at the Etihad, we'll be almost home and dry in terms of the title.

'As for Madrid, there's not really much more to say than it's going to be very, very tough. They're a brilliant team and we'll have to be at the top of our game to beat them. But, it's on our territory and it will be in our hands whether or not we pull it off!

'We're in the final sprint with the chance to win lots of trophies, which is exactly where we wanted to be. Their legs may be a bit tired but that happens to everyone at this stage of the season and the excitement can actually make you forget that tiredness. The players are all going to fight tooth-and-nail for everything. Pep's on a roll now … and he's not going to let up. We're facing outstanding opponents, but we know how good we are too. It's going to be a brutal fight but that's what we're here for – to keep fighting till the end.'

SCENE 31. SIMPLICITY
Manchester, 16 May 2023

It's a cool, sunny day – Txiki Begiristain and Juanma Lillo are sitting on a mat they've pulled up against the wall of the training ground, chatting animatedly while the players do warm-up exercises, when Guardiola and Estiarte join them. Everyone, coaching staff and players alike, is noticeably much more relaxed than they were before facing Bayern. Pep, in particular, is a picture of calm confidence as if tomorrow's game was just a fun kickabout rather than City's long-awaited chance to avenge the all-time calamity suffered last year.

These two great sides meet on equal terms tomorrow – it's anyone's game. Real Madrid need just one unanswered goal for history to repeat itself. But why ruin a pleasant afternoon by dwelling on harsh reality?

Pep's issued very few instructions. The game plan is simplicity itself. He's going with the same starting 11 he used at the Bernabéu, with Akanji at left-back again, given that Aké still hasn't recovered from the injury sustained in the Leeds game. Apart from this one variation, it's the same team that whipped Leipzig, knocked Bayern out and wiped the floor with Arsenal, a hybrid of defensive strength and aggressive attacking that plays with the level of harmony and equilibrium he instils in all his teams. Guardiola has made one or two small alterations for tomorrow's game though: 'Gündo … 15m higher up! Kevin, start your sprints from outside the area; Manu and John, go in through the half-spaces; Erling, you're going to have two men on you at all times … so we're going to take advantage of the superiority that will give us in other zones.' Lillo 'translates' Pep's instructions for me: 'By marking our two interior midfielders man-to-man, Madrid is effectively inviting us to position them at completely different heights of the pitch – make it uneven. Gündoğan is more likely to do damage when he's played much closer to Madrid's penalty area and De Bruyne has to do exactly the opposite. He'll need to pull his marker out of position and then break through when Silva sends him the ball deep.

'Madrid's formation will give Akanji and Stones loads of time and all they have to do is use it well. Nothing more. Everything will happen naturally from there. All our opponents worry about Haaland, which is why he's going to have two men on top of him the whole time. But we can turn that to our advantage and exploit our consequent superiority of numbers in other parts of the pitch.'

Pep's already said in his press conference that he won't be overthinking the game. It's one of the accusations that are thrown at him whenever one of his tactical decisions doesn't pay off. He's bluffing of course. Pep always overthinks their games – it's second nature to him. And this one is no different. He's revised the first leg twice, has studied Madrid's weak points and come up with a detailed strategic game plan. As long as they're mentally prepared, there's no better way of understanding how to deal with an opponent than playing them repeatedly. Smart players and intelligent coaches learn from their opponents.

İlkay Gündoğan, newly nicknamed Mr Whippy by the fans, stands out for his anticipation and intelligence.* The captain always seems to come into his own in the month of May. Remember his performance in the final, decisive, league game of last season? He's just finished his 300th game as a Citizen, celebrating in style by scoring twice against Leeds, providing De Bruyne with the assist for his goal in the Bernabéu and, two days ago, scoring twice again – the second an extraordinary juggling action – plus giving Haaland an assist to net City their decisive win against Everton (0–3) in the club's 500th Premier League victory.

On Sunday, at the end of the Goodison Park game, Guardiola reminds the fans that they're just two victories away from winning the title again but, shortly afterwards, Arsenal are hammered by the mighty Brighton at the Emirates (0–3) and, suddenly, the Premier League turns sky blue again. His team watch the game on their bus journey home from Merseyside and, by the time they arrive at Sportcity, there's absolutely no doubt: a third consecutive

---

* Mr Whippy is a whipped ice-cream brand: Gündoğan's new nickname is related to the fact that, with 17, he was the team's top goalscorer in the 2020–1 season, and in particular due to a curling shot he whipped in against Palace.

Premier League title is almost theirs. Something strange happens this Sunday. Usually when they get back from an away game, the players nip into the dressing room to get whatever they've left in their lockers and then hit the road. The coaching team stay on to go over the following day's schedules and, by the time they're done, the car park is pretty empty. Tonight, however, when Planchart leaves the building, the players' cars are still there. Surprised, he heads straight for the dressing room, wondering if something's happened. It's empty. Next, he checks the sauna and the swimming pools. No luck there. Then he tries the physios' zone. Bingo! Ten players receiving much-needed massages from the club's recovery specialists. Nobody's actually gone home – all of them are so intent on being in the best possible shape for the Madrid game.

Gündoğan is one of the players Pep gives specific instructions to with regard to tomorrow's game. He wants him to advance his position by 15m when the team attacks. The coach has also changed the formation of the three guys in midfield compared to the first leg: a 1+2 instead of the 2+1. The idea is that Gündo is positioned close to the area so that he can attack aggressively from a short distance. De Bruyne will then play deeper in order to draw his marker away from the danger zone and, in tandem with Silva, hopefully distract and confuse him. Stones and Akanji are asked to take advantage of Gündo's and De Bruyne's horizontal movements to open up channels of space between Madrid's full-back/centre-back partnerships. Pep's fourth instruction is for Haaland, although it's more of a reminder – he wants the big Norwegian to stay as calm as possible despite the double marking Madrid are likely to inflict on him.

I chat this last point through with Joan Patsy, who, having worked for years with Johan Cruyff, knows everything there is to know about the false 9. 'It's weird because Haaland is actually the complete opposite of a false 9 but, tomorrow, he has a similar objective to that of anyone playing that specific role: to get Madrid's centre-backs focusing entirely on him so that space opens up for his teammates to run into.' Half-jokingly, we decide to name Haaland's new role as a 'false true 9'.

Pep ties up the session having offered no more tactical instructions. He seems totally at ease and wants to keep things as simple and as calm as possible for his men. 'Tomorrow is business as usual' seems to be his key message. Lillo puts it like this, 'Everything should be as normal as possible. All we're asking them to do is press any imbalance Madrid have on either side, even though that's what we did last year. It's not about great tactical ideas now.'

By now you're probably wondering what on earth Lillo is doing in the middle of a training session on the eve of their big match. The Qatari season has actually already finished and he's here as Pep's guest. The coach called him last weekend and asked him to come over to support the team and City duly arranged a private flight to Manchester. He arrived this morning to a huge, warm welcome from staff and players, and will bunk up, as usual, in room no. 30 of Sportcity.

Old habits …

SCENE 32. A WORK OF ART

Manchester, 17 May 2023

Tonight, Pep's realised one of his long-standing ambitions: 'I've always wanted to force all 11 players in the rival team back into their penalty area from minute one and then not let them get out of their half the entire match.'

And, what do you know? Not only has he finally brought that dream to life, but it's against the most unlikely of all opponents: Real Madrid – in the Champions League semi-final. It's been a wonderful panacea for the horrors of losing 0–4 to Madrid in another Champions League semi-final – that time as Bayern coach. It's the same score, in reverse this time – against the same club and, coincidentally, with Los Blancos coached by the same guy (back in charge for a second spell). All of which combines to banish any residual pain from the original wound.

We've just witnessed an absolute work of art. Matches are ephemeral, of course, but this is the fullest artistic expression of a hard-nosed, long-developed football ideology, and to put on this 94-minute symphony it has required everyone to be at their physical, technical, tactical and emotional best. A choral work of soaring loveliness – it will be talked about for generations to come. Football as a work of art.

Just before kick-off, there's time for the group's usual moment of stillness and unity. Gündoğan leads: 'We need serenity. Let's play calmly, let's be ourselves.' Then the German midfield dynamo takes the kick-off and sends it directly back to Ederson, as is becoming a regular habit. From the beginning, City play out with a 3+2 structure against an unusually timid Madrid press of 1+3. The deal is that, if Stones crosses the halfway line, then Walker drops back to give him cover. If Stones stays in a defensive position, his England colleague has a good deal of liberty to move forward. In fact, it's Walker who hits the first potshot. Well wide, no threat, but it's an indication that Madrid aren't closing City down and there is really evident space around the edge of the penalty box. Things develop with Haaland dropping deep to help Akanji move possession forward; meanwhile, Gündoğan and even Stones are playing really high up – the German on the edge of Madrid's box, Stones higher up than Rodri. You could say he's patrolling De Bruyne territory. In the sixth minute, Courtois punts the ball long only for Rodri to beat all the Madrid players to it and send it back up the pitch. De Bruyne unleashes his creativity, Haaland takes advantage by nipping around Madrid's Belgian keeper … but there's no one in blue there to take advantage. City's domination is absolute – the European champions are corralled into their own penalty box. Rodri beats Kroos and Modrić but his diagonal shot neither goes in nor finds a teammate to finish it. Guardiola waves his arms up and down like the flapping of a condor's wings – exhorting City's supporters to roar and bay. The coach wants everyone pulling together in order to defeat the champions. Rúben Dias robs Benzema close to Madrid's area, Stones shoots at goal … As intended, City are playing like an enormous snowplough, pushing Madrid back against their own goalmouth.

In the first leg, Pep saw how Madrid left huge corridors of space in between their centre-halves and the two full-backs. Los Blancos 'blocked off' those corridors of potential advantage to City using Kroos, Modrić and Federico Valverde. Pep knew that this could be exploited but that it would need very smart, daring positional play by Walker on the right and Akanji on the left – both pushing forward sufficiently to 'pin' Vinicius and Valverde. Given that, in theory, Kroos is supposed to cover Rodri and Modrić is up against Stones, it then means that there's a free man: İlkay Gündoğan. Of course, if a Madrid man sees the threat and moves to close Gündo then, by definition, that will open up space for De Bruyne or Silva depending on the area of the pitch the covering Madrid player comes from. This has been the plan and it's working to Swiss-watch perfection. Ten minutes in and

City press and retain possession to the extent that Madrid can't get over the halfway line.

Rodri and Stones interchange a series of passes and Grealish is the beneficiary, but when his cross is headed into what looks like a gaping net, Courtois manages to make a fabulous save. Quarter of an hour passes and the numbers tell the story. City have made 124 passes – Madrid only 13. It's the biggest difference, at this stage, in the history of Champions League semi-finals.

The only way Los Blancos get the ball over the halfway line is by kicking long – usually from Courtois. But because the visitors are camped in at the back, these long clearances inevitably land at the feet of one of Pep's players who, free of pressure, can drive up the pitch and put Ancelotti's team under the cosh again. City's press is asphyxiating. Akanji's splitting Carvajal and Rodrygo positionally – running between the two of them. Everyone else is marking man-to-man – the key thing is to prevent them gaining momentum or creativity down their left, where, in the first leg, Vinicius, Modrić, Benzema and Camavinga created lots of danger for City. De Bruyne presses Kroos, Grealish takes on Militão and Courtois, Haaland covers Alaba, Silva's on Camavinga and Gündoğan covers Valverde. City steal the ball back from Madrid 12 times in Los Blancos' defensive third of the pitch (Silva wins 5, Rodri 3), and the more Courtois is forced to thump the ball long, the more it's guaranteed that possession is going to drop right back into City's lap. Over and over again. (Madrid only win the ball back in City's defensive third once in the whole tie.)

Seventeen minutes in, De Bruyne sends a direct freekick very narrowly wide. Three minutes later, a short corner between Silva and De Bruyne allows the Belgian to cross, and when Akanji nods it towards Haaland it seems, again, that this is a 'must score' situation – except that Courtois absolutely excels again. He's going one way, but twists and saves. But for him, this tie would be over already.

Minute 22.42 – breakthrough.

Silva gets it and the chance comes after a flood of quick passes and then a piece of chaotic madness created by Stones. The defender pops up wide, dragging Camavinga, Kroos and Vinicius with him, thereby disorganising all of Madrid's coverage. De Bruyne takes advantage, filters a neat pass to Silva and the net bulges.

Prior to the ball going in, City have had 81 per cent possession and have made 202 passes – Madrid just 28. Rodri and Silva, alone, have made more passes between them than Madrid's team as a whole. More remarkably still, neither Valverde nor Vinicius has completed a pass during those 22 minutes. Play distribution across the three thirds of the pitch tells the story. The ball's been in the third of the pitch nearest to Courtois 59 per cent of the time, the centre third 34 per cent, and in the third nearest Ederson ... 7 per cent. The Brazilian's barely had a touch of the ball. When Madrid take the kick-off after going 1–0 down it's the first pass they make in City's half of the pitch. Carvajal to Rodrygo ... who's immediately robbed by Akanji. Within three seconds the ball's back in front of Madrid's goal.

Ancelotti's team completes another pass in City's half by minute 25.10 – Valverde and Modrić. After 30 minutes, the European champions still haven't made two consecutive passes in City's half. Pep's team have 76 per cent possession via 273 passes compared to Madrid's 45.

Rodri's at the heart of everything, he's setting the tempo, directing the play, bossing his teammates – and when his promptings help City move Madrid from one side to another, big spaces open up, which Stones and Akanji repeatedly punch through. Haaland's causing panic wherever he marauds and, while he'll end up not scoring across the semi-final legs, the chaos he leaves in his wake helps teammates hugely. Madrid's double marking on the Norwegian costs them and everyone at City understands that and uses it. They say that great judoka use the strength of their rival against them. With Haaland at the club, the dictionary definition of a no. 9, there's obviously no regular need for a false 9 but, with Madrid trying to throw a cage around the striker, dedicating player resources to patrolling him, it achieves some of the things a false 9 was designed to – opponents following a player into spaces they really shouldn't be and City teammates ready and alert to turn the damage he's doing, positionally, to their advantage.

Anyway, back to the action. Madrid's first corner ends with Kroos thudding a long-distance shot off the crossbar. Just a few inches lower and, absurdly, it would have been 1–1.

One of the standout sideshows of the entire City exhibition is how Walker swallows up Vinicius. He accepts the challenge of outsprinting the Brazilian and steals the ball from him whenever the Madrid forward makes it into the box. Post-match, Walker will explain that he's used up every single spare minute for over two weeks watching and rewatching videos that City's analysts have prepared for him. Everything he might need is in there but there's a section dedicated to how Vinicius will sometimes let the ball run between his legs in order to trick his marker. In other words, precisely the fast one he pulled on Fernandinho last season. 'I was constantly pegged to my mobile – using every free moment to learn how best to defend against him.' Time well spent because, by the end of the tie, Walker's been sublime – Vinicius hasn't been able to influence things at all.

Grealish, too, is performing like his career rests on this display. Pressing, closing down, diverting opponents into City traps – Courtois must be sick of him pressurising any simple pass out. He shuts down the passing line between Courtois and Militão and, somehow, manages to harass Carvajal in the same pressing action.

The two–nil goal comes ten minutes before half-time and stems from Silva and Grealish managing to draw Camavinga too far to the right – a pebble-in-the-pond ripple, which leaves the other side of Madrid's structure imbalanced. Gündoğan is the one who takes advantage of the space created, De Bruyne draws rivals away from him and the German shoots. The effort bounces up off a defender and Silva is there, calm amid chaos, to carefully nod the ball past Courtois. By the break Silva, double goal hero, has won the ball back five times near the penalty area, has pulled off three of his four dribbles, shot at goal three times and scored twice. Only two other men have put a brace past Madrid in the first half of a Champions League semi-final – Messi in 2011 and Lewandowski in 2013.

The minute before the break summarises this remarkable match quite nicely. Modrić, trying to get a pass off to Camavinga, is chased and harassed by up to nine City men and, with the whistle imminent, Pep's team goes about trying to get a third. In that last minute, City have three big goal chances and, while none of them are tucked away, this has been spectacular. By half-time, every City player except Ederson and Dias has had a shot at Courtois' goal. By now, the pass count has ascended to City 351, Madrid 137. As far as passes made in the opposition half, it's City 200, Madrid 19.

Half-time brings a sober realisation of what's just happened. City need to preserve the lead and not take unnecessary risks. Ancelotti wants Madrid to play higher up the pitch, to be in positions where, if City should make mistakes, his men are in the right area to immediately take advantage. Nothing crazy – just a better attitude and better positioning. All of which means that when the second half kicks off, somehow the atmosphere has shifted slightly.

Gündoğan, after six seconds, loses the first ball in a danger zone. Half a minute later, Walker has to dive in and make a terrific tackle to cut off a run by Vinicius, after which De Bruyne misses a pass that looked very promising. Sixty seconds later, the Belgian player rushes, misses a simple control and the opportunity to give a golden pass to Haaland. At this minute, 49.01, there is a loud exchange of shouts between player and coach.

Guardiola yells at him: 'Pass the ball! Pass the ball!'

De Bruyne replies angrily: 'Shut up! Shut up!'*

Guardiola's desperate for De Bruyne to calm the game down. In a few brief moments, it's gone a bit crazy due to Madrid's vastly improved dynamic. Los Blancos required 45 minutes of the first half to rack-up 19 passes in the opposition half, but now it's only taken 4 minutes and 30 seconds to accumulate the same number, even if the majority have occurred near the central circle and with little risk, the ball shuttled between their defenders, who don't cross the halfway line. City have possession but aren't holding it even for a few seconds, nor making three passes in a row. This bears no resemblance to the first half. So, Pep is out on the touchline yelling at his players – demanding calm and ordering that City start passing again. A simple request. But, as you well know, nothing is as simple as it seems.

De Bruyne has been having a hard time of late. Someone close to him has personal problems and it's taking a toll on the player. Since mid-April he's also been having significant hamstring issues. The medical staff have done everything possible and the coach has spared overusing him to avoid a tear, which would be a disaster at this stage of the competition. Since 11 April, when he played in the first leg of the quarter-finals against Bayern, a match he wasn't able to finish, De Bruyne has only started five of City's nine matches: on the bench twice and in the stands for the other two (Fulham and West Ham). Of the 810 competitive minutes, the brilliant Belgian has

* The player's response to Pep is due to the extreme stress he's under at that moment.

only played half (409), making the club's concern about the player extremely clear. It's also obvious that tonight he's struggling physically and emotionally.

If you like stats to confirm visual impressions, Madrid's hugely improved dynamic is underlined by them having 60 per cent possession during the start of the second half (45–60 minutes). They've used that to put a good free kick on target (Ederson saving from Alaba). City have temporarily lost their compass. Gündoğan and Rodri are haring after the ball instead of doing smart things with it and De Bruyne keeps losing possession over and again. Before a corner, Dias approaches the Belgian, hugs him and whispers affectionate words in his ear to encourage him.

De Bruyne's performance between minutes 52 and 71 is unlike anything we've ever seen from him. He misses simple passes and, for the second time in the game, he launches a low free kick from a wide position, which he wastes badly. From the 59th minute onwards, he appears totally exhausted – repeatedly bending his body over in order to place his hands on his knees – even after an easy run. No one's seen De Bruyne as bad as this. Ever. He even has to break off during two good City attacking actions to lean down and rest both hands on his knees, despite being at the edge of the Real Madrid penalty area. On 68 minutes he massages the hamstrings of his left leg; 11 minutes later he suffers a cramp in his right calf. By now, nobody's in any doubt that Kevin's in bad shape, possibly ill. (Over the next three league games, against Chelsea, Brighton and Brentford, City's key creative player, Pep's brain on the pitch, will only play a total of 70 minutes, with the express aim of preserving him for the two finals.) His last act is a good pass to Haaland, but off his left foot because of the cramp he's suffering. He asks to be taken off, which will still take three minutes to happen, during which time he runs down the field with a last, obviously agonising effort. When Foden comes on for him, it's to the sound of a huge ovation from the entire stadium. Then, just to put the heat of the night to bed, Pep goes to him, grabs him and gives him a huge embrace. Body language tells you everything – this is a 'thank you' for the huge, debilitating effort City's superstar has put into a fantastic first half but a sharply declining second. Doing any of this, given his physical and emotional state, understanding the damage he could have done to his leg … it's impressive. As Guardiola often says: 'What really defines the best sportsmen and -women is how they react in the bad moments.' De Bruyne has committed a good few errors today but the courage he's needed to put himself on the line, physically and emotionally, is the thing that makes him the extraordinary sportsman he is.

While De Bruyne has been going through his own personal nightmare, his teammates have managed to calm the game. Grealish, the team's 'rest area', does brilliantly, managing to combine his innate desire to attack with the team's need to settle the pace and to try to put the game to bed. Grealish is so dedicated to keeping the ball that Pep ends up blowing him kisses from the sideline. With this tactic, City manage to destroy the rhythm that Madrid were beginning to impose. Los Blancos, in the entire match, will only manage to get into the home penalty box twice with the ball at their feet. You can't call that danger. All they can really muster are two consecutive shots by Benzema and Ceballos in the 82nd minute, which Ederson easily copes with.

Slightly earlier, Gündoğan pulled off a golden backheel for Haaland's point-blank shot, off his right foot, but Courtois once again denied what seemed a sure goal, tipping the ball onto the crossbar. The huge Belgian has prevented three goals from Haaland tonight (minutes 12, 21 and 72) and has stopped his team from leaving the Etihad having been walloped. What he cannot prevent is Akanji heading in a well-taken 75th-minute free kick (maybe there's some involuntary help from Militão via a deflection?).

The relief watch, Mahrez, Foden and Álvarez, add glory to a war already won. Particularly the latter two. The Argentinian World Cup winner only plays four minutes and three seconds but, in that time, he produces five top-speed sprints – four of them in the first minute and a half. Just after the 90th minute he steals the ball off Vinicius and it's Álvarez's first touch of the ball – ten seconds after doing so, he scores City's fourth. Mahrez and Foden are his co-conspirators in the move. The goal is only his second touch and it follows his fifth top-speed sprint since coming on.

Four is the magic number. That's the semi-final dealt with. Even Madrid aren't coming back from that … and the fans are already on their phones booking tickets to Istanbul. It'll be Internazionale Milano waiting there – and they'll have been watching this work of art created to defeat the reigning champions. Wayne Rooney, credit to him, had predicted this ('City won't beat Madrid … they'll destroy them'). Another red-letter night in Pep's reign and another high-scoring win at the Etihad* where they're unbeaten in the Champions League since 2018.[†]

This constitutes Guardiola's 13th win over Madrid in 23 meetings.[‡] It's also his 100th win in the Champions League: 47 with City, 23 with Bayern and 30 with Barcelona. It's a competition record, given that he's earned them in just 160 matches – 20 fewer than Ancelotti, 24 fewer than Sir Alex Ferguson.

For Madrid, Courtois has been special. But the list of big, big performances for City is a long one. Rodri was involved in the play 124 times, won the ball back 11 times and won 7 of his 9 duels. Grealish created 9 of City's goal chances across both legs of the tie. And Stones ties a ribbon on his transformation: now he mustn't be considered a defender who occasionally moves into midfield – he's a pivot/organising midfielder who also defends. Again, stats help. Across the semi-final City have played a defensive line 53m ahead of Ederson ... Madrid 39m away from Courtois.

With the Premier League almost in the bag and qualification confirmed for the FA Cup and Champions League finals, for the first time there is unashamed talk of winning the treble in a very, very happy dressing room. Guardiola celebrates the success with his family and the club's management until well into the early hours of the morning. To think, just three years ago Pep said that all of this was impossible.

---

* City's biggest hammerings of teams at the Etihad Stadium this season have been 6–3 Manchester United; 5–0 Copenhagen; 4–0 Southampton; 4–0 Chelsea; 4–2 Tottenham; 7–0 Leipzig; 6–0 Burnley; 4–1 Liverpool; 3–0 Bayern; 4–1 Arsenal; and, now, 4–0 Real Madrid.

† They're 26 unbeaten in their home stadium in the Champions League (2018–23), beating Arsenal's record of 24 matches (2004–9) and closing on Bayern's 29 (1998–2002) and Barcelona's 38 (2013–20).

‡ Of those 23 meetings with Madrid, Pep has 13 wins, 5 draws and 5 defeats; scored 47, conceded 27. His worst defeat in that sequence was the 4–0 home loss when in charge of Bayern Munich in 2014. Biggest victories against Los Blancos? Beyond tonight's 4–0: 5–0 in charge of Barcelona in 2010 and the 6–2 win at the Bernabéu in 2009. His teams have knocked Madrid out of the Champions League in 2011, 2020 and 2023 but suffered the reverse fate in 2014 and 2022.

SCENE 33. SERIAL WINNER

Manchester, 20 May 2023

They've done it!

For 247 days and nights, Arsenal reigned supreme but tonight, three days before the end of the season, City have become champions again. No one in their right mind would have predicted this four months ago when City trailed the Gunners by eight points after their defeat at Old Trafford. Back then, Arteta's men looked absolutely unstoppable and you'd have had to be mad to predict such a glorious end of season for the Citizens.

Totally bonkers, like Carles Planchart, who declared: 'We're going to do it. We're going to win. Arsenal are bound to slip up sometime!' (22 January.) Or, mad as a hatter, like Domènec Torrent, who said: 'Arsenal will mess up. They're a great team and Mikel is brilliant but I think City will end up on top because they've got so much more experience of the end of season sprints.' (25 January.) The truth is, of course, that both of these men have a detailed knowledge of, and extensive experience in, the Premier League. They knew they'd called it right.

City's ascendancy (and Arsenal's slide) began after their defeat at Tottenham Hotspur Stadium on 5 February. Since then, Pep's men have played 14 games, won 13 and drawn 1, for a grand total of 40 points. In contrast, the Londoners have played 17, won 9, drawn 4 and lost 4 for a total of 31. The Citizens have scored 39 goals and conceded 10 compared to Arsenal's 32 scored and 26 conceded. As City have become stronger and increasingly consistent, so Arsenal's performances have continued to deteriorate.

Arteta's had a miserable time of late. Defeated at home by Brighton and, today, 20 May, in Nottingham by Forest, he's had to accept that City will be crowned Premier League champions again this season. The entire City squad have watched the second half from Sportcity, squeezed in to the canteen to watch the beleaguered Gunners come out after half-time, already trailing the home side. What they see is an impotent Arsenal, fighting to come back against a Premier League struggler – albeit the only side to have taken a point from City since February. At precisely 7.31pm, after 11 minutes of added time, the final whistle blows in Nottingham. Arsenal have lost and City have won their third consecutive domestic treble. The men and women gathered in the Sportcity canteen erupt in euphoric celebrations. They've just become 'three-peat' champions.*

In retrospect, the dash to the end of season has been very different from what we all expected. Most people predicted a tight, tense sprint to the finish line, Sebastian Coe vs Steve Ovett style, with a photo-finish decider on the last day. But City have actually won the title with three games in hand and with relative ease. Which seems ironic, particularly when you consider that Arsenal were on top for 70 per cent of the season. No other team in history has led the Premier League table for 247 days only to miss out on the title at the end of the season.†

. . .

Twenty hours later, the Citizens are back doing what they do best: beating a mighty rival in the Etihad. On this occasion, it's Chelsea who receive a whipping in front of a euphoric home crowd who've come to witness the coronation of their own king of England. It's a triple celebration: City's youth team, which plays in Premier League 2, and their U-18 Academy side have won their own league titles for the third year in a row. City's consistency and quality are reflected in their stats across the last three seasons. They've won 84 of the 114 games they've played, drawing 16 and losing just 14. They've won 73.68 per cent of their Premier League games with an average of 2.42 goals per game (276 in total) and have conceded an average of 0.79 (91). Remember Lillo's zero point something? Fittingly, Álvarez's 11th-minute goal against Chelsea is City's 100th of the season at home.

---

* Three consecutive league titles have been won only five times: Huddersfield Town 1923–6, under Herbert Chapman and Cecil Potter; Arsenal 1932–5, managed by Herbert Chapman until his death and by George Allison thereafter; Liverpool 1981–4, under Bob Paisley and then Joe Fagan; and Manchester United on 1998–2001 and 2006–9, both under Alex Ferguson.

† Other teams that topped the league for a sustained period but failed to win the title include Newcastle, 1995–6, 212 days at the top (champions, Manchester Utd); Arsenal, 2002–3, 189 days (champions, Manchester Utd); Manchester Utd, 1997–8, 187 days (champions, Arsenal); Arsenal, 2007–8, 156 days (champions, Manchester Utd); Liverpool, 2018–19, 141 days (champions, Manchester City); and Arsenal, 2013–14, 128 days (champions, Manchester City).

Pep's gone for an unusual lineup: Phillips in organising midfield, Lewis in the attacking right midfield, Ortega in goal and a left flank made up of Gómez and Palmer. The victory is really just the aperitif for City's supporters' massive celebrations and it also marks another of City's winning streaks: it's the fifth time the team has won 12 or more games in a row.* Now, as Gündoğan lifts the trophy, the entire stadium bursts into rapturous cheers – men, women and children embrace each other and weep with joy. Amid the cheers and the tears though, Citizens' minds are already turning to the next big challenge. They've won the league, now they want the treble.

EIGHT MINUTES OF HISTORY

Since becoming a coach, Pep Guardiola has won 11 league titles out of 14 (although it's actually 12 out of 15).† He's the only person to have achieved this extraordinary feat, a fact which in itself speaks volumes about his obsessive, pedantic, workaholic nature. For Pep, the league title is the holy grail, the yardstick by which to measure his ability and talent, the ultimate prize for which he battles day in, day out. And, to those who peevishly suggest that he might not fare so well in charge of a small team, I say this, Pep's first job as a coach was in charge of Third Division Barça B, a team that was hardly more than a handful of kids. In 2008 he led them to victory in the league.

If you could make a 90-minute film that recounts the history and evolution of football throughout the last 179 years (1863–2023), Pep Guardiola would feature in the last eight minutes. Think about it. Pep only appears in the last few minutes but his influence on football has been enormous. He is the man who, in the twenty-first century, has transformed the way we play the sport. With Barcelona he achieved excellence by playing a very specific type of game. Then, at Bayern, he absorbed new ideas and expanded his understanding of the many ways to play football. At City, he's

---

* City's five longest winning streaks in the Premier League are August to December 2017, 18; February to August 2019, 15; December 2020 to March 2021, also 15; November 2021 to January 2022, 12; and between February and May 2023,12.
† Guardiola's league titles: Spanish Third Division 2007–8 (Barcelona B); La Liga 2008–9, 2009–10 and 2010–11 (Barcelona); Bundesliga 2013–14, 2014–15 and 2015–16 (Bayern Munich); and Premier League 2017–18, 2018–19, 2020–1, 2021–2 and 2022–3.

fused everything he's learned and experienced in order to create something incredible. In the process he's also gone through a personal transformation, leaving behind the devoted disciple of traditional positional football and becoming the eclectic master of a kind of hybrid football that has absorbed and applied the greatest concepts of football through the ages. And in all this, he's seen his mistakes and missteps as nothing more than the gasoline he needs to power continued growth and forward momentum.

The best memory I have of our friendship is sitting on the sofa in his house in Barcelona in 2016 going over a list of his faults. I was writing *Pep Guardiola: The Evolution* at the time and had dedicated an entire chapter to what, in my humble opinion, were his 'deficiencies'. I won't lie, I was nervous that evening – it was a tough thing to do and I was expecting him to react badly to my criticism. Not a bit of it. Pep's always said that he's not going to read my books: 'You do know that I'm not going to read any of the books you write about me? I'll probably really enjoy them in 20 years' time. I'll sit down by the fireside after a good game of golf, with a nice glass of wine and have a read. It'll be so good looking back on everything we've done. But only when I'm older. Now's not the time.'

Anyway, the only thing he was interested in was the chapter about his shortcomings and he asked me, in fact, he insisted, that I share them, warts and all. So, we spent a large part of that afternoon in Barcelona going through it all: the clumsy way he'd handled the Bayern doctor; the lack of empathy he showed his players; and his habit of letting his internal stress build up, like a pressure cooker, ready to burst … It can't have been pleasant for him but he took it on the chin and has never once reproached me for it, then or since. Looking back, the key takeaway from that afternoon was that this was a man big enough to listen to and accept constructive criticism. Not only did my comments have no impact whatsoever on our friendship but Pep has allowed me even greater access to the inner workings of his professional life in the subsequent years. A truly great man.

And one who is fully prepared to work on his faults. Absolutely determined to avoid repeating the same mistakes in Manchester, on his arrival he looked for new ways of doing things. There were lots of immediate practical modifications, including the establishment of a team of medics and physios he knew he could trust, without question. But he also made huge personal changes. No more 'Mr Stiff Upper Lip', nowadays Pep puts it all out there and, if he thinks he needs to call something out, whether within the club or elsewhere, he does it. He's much, much less standoffish with his players too and has lost the suit and tie – an elegant but anachronistic symbol of the hierarchy, which only served to create a barrier between himself and his men. From the get-go, Manchester Pep was a different beast entirely from Munich Pep: hugging his players and the fans; giving one rousing speech after another; boldly declaring that his first and main priority was to create a strong team spirit; and promising that anyone who came on board the 'Good Ship Guardiola' would have a whale of a time – tough, challenging and, yes, painful at times but, overall, bloody good fun. And that they were going to win everything too. Of course.

Manchester was his 'mission impossible'. He was going to take his game to the Premier League, to the home of football: domination through possession; relentlessly attacking football that seeks to control the game and minimise the threat of the unexpected; establishing your presence in the opposition's camp against the biggest, meanest clubs in England. A suicide mission. Total catastrophe. Or at least, that was the prediction made by many an 'expert'. For sure, he'd founder in the stormy waters of, say, the Britannia Stadium on some wild, wet winter's night. Not the first man-of-war to sink without a trace … And then, of course, there were those who condemned his 'arrogance and conceit', 'the sheer gall of the man …'

As it turns out, Pep sails through his first outing in Stoke-on-Trent mid-August 2016. A pleasant enough day – no rain, no howling gale … His team? Ten men he's inherited plus John Stones. They play his game, dominate all the phases of the match and defeat Stoke without a lot of problems. It's their first game of the league season and the first of his initial streak of ten consecutive victories. Unbeknown to the rest of us, it's also the launch of a campaign that will lead to the extraordinary, record-breaking, golden era of Guardiola football in the Premier League.

Guardiola is a member of that most exclusive of clubs: world football's serial winners. Through his 15+ years as a coach he's developed, and adapted, a single, clear idea: playing attacking football that achieves domination through possession. It's this that has allowed him to be consistently excellent and constantly victorious. And he's faced the best and brightest while doing so: Klopp, Mourinho, Ancelotti, Conte, home and away, Tuchel, Arteta, Potter, Bielsa, Wenger, Howe, Emery, Sarri, Moyes, Rodgers, Hasenhüttl, Benítez, Pochettino, Hodgson, Ranieri, Solskjær, Ten Hag, De Zerbi … Not a man among them who isn't exceptionally talented, prodigiously successful … and as tough as old boots. Even the monstrous talents of Jürgen Klopp haven't been a match for him (between 2016 and 2023 Pep amassed 625 points with City, to Klopp and Liverpool's 575).

• • •

Professor Sergio Lara-Bercial, co-author of *Learning from Serial Winning Coaches*,* is an expert on the phenomenon of the 'serial winner'. His research has taken him to 10 countries where he's studied the behaviour of 17 different coaches who, between them, have amassed more than 150 Olympic gold medals or World Cup trophies across a range of sports. We meet up for a coffee one blustery, wet Manchester afternoon and he's kind enough to share his findings with me: 'What sets a serial winner apart is the relentless pursuit of excellence balanced with genuine and compassionate support for others, for athletes and oneself. They want to win, nothing else matters. And they always want to win. We've identified five typical characteristics and behaviours they share: unwavering high standards; a high sense of purpose and duty; a pathological desire to win, all-in commitment and 20/20 vision. In the personality tests we did, we found that this group of coaches, in contrast with their athletes, had relatively stable psychological profiles. It was something that we could see with our own eyes. Sixteen out of 17 coaches have been married for 20 or 30 years, have children and lead relatively normal lives.'

Guardiola fits this psychological profile to a tee and, if we need further proof of his serial winner status, then a glance at his stats tells us all we need to know. Over 15 years he won 1 trophy with Barça B, 14 with Barcelona, 7 with Bayern and (at time of writing) 14 with City. An astonishing 36 trophies. In Manchester his winning average is 72.64 per cent, almost identical to his numbers with Barcelona (72.47 per cent) and slightly less than his average with Bayern (75.78 per cent). Across his career his winning average is 72.77 per

---

* Sergio Lara-Bercial and Cliff Mallett, *Learning from Serial Winning Coaches: Caring Determination* (Routledge, 2023). I highly recommend it.

cent. In other words, in his 15 years as a coach, Guardiola has consistently won seven out of every ten matches, and this track record of continual victories and repeated success confirms his most fundamental characteristics.

Once upon a time, though, Pep was tormented by his greatest enemy: himself. Always under pressure, he refused to take time out for himself, through worry, anxiety or because of the bad experiences he'd had. Even his early success tormented him, causing him to doubt his ability to scale similar heights again. Over the years, this is something he's changed and these days he makes an effort to carve out personal time for himself. It's probably the best decision he's ever made.

SCENE 34. FOOTBALL WITH INTENTION

London/Manchester, 3 June 2023

It's 80 minutes since Elton John finished his second concert of the week at the AO Arena in Manchester. He's resting now, comfortably seated in his private plane waiting for the OK for take-off from Manchester Airport in Ringway. One of his assistants rushes up to announce that the Manchester City players have just landed en route from London after beating their great city rivals, Manchester United, and winning the FA Cup. Instantly, Elton John gets up and asks urgent permission from his pilot to disembark the jet. Three minutes later, the world-famous English musician is on the tarmac and embracing each of the 70 members of the Manchester City expedition headed by Pep Guardiola – a huge fan of the singer. In fact, by chance, Pep was at Elton's concert on Wednesday, the first time he'd seen him live (coincidentally at the same time as various of his players, Gündoğan, Grealish, Silva, Aké, De Bruyne and Akanji, went back to the Etihad to enjoy a Coldplay concert). Maybe it's surprising to think of players being at big public events like that in the middle of Cup final week but the coach reckoned that, after so many months of tension, it would be good for the players, and for him, to push football to one side – just for a brief instant. On the airport runway it becomes evident that Elton is a big City aficionado. He takes selfies with every member of the staff, hugs all the footballers and raises the FA Cup above his head as if he's just one more Manchester

City supporter. To top it all off, he begins to sing with groups of the City expedition. Pep, all the while, looks like the happiest Elton John fan ever. For 15 minutes, Manchester Airport's empty Runway No. 3 stages a scenario unimaginable to anybody who doesn't know how much Pep adores Elton John – this impromptu concert between the musician and Manchester City.

Pep's already told everybody that they are getting two full days of fiesta after winning at Wembley. It's a habitual trick of his given that he doesn't like to schedule coaching sessions for more than three consecutive days. In his view, the players, at this stage of the season, are overloaded with information and need less rather than more training.

'In pre-season training, yes! We work hard! But during the season, I don't like them training more than three consecutive days. I'd much rather give them rest. I want them to be with their families and I want them to clear their minds. After resting, I want three hard days of training – and then we compete!' He did the same last week after the Premier League ended with a draw at Brighton and then a defeat at Brentford – in this last instance with a lineup composed of the least-used players.

Sunday and Monday are rest days even though some players need to come into the City Academy to receive physiotherapy – especially Haaland, who will spend almost all of both days stretched out on the physio's table. Tuesday, Wednesday and Thursday will be preparation days focusing on how to play and beat Inter. Thursday means the flight to Istanbul in two separate aeroplanes, one for the team and another for the families of everybody at the club. Friday's training session at the Atatürk Olympic Stadium will be really light – maybe no more than 30 minutes of getting a feel for the ball and the pitch. Next day – their second Champions League final in only three years.

Right now, though, it's everybody back to their houses after securing the second trophy of the season. Having wrapped up the Premier League, City have won the FA Cup. It's the second double that City have ever won (both under Pep),* and the 13th in the history of English football.† This

---

* In 2018–19, City won all four domestic titles: Premier League, FA Cup, League Cup and Community Shield.
† Preston North End (1888–9), Aston Villa (1896–7), Tottenham (1960–1), Arsenal (1970–1, 1997–8, 2001–2), Liverpool (1985–6), Manchester Utd (1993–4, 1995–6, 1998–9), Chelsea (2009–10), Manchester City (2018–19, 2022–3).

triumph stands out because it was the first Manchester derby in an FA Cup final – something that had been a huge stimulus for United. They wanted to stop City winning this and destroy their chance of competing for the treble. Nobody at United wanted their 'noisy neighbours' to win the treble 24 years after they themselves had become the first English club to do so.

But, 12 seconds into the final at Wembley, İlkay Gündoğan scores the quickest goal in FA Cup final history. The captain takes the kick-off and sends the ball back to the keeper, as has become the norm for the team since March when the coaching staff adopted this idea as a structural tactic in the game against Newcastle. Ortega is in goal today. He looks up, scans the pitch and bangs the ball long towards Erling Haaland, who charges on the right-hand side and beats Casemiro to the ball. Possession is now a scrap between Lindelöf and De Bruyne, who gets a nice nick off his head. Suddenly, Gündoğan is in the box and, instead of trying a diagonal shot, the German volleys straight, a much more difficult technique, but it completely catches United keeper David De Gea wrong-footed. It's a dynamite way for City to begin the final. Everyone expected that City would take the initiative and that United would press to try and rob the ball and counterattack, and that's how it goes, to a degree, but the fact that City are one-up so early amplifies their dominance. United press with a 1+3 using Christian Eriksen a little bit ahead of Fernandes, Rashford and Sancho – their intention is to close the passing channels, so that Rodri and Stones can't be on the ball with any degree of comfort. Seven times Erik ten Hag's players manage to ruin City's playing out, a high number, even if none of the disruption turns the move into a dangerous attack for the Reds. City are trying to play out in a 3+2 style, moving to 3+3 when necessary, with Ortega moving out to be the third defender between Walker and Dias if Akanji goes up into the midfield as another pivot. In both these variants, Pep's men try to go wide and do so with some ease but without creating enough danger. On the right, Walker's combining well with Silva and De Bruyne, but down the left neither Grealish nor Gündoğan can get free.

By half-time Pep tells Silva to start from a deeper position and asks Walker to play more centrally. He also instructs De Bruyne to play open and he tells Stones to be tight in at the back of United attackers. These changes have an immediate impact and allow Silva to be more free on the right side and to find Stones directly through the central channel. The more that United players tire, the less effective their pressing is. The only thing they're managing is to chase after City players until, inevitably, Silva and Stones find freedom and City play out with ease and accuracy.

The final is over as a contest not long after the break because Gündoğan scores his second – this is his tenth brace for City, a record in the club's history for a player who has yet to score a hat-trick. The captain's scored three of these braces since May – 35 per cent of the goals scored in the last eight matches. We already knew that Gündoğan tends to come alive in May and June ... and on this occasion United's defending really helps him.

Six men in red are in their own small box to defend a wide free kick taken by De Bruyne. They're marking just three City attackers: Stones, Haaland and Aké. A few metres back, Fred is marking Dias and Shaw is touch-tight with Rodri, so, when both these City players push forward, the result is to press the entire defensive line into eight against five, leaving Silva, Gündoğan and Grealish alone on the edge of the penalty area. De Bruyne's free kick finds Gündoğan, with his body shape angled so that he has to shoot from his weaker foot, the left. He's also hampered by the fact that the referee, Paul Tierney, is too close to him and only in the last split-second does the official get out of the damn way so that City's captain can score. This is the 28th goal-assist given by De Bruyne this season.

City haven't felt in any real danger for the entire game. Scoring after 12 seconds certainly helped, but neither United's penalty equaliser nor their last all-out attack in the dying seconds have worried City. Even so, Pep breathes a sigh of relief when the final whistle goes – he'd come to Wembley believing that this test might be even more complicated than the Champions League final itself. As the realisation sinks in that they've won their second trophy and that the treble is on, Pep's overcome by emotion. His eyes well up, just as happened when he won the Club World Cup with Barcelona in 2009 and the German Cup with Bayern in 2016. It's a result of the tension everybody's been under for the last few months. The seemingly impossible fightback against Arsenal, the massive European battles with two colossus teams, Bayern and Real Madrid, and now the FA Cup final against City's great historic rival. Lingering in his mind is that moment in January when he banged his fist on the table after the fightback against Tottenham. It's tough calling out your own players … and then the run of 30 consecutive matches that have been treated like 30 finals, of which City have won 23 and drawn 5. Except for the last three league matches, with the title already in the bag, all of those encounters have been 'life or death' experiences and now Guardiola is overwhelmed by the impact. This is Wembley, his personal playground. He really wants to enjoy the moment.*

City's captain lifts the cup high above his head. It's their second trophy of the season and they're now only one victory away from what will be a historic treble if City can pull it off. But it's not Gündoğan who walks down the famous Wembley steps with the FA Cup in his arms, it's Rúben Dias. Undisputed team leader and likely future captain.

Then they're off to the Hilton Wembley hotel to celebrate the triumph, toast their families and take photos with the two trophies. They now have a two-day break to refresh minds and legs before the ultimate match. Everyone's euphoric. They've handled the tough final sprint to the tape with a maturity very few could have predicted just six months ago. Arguably, we're watching the greatest work of Pep's entire coaching career.

Even above the positional play his team is famous for, this has been 'intention football', which has needed the incorporation of a series of important functions while others are discarded. This City don't really have full-backs, no single pivot, nor traditional inside-midfielders compared to other Pep teams – they don't even really have supposedly obligatory wingers. His team does use the traditional elements of positional play, like repeating pass after pass, looking to establish numerical superiority in behind opposition lines, disrupting opposition lines, and pressing as if your life depended on it, in order to recuperate possession. But these traditional elements have been reduced to 'basic' tools. The nucleus of City's play since February is in the rhythm and the intention that they show – just like Lillo said a couple of years ago: 'When and with what idea? At what rhythm and with what intention?' The team's dominated these important elements. They now know, instinctively, what tempo each action, each

---

* Guardiola has played 19 matches at Wembley, won 14, lost 5. It was at Wembley he won his only Champions League as a player (1992, Barcelona 1 Sampdoria 0) and his second Champions League as a coach (2009, Barcelona 3 Manchester United 1).

movement, each moment of the game needs. They understand the idea behind every pass, every long ball, every phase of play. Dias is the leader of the horizontal axis – with a bodyguard who's not prone to venturing forward and who can man-mark if needed (Akanji or Aké) and another teammate who's super-quick and can whizz in to correct errors or save everyone's bacon. John Stones is the leader of the vertical axis, to which he brings a remarkable new capacity to play as a pivot – alone or in a pair with Rodri. He's also got, vertically, the ability to completely shock City's rivals by popping up as a no. 10, or a right- or left-sided inside-forward, plus a superb passing range in and around the opposition box. In City's own defensive zone, Rodri is first among equals in how the ball's distributed – closely backed by Gündoğan. Around the rival penalty area, Rodri distributes horizontally, Gündoğan vertically and De Bruyne is asked to improvise. Silva and Grealish are defenders pushed forward into the winger position. Haaland is an inverted pivot.

Think about it: nothing is what it seems. We don't need to speak about defenders, full-backs, inside-forwards or wingers – instead we can talk about the vertical leader, the horizontal leader, the distributor, the connector and the cooperator. Let's move on from 'positions' and traditional functions, and concentrate on these roles, which are applied with a deliberate intention, sometimes only in a very specific game. Pep hasn't invented any of this, but combining all these ideas and seeking to hone them into a collective harmony is an extraordinary innovation by the Catalan coach. These days, we don't say that City play 'positional football'. They play 'football with intention'.

• • •

Around 11pm, on the tarmac of a Manchester airport runway, most of the staff, Pep and his players can be heard roaring about how wonderful life is at the top of their voices. Elton John responds by cupping his hands around his mouth, as if he has a loudspeaker, and ends the evening with a shout of his own: 'One more! One more … one more trophy!'

And then he nips back up the stairs to his private jet.

SCENE 35. JUST ONE MORE GAME

Istanbul, 9 June 2023

The JW Marriott Hotel is an imposing building right on the edge of the Marmara Sea, where Europe and Asia meet through the straits of the Bosphorus and the Dardanelles. We're talking about an enormous inland sea, 200km long and 75km wide, under whose waters runs the northern Anatolian fault, the cause of terrible earthquakes. Much of humanity's history has been written on these shores.

This is where the Argonauts, led by Jason, supposedly landed in search of the Golden Fleece. Herman Melville was inspired to write *Moby Dick* by the ancient whales that swam in the Marmara Sea and it was also in these same waters that the amphibious part of the Gallipoli campaign, a disaster that caused the resignation of young Winston Churchill, then First Lord of the Admiralty, foundered. It was around this sea that Sultan Mehmed II had the audacity to move his ships overland to deal the final blow to the siege of Constantinople, which, in practice, meant the end of the Byzantine contin-uation of the Roman Empire in 1453.

A sea full of salty history.

From the night of Thursday, 7 June, Pep and his troops have occupied this hotel – rooms with stunning vistas of the Marmara. It's about half an hour's bus journey over to the Atatürk Olympic Stadium, where Saturday's final will be staged. The week has slid smoothly by, no bumps or surprises, and the most satisfying thing is that the planned 'high-quality' training sessions have turned out to be just that. The balance is right – Wembley final won, two 'disconnect' days for everyone, then three proper training days. Tuesday's been the most draining – and not because Lorenzo Buenaventura has cranked up the pressure on tired bodies. No, it's because there's a 90-minute tactical briefing to show, in exhaustive detail, how Inter play and how City need to cope with, and beat, the Italians. Some of Pep's guys have already been studying Inter on their own – they want to turn a fantastic season into a historic one as much as the coach does. Everyone knows that Internazionale will have three centre-backs and two wing-backs. Their midfielders stay tight to you, they're tough and frustrating. Lautaro Martínez boasts terrific vertical movement, Edin Džeko's aerial ability is still top-class – Inter will look for second-ball action off his knockdowns. The preparation needs to start with this forensic dissection of City's Serie A opponents.

It's too early in the week for Pep to be fretting over the starting 11 but he mulls over ideas like … might Foden take Grealish's place? For months now, Grealish has been first choice for three reasons: he creates danger, he brings control and 'pause' to City's play (remember Guardiola blowing him kisses during the second leg against Madrid?), and he does colossal defensive work. All the same, Foden's form has been irresistibly on the rise – so much so that the coach has some questions in his mind about who should play on the left wing on Saturday night. Pep's residual idea is 'still Grealish' … but he's quite clear in his own mind (and tells his staff) that Foden's work in the training sessions this week has brought the possibility of changing his mind. The rest of the team is likely to be very similar to those on the biggest nights of recent months. Akanji right-back, Aké left. Inter don't have a Vinicius for Walker to gobble up and the Englishman has been given an extra day's rest after his exertions at Wembley – in the hope that his sore back will mend.

Tuesday: enemy analysis. Wednesday: battle plan. Pep hasn't told his squad the 11 yet but most of them assume that the lineup will be nearly identical to when they knocked out Leipzig and Bayern. So … the players' supposition is that Walker will be on the bench and Foden will have to fight hard to leapfrog his way into the starting team. Part of today's training has been to hone the players' explosive speed and there's been an emphasis on how to bring the ball out vs Inter – 3+1+3, a variation on recent weeks. Inter usually press using a diamond shape on their opponent's build-up and Pep thinks that starting 3+1+3 gives City the best chance of success.

FOUR CENTRE-BACKS

The decision to line up with four centre-backs is the culmination of a long innovation process that Pep started in Munich nearly a decade back. The evolution hasn't been linear, or strict, but natural and organic – deductions and preferences worked out on the hoof. That evolution started with moving the full-backs (initially Rafinha, Alaba, Lahm) towards and around the organising midfielder/pivot. Once in Manchester, this idea became a more attacking one (in Munich he'd wanted a defensive wall) because of the characters of the players initially available to him: Danilo and Mendy, both of whom had eyes firmly trained on the offensive part of the pitch, not the defensive. Cancelo was a different proposition – full-back/creative midfielder/organising midfielder – capable of constructing attacking play from central midfield. Then Rico Lewis arrived. Small, apparently fragile but adding something extra: full-back/pivot/inside-forward/no. 10 around the opposition penalty area, then fast and diligent enough to sprint back and defend again. Young Lewis, capable of performing in four different positions, moving from one to another without hesitation.

The coaching idea that emerged in Munich reached another dimension in Manchester, thanks to this kid who served as an inspiration to his colleagues. The only problem is Lewis's physique – he's small and light. At the moment, his slight frame means that going up against the tough, battle-seasoned players of the Premier League is going to be difficult and Pep has another player in his squad who can replicate the kid's full-back/ attacking midfielder/pivot/no. 10 role, which so few could even dream of attempting – John Stones.

If you're Pep and believe in his particular vision of football, especially in creating superiority of numbers across the pitch, then a guy like Stones (and Lewis) can be absolutely vital. The last two seasons have seen City trying to win superiority in the danger zone near the opponent's box, or at least between the lines, by using the false 9 concept and Silva's played a key role in this. But Haaland's arrival has changed the structure and the ideology. No room for a false 9 now, but Stones, capable of just about anything he's asked to do, can move in and out of so many positions and interpret them brilliantly that he, now, is almost perpetually the 'free' man who gives City superiority of numbers in creative and defensive zones.

The unexpected bonus of Stones's multi-functional status is that, now, Pep can, if he chooses, line up with four centre-backs in his defence. The exception being when Walker is needed as a full-back for a specific tactical reason – like opposing Martinelli against Arsenal or Vinicius when it's Real Madrid. If there isn't a specific threat like that then Guardiola now goes with four centre-backs: 'These are guys who've spent their careers defending, who enjoy defending, who are diligent about holding the defensive line we've set.' This four-man wall concept has brought City defensive consistency to an unparalleled level. In the six matches these four centre-backs have played together, City have conceded three – half a goal per match. These four musketeers have been central to City's progression to Istanbul.

LINEUP ANNOUNCED AND BARBECUE TIME

They travel to Istanbul on Thursday. The morning session consists of a few minutes of free mobility and technical exercises with the ball, followed by rondos in which the coaching staff demand maximum precision at the highest possible speed, as well as keeping the ball. Next, two exercises to reaffirm how to achieve overloads down the flanks and damage Inter, with all possible variants. Some finishing practice concludes the general part of the session – penalty practice is added. Then it's a massage session, and lunch in Sportcity before setting off.

They arrive six hours later at the hotel bathed by the waters of the Marmara. Before dinner there's a major surprise. Minutes after reaching their rooms, Pep calls for a massive meeting in one of the hotel lounges with the entire expedition of 70 who have travelled from Manchester on the official plane: players, coaching staff, the sports management, all the auxiliary bodies, doctors, physiotherapists, kitmen, logistics and administration staff – even the cooks. Everyone is called to a surprise meeting that only Estiarte knew was coming.

Everyone's in the huge salon with gigantic windows and beautiful chandeliers lit by lots of little LED bulbs. There's a rug in all kinds of light blue over the floor but the dominant feature, by far, are those beautiful big windows that allow you to view the sea. As soon as he can establish silence among the group, Guardiola begins to talk about Jorge Gutierrez, head chef at the club.

'I want to tell you the bad news that Jorge is leaving us after this final! His work for the City Group has been formidable and he's got all our gratitude for these long, tasty years he's been with us. We're going to celebrate his brilliance with a barbecue now. I'd ask you to give Jorge applause to show your appreciation!' The entire group roars with explosive appreciation: 'Jorge, Jorge, Jorge!' followed by an extended minute of applause.

Now that he's achieved an upbeat atmosphere, Pep changes direction radically. 'Listen up, I'm going to break with tradition and announce the team! On Saturday night the team will be Eddy, John, Manu, Rúben, Nathan, Rodri, Kevin, Gündo, Bernardo, Erling and Jack.' He says it as quickly and naturally as if he was reciting the evening's barbecue menu and without seeming to attach the normal level of importance to it ... but he nevertheless leaves everybody present with their mouths gaping. Guardiola has just broken one of his most sacred rules – he always, always keeps the lineup secret until a couple of hours before the game. Now, 48 hours before the match, and barely arrived in Istanbul, he's ripped up the rulebook and confirmed what most of his players had already intuited. The players who in recent months have defeated Leipzig, Arsenal, Bayern and Madrid will start against Inter. The only difference, obviously, is the reincorporation of Nathan Aké, who's recovered from his injury. So, Walker is benched.

Beyond simply being surprising, this is a demonstration of Guardiola's conviction ahead of the final against Inter. This time he's got no doubts about which of his different variants of team should start the final. He's got no questions in his mind about any position or the form of any of his football-ers, including whether or not some of his key men like Haaland, De Bruyne, Grealish or Rodri are already beyond the limit of their stamina. Guardiola believes that this starting lineup brings balance and he's convinced it's the right one. Privately, he's suffering a little bit for having to leave out Mahrez, one of his favourite forwards, but someone who rarely gets a start in the most important games. He's feeling bad for Foden, his 'second son', and poor Álvarez, in whom Pep has blind confidence. But, above all, it's sore to disappoint his always-loyal personal gladiator, Walker. A couple of minutes before this big reunion Pep's taken Walker aside and spoken to him, explain-ing the reasons why he won't be in the team. Yet another unusual detail from the Catalan but he firmly believes Walker deserves this explanation. Against Inter, Pep doesn't believe that Walker's extraordinary speed is going to be essential. Walker, this man for special operations, isn't a 'must pick' because there are no specific players in the Italian team that need hunting down in the way that has made him so special. For the defender, it's a hard blow, but he accepts it with typical British sportsmanship.

Before the surprise meeting is finished Pep demands one thing from the entire group: 'Now that you all know the lineup I would ask you that we all go forward together ... every one of us! We only win the Champions League if we do this ... if we're all together. Those who are playing, those who aren't starting and all of us whose work is outside the pitch. This is the only way we win. If every one of us puts all their effort into helping one another so that this thing is possible, then it will become possible!'

Right now it's in the group's subconscious memory that, two seasons ago, against Chelsea, not everybody was pulling in same direction. The majority were in favour of the ideas put forward for that final but there were a few who were sceptical or who stepped back from the collective interest. Pep has always said that a key factor in great victories is total unity. The collective need to win. And he thinks it's enough if just one person isn't rowing in the same direction for the boat not to reach harbour safely. He's got one last message: 'The team talk in the dressing room before we go out to play won't be given by me. On Saturday night, a couple of minutes before you go out, it will be our own Kyle Walker who talks to you!'

There's another explosive ovation at this news and then, out on the terrace, the barbecue prepared by Jorge Gutierrez and his team can begin. There are gas heaters out to protect the players from the fresh Istanbul night, and small tables have been replaced by four larger ones where the staff and the players eat together. While the players queue up for the food, Pep starts messing around filming a video with his mobile phone – almost as if he were a cameraman from the documentary that the club makes every season. As Joan Patsy will explain some days later: 'All week the conviction has been growing that the final was ours: we began to talk about how this would be Pep's 14th trophy, which would be 14 years after his first treble with Barcelona and that would tie in with the number 14 on the back of Johan Cruyff's football shirt. All of this helped our conviction grow – we were meant to win. You could begin to hear people saying, "It's written in the stars this year." And that began to create a powerful feeling, an inner belief that began to make us feel invincible!'

Friday training is about loosening muscles and getting to know the quality of the stadium pitch. It's a moment to check how the ball feels, what the grass is like, make sure the correct boots are prepared, work out what the dimensions of the pitch are like and get ready to fulfil City's great dream. In fact, the quality of the playing surface is a bit worrying and Lillo explains to me that evening: 'As soon as we arrived at the Atatürk stadium, Pep and I went to look at the grass and discovered that it was a little tall and a little too dense, making it a pitch where your muscles tire quickly and you can hurt your calves. I told Pep that they hadn't watered it enough. He had been assured that, before the final, the pitch would be properly watered. However, in these circumstances, when the grass is so thick and dry, watering doesn't necessarily filter through, it stays on the surface, and you need to water it super-heavily to make a difference. It's the type of surface that is so dense that sometimes your studs don't enter properly and you can end up slipping all the time.' They both warn the players of this problem.

During the session there are warm-ups, stretching and mobility exercises, rondos, some practice of positional play, crossing, heading.

As I mentioned, Lillo is now back … part of the grand expedition, as he was against Madrid. He brings an extra touch of calm serenity to a team that actually bears little resemblance to the team that reached the final in Porto two years ago. That group experienced an ultra-tense final and struggled with serious doubts. This bunch is much more mature, much more sure of themselves, and laidback about the challenge that lies ahead – although they're still full of hunger.

Pep sets the tone – he's serene, happy. He feels that his team is in top form at exactly the right moment and that's the message he gives me on the bus on the way back to the hotel: 'The rhythm of the ball in our positional play this morning was really excellent – that's a very good sign.' The Catalan is far from the type of coach who puts his own emotions ahead of his players. The Guardiola who showed his players an 'inspirational' video based on the *Gladiator* movie before the final of the Champions League in 2009, trying to provoke a great wave of emotion among his team but only making them tearful, going out to face Manchester United in pieces, has disappeared, leaving behind a man whose only goal is to help his team give their absolute best. He's so laidback and serene during the pre-match meal that people are genuinely shocked. Club president Khaldoon comes up to him to say hello during the dinner and Pep ends up spending an hour with him and other directors, seated at the table just talking about everything calmly, without nerves, in no hurry.

This doesn't seem like Pep at all – the days before a game his nerves are usually on edge. I reckon this is the most significant change he's made during his 15 years as a coach. He used to believe that he needed to make his players emotional. Now he understands that he needs to help facilitate them expressing how they feel. This is the reason that he cut down all his motivational speeches. Instead, he's now a fan of calm chats aimed at relaxing the general atmosphere so that the players can focus on giving their best. From emotional to calm. That has been the great metamorphosis.

The coach wants this to feel like a normal day. Just another matchday. The objective is that the players go into the match thinking about it as one more task, and that they play in the same way as the last 20 or 25 matches of the season, calmly and confidently, constructing their play well, building from the back, defending like Yugoslavians. He wants wingers testing Inter's defenders and Haaland participating on the ball and drawing their attention. De Bruyne sums things up well: 'We don't have to do anything outwith the normal. It's been a week with a little bit more going on but we haven't done anything special and we've striven to be as normal as possible.'

Pep adds one more detail about the need to stay patient: 'In this type of match one of the absolute keys is patience … *not* thinking that because we're at 0–0, somehow we're losing the game. Italian teams at 0–0 *always* think they're winning even though that's not true.' For the second time in seven years – the first was a week ago at Wembley – every man in Pep's squad is fit and in form, ready for battle. Mission achieved for Dr Mauri. City's leaders, Gündoğan and Rodri, give the last shout of defiance as they trot out to play.

Everyone knew it was coming. 'One more, guys … one more!'

It's just one more game. Everything's ready. Everyone's calm.

SCENE 36. WRITTEN IN THE STARS

Istanbul, 10 June 2023

Lorenzo Buenaventura is a guy with radical perspectives and his reactions often bump up against more established thinking. For example, every season, while the rest of the coaching staff constantly speculate about the possibilities of winning the league and the strengths of direct rivals, Lorenzo will ask the same question every single Monday: 'How many points are we away from fifth place?' No joke. He's serious. He's fixated with the precise point-advantage City have over the fifth-place team because he's thinking about precisely how much effort the squad will have to expend in order to qualify for the Champions League next season. This might seem an irrelevance to you and me, but Buenaventura genuinely puts enormous value in ensuring that City are, without fail, in the biggest European tournament every single season. Others take it for granted. He doesn't. But there's method in his madness: 'Playing in the Champions League every single year, over and over again, is the only true way to measure what level your team's at.' Pep's always believed that Lorenzo is blessed with a deep kind of practical, no-nonsense wisdom, so he listens every Monday when the question comes up. He's also noticed that the greater the point-gap between City and the fifth-place team, the greater his men's self-belief.

This evening Buenaventura has fired off another of his idiosyncratic sayings: 'What makes a team truly great is winning when they're far from being in good form.' City have arrived at this climatic finale to the season if not quite clinging on, then certainly very low on gasoline and conserving both mental and physical energy wherever possible. The full squad is available but the condition many of them are in is definitely not ideal. Since January, without respite, the team has visibly 'left it all out there' game after game after game. Haaland has been under the vigilant control of a team of physios all week long – five hours of treatment every single day with the aim of healing his abductor muscles, which are screaming out for him to stop playing and rest properly. Realistically, Rodri was close to burnout by the end of April and what energy he has left is limited. De Bruyne's hamstrings are seriously threatening to 'ping' – frankly they've been hanging on by a thread for the last six weeks. Aké's another example – he's only been fully fit to play for 60 minutes in the last month. Stones and Grealish keep soldiering on but they're running very close to empty. Both lack that key spark which makes them special.

So, touching down in Istanbul, the group's batteries are at a low ebb. Little wonder. They've played 60 games to get where they are, with two trophies in the bag. It's only their competitive drive that's sustaining them and they're focused squarely on conquering the Champions League, once and for all, and then achieving that rarest of feats, winning the treble. Buenaventura may well be right: truly great champions win, even when they're at their lowest ebb.

Fortunately, the team's problems are weighing more heavily on the staff than the players themselves. They're entirely focused on, and hugely excited about, the upcoming final and will have tucked the difficulties away in a corner of their minds. Kyle Walker, of course, is dealing with a whole host of different emotions at the minute. Absolutely gutted not to be starting, hugely appreciative of Pep's decision to break one of his own rules and give him the bad news personally and privately, and intensely proud that he's been asked to give the team talk tonight. He's taking that duty very seriously indeed and has spent two days coming up with exactly the right words.

Moments before kick-off, he gets to his feet and addresses his team-mates, his words resonating round the silent dressing room like the crack of a whip: 'Lads, you all know that I've dreamed about winning the Champions League my whole life. I've dreamed about being out there playing today. It's what gets me up in the morning. It's what makes me work so hard in train-ing. It turns out that I'm not going to be able to make that dream come true on the pitch today so I need you to do it for me. Go out there, relax and be fearless. I'm depending on you. Make my dream come true!'

Pep simply tells them: 'Tonight, you're playing to become immortal.'

As a match, the final isn't the prettiest. The flow of play is slow and lacking brilliance. It's not an ugly contest, because Inter are a tremendous opponent – they play to win but it's with sporting aggression rather than anything else. They want the ball, they have the resources to play, too. But there are few really memorable moments other than the scintillating winning goal, which Rodri smashes home, diagonal shots from Haaland and Foden, which André Onana saves, plus headers from Federico Dimarco, Lukaku and Robin Gosens – none of which find the net.

Inter press via Džeko and Martínez with either Denzel Dumfries or Dimarco backing them up by, respectively, pushing up to close down whoever City's backline are sending the ball to in the build-up. City play out with a 3+1+3, with a 'diamond' shape in midfield – Rodri at the base, Gündoğan at the tip with De Bruyne and Stones on either side. Tonight's task is a tough one for Stones – defend like a full-back, but push on, in front of Rodri, to be the 'free man' whom City feed in the build-up to create superiority. Over on the left, De Bruyne's really not seeing the ball and is disconnected from Gündoğan. This is resolved, however, after 20 minutes when they alter their positions – Gündo deeper, De Bruyne higher up. City press high in a 4–2–4 but it doesn't become a big factor in the game because

Inter's keeper, Onana, is genuinely excellent in how he uses the ball when it's at his feet. The Cameroon international has very good peripheral vision and his teammates know they can depend on him for a little rest when things get a bit turbulent.

The Inter coach, Simone Inzaghi, has made a few unexpected but minor tweaks to his playing strategy and, initially, it's a little disconcerting for Pep's men. For example, today, Dimarco is much further forward when Ederson is trying to play out via a goal kick. Alessandro Bastoni is also making many more attacking runs high up the pitch. In contrast, Rodri, Akanji and Aké all look a metre or so off their normal sharpness, physically and mentally, and their passing is poor.* From the outset it's clear that City aren't nailing the fundamentals of their game. Bad news for a team whose identity depends on getting those basics right. Their passing is sluggish and they're not managing to shake off their markers or find the free man. The playing surface is also slow and unreliable – a horrible additional disadvantage in a situation like this. Time and again, De Bruyne, Dias, Onana, Haaland and Ederson (twice) slip and fall as the playing surface gives way under their studs. Not good enough.

It's as if the team has forgotten that Stones is delineated as the free man and it takes until the 24th minute for Ederson to make a meaningful pass to him. Does Stones make himself visible enough during those initial minutes? Perhaps not, but the key flaw is the time wasted in meaningless, risk-free passes around an overpopulated part of the pitch while Stones is often free on the right. This is far from the level of play we're used to.

Some of this has been anticipated. Pep figured that the excellent Marcelo Brozović would man-mark Rodri while Nicolò Barella, Martínez and Džeko would press City's passers and ball carriers as they play out from the back. In effect, when Gündoğan drops deep to try and provide options, he's hotly pursued by Hakan Çalhanoğlu. Making it all the more frustrating for the staff since they, at least, can see that Stones is finding free space on the right. Last night they'd joked, 'If we get our system right and apply it well then John's going to be so freed up that he'll have time to grab a quick

---

* City's passing accuracy overall in the final is only 84.4 per cent, 5 percentage points lower than the season average.

coffee while he's waiting.' It's not *quite* as bad as that but there's no doubt that Stones has time and space to move but, for some reason, isn't communicating well enough and his teammates aren't finding him. And Inter's relentlessly good organisation and discipline aren't helping matters any.

The first 25 minutes are blemished by three Ederson errors: sending the ball too far down the wing and losing possession when a break is on; leaving a long cross, which he thought was over the byline but Martínez manages to recover and keep in play; then an awful attempt to distribute to Dias, which goes straight to Barella, the danger man. His instant shot goes well wide but it's a catalyst for Pep to yell to his keeper: 'Relax! Relax!' It's obvious that his men are not in control of their emotions, any more than they're in control of the ball. Only a nice jinking run by Silva into Inter's box and a shot which goes narrowly past offer any hope during those bleak first 25 minutes. City are their own worst enemies so far.

Sport is strange, though, and, as often happens, the impact of the huge blunder from Ederson liberates the team from their collective freeze. Almost instantly, Gündoğan and De Bruyne slice open Inter's defence and feed Haaland to breach the Italian penalty box and rake in a decent diagonal shot. Onana's outstretched left hand makes the save, but in the next breath he has to parry again, from De Bruyne this time. From a wasteland, City have suddenly conjured up two solid minutes of superb attacking play, but then, just when Guardiola's team are beginning to tip the balance, De Bruyne's hamstring abandons him. He fights on, valiantly, for five minutes but it's no use. Second Champions League final, second time he's had to go off, miserable, frustrated and unable to bring his particular brand of genius to City's Holy Grail pursuit. Of course, the solution is Foden. He slots into the position at the top of City's midfield diamond – and as he's doing so your eye can't help but be drawn to poor old De Bruyne, an icepack now tied to the injured area, seated between Ortega and Walker. Utterly devastated. The half-hour he's managed here is a mini-miracle – his body's been telling him for months that it's in the red zone and nobody should ever forget the mammoth effort he's made to get this far in the showpiece match. Quiet heroism.

A more evident hero's performance is evolving in front of us as Dias intervenes three times to ensure that Inter don't take what might be an untouchable lead. It's Martínez and Džeko he thwarts and there's no question that the Portuguese is, so far, City's standout man – by a long way. If Walker's dream is in anyone's hands, it's big old Rúben. City's defence doesn't look as unbeatable as usual but he's patently in the zone, in charge of his emotions and evidencing that he will not let this opportunity pass him by. Stones catches the bug. Suddenly, he's finding not only the ball but a way to dribble with it and punch through Inter's fierce press. But, at just 42 minutes in, he also looks exhausted. The first half has been bumpy and slow, and City are running on empty. Their prospects for the rest of the match aren't looking great.

'You're playing shit!' Pep's decided to give it to them straight. But it's directed pretty specifically to Rodri. The standout player over the previous 60 matches this season, often superb, always reliable, often the margin between defeat and victory. But even that doesn't protect him from hearing precisely what Guardiola's verdict is. Maybe he's made his bed and must lie in it. The very fact that his dynamism, his brilliant use of risk and reward, his playmaking, his incessant implementation of Pep's wishes on the pitch are all lacking tonight has highlighted just how badly he's playing. He's a shadow of the extraordinary player we know him to be. The accuracy of his passes isn't the problem (92.4 per cent) but two-thirds of them have been sideways to his wide defenders and only the remaining third have been forward and creative. Pep spells it out in the bluntest of terms. This is a final, the opposition is dangerous – there's no time to mince words. The coach then lists the changes he wants to make. Gündoğan is instructed to play much closer to Rodri with Silva dropping a little deeper. He also re-tweaks their pressing – from 4–2–4 to 4–3–3. Foden will play just in behind Haaland and the two wingers will play less open than in the first half.

Stones is the first to show that the half-time break has had an impact. He's showing for the ball, loudly and clearly, and his mojo is definitely working again. His teammates respond and find him repeatedly. That means Rodri needs to move around less and, as pivot, distributes the ball with increasing impact and threat. Gündoğan being closer to him means that there's a better, quicker, passing option always available when the Spaniard is pressed. Fluidity reigns. Ten minutes after the restart, Stones is starting to play like an old-fashioned Italian *trequartista* (a 'three-quarter', indicating an advanced playmaker) of the 1990s – four consecutive daring dribbles on the ball, elegant, confident and marking out territory. City have arrived, they're in the final and everyone needs to pay attention. In playing like this, Stones is the opponent who's most upsetting and disconcerting for Inter. He's doing the unexpected and keeps popping up as the free man. But he's clearly in pain and keeps touching his knees, just as De Bruyne did. Worried, the coaches tell Walker to start warming up. This isn't great but sport is often chaotic, always uncertain. The great talent is coping with it, reacting well to it – deciphering it.

Ederson hasn't had to save anything until now because Inter haven't been hitting the target. So far, he's been nothing more than an 11th footballer, receiving and recycling possession as if he were, exclusively, a spare sweeper. An experience he's pretty used to. 'Of course, it's complicated to maintain absolute concentration when you barely have contact with the ball,' he'll admit. 'I'm constantly in contact with my teammates, talking, listening, but there's no question that if you're not asked to make saves and catches all the time then it wears you down mentally.'

Half an hour before the end, the Brazilian is offered the chance to show his powerful mentality and strength of concentration. Silva has the ball on the right touchline and sends it back. While Akanji clearly interprets it as a pass aimed at Ederson, the fact is that the keeper's too deep. Plus, it's badly executed. The Swiss takes a couple of crucial seconds to realise that disaster is looming, by which time Martínez has pounced on the confusion and is heading towards City's goal. Lukaku's bursting up to support him, pursued by Dias and Rodri, which means that, as chaos erupts, Brozović is being ignored and he's slotting in behind the first line of action. Ederson bursts out to close down the angles and makes a top block, with his left arm, to stop what looks like being an Inter goal for 1–0. It's all come from a horrible City error, bad thinking, poor communication, but this is the first warning that Ederson's going to need, and will produce, a brilliant night.

Stones maintains his role as the free man and City's most threatening, anarchic player in this tense final as he keeps dribbling past Inter players – 100 per cent success in each of his risky ventures. By the end, his achievement is second only to the mighty Leo Messi, who produced superior dribbling numbers in the 2015 final against Juventus. That said, it is, in due course, Akanji who smashes the Italian great wall.

History will show that the goal goes in on minute 67.31, but its genesis comes 20 seconds earlier when Grealish balloons the ball into the area from the left, looking for Foden. Brozović wins the duel but doesn't control the ball, and Gündoğan pops up in one of those 'where did he come from?' moments. City's captain wins the ball, feeds Foden, who's covered but works back metre by metre. To the less well-versed, it might look like the attack's dying at Foden's feet but, instead, he's being smart and finding a way to make the switch to the other side and find Akanji. The Swiss defender's push up the pitch has caught Inter a little dishevelled positionally and Bastoni takes the decision to push out towards Akanji. Silva instantly anticipates there'll be space, even as Bastoni's still deciding to break with his position and press City's attack, and makes a run that is super easy for his colleague to feed. Akanji's pass is given the perfect weighting – De Bruyne would have been proud of the precision – and pushes Inter (eight of them) to drop deep. Their defensive wall has been breached. And they've misjudged. It's a basic human instinct in sport to run to where the danger seems to be, not necessarily where it's about to be. So, Silva cuts the ball back. It takes a little nick off Francesco Acerbi and drops sweetly for Rodri. His strike for the ages is enough to beat Onana, to win the Champions League and to seal the treble.

The splendid, infinite ironies of football. The guy who'd produced a 'shit first half', according to his boss, is the one who wins the match, who earns infinite glory. It's a work of art, it's going to be dissected and celebrated and recounted for hours and hours tonight. Rodri's connection with the ball is like a Major-winning golf swing; his distance from the goal gives him room to move it in the air, around Çalhanoğlu and Matteo Darmian, in a trajectory that buries it inside Onana's left-hand post. The Italian keeper just looks on helplessly, turned to stone for those few grim moments. Rodri: 'My first thought was to hit it hard but my peripheral vision saw lots of Inter shirts in front of me so I opted for direction and I tried to bend it from out to in.' So precise is his shot that the ball almost grazes Darmian's left hip. It's an iconic moment.

There's a little detail hidden in all the glory. Minutes before, as Foden, under pressure from Brozović, works his way back out of the Inter area, no doubt to the displeasure of many City fans, Rodri's directing operations from midfield and ordering him to play over to the other flank. As

Foden begins to move backwards with the ball, the Spaniard's surveying the breadth of the pitch and sees that Stones is wide and open, but that Akanji is more 'inside' and, therefore, the better, more dangerous option. Rodri immediately stretches his arm out to point to the Swiss and roars at Foden to switch. A small detail but it plays its part in winning the final. It won't be the only minuscule moment upon which victory balances. There's going to be a crossbar, a clearance, a header to an open goal and a punch clear …

Walker celebrates Rodri's strike by running over to embrace his team-mates, beating Kalvin Phillips to the pile-on by about a second. Over in sector 203–B of the Atatürk main stand, Màrius Guardiola has gone wild with joy, hugging his mum, Cristina, and both his sisters – Maria and Valentina. They are roaring to the Turkish night sky, convinced that this is the time, this is Pep's moment, that it's written in the stars – vindication and victory at last. Or that's how it feels when the ball bulges Inter's net.

On the sidelines, Pep's much more moderate in his jubilation. Closed fist, a punch of satisfaction and then, as if demanding calm from himself, the moment of celebration dissipates. He's got an eon of experience, enough to know that what remains of the final is long enough for empires to fall, be rebuilt and fall again. He knows Italian teams – only too well. City, dead on their feet despite leading 1–0, are, no doubt, about to face a bombardment – strategy, unpleasant surprises, all-or-nothing heroics … it's all coming their way. It's imperative that City show cold-blooded ruthlessness to win. Walker makes it back from the frenzied celebrations and is immediately told to get on with his warm-up. Fast. They need him, with all his strength, pace and self-belief. And Stones is patently on his last legs.

Just a handful of metres behind the bench, in the seats at the bottom of the stand, Estiarte has also calmed down after all the excitement and is now tensed for whatever stunning response the Italians are sure to produce. Twenty metres behind him, Màrius Guardiola recalls his dad's explanation of the difference between producing a 'moment' and doing something 'heroic'. He's got goosebumps thinking about his father talking about Bayern's preparations for a Juve game.

'We know they'll seek a "moment" – an episode, a corner, a free kick: anything which has the potential to flick a switch and change the match in an instant. Juve will seek to stay alive in the match until the 75th minute and then they'll go with three forwards and if we [Bayern] haven't managed to finish them off by then you can be sure that the final quarter of an hour will be horrible. They'll look to catalyse a single "moment". They're Italian and if they find the "moment" doesn't work, they'll change and try to produce something "heroic". And then we'll suffer like dogs!'

Tonight, in Turkey, as soon as Rodri scores, Pep, Estiarte and Màrius, in unison, cast their minds back to that dinner in 2016 when they analysed the Italian sports mentality. Each of them watches intently, fully prepared for what the boys in black-and-blue are about to produce. They don't have long to wait.

It's no more than two minutes after play restarts that Dimarco smacks an effort off City's crossbar. Inter have gone to three up front but their chance doesn't come from clever play – it actually stems from a poor cross by Brozović, which glances off Çalhanoğlu, deflects off Grealish and pinballs around City's penalty area.

Akanji collides with Lukaku, bending his ankle, and Stones is unaware that, behind him, Silva has let Dimarco go and danger is arriving. He looks offside but he's not, so, when Dimarco gets his head on the ball, it's going be a legal goal if he can keep the effort down … but he can't. The ball bounces back to him directly off the crossbar and this time it looks like he's got time and space to finish, but Lukaku's slow to react. He's watching the action instead of moving out of the way and the ball hits him. It looks, in the frenzy of the instant, like the Belgian has denied his own team an equaliser – but calm review shows that Dias is on the line and would without question have blocked Dimarco's second effort.

It's definitely a 'moment' but it's not *the* moment. Guardiola breathes again but there, standing alone on the touchline, he's sure that *This is an Italian team – they'll reach for the heroic now* … It's Walker's time. They need his energy and strength. Now, more than ever.

History beckons.

Akanji isn't doing well against Martínez, which leads to Lukaku shooting from distance. The Swiss is feeling that his ankle's giving way after that collision a moment ago and so Walker takes his place. Or nearly … the sign-board is up, 25 coming off, 2 coming on, but, just as that's about to happen, Pep sniffs a problem.

'Wait, Kyle, wait. Sorry, not yet.'

Guardiola can see that Akanji is in pain but he can also see, just as clearly, that Stones looks empty. Finished. Guardiola doesn't want to make a raft of changes – neither Haaland nor Grealish have shone but what's the answer? Put Álvarez and Mahrez on? Neither of them have performed well but Haaland's aerial power might still be decisive. Do we really want to sacrifice Grealish's willingness to help out his defenders? And what if there's extra-time because Inter equalise? The Akanji/Stones thing is agonising in that context … the Swiss hasn't been City's best defender tonight, notwithstanding his role in the goal, but taking him off means asking Stones to dig deeper than ever before and get through the last 10 or 15 agonising minutes. What to do?

Just for a moment Pep's not sure of the answer and he puts the brakes on the planned substitution. Smart decision. Walker's agitated, understandably, because he's desperate to get on. Against the backdrop of this little brain freeze on the touchline, drama erupts on the pitch. Foden takes possession from Rodri, easily drifts away from Dimarco with a lovely twist and the Stockport Iniesta is suddenly on the charge towards Inter's goalmouth. He's sprinting, touching the ball forward twice off his left foot and then he shoots. It looks like the moment to kill Inter off, to seal the win. Two Inter men have dived in, three more are watching impotently, City's strikers hold their breath collectively and Foden angles his drive across the goal towards the far post, but Onana reads it and gets there. Maybe dummying a shot to the far post but cutting it inside the keeper's near post would have been the percentage execution – who knows? In any case, it's a big opportunity gone abegging. Two minutes later, Foden's breached Inter's penalty box again and the hangover of shooting but not scoring conditions his choice to cede the ball to Haaland instead of finishing himself. Anyone who's followed City across the long, brutal season can begin to see the scars now – they're ahead, they're competing like beasts, but they are running on empty. Individually and collectively.

In the stand behind the dugout, 15 minutes away from full-time, Juanma Lillo turns to Pablo Barquero, Rodri's agent, and says: 'These lads are carrying 60 matches in their legs and they're knackered. They already were in the

FA Cup final but now, here, right now, they're absolutely empty. There's not a drop of energy left in them.'

Stones has had to come off, in pain and with his shirt ripped from top to bottom. Walker's on in his place, finally, and there are eight minutes left. Having Walker on the pitch means that Silva can move infield a little to help his fellow midfielders. The seconds tick past ... Ederson slips, without punishment. He slips again, still nothing, and it feels like the game is ebbing away from Inter. But when you know you know ... Pep's conviction that an Italian side will always do something absolutely heroic when all seems lost is right. Nobody ever knows how the Italians do this, but they do.

By now, it's as if City are using a double full-back system, Silva and Grealish in front of Walker and Aké – aimed at bailing out the defence now that Inter are desperate and throwing seven men into attack every time they get the ball. Gosens flings in a cross, inexact but in the danger area nonetheless. Raoul Bellanova picks it up, sees that he's got no space, so punts it to Brozović, who goes back to the beginning. Gosens gets past Silva on the left and bumps the ball to the centre of the area. Even now, City have numerical superiority (eight vs five) but Akanji and Rodri don't properly contain Lukaku, who receives from Gosens. The Belgian striker has time and space to head at goal – 4m out. His header is good, firm, well-aimed. It bounces up and is brutal to save but, because this is meant to be, Ederson has a moment of pure inspiration and, somehow, gets his outstretched leg to the effort and saves what was a certain equaliser. The rebound heads towards Dias, he contorts himself, more instinct than judgement, and puts it behind for a corner. They can't be 100 per cent sure yet but City have just survived Inter's 'moment of heroism'. No one in black-and-blue can believe what's just happened, nor can poor old Inzaghi. Their big chance to equalise, to cripple City, just went down the drain.

There's one last blip, from the corner. Time's actually up. So is added time, but Polish ref Szymon Marciniak wants the corner taken. Dimarco obliges. This is it. Glory or a punch in the guts. It's played in for a backward glancing header by Gosens, who's shaken off Gündoğan. Without intervention, the effort will go in but this time it's Ederson who produces a heroic response. He punches clear with both fists and every last ounce of defiance and strength in his body. The ball soars away from the red zone and the whistle goes. Minute 95.46.

The agony's over. City are European champions. They've won the treble. Guardiola has, once again, won the Cup with the Big Ears.

It was written in the stars. As Lorenzo would say ... *does* say: 'What makes a team truly great is winning when they're far from being in good form.'

SCENE 37. 'WE'VE DONE IT!'
Manchester, 12 June 2023

Forty-eight hours of celebration. Several iconic images: Jack Grealish, a beer in one hand, the microphone in the other, cracking jokes. Pep smoking a cigar, and declaring that he was the best dancer among his staff.

It's been two solid days of partying for the Citizens, from the moment Gündoğan lifted the cup up to the sky in Istanbul to their triumphant parade through the streets of Manchester as the heavens open and Catherine wheels paint the Manchester gloom in a dazzling azure. It's great fun and hugely cathartic after 11 months of stress, tension and bloody hard work.

The newly crowned champions of Europe party the night away in Istanbul's Marriott Hotel: good food, lots of booze and great company. Everyone's hugging, embracing each other for the sheer joy of what they've achieved together. They dance and sing until dawn, with Grealish, Haaland and Walker leading the celebrations and happily mingling with any fans who've managed to make it into the hotel's gardens.

Nobody gets much sleep and, by 2pm the next day, they're boarding a Boeing 787-9 Dreamliner, which is suitably adorned in club colours. It's four hours back to Manchester. Just enough time for 40 winks before the festivities recommence. Back home, it's a mad dash to pick up a change of clothes and the City expedition's off again. To Ibiza. They've got an entire floor to themselves in the Ushuaïa Beach Hotel and, despite having flown 5,000km in one day, the champions dance until dawn once more. A hearty breakfast and they're heading homewards again, back to the club for some food and then on to 'the best party Manchester has ever seen' (De Bruyne).*

And this party's all about the fans. Their supporters, who've kept the faith during the long hard months of shredded nerves and weary legs, who've sung their hearts out, even in defeat, and who came to the Atatürk yesterday, raised the roof and cheered their boys on, offering their support in their own inimitable way, by turning their backs to the pitch, linking arms and 'doing the Poznań' as the first notes of the Champions League anthem sounded.

It was a tough game. Not just for the players but for the City faithful too: the tension of the game, Inter's late push and, as for UEFA's disastrous organisation, which left some City fans stranded without transport for hours after the match … It's not the first time the powers-that-be have made a total hash of things, to the extent that, these days, attending European games can be a logistical nightmare. Of course, those safely back home in Manchester were with them every step, and pass, of the way, and, as the final whistle blows, their roar of pure, sweet joy reverberates across the city streets, while, almost 2,000 miles away, Rodri cries a triumphant, 'Manchester is blue!'

It's still pouring, so Pep & Co tuck their celebratory Partagás cigars back in their pockets. Thousands of supporters are still streaming into Deansgate, anxious to salute their all-conquering heroes and, seemingly, impervious to the torrential rain. Wave upon wave of blue shirts, confetti, music, lots of singing and decibels of rapturous, happy celebrations. The squad, also getting soaked on the open-top bus, drink and party like there's no tomorrow.

There's one person missing today: Manel Estiarte didn't come back to Manchester with everyone else. His eldest daughter was about to give birth and he left Istanbul to be at her side. Happily, before the day is out, we hear that baby Sophie has arrived safely and mother and daughter are doing well. Grandad Manel's pleased as punch.

So, how does it feel to be crowned kings of Europe? Well … let's ask the experts.

---

* De Bruyne's injury was diagnosed on Tuesday in Manchester as a grade 3 hamstring tear. The following day the player started his summer break accompanied by one of the club's physios, who worked with him every day for several weeks in order to support his recuperation.

Captain İlkay Gündoğan, in his third final and ... finally a winner: 'We've made history lifting the treble despite the fact that we let ourselves down a bit in the first part of the final. We knew that we had to do much better in the second half. It was a 50–50 game and we were very lucky that things went our way.'

Rodri: 'It wasn't easy. They're an incredible team, the way they defend and counterattack! We gave it everything we had. We didn't play well in the first half but finals are like that ... very stressful, nerve-wracking. You can't expect to play brilliantly all the time but we fought like lions. These people [the fans] have waited, I don't know how many years. They deserve this. We deserve this. We got so close the last few seasons ... I just want to thank them all. We want to go on winning. Keep aiming high. Dreaming big!'

Kyle Walker: 'This is a dream come true. My mum and dad were in the stands today. I'm from Sheffield and tickets for a Champions League final are way beyond the reach of people like us. I remember times when my mum didn't have enough money to even buy me an ice cream. Right now, we're going to have the biggest party ever. We were the Centurions, the first team to reach 100 points in the best league in the world. Then we were the Fourmidables ... the first ones to win all four domestic trophies. Now we've won the treble, we're the Immortals.'

To general hilarity, Scott Carson declares, straight-faced, 'Every time I go to Istanbul, I come back with a European Cup.'*

Jack Grealish: 'This is what you work your whole life for. I was rubbish in the final but that doesn't matter now. It's such a special feeling to have won the treble with this group of players. Anyone who knows me understands how much I love football and how hard I've worked my whole life to get here. It was amazing to see my family there in the crowd in Istanbul. Pep's shown such faith in me. He's an absolute genius.'

Pep hasn't partied quite as much as his men. He and the family were pretty low-key at the Istanbul celebrations although he's let his hair down a bit more in Manchester with Màrius. At one stage of the proceedings, Pep, dedicated sun-worshipper that he is, is to be heard shouting, 'We want rain,

---

* Carson won the Champions League with Liverpool in 2004–5. The game is known as the 'miracle of Istanbul': AC Milan were winning 3–0 at half time but the Reds fought back to a draw in the second half and then won the penalty shoot-out (3–2).

rain, rain!' to the delight of the gathered fans. Today, they couldn't love him more! One of his first priorities on the night was to get a selfie with Domènec Torrent holding the cup. Dome has been his constant companion and trusted lieutenant all these years and he wanted to recognise how much he has meant to him. And the admiration is mutual. Torrent: 'Pep is the best coach ever in the history of football.'

Pep: 'Inter were as tough to beat as we expected. Very, very difficult. You never know what to expect with Italian teams, they can suddenly produce something unbelievable from nowhere and they play with such guts and courage. But that's what the Champions League is all about. It can so easily slip through your fingers and it's brutally hard to win. At times, it's seemed mission impossible. But we've done it!'

'And that's it then?'

'Yes, that's enough.'

It sounds an awful lot like the end of an era …

City is the first Champions League winner for 15 years not to have lost a single game on their way to the final. They won 8 matches and drew 5, scoring 32 goals and conceding just 5. Interestingly, the last team to win the Champions League without any losses were their city rivals, Man United, in the 2007–8 season, also with 8 wins and 5 draws.*

Thirty years ago, Joan Patsy, with Johan Cruyff, won Barcelona's first-ever Champions League trophy, when the final was held at Wembley. He's just relived that experience with Pep, Cruyff's protégé. 'Memory can play tricks on you but I definitely remember that campaign being very similar. Johan took the burden of all the stress so that the players didn't have to. I remember that he said that day in the dressing room at Wembley, "Go out and enjoy yourselves!" He made the players feel that it wasn't a big deal, that we were only at the start of the cycle. Pep and Txiki were both in that squad. They'll tell you, Johan made them feel like, "If we don't win this year, we'll win it another year." The European Cup final was virgin territory for them. Koeman's goal opened the floodgates. Everything changed at Barcelona that day. Now the same thing's happened here at City.

---

* Bayern Munich also won the Champions League in 2020 without losing, but the competition was reduced to 11 games because of the pandemic.

'For those of us who have been here for 10 or 12 years, for Txiki and Ferran [Soriano], this is the culmination of all our projects and our dreams. We've done it. We've achieved what we set out to achieve. It's more than likely that we wouldn't have done it without Pep but he was generous enough to join our project and make it all possible. And now that's it. *Feina feta* [job done]. Mission accomplished. So, what next? More of the same, actually. There will be seven trophies up for grabs next season: the four usual ones and three more that we're now qualified to play for. Knowing Pep, he's going to want all of them. It's in his genes. He just wants to keep on winning. We'll need new blood, for sure. Some people will go, new guys will come in. And everyone will have to run even faster than before. We've realised Pep's dreams and the club's ambitions. Nothing left undone. We've won the Champions League, the treble, the three-peat of the Premier League …'

It's been a long, hard journey, full of ups and downs, setbacks and bumps along the way. They've needed patience, tenacity, strength of character and endurance. They've worked hard to create and foster team spirit, build a clear identity, stay loyal to the fundamentals of their game, they've understood that each victory was just a small step in the process and they've taken the losses on the chin. They've suffered the pain of defeat and gloried in the joy of victory.

It's been seven years, although it's felt like several centuries. During those years Pep and his assistants have dedicated all their energy, their expertise and their time to developing the team with patience, care and passion.

'It is the time you have wasted on your rose that makes your rose so important.'

STATS 2022–3

	P	W	D	L	GF	GA
Community Shield	1	0	0	1	1	3
Runners-up						
Premier League	38	28	5	5	94	33
Champions						
League Cup	3	2	0	1	5	4
Fifth round						
FA Cup	6	6	0	0	19	1
Champions						
Champions League	13	8	5	0	32	5
Champions						
Total	61	44	10	7	151	46

- 72.1 per cent victories in matches all season
- 73.7 per cent wins from all Premier League matches
- 2.47 goal average per match scored in the entire season
- 2.47 goal average per match scored in the Premier League
- 0.75 goal average per match conceded in the entire season
- 0.87 goal average per match conceded in the Premier League
- 105 positive goal difference across the whole season
- 89 points in the Premier League
- 19 efforts off the post in the Premier League (4 Foden and De Bruyne)
- 63.2 per cent possession in the entire season
- 64.7 per cent possession in the Premier League
- 82 per cent highest level of possession (vs Leeds, May 2023)
- 36 per cent lowest level of possession (vs Arsenal, February 2023)
- 660 average number of passes per match
- 850 highest number of passes (vs Copenhagen, October 2022)
- 89 per cent completed passes per match
- 15.1 shots at goal per match/6.2 on target
- 8 shots at goal conceded per game/2.5 on target
- 12 best run of consecutive wins in the Premier League
- 52 top goalscorer: Erling Haaland (36 in the Premier League)
- 28 most assists: Kevin De Bruyne (16 in the Premier League)
- 56 most appearances: Rodri (36 in the Premier League)
- 7–0 biggest win (vs Leipzig)
- 1–3 biggest defeat (vs Liverpool)

Epilogue: In Pep's Words

Barcelona, 12 July 2023

When you read this book, season 2023–4 will be over. We will know the destination of the seven trophies in play during Pep's eighth season in England.* Across the previous seven, City played 413 official matches with 300 wins, 55 draws and 58 defeats. In other words, a 72.64 per cent win rate – rising to 74.06 per cent in the Premier League. They've scored 1,015 goals (2.46 per match) and conceded 336 (0.81).

Guardiola's success can't be fully explained without understanding the level of support the club has always given him. Khaldoon Al Mubarak has been the ideal president for a coach like this – a mixture of serenity and audacity, and someone who, every time a big decision has been needed, has called it right. Ferran Soriano, as CEO, has acted with courage and great caution, generally putting prudence before risk. And Omar Berrada, head of the football division, has provided an unusual level of clairvoyance in his work. From the top leadership to the humblest of employees, everyone at City has worked together, supporting the coach without question in the good and, above all, the bad times.

Txiki Begiristain has been like Pep's big brother throughout. He's carefully constructed a perfect ecosystem around his old teammate from Barcelona, ensuring that the best people, most useful technology and every

---

* Manchester City won three of the seven trophies in 2023–4: on 6 August 2023, City lost the Community Shield against Arsenal on penalties after a 1–1 draw; on 16 August, they won the European Super Cup, defeating Sevilla, also on penalties, after another 1–1 draw; on 27 September, they were beaten 1–0 by Newcastle in the League Cup third round; on 22 December they won the FIFA Club World Cup, beating Fluminense 4–0; on 17 April 2024, they were beaten by Real Madrid on penalties in the Champions League quarter-finals; on 19 May they won the Premier League; and on 25 May they lost 2–1 to Manchester United in the FA Cup Final.

resource possible are at the disposal of the coach, his staff and the playing squad. Year in, year out, he's been adept at seeing off big names from the squad and replacing them with fresh, stimulating talent without ever allowing incoming players or their agents to think that it's a seller's market. City don't let the market dictate to them, even though that can sometimes leave Pep with a headache or a dark countenance after Txiki has convinced him that they can't sign a desired player because of wage demands, a transfer price or an agent's commission is €5 million too high. Some of those brought in don't quite make the grade – but the huge majority of Txiki's signings have brought talent, the ability to adapt and success to City.

Every single new player coming in has made significant improvements under Pep. And Txiki has always reacted fast and flexibly to the comings and goings: compensating for the loss of Dome Torrent and his much-valued experience and expertise; backing the selection of young but talented guys like Arteta and Maresca – then replacing them when they leave; holding on to and promoting the highly talented Rodolfo Borrell; accepting Lillo's need to leave, then Pep's need to have him back. Txiki has guided City through huge investments over the years and he's guided them well. From Guardiola's arrival in summer 2016 until the beginning of the 2023–4 season the club has spent €1.24 billion (approx. £1.066 billion) on 180 players (€6.8 million per player) – a total sum that is practically identical to Manchester United's spend on 98 footballers in the same period and €400 million less than Chelsea, who bought 195 players. With respect to the other great English clubs, City spent €220 million more than Arsenal and €500 million more than Liverpool and Spurs, who invested in around half the amount of players Pep and Txiki brought in to their squad.

It's clear that you can't usefully analyse expenditure without balancing it by looking at what's been earned by sales: the 'net spend'. Chelsea, over the period, have sold 193 footballers for a total of €817 million, City have sold 177 players and brought in €575 million (approx. £495 million) – they are the two clubs that lead the English market in business conducted.

So, the net spend in euros looks like this in 2016–23:*

---

* Source: Transfermarkt.

Manchester United	903 million
Chelsea	805 million
Manchester City	668 million
Arsenal	643 million
Tottenham	426 million
Liverpool	267 million

If you compare net spend to trophies won by each club over the seven seasons in question you get the following 'cost per trophy'.*

Liverpool	38 million
Manchester City	47 million
Chelsea	134 million
Arsenal	160 million
Manchester United	225 million

It's clear that the spend-to-trophy ratio of both City and Liverpool is very good over that seven-year period but it's more enlightening still if we look at the 'mid-term', which is often, in business, considered to mean a five-year span.

In which case the net spend in 2018–23, in euros again, has been:[†]

Chelsea	716 million
Manchester United	613 million
Arsenal	549 million
Tottenham	378 million
Liverpool	284 million
Manchester City	259 million

In that period, Manchester City have won 12 trophies at a net spend of €250 million or €21 million per trophy – which is less than any of their rivals: Liverpool €€40 million per trophy, Chelsea €179 million, Arsenal €274 million, Manchester United €613 milliom.

---

* In 2016–23, City won 14 trophies; Liverpool 7; Chelsea 6; Arsenal and Manchester Utd 4. Spurs 0.

† Source: Transfermarkt.

Taking all these statistics into account we can conclude that Begiristain and Berrada have done sensational work.*

The preceding analysis makes clear that a club's success isn't just related to the spend (net or gross) Spurs and United are good examples of that. There are so many other factors beyond financial power. City have had the same coach for those previous seven years while Chelsea and Spurs have had six and United five. Looking closely at the Begiristain and Berrada tandem, it's also clear that they don't really go in for 'superstar' signings – Haaland, perhaps, aside. Of all those they brought in, only Gündoğan had previously played in a Champions League final (and Bernardo Silva in a semi-final) before being brought to City. Pretty much every footballer signed in this seven-year period has had a specific profile identified in their play and personality, and come to the club with the potential to be moulded and perfected. Most of the selling clubs aren't in the world top five – Benfica, Dortmund, Wolfsburg, Everton, Athletic Bilbao, Leicester, Villa, Monaco, Bournemouth, Bielefeld …

A huge part of the merit is owed to the fact that most of these players wanted to be part of a challenging project and were willing to take risks, expend huge amounts of physical and mental effort and submit to an almost perpetual load of competitive tension. Those who've succeeded under Guardiola have accepted his vision and trusted him enough to take a risk: Silva agreeing to play at left-back; Stones being willing to try half a dozen positions and to develop into a pivot who can be a defender, rather than the other way around; Grealish understanding that he'd need to develop into the team's 'rest area', that team objectives were more important than his capacity to try and wreak one-vs-one havoc; Aké and Akanji taking on their roles as 'firemen' who might be called in to rush to various areas of the pitch in order to douse the flames of a situation going wrong; and Rodri, who accepted the counsel that, sometimes, holding the right position was much more important than what his gut instinct told him he should be doing. All the way through to Rico Lewis, an outright inspiration when, in Christmas 2023, a nightmare was looming for the team. All of these players have got fully on board with their talented, demanding coach.

---

* In the last two markets, City have brought in €275 million through selling graduates of their youth academy – most of them with built-in buy-back clauses.

It's best expressed by Rúben Dias: 'When you buy a footballer you need to know, in advance, what type of profile you're looking for. Since I arrived in Manchester I've watched City seek out players with very specific identified qualities, whether they are good dribblers, have a great shot, are a lightning-fast full-back, are really good defenders. Right from the start, though, I saw clearly that ability and quality weren't enough – City look for personality too. They won't buy the wrong kind of guy – and that's why continuous ambition will never be a problem in this team.'

• • •

It's brutally hot in Barcelona. Pep takes to the swimming pool for a bit then, having cooled off, ambles back to the TV screen to watch the final stages of Wimbledon. He's approaching the end of his own summer holidays and, within 72 hours, will swap the Catalan sunshine for the rain and grey skies of Manchester. Back with his 'old friends'. For a month now, he's totally disconnected – a family visit to the Egyptian pyramids, he's played golf, gone out to dinner with friends, given some classes and, happily, totally recharged his batteries. He's put on a couple of kilos and he's let the sun turn him a little browner. Not quite as successfully as Estiarte, who's been toasting himself on the Pescara beaches every morning – before spending the afternoons with his precious new granddaughter.

It's ten years since Pep and I first got together in Trentino, during Bayern's pre-season, when he first opened not only the door of the dressing room to me, but his home and his head. From that moment forward he's allowed me to witness everything going on around him during three vibrant years at Bayern, and these seven passion-fuelled seasons in Manchester. We're reaching the end of our mutual journey.

• • •

Q: 'Pep, time to weigh up these seven seasons in Manchester, full of success, failure, drama and happiness. When I first came to you to propose these books covering your move to City, what did you really expect from your new job and what you could achieve?'

A: 'I really didn't expect to stay for seven years – of course. I'm starting an eighth now and I guess it'll likely be nine years in total by the end. I probably didn't expect to win the Premier League as often as we've managed to do. But what I did fervently trust and, what has come true, was having the confidence and backing of Txiki, Ferran, Omar ... and if you have that backing that means you've automatically got the confidence and trust of 80 per cent of the players. The other 20 per cent of the footballers you have to just go out and win their confidence – day by day in our training ground work. It's absolutely key that everyone knows that results alone won't be the reason for whether I stay or go and that I won't be sacked if we have a blip, which would be the case for at least 90 per cent of the other clubs around the world – that helps a huge amount. It means that I don't have to spend time and energy negotiating with my employers to see whether I'm staying or not.

'I don't think that during the process we've been through I ever reckoned that by season seven we'd be playing as we are now. Things have developed naturally. Paco [Seirul·lo] and Juanma [Lillo], the two genuinely smart guys in this field, always say: "Let's start training, let's start playing, let's start playing matches and then we'll see what kind of players we've got. We'll watch, learn and act." When I arrived here I'd no concept that, for example, Zinchenko would end up being a fundamental player because, then, he was playing no. 10 for his national team. He wasn't bad in that position and after the first training rondo under my management he looked pretty good. Despite that, in the first friendly we played in Germany, Zinchenko didn't touch the ball once! In that moment there's no way I could have imagined he'd play a key role in some of the league titles we won nor imagine how flexible and important he'd be in a range of positions.

'With the passage of time, of course, you view things differently. Which is a lovely thing to be able to do. It's because we've won a lot that I've been here seven years. Without trophies I'd not have been at City for this length of time. As for the team building, it's just like I said – we go along and pay attention to how each of them reacts to my needs, but to the pressures they are under too. We put our finger on the pulse and see who's healthy and who's not.

'Who knows, maybe next year I'll find a player producing performances I didn't expect. Here's another example. Before the last pre-season, in China, I wasn't going to list Rico Lewis in the travelling squad simply because I didn't really know him. But Carlos Vicens, who'd been a youth-team coach, asked me: "Why aren't you calling on Rico for the China tour? He can play full-back on either side of the pitch and he'll be well capable of handling your concept of the 'inside full-back'."

'My logic was that if Carlos felt that strongly and the squad wasn't yet sealed off, and it was going to be hot and tiring out in China, then it might be a good idea to listen and to add the kid to the travelling party. He got a little bit of time against Bayern and, immediately, I was like "Shit! Look how well this guy plays!"

'The overall result is that this last season it's been him who's shown all of us precisely what the process of learning and developing and apprenticeship should be like. When Rico's played or in training he's been demonstrating to all of us, players and staff, exactly what movements an "inside" full-back should make. Honestly, he's even invented a few movements which have helped refine our understanding of how the role can work at its best. Stuff we weren't doing before. But football's like that – sometimes remarkable things happen.

'I really believe that this is how a football team should be – open. Ready to be fluid if the circumstances dictate. Even when you least expect it.'

Q: 'What's been your biggest, most meaningful triumph in Manchester?'
A: 'Playing such high-level football for such a long time despite people always saying, and continuing to say, that you can't play that way in a league as tough as the Premier.

'Obviously, with each big trophy won it's easier to earn respect and admiration for how we play and win. But that's not been simple to gain. Imagine if we were starting right now, all over again, and you begin by saying that you are definitely going to win five of the next six league titles? Nobody will believe you. It's hard even to imagine, right? But that's what we've done. Everyone was saying, "Pep can't do this or that … his style can't work in England." Well, just look now! And we've done it with Rico Lewis and we've done it with Erling Haaland!'

Q: 'It's that old chestnut where they were saying, "His team won't be able to play like that in Stoke on a wet, windy Wednesday night without being blown away …"'

A: 'Exactly that. And, basically, we've been showing that the opposite is true for quite a long time now. Because … you can move to England and win things for one season. Or, perhaps, win things for two years. But when you do it for as many consecutive years as we have it's a demonstration of the strength of your ideas, your club, the staff, the "identity" and the philosophy of a club wanting to scout talented young kids, develop their talents and then bring them into the first team at the right stage. That's when it'll be you, the club, who dictate prices – not the agent or the other clubs. Over my time here, the club has done many, many things very well – their solidity and loyalty have been the basis for success.'

Q: 'If we analyse this treble season and look at the way City have played, has it been the defending which has been standout rather than the associative teamplay or the outstanding quality of the overall football which has maybe been slightly less brilliant than previous years?'
A: 'I don't think we've played badly. Once you add Haaland in then, of course, we have needed a slightly longer process of adjustment and adaptation but I don't think that's affected our play. Nor am I agreeing that we've defended so much better or differently – we've always defended well. The statistical analysis we do suggests that teams don't create many chances against us – but they do score all the same!

OK, we did play a good chunk of the season with four central defenders across the back and the key is that each of them lives to defend, loves to defend. That's an element in our overall play where we have made a step forward. True. This might be the season when we've defended in our penalty box better than ever.

Q: 'Can we view what's happened recently with John Stones and his role in your team to be part of a process which actually started a few seasons ago at Bayern with Lahm and Rafinha to the point that, now Johnny is a pivot who defends rather than a defender who can stand in at organising midfielder? In your head are the things you developed in Munich linked to what you've done with Stones here?'
A: 'No, no, no. In Germany I never even imagined doing things like we've achieved with Stones here. OK, there might be a central thread to it all,

knitting ideas together. Finding an extra man in midfield. You can achieve that with the forward who drops back or the defender who moves forward. But I'll always look to have one more man than the opponent in midfield. Now that Haaland is our striker we can't use him for that, meaning that it's imperative we use one of our backline to provide us with that superiority by moving forward.

'Depending on what's going on we can do that with one of the two full-backs – across the time here, Delph, Zinchenko, Cancelo, Rico, or via a central defender like Stones. What does that depend on? Well, on the quality of the footballer, how he handles the adaptation from one role to a much more complex and demanding one. But the fundamentals don't change – two inside full-backs, an extra man in midfield so that we have four in that zone … a false 9 if appropriate. More or less, I've always played with the same ideas.

Q: 'Which part of football history do you imagine the figure of Pep Guardiola will occupy?'
A: 'Not a clue. None. You have to live history. You have to live it yourself. *Live* it! There's no way you should live so as to be "remembered". I'm not into that idea at all. And, now, have we done well, have we enjoyed ourselves? No question! Listen, before the semi-final second leg against Madrid where we played so, so well, they were asking me if getting to the final would signify doing something historic and, again, I told them that I really had no idea if that would be the case or not. But one thing is sure – we've had the best time doing it. I promise you that's the truth. It's been marvellous. If anyone envies us for anything at all it should be that – it's been an absolute ball!

'Life is the day to day and how you live it. It's today. When we die nobody's going to come and tell you, "This is the place in history you occupy …" When you're dead you're dead and history won't matter a damn.

Q: 'So that's why you fixate on the day to day and you neither think about the mid-term nor about what there is left for you to achieve in your career?'
A: 'Right now I'm on holiday and the only thing I'm thinking about is getting to Manchester and finding out which players I've got available for the first training sessions. That's it. I don't bother too much about the micro-planning,

the micro-programming or the macro-programming. I used to, back when I was coaching at Barcelona B – but Juanma Lillo taught me that all that wasn't worth it. He was right then and he's still right. The idea is to get to training and say: how many have we got today and who are they? If we've got "so many and such and such" then we use that to put on a good session, reminding them about our principals of playing, our fundamentals and everything that flows from that and we'll work on day by day until the first friendly comes along. We'll try and win, reminding the players how we did it in the past, improving bits and pieces, and that's about it. Then the second friendly comes along and we'll do the same but hopefully better, then the third, then the competitive matches. We focus on what's next, nothing more.

Q: 'You've coached 413 matches with City but with only 58 defeats – that's a rate of 14 per cent. If you've to pick the three which have stung the most, I think they'd be the 4–0 at Goodison in January 2017; in Lisbon against Lyon in the pandemic Champions League restart; and Madrid's comeback victory in the Bernabéu Champions League semi-final. Would they be the ones?'
A: 'The Everton one, yes. I hadn't quite "found" the team yet – that was painful medicine. But later that year we finished third but, above all, playing really well. And that summer the club took a quantum leap forward, investing well in the resources we needed, because that was a squad which had become too "veteran". Still good, but ageing. Eleven of my players were over 30 and the updating/reset was totally needed.

The second one, losing to Lyon in Lisbon, hurt badly because the Champions League is always a special prize. We lost because of details. Basically defensive errors. Not because we played hugely worse than our opponent. That was a night which demonstrated the club's strength and character – the president, talking to all the players and staff, said: "We'll be back and, sooner or later, we'll win this competition!" That's the type of moment you never forget. In the middle of a post-defeat dinner, when everyone's morale is in their boots – Khaldoon stood up and told them all: "Next season we'll be back again and one day we'll win the Champions League."

'Actually, the Madrid defeat hurt much less. It was a tough blow to take, that night in the Bernabéu, but the tie was lost at home in my view. It was one of those nights when the heavens didn't want the semi-final to be completely over in the first match. If you spend your life in football you know that this is a sport which plays these tricks on you!

'But the team did good things home and away – OK, a little less so in Madrid. But don't believe that that was a defeat which cost me a lot to get over. In fact, it was a loss that helped us do what we've done subsequently – reach the final the following year and then win the trophy. All of that can happen in football.

'So, without a shadow of doubt, that 4–0 loss at Everton is the defeat which hurt me most because it was a blow right in the middle of a time when I was still struggling to find the right way for the team to be and to play.'

Q: 'That was your most difficult Christmas (2016–17) because it felt like one thing after another – away defeats at Chelsea, Leicester, Liverpool and then to Everton.'
A: 'Yes, yes … it was a moment when I hadn't quite got to grips with the team and what I wanted to do with it. But in those brutal moments my staff supported me so well and I received phone calls from people I admire, all of which raised my spirits greatly. Good things cost – and those tough times simply make you value the achievements still more.'

Q: 'Across the seven years there have been so many wins, 300 in total, which is more than 72 per cent of the matches played. Which wins have been the most emotional or impactful?'
A: 'The wins which make me proudest were the Premier League titles. In England, being champion is very special because it's so tough to do. Then, when you've won one you think, *That's that done*, but you win another and then Liverpool walk right over you for the next one and it's important to discover what we're made of and what our character is. Getting our act together and then winning again made us consistent winners – the platform for the next two.

'The need for day-to-day quality of work, consistency, is what makes the league special. When you face a test that won't let you have time to think or breath and you overcome it – that's when the most satisfaction comes. But I'll add an important detail – the four consecutive League Cup wins. It's a competition that people think no one cares about but you winning it four times on the bounce shows how much detail you put into your work, how importantly you treat every training session, every detail, every single match preparation. No slacking. I've always thought that actually winning a so-called "lesser" trophy is a test of your humility. It demonstrates to everyone that this Premier League-winning club also works hard to win the Carabao Cup and that you don't gift any match away to anyone ever. There's the concept that not being in it gives you longer weeks to recover, fewer matches, a chance to let injured players heal and that, overall, you'll be fresher if you're knocked out – more tired if you tilt at winning it. But, no! You put effort into winning everything, you try to win all domestic trophies and then you do it four consecutive years. That made me proud. It said so much about the club and the squad. Our character and our competitive culture – something that we wanted to instil at the club.

'Everyone who's been here these seven years, players, staff, we've all raised our level. Right now City's competitive level is very high – which is something we need to maintain not just in the coming years but for decades in the future.

'I believe that so long as Khaldoon is there, pressuring everyone, we'll still be competitive all the time. When I'm not there it'll be someone else trying to hit the same standards. It's a culture.

'Trophies are very important but ensuring that there's a competitive character is even more so. In the future, people will look back and comment that we competed for everything all the time. That we lost four [FA] Cup semi-finals but we won the trophy twice. And that in the Champions League it was like a pattern – semi-final, final, semi-final … until finally we won the final.

'When you set the bar that high then it's a bit of a bugger to maintain but that's what you have to do. Nobody here thinks it's enough to reach the summit one year and win the title or the Champions League – we have to be consistent and be competitive every single season.'

Q: 'Let's talk about the "that'll do, that's enough," which you said in Istanbul. I guessed that it only meant that you'd finally culminated the work of rescaling the heights. That the achievements of winning the treble back in 2009 had been a heavy weight to carry all these years but no longer now?'

A: 'Winning the treble in your first season at Barcelona seems to suggest that you can dream of winning it every year. But that's really not possible. I'm a good coach but not *so* good as to be able to win the treble every year. That's never been something I imagined doing or set as our goal. But it's true that, having won five Premier Leagues, you still yearn for City to be recognised as a European great – then, obviously, you have to win the Champions League too. Winning the biggest European trophy has added sheen to the five Premier League victories. In Istanbul we'd finally done what we'd set out to do. That's why I said: "That's it, we've done it!"

'We'd played well, we'd won the English title and, finally, we'd won in Europe too. That's that. But you go on holiday, you rest, you switch off, you feel strong again, you get back and instantly you find yourself pushing hard to do all of it over again. But, let's not kid about that night in Istanbul, the dominant emotion was "We've done it!"'

Q: 'Throughout the years you've repeated to me that it would be impossible to do it again, that the achievement at Barcelona was unsurpassable … but you did it!'

A: 'Look, if winning the Champions League is difficult then you can barely imagine how hard it is to win the treble. These are things that might happen once in your lifetime – which is why I talked about it being impossible to you. It had happened to me once at Barça! It's a once in a lifetime thing, which has happened to me twice. I can't ask for more!

'When you're working at a club your day to day is train–play–compete–think about your rivals–which rival is good–which is weak–where are our weak points–where must we improve?, and repeat over and over. In summary it's trying to work out how we can maintain a team that has won the treble at the same standards – but not just maintain it, which is a huge task, but try to improve it if that's even possible. But when you leave your club and sign-off on what you've achieved it's then when you weigh things up and take account of what you've genuinely achieved or failed to. When I left Barcelona I was struck by the magnitude of what we'd actually done. At Bayern we were left with the pending task of winning the Champions League. And at City, it's like Barcelona. What we needed to do and what we've actually done. But the true balance can only be added up with certainty when you actually leave.

Because, I'll tell you one thing, while we are still here we'll still be working flat out to achieve even more.

'When we arrived, City hadn't ever won the Champions League. We took seven years but we did it. That's that. Right, now, how many clubs have won the Champions League? Lots of them. And quite a few have even won two or three or four. So, by definition, what we've achieved is massive for the club but not exceptional in football terms. Exceptional is winning 14 Roland-Garroses like Rafa Nadal, or 8 Wimbledons like Roger Federer – *that* is exceptional. So would winning 11 out of 14 leagues. Conquering the Champions League is great, we're content, but it's simply not exceptional. *If* we win two or three more then everything changes and perhaps that'll make us exceptional.'

Q: 'There's still time to win the Champions League again! It's my impression, knowing you, that the greatest change you've effected as a coach over the last seven years, no doubt influenced by maturing as a man, is much more to do with managing your emotions, your players' emotions, rather than anything related to football on the pitch. Might that be true?'
A: 'Yes, that's undoubtedly true. I fully agree. It might not seem that way but I'm much more patient now. Much more optimistic in the build-up to games. More clear-headed and calm in post-match analysis. Less emotional. Even if some of my tactual leaps are still based a lot on how I feel – what my emotions tell me. No matter how much AI or "big data" reaches us. The majority of my tactical decisions I make on instinct. For "how the grass smells", for how you feel in a given situation.

'But it's fair to stay that even if emotion still governs a lot of my tactical work I've still changed a lot. The anxiety and anguish pre-match are hugely diminished. I'm much more optimistic, much easier on myself than I was. I've done away with a lot of negativity and bad stuff like that. I take it all just like another piece of our lives – part of the process of being involved in sport. So I'm much more tolerant because I cope better with certain things. And because I'm more optimistic and positive as the games approach, I enjoy it all a lot more and it affects me less. This is the factor that has already prolonged my coaching career in England. If I hadn't changed this radically I'd already be long gone.'

●　●　●

Time, it's always about time. Nobody chooses how long they're given to live. No sportsperson decides what era they compete in or who's alive at the same time to compete against. These are the whims of life, which you just have to accept without regret or protest. Nor is it feasible to choose whether your sporting growth bubbles gently along or erupts explosively. In simple terms, it happens. You can't 'own' time, nor can you shape it to your wishes, domesticate it, beat it – only administer it.

Choosing 'how I'm going to compete' is the only thing a sportsperson can control. How to face the challenges and compete with the rivals who've been thrown in my path. What will be my attitude, my style and my 'intention' against those who are up against me? That's the real power in sport – and in understanding/managing it lies the real key to success. Choose the 'how' and accept that time will help you reach your destination.

Guardiola never imagined he'd win every trophy available in his first year as coach, but it happened. He later tried to ascend that summit again, but suffered innumerable setbacks, just like a Sisyphus punished by the gods to push the boulder, again and again, to the top of the mountain only for it to inevitably fall back. Stubborn as he is, Guardiola insisted on fighting – increasingly aware that he could not choose the times, but he could choose the ways. 'Time will always defeat us,' Garry Kasparov warned him years ago in New York. Time is the water that slips through our fingers.

Today Pep and I talk about time, that great sculptor which shapes us and decides our fate, and I can testify that he has finally understood the magnitude of the great rival of every living being:

'Life is today. When you die, you are dead, and the story you've made doesn't matter.'